Looking Back

A Reader on the History of Deaf Communities and their Sign Languages

International Studies on Sign Language
and Communication of the Deaf
Volume 20

Renate Fischer • Harlan Lane (eds.)

Looking Back

A Reader on the History
of Deaf Communities and their Sign Languages

SIGNUM

International Studies on
Sign Language and Communication of the Deaf

edited by Siegmund Prillwitz
on behalf of the *Society* and the *Center*
for German Sign Language and Communication of the Deaf
University of Hamburg

Volume 20

Die Deutsche Bibliothek - CIP Einheitsaufnahme

Looking back : a reader on the history of deaf communities and
their sign languages / Renate Fischer ; Harlan Lane. - Hamburg
: Signum-Verl., 1993
  (International studies on sign language and communication of the deaf
  ; Vol. 20)
  ISBN 3-927731-32-3
NE: Fischer, Renate [Hrsg.]; Internationale Arbeiten zur
  Gebärdensprache und Kommunikation Gehörloser

© 1993, SIGNUM - Press
  Hans-Albers-Platz 2 • D 2000 Hamburg 36
  Tel.. ++49 - (0)40 - 319 2140 • Fax ++49 - (0)40 - 319 6205

Editor: Tomas Vollhaber
Word Processing: Trixi Flügel • Katharina Kutzmann
Reader: Amanda Lee
Cover and DTP: Tomas Vollhaber
Cover illustration: *2-year-old Carl Max Löwe* (later a Deaf teacher and chronicler of the Deaf in Leipzig),
             painting by E. Weser, 1836.
             Samuel-Heinicke-Schule, Leipzig. Photo: Hans Ballschuh
Print: Fuldaer Verlagsanstalt

Printed in Germany
ISBN 3-927731-32-3

Contents

Deaf Biographies

Deaf Communities

Sign Languages and Signed Systems

Deaf Education in the Context of Oralism

Issues Concerning Medicalization, Sociology, and Philosophy

Methodological and Theoretical Issues of Deaf History

We find it a privilege to have edited the first international reader on Deaf History with the cooperation of so many outstanding researchers in various fields.

We'd like to thank all of them and hope readers will find the book useful, inspiring, and provocative.

Renate Fischer • Harlan Lane

Hamburg • Boston, september 1992

The authors wish to salute Dr. Siegmund Prillwitz,
Director of the Centre for German Sign Language and
Communicationof the Deaf, University of Hamburg,
a champion of the rights of Deaf people,
on the occasion of his 50th birthday.

Deaf Biographies

Bernard Truffaut
St. Jean de la Ruelle, France

Etienne de Fay and the History of the Deaf

Summary • Résumé

When talking about the history of the Deaf in France we usually mention the name of a hearing person first: abbé de L'Epée. Why not start with a Deaf person: Etienne de Fay?

Born about 1669, he was educated in the abbey of Amiens where he stayed for the rest of his life, more than 70 years, and was named *the old deaf-and-dumb man* from Amiens. Etienne de Fay was fortunate to receive a good education in the abbey and to lead a life without material deprivation. He had social support and helpful patronage. But he was Deaf - like we are - and had to cope with the same difficulties as we have today. We should be proud of him, his life serves as an example: we can become responsible and independent through education.

Etienne de Fay was a skilful architect. When the abbey had to be reconstructed, the monks asked him to make the plans. It was a great success. We can still admire the buildings today in spite of destruction during wartime. Like the monks from Amiens in the past, hearing people of today should see in us our skills and not a handicap.

Etienne de Fay was also a teacher. He communicated very well through signs and educated several Deaf students using signs and writing. At the same time in France Pereire was teaching his own Deaf students to use speech. History has only preserved the name of Pereire and nearly forgotten Etienne de Fay. Thanks to Théophile Denis and his research on Deaf history, *the old deaf-and-dumb man* from Amiens was identified and is still remembered today.

The memory of history is very fragile. Achievements of the Deaf have often been neglected from ignorance and suppression that we all know so well. Therefore it is our task to save and take care of our historical heritage. The life of Etienne de Fay is closely connected to the history of the Deaf in France and we may grant him the honor of calling it the starting point.

En France, on a l'habitude de faire commencer l'histoire des Sourds avec l'abbé de L'Épée, une personne entendante. Pourquoi pas avec un sourd: Etienne de Fay?

Né vers 1669, il a été instruit dans une abbaye, à Amiens; il y est resté toute sa vie. Il était très habile à communiquer par signes. Il a vécu plus de 70 ans et on l'appellait le *vieux sourd-muet* d'Amiens. Etienne de Fay a eu de la chance d'être instruit, de vivre facilement et d'avoir un belle promotion sociale. Mais il était comme nous, sourd(e)s, avec les mêmes problèmes. Il nous laisse son exemple: par l'instruction, on devient autonome et responsable. Nous pouvons être fiers de lui.

C'était un bon architecte. Les moines d'Amiens l'ont chargé de faire les plans pour reconstruire leur abbaye. Ce fut une réussite. Les bâtiments, malgré les destructions de la guerre, sont encore visibles aujourd'hui. Comme les moines d'Amiens, les entendants doivent voir en nous, non le handicap, mais les aptitudes.

De Fay a été aussi professeur; il a enseigné plusieurs sourd(e)s en utilisant les signes et l'écriture. Mais à la même époque Pereire apprenait aux sourd(e)s à parler. L'Histoire a retenu le nom de Pereire et presque oublié celui d'Etienne de Fay. C'est une forme d'oppression, parmi les nombreuses que nous sourd(e)s, nous connaissons.

Le *vieux sourd-muet* d'Amiens a heureusement été identifié par Théophile Denis. Cela montre que notre histoire est fragile. Sauvegarder notre patrimoine doit être notre souci à toutes. L'histoire d'Etienne de Fay est étroitement liée à celle des sourd(e)s. Il mérite bien d'en être le point de départ.

The dawn of history

For the last ten or fifteen years, in France, there has been some discussion of the history of the Deaf when previously and for nearly two centuries, it was especially the history of Deaf people's education upon which attention and research was focused . In this earlier period, scholars were concerned with social history in general; that of Deaf people was of limited interest. Nevertheless, this marginalized history had a sociological aspect: the deaf community and its identity, its culture, its initiatives for the recognition of its rights, its artists and militants; and a linguistic aspect: the sign language and the vagaries of its acceptance, its analysis, its writing and its applications. Here was a great and rich field of study, which remained practically unexplored because of a lack of pioneers. However, the history of education couldn't take the liberty of neglecting these sociological and linguistic aspects. But education was the field reserved for hearing people, where they played the major role as inventors, theoreticians, practicioners and historians. So the history of Deaf education written by hearing people stood in for true Deaf history. Today we can say that the perspective has been corrected and the vision broadened, in France at least.

Every history has a beginning, the moment when the record of events takes shape thanks to the written tradition. Upstream from this point, is prehistory. When the history of the Deaf was that of their education, the curtain opened on the first teachers: Fray Pedro Ponce de León in Spain, the abbé de L'Epée and Pereire in France. Then where were the Deaf at the dawn of their intellectual emancipation, if not among the crowd? It's true that their social advancement depended on their education, and this couldn't be spontaneous. They needed, at the beginning, hearing educators. But does the history of a people begin with the arrival of the first colonizers and missionaries?

This is why, as our historical perspective has been corrected, I would like, with regard to France, to put the first milestone not at the advent of the abbé de L'Epée, in spite of all the credit we must grant him, but at the advent of a deaf person: Etienne de Fay. With him, the dawn breaks, announcing the day.

Biographic references

Many written testimonies allow us to describe with sufficient precision the life of this man who stands out as a guide.

We can determine his date of birth from a comment he made about his collection of coins and medallions. *I only learned about the medals two years ago, I will be 70 years old in 1739 (Il n'y a que deux ans que je scay ce que c'est que médailles et j'ay 70 ans en 1739;* De la Faye). Thus he would have been born in 1669. He was deaf from birth. We don't know

14

his family roots, but because of his handicap,when he was five years old, he was placed in the Abbey of Saint-Jean d'Amiens, run by the Prémontrés monks.

He was given a good basic education. By whom and how? We don't know. The Jesuit Father André, a well-known writer at that time, spoke of this

> *deaf-and-dumb scholar from Saint-Jean d'Amiens who, besides reading and writing, knew arithmetic, Euclidean geometry, mechanics, drawing, architecture, holy and profane history, especially of France.* (André 1766)

No doubt this basis allowed Etienne de Fay to continue to educate himself.

De Fay spent his whole life as a boarder in the abbey and contributed to the brothers his talents as architect, sculptor, librarian, procurator (25 years), and teacher for Deaf mute children. No testimony reports that he learned to speak. It is pointed out that he was *very skilful* (*très habile;* Cazeaux 1774) at communicating with signs. His pupils also expressed themselves with sign language.

The date of his death is unknown. Up to about 1745 ,when he was 76 years old, he taught Azy d'Etavigny. According to his contemporaries, such as Cazeaux, in 1746, he was called *the old deaf mute (vieux sourd-muet;* Cazeaux 1747). When, later on, the name Etienne de Fay disappeared in the oubliettes of time, this nickname remained.

Etienne de Fay's life is not a loose thread in the history of the Deaf. In 1746, the instruction of his pupil Azy d'Etavigny was taken over by Pereire. A fabric was begun, soon to be reinforced by the work of the abbé de L'Epée, work that has propagated to the present. Deaf people at the end of the 20th Century are thus connected, across three centuries, to our ancestor, this *old deaf mute* from Amiens. His life is exemplary of ours and we can identify with him. We propose, moreover, to examine some of his, in many ways, distinctive qualities.

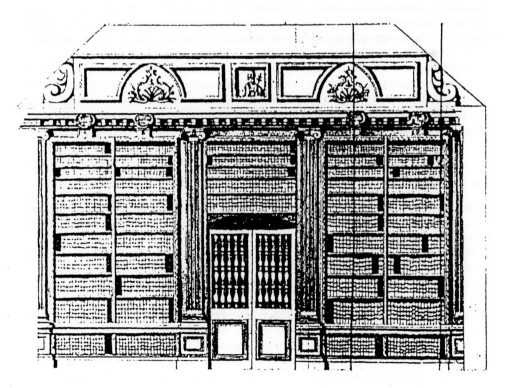

Ill. 1: *Library of the Abbey of St. Jean d'Amiens, drawing by Etienne de Fay*

Grass-roots or elite?

The history of the world of the Deaf is marked by a rift between the masses and the elite. Most certainly, this same rift is found in the hearing world, but in the Deaf world the phenomenon is more pronounced for several reasons: the members of this minority are less numerous; the choice of educational methods has stronger repercussions for them; a preferred mode of communication is imposed on them – sign language or speech – which is often reflected in a problem of cultural identity to such an extent that the elite, if they break away from Deaf people as a group, consciously or inconsciously deny themselves the right to be Deaf people.

What about Etienne de Fay? He embodies these contradictions. Descendend from a noble family, as we can see from his name *de Fay* or *de la Faye;* boarder in an abbey, a privileged situation, much better than that of most Deaf people of his time; having had the luck to find along the way a competent teacher to instruct him and enjoying ideal conditions in which to develop this instruction and so to reach positions of responsibility on his own and without any visible bonds with the deaf communitiy, he can rightly be considered among the elite.

But his life was also marked by the common destiny of the Deaf. Born deaf, separated from and perhaps rejected by his family because of his deafness, he surely lost a great part of the rights conferred by his name. He was deaf and mute, he used sign language with dexterity and employed it to educate his pupils, creating with them a linguistic mini-community. His communication with the outside world was undoubtedly limited, and he had interpreters among the members of the abbey. With these circumstances taken into account, we must place him as belonging completely in the deaf community.

In him the Deaf can not only recognize themselves but also find a model. If, at first, his intellectual awakening was dependent on others, afterwards, it was by his assiduous personal work that he achieved his erudition; so he mastered the hearing culture. He was the proof that instruction leads to autonomy: as the abbey's procurator, Etienne de Fay left the abbey to buy necessities and without doubt to bargain in writing, just as before him, in 17th century Toulouse, the Deaf Mute Guibal had done. His intellectual emancipation permitted him to reach positions of trust: he participated in the rebuilding of the abbey as an architect, he was employed as procurator, he furnished the library with *thousands of excellent books* (*milliers de livres excellents;* De la Faye n.d.). Socially handicapped, he proved that a Deaf Mute can reach the same level that hearing people can and can even go beyond it. Etienne de Fay, with his performance, is the pride of deaf people.

The architect

When the Prémontrés monks rebuilt a part of Saint-Jean d'Amiens Abbey in 1706, the plans of the new buildings were created by Etienne de Fay, who was *known as a skilled architect* (*réputation d'habile architecte;* Daire 1757).

At this point we must stop and take notice: hearing people appointed a Deaf Mute architect of a major building, and this in the 18th century! To give such a responsibility to a 'non-normal' person is a great mark of esteem and trust. With this act the Prémontrés showed a particular broadness of mind and solid judgement. They did not see only the handicap, but competence. Besides, they had known Etienne de Fay well for the thirty years that he had been living with them.

De Fay participated very closely in the construction of the new building. On the 8th of March 1712, Father Postel, the sub-prior, wrote in his diary: *This afternoon, Brother Claude, Monsieur de Fay and I went to the quarry on our lands, (…) and we have decided on the stones for the building* (Postel 1708–1733, pp. 4-5). In 1714, the construction was

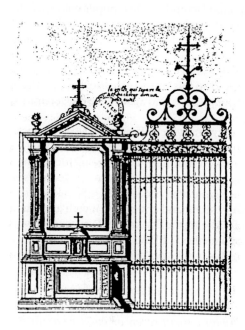

*Ill. 2: Pieces in the church of the Abbey de St. Jean d'Amiens,
drawings by Etienne de Fay*

almost ended. *The good architecture of this edifice is from Etienne de Fay*, said a chronicler
(*la bonne architecture de cet édifice est due à Etienne de Fay;* Daire 1757). And another: *a
superb house, built with the drawings and under the supervision of Etienne de Fay* (*Maison superbe, bâtie sur les dessins et par les soins d'Etienne de Fay;* Devermont 1783).

In 1718, the Bishop of Amiens visited the rebuilt abbey and expressed his admiration
saying, Father Postel writes,

> *that it was the most beautiful house in the town. He wanted to see Monsieur de Fay, our
> deaf mute boarder, to witness himself all of the good things he had heard about him:
> and after having seen his talent and capabilities he ought to say that we had a true miracle among us.*

The buildings of the abbey of St. Jean will last the centuries. During the second world war all
of the abbey but the walls was completely devastated by fire. Fortunately, the Amiens community restored it according to the original design. Therefore we can still admire Etienne de
Fay's architectural work.

These vestiges remind us of the lesson given by the Prémontrés in the 18th century to all
future generations. We must, as they say, allow the Deaf, from childhood, to fully develop
their abilities and, once they are skilled, we must have confidence in them. That is a question of perspective, a point of view that does not focus on handicap, but on the positive
aspects of the person. Success requires this. We hope that this message will be heard!

Oppression

The Deaf, throughout their history, have figured as an oppressed minority. Etienne de Fay's
destiny does not escape this rule.

The 18th century saw the growth of the education of the Deaf in France. Two methods
were established but over the course of time, one vied for ascendancy at the expense of the

other. The first method, represented by Pereire, aimed to endow Deaf pupils with speech—to change the Deaf Mutes into Deaf Speakers (and later, when the advances of medicine and technology would allow it, to let them hear), in order to bring them, as much as possible, nearer to the hearing model. The other method, personified by the abbé de L'Epée, was to accept the Deaf Mutes as they are, with the abilities they have, in particular the sign language which is their natural means of communication, and in this way to give them access to the dominant language and culture, that of hearing people. We find again here the separation between the elite and the mass.

Etienne de Fay used this second method, the only one which offers to the Deaf the possibility to be teachers and to shape their own destiniy. He taught Azy d'Etavigny in this way for seven years. D'Etavigny's parents, however, removed him from de Fay's instruction and placed him in the care of Pereire so that he might learn to speak. For at that time, a deaf person taught with signs was not so remarkable; but a Deaf Mute who had learned to speak was singular, all the more so since Pereire kept his method secret and enveloped it with an aura of mystery. For this reason Etienne de Fay, in spite of his being the first known Deaf teacher, was eclipsed by a more sensational rival. Thus did one method of Deaf education prevail for a time. Father Cazeaux, who introduced Pereire and his pupil Azy d'Etavigny to the *Académie Royale des Belles-Lettres* of Caen, said:

> *Monsieur d'Etavigny sent his son to Amiens to be taught with four or five other Mutes who were there, and who were directed by an old Deaf Mute who was very skilled at explaining himself in signs. The young Etavigny spent seven or eight years in this school; he learned to ask with signs for the things which are the most necessary to life.* (Cazeaux 1747)

The teacher's name is not mentioned and it is implied that the pupil learned practically nothing during these seven or eight years, which is hardly probable. No doubt this is disinformation, Cazeaux devaluating Etienne de Fay's work in order to exaggerate Pereire's achievements. Father André had spoken, as we have seen, of the *learned Deaf Mute from Saint-Jean d'Amiens (savant sourd-muet de Saint-Jean d'Amiens)*, and Cazeaux mentioned the *old Deaf Mute (vieux sourd-muet)*. For a long time, these two statements were the only testimonies concerning Etienne de Fay, whose name remained scarcely known. The Baron de Gérando, who published his work *De l'éducation des sourds-muets de naissance (On the Education of the congenitally Deaf Mute)* in 1827, the first thorough study of the history of the education of the Deaf, was content to accept these testimonies without verifying them and without seeking to know more.

Etienne de Fay, with his name, his life and his work passed on, became, as have many deaf people, lost and forgotten in history. He was indeed a member of a minority which has been oppressed in all eras.

Survival

The arbitrary judgement of many hearing people concerning the history of the Deaf – reminder of the difference between 'great' and 'little' history – involves unreliable initiatives on their part and, it follows, precarious conservation of written and iconographic archives. One of the most famous and saddest examples is the fate of the Musée Universel des Sourds-Muets at the Institut National des Jeunes Sourds in Paris. This rich and splendid memorial, created in 1889 by Théophile Denis, an official in the Ministry of the Interior who was responsible for deaf issues, was first settled in a spacious gallery with display windows, then was moved to a smaller room, then the collection was scattered in part to various locations and in part dismantled and stored in the basement.

It is the same Théophile Denis, open-minded and interested in all aspects of deaf people's lives, who first undertook research into the *old Deaf Mute from Amiens* about whom there was so little information and who brought his name and his biography up to date. In the archives at Amiens, he discovered:

– the chroniclers reports which attributed the architectural conception of Saint-Jean d'Amiens to *Etienne de Fay, deaf mute from birth, educated in the monastry since the age of five (Etienne de Fay, sourd-muet de naissance, élevé dans le monastère depuis l'âge de cinq ans;* Daire 1757);

– Father Postel's manuscript, called *A historical Diary written in the Abbey of Saint-Jean d'Amiens (Journal historique écrit dans l'abbaye de Saint-Jean d'Amiens)* about the period between 1708 and 1733 and citing often Etienne de Fay, as either architect or teacher of young Deaf Mutes;

– finally, a crucial document, two manuscripts of about 750 pages, covered with drawings by Etienne de Fay, sometimes annotated and representing façades of the Saint-Jean Abbey, the furniture in the church and the library and the riches of the abbey museum. A veritable illustrated catalog.

It almost came to pass that *the old Deaf Mute* from Amiens was forever anonymous, with a slim biography. What saved him from being completely forgotten were his architectural abilities, his passion for drawing, Father Postel's chronicle, Théophile Denis' curiosity

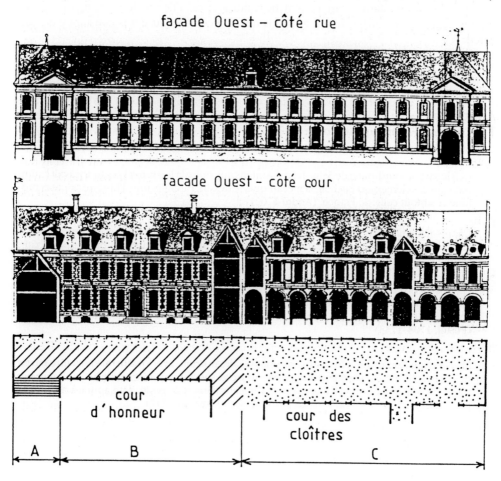

Ill. 3: *Views of the western façade of the abbey, drawings by Etienne de Fay*

and the concern of the town of Amiens to recover archives dispersed after the abbey was closed at the time of the Revolution.

Yes, the history of the Deaf is a very precarious thing for its sources are at risk since they are at the whim of individuals. The safeguard of the legacy of Deaf people ought to become among all people, Deaf and Hearing, an essential concern, following the example of Théophile Denis.

Conclusion

The history of the Deaf is no longer only that of their education or of their hearing teachers. It is the history of the Deaf people in its long march, with its hopes, its sufferings, its joys, its angers, its defeats and its victories. The history begins not with the abbé de L'Epée but with the deaf mute twins who, first, won him to their cause. Still earlier, Deaf history began with Azy d'Etavigny, driven from one educational method to another, Pereire's pupil, after having been Etienne de Fay's pupil. Before Etienne de Fay, the darkness is crossed by sparse fugitive gleams, such as Guibal's brief cometlike passage.

Therefore Etienne de Fay stands at the door of our history, around him his pupils: Jean-Baptiste des Lions, François Meunier, François Baudrant, Azy d'Etavigny. In him as in them, we can read the whole tragedy of the Deaf people, but we can also see its struggles and its triumphs. Deaf generations march down the centuries from Etienne de Fay to us, their faces serious, reaching towards a future which is never secure because it is constantly endangered.

Such is the History of the Deaf.

Appendix
The original French quotations:

p. 15
(…) le savant sourd-muet de Saint-Jean d'Amiens qui, outre la lecture et l'écriture, savait l'arithmétique, les éléments d'Euclide, la mécanique, le dessin, l'architecture, l'histoire sainte et profane et surtout celle de France. (André 1766)

p. 16
L'après-midi, nous avons été, le frère Claude, M. de Fay et moi, à notre carrière située sur nos terres au chemin de Beauvais, et nous sommes convenus de faire tirer des pierres pour bâtir. (Postel, 1708–1733, pp. 4-5)

p. 17
(…) disant que c'était la plus belle maison de la ville. Il a voulu voir M. de Fay, notre pensionnaire sourd-muet, pour être témoin de tout le bien qu'on lui en avait dit; et après avoir connu son mérite et sa capacité, il n'a pas feint de dire que nous avions chez nous un vray miracle. (Postel, 1708–1733)

p. 18
M. d'Etavigny envoya son fils à Amiens pour le faire instruire avec quatre ou cinq autre muets qui s'y trouvaient, et qui étaient dirigés par un vieux sourd-muet, très habile à s'expliquer par signes. Le jeune d'Etavigny a passé sept ou huit ans dans cette école; il y a appris à demander par signes les choses les plus nécessaires à la vie. (Cazeaux 1747)

Scenes from the life of Etienne de Fay
drawn by Bernard Truffaut for the *Cahiers de l'Histoire des Sourds*

Etienne de Fay is born around 1669.

At the age of 5 he enters the Abbey of St. Jean.

Etienne is given a good basic education.

After the age of 20, he continues to live at the Abbey.

Etienne teaches his Deaf pupils using signs.

Etienne works as an architect.

Etienne is a sculptor himself.

Going to the quarry.

In 1718, the Bishop of Amiens visits the Abbey
of St. Jean after its reconstruction.

The Bishop of Amiens communicates with
Etienne by means of an interpreter.

Between 1722 and 1727, father André goes to see Etienne de Fay.

Around 1738, Azy d'Etavigny enters the school of Etienne de Fay.

Etienne teaches Azy d'Etavigny for about eight years.

Around 1746, Azy d'Etavigny has to leave Etienne and receives speech lessons from Pereire.

Father Postel writes the historical Diary of the Abbey.

23

References

André, Père (1766): Discours ou divination sur la manière dont on peut apprendre à parler aux muets; in: *Œuvres complètes*, t.III.

Bézagu-Deluy, Maryse (1990): *L'abbé de L'Épée, instituteur gratuit des sourds et muets*. Paris: Seghers. (On de Fay, see pp. 141-143).

Bonnet, Philippe (1983): *Les Constructions de l'Ordre de Prémontré en France aux XVIIe et XVIIIe siècles*. Paris: Arts et Métiers Graphiques.

Borée, Père (n.d.): Le portrait historique de l'abbaye de Saint-Jean d'Amiens. B.M. de Laon, ms. (On de Fay, see 406bis).

Cazeaux, Père (1747): Discours à l'Académie royale des Belles-Lettres de Caen, le 22 novembre 1746; in: *Journal des Sçavans*, juillet 1747, p. 345.

Daire, P. (1757): *Histoire de la ville d'Amiens depuis son origine jusqu'à présent*. Paris. (On de Fay, see vol. 2, pp. 236-244).

De la Faye (n.d.): Description d'un cabinet et d'un médailler. B.M. d'Amiens, ms. 400, 2 vol. in 4°.

Denis, Théophile (1887): Le premier instituteur des sourds-muets en France; in: *Revue Française de l'Education des Sourds-Muets*, no. 10, janvier 1887, pp. 217-219; no. 11, février 1887, pp. 242-246.

Denis, Théophile (1893-1894): Etienne de Fay. Nouveaux renseignements sur cet Instituteur de Sourds-Muets; in: *Revue Française de l'Education des Sourds-Muets*, no. 6-7, décembre 1893; janvier 1894, pp. 137-141.

Denis, Théophile (1894): Etienne de Fay (IIIe article); in: *Revue Française de l'Education des Sourrds-Muets*, septembre-octobre 1894, pp. 124-128.

Denis, Théophile (1905-1907): Etienne de Fay, dit le 'Vieux Sourd-Muet d'Amiens'; in: *Bulletin mensuel de la Société d'histoire et d'Archéologie du Vimeu*. Vol. 1, 1905-1907, pp. 55-60 and 75-79.

Devermont (1783): *Voyage pittoresque ou notice exacte de tout ce qu'il y a d'intéressant dans la ville d'Amiens*. Amiens.

Dictionnaire de Biographie française, t.XIII, p. 882.

Dubar, Luc (1899): *Les derniers jours de l'Abbaye de Saint-Jean d'Amiens*. Amiens.

Dubois, Pierre (1910): *Le Lycée d'Amiens, esquisse historique*. Amiens. t.I.

Du Pré, Père Maurice (1899): *Annales de l'Abbaye de Saint-Jean d'Amiens (...)*. Amiens.

Duthoit, A. et L. (1874): *Le vieil Amiens dessiné d'après nature*. Amiens.

Gérando, Joseph-Marie de (1827): *De l'Education des Sourds-Muets de Naissance*. Paris, 2 vol. (On de Fay, see vol. 1, p. 400)

Goze, A. (1861): *Histoire des rues d'Amiens*. Amiens, vol. IV. (On de Fay, see p. 147)

Grenier, Dom (n.d.): *Mémoires historiques d'Amien*. B.N. coll. Picardie, t.II. (On de Fay, see pp.137 sq.).

Pagès, Jean (1856): *Manuscrits de Pagès, marchand d'Amiens, écrits à la fin du XVIIe et au commencement du XVIIIe siècle sur Amiens et la Picardie*. Amiens. (On de Fay, see vol. 1, pp. 205-216)

Postel, Père (1708-1733): Journal historique écrit dans l'abbaye de Saint-Jean d'Amiens (1708–1733). B.M. d'Amiens (Ms 532). 5 vol.

Roy, Paule (1983): *Chronique des rues d'Amiens*. t.7, Amiens: C.R.D.P., vol. 2.

Samson, C. (1978): *Présence prémontrée en Picardie*. Amiens.

Sartre, Josiane (1972): L'architecture de l'Abbaye de Saint-Jean d'Amiens; in *Bulletin de la Société des Antiquaires de Picardie*, 3e trim., pp.396–405.

Séguin, Edouard (1874): *Jacob-Rodrigues Pereire*. Paris. (On de Fay, see pp. 244-247)

Truffaut, Bernard: *Cahiers de l'Histoire des Sourds*. 1/1989 sq.

Maryse Bézagu-Deluy
Ivry-sur-Seine, France

Personalities in the World of Deaf Mutes in 18th Century Paris

Summary • Résumé

Personalities in the World of Deaf Mutes in 18th Century Paris presents profiles of significant Deaf personalities from a time when their world was emerging from its prehistory. Elements of a new situation were being defined: reflections about the status of the Deaf had increased, changes in their social and personal perspectives had become possible. The abbé de L'Epée opened France's first free public school at his home in Paris. He contributed to the recognition of sign language as a natural language and of the Deaf as citizens equal to all others.
The Meusnier brothers were sons of a bourgeois with strong ties to the court of the French King. Claude-André Deseine, son of an artisan carpenter, became a recognized artist. Pierre Desloges, the bookbinder, came to Paris and published a book which is essential to a history of the Deaf. All of these figures played significant roles in their times. They were men of character, remarkable men; passionate personalities - a bridge between us and the other Deaf of their century: those who were unknown, nameless, locked away in hospitals. These men can serve as examples to us. The Meusnier brothers were minors, banned and cloistered; we are left with only what others have to say about them. Claude-André Deseine and Pierre Desloges – a generation after the Meusniers – spoke, in diverse forms, for themselves. Their lives and works show that they were active in the life of their times and in the French Revolution.

L'article présente les portraits-caractères de quelques-unes des personnalités fortes ou particulièrement significatives du monde des sourd(e)s au moment où ce monde sort de sa préhistoire; au moment où se mettent en place les éléments d'une situation nouvelle; des réflexions s'élaborent sur le statut des personnes sourdes, un changement s'amorce dans leurs perspectives sociales et leur vie personnelle: l'abbé de L'Epée ouvre pour elles la première école publique et gratuite française, chez lui, à Paris. Il contribue à ce que la langue des signes soit reconnue comme langue à part entière, à ce que les sourd(e)s soient reconnu(e)s comme des citoyen(ne)s à part entière.
Les frères Meusnier sont les fils d'un bourgeois bien placé à la cour du roi de France. Claude-André Deseine, fils d'un artisan menuisier, devient un artiste connu. Pierre Desloges, relieur, 'monte' à Paris et publie un livre qui fait date. Chacun d'eux a joué durant cette période, directement ou indirectement, un rôle non négligeable.
Ils furent des hommes de caractère, des hommes hauts en couleurs; des individualités passionnantes; un pont comme jeté entre nous et ces autres sourd(e)s de leur siècle – des inconnu(e)s, sans nom, enfermé(e)s à l'hôpital. Ils ont une valeur d'exemple. Les deux premiers, les frères Meusnier, sont mineurs, interdits et cloîtrés; on ne sait d'eux que ce que les autres en disent. Les deux derniers, Claude–André Deseine et Pierre Desloges, d'âge à être leurs fils, prennent – sous diverses formes – la parole eux-mêmes. Leur vie, leurs oeuvres, témoignent qu'ils sont partie prenante dans l'histoire du siècle et de la Révolution française.

I Introduction

'In homage to the Unknown Deaf Mute': such should be, one day, the formula inscribed on a tombstone for all unknown Deaf Mutes,[1] those who were lost in the night of time, abandoned to the original terror of difference. In the same manner, the Tomb for the Unknown Soldier in Paris is a symbolic homage to the dead in all wars. For, up until recent times, the heros in the history of the Deaf and Dumb were the forgotten ones: women and men, children and adolescents deprived of hearing, destined to an early death on the straw of villages and on the cobblestones of cities. They were most often homeless and in need, in pain and suffering. Exhausted and at loose ends, they were reduced to begging and charity, abandoned to misery and poverty, subject to distress and imprisonment, self-imprisoned in a charity home or asylum. Each and every one, unimportant, little people, as we say, who may have known happiness and *joie-de-vivre*, but who, most often, once they escaped extreme poverty, lived a life of need in menial conditions, distraught and humiliated.

They were not the sons and daughters of those in power nor children of the wealthy, nor of those who had their hands full and knew how to keep them that way. Until the second half of the 18th century when a new situation surfaced, they were less than nothing: the dust of pathways... They have no names.

The formula used by hospitals to register the Deaf can serve as a graphic illustration of the exclusion the deaf were subject to: 'a deaf mute whose name is unknown'. Other 'little people' among those who speak and hear did not know how to read or write (they were numerous); yet they had names and could almost always say them. For Deaf 'little people' there is nothing left, nothing that could constitute a memory, nothing recorded, engraved or imprinted. Nothing or almost nothing. It is only by escaping shortage and need, only when the family could offer some guarantee of survival that the Deaf-and-Dumb child came into a story which can be told, which one can seek in archives, or on the shelves of notaries, in sheaves and piles of paper. The characters whose lives I will recount are relatively privileged children: sons of the bourgeoisie, artisans or gentry, newly wealthy and recognized, or even children from the families of prosperous workers. The Meusnier brothers, Claude-André Deseine, Pierre Desloges - among those who have left behind traces – were gifted with remarkable destinies over a period of a few remarkable decades when pedagogical, ideological and social conditions were established to help bring about significant changes in the lives and futures of the Deaf and Dumb.

II The Meusnier brothers
History of an inheritance

The father of the Meusnier brothers, François Meusnier, was born in 1675. He became Usher to the King's chamber in 1702 (the position was purchased by his mother). As holder of this position, he thus became a squire. He was married in 1705. Four years later, in 1709, Louis XIV went into mourning: his second cousin Emmanuel Philibert Amédée de Savoie, Prince of Carignan, a famous Deaf Mute of the times, had just died; and François Meusnier's wife Louise Jouan gave birth to a son: our François Meusnier. Four years later, in 1713, a second son was born into the Meusnier family: he too was named François. In 1715, the king granted the father a royal warrant which was increased the following year. In 1723, another royal warrant was granted to the two children, then aged fourteen and ten respectively: this was the first official

---

1 For the purposes of this essay I will use the terms 'Deaf and Dumb' and 'Deaf Mute'. They were the terms most frequently employed in the 18th century. – I allow myself here to refer the reader to my book (Bézagu-Deluy 1990); one can find therein the stories of many who defined the terms of this epoch.

mention of the Meusnier brothers (to our knowledge). They were designated: *two sons born deaf and dumb (deux fils nés sourds et muets;* Archives nationales: O^1 67 fol. 227).

Traces of the Meusnier brothers can be picked up again in 1728 in Amiens at the Abbey of St. Jean. Their teacher was the architect and draftsman Etienne de Fay: he too was Deaf and Dumb. On the 19th of June of the same year, the eldest François was designated as the bell godfather, in appreciation of his studious conduct.

Three daughters were born into the Meusnier family after the two sons: they were not deaf and dumb. In 1733, the eldest of the daughters, Marie-Louise, was married. Her husband shared her father's title. Ten years later, in 1743, another royal warrant was drafted for Sieur Meusnier's two sons. As early as April,1745 the father hand-drafted a last will and testament. His second will, written in 1748, contains more details than the first. (Archives nationales: Y 56 fol. 120 et 121)

On March 25th, 1749, François Meusnier (the father) died. The eldest son François was forty years old, the younger François, Sieur de Baudran, was thirty-six. All we know about them up to the year 1749 is indistinguishable from many other handicapped children of families belonging to the same class. The particularities and contour of the Meusnier last will and testament allow us to continue our story.

Though the Meusnier brothers were in mourning (each wore vestments of black wool; mourners-strips of thin white linen fabric around the collar and cuffs of their clothes; jackets severely buttoned-up; full-body overcoats draped over their shoulders; black mourning crêpe hanging off the brim of their hats...), we do not know if they took part in their father's funeral. On the burial register at the Saint-Louis Cathedral where the ceremony took place there were four signatures: those of a son-in-law, a brother-in-law, a gentleman in the queen's service and the priest of the king's chapel (Archives des Yvelines: 5 MI 191). The obligatory signature of the presiding priest was also present. There is no trace of the brothers, though custom would have necessitated their signatures.

The day following the burial, one of the notaries of Versailles, where the father had died, went to the Rue de Satory, near the château, to the house where the Meusnier family lived. The widow handed him two hand-written pages on notarized paper: the last will and testament. The father disposed of his possessions, and wished – he insisted – that the peace which had until then reigned in his family be preserved. To this point came a very fatherly recommendation: *I wish my two sons and my three daughters to live together in peace and union and submission to their mother.* Then came his last wishes, expressed in precise terms without useless details:

> *I want and demand, that François Meusnier the eldest of my sons, and François Meusnier de Baudran, the youngest, also my son, be entitled to inherit only their legitimate due. I have reduced these claims to the possessions which belong to me at the time of my decease. In addition, I bequeath to my two sons all that my wife their mother shall decide to give them from my wardrobe and my weapons (...).* (Archives nationales: Y 56 fol. 120-121; Minutier central des notaires de Paris: Etude II, liasse 524)

The two brothers were thus entitled to inherit only half of what they would have received without a will. Why? This was not an example of paternal anger being exercised upon unworthy sons: the personal possessions that were left – clothes and weapons – attest to an obvious tenderness. The two youngest daughters, Marie Magdeleine and Marie-Jeanne, each inherited half of the remaining possessions (the eldest daughter had already received her share in the form of the function her husband shared with Sieur Meusnier). But Marie-Jeanne only had access to the usufruct of the bequeathed capital; only her children – were she to marry – could inherit the property; if she were to die without children she could not bequeath her inheritance with a testament of her own; her possessions would go to her sisters or to their yet-to-be born children.

All of this is clear, straight to the point, with neither justification nor explanation. Not once is there mention of the children – already born or not – of the Meusnier sons. They were deaf, they were mute, they were kept apart.

A mute usher?

François Meusnier (the father) was without doubt always a man of order. His parchments and papers were carefully arranged in his bedroom on the second floor of the house he rented: all that gave meaning and value to his life, namely his position and his title.

Meusnier was a commoner, son of a bourgeois gentleman from Orléans, but on the fringe of the nobility. He was bourgeois but of noble appearances – which is confirmed by his dress in the accomplishment of his employment at the court: he stood before the doors to the King's chambers, bearing a sword. He preceded the King to church, walked alongside the Constable, dressed in white satin and royal apparel. His place was marked for all ceremonies and feasts.

He wanted to see his sons pursue his career in the same manner. No doubt he wished this before his sons were even born. One need only look at how carefully he preserved the different letters patent from Kings Henry IV, Louis XIII, Louis XIV which confirmed his title of Squire, employed as Usher to the King's Court, a title that also belonged to his children. François the eldest, and François the youngest, however deaf and mute they may have been, thus held the title of Squire. They had the right, as did their father, to wear a sword. They shared this privilege with the sons of nobles. Yet while they could wear a sword, and they did, they could not assume the role of usher: could one imagine a mute usher? The gesticulations of the mutes of the Seraglio were but clowning for theater plays in need of gross misunderstanding; moreover, these mutes were not even deaf: their tongues were cut out! So the Meusnier brothers were not ushers. No one so much as considered the idea. Despite their ages, their father was legally responsible for them. The law considered them incapable of managing their possessions and of caring for their persons. Their father exercised the same paternal authority over them as he would have exercised over minors.

The position of court usher remained in the family. It served as the dowry of the eldest daughter. The title and the sword were left to the Meusnier sons: this is largely the staging of appearances, the staging of illusion (even if this formal aspect is not without psychological importance).

The sons were not only deemed incapable of holding the position of their father, with them the family lineage was interrupted. Did the father ever show them his marriage contract – some ten pages tied by a now faded blue ribbon? The Meusnier sons would have read three signatures: Louis, signature of his Majesty Louis XIV; Louis, signature of Monsignor the Dauphin, son of the king; Louis, signature of the eldest son of the Dauphin, grandson of the king.

Three Christian names for a dynasty.

François-the-father, François-the-elder, François-the-younger, a dynasty perhaps, though bourgeois? No. For the question of a family lineage was settled. The Deaf did not marry. Their deafness condemned them to a childless life.

Yet the Meusnier sons were not left without resources. Their father, in addition to his own income, had acquired substantial *assurances* (Archives nationales: O^1 59 fol. 94 O^1 60 fol. 89) for them. After the death of Louis XIV, the Regent accorded a supplementary pension to the father for the care of his sons. Louis XV, upon his ascension to the throne, manifested this agreement:

(...) April the 8th, 1723 (...) Sieur Meusnier (...) suffering the ill fortune of having two deaf and dumb sons, has already been favored by his majesty to receive 500 pounds in annual gratification for their subsistence. As they are already of an age which demands that he

supervise their conduct and unable to do this himself because of the service he owes to the king(...) Sieur Meusnier has begged the court to have compassion for such an affliction and to kindly augment his pension so that he may place his two sons in a religious community, where they may receive care suitable to their condition (...). (Archives nationales: O[1] 67 fol. 227)

The royal favor was granted in 1723, as soon as the young king became an adult. Such was the law: the kings of France were adults at the age of fourteen years. The king's subjects were theoretically adults at the age of twenty-five years. The deaf and dumb were never adults. They had a father, then at his death, a tutor and guardian who managed their possessions and supervised their persons. The Meusnier brothers would most likely never leave the religious communities they lived in – first in Amiens, then in Orléans. At the Abbey of Saint-Jean in Amiens, they learned how to read and write. They studied, as everywhere, the catechism, and all that one usually studied at boarding schools. Their teacher, Etienne de Fay, himself Deaf, taught them in sign language.

Saint-Jean was an exceptional though peculiar school: the grounds were enclosed and the main structure was a cloister. It probably was the only school of the time known in France to have Deaf and Dumb students. The school was private and costly.

The Meusnier sons were receiving a royal pension. They would also inherit a part of their father's belongings (a part deliberately reduced by the father in order to care for the two youngest daughters who could both hear and speak). They were assured of living without financial difficulties. They were granted this privilege. But, given this privilege, the injustice inflicted upon them by the law appeared all the greater.

The inheritance procedures began (lasting a year and a half which was long even for the time): judgements and sentences in Paris and in Versailles, pages on top of pages, signed by judges, attorneys, etc. – the framework of an omnipresent judicial power structure. Behind the writings, between the lines, traces of the brothers can be found: outside of the family as if excluded from it, yet still a part of it, despite everything. They were not given the chance to testify on their own behalf, nor to respond to the situation imposed upon them (Minutier central des notaires de Paris: Etude II, liasses 523, 524, 526). Thousands of lines were accumulated by the clerks – rigorous scribes of sacrosanct language – which assigned a kind of existence to the Meusnier brothers, lines from which their lives surge forth, 'fragments' of their lives. Paradoxically, it is because of this staged judicial process that we can see into their lives, that we can learn something about them which only the archives can shed light upon.

Minors, absent, and banned?

The Meusnier brothers were assigned a tutor and a guardian. The law was the same – however unjust and outrageous it may appear to us today – for minors, the insane, the demented ... and other persons. The Deaf and Dumb were 'other persons'. They were in need of a tutor and a guardian. The nominations for this position necessitated a judicial decision. A judge would convoke a precise number of relatives and friends to seek their advice. In the present case, eight persons were called to the Versailles bailiwick (which was also a prison): the mother – the only woman and guardian to be – a maternal uncle (court usher), other ushers, a guard at the archives, a parliamentary advocate, a dashing cavalier, a member of the Household Cavalry, tutor to be.

Other decisions followed in Paris and Versailles, always in the absence of the Meusnier brothers, always before a judge and notaries. The brothers were referred to as 'deaf and dumb'. The Meusnier children – the two brothers and the youngest daughter, who needed a tutor on account of her minority – were categorized under the succinct formula: *children: minors, absent and banned (les enfants: mineurs, absents et interdits;* Minutier central des notaires de Paris: Etude II, liasses 523, 524, 526).

Curiously, we can find no trace of an official ban of the Meusnier sons. They were banned, in effect, since they had no legal rights of their own. But no written document established the ban. To have been banned, they would have had to appear in person before the judge. The Meusnier relatives, it seems, did not ask that they be banned. Was it because the brothers knew how to read and write, and had received an education? Was it because their deaf and dumb condition kept them so resolutely apart that there was no need to ban them?

The nuance was taken into consideration by the law: a person whose simple-mindedness approached imbecility yet who was not so slow as to be classified with the insane and the demented... such a person was not to be banned. Such persons suffered a diminution which did not absolutely make them unable to distinguish good from evil.

The Meusnier brothers could, no doubt, distinguish good from evil. Opinions of relatives and friends, sanctions, sentences, diverse judicial procedures, statements deposited with notaries – it all goes on and on – attest to this fact (Minutier central des notaires de Paris: Etude II, liasse 523).

And these procedures, which were meant to resolve the problem of assigning to the Meusnier brothers their rightful possessions – were, in fact, asking essential questions of their being, of who they were. Minors, absent and banned, in effect, they would never become the subjects of their own history. It was always others who would determine the main directions of their lives.

They received their father's legacy (their tutor did) in 1750. One can safely guess that they also received what was left of their father's wardrobe. And a derisory list that was: 5 suits, 10 jackets, a bathrobe, an overcoat, a frock coat, 6 knickers, and court clothing – all to live in a cloister? A form of compensation to fill up a closet...

Though of the same generation as Jacob Rodriguez Pereire and the abbé de L'Epée, nothing leads us to believe that the Meusnier brothers benefited from these men's teachings. Perhaps they met in passing one day? In 1749, Jacob Rodriguez Pereire gave a lecture on the deaf and dumb at the French Academy of Science in Paris. He presented one of his Deaf students to demonstrate his principles: push the deaf and dumb to speak like everybody else, then, instruct them. It would be another few years before Charles Michel de L'Epée would meet the two Deaf sisters who would inspire him to pursue the distinguished career he had as a teacher.

The children the Meusnier brothers might have had (we lose trace of them after the inheritance story) could have become the abbé de L'Epée's students on the Rue des Moulins where new clothes were laid out for Deaf children in the 1760s – whether or not they happened to be the children of squires.

III Claude-André Deseine
The banned sculptor

Claude-André Deseine's father, Louis-André, was, to the best of our knowledge, born in Paris (birthdate uncertain). He was a carpenter. His father was a carpenter. His brother became a carpenter. A kind of dynasty. A dynasty of carpenters, a family of artisans. In 1738, Louis-André married the daughter of a locksmith, Marie Madeleine Potier. Artisans in the neighborhood which has become a part of the 2nd and 3rd districts of Paris were not uncommon.

Two years after their marriage on the 12th of April, 1740 the hero of our narrative was born. He was the first – perhaps – of the fifteen to eighteen children born into the Deseine family. The father was not a simple worker. We can find traces of the respect and authority he wielded in the community of carpenters in Paris. This fact attests to a certain social standing, however relative it may have been. The Deseine father was an artisan, but he was also a

par deseine, bonaffe, sourd-muet

Ill. 1: *Claude-André Deseine – self-portrait*

bourgeois. At his death on the 29th of April, 1777, he had possessions, including a house in the neighborhood where he lived.

In the year of his death, only six of the fifteen to eighteen Deseine children were still living: three boys and three girls. The girls were minors, aged 17, 18, and 20 years. The youngest of the sons, Louis-Pierre, was 28 – a sculptor. Louis-Etienne, 36, was an architect who won the Grand Prize of Rome in 1777. The eldest son, Claude-André was 37. All that was known about him then was his age and that he was deaf and dumb from birth. It is interesting to note another form of social and cultural standing due to the three sons' roles as 'artists'.

The father's death led to the bequeathing of his property; an inventory had to be drawn of his belongings, which would then be left to the widow and their six children. It was also necessary to take care of a particular case: the deaf and dumb son. The family followed procedures to establish an official certificate which designated Claude-André as 'deaf and dumb from birth'. An official certificate, which is to say, in accordance with the laws of the time, a judicial certificate. A meeting was set with the magistrate.

The staging of an engagement

On the 16th of May, 1777, a little over two weeks after the death of the father, Claude-André Deseine, accompanied by about ten people, went to the Châtelet de Paris, the most

31

important, the most celebrated of the capital's courts. The building was an old fortified castle situated on the present day site of Châtelet square. The imposing locale housed a morgue, prison cells, and courtrooms. The edifice was sinister. Sight and smell were more than enough to know that the neighboring streets and alleys were equally detestable, equally lamentable. Here the throats of cattle and sheep were slit, and there was a large fish market nearby. The cries and insults, bellows and moans did nothing to improve the atmosphere.

The small group surrounding Claude-André turned its back on the Rue Saint-Denis and hurriedly, though with caution, wound its way through the puddles of blood and wastes of all kinds littering their path. They headed toward the right wing of the Châtelet. The civil lieutenant was there, waiting in his 'council chamber', the judge's chambers. He, Judge François Angran D'Alleray, was in fact the veritable head of Châtelet, a person of the utmost importance: he was the man in the red robe, a well-known man, from a 'good' family – nobles for 150 years! – with a strong reputation, respected for his uprightness and education. A prosecutor and three councilors were in the chamber with him.

Claude-André knew why he was in the judge's chamber. He had for a long time been *adult, but deaf and mute from birth (majeur, mais sourd et muet de naissance)* as Judge D'Alleray had inscribed on the register, to which he added: *It is necessary to make a decision relative to the state of Claude Deseine* (Archives nationales: Y 5029 B). The presence of family had no other meaning but to offer their advice as to the type of decision to be made. Claude-André's mother was there, his two brothers, four uncles, two cousins, and a friend of the family. Each stated her or his family name, first name, and trade. Carpenters, locksmiths, a tailor, and haberdashers. Claude-André's two brothers were 'artists' as opposed to artisans. The man in the red robe made each of them take an oath: they were to state their opinion from the bottom of his soul and conscience. He transcribed the resulting decision in the customary terms: '(those present) *are unanimously in favor of the ban of Sieur Claude Deseine, deaf and dumb from birth, as being incapable of managing and administrating his person and possessions* (Archives nationales: Y 5029 B). The mother was proposed as guardian and one of the uncles, Claude-André's godfather, a carpenter, as tutor. Upon the advice, then, of what today might be referred to as a family council, it was proposed :

1) the ban of Claude-André, given his condition of deafness and muteness;
2) the names of those who would manage the ban.

The hearing

The man in the red robe then addressed himself directly to Claude-André and transcribed what he could of this singular dialogue:

> *Claude Deseine, deaf and dumb, whom we have brought into our cabinet (...) accompanied by his mother, and to whom we addressed several questions responded with gestures to make apparent that he could not hear, and perceived that we were speaking to him only by the movement of our lips. He then made conspicuous efforts to articulate sounds but was unable to proffer any speech, though he managed to indicate by gestures that he could neither hear, nor talk, nor write (...).* (Archives nationales: Y 5029 B)

François Angran, the man in red, did not doubt having understood. But he was in the process of accomplishing an unfamiliar job: translation. Therein resides one of the most interesting points of this document: it was a new type of translation; he was transcribing that which was said to him in sign language – a language which had, until then, been scarcely recognized as language by hearing people.[2]

---

2   In 1991, two hundred years later, in France, no law (despite several proposals) has been drafted that officially recognizes what is now called French Sign Language (Langue des Signes Française, L.S.F).

Judge François Angran translated the signs made by Claude-André: his minutes were a written report of the oral interviews he held with all those present at the time. All. He asked questions; Claude-André followed the movement of his lips; between one and the other communication was established. However brief or fragile and insufficient, it was nevertheless communication.

When reading the rendered judgement, one can ask if the communication between the two men (two mature men, the 61-year-old judge could have been the father of the 37-year-old deaf mute)... one can ask if the exchange was not subtler than it first appears. François Angran could have limited himself to remarking that:

1. Claude-André was deaf;   2. he was mute;
3. he did not write;   4. he did not read;
5. thus he was incapable of managing his possessions and his person.

The judge drew his conclusions: he – as did the assembled family members – favored the ban and the naming of the proposed guardian and tutor.[3] He did just that.

But the case was far from being closed.

A clear note

And here is what gives, all of a sudden, a new turn to the case: there was a short note (clearly written!) that followed the announcement of the ban. A note of apparently no importance, on a separate piece of paper, which no one thought worthy or indispensable, or even useful to read and attach to the sentence. A separate piece of paper that could have been lost, but one that was not lost. A few words on paper as if to give time for reflection, for hesitation: the only manifest traces found today – two centuries later – of a moment of indecision before the definitive drafting of the sentence. One can see in this exceptional document that before having written *he does not know how to read or write (il ne sçait lire ni écrire)*, the word *cannot (ne peut)* was written then struck by the judge. He does not know how to read or write, 'he cannot read or write', neither formula nor meaning are the same. Can(not), know how to? The choice is not as easy as it seems. The man in red wrote, *He does not know how.* Which meant, in the judge's opinion, that although Claude-André did not know how to read or write, he had the ability to know how (he could come to know how, he could attain the knowledge of reading and writing if someone taught him, if he learned) despite the fact that he was deaf and mute.

This glance at a small note calls for a remark, a point of history, which is not without relationship to our subject. Exactly ten days before the hearing – the 6th of May, 1777, during one of his visits to Paris, the Austrian Emperor, Joseph II, brother-in-law of King Louis XV, paid a visit to the abbé de L'Epée and his Deaf students on the Rue des Moulins, home and teaching site – in the words of the abbé de L'Epée himself – of the first *free teacher of the deaf and mute (instituteur gratuit des sourds et muets;* L'Epée, 8 août 1779 (ms dedication, see Bézagu-Deluy 1990, p. 183 and ill.) and repeatedly). A visit which was widely discussed, if one can put it that way: deaf mutes from birth who could talk and make themselves heard, and who could thus be educated. Paris rediscovered the school thanks to this imperial visit. Rediscovered is the word ... because Paris already knew or could have known for at least six years, when the abbé had begun inviting people to view 'public exercises' by his Deaf students in order to tirelessly demonstrate that they, as much as other children, adolescents or adults, could be educated.

This aside throws light on the period and climate in which the judge wrote his decision

---

3   Claude Deseine – Claude-André Deseine's paternal uncle and godfather – was named tutor. As we can see, it was not yet the youngest of the brothers – Louis-Pierre Deseine – who was named tutor, as the biographer of the brothers, Georges Le Chatelier, wrongly states (1903, p. 49) – and as I had thought before finding and reading the document of the 'ban'.

and worked over the rough draft. We can see that what gave the 'ban' a new definition was the recommendation, the actual term used, of taking into account the *intentions (ses intentions)* and the personal *will (sa volonté)* of Claude-André, deaf mute.

In effect, it was suggested that the mother (his legal guardian) employ the banned one's (Claude-André) revenues *(...) in accordance with the intentions of the banned one, insofar as he can make them known: even to give him sums from his revenue to dispose of as he wishes (...)* (Archives nationales: Y 5029 B).

Claude-André, the banned one, was thus recognized as having the right to possess and exercise a personal will. That is no little acquisition. Something, one can see it, and the relationship to the activities of the abbé de L'Epée accentuate it, was in the process of changing. A place for liberty was opened, including the new interpretation of what a ban meant when applied to a person who was deaf and mute from birth. Claude-André Deseine did and could manifest his intentions and his personal will. He was judged incapable of managing his possessions, but capable of – and authorized to dispose of his income.

Something happened between Deseine and Angran; something that attenuated – above and beyond the words and signs exchanged – the violence of the law. From the sturdy and adult man facing him, the man in the red robe seized something of his person, of his being, of his presence in the world.

Thirty-seven years after his birth, the ban, with its particular character, was for Claude-André a kind of second baptism. The same actors were present: the father, now dead but present by virtue of his wishes and the terms of his inheritance; the mother, who, as was often the case, was designated his guardian; the godfather, the uncle Claude Deseine, carpenter, who held his godson during the baptismal ceremony and who was designated his tutor. The godmother was the only one absent, she was his maternal grandmother, but eight of her grandchildren were there in her stead!

Let us now take another detour to shed light upon the situation. We do not know if, in 1777, Claude-André was already a student of de L'Epée (who accepted both young and adult students). Though we know for certain that he was at one time a student, we do not know when he first started attending courses. We know only that he dated the bust he made of his *instituteur* in 1786.

Another detail for our narrative underlines the convergences in and the progress of the times: the same François Angran, the man with the red robe who 'banned' Claude-André in May, 1777, made the abbé de L'Epée take an oath six months later: to rightfully and faithfully exercise the role of interpreter for the minor Joseph. This minor Joseph, one of the abbé's deaf mute students, would become the hero of a case that had just begun and which would last for years, the celebrated 'Solar Case'.[4] And the language for which de L'Epée became interpreter, the language he had to translate, was sign language.

Whatever he must have felt at the time, Claude-André was not about to forget the date of May 16th, 1777. It is also a date which is important for our story: it is around this time that Claude-André began leaving traces of his existence, of his existence and of his activities, of his activities and their artistic character.

We know that in 1778 Claude-André was a student at the Royal Academy of painting and sculpture in Paris (Le Chatelier 1903, p. 49). His great-great-nephew, who is also his biographer, proves this to us. Claude-André was a student of Pajou, as was his brother Louis-Pierre. That year he was awarded the 'third medal' as a sculptor, in recognition of his work, while his brother, 29-year-old Louis-Pierre, won a 'grand prize'.[5]

---

4 'Joseph' was abandoned on the side of a road. He seemed to be, for a number of reasons, the son of Count Solar. The abbé de L'Epée began a judicial procedure to give back the rights and name to the young man (who was fifteen in 1777). The trial, in many episodes, is one of the century's most important ones.

5 Louis-Pierre was not yet, as we have noted, his tutor.

In June of 1782, Claude-André exhibited five works at the Salon de la Correspondance on the Rue Saint-André des Arts, a salon where artists who were not members of the Royal Academy could exhibit. We also know that between 1782 and 1785 he made busts of the Baron of Besenval, the Viscount of Ségur, the Count of Argental, and the Duke of Richelieu, which were, no doubt, private commissions.

Thus, he was from then on recognized as an 'artist'. 'Artist' or 'artisan', the difference between the two then was not as clearly marked as today. His social status remained ambiguous. Sculptors and carpenters, artists and artisans both formed communities (called 'corporations' at the time). Produce and sell: their purpose was a common one.

Jacobin encouragement

1789 is the year of the French Revolution. In 1791, fourteen years had passed since the banning of Claude-André Deseine. He was fifty-one years old. He began a series of busts which expressed his sympathy toward the revolutionary cause (whereas his younger brother, Louis-Pierre, was a quasi-official sculptor for the Prince of Condé and was received into the Royal Academy in March of that year; he was an affirmed Royalist). 1791 was also a great year in the career of the sculptor Claude-André. A contest[6] was organized by the Jacobin Society: its purpose was to place a marble bust of Mirabeau (who died on April 2nd, 1791) in the meeting hall of the Society.

There were four contestants. One of them was Claude-André Deseine. Another, already celebrated at the time, was Houdon. Claude-André had to speak in public – if we can put it that way – for the first time. And it was not a matter here of a public of enlightened amateurs who frequented the Salon de la Correspondance, or of aristocrats who did him the favor of commissioning a bust! The public address was to take place before the representatives of the National Assembly (Mirabeau's day of death had become a national holiday).

An entire delegation expressed its support of Claude-André. It was announced in the press that Claude-André had taken a cast of Mirabeau's face:

> *The famous Mr. Houdon is not the only sculptor to have taken a cast for the bust of de Mirabeau. Sieur Deseine, figurist sculptor, deaf mute, known for his talent, also merits a place in your papers. On the 2nd of April, a day of mourning for all of France, a deputation (...) went to the house of (...) one of the executor-testators of the deceased to obtain permission for Sieur Deseine to take a cast of this great man (...) signed: Corbin, a citizen member of the delegation.* (Corbin 1791)

Since Claude-André could not talk, others talked for him; they were his 'interpreters'.

On the 14th of May, 1791, Claude-André appeared before the National Assembly to offer a plaster-of-Paris copy of Mirabeau's bust. The other three candidates did the same. On the 30th of July, he offered a second bust to the same Assembly: that of his *instituteur*, the abbé de L'Epée, who had died in December of 1789 and who had been proclaimed *Benefactor of humanity and of the Nation (Bienfaiteur de l'humanité et de la Patrie)* by the National Assembly. This bust was a copy of his original, and was accompanied by a protest against a fraudulent copy of his bust, which was claimed to have been done by a certain Abert, mirror cutter.

The Assembly conferred honors upon him. No doubt he could not, did not know how to, articulate sounds or proffer any speech, but he knew how to present himself and let others intervene in his name: a woman whom his biographer assumes to be his sister, and

---

6   The Contest was a new principle, born of the Revolution, tied to the notion of the encouragement of artists, to try and avoid the risk of arbitrary judgements. The Jacobins, from 1789 on, were among the most zealous of revolutionaries; they supported Robespierre to the very end. Their 'club' was situated in the old Jacobin convent of the Rue Saint-Honoré in Paris. It was closed in 1794 after the fall of Robespierre and his friends.

who is sometimes taken (to no surprise) for his wife; later on, he had an interpreter, citizen Bergurieux (Le Chatelier 1903, p. 58).

Claude-André Deseine's *Mirabeau* was finally awarded the Jacobin prize: *He combined a perfect likeness with expression and energy (Il a réuni à la ressemblance parfaite, l'expression et l'énergie;* Société des amis de la constitution 1791).

Curiously, the critics were at one in underlining that the bust made by the deaf mute was the best at communicating the oratory power of the great man.

Houdon's bust was judged somewhat 'dull'. He had removed himself from the competition, humiliated at having to compete with such little-known artists. But it is not out of the question that Claude-André felt he had also resolved a subject of great contention: his professor at the Academy, A. Pajou, was considered one of Houdon's enemies (a somber story of rivalry) and, what's more, his brother Louis-Pierre had competed against Houdon in 1790. (An interesting aside is to note that Houdon too would one day do a bust of the abbé de L'Epée, a bust which to this day has never been found.)

In this year of awards and homages rendered to him by the National Assembly and the Jacobin Society, our hero Claude-André Deseine exhibited at the Salon du Louvre. For the first time in its history, the salon was open to all artists; it had been reserved for members of the Royal Academy, of which Claude-André was merely a student. He exhibited his *Mirabeau*, an allegory of liberty, and a bust of Jean-Jacques Rousseau. During the same period he made busts of two celebrated Jacobins: Maximilien Robespierre[7] and Jérôme Pétion de Villeneuve, the future mayor of Paris (who would replace J.S. Bailly, a bust of whom was made by Louis-Pierre).

Among the important works of these years in the oeuvre of Claude-André, one should note the busts of Augustin Robespierre, Maximilien's brother, Le Peletier de Saint-Fargeau, Marat. These sculptures make it obvious that Claude-André was an 'engaged' artist, clearly manifesting his *intentions* and his *personal will* to again make use of the terms of the judge in the red robe.

Of the forty works from his hand that we know of,[8] three-quarters of them were produced between 1791 and 1794. He who did not seem to know how to write in 1777 during the judicial hearing in which he was 'banned', now signed his works: *Deseine, deaf mute (Deseine, sourd et muet),* or (on his self-portrait) *Deseine, Meek, deaf mute (Deseine, Bonasse, sourd-muet). Meek (Bonasse),* according to his biographer, was the nickname given to him by his family (Le Chatelier 1903, p. 58). Never did he sign his works with another name his family called him: the mute.

The end of an exceptional life

The Salon of 1793 was the last salon Deseine exhibited in. From then on silence engulfed him as it did many of the Jacobins or Jacobin-sympathizers after the death of Robespierre. We only know that around 1797 he made a bust of General Bonaparte, then an officer of the Revolution who had earned the admiration of Augustin Robespierre. Thereafter, he received some little aid (in January 1795, the Public Education Committee granted him 2,000 pounds). He received no official commissions. He wrote himself, or had someone write for him:

> *(...) the petitioner is without work, has no means of existence, is crippled, abandoned to himself, he is one of the Republic's most famous sculptors (...) Deseine is seeking a quick and provisional grant proportionate to his situation (...).* (Le Chatelier 1903, pp. 47-48)

---

7 This is the only existing bust of Robespierre. The original has been kept, since 1986, at the Museum of the Revolution in Vizille, near Grenoble. A casting exhibited since the beginning of 1991, is still on show at the Conciergerie Museum in Paris.

8 They were produced between 1782 and 1797. Some are preserved in public or private collections, others are only mentioned without our knowing whether or not they still exist.

The signature on the petition is not without interest: *Regards, respectfully, Claude Deseine (Salut et respect, Claude Deseine;* Le Chatelier 1903, p. 48).

Another brief aside: Houdon got his revenge when in 1800 the Ministry of the Interior commissioned a marble bust of Mirabeau from him!

In 1822, Claude-André was 83 years old. One of his nephews was appointed as his new 'tutor' after the death of his brother Louis-Pierre that same year. Our sculptor was still 'banned'. He died the following year in a bourgeois 'pension', in Gentilly, near Paris, on December 30th.

IV Pierre Desloges
The Jacobin bookbinder

Pierre Desloges was born in the Touraine region, in the town of Grand Pressigny. The parish registers from his home town tell us that he was baptized on the 21st of September, 1742[9] in the parish of Saint-Gervais. The precise date of his birth is not given though we know that it was customary then for children to be baptized on the day of their birth, or one or two days later. Pierre was, then, born between the 19th and 21st of September, 1742. His father, Pierre Desloges (the first child often had the same first name as the father), had married Geneviève Noël. The couple had not been in Grand Pressigny for long; the father had declared, upon the birth of his son, 'bourgeois of Paris'.

The godfather of the young Pierre was lord and baron of Grand Pressigny; his godmother, the wife of a squire. The godfather and godmother were absent from the baptism and were represented by the local assessor, who was charged with the assessment and collection of taxes – he was accompanied by his wife. Grand Pressigny was a lordly burgh in a region of France which was for a time the favorite, privileged site of kings; one can find there one of the Loire Valley châteaux which was a princely residence, erected near the river at a time when the royal court frequented the region. The landscape is spread between two hills: on one of the slopes stood a fortress (which must have been formidable in the Middle-Ages), a square dungeon and watchtower and a château which, in the 18th century, was grandiose, imposing and revered.

The young Pierre was raised in this modest village. A year after his birth, his father was appointed *tax collector general of Grand Pressigny (receveur général de la baronnie du Grand Pressigny):* he was in the service of his lord-baron, Messire Masson de Maison Rouge (Archives contemporaines d'Indre et Loire: Grand Pressigny, paroisse Saint Gervais, Baptèmes - Mariages - Sèpultures, années: 1700-1750).

Little Pierre was four years old in 1746 when a daughter was born into the family: Marie-Anne (baptized on August 2nd). Many of the same people who were at Pierre's baptism were at hers. There probably wasn't much choice, nor the possibility of doing otherwise in the small village. The existence of a parish register creates this peculiar situation: we have details of the first days, and even the first steps, of Pierre Desloges, and yet we know but very little afterwards. We would probably know nothing at all if Pierre hadn't kept a kind of register himself, presented in the form of writings.

Apprenticeship

Pierre learned how to read and write. This was somewhat easier for him than for most of the children of his age, since he did not live under conditions of the great majority (his parents were not indigents, nor truly poor). Then sickness befell him and with it came a veritable,

---

9 *born in 1747,* in Desloges (1779a, p. 1 of the preface); *born in 1742,* in Desloges (1790, p. 16). I wrote *born in 1747,* which was the only date cited by authors, until I had a chance to consult parish registers.

profound and dramatic modification of the life of the young boy: Pierre Desloges, between the seventh and ninth years of his life – it is not possible to be more exact – went deaf. He contracted smallpox, scarlatina or some other infectious, irruptive disease which leaves scars:

> *I became deaf and dumb following a terrible case of smallpox which I caught at the age of seven. The two accidents of deafness and muteness came upon me at the same time and, in a manner of speaking, without my having noticed.* (Desloges 1779a, p. 6 of the preface)

Pierre was very deaf: he could perceive only the vibrations of a rolling carriage or a drum. His speech was also greatly affected; his pronunciation became unintelligible, his voice very low.

He was the only Deaf person in Grand Pressigny and had to write to make himself understood.

After his illness comes a period in his life of which we know nothing. We pick up Pierre's track again in 1761-1762 when he was nineteen years old. He made his *residence in Paris (demeure à Paris;* Desloges 1779a, p. 13 of the preface) at the same time as the abbé de L'Epée was establishing teaching practices for Deaf people, when he began to learn the rudiments of their sign language from them. Pierre left his family, no doubt on his own accord. His situation had become worse and he used only *scattered, isolated signs without development or relations (signes épars, isolés, sans suite et sans liaison;* Desloges 1779a, p. 12 of the preface). He wrote:

> *(…) placed in apprenticeship* (with whom?) *against the wishes and advice of my parents who deemed me incapable of learning; without support or revenue; reduced twice to the hospital since I had no employment, fighting unceasingly against misery, opinion, prejudice, insults and violent injurious remarks from relatives, friends, neighbors, and others who treated me as beastly, imbecilic, insane who was pretending to be the thinker with a superior intelligence but who would some day end up in the Petites-Maison* (with the insane!) *(…).* (Desloges 1780a)

In 1776 he became a bookbinder – or more exactly a bookbinder and upholsterer (at that date a parliamentary edict united bookbinders and furniture upholsterers, as opposed to their previous grouping with booksellers, and, before that, with writers). We do not know whether he learned his trade in Paris or elsewhere. We do know, however, that in 1769 or 1770, he met an Italian, who was deaf mute from birth, and who, while not knowing how to read or write, possessed sign language and taught it to Pierre Desloges, then aged twenty-seven.

The only book authored by a deaf mute

1779 was a landmark year for Pierre Desloges. His life changed. He became a writer, and the author of the century's only book written entirely by a Deaf author (Desloges 1779a): a book, not merely an almanac or journal publication. It is a book that tells of his experience, a self-analysis we might say today, and a book that was interventionist in its time. In a book in 1779, the abbé Claude François Deschamps told of his own experience of teaching Deaf children, and did not fail to mention the abbé de L'Epée. (Deschamps 1779) He wrote that he was as important as his predecessor in the world of deaf mutes, Jacob Rodriguez Pereire. The abbé Deschamps also believed, as did many, that abbé de L'Epée 'had invented' the language of signs. Pierre Desloges – and this shows that he was aware of current events of the time – responded to Deschamps' book in his book which was published that same year in Paris: *Observations of a Deaf Mute on An Elementary Course of Education for Deaf Mutes,* where he wrote:

Monsieur abbé Deschamps is not the only one who believes that the abbé de L'Epée created and invented the language of signs (...). (and he gives some details) *(...) de l'Epée did not create and invent this language: on the contrary, he learned it from deaf mutes; he merely rectified that which he found defective in this language; he developed it, and gave it methodical rules (...).* (Desloges 1779a, pp. 39,7)

These remarks show a strong critical sense, both admiring of and attentive to the true character of what de L'Epée was setting up. Pierre Desloges was not then and never became a student of de L'Epée. Yet his book can be read as a defense and illustration of the fundamental theses of the abbé's teachings – with the authority of experience and emotion that comes from a difficult life. An ardent plea against the miserable situation created for the Deaf, the book is also an ardent plea for sign language and its teaching. It was another attempt to exhibit the situation of the Deaf to the majority, to the non-deaf, to explain the state of things at the time for Deaf people in terms of exchange and communication. *Everybody has formed false ideas of our condition (Tout le monde s'est formé les idées les plus fausses sur notre compte;* Desloges 1779a, p. 2 of the preface) he wrote.

Ill. 2: *Pierre Desloges, autograph*

In February of the following year, 1780, the *Journal encyclopédique* reviewed Pierre Desloges' book followed by a letter from its author. The letter is a kind of sequel to his book. It tells us more about his person and his situation – *the condition of the strange deaf mute author (la situation de l'étrange auteur sourd et muet;* Desloges 1780a). Even more than in his book, here one can read of the rejection he experienced from others – especially when he pretended, despite being Deaf, to be their equal and to live like everybody else.

A deaf mute French citizen

The 1789 Revolution did not catch Pierre Desloges unawares. Almost from the beginning he participated in the Revolution through his writings. On the 28th of June he wrote a seven-page text which was printed on the 15th of July – the day following the storming of the Bastille. The text is entitled *Letter Addressed to the Voters of Paris* (Desloges 1789). We can say without without exaggeration that between these two dates the world had toppled over. The letter is a brief but eloquent monument to the glory of the Gardes Françaises for their behaviour during those days; it is signed, simply, *a deaf mute French citizen (un citoyen français sourd et muet;* Desloges 1789, p. 1). It was widely read, and talked about – so much that de L'Epée thought it necessary to release a statement saying that its author was not one of his students (L'Epée 1789, p. 906). But this small celebrity did not go far: we know that in 1790 as in 1789, Desloges still lived at the hospital-prison Bicêtre as a 'good pauper'. One can imagine him there in his homespun frock, with knickers and stockings of the same fabric, wooden clogs, a wool bonnet and white shirt. Bicêtre, located near the town of Ville-juif, crammed in as many as 4,000 patient-prisoners, sometimes more.

But this did not stop Pierre Desloges from publishing a new opuscule, dated *the second year of liberty (l'an second de la liberté;* Desloges 1790) and dedicated to La Fayette. In

1793-1794 he wrote again (which lets us know that he was not slaughtered in the Bicêtre September massacres), while still in the 'hospital'. He published a 37 page almanac *for year two of the French republic, one and indivisible (pour l'an deux de la république Française, une et indivisible;* Desloges 1793-1794) with the epigraph, *Honor Old Age, Respect Unhappiness (Honorez la Vieillesse, Respectez le Malheur)*. The dedication is addressed to the *Society of Friends of Liberty and Equality (Société des Amis de la Liberté et de l'Egalité)*. The almanac was designed entirely by Desloges but with additions and montages of texts which were not written by his hand (there are texts on calendar reform, hymns to liberty and reason, an abridged political and moral catechism for republican education, the Human and Citizens' Rights...).

The almanac is signed in a somewhat mysterious and symbolic manner: *Esope* (= *Aesop) - Desloges*, a pseudonym which evokes a then fashionable fascination for Greece, but which also evokes an extraordinary character: a storyteller, a legendary figure, deformed and stammering, a slave before being emancipated. The symbolism was not enough for Desloges; on the book's cover were his traditional symbols: the red bonnet and lances. The dream of a world without injustice and discrimination, of an egalitarian world open to all and for the happiness of all – the Jacobin dream joined to the dream of the Deaf and of all those who were different, marginalized or shunted aside.

Pierre Desloges was a Jacobin, there is no doubt about that. As another symbolic proof of this, he disappeared – which is to say, we lose trace of him – after the fall of the Jacobins. Silence.

(Translated by Joseph Simas)

Appendix
The original French quotations:

p. 27

J' invite mes deux fils et mes trois filles de vivre ensemble en paix et union et soumission envers leur mère.

Je veux et ordonne que François Meusnier l' ainé de mes fils et François Meusnier de Baudrant son cadet aussy mon fils ne puissent prendre dans ma succession que leur légitime de droit à laquelle je les réduis dans les biens qui se trouveront m'appartenir lors de mon décès. Je lègue et donne de plus à mes dits deux fils tout ce que ma femme leur mère jugera à propos de leur donner de ma garde robe ainsi que mes armes (...). (Archives nationales: Y 56 fol. 120 - 121; Minutier central des notaires de Paris: Etude II, liasse 524)

p. 28 / p. 29

(...) le 8 avril 1723 (...) le Sieur Meusnier (...) ayant le malheur d'avoir deux fils sourds et muets, il a plu déjà à sa majesté de lui accorder 500 livres de gratification annuelle pour leur subsistance. Comme ils sont déjà d'un âge à l'obliger à faire suivre à leur conduite, ne le pouvant lui même à cause du service qu'il doit à sa majesté (...) le Sieur Meusnier suppliait d'avoir compassion d'une telle affliction et vouloir bien augmenter sa gratification pour qu'il place ses deux fils dans quelque communauté de religieux, où ils soient soignés d'une manière convenable à leur état (...). (Archives nationales: O^1 67 fol. 227)

p. 32

Il est indispensable de prendre un parti relativement à l' état du dit Claude Deseine. (Archives nationales: Y 5029 B)

[les présents sont] tous unanimement d'avis de l'interdiction du dit sieur Claude Deseine sourd et muet de naissance comme incapable de gérer et administrer ses personne et biens. (Archives nationales: Y 5029 B)

Claude Deseine sourd et muet que nous avons fait entrer dans notre cabinet, (...) amené par sa mère, auquel [nous] avons fait plusieurs questions qu' il nous a témoigné par gestes ne pas entendre, s'apercevant seulement au mouvement de nos lèvres que nous lui adressions la parole, ayant notoirement fait quelques efforts pour articuler des sons mais n'a pu proférer aucune parole nous aurait même indiqué par ses gestes qu' il ne pouvait ni entendre ni parler ni écrire (...). (Archives nationales: Y 5029 B)

p. 34

(...) conformément aux intentions du dit interdit, autant qu'il pourra les lui faire connaître (…) même de lui remettre les sommes provenant de ses revenus pour en disposer à sa volonté (...). (Archives nationales: Y 5029 B)

p. 35

Le célèbre Mr. Houdon n'est pas le seul qui ait coulé sur nature le buste de feu M. de Mirabeau. Le Sieur Deseine, sculpteur figuriste, sourd et muet, connu pour ses talents, mérite aussi d' avoir une place dans vos feuilles. Le 2 avril, jour de deuil pour toute la France une députation (…) s'est rendue chez (…) l'un des exécuteurs testamentaires du deffunt, pour obtenir la permission de faire prendre par le dit Sieur Deseine l'empreinte de la figure de ce grand homme (...) signé: Corbin, l'un des citoyens qui composait la députation. (Corbin 1791)

p. 36

(...) le pétitionnaire est sans ouvrage, sans moyen d' existence, infirme, abandonné à lui-même, il est l'un des plus fameux sculpteurs de la République (…). Deseine demande un secours provisoire prompt et proportionné à sa situation(…). (Le Chatelier 1903, pp. 47-48)

p. 38

Je suis devenu sourd et muèt à la suite d'une petite vérole afreuse que j'ai éssuyée vers l' âge de sept ans. Les deux accidens de la surdité et du mutisme me sont survenus en même-tems et, pour ainsi dire, sans que je m'en sois aperçu. (Desloges 1779a, p.6 of the preface)

(…) mis en apprentissage [par qui?] contre le gré et l'avis de mes parens, qui me jugeaient incapable de rien apprendre; (...) sans appui, (...) sans ressource; réduit deux fois à l'hôpital, faute d' ouvrage; forcé de lutter sans cesse contre la misère, l'opinion, le préjugé, les injures, les railleries les plus sanglantes, de parens, amis, voisins, confrères, qui me traitent de bête, d'imbécille, de fou qui prétend faire le raisonneur et avoir plus d'esprit qu'eux, mais qui sera mis quelque jour aux Petites-Maisons [chez les fous!] (...). (Desloges 1780a)

p. 39

Monsieur l'Abbé Deschamps n'est pas le seul qui s'imagine que M. l' Abbé de l'Epée a créé et inventé le langage des signes (...) [et il précise:] Ce n'est donc pas M. l' Abbé de l'Epée qui a créé et inventé ce langage: tout au contraire, il l'a apris des sourds et muèts; il a seulement rectifié ce qu'il a trouvé de défectueux dans ce langage; il l'a étendu, et lui a doné des règles méthodiques (...). (Desloges 1779a, pp. 39, 7)

References
unpublished

Archives nationales Paris

AA 12 (Letter dated august 25, 1790, addressed by Pierre Desloges to garde des sceaux de France).

D IV 49, item no. 1398, Pétition du sieur Deseine à l'Assemblée nationale afin d'exécuter en grand le buste de l'abbé de L'Epée, 28 juillet 1791.

O[1] 46 fol. 188, Meusnier Francois. Retenue d'huissier de la chambre du roi, 4 décembre 1702.

O[1] 59 fol. 94, Meusnier Francois, huissier de la chambre du roi. Brevet d'assurance, 10 juin 1715.

O[1] 60 fol. 89, Meusnier Francois, huissier de la chambre du roi. Brevet d'augmentation d'assurance de 5000 livres, 22 juin 1716.

O[1] 67 fol. 227, Brevet de 500 livres d'augmentation de pension pour faire 1000 livres en faveur des deux enfants du sr. Meusnier Francois, huissier de la chambre du roi , 8 avril 1723.

Y 56 fol. 120 et 121, Testament de François Meusnier (dated december 23, 1748).

Y 5029 B, Avis Deseine. Interdiction Claude Deseine, 16 mai 1777.

Minutier central des notaires de Paris (Archives nationales)

Etude II, liasse 523 (Inventaire de M. Meusnier, huissier de la chambre du roi, 15 décembre 1749); liasse 524 (Renonciation par la dame Jouan Meusnier à la communauté de son mari, 26 mars 1750; Renonciation à la succession de M. Meusnier, par les Sr. De et delles ses enfants, 12 avril 1750; Consentement d'exécution testamentaire et délivrance de legs, par M. de Bongard, tuteur des sieurs Meusnier, 12 avril 1750); liasse 526 (Consentement par les enfants et héritiers de M. Meusnier à madame leur mère, 3 septembre 1750).

Etude XI, liasse 381 (Contrat de mariage, François Meusnier et Louise Jouan, 14 juin 1705).

Etude XX, liasse 252 (Contrat de mariage, Mr. Tarlé et Mademoiselle Meusnier, 21, 23 et 26 juin 1733).

Archives contemporaines d'Indre et Loire

Grand Pressigny, paroisse Saint Gervais, Baptèmes-Mariages-Sépultures, années: 1700-1750.

Archives des Yvelines

5 MI 191, registre des sépultures de la paroisse Saint-Louis, à Versailles, année 1749.

Bibliothèque municipale d'Amiens

ms. 532, Journal du P. Postel (vol. 4: 19 juin 1728, 29 novembre 1733).

published

Bézagu-Deluy, Maryse (1990): *L'abbé de L'Epée, Instituteur gratuit des sourds et muets, 1712-1789.* Paris: Seghers.

Corbin [?] (1791): (no title); in: *Annonces, affiches et avis divers (…)* 106, p. 1422.

Deschamps, Claude -François (1779): *Cours élémentaire d'éducation des sourds et muets (…).* Paris: Debure.

Desloges, Pierre (1779a): *Observations d'un sourd et muèt sur un cours élémentaire d'éducation des sourds et muèts publié en 1779 par M. l'Abbé Deschamps.* Amsterdam et Paris: B. Morin.

Desloges, Pierre (1779b/1882): (Deux entretiens avec J. R. Pereire (31 oct.1779, 6 nov.1779)); in: La Rochelle, E. (1882): *J. R. Pereire, (…) sa vie et ses travaux.* Paris: P. Dupont, pp. 405-410. Reprints: *Cahiers de l'Histoire des Sourds* 1, 1989, fiche 7.

Desloges, Pierre (1779c): Lettre à M. le Marquis de Condorcet; in: *Mercure de France,* 18 décembre 1779, pp. 142-150.

Desloges, Pierre (1780a): Lettre [to the editors]; in: *Journal encyclopédique,* 1, p. 463.

Desloges, Pierre (1780b): Lettre à M. Bellisle (…) en réponse à celle que lui a écrite M. l'abbé Deschamps au sujet des observations de M. Desloges; in: *Journal encyclopédique,* 6, pp. 125-132.

Desloges, Pierre [1789]: Lettre adressée à MM. les électeurs de Paris, par un citoyen français, sourd et muet, n.p.n.d. ('composé le 28 juin et imprimé le 15 juillet [1789] ', based on the British Museum copy).

Desloges, Pierre [1790]: *La prédiction des astronomes sur la fin du monde accompli, ou la Régéneration de l'Europe en travail.* Paris: Garnery.

Desloges, Pierre [1793-1794]: *Almanach de la raison. Pour l'an deux de la république Française, une et indivisible.* Rédigé par le Républicain Esope-Desloges, sourd et muet (…). Paris, chez le Citoyen Desloges, rue des Noyers.

Le Chatelier, Georges (1903): Deseine le sourd-muet. Claude-André Deseine, statuaire; in: *Revue Générale de l'Enseignement des Sourds-Muets,* 3, pp. 45-59.

Le Chatelier, Georges [1906]: *Louis-Pierre Deseine (…) (1749-1822), sa vie et ses oeuvres.* Paris: Librairies-imprimeries réunies.

L'Epée, Charles-Michel de(1789): Lettre aux auteurs du Journal (…); in: *Journal de Paris* (20 juillet 1789), 201, p. 906.

La Révolution Française et l'Europe 1789-1799 (1989). Catalogue d'exposition. Galeries nationales du Grand Palais, Paris, 16.3.-26.6.1989. Paris: Editions de la Réunion des musées nationaux. (*Deseine Cl.-A., sculpteur.* pp. XXVIII, 444, 445, 448, 894, 896.)

Société des amis de la constitution (…) [1791]: *Annonce.* Paris: Imprimerie du Patriote français (on Mirabeau's bust).

Deaf People

Ill. 1: In 1930, at a Deaf masked ball in Berlin, 20-year-old Miss Hetzler was crowned Berlin's first Deaf Queen of Beauty.

Imprimé à l'Institution   *Cliché Payeur*

Mademoiselle MARIE MEUNIER
(1806-1877)

Sourde-muette indigente, élève, puis monitrice, puis 1ʳᵉ ouvrière lingère à l'Institution nationale, à laquelle elle a légué une rente annuelle et perpétuelle de *sept cent quarante et un francs*, unique fruit de ses économies, c'est-à-dire de ses longues et persévérantes privations.

Ill. 2: A typical Deaf female career...? The comment on Marie Meunier (1806 - 1877) says that she was poor, a former pupil of the Paris Institute, then working there as a monitor and as head of the school's laundry; she gave regular gifts of 741 francs to the Institute, these savings representing 'the only fruit (…) of her long and unceasing privations'.

Ill. 3: Eliza Boardman Clerc (1792 - 1880), wife of Laurent Clerc, with their daughter.

Ill. 4: Sophia Fowler Gallaudet (1798 - 1877), wife of Thomas Hopkins Gallaudet.

Das erste gehörlose Fräulein Doktor.

Frl. Suzanne Lavaud in Paris

erwart an der Sorbonne (Universität zu Paris) den Doktortitel. Sie ist wohl die erste taubstumme Frau in Frankreich und Europa, die den Doktortitel erwerben konnte.

Ill. 5: In1932, Suzanne Lavaud (born deaf) received her Ph.D. in Paris. The caption says that she probably was the first deaf mute woman in France and Europe to do so.

Lavaud Suzanne, Docteur ès-lettres de l'Université de Paris (1932). A publié un étude sur Marie Lenéru, femme de lettres également sourde (voir plus loin): «Marie Lenéru, sa vie, son journal, son théâtre» - Paris, Société Française d'Editions Littéraires et Techniques, 1932 - In 8°, 281 p.). D'un autre côté, elle a édité des ouvrages de bibliographie: «Catalogue des publications de congrès» (1954), «Catalogue des thèses de doctorat ès-sciences naturelles soutenues à Paris, de 1891 à 1954» (1955), «Catalogue des thèses de pharmacie de l'Université de Paris de 1895 à 1959» (1960).

Ill. 6: In a 1964 article, Suzanne Lavaud gives informations about Deaf artists and scientists, among them, herself. She lists some of her publications, e.g. her work on the Deaf author Marie Lenéru (1875 - 1918) deafened at the age of 14.

Sunny home Aug 21st 1850.

My dear friend Miss Six

I was very glad to
receive a long letter from you
the 7th of Aug.
I thank you most sincerely for
the card which you sent to me.
I am very glad to think of your
very pleasant acquaintance with
Miss Bowman. I trust that she
will meet with the very good &
pleasant people at Cape May.
I prize my book very highly
which Miss B. presented me.
with...........

Yours truly

Oliver Caswell Laura Bridgman.

Ill. 7: Deaf blind Laura Bridgman (1829 - 1889) giving lessons to deaf blind
Oliver Caswell (born in 1829).

Ill. 8: Facsimile (incomplete) of a letter written by Laura Bridgman to her
friend, Miss Six, on August 21, 1850.

Many Deaf female pupils (or pupils-to-come) had a decisive influence on the career or the renown of their hearing teachers. Rare are those whom we know by name, such as Marie Marois (see ill. 75, p. 328) or Alice Cogswell:

Ill. 9: Statue of Alice Cogswell and Thomas Hopkins Gallaudet, Washington, USA, 1889.

The incentive the two 'nameless' French sisters gave to the abbé de L'Epée and which made him a teacher of the Deaf, has become a prominent topic, even a myth, in Deaf history and has repeatedly been represented by Deaf artists:

Ill. 11: The abbé de L'Epée teaches the Deaf sisters.

Ill. 10: Providence arranges a meeting between the abbé and the two sisters...

Ill. 12: The first contact is also represented on the monument in honour of the abbé de L'Epée, which can still be seen in the courtyard of the Paris Institution.

* * * * *

il y a entre nous deux Confra
ternité de malheur. Préférez
vous être Sourd-muet à être aveugle

Je pense que les Aveugles-nés ne sont pas malheureux,
au lieu que les aveugles d'accident le sont davantage;
La vue est le plus agréable de tous les sens,
mais l'ouïe est très instructrice.

Vous ne répondez pas directe
ment à ma question,
j'préfère d'être Sourd=muet; mais si j'étois
aveugle-né, j'en auterois par affligé.

moi, je préfère ma Cécité
complète au Sourd-muets
-me.

j'ai vu à Paris une Sourde—muette—aveugle.
elle n'étoit pas fâchée, elle étoit gaie.

Ill. 13: A conversation was conducted in writing by Alexandre Rodenbach (blind, 1786-1869) and Jean Massieu (deaf, 1772-1846) in Lille, France, at the time when Massieu was the director of a school for the Deaf there. Rodenbach asked questions, and Massieu replied. Questions Rodenbach put, were for example those 18th century stereotyped ones about intellectual capacities of deaf people ('What idea did you have, prior to instruction, of audition and speech?') or whether Massieu preferred being deaf mute to being blind... 'I prefer being deaf mute', Massieu replied, 'but if I was born blind, I wouldn't mind either.'

Ill. 14: A fictitious portrait of Deaf Quintus Pedius, represented with his mouth bound. He lived in the 1st century, a contemporary of Julius Cesar who designated Quintus Pedius one of his heirs. His career as a painter was ended by an early death.

Ill. 15: Honoré Trézel was born deaf in Paris on June 4, 1815 and presented to the Academy of Sciences on April 25, 1825 by Doctor Deleau who claimed having 'rendered back' (!) audition and speech to him.

Ill. 16: J.L. Hyppolite Bertrand (Deaf?), at the age of 11, saved a woman who attempted to drown herself in the river Seine in Paris, France, in 1826. – Based on an historical event of this kind, a Deaf person rescuing a hearing person was a theme in several French 19th century dramas.

Susan Plann
Los Angeles, USA

Roberto Francisco Prádez[*]

Spain's first Deaf teacher of the Deaf

*Who can possibly calculate the utility brought to a kingdom
by just one man dedicated to public or private teaching?*

José Miguel Alea

Summary • Resumen

This article examines the developments leading up to the foundation of the Madrid school for the Deaf and the role played by Roberto Prádez, Spain's first deaf teacher of the Deaf, during the school's first three decades of existence. Although he has been historically neglected, Prádez is a founding father of Deaf education in the nineteenth century, a heroic figure who contributed crucially to the establishment and operation of Spain's first state-sponsored school. This study underscores the need for a reexamination of the historical record and for the recovery of Spanish deaf history.

Este artículo analiza los sucesos que conducen a la fundación del Real Colegio de Sordomudos de Madrid y examina el papel de don Roberto Prádez durante las primeras tres décadas de existencia de aquel establecimiento. Aunque ha sido totalmente olvidado e ignorado por la historia, Prádez es muy importante por ser el primer maestro sordo de sordos eñ Espana. Es uno de los fundadores de la educación del sordo en el siglo diecinueve, una figura heróica que ha contribuido crucialmente al establecimiento y operación del primer colegio estatal español. Este estudio subraya la necesidad de reexaminar la documentación histórica y de recuperar la verdadera historia de los sordos españoles.

* This article is dedicated to Mar Caso Neira. Her friendship and assistance have contributed immeasurably to this research.
This work was made possible by grants from the University of California at Los Angeles and the Council for the International Exchange of Scholars.

I Background

The year 1805 marked the opening in Madrid of the Royal School for Deaf Mutes. Although this was the nation's first state-sponsored school for the deaf, Spain was no stranger to the art, for in the mid-sixteenth century Pedro Ponce de León, a Benedictine monk, had taught the deaf sons and daughters of the Spanish nobility, thus giving the lie to the long held belief that Deaf people could not receive instruction. During the early decades of the seventeenth century Manuel Ramírez de Carrión, Spain's first professional teacher, continued to instruct deaf children of noble birth, and the soldier and statesman Juan Pablo Bonet published the first book on the education of the Deaf (Bonet 1620). Around this same time a Spanish physician, Pedro de Castro, carried the teaching to Italy.

Word of the Spanish invention spread gradually throughout much of Europe, but even as it was disseminated and perfected abroad, it met with decline and abandonment in the land of its birth. Spain reacted to this state of affairs with a wounded sense of national pride, and this reaction, first manifest in the early decades of the eighteenth century, would help prepare the way for the eventual reestablishment of Deaf education. In 1730 a Benedictine monk, Benito Jerónimo Feijóo y Montenegro, became the first to inveigh against Spain's abandonment - and Europe's appropriation - of the teaching:

> *Here there is motive to lament the common fatality of the Spaniards during the last two centuries that the riches of their country, including those that are the product of the creative faculty, are enjoyed more by foreigners than by Spaniards. The art of teaching the deaf to speak was born in Spain and I believe that there is not nor has there been for a long time in Spain anyone who wishes to cultivate it and avail himself of it, while foreigners have made and are making great use of this invention.* (Feijóo y Montenegro 1730, p. 419)[1]

Moreover, not only had the instruction been appropriated by foreigners even as it had ceased to be practiced in Spain, but the names of the early Spanish teachers had been eclipsed by those of their European successors. Thus the indignant Feijóo hastened to remind a forgetful Europe that the first teacher of the Deaf had been none other than his fellow Benedictine, *our monk Fray Pedro Ponce (nuestro Monge Fr. Pedro Ponce;* Feijóo y Montenegro 1730, pp. 417-418).

Feijóo's account of Ponce served to inspire another Spaniard, Jacobo Rodríguez Pereira,[2] whose teaching of the Deaf in Paris, La Rochelle, and Bordeaux would win the acclaim of France's intelligentsia, the Royal Academy of Science, and the French king himself. But Feijóo was apparently unsuccessful in his efforts to revive Ponce's fame, for several decades later he again felt compelled to take up his pen in Ponce's defense, deploring the fact that

> *(...) from Paris to Amsterdam and from Amsterdam to Paris, people are cannonading each other over who is the inventor of the art, and no one remembers Fray Pedro Ponce, who was indisputably the inventor.* (Feijóo y Montenegro 1759, p. 95)

Feijóo's complaint was more than justified, for during the last decades of the 1700s all Europe toasted not Pedro Ponce but its most famous teacher of the Deaf, the French abbé de L'Epée.[3] Indeed, many mistakenly took de L'Epée to be the inventor of the art, and in 1793 Feijóo's voice was joined by that of a Spanish Jesuit writing in exile in Italy,[4] Juan Andrés

---

1 Feijóo (1676-1764), known as the Spanish Voltaire, was the 'vulgarisateur' of the Spanish Enlightment, the first to popularize ideas of experimental science in the early eighteenth century.
2 Jacobo Rodríguez Pereira (1715-1780) was a Spanish Jew whose sister's deafness first led him to contemplate the instruction of the deaf.
3 Charles-Michel de L'Epée (1712-1789), known as the 'spiritual father of the Deaf'.
4 The Jesuits had been expelled from Spain in 1767.

Morell, who also took umbrage at the slight. Europe's adulation of de L'Epée was now at its height, but as Andrés reiterated, the art of teaching had first been invented, practiced, and disseminated by Spaniards (Andrés Morell 1794). Feijóo's writings had by this time been translated into various tongues and the Spanish version was readily available, yet according to Andrés, each new teacher claimed to be the inventor of the art, and not one mentioned Pedro Ponce. Writing in eloquent defense of Ponce, Bonet, Ramírez de Carrión, and Pereira, he concluded that the teaching of the deaf, which for many years had been celebrated as the invention of the French abbé de L'Epée, was in reality *an entirely Spanish art (un arte enteramente español;* Andrés Morell 1794, p. 19). Andrés Morell's essay, translated into Spanish, appeared in Spain one year after its publication in Italy.

But Feijóo's and Andrés's protestations nonwithstanding, well might Europe celebrate Charles-Michel de L'Epée. The French abbé had founded the first public school for the deaf in Paris in the early 1760s, and in the decades that followed, he and his successor, the abbé Roch-Ambroise-Cucurron Sicard, trained many others who in turn continued to spread the teaching. By the end of the 1700s, schools for the deaf had been founded in many European countries, due in great measure to the efforts of de L'Epée and Sicard. The fame of the two abbés was by this time widespread in Spain as well, but no school for the deaf had as yet been established there.

As the eighteenth century drew to a close, impetus for the creation of a school reached Spain from other European nations, and the teaching of the deaf, that eminently Spanish invention, was in effect imported from abroad. In 1793, the same year in which Andrés Morell sought his nation's revindication as inventor and propagator of the art, another Spanish Jesuit exiled in Italy, Lorenzo Hervás y Panduro,[5] wrote a book urging the establishment of public education for deaf in Spain. Hervás had learned of the teaching in Rome, where his lawyer friend Pascual di Pietro had sponsored the first Italian school (the teacher, Tommaso Silvestri, was a disciple of de L'Epée). Hervás's book appeared in Madrid in 1795.

Four years later Hervás himself journeyed to Barcelona.[6] There he met the French presbyter Juan Albert Martí,[7] who had read his book on the teaching of the deaf. During his brief stay in Barcelona, Hervás collaborated with Albert to establish Barcelona's first school for the deaf, under the auspices of the municipal government. Albert, guided by the writings of Hervás and de L'Epée,[8] began teaching in 1800, but this endeavour was short-lived: Just two years later he returned to his native France and the school, now left without a teacher, was forced to close.

Attempts to reestablish the education of the deaf in Spain were not limited to Barcelona, however. During these same years, Madrid would also take steps to reinstitute the teaching, and here too the impetus would come from abroad. In 1793 Carlos IV, upon learning that the Piarist father José Fernández Navarrete was in the Spanish court, directed him to undertake the teaching of the deaf.[9] Fernández Navarrete, like Hervás, had studied in Rome under

---

5 Lorenzo Hervás y Panduro (1735-1809), *the last man who knew everything,* was born in Horcaja de Santiago in the province of Cuenca, Spain, and entered the Company of Jesus in 1749. He was better known as an intellectual than as a teacher of the deaf, and was reputed to know more than any other man of his time. The author of some ninety volumes (not including pamphlets and unpublished manuscripts) on topics as diverse as mathematics, history, geography, ethnology, astronomy, and linguistics, Hervás is best remembered as the father of comparative philology.

6 The Jesuits had been allowed to return to Spain in 1798.

7 That Albert Martí was a Frenchman is mentioned in a letter from Rouyer to the Marquis de Fuerte-Hijar, Director of the Economic Society (ARSEM, legajo 175, documento 3, 5-30-1802).

8 It is widely acknowledged that Albert was a disciple of Hervás; according to M. Ainaud, he was also influenced by de L'Epée (Ainaud 1919, p. 2).

9 José Fernández Navarrete de Santa Barbara was born in Murcia in 1758. He joined the Piarist fathers in 1774 and left the Order in 1804.
   Manuel Godoy, Prime Minister to Carlos IV, sought to claim credit for the reestablishment of deaf

Tommaso Silvestri,[10] and at his sovereign's behest he established a class for the deaf at the Piarist fathers' school of San Fernando in 1795. But Navarrete was able to attract only a few pupils - perhaps because, as one contemporary hypothesized, the art had been so long neglected in the land of its origin that it had come to be viewed with suspicion. In this writer's words, *The deaf mutes of the Spanish court do not attend* (Navarrete's) *school, in my opinion, because of people's concern about the safety and certainty of the principles of the art* (Alea 1795, p. 262).[11] Be that as it may, in 1802, just seven years after the school's inauguration, instruction there ceased entirely when Fernández Navarrete left Madrid for Almendralejo, in the province of Extremadura, to teach Lorenzo Golfín, the deaf son of the Marquis of Encomienda. In Madrid, as in Barcelona, the brief experiment with public instruction had ended, and the education of the deaf in Spain was once again the exclusive domain of the privileged.

II Foundation of the Madrid school

The hour for establishing an official school was at hand, however. Spain, for her part, was now ready, but this time too, as on previous occasions, the crucial stimulus would come from abroad. In 1800 Navarrete's class at the school of San Fernando had come under the protection of Madrid's Royal Economic Society of Friends of the Country. The Society's members, a reform-minded elite who were influenced by the thought of the European Enlightenment, sought to encourage their nation's development and prosperity through industrial and scientific progress, and through education.[12] In 1801, one year before Fernández Navarrete was to abandon the Spanish court, a French disciple of the abbé Sicard, one Antoine-Joseph Rouyer,[13] approached the Economic Society with a proposal to

education in Spain, and his version has been cited often (and uncritically): According to Godoy, in July or August of 1794 he suggested to Carlos IV the establishment of the teaching, and this proposal caused the monarch to decree the foundation of the school at San Fernando the very next day. (Godoy 1956, pp. 211-212)

It is quite possible that the efforts of one Antoine-Joseph Rouyer to found such a school antedated Godoy's, however (see note 13 below). At the very least, Godoy's recollection of the date cannot be correct, for a letter of October 24, 1793, not 1794, communicated to the Provincial Father of the Piarist Order of Castile Carlos IV's desire that Fernández Navarrete dedicate himself solely to the instruction of the deaf. The letter is signed by the Duke of Alcudia, that is, none other than Godoy himself. (The document is to be found in the Archives of the Order of the Fathers of Pia, Madrid; a copy was provided to me by Father Vicente Hidalgo.)

10 According to some, Navarrete had also studied in Genova under the Piarist father Bautista Ottavio Assarotti, a disciple of Sicard. The primary documentation I have consulted refers only to Navarrete's having studied in Rome, however, and those who maintain he studied in Genova cite no sources for this claim.

Documentation at the Madrid's Economic Society and at the archives of Navarrete's order reveals that he had studied in Rome under Silvestri (ARSEM, Actas, 5-28-1803; this is also stated in a letter of October 24, 1793 from the Duque de Alcudia to the Padre Provincial of Navarrete's Order; the latter document pertains to the Archives of the Order of the Fathers of Pia, Madrid, and was provided to me by Father Vicente Hidalgo).

Sources claiming that Navarrete was a disciple of Assarotti are: Granell y Forcadell 1936, p. 3 and Perelló/Tortosa 1972, p. 8.

11 Alea, writing in June of 1795, observed that to date Navarrete had had but two disciples, only one of whom was from Madrid. Both had left after one or two months of instruction. At the time of Alea's article, Navarrete had just one student, a girl, though he was awaiting the arrival of two other deaf children from Galicia (Alea 1795, p. 262).

12 For a discussion of the labor of the Economic Society and educational policy in general during the early nineteenth century, see Ruiz Berrio 1970.

13 Although a native of Paris and a graduate of the University there, Rouyer had lived much of his life in Madrid, where his father was the king's dentist. After having studied under Sicard in the French

establish a school for the deaf in Spain. Now, the Friends of the Country held an abiding faith in the redemptive value of education – their motto was 'Help by teaching' *(Socorre enseñando)* – and by this time they had already founded various 'patriotic schools', where the socially marginalized – beggars, vagrant children, the unemployed – might learn a trade, acquire a rudimentary education, and become 'useful citizens'. It was not surprising, then, that they should be interested in the schooling of another of society's marginal groups, the deaf. Through education, they reasoned, deaf people too could become productive citizens. Thus, they secured royal approval and support for Rouyer's proposal, then sent the Frenchman back to Paris to perfect his knowledge under Sicard. But when Rouyer returned to Madrid in 1804, the Friends of the Country presented him with a startling proposition: To cope with a shortage of funds, the Society proposed to reduce its expenses by halving the number of pupils it would support, and paying Rouyer half his agreed-upon salary (ARSEM, leg. 178, doc. 6, letter to Antonio Rouyer, 1-16-1804). Rouyer's response to this turn of events was to tender his resignation before the school ever opened,[14] leaving the Economic Society without a teacher.

The Friends of the Country shed no tears over Rouyer's resignation, however, for by their own admission, they had deplored *the hard necessity of begging among foreigners when it came time to look for a teacher (la dura necesidad de mendigarlos entre entre los extrangeros, quando fuese preciso buscar Maestros).*[15] Clearly, if Europe was indebted to Spain for the invention of the education of the deaf during the sixteenth century and for its propagation during the seventeenth, in the late 1700s and early 1800s Spain now found itself indebted to Europe (and most notably to France) for its reintroduction, and this bitter irony was not lost on the members of the Economic Society. It could hardly have escaped their notice that all the efforts that would culminate in reestablishment of the Spanish art – Hervás's advocacy of education for the deaf, Albert Martí's short-lived school in Barcelona, Navarrete's class at the school of San Fernando and Rouyer's endeavours to found a school in Madrid – all had originated abroad. Moreover, every one could be traced either directly or indirectly to France and the abbés de L'Epée and Sicard.

Thus, the Economic Society was understandably pained at its dependence on foreigners to implement the teaching that had originated in Spain. The nation that had invented the art was now faced with the need to import a teacher from abroad; nevertheless, there appeared to be no alternative. It is only in this context that we can understand the Friends of the Country's reaction when, in 1803, they were contacted by a certain Juan de Dios Loftus y Bazán, who offered his services as a teacher of the deaf. Now, the Society believed it already had a teacher at this time – Rouyer, who was soon to return from Paris. Moreover, Loftus was by profession not a teacher at all but rather a military man, an infantry captain brevetted to lieutenant colonel, and as the Society was later to learn, he was an admitted embezzler to boot.[16] But while stationed in Ceuta he had had some success at teaching a deaf child, one

capital, he had journeyed to Madrid early in the 1790s with the intention of founding a school for the deaf, but had been unable to bring his plan to fruition. Having failed in his attempts to establish a school for the deaf on his own, Rouyer then presented his plans to the Economic Society in 1801.

14 The Society was informed of Rouyer's resignation on February 11, 1804 (ARSEM, Actas). Rouyer himself related the circumstances of his resignation in a letter of March 11, 1804 (ARSEM, leg. 178, doc. 6).

15 ARSEM, leg. 176, doc. 9, "Relación de lo hecho por la Comisión de sordo-mudos después de la última Junta de premios," n.d.
Even when the Economic Society had thought to employ the Frenchman Rouyer as head teacher, they must have done so with extreme reluctance, for in a letter to the Marquis de Fuerte-Hijar, director of the Economic Society, Rouyer recalled his promise that whenever he was consulted concerning teachers of the deaf, he would never permit the selection of a foreigner (ARSEM, leg. 175, doc. 3, 5-30-1802).

16 Loftus had been accused of embezzlement by his former regiment and he recognized the truth of

Juan Machado, and best of all, he was a Spaniard. The Society, leaving better judgment aside, so it would seem, asked him to stay in touch. That the members would even consider one whose credentials were so dubious would seem to be a measure of the nationalistic mood of the times, as well as an indication of the scarcity of qualified Spanish teachers. But be that as it may, when Rouyer resigned in 1804, the Friends of the Country hastened to secure royal approval to replace the French disciple of de L'Epée with the Spanish lieutenant colonel and embezzler, Juan de Dios Loftus y Bazán.[17] (They would soon regret the decision.)

And so it was that when Madrid's Royal School for Deaf Mutes finally opened on January 9, 1805, instruction was in the hands of a Spaniard. With the foundation of the first state-sponsored school, Spain rededicated itself to the teaching of the deaf. Their public education had at long last been established in the cradle of the art, where the teaching had originated some two and a half centuries earlier, and poor deaf children – albeit only six of them, initially – were given free access to an education.[18]

III Roberto Prádez

In the decades preceding the school's establishment, education of the deaf in Spain had apparently been limited to a few isolated experiments. The product of one such experiment was Roberto Francisco Prádez, Spain's first deaf teacher of the deaf and a key figure in deaf education during the early nineteenth century.[19] It was to his efforts that the Royal School for Deaf Mutes owed much of its success, and at times its very existence, during its precarious first three decades.

Prádez approached the Economic Society in May of 1805 requesting to teach either reading and writing, or drawing at the newly established school (ARSEM, Actas, 6-1-1805). Reading and writing were already being taught, but members of the school's governing Junta gladly accepted Prádez' offer to teach drawing, for they realized that such a skill would be most useful to their charges. Moreover, they recognized in Prádez' deafness a highly desirable qualification. Their new teacher, they reasoned, would be *much more appropri-*

---

the accusation, although he assured the Economic Society that he had repented and that his conduct since then had been above reproach (ARSEM, leg. 160, doc. 12, e, cited in Negrín Fajardo 1982, p. 25, n. 67).

17 The appointment was made by *Real orden* of June 19, 1804 (ARSEM, leg. 160, doc. 12, c, cited in Negrín Fajardo 1982, p. 25).
We have no record of how Loftus came by his knowledge of the instruction of the deaf, and foreign influence cannot be discounted.
When the school first opened, Atanasio Royo Fernández was hired as Loftus' assistant. Royo was another Spaniard who had some experience in the education of the deaf, for he had been teaching two such pupils in Madrid (anon. 1805, p. 62). Royo was soon to be replaced by Angel Machado, the father of Loftus' prize student Juan Machado.

18 The six who were supported by the school were provided lessons and room and board. Other boarders could attend for fifteen *reales* a day, and day students would pay one hundred *reales* a month (*Reglamento*, 1804, chapters VIII-XI).

19 Another example was Prádez' contemporary, Gregorio Santa Fe, who had been educated by a mysterious Jesuit, Diego Vidal, at the Piarist Fathers' school of Santo Tomás in Zaragoza. When he arrived in Madrid in 1795 at the age of twenty-two, his story was related in the press by José Miguel Alea (Alea 1795).
The similarities between the two deaf men are striking: Both were from Zaragoza, both were of the same age - Alea gave Santa Fe's age as twenty-two in 1795, Prádez' age was listed as twenty-four when he enrolled in the Royal Academy of San Fernando in 1797 (ARABASF, leg. 3/302, Libro de matrícula de la Real academia de San Fernando que principia en primero de septiembre de 1795), and within two years of each other both journeyed to Madrid to study art. But while Prádez went on to an illustrious career as a teacher, I have been unable to learn anything of Santa Fe's fate.

ate for (this instruction) *than any other, in view of the conformity of organization that exists between him and those he would teach* (ARSEM, Actas, 8-3-1805).

The Friends of the Country welcomed Roberto Prádez for another reason as well: In him they had found that exceedingly rare commodity, an educated deaf Spaniard, and one who had never left the Iberian Peninsula at that. In an era in which the teaching of the deaf had been virtually extinguished in Spain and national pride had made these men loath to resort to foreigners, this was a stroke of good fortune indeed. Thus, the Friends of the Country congratulated themselves on the new addition to the school, and understandably so. Prádez, for his part, must have also been eager to collaborate in the enterprise, for when initial efforts to secure a salary for him were unsuccessful, the art teacher was undaunted, and offered his services for free.[20] And so began the career of Spain's first deaf teacher of the deaf.

Despite his lack of hearing, Prádez had no trouble communicating with his colleagues at the Economic Society. He could, according to members of the school's governing Junta, *read on the lips the majority of words addressed to him, and comprehend perfectly all that was said to him in writing or in the manual alphabet, and respond in either fashion with complete propriety* (ARSEM, Actas, 2-2-1806). Prádez himself described his pronunciation as *unintelligible (confusa)*,[21] but his ability to lipread must have been nothing short of remarkable, to judge from the account of one member of the Junta:

> *The deaf mute Roberto Prádez answers anyone who speaks to him; and I have taken the trouble to experiment* (to see) *if while I was seated below* (the level of his gaze) *and he was standing he could understand me. I have seen that he understands even this way, and the most he does is look more closely so he can see what the mouth reveals naturally upon speaking; but he does not need to inspect the inside* (of the mouth) *(...).* (Hernández 1815, p. 104)[22]

In a time when there were no schools for the deaf in Spain, how could a deaf Spaniard who had never been abroad acquire an education? Prádez himself tells us that he learned to read and write at home – on one occasion he attributed his instruction to the efforts of *his caring mother (su cuidadosa madre)*,[23] on another, to both his parents (ARABASF, leg. 1-49/3, petition from Roberto Prádez, 3-2-1804). Prádez' father, Pedro, had been born in Béziers, in the Languedoc region of southern France, and his mother, María Gautier, was most likely of French origin as well, to judge by her name. Once again, the link with France. Did Prádez' parents learn of the teaching of the deaf while living there?

Whatever the debt to France, it was most likely substantial, to judge from the reticence of the Economic Society. The members took obvious pride in this educated deaf man who has never been abroad and there can be no doubt but that they knew the circumstances of his education, yet they never made any reference to how he had been taught, and not once did they mention his mother (or both his parents, as the case may be). If the teacher was French, and a woman at that, no acknowledgment was called for, it seems.[24] Nevertheless, if

---

20 ARSEM, Actas, 2-2-1806. Prádez was not assigned a regular stipend until August of 1807 (Granell y Forcadell 1932, p. 47), and not until 1810 did he begin to receive a salary. Eventually, he would receive a salary and room and board at the school.

21 ARABASF, leg. 1-49/3, Memorial de D. Roberto Prádez al Señor Protector solicitando la continuación de una pensión que obtiene de nueve reales diarios, 7-28-1801.

22 This same author noted that Prádez had trouble with the use of prepositions, however, and that the weekly reports he wrote for the school contained *an abundance of sentences that cannot be understood because of their lack of connectives.* (Hernández 1815, p. 83) Yet even this writer found merit in Prádez' achievements: *(..) if lacking instruction in the* (Spanish) *language he has achieved* [all that he has], *his intellectual progress would be admirable if he had had more perfect teaching.* (Hernández 1815, p. 104)

23 ARABASF, leg. 1-49/3, Memorial de D. Roberto Prádez al Señor Protector solicitando la continuación de una pensión que obtiene de nueve reales diarios, 7-28-1801.

it is fair to judge teachers by the achievements of their students, María Gautier and Pedro Prádez were indisputably among the most successful, for their son would go on to become first an award winning artist, then a teacher of the deaf who would teach many, many deaf students over the course of more than thirty years.

At the beginning of the nineteenth century, when Prádez was in his late twenties, he provided the following account of his early life: He was a native of Zaragoza (in northeastern Spain), and deaf from birth. He was from a *distinguished (distinguida)* family,[25] for his father, Pedro Prádez, had built the Imperial Canal of Aragón (the greatest public work of the eighteenth century).[26] But his fortunes took a turn for the worse when *at a tender age (de tierna edad)* he was orphaned and left *destitute of resources which would permit him to subsist (destituido de medios para poder subsistir)* and with only the a knowledge of reading and writing, obtained *by virtue of extraordinary effort (a fuerza de extraordinario trabaxo)*. On account of his deafness, he could not aspire to a position corresponding to his station in life, and thus, *with no more support than that of his poor sisters (sin tener mas amparo que el de sus pobres hermanas),* he turned to the study of drawing and engraving. In 1789, when he was sixteen years old, Prádez enrolled at the Royal Academy of Fine Arts of San Carlos in Valencia, where he studied for seven years under the direction of Manuel Monfort.[27] The best teachers, however, were to be found not in Valencia but in the Spanish court. So the young artist, despite his precarious economic situation, journeyed to Madrid in 1797, in order to perfect his skill at drawing and engraving. There he was accepted to study under the direction of a well-known professor of engraving, Fernando Selma, of the Royal Academy of Fine Arts of San Fernando.[28]

By the following year Prádez' economic situation was critical, and he turned to Carlos IV, the Spanish king, requesting a pension that would allow him to continue his studies at the Academy of Fine Arts. Fernando Selma, Prádez' teacher, wrote in support of his petition. Selma clearly held his deaf pupil in high esteem. He praised his disciple's talent – *how pleasing to me are his skills,* he wrote, *as well as his diligence and his judgment (cuan gratos me son sus preceptos)*– and noted that the work he had already presented at the Acad-

---

24 In contrast, a member of the school's Junta, in an account of an educated deaf contemporary of Prádez' (see note 19 above), had gone so far as to suggest that a monument should be erected in honor of the man's teacher, one Diego Vidal (Alea 1795, p. 359). Significantly, Vidal was a Spaniard - albeit one who had probably learned of the teaching of the deaf in Italy and had begun his teaching with the methods of the Englishman John Wallis.

25 Prádez must have been born in 1772. In March of 1797 he was twenty-four years old (ARABASF, leg. 3/302, Libro de matrícula que da principio en primero de septiembre de 1795), and in July of 1799 he was twenty-seven (ARABASF, leg. 2-3/5, Opositores que han presentado obras para este año de 1799).

26 The Imperial Canal extended and intensified older areas of irrigation. A *Real cédula* of 1775 granted Pedro Prádez and his company permission to build the canal at his own expense (AHN, Sección Estado, leg. 4900, Real cédula de su Magestad (…) aprobando la propuesta hecha por Don Pedro Prádez, para hacer a su costa, y la de su compañía, un canal de riego, y navegación, (…)).

27 Prádez enrolled at the Royal Academy of Fine Arts of San Carlos in Valencia in November of 1789. His name is erroneously recorded as *Norberto Prádez,* but the names of his parents, Don Pedro and Doña María Gautier, leave no room for doubt (Archives of the Real Academia de Bellas Artes de San Carlos, Libro I, Matrículo de discípulos de la Real academia de San Carlos (desde 18 de febrero hasta abril de 1799)). This information was provided to me by Francisco-Javier Delicado Martínez, Archivist of the Royal Academy of Fine Arts of San Carlos, in Valencia.

28 For Prádez' account of his early years, see ARABASF, leg. 1-49/3, Memorial de D. Roberto Prádez al Señor Protector solicitando la continuación de una pensión que obtiene de nueve reales diarios, 7-28-1801, and a petition from Prádez of 3-2-1804.
  Prádez enrolled at Madrid's Royal Academy of Fine Arts of San Fernando on March 5, 1797, at the age of twenty-four (ARABASF, leg. 3/302, Libro de matrícula de la Real academia de San Fernando que da principio en primero de septiembre de 1795).

emy showed how much he promised in the future. Moreover, he revealed a personal concern for the young artist when he hastened to point out *the interest I have in his further development (el interes que tengo en su mayor lucimiento).*[29] Members of the Academy agreed that Prádez, *in virtue of his diligence, conduct, and natural circumstances (por su aplicacion, conducta y circunstancias naturales),* was fully deserving of royal favor. The king was persuaded, and he granted Prádez a pension of nine *reales* a day and charged the members of the Academy, and the master engraver Fernando Selma in particular, with seeing to his continued application. [30]

In 1799, two years after he had enrolled at San Fernando, Prádez entered a contest sponsored by the Academy. Although four contestants had signed up for the category of engraving, on the day of the contest only two would present themselves: Roberto Prádez and Estevan Boix. Boix had studied at the School of Fine Arts in Barcelona before enrolling at the Academy of San Fernando in 1796, a few months prior to Prádez' arrival.[31] At the time of the contest, Prádez was twenty-seven years old; his rival was two years his junior.

On the appointed day, each contestant delivered to the Academy his rendition of Mengs' (Anton Raphael Mengs, 1728-1779, German artist and court painter to Carlos III) painting of the Virgin, which hung in the king's oratory in the royal palace. Then Prádez and Boix, in the presence of twenty judges, were given two hours in which to produce a drawing of a statue of the Greek youth Antinous, antiquity's ideal of masculine beauty. When the contest was over, the judges declared Prádez the winner; voting by secret ballot, they had awarded him thirteen votes to his rival's seven (ARABASF, leg. 3/86, Junta general, 7-4-1799). A few days later the Crown Prince himself would bestow the first prize on Roberto Prádez. On bended knee, the deaf artist kissed his future sovereign's hand as he accepted his reward, a gold coin of one ounce (ARABASF, leg. 3/86, Junta pública, Distribución de premios, 7-13-1799).

Not everyone at the Academy was satisfied with the outcome of the contest, however, and some accused Prádez' teacher, Fernando Selma, of having assisted his pupil more than he should have, and of perhaps even having gone so far as to touch up Prádez' engraving of the Virgin. (ARABASF, leg. 3/125, Actas de juntas particulares, 8-4-1799) Without bothering to conceal his anger at these accusations, Selma issued his denial:

> *I understand the Academy is displeased because I have taken too much interest in carrying out their commission. The Academy saw fit to charge me with the direction and teaching of the disciple Don Roberto Prádez. I have tried to lead him on the path that I consider most advantageous for his progress. (...) I have helped him to the extent that I consider normal; just as in all the Academy's contests it has been customary to practice regularly with the disciples who have taken part in them. If the contestant Don Estéban Boix did not know how to take advantage of the help that has been liberally offered to him, it is his own fault. Boix may know more than Prádez, but Prádez has shown more intelligence, both in the work prepared in advance and in the extemporaneous work done in the judges' presence. (ARABASF, leg. 1-49/3, letter from Fernando Selma, 7-11-1799)*

The dispute was not to be resolved until the Academy, desirous of recognizing Boix's considerable talent and of encouraging him in his future work, agreed to award him a special

---

29 ARABASF, leg. 1-49/3, letters from F. Selma to Isidoro Bosarte, 8-2-1798 and 10-9-1798.

30 By *Real orden* of October 4, 1798, Prádez was awarded a pension for two years (ARABASF, leg. 3/125, Actas de juntas particulares, 10-7-1798.). It was renewed on subsequent occasions for a total of some six years.

31 Boix enrolled at the Academy of San Fernando on November 18, 1796, when he was twenty-two years of age (ARABASF, leg. 3/302, Libro de matrícula de la Real academia de San Fernando que da principio en primero de septiembre de 1795).

prize, equal in value to Prádez' (ARABASF, leg. 5-19/2, Borradores de actas, 1779, Concurso de 1799: Gravado de láminas).

In spite of his initial success at the Academy of San Fernando, however, Roberto Prádez was not destined to become an engraver. While the Academy noted progress during his first few years there, they soon began to complain of the paucity of works presented, and of a lack of application. *He's slackening up (va aflojando), He's doing poorly (va mal), He's doing all right, but he needs to apply himself (va bien, pero que se aplique)*, were typical reactions to his work during his final years at San Fernando.[32] Did economic necessity leave little time for art studios? Already in 1801 Prádez had referred to himself as *totally destitute of means by which to subsist, and faced with having to beg (totalmente destituido de medios para poder subsistir, y expuesto a mendigar).*[33] To supplement his pension, he found private employment, but this seemed to leave little time for his studies: *Prádez should present works in the design studio and in engraving in addition to those he does by private commission (Pradez debe presentar obras de estudio en el diseño y en el grabado ademas de las que haga por encargo particular)*, was the judgment of the Academy.[34] The young artist also ceased to frequent the studio of Fernando Selma, and the teacher who had once so warmly praised his ability, his diligence, and his character now soured on his former disciple. Selma's comments at this time contrast dramatically with his opinion of just a few years earlier:

> *In the time that he was under my direction, he was fairly diligent; and despite being a deaf mute, he progressed sufficiently, as the Academy could observe from the various studies he presented (...). What can be determined of his talent is that, if he applies himself a lot, and if whoever directs him contributes an equal amount of care, it will be possible to obtain a mediocre professor.* (ARABASF, leg. 1-49/3, letter from Fernando Selma to Isidoro Bosarte, 9-20-1801)

Then Selma went on to reveal the depth of his prejudice against the deaf: *Since he is a deaf mute, he lacks ideas, and it is impossible to make him comprehend various principles of the Art* (ARABASF, leg. 1-49/3, letter from Fernando Selma to Isidoro Bosarte, 9-20-1801). Three years later, in 1804, Selma's appraisal remained unequivocally negative:

> *His application could be much greater; his subsistence I do not consider possible with only what the works he is capable of executing can produce, and it is even less possible for him to make progress in his profession.* (ARABASF, leg. 1-49/3, letter from Fernando Selma to Isidoro Bosarte, 5-10-1804)

There is no further record of Prádez at the Academy of San Fernando after 1804.

Upon leaving the Academy, Prádez turned to his true calling, his life's work as a teacher of the deaf, and in 1805 he began his career as art teacher at the Madrid school. (The students received this instruction *with the greatest pleasure (con el mayor gusto)*,[35] and the archives of the Economic Society still contain their pencilled sketches of eyes, lips, noses, ears – mute tribute to their teacher's efforts.) During his early years at the school, Prádez did much more than teach drawing, however. Indeed, the record reveals a flurry of activity: In December of 1805 Prádez, together with Lieutenant Colonel Loftus, the head teacher, presented a curriculum for the school (Granell y Forcadell 1932, p. 42), and in 1807 and 1808 Prádez joined

---

32 For records of Prádez' works presented to the Academy and accompanying comments, see ARABASF, Juntas ordinarias, leg. 3/86, leg. 1-23/4, and leg. 1-21/1. The years covered are 1798-1804.

33 ARABASF, leg. 1-49/3, Memorial de Don Roberto Prádez al Señor Protector solicitando la continuación de una pensión que obtiene de nueve reales diarios, 7-28-1801.

34 ARABASF, leg. 3/86, Junta ordinaria, 12-4-1802. A similar admonition occurs in the minutes of a meeting of September 5, 1801 (leg. 3/125, Actas de juntas particulares).

35 ARSEM, leg. 203, doc. 6, Relación de las tareas y ocupaciones de la Real sociedad económica en el año académico de 1807.

Loftus, a teaching assistant, and the school's spiritual director in examining the students (Granell y Forcadell 1932, pp. 47,49). In the fall of 1808 the school's governing Junta accepted Prádez' offer to teach writing and appointed him acting teacher of caligraphy (Granell y Forcadell 1932, p. 50).

During these same years, the Junta clashed repeatedly with its head teacher, Lieutenant Colonel Juan de Dios Loftus y Bazán. True, Loftus had undertaken the instruction of the deaf child Juan Machado while stationed in Ceuta, but he was first and foremost a military man, enamoured of his rank, which in his words entitled him to be treated *with the respect that I am due (con el decoro que me compete)*, and made him *distinguished among persons of status (distinguido entre todas las personas de caracter)*.[36] It was no doubt because of such sentiments that Loftus was ill-disposed to submit to the authority of the school's Junta. In the words of its members, although the regulations (...) state that he is an employee and under the authority of (the Junta), he could never conceive of the possibility that a military man of rank might be subordinate as head teacher to men of another social class (ARSEM, leg. 206, doc 7, report of the governing Junta, ??-2-1810 [month illegible]). And when it came to dealing with the students, Loftus would be content with nothing less than absolute power over them – the children should know that *their reward or their punishment depends on me (su premio o su castigo pende de mi)*, he proclaimed (AGS, Gobierno intruso, leg. 1182, letter from Loftus to Miguel Ruiz de Celada, 4-29-1809) - and he resented any intervention on the part of the governing body. As could be expected, Loftus' refusal to acknowledge the supremacy of the Junta was a source of continual conflict.

In addition to the dispute over authority, there was the question of Loftus' teaching: The Junta could find nothing good to say about it, and Loftus, for his part, was not about to accept any suggestions. His method, the Junta complained, *served only to obfuscate the students' understanding (no sirve sino de ofsucar el entendimiento de los alumnos;* AGS, Gobierno intruso, leg. 1182, report of José Miguel Alea, 3-26-1809). And all attempts at methodological discussion were useless, for in the Junta's estimation, Loftus regarded any such effort as *an abuse of power (un abuso del poder;* ARSEM, leg. 206, doc. 7, report of the governing Junta, ??-2-1810 [month illegible]). Although at times he might feign submission, the Friends of the Country were convinced that given his *military character (caracter militar)*, Loftus *would never submit to anyone else's plans (jamas se sujetaría a a plan ageno;*ARSEM, leg. 206, doc 7, report of the governing Junta, ??-2-1810 [month illegible]). They could only conclude that their head teacher suffered from a *defect of aptitude and docility (defeto de aptitud y docilidad)*.[37]

Loftus' rigid military character and his ineptitude as an instructor were bad enough, but worst of all was his mistreatment of the students. In 1806, just one year after the school's opening, one student, Francisco de Sales Entero, wrote to the Junta in desperation: *The head master threatens me at all hours and I have resolved to run away if you do not put an end to it (El Maestro Director me amenaza a todas horas y estoy resuelto a dejarle si V.M. no lo remedia);*[38] the following year he made good his threat (Granell y Forcadell 1932, p. 47). (Expulsion eventually ended Sales Entero's travails at the Madrid school, but not before he had made an unsuccessful attempt to take his own life; ARSEM, leg. 202, doc. 14, 8-21-1807). By 1809 the pupils were complaining *all with the same voice (todos de una voz)* of the cruelty with which their teacher punished them; in reality, this complaint had existed since the opening of the school (AGS, Gobierno intruso, leg. 1182, report of José Miguel Alea, 2-26-1809).

---

36 ARSEM, leg. 209, doc. 18, letter from Loftus to the Subdirector of the Economic Society, 12-7-1810.

37 ARSEM, leg. 205, doc. 1, Representación hecha al Rey sobre la enseñanza del Maestro Director del Colegio de sordo-mudos D. Juan de Dios Loftus, 2-11-1809.

38 AGS, Gobierno intruso, leg. 1182, note of 12-4-1806 from the student Entero, reproduced in a letter from José Miguel Alea, 3-26-1809.

The students were in open insubordination, they refused to respect and obey their teacher, and according to Loftus, it was all because the Junta had undermined his authority. He claimed that when he admonished his pupils for some misdeed and threatened them with punishment – deprivation of food and being made to kneel in the classroom were the only ones he acknowledged inflicting – his charges became so arrogant, they threatened to run away from the school, or they seemed disposed to strike their teacher. Hurling invectives from their fingers, they signed that they would not obey Loftus and his assistant, and that they shat on them. If punished, they jeered, they would go to the Junta, and as if to emphasize the point, they proceeded to reel off the names of the members, using the name signs they had invented for each one.[39] One student, José Hernández, had gone so far as to raise his hand menacingly to the teacher, signing that he despised him and would not obey him, and threatening to throw an inkwell at him. Loftus ordered the unruly pupil confined to his room and deprived of meals, but Hernández countered that the cook would give him food anyway, then repeated that most galling taunt: If punished, he would go to the Junta. Loftus, *to avoid vexations (por evitar desazones)*, as he put it, let Hernández go unpunished (AGS, Gobierno intruso, leg. 1182, letter from Loftus to Miguel Ruiz de Celada, 4-29-1809).

Clearly, this situation could not be allowed to continue. The Junta would have liked nothing better than to fire the intractable head teacher, but it was frustrated in its attempts to do so. In 1809 the Junta suspended Loftus, but because the lieutenant colonel was an *afrancesado*, a supporter of the French government that ruled Spain at that time, his ties to Spain's French ruler, Joseph Bonaparte, kept him at his post. By 1811, however, Loftus himself had had enough. He wished to resume his military career, and declared that after six years of *this job and this painful work (este destino y penoso trabajo)*, he was *tired of contending with children, and more so those of this class (cansado de lidiar con ninos, y mas de esta clase;* AGS, Gobierno intruso, leg. 1182, letter from Loftus, 2-22-1811). A member of the governing Junta, the intellectual abbé José Miguel Alea, then offered to teach the children for free and was named to replace Loftus. (ARSEM, leg. 212, doc. 21, 3-28-1811)[40]

During these years of crisis, Prádez' importance at the Madrid school increased greatly. His official duties expanded to include the teaching of writing and arithmetic (ARSEM, leg. 206, doc. 7, report of José Miguel Alea, 10-20-1810), and unofficially he seems to have been doing a good deal more as well. This expansion of his role at the school was facilitated by the problems between Loftus and the Junta. As the disputes escalated, the lieutenant colonel responded by neglecting his teaching duties, and for long periods of time he did not bother to go to class at all.[41] The Junta was faced with a difficult situation indeed: A head teacher who often would not deign to go to class, yet could not be fired. A void had thus been created which allowed Prádez to take over the teaching at the Madrid school, and on many occasions it was the deaf artist, not the infantry officer, who taught the children.[42] Although Loftus continued to hold the title of head teacher until 1811, in reality Prádez alone often did

---

39 ARSEM, leg. 206, doc. 7, Expediente formado en la Real sociedad económica sobre la inasistencia a la clase del Maestro Director del Colegio de sordomudos D. Juan de Dios Loftus y Bazán. The complaints summarized here appear in the aforementioned document, as well as in letters from Loftus to Miguel Ruiz Celada (AGS, Gobierno Intruso, leg. 1182, 3-11-1809, 4-29-1809).

40 Already in 1809 Alea had replaced Loftus when the latter had been temporarily suspended from his post (ARSEM, leg. 206, doc. 2, Copia del informe que dio al Ministerio del interior, la Junta de dirección y gobierno del Real colegio de sordo-mudos, 1-16-1809).

41 For instance, at one point the Junta complained that Loftus *has been absent (…) or has attended* (class) *without any formality concerning his teaching from August 26, 1809, until October 17, 1810* (ARSEM, leg. 206, doc. 7, Extracto de los documentos (...) que prueban la poca asistencia del Mo Don Juan Loftus (...), n.d.).

42 For example, various references to Prádez taking over for Loftus appear throughout the documents of ARSEM, leg. 206, doc. 7.

the teaching. Roberto Prádez contributed greatly to the school during these years, but in the years to come, his contributions would be even greater.

The year 1808 marked the beginning of Spain's War of Independence. Under cover of the treaty of Fontainebleau, Napoleon's troops had secured the partial occupation of Spain in 1807, supposedly for the purpose of a joint war against Portugal. In March of 1808 Carlos IV was forced to abdicate in favor of his son, who became Fernando VII, and the following month Napoleon lured both father and son to Bayonne, where he obliged them to abdicate in favor of his brother Joseph. One month later, on May 2, 1808, a popular uprising in Madrid marked the beginning of the insurrection against the French occupation, but not until 1813 would the French troops withdraw from Spain; Fernando VII, converted by his absence into the Desired One, would return the following year.

The war years brought great suffering and deprivation to Madrid. The year 1811, which was known as *the year of hunger,* saw more than 20,000 residents perish from hunger and infectious diseases. As the price of a loaf of bread soared to thirteen *reales,* the populace ate all existing animals, beginning with those that were edible and turning next to those that were not, and many people died in the streets from starvation. (Corral 1985, p. 75) These were years of hardship for the Madrid's Economic Society as well. The Junta was faced with a severe shortage of funds for the school, and in 1808 members resorted to taking the children to their homes for their midday meal (ARSEM, Actas, 9-17-1808). The worst was yet to come, however, and neither the students nor Roberto Prádez, their teacher, would be spared the suffering of their fellow *madrileños.* By February of 1811 the school was in debt and, although the head teacher, José Miguel Alea, had already agreed to teach the children for free, the Junta had fallen behind in paying its other employees. There were no funds with which to provide for the children, either, and Spain's first deaf teacher of the deaf, the award-winning artist of *distinguished* birth, was reported to be *without exaggeration, stark naked (sin exageracion en cueros;* ARSEM, leg. 212, doc. 11, 2-26-1811). Desperate because of the school's financial situation, the Friends of the Country at last found a way to eliminate housing expenses and the positions of the *mayordomo* and other employees: They would lodge Prádez and the six students supported by the Society at the municipal school of San Ildefonso.[43]

On the night of April 30, 1811, Roberto Prádez and his students moved to San Ildefonso. A chilly reception awaited them there. Because the deaf youths were somewhat older than the children at the municipal school,[44] it was feared they might exert a bad influence.[45] Thus, total separation of the two groups was rigorously enforced. The door that connected the deaf students' room to the rest of the school was locked from the outside, the key was taken away, and for good measure, a bolt was nailed on the outside. (AGS, Gobierno intruso, leg. 1182, 1-5-1811) Although the school had a fountain within its grounds, Prádez and his students were denied access to it and were forced to fetch water from a public fountain in the neighborhood. (ARSEM, leg. 213, doc. 6, 6-17-1811, and leg. 213, doc. 7, 6-14-1811) They were forbidden to eat in the school's refectory, and their food, two meager meals a day, was prepared in a public inn. (ARSEM, leg. 213, doc. 6, 6-17-1811, and leg. 213, doc. 7,

---

43 AV, Secretaría, leg. 2-371-6. For a discussion of events leading up to the move to San Ildefonso, see also ARSEM, Borradores de actas, 3-2-1811, 3-16-1811, in leg. 212, doc. 11, and in leg. 213, doc 17.

   At San Ildefonso they would eventually be joined by a seventh deaf student and a hearing employee, Antonio Ugena. The school of San Ildefonso, known also as the Niños de la Doctrina, was for children of Madrid who were either orphans, or fatherless.

44 In one document the deaf youths were said to be between the ages of seventeen and thirty (AGS, Gobierno intruso, leg. 1182, 7-11-1811); in another they were said to be between fourteen and nineteen (AV, Secretaría, leg. 2-371-6).

45 AV, Secretaría, leg. 2-371-6; AGS, Gobierno intruso, leg. 1182, letter from various members of the Economic Society, 10-30-1811.

6-14-1811) The children were barefoot, their unwashed clothes reduced to rags. (ARSEM, leg. 213, doc. 6, 6-17-1811) Confined to a single room, they were virtual prisoners at San Ildefonso. In such conditions, one observer found it

> *not (...) strange that they amuse themselves by ruining their quarters, throwing in the privy whatever they have at hand, after having broken it to bits and filled its drain with bones, rocks, and debris (...).* (AV, Secretaría, leg. 2-371-6)

The Economic Society was moved by the plight of the children whose education they had sought to establish, and in a petition to the Ministry of the Interior, the members denounced the insalubrious conditions at San Ildefonso and pleaded for improvement.[46] Their pleas, however, were accompanied by what was clearly an ultimatum: *If no remedy is possible, it will be necessary for the Society to exempt itself from the distress that such misfortune creates at every turn* (ARSEM, leg. 213, doc. 7, Representación de la Sociedad al exmo. Ministerio del interior, 6-17-1811). Improve the situation, or we will wash our hands of it. Clearly, the school had become a stone around the Society's enlightened neck.

While the sensitive members of the Economic Society prepared to relieve their anguish by walking away from the problem, Prádez, who continued to live with the students, provided an account of conditions at San Ildefonso. Each day, he wrote, there was less food, and when the complaint was voiced to the innkeeper who prepared it,

> *he responded (with deceit) that it was not his fault,* (and) *that if the midday meal was somewhat scanty, it was also better prepared, and* (as for) *the meat and the salt pork, it seems that there is little because it disintegrates in the kettle after the bones have been removed from the meat, when really it is just the opposite, because most days the meat and salt pork are so hard that one's teeth creak upon biting into it, and furthermore, as if that weren't enough, there is no lack of bone: in spite of this and in spite of having told him to put in more salt pork and more meat, of the former he puts in the same as before, but of the latter he has now started (in order to make us see how much meat he puts in) to include so much bone in the stew that an experiment in a scale we have has made us see that on one day, of three pounds of meat in the midday meal and supper, there was a good pound and a half of bone.* (ARSEM, leg. 213, doc. 6, 8-21-1811)

Not surprisingly, the meager rations had begun to take their toll, as Prádez related: *One begins to see and experience in the deaf mutes a weakness and stomach pains so excessive that they do not permit them to write, draw, or attend class most days* (ARSEM, leg. 213, doc. 6, 8-21-1811).

By the fall of 1811 the Economic Society had no funds with which to meet the needs of the school. The children were being housed at San Ildefonso at no cost, but they still needed to be fed and clothed, they needed school supplies, and Prádez, their teacher, needed to be paid. The Society could provide for none of these things, and it began to look for ways to rid itself of responsibility for its creation. It was in this context that the members reconsidered the goals of deaf education and concluded:

> *(...) we have committed the error of directing* (the teaching of the deaf) *solely toward literary knowledge, neglecting what they will most need, which is to be able to support themselves and learn a trade that could provide for their future subsistence. The few that remain today are no longer children, and they find themselves no less in need of assistance and the charity of others than when they were in their infancy: and so if we continue in this fashion, our efforts will only produce lifelong beggars, who will increase the burden of the State, and perhaps the work of the Criminal Courts.* (AGS,

---

46 Specifically, they requested that the government provide six hundred *reales* per month for the support of the students (ARSEM, leg. 213, doc. 7, Representación de la Sociedad al exmo. Ministerio del interior, 6-17-1811).

Gobierno intruso, leg. 1182, letter from various members of the Economic Society to the Minister of the Interior, 10-30-1811)[47]

To the Friends of the Country, the solution was obvious: lower your expectations. *It is necessary,* they concluded, *to regard as a chimera the desire to make of them sages or sublime artists. In all times and with all possible assistance, it would be a marvel to produce even one of the former, and a few examples of the latter* (ARSEM, leg. 213, doc. 17, 6-18-1811). The nation was at war, the Society had no funds with which to support the school, and goals of the education of the deaf were redefined accordingly: Forget about reading, writing, and arithmetic, and apprentice these students out to learn a trade. Not coincidentially, the Society would then be relieved of its financial responsibility, for as the members envisioned it, the apprentices would live in the homes of their employers, where they would do double duty as servants.[48]

The Friends of the Country were never to implement this plan, however. Instead, they persuaded the municipal government of Madrid to provide for the deaf students (ARSEM, Actas, 9-21-1811, 9-28-1811, 10-26-1811, 11-9-1811). It had not been easy – one member noted that only *with the greatest difficulty and* (after) *many attempts did* (the Society) *rid itself of the ruinous administration of that establishment* (ARSEM, leg. 213, doc. 34, comments of the Society's censor, Tiburcio Hernández, 4-30-1812) – but at last they were free of financial responsibility for their charges. Under the Municipality, Prádez and his students were moved from San Ildefonso to the Hospicio, the poorhouse. At the Hospicio, deaf education was redefined in yet another way: The children were set to weaving cloth (AV, Secretaría, leg. 2-371-6).

By 1812 Prádez' lot had been reduced to extreme misery, and he found himself *in desperate need of both undergarments and outerwear, for the decency of his person (sumamente necesitado de ropa tanto interior como exterior para la decencia de su persona;* AV, Secretaría, leg. 2-371-4, letter from Prádez to Manuel García de la Prada, Corregidor de la Villa de Madrid, 6-7-1812). In 1810 the Economic Society had granted him a salary of six *reales* per day – three *reales* less than the pension he had received twelve years earlier during his student days at the Academy of San Fernando – but he had not been paid for several years (AV, Secretaría, leg. 2-371-4, letter from Prádez to Manuel García de la Prada, Corregidor de la Villa de Madrid, 6-7-1812). Although the Society had repeatedly recognized Prádez' *merit, diligence, and good conduct (merito, aplicacion y conducta;* AGS, Gobierno intruso, leg. 1182, note that accompanied Prádez' petition of 1-29-1811 to the Ministry of the Interior), his singular worth and his many contributions to the school seemed to count for nothing when he requested his back salary. The Friends of the Country acknowledged that his claims were *extremely just,* but they pointed out that they were no longer responsible for the economy of the school. Besides, they observed, Prádez and his students were at least being fed, which was more than could be said of others in these times. Thus, Prádez' request was denied and he was advised to go elsewhere (*justisimas*).[49]

---

47 In 1803 the Economic Society had proposed to teach the students reading, writing, arithmetic, and grammar. Geometry, geography, and history would also be taught to those who should study them *because of their circumstances and class,* and religion would be taught as soon as students were sufficiently prepared to learn it (*Reglamento,* 1804, cap. V, art. 2, 3). But the king complained that while the school established two classes of students, rich and poor, they were given the same instruction, and no trade was taught to the poor (ARSEM, *Actas,* 11-5-1803). The Economic Society agreed to teach a trade to the poor students, but by 1811 this provision still had not been implemented.

48 The Society, however, would continue to fulfill certain obligations towards the students, for instance, seeing to it that they received religious instruction (ARSEM, leg. 213, doc. 17, 6-18-1811).

49 ARSEM, leg. 213, doc. 34, Prádez' petitions to the Economic Society for back pay, 3-22-1812 and 4-24-1812; comments of Tiburcio Hernández on Prádez' request, 4-30-1812.

Although the Economic Society maintained that the children were being fed at the Hospicio, in truth they were, according to one observer, *reduced to an extremely meager ration and suffering continuous hunger, sickness of the stomach and nudity.* (ARSEM, leg. 213, doc. 34, letter from Antonio Ugena, 8-11-1812) Eventually, necessity drove them to the streets to beg for food. (ARSEM, leg. 218, doc. 3, 12-26-1813) By August of 1812 three of them, Domingo Pérez, Manuel Muñoz, and José Hernández, who in better times had threatened Lieutenant Colonel Loftus with an inkwell, had died, and the others were about to suffer the same fate. (ARSEM, leg. 213, doc. 34, letter from Antonio Ugena, 8-22-1812)

The War of Independence ended in 1813, and the Madrid school for the deaf reopened the following year, once again under the auspices of the Economic Society. By this time, however, a majority of the students had died from hunger and exposure (ARSEM, leg. 216, doc. 11, 11-9-1813, and leg. 221, doc. 4, 12-20-1814), despite the efforts of Prádez and the Municipality to provide for them at the Hospicio. In the words of one eyewitness, *such was the scene of horror and desolation of those days of mourning for all of Spain* (ARSEM, leg. 221, doc. 4, 12-20-1814).

Prádez' behavior during the war years had been nothing less than heroic. The Friends of the Country had in effect turned their backs on the deaf, but Prádez, in contrast, had never waivered in his devotion to his charges. Despite the hardships at the municipal school of San Ildefonso, despite the inhuman conditions of the Hospicio, he had remained with his students, pleaded for the betterment of their conditions, shared their misery, and continued to teach them. It is fair to say that from the move to San Ildefonso in 1811 until the school reopened in 1814, what education of the deaf there was in Spain was due in large part – if not solely – to the efforts of Roberto Prádez.[50]

During the first third of the nineteenth century, instability would be the hallmark of the Madrid school, in large part because it was from its inception sponsored by the State (unlike many other European schools for the deaf, which were run by the Church). Thus, its fate was directly affected by the major political upheavals of the time, and head teachers and governing bodies fell victim to political events with predictable regularity. During the War of Independence, José Miguel Alea, who in 1811 had replaced Lieutenant Colonel Loftus as head teacher, collaborated whole-heartedly with the invador and came to be counted among Joseph Bonaparte's intimate advisors. (Juretschke 1962, p. 156) At the war's conclusion in 1813, Alea emigrated to France, along with 12,000 Spanish families who had served the French king.[51] He was succeeded as head teacher by another member of the school's gov-

---

During the war years Prádez pleaded for financial assistance from a number of sources in addition to the Economic Society, among them, the Ministry of Interior (AGS, Gobierno intruso, leg. 1182, 3-22-1812), the Magistrate of Madrid (AV, Secretaría, leg. 2-371-4, 6-7-1812), and the Municipality (AV, Secretaría, leg. 2-371-6, 9-2-1813).

50 During the war years, José Miguel Alea continued to hold the title of head teacher, but I have found no evidence to suggest that he actually did any teaching. Indeed, what documentation I have seen suggests just the opposite: In 1810 Alea was in Seville, where he formed part of a commission whose task it was to select those paintings from Seville's churches and convents that were to be handed over to the occupation government (*Gazeta de Sevilla*, February 11, 1810, cited in Gómez Imaz 1910), and in 1811 it was reported that he had been and continued to be *indisposed*, and thus unable to attend to the teaching of the children (ARSEM, leg. 213, doc. 31, petition from Antonio Ugena, 11-30-1811). In August of 1812 Alea and Domingo de Agíero, who were nominally in charge of the administration of the school at that time, were both reported to be out of town (ARSEM, leg. 213, doc. 34, letter from Ugena, 8-22-1812). In addition to Prádez a hearing adult, Antonio Ugena, also lived with the children at the Hospicio. Ugena originally joined the school in the capacity of a servant, but eventually came to occupy the position of teaching assistant.

51 All who accepted employment under the French government were officially considered as collaborators, even though many had done so more out of necessity than conviction. As a teacher at the Madrid school, Prádez too had been in the employ of the invador, and at the close of the

erning Junta, the liberal lawyer Tiburcio Hernández. When Fernando VII returned to Spain in 1814, he lost no time in abolishing the constitution the liberal Cortes had written in his absence, and the return to absolute monarchy went hand in hand with the persecution of those of liberal ideas. The liberals regained power in 1820, however, and during the liberal triennium that followed, the school for the deaf (along with all other teaching establishments) was placed under the *Dirección General de Estudios*. Fernando VII reestablished his despotic rule in 1823, with the help of armies sent by Europe's other absolute monarchies, and persecution of the liberals began anew. Many liberals fled Spain at this time, among them head teacher Tiburcio Hernández, whom the government had condemned to death. The *Dirección General de Estudios* was dissolved, as was the Economic Society, and the administration of the school for the deaf was for a few years left to its spiritual director, Vicente Villanova, until Fernando VII entrusted it to a dandy courtier, the Duke of Híjar, in 1827. There ensued a chaotic interval of eight years, during which brutal mistreatment of the students was met with insubordination and finally open rebellion. When Fernando VII died in 1833, the Economic Society was reorganized, and in 1835 the school for the deaf was once again entrusted to its care. That same year Juan Manuel Ballesteros was named director, ushering in a new era of stability that was to last nearly thirty-five years.

Roberto Prádez remained at the Madrid school throughout the tumultuous first third of the nineteenth century. As changing political tides swept aside a succession of head teachers and administrations, the school lurched from crisis to crisis, and during those troubled times, Prádez provided much needed stability and continuity. For an uninterrupted period of more than three decades, he participated fully in the life of the institution, teaching, producing materials for use in the classroom, providing the Junta with regular reports on the goings on at the school, and serving on commissions with his hearing colleagues. Prádez' name continued to appear in documents from the school up through late 1836,[52] but it appears that towards the end his importance declined and he was somewhat marginalized. To judge from the record, he participated less in the life of the school during his final years there, and although he continued in the position of writing teacher, in his last year at the institution a young hearing man, Francisco Fernández Villabrille, was appointed art teacher.[53] Villabrille would go on to a distinguished career as a teacher and writer, but there is no record of his having any credentials whatsoever as an artist.

Roberto Prádez' life ended on December 7, 1836, at number 14 on the Calle de Santiago, where he was living with his wife, Modesta Sierra.[54] His death certificate records that he died without receiving the Holy Sacraments of the Catholic Church and was afforded a free burial outside the walls of the cemetery of the Puerta de Fuencarral, *out of pity (de misericordia;* Archivo parroquial de Santiago y San Juan Bautista, diócesis de Madrid, Alcalá,

---

war, both his name and that of Alea's successor, Tiburcio Hernández, appeared on a list of *purification agreements* pardoning certain individuals who had been associated with the government of Joseph Bonaparte (AV, Secretaría, 2-4-1-56, Indice alfabético de acuerdos de purificaciones del Ayuntamiento constitucional al contado desde 28 de junio de 1813 a 9 de mayo de 1814).

52 In August of 1836 Prádez was among those at the school who swore their allegiance to the constitution of 1812 (Granell y Forcadell 1932, p. 173), and in November of that same year his name also appeared in the school records (ARSEM, leg. 294.1, Relaciones para la Guía de forasteros de 1837, 11-24-1836), but one month later his name was absent from a list of employees. (Granell y Forcadell 1932, p. 174).

53 In November of 1836, Prádez was listed as writing teacher, and Fernández Villabrille as art teacher. (ARSEM, leg. 294.1, Relaciones para la Guía de forasteros de 1837, 11-24-1836).

54 In 1815, when the War of Independence had ended and he had begun to receive a regular salary once again - now raised to nine *reales* per day - Prádez had requested the Junta's approval to marry. The Junta consented and extended a personal invitation to the judge of the ecclesiastical tribunal of spolium. (Granell y Forcadell 1932, p. 80). I have been unable to locate Pradez' marriage certificate or to ascertain if he indeed married Modesta Sierra in 1815.

Libro de defunciones, libro 12, folio 101). The life of Spain's first deaf teacher of the deaf had ended without fanfare in a pauper's funeral.

IV Conclusion

Prádez' death marked the end of an era. In times of crisis, a deaf man had been able to educate his fellows and had attained a position of influence and importance at the Madrid school. For more than thirty years, he had taught and served as a role model for many, many deaf students, and had won the acclaim and gratitude of the Friends of the Country. But once order was restored at the institution, his importance apparently diminished, and his position as art teacher was eventually awarded to a hearing man. Never again would a deaf person achieve comparable stature and prominence at the Madrid school.

Prádez had lived to see the dawn of a new day, which commenced with the appointment of Juan Manuel Ballesteros as director. Ballesteros' tenure, which began in 1835, one year before the art teacher's death, would span the second third of the 1800s. In sharp contrast to the first third of the century, this second third would be a period of stability, characterized by the expansion of the education of the deaf and by the professionalization of their instruction – but also by the systematic exclusion of deaf teachers. In the decades to come, the teaching would no longer be entrusted to infantry officers, intellectual abbés, liberal lawyers – or deaf people. Instead, deaf education would be in the hands of professionals, hearing professionals who would systematically exclude the deaf from their ranks. The founders of the Madrid school had been open-minded, sympathetic intellectuals who could accept a deaf colleague and recognize the advantage conferred by the *conformity of organization* he shared with his pupils; they believed that deaf people, like everyone else, could be redeemed through education. In the second third of the nineteenth century, however, these men were succeeded by others of lesser statue, 'professionals' who declared the deaf unfit to become teachers of their own kind.

This policy was clearly articulated by the school's new director, Juan Manuel Ballesteros.[55] *The difficulties and complications of this teaching do not make us expect in the deaf the set of requirements they need to be teachers of* (their) *companions in misfortune,* he wrote. *For this,* he concluded, *they need to have received a very special education* - and it was apparently inconceivable that they would receive it at the Madrid school (Ballesteros in Ballesteros/Villabrille 1845, pp.107-108).[56] Under Ballesteros, deaf people would be relegated to the school's workshops, there to teach the students a trade.[57]

---

55   Ballesteros had been trained as a medical doctor (he had formerly served as the school's physician), and it may be that his medical background led him to view the deaf merely as less-than-perfect versions of hearing people.

56   Ballesteros did allow that deaf people might be employed as *teaching assistants,* however, subordinate to *professors of unhindered senses,* and he also conceded that deaf people might be teachers of writing and drawing, disciplines he considered to be *up to a certain point (...) purely mechanical* (Ballesteros in Ballestero/Villabrillev 1845, pp. 107-108). Nevertheless, shortly after he was named director, a hearing man, Francisco Fernández Villabrille, replaced Prádez in the position of art teacher.
      In barring the deaf from teaching positions, Ballesteros invoked the argument that they were not suited to teach speech, but this was clearly a pretext because the teaching of articulation was not emphasized at this time. Contrary to popular belief, oralism was not implemented in Spain until the very end of the nineteenth century.

57   There was also an occasional deaf assistant to hearing professors, though apparently none who reached a position of any importance. In 1886, half a century after Prádez' death, another deaf man, Daniel Perea, would be hired as the school's art teacher. Perea was a former student of the Madrid school and a well known artist of the day, but he never attained Prádez' stature and importance, and the record suggests that at no time did he participate in the life of the school to anywhere near the extent that his predecessor had.

Ballesteros' views and those of other 'specialists' of his ilk went unchallenged, allowing them to consolidate control over deaf education exclusively in the hands of the hearing. The hold of the hearing upon the education of the deaf has been so tenacious that to this day, deaf people in Spain continue to be barred from teaching positions.

It is perhaps for this reason that it has been historically convenient for Spain to 'forget' about Roberto Prádez, the nation's first deaf teacher of the deaf, for the exclusion of deaf people from the ranks of educators of the deaf has been accompanied by their erasure from deaf history. In Spain today, a century and a half after Prádez' death, to speak of deaf education in the 1800s is to speak of hearing men (Alea, Hernández, Ballesteros, ...), but there is virtually no recollection of the deaf artist turned teacher. His role as a founder of deaf education in the nineteenth century, his heroic conduct during the War of Independence, his three decades of contributions to the Madrid school – all are unknown and uncelebrated. Indeed, in the land of his birth, it is now 'common knowledge' that Spain has **never** had any deaf teachers of the deaf. Hence, the need for reexamination and rearticulation of the historical record, and the special importance of paying homage to Roberto Francisco Prádez and of restoring him to his rightful place in deaf history and culture.

Appendix
The original Spanish quotations:

p. 54

Aqui ocurre motivo para lamentarnos de la comun fatalidad de los Espanoles, de dos siglos à esta parte, que las riquezas de su Pais, sin exceptuar aquellas, que son produccion del ingenio, las hayan de gozar mas los Estrangeros que ellos. Naciò en España el arte, que enseña à hablar los mudos; y pienso que no hai, ni huvo mucho tiempo ha en España quien quisiesse cultivarla, y aprovecharse de ella; al passo que los Estrangeros se han utilzado y utilizan mui bien en esta invencion. (Feijóo y Montenegro 1730, p. 419)

(...) de Parìs à Amsterdàn, y de Amsterdàn a Parìs se estàn cañoneando sobre quien es el Inventor de el Arte, sin que nadie se acuerde de Fray Pedro Ponce, que lo fuè indispensablemente. (Feijóo y Montenegro 1759, p. 95)

p. 56

(...) no concurren á la Escuela [de Navarrete] los sordos y mudos que hay en esta corte, por la preocupación, á mi parecer, en que viven las gentes en cuanto á la seguridad y certeza de los principios del arte. (Alea 1795, p. 262)

p. 58 / p. 59

(...) mucho más aproposito para [esta ensenanza] que otro alguno atendida la conformidad de organizacion que concurren entre él, y los que habia de ensenar. (ARSEM, Actas, 8-3-1805)

p. 59

(...) percibe por el movimiento de los labios la mayor parte de las palabras que se articulan dirijidas a él, y comprende perfectamente quanto se le dice por escrito o por el alfabeto manual, y responde de uno y otro modo con toda propiedad. (ARSEM, Actas, 2-2-1806)

El sordo-mudo Don Roberto Pradez contesta á qualquiera que le habla; y yo he cuidado de experimentar si estando sentado en baxo y él de pie me entendia. He visto que entiende aun asi, y que lo mas que hace es acercar la vista de modo que vea lo que la boca presenta naturalmente al hablar; mas no necesita reconocer lo interior, ó sea verlo (...;Hernández 1815, p. 104)

p. 61

Tengo entendido que la Academia se ha disgustado por interesarme demasiado en desempeñar su comision. La Academia tuvo a bien encargarme la direccion y enseñanza del Discipulo Dn. Roberto Pradez. He procurado dirigirle por el camino que considero mas bentajoso para sus adelantamientos. (...) Le é auxiliado lo que me á parecido regular; como en todas las oposiciones de la Academia se á practicado regularmente con los Discipulos que an concurrido á ellos. Si el Opositor Dn. Estevan Boix no se á sabido aprobechar de los auxilios que le an franqueado, el tiene la culpa. Podra saber mas Boix que Pradez, pero este á manifestado mas inteligencia, tanto en la obra de pensado como en la de repente. (ARABASF, leg. 1-49/3, letter from Fernando Selma, 7-11-1799)

p. 62

En el tiempo que estuvo en mi direccion fue bastante aplicado; y sin embargo de ser sordomudo, adelantó lo suficiente, como la misma Academia a podido adbertir por los barios estudios que subcesibamente fue presentando (...) Lo que se puede juzgar de su talento es, que aplicandose mucho, y poniendo a su parte otro tanto esmero que le dirija, podra lograrse un Profesor mediano. (ARABASF, leg. 1-49/3, letter from Fernando Selma to Isidoro Bosarte, 9-20-1801)

Como es Sordo-mudo, carece de ideas, y es imposible acerle comprender barios preceptos del Arte. (ARABASF, leg. 1-49/3, letter from Fernando Selma to Isidoro Bosarte, 9-20-1801)

Su aplicacion bien pudiera ser mucho mas; su subsistencia no la consider posible con solo lo que le pueden producir las obras a que es capaz desempeñar [sic], y menos acer adelantamientos en su Profession. (ARABASF, leg. 1-49/3, letter from Fernando Selma to Isidoro Bosarte, 5-10-1804)

p. 63

Aunque el reglamento (...) le enseñaba que era un dependiente y un subdito de [la Junta], nunca pudo concebir la posibilidad de que un Militar de graduacion estuviese sometido en el concepto de Maestro director a gentes de otro rango. (ARSEM, leg. 206, doc 7, report of the governing Junta, ??-2-1810 [month illegible])

p. 66

(...) no es extrano que se diviertan en arruinar el piso que habitan, echando en el lugar común cuanto les viene a mano, despues de haberle destrozado y llenado su conducto de huesos, piedras y escombros. (AV, Secretaría, leg. 2-371-6)

(...) si no fuese posible el remedio, se verá precisada la Sociedad a pedir el quedar eximida de las angustias que tales desdichas la originan a cada paso. (ARSEM, leg. 213, doc. 7, Representación de la Sociedad al exmo. Ministerio del interior, 6-17-1811)

(...) ha respondido (con engaño) que el ni tiene la culpa, que si la comida y la cena viene algo escasa, tambien viene mejor compuesta, y que la carne y tocino parece que hay poco, porque se deshace en la marmita, despues de que la carne esta mondada de todo hueso, siendo todo lo contrario, porque la carne y tocino vienen los mas de los dias tan duro que rechinan los dientes al tiempo de partirlo, y ademas poco que mucho no ha faltado hueso: con esto y con haberle dicho que heche mas tocino y mas carne, de lo primero hecha lo mismo que antes, pero de lo segundo ha empezado ahora (para hacernos ver la mucha carne que hecha) a hechar tanto hueso en el cocido y guisado que la experiencia, en un peso que tenemos de tres fieles nos ha hecho en un dia que de tres libras de carne en comida y cena ha habido libra y media larga de hueso. (ARSEM, leg. 213, doc. 6, 8-21-1811)

se ha empezado a ver y a experimentar en los sordomudos un descaecimiento y unos dolores de estomago tan excesivos, que no los dexa escribir, dibujar ni asistir los mas de los dias a la clase de ensenanza. (ARSEM, leg. 213, doc. 6, 8-21-1811)

p. 66 / p. 67

(...) se ha cometido el error de dirigir [la educacición de los sordomudos] solo hacia algunos conocimientos literarios, descuidando lo que mas falta podrá siempre hacerles que es el valerse a si mismos, y aprender un arte que pudiera proveer a su futura subsistencia. Los pocos que existen hoy han llegado ya a una edad crecida, y se encuentran poco menos necesitados del auxilio y caridad agena, que lo estuvieron en su infancia; de suerte que siguiendo asi solo produjeran nuestros cuidados unos mendigos de por vida, que aumentasen la carga del Estado, y acaso la ocupacion de los Tribunales criminales. (AGS, Gobierno intruso, leg. 1182, letter from various members of the Economic Society to the Minister of the Interior, 10-30-1811)

p. 67

Es menester partir del principio de mirar como una quimera el querer formar de ellos unos sabios o unos artistas sublimes. En todos tiempos y con todos auxilios sera un fenomeno lograr uno de aquellos, y de pocos exemplos los segundos. (ARSEM, leg. 213, doc. 17, 6-18-1811)

(...) a duras penas y muchísimas diligencias [la Sociedad] se desprendio de la administracion ruinosa de aquel establecimiento. (ARSEM, leg. 213, doc. 34, comments of the Society's censor, Tiburcio Hernández, 4-30-1812)

p. 68

(...) reducidos a una cortisima racion [y] padeciendo continuos hambres, enfermedades de estomago y desnudeces. (ARSEM, leg. 213, doc. 34, letter from Antonio Ugena, 8-11-1812)

(...) tal era el cuadro de horror y desolacion de aquellos dias de luto para toda Espana. (ARSEM, leg. 221, doc. 4, 12-20-1814)

p. 70

Lo dificultoso y complicado de esta enseñanza, no hace suponer en los sordo-mudos el conjunto de requisitos que necesitan para ser maestros de otros companeros de desgracia. Para esto necesitaban haber recibido una educacion muy especial. (Ballesteros in Ballesteros/Villabrille 1845, pp.107-108)

Abbreviations of unpublished sources

AGS   Archivo general de Simancas
AHN   Archivo histórico nacional
ARABASF Archives of the Real academia de bellas artes de San Fernando
ARSEM   Archives of the Real sociedad económica matritense de Amigos del país
AV   Archivo de la Villa (Madrid).

References

(anon.) (1805): Historia del establecimiento de un colegio de sordomudos en la corte de España, baxo la inmediata protección de la Real sociedad patriática matritense de los Amigos del país; *Efemerides de España*, 1-11-1805, pp. 54-55, and 1-15-1805, pp. 56-64.

Ainaud, M. (1919): La primera escola de sords-muts establerta a Barcelona; *La paraula*, year II, number 1, January-March, pp. 1-8.

Alea, José Miguel (1906/1907): Carta dirigida al editor del Diario de Madrid, 1795; *La Academia calasancia*, XVI, pp. 256-263, 286-290, 322-326, 353-361.

Andrés Morell, Juan (1794): *Carta del abate don Juan Andrés sobre el origen y las vicisitudes del arte de enseñar a hablar a los mudos sordos;* translated by Carlos Andrés Morell. Madrid: Imprenta de Sancha..

Ballesteros, Juan Manuel/ Francisco Fernández Villabrille (1845): *Curso elemental de instrucción de sordomudos.* Madrid: Colegio de sordo-mudos y ciegos.

Bonet, Juan Pablo (1620): *Reduction de las letras, y arte para enseñar a ablar los mudos.* Madrid: Francisco Abarca de Angulo.

Carr, Raymond (1982): *Spain: 1808-1975.* Second edition. Oxford: Claredon Press.

Corral, José del (1985): *Madrid de los Borbones.* Madrid: Avapiés.

Feijóo y Montenegro, Benito Jerónimo (1730): *Teatro crítico universal,* tomo IV. Madrid: Viuda de Francisco Hierro.

Feijóo y Montenegro, Benito Jerónimo (1759): *Cartas eruditas y curiosas,* tomo IV. Madrid: Imprenta del Supremo consejo de la Inquisición.

Godoy, Manuel (1956): *Memorias;* Biblioteca de autores españoles desde la formacion del lenguaje hasta nuestros días. Madrid: Ediciones atlas.

Gómez Imaz, Manuel (1910): *Los periódicos durante la guerra de la independencia (1808-1814).* Madrid: Tipografía de la Revista de archivos, bibliotecas y museos.

Granell y Forcadell, Miguel (1932): *Historia de la enseñanza del Colegio nacional de sordo-mudos desde el año 1794 al 1932.* Madrid: Colegio nacional de sordomudos.

Granell y Forcadell, Miguel (1936): El Padre José Fernández Navarrete; *Gaceta del sordomudo, no. 10,* April, pp. 3-4.

Hernández, Tiburcio (1815): *Plan de enseñar a los sordo-mudos el idioma español.* Madrid: La Imprenta real.

Hervás y Panduro, Lorenzo (1795): *Escuela española de sordomudos, o arte para enseñarles a escribir y hablar el idioma española.* Madrid: La Imprenta real.

Juretschke, Hans (1962): *Los afrancesados en la guerra de la independencia.* Madrid: Ediciones Rialp.

Negrín Fajardo, Olegario (1982): Proceso de creación y organización del Colegio de sordomudos de Madrid (1802-1808); *Revista de ciencias de educación,* 109, January-March, pp. 7-31.

Perelló, Jorge/Francisco Tortosa (1972): *Sordomudez,* second edition. Barcelona: Editorial cientifico-médica.

Reglamento del Real colegio de sordomudos, formado por la Real sociedad económica matritense y aprobado por S.M. (1804). Madrid: Imprenta de Pacheco.

Ruiz Berrio, Julio (1970): *Política escolar de España en el siglo XIX (1808-1833).* Madrid: Consejo superior de investigaciones cientícas.

Yves Bernard
Paris, France

Silent Artists

Summary • Résumé

This article is a survey of two periods dealing with Silent Art:

The dumb woman: during the Renaissance, the great masters tried to achieve a better psychological atmosphere for human actions in their paintings; they studied physiognomy, gestures and the language of deaf people. Then a number of silent artists appeared, some of them very successful illuminators, copyists and painters.

Memories of the heart: As the abbé de L'Epée died in 1789, the Bicentennial of the French Revolution was an opportunity to record how silent artists expressed their gratitude to their 'Spiritual Father'. Silent artists won prizes and worldwide acclaim, achieving the same honors as hearing people. At the same time they were very influential in the French Deaf Community, and helped to develop legal aid and social welfare for the Deaf.

Cette étude porte sur deux périodes de l'art silencieux:

La femme muette: au cours de la Renaissance, les grands maîtres recherchèrent une expression psychologique plus fine des actions humaines dans leurs peintures; ils étudièrent la physionomie, l'expression corporelle et le langage des sourds. C'est alors qu'apparurent de nombreux artistes silencieux, dont certains devinrent des enlumineurs, des copistes et des peintres renommés.

La mémoire du coeur: L'abbé de L'Epée étant mort en 1789, le bicentenaire de la Révolution fut pour nous le prétexte d'évoquer comment les artistes silencieux témoignèrent leur reconnaissance envers leur 'père spirituel'. Des artistes silencieux remportèrent concours et grand prix artistiques, leurs talents furent universellement reconnus. Simultanément ils eurent une profonde influence sur la société silencieuse française afin qu'elle acquière sa liberté par le droit et l'aide sociale.

The dumb woman

Under Roman Law people born deaf remained under legal guardianship for their entire lives. In the second century, a Greek surgeon practicing in Rome, Galen, wrote that speech is the *actio nobilissima voluntaria*; he naturally concluded that the deaf had little native ability. In fact, that mournful assertion could have been contested: a congenitally deaf painter, Quintus Pedius, was highly successful during the first century. He was in fact the grandson of Claudius Pedius, an honored general who had been jointly nominated with Augustinus to succeed Caesar. In the Augustan Age, Rome grew more beautiful, art and literature developed substantially. Although Quintus Pedius died early, and was discriminated against in that highly cultured society, he was able to bring his life to a fruitful conclusion.

Until the 15th century art history kept silent about deaf people. We cannot understand such an unacceptable lack. During the Renaisssance, however, new philosophical and cultural streams propitious to deaf people were developed.

Ill. 1: *The Coronation of the Virgin by Bernardino di Betto Biagi*

Ill. 2: *Siena Duomo – View of the Libreria Piccolomini, with the three Graces by Bernardino di Betto Biagi*

Bernardino di Betto Biagi (1454 Perugia -1513 Siena) became deaf in his youth. Some friends saved him from an overwhelming depression. Surnamed *il Surdicchio* and *il Pinturicchio*, he learned to paint with another well-known student, Raphaël (1483-1520); their famous master was Pietro Vanucci, *il Perugino* (1446-1523).

With his own assistants and students Bernardino painted *The Miracles of Saint Bernardin* in San Francesco al Prato (Rome). He and *il Perugino* painted some frescoes of Moses' life in the Sistine Chapel. He became the favorite painter of the Curia: in Rome, the papal apartments of Innocent VIII and Alexander VI were decorated by Bernardino; in Siena he worked on the wonderful ornamentations of Piccolomini's library (Piccolomini became Pope Pius II).

In the Renaissance, inventive masters attempted to discover true human nature. Leonardo da Vinci (1452-1519) called for the study of physiognomy, bodily gestures and deaf language so that painters could intensify feeling in their works. Da Vinci trained a very skilled painter, Ambrosio de Predis, whose deaf father Christoforo was one of the well-known illuminators and miniaturists in Milan.

Ill. 3: *The Dumb Woman by Raphaël*

In that period, artists studied architecture, sculpture and painting at the same time: *il Perugino* tried to portray psychological atmosphere in his paintings, so that characters, human groups and architectural backgrounds could harmonize with each other. At last, both Raphaël and *il Pinturicchio* solved the technical difficulties that stood in the way and they grew more skilful than their teacher *il Perugino*. We read in *Histoire de l'Art: In reality, Pinturicchio's painting became by degrees more refined than his master's* (Cassour/ Vicens (eds.) 1974, p. 228).

The study of physiognomy resulted in an age of authentic portrait painting: in 1506 Raphaël painted *The Dumb Woman* (in the National Gallery of Urbino), his most elaborate portrait in that genre, while da Vinci won immortality thanks to *Mona Lisa* whose enigmatic smile is still the subject of debate.

Though deaf people had given proof of their artistic abilities under certain circumstances, deaf children remained a philosophical casus belli: for the hearing person, their intelligence was proportional to their ability to speak and to write.

From the Renaissance we find in Italy: Hercule Sarti from Ferrare (about 1598) also called *Muet de Ficarolo*, a born deaf successor to Scarsellino, raised signing; and François Comi (1682 Bologna - 1737 Verona) *il Fornaretto* or *the Mute from Verona*, painter of historical and religious subjects.

Except for some deaf mimics who undoubtedly would have performed during the Roman Empire, painting seems to be the favorite form of expression in the first period of the artistic silent community. The fact that some deaf people reveal early a kind of vocation for drawing convinced some observant monks that it would be unfair to neglect their education and thus were cultivated some of the finest illuminators of manuscripts.

Ill. 4: *Decapitation of Jacob by Juan Fernandez Navarette*

So in Spain, Juan Fernandez Navarette (1526-1579), who became deaf when he was three years old, earned a living by drawing. After his education in the Monastery of Estrella near Logrono, his birthplace, he studied for twenty years in Italian masters' ateliers in Rome, Florence and Venice: he became the *Spanish Titian* and his nickname was *el Mudo*. King Philip II called on him in 1568 to help decorate the Escurial. A friend translated Spanish into signs for him. He trained Herrera, a painter who married his daughter. He was very knowledgable about mythology and history because he read widely.

In Madrid also lived: Jaime Lopez (16th century), called *el Mudo*, who painted frescoes in the Hermitage of Notre-Dame (Prado); Pedro *el Mudo*, experienced colorist; Del Arco (1620-1700), surnamed *el Surdillo de Pereda* (his master Pereda) who painted the Baptism of Saint John the Baptist in the Church of Toledo.

Among deaf students of the benedictine monk Pedro Ponce (1520-1584) who was a pioneer in deaf education, there was Fray Gaspar from Burgos, a congenitally deaf priest who spoke poorly but wrote well. Ponce used to teach by writing. Gaspar distinguished himself as an illuminator and a copyist.

The refinement of the works of Bernardino di Betto Biagi painter of Popes, leaves not the slightest doubt that he had first been an illuminator. Cristoforo de Predis (Milan), a deaf illuminist and miniaturist, and Gaspar from Burgos exemplified that aesthetic age of writing responding to newly invented printing.

In Holland a deaf painter, Hendrik van Campen (Avercamp or den Stamme van Kampen, 1585-1634) painted a splendid *Icy landscape with Flemish skaters;* though he

Ill. 5: *Icy landscape with Flemish skaters by Avercamp (Hendrick van Kampen)*

was an orphan, he became a geometrist and a painter in Francker. About 1776, Elzenerus Helmich, a deaf artist, lived in Goordrenthe; he was a landscape and portrait painter. In 1783 there died in The Hague a Frenchman, born deaf, Delacroix, a self-taught painter who completed portraits of Prince William V and his sister Caroline.

Memories of the heart

Silent artists frequently honor their 'Spiritual Father' Charles-Michel de L'Epée as well as his rival, Jacob Rodrigues Pereire. Paul Choppin (1856-1937), a French sculptor, who became deaf when he was two years old, sculpted two marvellous plaster statues of Pereire. Félix Martin (1844-1917), a deaf sculptor, created in 1879 the statue of de L'Epée which still stands in the courtyard of the Institut National de Jeunes Sourds (National Institute of the Deaf), rue Saint-Jacques in Paris: at the unveiling of the statue, he was presented the Legion of Honour. The Martins were three deaf brothers: the oldest, Ernest, depicted soldiers and army maneuvers and Georges cut cameos and precious stones. Félix Martin produced a series of twelve bronze plates of de L'Epée's life.

We know what de L'Epée looked like thanks in part to works from two of his students. The first, Paul Grégoire, drew several portraits when de L'Epée was alive: *The*

Ill. 6: *Jacob Rodrigues Pereire and a pupil by Paul François Choppin*

Ill. 7: *The Master in profile*
by Paul Grégoire

Ill. 8: *Mirabeau*
by Claude-André Deseine

Master in profile (1776) was reproduced in 1898 by Auguste Colas, a deaf engraver and a teacher at the Paris School. Auguste Colas had a deaf brother, Victor, an engraver, as well, who distinguished himself in lithography; Auguste Colas trained his hearing son with other hearing students who frequented his atelier. Claude-André Deseine (1740-1823), *le Sourd-Muet*, also a de L'Epée student, was a sculptor who made a tinted plaster bust of his teacher in 1786. He was born into a large family of about eighteen children: four of them were artists – two sculptors: Louis Pierre, who won the Prix de Rome, and Claude-André, the only deaf child; another son, Louis-Etienne, also won the Prix de Rome in architecture, and a daughter, Madeleine-Anne, was a painter.

Claude-André Deseine showed the prominent influence of such an artistic environment compared to the relatively small part played in his development by education: in fact de L'Epée began to teach Deseine only when the future painter was at least twenty years old; *le Sourd-Muet* produced his first work when he was forty years old. Among his various works commissioned by the state we find a bust of *Mirabeau* (1791), now in the Musée d'Art of Rennes: this bust had been exhibited in the Salle des Jacobins and destroyed after Mirabeau's treachery. In the Musée of Troyes we can see a bust of Danton's first wife by Deseine (1793).

Silent artists gave free rein to their gift encouraged by de L'Epée's statement in 1773: *Deaf people can practice any of the liberal arts with distinction* (de L'Epée 1773/1776, Lettre III, p. 52).Claude-Augustin Wallon (1790-1857) drew a charcoal portrait of de L'Epée. He was born deaf, admitted to the Paris School when nine for a six year course, first trained in the tailoring shop. Then, an Italian master invited to France by Napoleon, Belloni, taught him mosaic work.

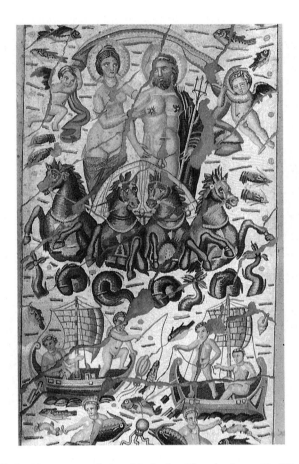

Ill. 9: *Neptune and Amphitrite by Claude-Augustin Wallon*

Belloni and four deaf students, Wallon, Gire, Page and Blondeau, made mosaics which are now in the Louvre: one of those works put into storage in 1936, is entitled *Minerva as Genius of the Emperor, mastering Victory and giving Peace and Abundance*. Wallon travelled through Europe attending famous ateliers.

In the 19th century silent artists were trained by Jouffroy, Falguière, Cavelier, Barrias, Bonassieu, Loison, Duret, Guillaume for sculpture and statuary, Girodet, Lefebvre, Boulanger, Desbrosses, Guillemet, Hillemacher, Cabanel, Michel, Detaille, Cogniet, Hersent, Ingres for painting. Deseine was Pajou's student in the 18th century. Because of these famous teachers, the best Arts Academies in Paris and everywhere in France admitted those hopeful silent artists. Nachor Ginouvier, a deaf student of Saint-Hippolyte-du-Fort (Gard, France) attended the Fine Arts School of Montpellier.

We also find some drawings of de L'Epée's house, 14 rue des Moulins, made after its demolition in 1876 when the Avenue de l'opéra was constructed: these works are from Félix Martin and A. J. Cochefer (1849-1923), a deaf architect and decorator in the famous firm of Mazarov-Ribalier; he drew a carved wooden door for the Hôtel de Ville of Paris. For the centennial of de L'Epée's death in 1879 he drew Saint-Roch Church, where de L'Epée is buried, and Baudeuf, another silent artist, drew the master's grave ornamented with a bust made in 1841 by S. Préault, the well-known romantic (hearing) sculptor.

To close this short iconography we have to mention a work from a great silent painter, Frédéric Peysson (1807-1877) who lived in Montpellier and who became deaf when he was

Ill. 10: *A lesson with the abbé de L'Epée by Nachor Ginouvier*

two and a half years old; he painted the masterpiece *Last Moments of the abbé de L'Epée*. In the Paris Fine Arts School, Peysson won distinctions and prizes from his masters – Hersent 1829; Léon Cogniet 1837; Ingres 1842. Every year the Montpellier Fine Arts School awarded a special prize, created by Peysson, for the best portrait painter.

Ferdinand Berthier (1803-1886), born deaf, was aware of social and cultural meanings of deafness. In 1818 the young Berthier gave a portrait of Henry IV to Louis XVIII. In 1829 he became a teacher. The Musée Universel des Sourds-Muets of the Paris School still has an engraving from him that seems to reveal a premonition: it shows a man who tears masks from his face; a giant snake gliding from his mouth seems about to attack him.

In 1834 Berthier organized the first public banquet of the deaf which can be regarded as a historic day for the French silent society. Fifty guests attended and the banquet initiated an unprecedented movement for legal aid and social welfare for the Deaf. In 1838 the Société Centrale des Sourds-Muets de Paris was founded, which in 1867 became the Société Universelle des Sourds-Muets.

At that time the deaf community wanted to organize a commemoration of de L'Epée, but no one knew where he was buried. Berthier supervised an inquiry, and in August 1841 Préault unveiled the Master's grave in Saint-Roch Church. Then, in 1843, Michaut, a hearing engraver of the Hôtel des Monnaies (the Mint) in Versailles, cast a statue of de L'Epée, which is today located on the left side of Saint-Louis Cathedral. The façade of the Hôtel de Ville in Paris showed another statue of de L'Epée, a bust made in 1841 by S. Préault, the well-known romantic hearing sculptor, but it was destroyed by a fire in the Commune civil war (1871).

Although a wooden door of the Hôtel de Ville designed by Cochefer was burnt in the

Ill. 11: *Charles-Michel de L'Epée by Marie Arbaudie, a deaf porcelain-painter*

Commune (1871), we can still see in the back courtyard two statues from Félix Martin: *Trudaine*, the founder of a Civil Engineering School (Ecole des Ponts-et-Chaussées) and Picard, an academician and playwright who became the Director of the National Theatre, Place de l'Odéon. In fact, Félix Martin was a grand-nephew of Picard and sculpted two other works of him for the foyer of the National Theatre and for the main foyer of the Opéra. Martin took second place in the 1869 Prix de Rome with *Alexander the Great and his physician Philip (Alexandre le Grand et son médecin Philippe)*. In the Hôtel de Ville, too, the Science Hall was decorated with frescoes rich in symbolism: we can see there a painting of a woman pulling a boat entitled *The Water,* painted by Berton (1854-1927), deaf from the age of nineteen, who took part in the Salons des Artistes Silencieux.

Several Paris streets were ornamented by Nicolas Gustave Hennequin, a deaf architect and decorator (1834-1918) who studied at the Nancy school for the Deaf and at the Paris Fine Arts School. The Sorbonne faces a square where we can see the Rector Gréard's monument sculpted by Hennequin. Starting from there and walking up Saint-Jacques Street towards the Institute National de Jeunes Sourds near Saint-Jacques Church we find the Oceanographic Institute, whose façade is decorated with the Arms of Monaco, also a work by Hennequin.

Paul François Choppin, whose wife was a skilful silent miniaturist, sculpted a *Marseillaise* which was on display in a court of the Invalides Monument; among his other statues we know the *Victor of the Bastille* (1888) for the Square Parmentier, Place de la Bastille; the 1792 *Volunteer* for Remiremont; the *Washerwoman* for the Lake of Montsouris Park. He won first prize in 1887 when he was twenty-nine years old with the *Doctor Paul Broca;* this statue was located on the Boulevard Saint-Germain. But, as bronze was very scarce in the war time, all these works were melted down during World War II.

Ill. 12: *The Rector Gréard's Monument and the Sorbonne, Paris,*
by Nicolas Gustave Hennequin

Fernand Hamar (1869-1943) became deaf at the age of one; he was admitted into a special school when he was ten years old, studied decorative arts, then fine arts from 1888 to 1890. From him we can see statues of the Field-Marshal de Rochambeau (1750-1813) who took part in the American War of Independence: the first statue stands in Vendôme, the sculptor's birth-place, and the second in the Garden of the Invalides in Paris, the third in a Newport RI park (USA) and the fourth on the grounds of the White House in Washington, D.C. (1902).

An engraving of Field Marshal Mac-Mahon, who became President of France in 1873, was exhibited in 1874 by a silent painter, René Princeteau (1843-1914). Princeteau won a golden medal in Philadelphia with an equestrian painting of George Washington. Prince-teau appears in biographies of a great hearing artist, Henri de Toulouse-Lautrec (1864-1901) whose father was a close friend of the deaf artist.

Toulouse-Lautrec became permanently lame after he had broken his legs twice in a year at about the age of fourteen. Princeteau taught him to draw animals, then Toulouse-Lautrec became a student of Cormon and Bonnat; he was in search of human nature, sought inspira-tion from singers, clowns and dancers and led a free Bohemian existence. He was a perfect caricaturist, attentive to gesture and physiognomy. At that time poster art developed; Tou-louse-Lautrec studied rhythms of Primitives, Japanese Arts, announcing modern style. But in his lonely work we find a lot of horsewomen, jockeys, animals and circus sights directly influenced by Princeteau.

To end this survey of silent art we record a thought of Paul Choppin. The Deaf proved to us that silent art is worth seeing, that Fine Arts Academies and Decorative Arts Schools had to admit them and eventually provide them deaf signing masters to enable communication between teacher and student.

> *If they learn that I am a deaf mute they will cry out against such a feat of skill; they won't think that I am an artist as gifted as those who are hearing and talking; or my rivals will assert that I reaped laurels not for my ability but only for my pitiful fate.* (in Boyer 1909)

85

Ill. 13: *Doctor Paul Broca by Paul François Choppin*

Appendix
The original French quotations:

p. 78

> En réalité le dessin de Pinturicchio se fit peu à peu supérieur en élégance à celui de son maître.(Cassour/Vicens (eds.) 1974, p. 228)

p. 81

> Il n'est point d'art libéral que les sourds-muets ne puissent exercer avec distinction. (Abbé de L'Epée 1773/1776, Lettre III, p. 52)

p. 82

> Génie de l'Empereur sous les traits de Minerve maîtrisant la Victoire et ramenant la Paix et l'Abondance.

p. 86

> Si l'on apprend que je suis sourd-muet, on criera au tour de force; on ne voudra pas croire que je puisse avoir du talent comme ceux qui entendent et qui parlent; ou bien mes rivaux affirmeront que ce n'est pas à mon mérite mais à mon malheur pitoyable que je dois d'être couronné. (cited in Boyer 1909)

Iconography

Ill. 1: The Coronation of the Virgin; by Bernardino di Betto Biagi.
Pinacoteca Vaticano.

Ill. 2: Siena Duomo – View of the Libreria Piccolomini, with the three Graces;
by Bernardino di Betto Biagi.
Pinacoteca Vaticano.

Ill. 3: The Dumb Woman; by Raphaël (1508).
Galerie Nationale d'Urbino.

Ill. 4: Decapitation of Jacob; by Juan Fernandez Navarette.
Patrimonio Nacional, Madrid.

Ill. 5: Icy landscapes with Flemish skaters; von Avercamp (Hendrick van Kampen).
Rijksmuseum, Amsterdam.
Photo: Studio de la Comète.

Ill. 6: Jacob Rodrigues Pereire and a pupil; by Paul François Choppin.
Photo: J.-L. Charmet.

Ill. 7: The Master in profile. Charles-Michel de L'Epée; by Paul Grégoire (reproduced in 1898 by
Auguste Colas).
Photo: J.-L. Charmet.

Ill. 8: Victor Riqueti, Marquis de Mirabeau; by Claude-André Deseine.
Photo: Studio de la Comète.

Ill. 9: Neptune and Amphitrite; by Claude-Augustin Wallon.
Photo: Studio de la Comète.

Ill. 10: A lesson with the abbé de L'Epée; by Nachor Ginouvier (from Frederic Peyson (1807-1877)).
Photo: J.-L.Charmet.

Ill. 11: Charles-Michel de L'Epée; by Marie Arbaudie (reproduced from Houdon).
Photo: J.-L.Charmet.

Ill. 12: The Rector Gréard's Monument and the Sorbonne, Paris; by Nicolas Gustave Hennequin.

Ill. 13: Doctor Paul Broca; by Paul François Choppin.
Photo: Studio de la Comète.

Ill. 1-2, 4-11, 13: *Musée Universel des Sours-Muets* and *Archives* of the *Institut National de Jeunes Sourds de Paris*, 254 rue Saint-Jacques, 75005 Paris.

Ill. 3 and 12 : Yves Bernard

References

Boyer, A. (1909): *Paul Choppin, artiste sculpteur sourd-muet, officier de l' Institution Nationale des Sourds-Muets de Paris*. Paris: Atélier typographique de l'Institution Nationale des Sourds-Muets.

L'Epée, C.M. de (1773/1776): Lettre III ; in: id. (1776): *Institution des Sourds-Muets par la voie des Signes méthodiques, ouvrage qui contient de Projet d'une Langue Universelle par l'entremise des Signes naturels assujettis à une Méthode*. Paris: Nyon L'aîné.

Cassour, J./Vicens, F. (eds.) (1974): *Histoire de l'Art: La grande aventure des trésors du monde en 10 volumes*. Paris: Editions de la Grange Batelière, vol. V.

Examples of Deaf Art

Illustrierte
Gehörlosen=Welt

6. Jahrgang | JULI 1932 | Nummer 3

Ruth Schaumann die gehörlose Dichterin

Eine gehörlose Frau erhält den Dichter-Preis

Die Dichterin Ruth Schaumann, die den Münchner Dichter-Preis erhielt, hat sich nicht nur durch ihre zarten lyrischen Werke, sondern auch als begabte Bildhauerin und Holzschneiderin einen Namen gemacht.
Aufn.: Aurel Schwabik.

Eine der erfolgreichsten Dichterinnen der Jetztzeit, ist die gehörlose Dichterin Ruth Schaumann, welche die erste Frau ist, die seit Bestehen des Dichterpreises der Stadt München diese hohe Auszeichnung erhielt. Ruth Schaumann ist trotz ihrer erst 32 Jahre eine sehr produktive Dichterin. Sie hat schon viele Gedichtsammlungen herausgegeben. U. a. „Der Rebenhag", 200 S. stark, „Der Knospengrund" 136 S. stark, „Das Pasional" 48 S. stark, „Die Kathedrale" 47 S. stark, zuletzt den Gedichtband „Die Tenne" 236 S. stark, welcher ihr den Literaturpreis der Stadt München einbrachte. Ruth Schaumann ist nicht nur eine große Dichterin, sondern auch ein Künstlerin von Format. Sämtliche Gedichtsamm-

lungen und Bücher hat sie mit schönen Titelholzschnitten ausgeschmückt. Auch hat sie mehrere handbemalte Holzschnitte in Form von Leporello=Albums herausgegeben, die viel Anklang gefunden haben. Ihre dichterischen Werke haben ihr die Anerkennung der Kritik ohne Unterschied der literarischen Richtung, Konfession und Partei eingetragen und das will in unrerer heutigen Zeit sehr viel sagen.

Ruth Schaumann wurde 1899 als Tochter eines Offiziers in Hamburg geboren. Durch eine Kinderkrankheit verlor sie ihr Gehör und besuchte die Taubstummenschule. Seit 1917 lebt sie in München. Wir Gehörlose können uns über die Erfolge dieser unserer Schicksalsgenossin nur freuen, tragen sie doch dazu bei, das Vorurteil gegen uns zu bekämpfen und zu beweisen, daß auch Gehörlose Großes leisten können.

Allen unseren Schicksalsgenossen empfehlen wir die Anschaffung von Werken Ruth Schaumanns. Sie sind zu haben im Verlag Josef Kösel & Friedr. Pustet, München und können auch durch den Taubst.=Verlag H. Dude Nachf., Leipzig O 5, besorgt werden.

Ill. 17: Ruth Schaumann (1899, Hamburg - 1975, Munich, Germany) was deafened in her childhood. She was an artist with many talents – sculptor, painter, woodcutter, and author (see also ill. 18, 19, 20, p. 90).

Ill. 18: 'And she wasn't aware of it.'   Ill. 19: 'This must be Father Adam.'

Ill. 20: 'And mourn over the saurian's little corpse at the walls.'

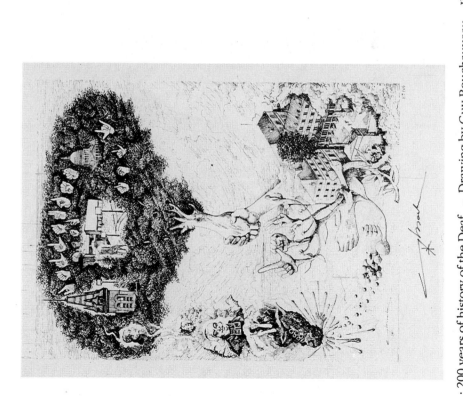

Ill. 21: 200 years of history of the Deaf. – Drawing by Guy Bouchauveau (Deaf), Paris, France, 1980.

Ill. 22: Nude of an old man. – Painting by José A. Terry, jr. (Deaf, 1878 - 1954), Santiago de Chile, 1902.

Ill. 23: Walter Scheffler (1880 - 1964) was born in Königsberg (which, then, was German). In 1956, he wrote a poem on 60 years of marriage to ... Madame Deafness (he was deafened in 1896).

Ill. 24: Directors and members of the Board of the Deaf Institute in Groningen, Netherlands, from 1790 to 1915. – Painting (1915) by Lucas Kisjes (1878, Amsterdam - 1951, Bussum) deafened at the age of 2 and former pupil of the Institute.

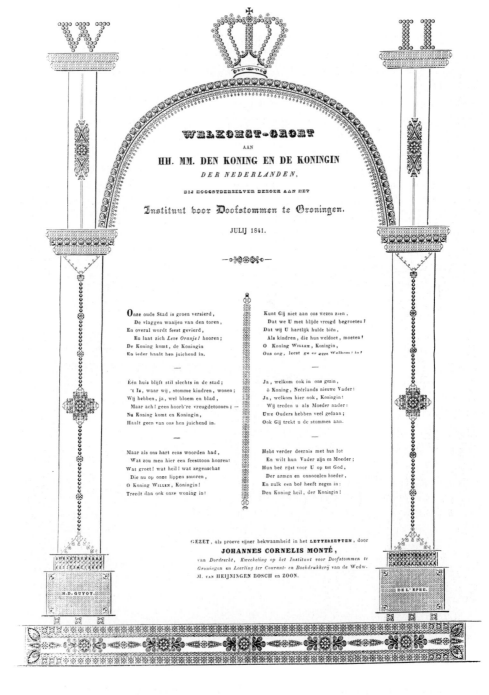

Ill. 25: Work by Johannes C. Monté (Deaf) for his final exam as master of typesetting at the Institute of Groningen, Netherlands, in 1841.

Ill. 26: Ferdinand Beure von Hilpoldstein, Deaf etcher in Nürnberg, Germany. The undated self(?)portrait is accompanied by, among others, two leitmotivs composed by two of his brothers and an 'ephphatha' scene in the upper left.

Brian Grant
Carlisle, Great Britain

Francis Maginn (1861-1918)

Summary

Francis Maginn, an Irishman, was the founder of the British Deaf Association (BDA), the oldest surviving national deaf organisation in Great Britain which began as The British Deaf and Dumb Association (BDDA) in 1890.

Ill. 1: *Portrait of Francis Maginn*

I

Francis Maginn, the founder of The British Deaf and Dumb Association, was born on the twenty-first of April, 1861 at Johnsgrove, near Mallow in Southern Ireland. His father – the Rev. Charles Arthur Maginn – died as Rector of Killanully near Cork, having previously been Rector and Rural Dean of Castletown Roche. His mother, a descendant of the 16th century poet Edmund Spencer, belonged to one of the leading families of the County of Cork. Francis's parents as cultured people were ambitious for their son and keen on giving him the best possible education. They therefore secured for him, while he was still an infant, a place at Christ's Hospital, London, which was one of the top schools in the United Kingdom at that time.

Some other child was to take up his place in due course, because Francis, at the age of five, contracted scarlet fever and lost his hearing. This illness, which has now ceased to be a danger, was in the past responsible for many cases of acquired deafness. When Francis rose from his sick bed, *he had almost lost his power of speech and forgotten many things, he once heard and learnt* (*The Deaf and Dumb Times* 1890, Vol. 1, p. 140). For this reason, instead of being educated at Christ's College, he received his education at the Asylum for the Education of Deaf and Dumb Children of the Poor in Bermondsey, South London.

This school had been opened in 1792 and was the first educational establishment in the United Kingdom which admitted deaf children regardless of social background and without payment of fees. Its name describes its character and the founder's intentions. It was not only a school but also a shelter from a harsh world. The institution was considered so successful that it established the pattern of deaf education in the United Kingdom during the Victorian era. It was not until 1903 that the state began to provide school for deaf children and attendance became compulsory (see below). Until then all ecucational establishments were private and less than two-thirds of the eligible children ever saw the inside of a school. Conditions in the asylums were grim, but must be judged from a historical perspective.

> *Those who gained admittance were fortunate. If by our standards their lot was a hard one, what they suffered inside was nothing to what they would have had to endure outside from a still brutalised populace. And if much that was done in those early days shocks us, we have to remember what had gone before was worse. Certainly the children admitted to the first asylums were those most in need. Deaf and dumb children who could manage by self-teaching alone through their eyes to make themselves useful and a source of income to their parents did not often find their way into the asylums. The children who were pushed in were the ones useless to their families, the backward and the troublesome, just the poor little wretches to provoke barbaric jokes and kicks and blows.* (Hodgson 1953)

Francis was nine years old when he was admitted to the Bermondsey Asylum. This school had been chosen as the Headmaster – the Rev. James Watson, a descendant of Joseph Watson, who had been the school's first Head and author of a famous early teaching manual – was considered outstanding. Francis escaped the full horrors of being an inmate of an asylum as he went to Bermondsey as a fee-paying pupil. This meant that he lived in the Headmaster's home as a lodger instead of inside the Asylum. It also meant that he was one of a handful of private pupils, whom Watson taught personally as a small select group. In other words, he had virtually private tuition in all subjects. All Heads of Schools for the Deaf were at that time paid as salary a mere pittance. Only the fees paid on behalf of private pupils enabled them to earn a decent living and to maintain a respectable standard of living. This curious system, which was forced upon them by the governors, who needed all available money for the upkeep of the schools and had none to spare for salaries, was of great benefit to the private pupils, as it gave them the chance of a proper education, which pupils inside the Asylum did not enjoy. The system had another significant side effect: It created within the deaf population an elite consisting of privately educated people. Francis Maginn was a member of that elite.

He was also exceptionally intelligent and eager to learn, which explains why, after only five years at the Asylum, he was offered the position of a 'pupil teacher' at a branch of the Bermondsey School in Margate, Kent, now known as the Royal School for the Deaf. Three years later, at the age of seventeen, he was promoted to a Junior Teachership. He remained in this post until 1883, when he left the teaching profession for good and returned home to Ireland.

How was it possible that Maginn from the age of fourteen onwards was a teacher of deaf children? The simple answer is that there was no qualification for this occupation at that time. Anybody willing was welcome to have a go. If he had aptitude, so much the better. Pay and conditions were so bad that only those for whom the instruction of deaf children was a vocation – and they were few and far between – and those, useless for any other job, stuck to it. The consequent standard of education for the ordinary inmates of the asylums was appallingly low. This was aggravated by the fact that the average length of school life in those days was only three and a half years. In the circumstances only the very intelligent and keen ones could hope to derive any benefit from what was available by way of education.

Dr. Richard Elliott was Headmaster of the Margate School during Maginn's years as a teacher. This important educator deserves to be remembered alongside Francis Maginn. He was the only one of the eight British delegates at the Milan Congress in 1880, who voted with the American delegation against the principal resolution adopted by this assembly. Five years later, he was co-founder with Dr. Stainer of the College of Teachers for the Deaf, which at last transformed such teachers into a professional body with proper qualifications, and thus paved the way for higher standards in deaf education. Maginn left the teaching profession with the following testimonial from Dr. Elliott:

> *During the time you were under me as a teacher, I always found you faithful in the discharge of your duties, an excellent teacher, and most anxious to promote the welfare of the pupils. You used to devote much of your leisure time to their benefit, and by that means materially aided in raising the moral and intellectual standard of the school. I and all the staff – with whom you were a favourite – regretted that your praiseworthy desire to gain all the intellectual advantages possible in your case, severed connections with us.*

II

So it was Maginn's desire to improve his own education, which made him give up teaching. Inevitably this meant going to America, the only place, where educational facilities existed to enable him to achieve his objective. Before enrolling as a student at the National Deaf Mute College in Washington, DC – now known as Gallaudet University – he stayed for one year in Ireland, where he got to know the appalling conditions in which most deaf mutes were living and took part in the formation of the Southern Branch of the Missions to the Adult Deaf and Dumb. Maginn had intended to take a three year course at the College, but his father's death necessitated his return before its completion. He left with the Principal's blessings, as shown by the following extract from a letter by Dr. E.M. Gallaudet:

> *It gives me pleasure to speak of the high regard in which you are held by all the members of the faculty and your friends generally here. You carry with you our most cordial wishes for your success in the important field of labour to which you are going. I commend you most heartily to the confidence of all with whom and for whom you are to put forth your efforts, believing fully in your fitness for the work, and in the sincerity of your motives.*

The field of labour, which Maginn was about to take on, was the Irish Mission to the Adult Deaf and Dumb with special responsibility for Cork in the South and Belfast in the North. He was only twenty-six years old when appointed to this position.

The years which Maginn had spent in the United States – from the autumn of 1884 until early in 1887 – were of seminal importance to his work in the next period of his life. Deeply impressed by the achievements of the American deaf mutes he had become convinced that progress *on American lines* – a phrase which he constantly used – was the way forward for the deaf of Great Britain. His principal goals were accordingly the introduction of state education for the deaf and the formation of a national organisation to look after the interests of the deaf population. The following extract from an article in the *Quarterly Review of Deaf Education* of January 1887 is typical of the eloquent and forceful style in which he expressed his plea for change and advance:

> *Is it not to be wondered at that Christian and philanthropic England is only beginning to recognise the equitable educational claims of deaf mutes, which have so long been*

treated with comparative indifference? And still more, that the Members of the House of Commons have failed to comprehend the fact, that it is the duty of the state to educate ALL her children? The state ought to assume this duty in order to protect herself and her resources (...). We deaf mutes have a right to object to calling Schools for the Deaf 'charitable institutions' and to the classification of the deaf with the inmates of prisons and insane asylums. Every teacher knows that deaf mutes are mentally equal to other people, save only in the lack of development, that they are as justly entitled to education as any child in the full possession of his faculties and have as much right to participate in the benefits of the 'Educational Fund' as other children. If they are denied this, the taxes of their parents and guardians should be remitted.

Throughout the United States, whatever may be the system of education pursued, the schools are maintained at public expense by the respective states. The College in Washington receives the liberal support of the general government (...).

Following a description of the American educational system the article continues:

Every deaf mute in the United States has it in his power to climb to a higher grade of attainment, and in the College at Washington the studious and earnest youth receives all encouragement. I never had the honour of mingling with such intelligent mutes until I entered this College. They discuss with facility literature, mathematics, history, philosophy and politics. They see before them a future bright with promises of usefulness, honour and influence (...). I attribute the wonderful results intellectually achieved by deaf mutes in the United States to the employment of efficient teachers and to the entire completeness of the system (...). Having taken special interest in the education of the Deaf, and having impartially compared the systems of Great Britain and the United States, I come to the painful conclusion that the education of the Deaf and Dumb in England is in a very unsatisfactory state, though things have improved of late (by the establishment of the College of Teachers).

I am hopeful that the Royal Commission may recommend legislation for the furtherance of the education of the deaf, and that they may be induced to approve the American system, which would greatly elevate and benefit deaf mute education in England. I do strongly advocate this, with a desire to see this education raised to a higher standard of efficiency and to give the deaf a better chance to take their part in the battle of life successfully.

While waiting for the publication of the Royal Commission's recommendations[1] Maginn was invited to become President of the first national organisation *to further and advance the interests of the Deaf and Dumb throughout the United Kingdom and the World*, which was formed on the 1st June, 1888. The invitation was a remarkable tribute to Maginn's standing within the deaf population. He was, after all, only twenty-seven years old and had been a missioner for only one year. The Secretary, Treasurer and moving spirit of the Deaf Mute Association, as this organisation was called, was one John T. Maclean, an accountant from Greenock, Scotland, who later moved to London. The Executive Committee included such well known names as Benjamin Payne from Swansea and Ernest Abraham from Bolton. The Association had twenty-five founder members including one woman and it published its own magazine: *The Deaf Mute*. The membership grew to 236 within fifteen months, which compares very favourably with the subsequent beginning of the BDDA.

It included George Healey, James Muir, William Raper, Wilhelmina Tredennick, James Dawson, Alexander Baird, Robert Semple and William Agnew, who all later became prominent members of the BDDA. Yet despite this support The Deaf Mute Association failed and the last monthly issue of its organ was published in August 1889. Why and in what precise

1 Maginn made written submissions to the Royal Commission, but was not invited to give evidence.

circumstances the Association ceased to exist is guess-work, but it is probable that John Maclean had to be eliminated before a national organisation could succeed. He and Maginn did not get on according to the gossip column of *The Deaf Mute,* written 'by one inside', and Maclean plays no further part in the history of the deaf after his brief involvement in the abortive Deaf Mute Association. Maginn, on the other hand, wasted no time to prepare the ground for a new organisation.

III

He first mooted its formation with the British delegates to the International Congress of the Deaf and Dumb, which had been convened in Paris in July 1889 in order to celebrate the 100th anniversary of the death of the abbé de L'Epée (*The Deaf and the Dumb Times* 1890, Vol. 1, p. 101). Maginn attended this gathering not only as missioner to Ireland but also as President of The Deaf Mute Association, then still in existence. A letter from Maclean to the President and members of the Congress, dated 29th June, 1889 and reprinted in *The Deaf Mute,* sends fraternal greetings, draws attention to the Association, invites international membership and introduces Maginn as President.

The Paris Congress, where Maginn was one of the speakers, coincided with the publication in Britain of the Report of the Royal Commission *on the condition and education of the Deaf and Dumb.* The Commission had been appointed in 1885 and the result of its deliberations had been eagerly awaited. The recommendation that deaf and dumb children between the ages of seven and sixteen should receive compulsory education, financed by the state, was naturally welcomed,[2] but there was general disappointment and bitterness about the Commission's support for oralism as a method of teaching and the absence of any recommendation for the provision of higher education. The Report also caused anger by recommending *that the intermarriage of the congenitally deaf should be strongly discouraged, as well as the intermarriage of blood relations, especially where any hereditary tendency to deaf-mutism prevails in the family.* The latter recommendation was not only outside the terms of reference of the Commission, but on the scientific and medical evidence, already then available, without foundation. It was based on the bigoted evidence to the Commission of Dr. Graham Bell, against whom Maginn had tried to warn the members of the Commission by writing in *The Deaf Mute*:

> We advise the Royal Commission to hesitate before accepting all which the Professor advances. Having been in America and knowing something of Dr. Bell, I wish to say that the deaf mutes of the United States recognise the fact that he is acting in all sincerity and with the best of intentions, and that their esteem for him is not lessened by the contempt in which they hold his theories.

Maginn returned from Paris with plans to hold a national conference for the discussion of the recommendations of the Royal Commission and of his proposal to form a National Deaf Association. *The Deaf and Dumb Times,* an influential monthly paper then edited by Charles Gorham, who was deaf and in due course became the first Secretary of the BDDA, backed Maginn's idea and helped with the arrangements, which led to the first British National Deaf Conference. This took place in the lecture hall of St. Saviour's Church in Oxford Street, London, during 16th -18th January, 1890.[3]

The first two days were given to debates about the Commission's Report. Maginn, who took a prominent part and dominated the proceedings, proposed the following resolution:

---

2 This recommendation was implemented by enactment of the Elementary Education (Blind and Deaf Children) Act in 1903.

3 The first church in Britain dedicated exclusively to the use of the deaf. It was consecrated in 1873 and demolished to make room for redevelopment in 1922.

> *That this conference is of the opinion that the combined system, as advocated by Dr. E.M. Gallaudet before the Royal Commission, is calculated to confer the greatest bene-fit upon the greatest number of the deaf and dumb.*[4]

All speeches were limited to ten minutes so that he had time for only the following points:

> *Before I went to America I was rather one-sided, and opposed the teaching of speech too much. But after entering the celebrated College in Washington, I saw that not only could speech be taught with much success, but that those educated on the combined system spoke better than those educated on the so-called pure oral method. I have come across deaf mutes educated by all systems and as I have met and conversed with the deaf in various parts of Great Britain and Ireland, France and the United States, I have not the least hesitation in saying that the combined method as advocated by Dr. E.M. Gallaudet before the recent Royal Commission certainly confers the greatest benefit upon the greatest number. I do not deny that some very good results have been reached by the oral method, and especially so in the case of those children possessing the natu-ral quickness of observation and retentiveness of memory which this method requires. I wish to correct a wrong impression that has gained some credence amongst the ignorant and unreasoning public, that sign language – the agency through which we interexchange thought and opinion – is calculated to do injury to the intelligence of the deaf and dumb. This language is to the deaf mute what the German language is to the German, or French to the French. I contend that the best evidence of the efficacy of the combined system are the attainments of the deaf mutes who have profited by it, and that the deaf mutes of America are far better educated than those of any other country. I defy the conclusions of the Milan Conference and of similar packed conventions. As to the advantage of the American combined system, let results speak for themselves. Sixty years ago there was not one educated mute in America, but now there are four who are principals of schools, three are editors of newspapers circulating among the hearing community, two are professors in the deaf mute college, three are chemists, six are ordained ministers, two have entered the civil service of the government; one of these, who had risen rapidly to a high and responsible position, resigned to enter upon the practice of law in patent cases in Chicago and Cincinnati, and has been admitted to practise in the Supreme Court of the United States. The number of those employed as teachers, artists etc. is too great even to mention.*

The motion was carried by a majority of twenty-one to three. Support for the combined system was to become one of the fundamental policies of the BDDA. Universal adoption of its modern development – Total Communication – remains to this day one of the BDA's chief objectives. Maginn also took part in the debate on the motion:

> *That it is satisfactorily proved to this conference that the intermarriage of deaf and dumb is conducive to their happiness and there is no reason to fear injurious result there from.*

The following quotation illustrates the flavour of his scornful speech, which according to the report in *The Deaf and Dumb Times* earned *loud applause:*

> *In Belfast I know of eighteen couples who live together happily, and only one couple has deaf children. Should the government dare to interfere with our private domestic life, let us rise to a man and protest and also let us get up a monster demonstration and march four deep to Trafalgar Square.*

---

4 Maginn wrote at greater length on this subject in two letters to *The Times* on September 25th and December 27th, 1890.

This motion was carried by a majority of twenty-four to two. The agenda for the third day of the Conference read:

> *Proposal to form the National Deaf Association on American lines, the objects of which will be the protection, and the educational and social elevation of the deaf of the United Kingdom.*

Francis Maginn had prepared the ground for this occasion – Saturday morning, January 18th – with an article in the *The Deaf and Dumb Times* of January, 1890, entitled *The Proposed National Association of the Deaf*:

> *Certainly no class of persons knows better than the deaf the after effects of their education. Their judgment is of necessity based not upon hypothetical conditions, but upon the evidence of incontrovertible facts. Those who saw the American delegates to the Paris Congress, must have been struck with the excellence and superiority of their education. The readiness with which the American delegates impressed their character and energy upon the Congress, leading its deliberations, influencing its thoughts, and even in some instances correcting its faults, is a quiet but signally effective illustration of their better preparation for a more thorough practical acquaintance with the work of deliberative assemblies. We should make a strenuous and united attempt to incorporate in the management of our institutions some of the features which have given the American schools the character they enjoy.*
>
> *In order to accomplish this, and to place the deaf before the public in their true light and proper position, as useful members of the community at large, the formation of an Association on American lines is most desirable.*
>
> *The want felt for such an organisation for the promotion of their intellectual, social, moral, temporal and spiritual welfare is very great. There is a wide field of usefulness for the proposed union. It should be recognised as the only organisation that the deaf mutes of the United Kingdom can look to as the protector of their interests, and they should have something they can depend on. The strife of local societies should have no place in its councils where all meet upon common ground, with the common end of mutual betterment. A periodical reunion of the deaf of Great Britain and Ireland should always occur, and there is everything to be said in its favour. It should meet biennially in some great centre. The Deaf and Dumb Times to be the exponent of the cause of the Association. The interests of the deaf in various towns should be watched by local agents, and grievances, if fully substantiated, be published in the organ of the Association.*

Maginn attached to his article a draft/constitution of the proposed national association. Two noteworthy features were that only deaf people were eligible for membership, and that the expression 'deaf mute' is used instead of 'deaf and dumb'. Neither of these features, as we shall see, found approval, which militated against the advance of the Association in the course of its history. (For details of the history see Grant 1990.)

Nineteen delegates were present that Saturday morning at the private meeting, which was chaired by the Rev. W.B. Sleight, a Church of England clergyman and hearing son of William Sleight, the respected Headmaster of the Brighton Institution of the Deaf and Dumb. Having grown up in the company of deaf pupils of the school, fingerspelling and signing were for him natural alternative modes of communication. Sleight had been a member of the Royal Commission and was considered a champion of the deaf and their causes. His dissent on two of the recommendations which had caused particular displeasure was much admired. The invitation to be President of the Conference was therefore a tribute to his partisanship.

All speeches on this historical occasion were delivered *in finger language, no signs whatever being permitted* (*The Deaf And Dumb Times 1890,* Vol. 1, p. 89). Francis Maginn proposed the motion advocating the formation of a national association:

The tendency of the trades nowadays is to seek co-operation and union. The dockla-bourers would never have won the day only for the sympathy the men showed each other, and for the co-operation extended to them. We all know of the great advantages that accrue from the meetings of the Church Congress, the British Association, and the Medical Association. In the kingdom there are about 20,000 mutes, and there is no organised association which should keep a jealous eye over their interests, educational, moral and social.

In almost every state of America there is an association of mutes and a National Society, organised and officered by the mutes themselves. We want an association formed on American lines. A wide-awake and intelligent class of people that numbers 20,000 in the Kingdom, as I said before, certainly has the power to command public respect and attention when by energetic work wisely directed to the building up of the association a vigorous organisation is secured.

What strength is there in union? What is it all worth? The mind that cannot conceive the benefits which accrue by a coming together and a binding by paternal ties by a people having common sympathy must be wayward indeed. The very foundation of our education rests in meeting under a common roof, whether it be the education of the classroom, the church or citizenship. An Association of the deaf, powerful in its members and unity, has before it the greatness of things to be done.

He concluded with the suggestion that a committee be formed to draft a constitution of the proposed Association for submission to a future gathering of potential founders. H.B. Beale from Gloucestershire seconded the motion and he was followed by seven more speakers, all in favour of the motion. The following resolutions were then passed unanimously:

In the opinion of this Conference it is advisable that a National Society be formed, the chief objects of which will be the elevation, education and social status of the deaf and dumb in the United Kingdom.

That the matter of this Association be referred to a special committee consisting of the President of this Conference (The Rev. W.B. Sleight) as Chairman, and twelve gentlemen (six deaf and dumb and six hearing). The Committee to have power to add to their number.

Maginn was one of the *deaf and dumb gentlemen* appointed to the Steering Committee, which disagreed with two fundamental aspects of his published draft and eventually decided on a constitution with the following main features:

1. Name: Maginn's suggestion had been the National Society of the Deaf. The Committee chose instead The British Deaf and Dumb Association. Maginn never used the expression *deaf and dumb* and would wholeheartedly have approved of the following comment on the choice of name in the *The Deaf and Dumb Times* of August, 1890:

(...)in deciding that the title should be the British Deaf and Dumb Association the Association would have done better had they omitted the objectionable word 'dumb' which is really unnecessary and has proved very misleading to the public. The term 'dumb' really implies that the person so called is incapable of making himself understood by his fellow creatures. It is true that this word is mentioned in the Bible, but it was rightly applied, for these unhappy creatures mentioned were not in a position to make themselves understood. The Americans have dropped the word altogether, and hinted to us to do the same (...).

There is no doubt that over the years many potential members were put off by the Association's name, but it took eighty-one years before, in 1971, a majority was found to change the name to the present title: the British Deaf Association.

2. Kind of Organisation: Maginn's draft envisaged an Association of members entitled to elect the officers and having considerable control of policy.The Committee adopted this pattern of self-government making democratic elections and membership influence outstanding features of the constitution from the beginning. In modern parlance the BDA is and always has been a democratic grassroots organisation.This is entirely in accordance with Maginn's original vision and due to his inspiration.

3. Membership: Maginn's draft provided that *any deaf mute of the United Kingdom*, and nobody else, should be entitled to be a member of the Association. He regarded the deaf as capable of running **their own** organisation, but the Committee, lacking his courage and self-confidence, recommended that membership should be extended to hearing missioners and *persons who can hear and take an active interest in the welfare and education of the deaf and dumb provided they are recommended by five ordinary members of the Associa-tion.The Deaf and Dumb Times* of August 1890 purports to explain the new membership rule with the following comment:

> *As it stands, it is a safeguard against the admission of unscrupulous persons, who might at some unexpected moment do harm to the objects of the Association. It being desirable and natural that the Association should be governed solely by bona fide deaf members, it was felt that it would be an act of selfishness to ignore those 'hearing friends' who take real interest in the cause and welfare of the deaf. Yet apprehensions were felt as to the wisdom of adopting such a course.*

Ill. 2: *The Church Institute at 5 Albion Place, Leeds,*
the birthplace of the British Deaf Association (contemporary engraving)

This comment merely hints at the real reason for the change, which was to allow a hearing person, namely the Rev. W. B. Sleight, to become the first President of the BDDA. His candidature, made possible by the change, was a last minute's surprise as *it had been generally inferred that the honour of the Presidency would be conferred upon a deaf person (The Deaf and Dumb Times* 1890, Vol. 2, p. 25). The favourite for the honour had undoubtedly been Francis Maginn, who would have made an effective leader. But when it came to the crunch, the founders preferred a hearing man of fourty-one to a deaf man of twenty-nine. A historical opportunity was thereby missed.

The Congress, which led to the formation of the BDDA, met in Leeds, Yorkshire in the summer of 1890. The address, where the founders met, was the Church Institute at 5 Albion Place. Although this building stands right in the centre of the City, it has miraculously survived with the exterior unchanged except for the fenestration on the groundfloor, which has become modern shop windows. The interior is now converted and used as office, and since Centenary year a plaque on the entrance porch commemorates the formation of the BDDA inside the building.

On 24th July, 1890, thirty-six founders, of whom four were ladies, assembled in the small lecture hall, where they were welcomed by the Rev. W. B. Sleight in his capacity as Chairman of the Steering Committee. After prayers he explained the outcome of the committee's deliberations and the particulars of the constitution, which was submitted to the founders for adoption. They unanimously did so and then paid their entrance fees and their first annual subscription to the acting treasurer. By doing so, in the words of the preamble to the constitution:

The Deaf and Dumb of Great Britain and Ireland agree to form themselves into an Association for the advancement and protection of their interests in every possible way.

In the elections of officers, which followed, the Rev. William Blomefield Sleight became the first President of the BDDA. Thus Francis Maginn's dream of a National Association came true, but he himself was denied the chance of leading it. He had to be content with one of the four regional Vice-Presidencies. This was an honorary position, but it gave him an ex officio seat on the executive. Maginn could therefore have continued to play his part and exert his influence in the running of the organisation, but he chose not to do so.

Maginn's withdrawal from participation in the affairs of the BDDA was gradual. In particular, he attended the first Congress in Glasgow in August 1891. This was honoured by the presence of his former principal Dr. E. M. Gallaudet and another famous member of the same family, Dr. T. Gallaudet. Both these distinguished gentlemen gave addresses, and Maginn was there to welcome them as a personal friend. But, although the Congress lasted three days and many subjects were debated, Maginn's sole contribution was to second a motion thanking the Glasgow Mission Committee for placing their rooms at the disposal of the delegates.

The explanation for Maginn's low profile is not difficult to find. He was simply at odds with the leadership of the BDDA. The *hearing friends* of the deaf, whose membership he and others had apprehended, were in charge and running the Association with benevolent paternalism, for which Maginn had no time. Care and kindness were all right for the performance of missionary duties, but ineffective for a national organisation aiming to improve the miserable lot of the deaf mute population. Such a body needed clout *on American lines,* which the BDDA under Sleight never had. Maginn, however, was not one for rocking the boat. Hence his withdrawal and concentration for the remainder of his life on his work as a missioner in Ireland, where he was held in high regard for his dedication, and became the first Superintendent of the Ulster Institute for the Deaf.

While remembrance of him faded in Great Britain and the BDDA failed to give him credit or to honour him for his leading role in the formation of the Association, his reputation abroad remained high. His former College in Washington conferred on him an honorary degree in recognition of his work for the deaf, the French Academy elected him one of its Officers, and the Indian government offered him the position of Headmaster in a new School for the Deaf in Calcutta, which Maginn declined.

One hundred years were to pass before research into the history of the Association during Centenary Year revealed Maginn as the founder and an outstanding figure in the history of the deaf of the United Kingdom. A headstone, erected on his grave in 1990, at last pays overdue tribute to his achievements and memory.

Ill. 3: *Members of the Ulster Institute for the Deaf at the graveside of Francis Maginn*

References

Grant, Brian (1990): *The Deaf Advance. A History of the British Deaf Association 1890-1990.* Edinburgh: The Pentland Press Limited.

Hodgson, Kenneth W. (1953): *The Deaf and their Problems.* London: Watts & Co.

The Deaf and Dumb Times (1890), vol. 1.

The Deaf Mute (1888-1889).

Howard G. Williams
Weston-super-Mare, Great Britain

Deaf Teachers in 19th Century Russia

Summary • **Резйоме**

Reference is made generally to historical trends in developments in Russia, with particular attention being given to those Deaf teachers of the Deaf who contributed significantly during the later 19th Century, those people whose work and endeavours remain relatively unknown outside of Russia; available sources and documentation are described as well as a coming publication which will cover the history of Russian work in education of the Deaf from about 1760 to 1975.

Справка дана восновном на исторические тенденции в развитии Росии, и особое внимание уделено тем глухим учителям глухих, которые успешно работали во второй половине 19 века; эти люди, их труды и планы почти неизвестны за пределами России; ниже описываются имеющиеся в нашем распоряжении источники и документы, а также публикующаяся сейчас книга, которая охватит историю русской работы в области обучениа глухих примерно с 1760 по 1975.

I

The history that relates to the Deaf in Russia can be traced back over many years. In the days of Kiev Rus and at the beginning of the emergence of the State of Muscovy, there were civil and canon laws which, though difficult to separate, did express specific attitudes towards the Deaf, or, as it was then said, the Deaf and dumb. These attitudes, like that latter phrase, might not be judged exemplary at the present day but, for their time, and possibly in comparison with what then prevailed in Western Europe, they seem quite progressive. Thus the Code of Tsar Alexei Mikhailovich in 1640 decreed that:

> *If there should remain Deaf and dumb children after a death and brothers and sisters cause them wrong and try to drive them out of their father's or mother's estates, then the estates of their father and mother are divided according to lot into equal parts for the children of the deceased, so that no-one should be seriously harmed.*

Again in 1733, a decree issued on 14th August, extended clerical protection to the Deaf:

> *The police, who keep mute poor for maintenance and mental correction, should refer them to the Holy Synod so that it can order them to be sent to a monastery.*

In the Code of Laws issued in 1833 the Deaf were protected under a legal system of wardship, which oversaw their rights of inheritance. Any criminal proceedings against a Deaf person had to be overseen by an advisory court. More importantly those who had gained access to education were accorded certain legal rights which recognised the value of that education, and possibly entrance to certain vocations. Admittedly there were very few Deaf persons, if any, being educated at all in Imperial Russia outside of the Institute at St. Petersburg, but, at least, by 1833, legalistic protection of a kind had been promulgated.[1]

Yet even if the history of the Deaf in Russia can go back for many years, we are relatively uninformed in the West about Russian development and its achievements.

Part of our ignorance is conditioned by the Cyrillic curtain that the Russian language and its alphabet raises before our initial glances, but there are also other difficulties of access. It is not necessary to dwell upon the unavailability of the relevant texts. One could dwell at length, however, on the political considerations that have inhibited close contact with work in this field, but it is to be hoped that such ideological considerations have been exorcised by both sides, and that, in a happier future, the due attempts at honest and critical appraisal of Russian work can go more expressly forward. If we want to expand our knowledge of Russian work, we no longer have to waste our time on, or have our time wasted by prejudice, sycophancy or pedagogic myopia. And now shortly, to begin, like Alice, at the Beginning.

II

There is a claim[2] by Soviet educationalists that there was a school opened for the Deaf in Pernau (Pärnu) before 1709 – this was in what is no longer to be designated the Estonian Soviet Socialist Republic. This arrangement run by one Jakob Wilde (Vil'dye) attempted to teach oral speech and was said to be the first school for the Deaf in Europe, and in the world. Given the fact that there is little or no documentation to substantiate this claim, however, one must hold over the chance of its originality the Scottish legal verdict of 'not proven'. But whatever the doubtful and meagre origins, it cannot be denied that, over the years of the

---

1   For information about the legal circumstances of the Deaf see Appendix A to D'yachkov and Dobrova 1949 from which the quotations are taken.

2   There is a short, largely uninformative reference to work on Pärnu in Basova 1965. A more extended account can be found in Hörschelmann 1903. Hörschelmann was director and *Anstaltsprediger* in Fennern.

19th century, Imperial Russia developed a rudimentary system for educating its Deaf people which bore many of the characteristics of what we might call Western attributes.

From 1806, the Dowager Empress Maria Feodorovna had sponsored work in St. Petersburg, and, given philanthropic support, the largest school in Russia, the Petersburg Institute, was to emerge there[3] – other schools took root in Moscow (1860), as early as 1817 in the city of Warsaw in what was then Russian Poland, and at various provincial centres like Kazan' on the Volga (1886). There was even a sprinkling of small private establishments, schools for Deaf children that were run by Deaf people themselves and whose value and importance will later be stressed.

It was generally the case though, as in Western Europe and USA at this period, that philanthropy of various kinds was the name of the game. Again, as it was abroad, so it was in Russia, that ideas about education for the Deaf were influenced by the considerations that flowed mainly from French or German inspiration. As the years of the 19th century tolled on, we find also that signing and gestural communication gradually became superseded (in the larger schools at least) by adherence to the pure oral method.

But it must not be thought that the Russian schools for the Deaf were just pale copies in imitation of whatever could be taken over from French or German models. There were significant teachers of the Deaf working assiduously and very effectively in 19th Century Russia; and our knowledge of teaching of the Deaf, and of special education, that history is all

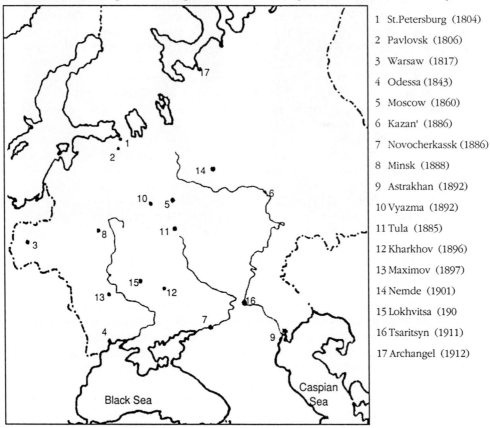

1	St.Petersburg	(1804)
2	Pavlovsk	(1806)
3	Warsaw	(1817)
4	Odessa	(1843)
5	Moscow	(1860)
6	Kazan'	(1886)
7	Novocherkassk	(1886)
8	Minsk	(1888)
9	Astrakhan	(1892)
10	Vyazma	(1892)
11	Tula	(1885)
12	Kharkhov	(1896)
13	Maximov	(1897)
14	Nemde	(1901)
15	Lokhvitsa	(190
16	Tsaritsyn	(1911)
17	Archangel	(1912)

Table 1: *Schools for the Deaf in Russia before 1917 (list not exhaustive)*

---

3   The original school was sited in the Fortress of Marienthal at Pavlovsk in 1806 and later moved to a house in Vyborgskaya in St. Petersburg itself. From 1810 it occupied the buildings on Gorokhovaya where it was to remain until about 1965. For a history of the institute see Lagovsky 1910.

the more impoverished because we have not allowed them the honour of the recognition they so richly deserve.

III

Merit of the highest degree is long overdue to Viktor Ivanovich Fleri (1800-1856) – he directed the St. Petersburg Institute and his thinking and practice about the possibilities of effective communication for Deaf children were very much ahead of his time. And the roll of honour must include Georgii Alexandrovich Gurtsev (1778-1858), whose *Encyclopaedic Course* of 1838 attempted to provide for the entire education of the Deaf; other names come to mind, amongst whom must be Aleksandr Fedorovich Ostrogradsky (1851-1907).

Ill. 1: *Victor I. Fleri*   Ill. 2: *Georgii A. Gurtsev*

Still one must be careful not to exaggerate the extent to which the educational needs of Deaf people were being given attention in Tsarist Russia. In 1902 Karth (writing from Breslau, which is now Wroclaw in Poland east of the Oder-Neisse line) could instance 17 schools in existence in Britain catering for 3073 pupils: in Russia (which then included most of what we now call Poland as well as the Baltic Republics) there were actually 20 schools, but serving only 885 pupils (Karth cited in Basova 1965, p. 62). In reality, if we break this number down, the St. Petersburg, Warsaw and Moscow schools (with possibly that at Kazan') held by far the greater majority of pupils, and the other 15 or so 'schools' were very small private institutions just about existing and sometimes providing only a pittance of education. For our purposes, however, attention should be given to these smaller schools for a few of them were run by Deaf teachers of the Deaf.[4] And there is one major exception to this general rule

---

4   Most of the material is derived from Basova 1965, Chapter III, especially parts of the section on :

about their smallness for the main school in Moscow itself, which in 1902 was second only to St. Petersburg – that school had been founded and run by a Deaf man, I. K. Arnol'd.

IV

Ivan Karlovich Arnol'd (1805-1891) organised the Moscow school for the Deaf and was amongst the most outstanding personalities working for the teaching of the Deaf in mid-19th century Russia. His road in life was one of continual and selfless endeavour to extend opportunities for the Deaf to be educated.

Arnol'd was born on 25th September 1805 and lost his hearing at the age of five. His parents originally sent him to the Petersburg Institute but soon had him transferred to a boarding-school in Germany with his hearing brothers. Though he resided at the boarding-school, he actually went to a school for the Deaf for his education and later, after leaving this school, his parents tried to develop his artistic talent by sending him to Dresden Academy of Art where he completed the course-work and obtained qualifications as a painter and artist. On finishing in Dresden, Arnol'd obtained a post as typographer at the Petersburg Institute but he was dissatisfied with these duties and aspired to open a school for the Deaf. In his application to the Ministry of Popular Education to open such a school, he wrote:

> (My wish is) *to occupy myself with the teaching and development of unfortunate Deaf and dumb children, like myself, of whom, as I have found out from travelling about Russia, there are very many in our empire, who, for the lack of educational institutions, are left in the majority of cases as if they were rejected by the world and men.*

It was with thoughts like these that, in 1850, Arnol'd entered upon his educational and philanthropic activities.

His first experience of teaching the Deaf was in a private household, and, after that, he opened a small private school in St. Petersburg. But he soon became convinced that this school could not possibly survive: it was precariously financed and the method of obtaining funds for its upkeep was rudimentary. Realising these difficulties, Arnol'd turned to V. I. Fleri, then director at Petersburg and suggested that his small school should be joined to the Petersburg Institute as a preparatory section for Deaf children aged from two to ten years. This suggestion was not acceptable to the bureaucratically-bound Board of Governors at the institute, however, although it was in fact supported by Fleri himself.

About 1860, Arnol'd wished to start up a school in Moscow and, to assist in this work, he made use of the official connections that his father had as director of a commercial academy. Official permission was soon granted to allow Arnol'd to open a school but again there were financial problems. Arnol'd turned for help to private and public charities in Moscow, wrote numerous letters to authorities he knew and to rich people and even went around with a bag, collecting money for the school.[5]

But not enough money was raised and Arnol'd was convinced by this experience that the school could not survive if it relied only on charitable contributions. There could be no question of free education for the Deaf and the children accepted by the school were to come mainly from well-to-do parents and the fees for their education and up-keep increased year by year. Arnol'd did manage to obtain some direct assistance from the Moscow Town Council and this funding allowed some poor pupils to be admitted to the school, but the council

The development of schools for the Deaf (and dumb) in outlying districts of Russia. The original texts are derived from this section of Basova's book.

5   This relict (and other items associated with Arnol'd and his school) had been placed in the Moscow Museum on the Education, Training and Care of the Deaf which had been founded about 1888 attached to the Polytechnical Museum. In the 1920s when the teaching side of the Polytechnical Museum was discontinued, the exhibits were all transferred to the custody of the Moscow Town Institute only to be destroyed during World War II (see Derdik 1971).

refrained from committing itself to large-scale support. In 1865 it suggested that a 'Trustee Society' for the school should be formed with duties to support existing links with the town council, to attract benefactors and *to maintain discipline at the school*. The payment of educational fees continued, however, and, in general, it was the children of the better-off who went on being taught there, though some pupils did get grants from the town council or benefactors. The Moscow school was only taken under the authority of the Moscow Town Council in 1900 and reliance on charitable support continued to play a significant financial role in the school's life until after 1917, when private education was abolished.

Amongst the school's benefactors was P. M. Tret'yakov, who founded the Tret'yakov Art Gallery – he was very interested in the problems associated with the teaching of Deaf people and, in 1875, at his own expense, provided a set of newer buildings at the school. It is for this reason that, at the end of the 19th century, the school was renamed the Arnol'd-Tret'yakov School in honour both of its founder and of its great benefactor.

As the school grew, its reputation spread and one of Arnol'd's intentions was that the school should specialise in training future teachers of the Deaf, but, though some of the pupils did actually become teachers, most of them either remained in the school's workshop or entered small business activities.

It is interesting to note that in this Moscow school, just as at Petersburg and Warsaw, there was a struggle to introduce oral speech, not only as a class-subject but also as a means of communication in social and working life. Compared to the other large schools, however, written and dactylic communication continued to play a significant part in the work of the Moscow school until the very end of the 19th century. It was only in the early years of the 20th century that oral speech dislodged fingerspelling from its eminence and that the role of written communication was diminished.

V

The Brothers Ivan Andreevich and Aleksandr Andreevich Burmensky were both born Deaf into the family of a priest, and both were to go to the Petersburg Institute.

Ivan A. Burmensky (1854-1936) finished his schooling in 1870 and worked in one of the government departments in St. Petersburg, then the capital city of Imperial Russia. In 1884, he left for Novocherkassk (near Rostov-on-Don, in Southern Russia) where, in the space of a year, he succeeded in setting up a section for the Deaf in the orphanage there. Burmensky himself writes about this in one of his many applications for help to the Mariinsky Foundation (which was supposed to cater countrywide for the needs of Deaf people):

> *In 1884 I arrived from St. Petersburg and discovered that, in the foundling hospital, there were abandoned Deaf-and-dumb children, and I had the good idea of serving the sacred cause by teaching and educating these children, so ill-treated by fate, to read and write, and giving them the opportunity of using human speech.*

I. A. Burmensky was to work in this section of the orphanage at Novocherkassk for 30 years.

During his first ten years there he wrote and published a number of textbooks for the Deaf pupils that were composed in simple language, within the grasp of anyone just about able to read. In 1894 he published a grammatical textbook covering a four year course of instruction. It has been said that this publication was not entirely original (because it was similar in style and content to books earlier written by I. A. Seleznev) but it did help Deaf pupils master grammatical forms and sentence structure. By contrast as a manual, his *Conversational Language for the Deaf-and-dumb with Questions and Answers* (1895) was both more interesting and innovative. In it, Burmensky tried to give a typical range of questions and answers useful for general social communication and for mastering some educational topics, in history and geography, for instance. In 1898, again at Novocherkassk, he published another textbook *A Primary School Vocabulary related to the concepts of everyday life*, which was in the form of lessons dealing with specific themes from everyday life and on history and geography.

Burmensky used natural gesture, mime and fingerspelling to instruct his pupils and these basic methods of imparting knowledge were supplemented with written speech. According to the testimony of the administrators of the orphanage, children were able to leave the orphanage, *able to read and write, and mentally developed.*

Aleksandr Andreevich Burmensky, Ivan A.'s brother, also worked in the educational field as a teacher in many different parts of Russia and has received particularly favourable comment for his work in Tsaritsyn (the City of Volgograd, also known to history as Stalingrad). A. A. Burmensky adopted the written method to teach language and made extensive use of a system of outside excursions in his lessons with pupils in order to acquaint them both with the natural life around them and the circumstances of urban living.

Ivan Osipovich Vasyutovich had been one of the teachers at the Petersburg Institute even though he was Deaf. In 1895 he started a private dayschool at Vitebsk in northern Belorussia, and, hoping to obtain funds from the local *zemstvo* or self-governing authority, he invested his savings in the school and wrote about it to the director at Petersburg as follows:

> *The school which you visited was started at my own expense in 1895 and still exists at the present time, supported from my own funds. It is true that my school is under the authority of the Board of Directors of People's Schools, but in spite of this fact, I have so far received no help or support from their exchequer, and, consequently, keep it going on the few pence that I manage to get for teaching the children.*

But such payments were so small that Vasyutovich had virtually no income. Only after much trouble and effort did he succeed in getting a grant of 400 Roubles a year from the proceeds of a house-to-house collection made on behalf of the school and it still remained small and very poor. Vasyutovich only taught the children reading, writing, arithmetic and calligraphy, but, in spite of being Deaf, also strove to give his pupils the ability to articulate some speech. According to reports from visitors to the school, he obtained favourable results in articulation, and organised some vocational training: needlework for the girls and bookbinding for the boys. Vasyutovich's devotion to his pupils amounted to his own self-sacrifice and it is said that his desire to develop the oral capacities of his Deaf pupils,which went alongside his wish to get them included in the community, attracted attention and aroused much respect.

VII

L. S. Vosnesenskaya was a Deaf teacher who kept a private school in the town of Tula from 1885.[6] She had been through the course of studies at the Arnol'd-Tret'yakov school in Moscow, which gave her the right to teach. A letter that she sent to the Guardianship of the Deaf, with a request for material assistance for the Tula school gives a picture of a hard unremitting life:

> *I, L. S. Vosnesenskaya, Deaf and dumb from birth, the daughter of a collegiate councillor, am the only teacher at my private school, which has no funds to support it, while I, a poor girl without any means to support myself, rent an apartment in a little wooden house, 21 feet wide by 32 feet 8 inches long (9 arshin x 14 arshin; 1 arshin = 28"/•71 m). The school is held in it and I live there myself and receive 2 to 4 Roubles a month from the parents for my teaching, on which I have to keep myself, as the children live with their parents who keep them. Pupils living outside the town live with me at my expense, paying up to 10 Roubles a month, with clothing and shoes from their parents.*

6   According to Basova 1965 but others give the date of this school from 1904.

Ill. 3: *At the Tula School for the Deaf and Dumb*

I receive no donation from anyone: I have sent a petition to His Excellency the Governor, the Mayor, the Marshall of Nobility, the President of the provincial district council and asked for help in the acquisition of a school and allocation of premises, but in the space of the four years from the day my school opened, I have only received 150 Roubles aid from the Tula provincial district council.

In this province there are up to 1500 Deaf and dumb altogether, and I have 10 of these in my school; there is no other school in the province. If I were given the means, I could have many pupils: there are poor parents, who cannot pay and I do not teach for nothing, because I myself have no means of support. But, with the help of others, I am ready to give my work for the benefit of society and the education of poor children. I have applied for help to all the local authorities, but in vain – nobody pays attention to the Deaf and dumb.

This long quotation should not be excused for it is important to have it on the record. The quotation comes from M. V. Bogdanov-Berezovsky's book of 1901 entitled *The Position of the Deaf and Dumb in Russia*. Basova (1965, p. 60) cites it in exemplary condemnation of what was being done (or rather what was **not** being done) for the Deaf in Tsarist Russia. By contrast, Inspector Ivan Moerder who oversaw the work of the Curatelle (or Guardianship) for the Deaf (in a report about the turn of the century) said that *Mlle Vosnéssensky in Toula* and others like her were *treasures in their self-abnegation, whom it is necessary to encourage, not only because of their own efforts, but as examples to others*[7] (Moerder 1899, p. 25). Which must have been little consolation to Vosnesenskaya because it appears that the

---

7   Moerder's reports can usually be found written in French, that was generally the language of court and official circles. I am indebted to Alexis Karacostas of the Institut National de Jeunes Sourds de Paris, for his assistance in finding copies of this report for me.

Curatelle did little to help her in any way. These few lines by Vosnesenskaya should be regarded objectively as a piece of documentary evidence that deserves to be recognised for what it is: a statement of fact about the devotion and honesty of purpose of a Deaf teacher of the Deaf. It is about a Deaf woman who struggled against tremendous odds, a Deaf woman who worked on her own for her own. It is about a Deaf woman who must not be forgotten from the pages of history.

VIII

And speaking of other teachers, we must not forget the brothers Sergei and Evgenii Zhuromsky, both Deaf from birth. As a teacher of the Deaf Evgenii Zhuromsky campaigned actively through the pages of the Curatelle's journal, *The Herald of Trusteeship*, that fingerspelling should be used in the education of the Deaf. His brother Sergei taught in the Mariinsky Institute in St. Petersburg. We also have some information about Evgenii Fedorovich Tomkeev, (1855-?), who had become Deaf in adolescence. He was educated at the Arnol'd-Tret'yakov school where he was later entrusted with teaching those Deaf juveniles who were considered backward in developing oral speech.To teach them he employed auxiliary means like natural gesture and fingerspelling. Tomkeev was a master of the grammar of Russian as well as a talented mathematician.

It has to be acknowledged that there is at present only a paucity of material available to us about these Deaf people. But it has also to be recognised that these Deaf teachers of the Deaf were making a significant contribution to the education of Deaf people in late 19th century Russia. While that system of education as a whole was then only nascent, this particular contribution was of significant value, over and above the number of the individuals concerned.

The contributions made by Deaf people to the education of the Deaf were to be limited as the pure oral method became the dominant mode of instruction in Russian schools for the Deaf.[8] But if one continues pedagogic (or, as the Russians call them, *surdopedagogic*) explorations of the Russian scene into the Soviet period, it is posssible to see VOG – All-Russian Federation for the Deaf – continuing to represent the educational needs of Deaf people. Episodes come to my mind like the 1930 investigations into the standards of instruction in schools for the Deaf.[9]

There is also the work of the Technicum for the Deaf at Pavlovsk. This establishment provides extremely well-oriented, high-level courses in vocational training and education for Deaf young people from all over the Soviet Union, and this Technicum is, of course, sponsored and supported by VOG itself.[10]

---

8   The general manner of this changeover is detailed in Basova 1965.

9   During the 1930s there was intense discussion in the schools about the methodologies that were to be employed to teach Deaf children. Ideas were sought from abroad, particularly from Germany but could not be effectively translated into practice.
Representatives of VOG were concerned that pupils leaving school to enter industry were undereducated and not properly prepared for life. Minakov, VOG director at Smolensk, voiced this concern in an article entitled *Za noviyu shkola* (Beyond the New School) in the journal *Zhizn' Glukhonemykh* (*Life of the Deaf and Dumb* 1932): *Our schools are our weak spot. We expect new staff from them, we expect replacements, but, in the majority of cases, the child who has spent eight to nine years at school emerges ignorant and unprepared for an independent life, without any qualifications...* A team was formed to enquire into the Moscow Institute for the Deaf (formerly the Arnol'd-Tret'yakov School) and it reported on the character of the work there... The team came to the opinion that it was necessary to introduce signing and gestural communication into the institute to remedy teaching there which was paying a lot of attention to speech techniques but not enough to the pupils' overall development (see Basova 1965, pp. 169-170).

10   The Technicum is situated at: 189623 Leningrad-Pavlovsk, LVTs, ulitsa Kommunarov 18 (Director in charge: Lydia Gerasimovna Sinitsyna).

It is important also specifically to draw attention to the very fine archive and exhibition at *VOG* headquarters in St. Petersburg in Krasnaya ulitsa 55, overlooking the Neva.[11] One can see there much about work for the Deaf over many years and it is excellently displayed.

Reference can also be made to a coming publication which will cover the history of Russian work in education of the Deaf from about 1760 to 1975. This is a full English translation of A. G. Basova's *Ocherki po istorii surdopedagogiki* of 1965, supplemented with additional information from the later text that Basova and Yegorov published in 1984. The translation is extensively annotated and provided with a range of illustrations and data taken from a large collection of Russian books and other sources about the Deaf that have accrued to my possession over the past 37 years.

It is possible to conclude with the philosophical statement that we have much to lose if our knowledge of Deaf history continues to be ignorant of the work that has been carried on for so long within Russia and the former Soviet Union.

Appendix
The original quotations:

p. 110

А будет после которого умершего останутся дети глухи и немы, а братья или сёстры учнут обижать их и отцова или материнова имения учнут их отлучать, и тем умершего детям имения отца их или матери разделите по жребьям всем поровну, чтоб из них никто изобижен не был.

Содержащихся в полиции безмолвных нищих для прокормления и исправления в уме их отослать в Святейший Синод, чтоб Святейший Синод повелел оных определить в монастырь (указ 14 августа 1733 г.) (Дьячков, А.И./Доброва, А.Д. (1949), стр. 378).

p. 113

Заняться обучением и развитием несчастных, подобно мне, существ, глухонемых детей, которых, как мне известно было из путешествия по России, родится в империи очень много и которые за неимением для них образовательных учреждений в большинстве случаев остаются как бы отвергнутыми от мира и людей (Басова А.Г. (1965), стр. 47).

p. 114

В 1884 г. прибыл из Петербурга и узнал, что в воспитательном доме имеются глухонемые дети из подкидышей, и мне пришла благая мысль послужить святому делу воспитания и обучения грамоте детей, обиженных судьбою, дав возможность им понимать человеческую речь...

выходили из приюта грамотными и умственно развитыми (Басова А.Г. (1965), стр. 58/59).

p. 115

Школа, которую вы посетили, открыта на мои собственные средства в 1895 г., на мои же средства существует она и по настоящее время. Правда, моя школа находится в ведении дирекции народных училищ, но несмотря на это, никакого посо-

---

11   The full address of VOG Headquarters in St. Petersburg is: St. Petersburg 190000, Krasnaya ulitsa 55. There is also an important archive of material in the School Library-Museum at Leningrad School for the Deaf No. 1.

бия от казны, ни содержания я до сих пор не получаю и, следовательно, содержу его на скудные лепты, которые приходится мне получать за обучение детей (Басова А.Г. (1965), стр. 59).

p. 115/ p. 116

В моей частной школе воспитательницей состою я одна, дочь коллежского советника, Л. С. Вознесенская, от рождения глухонемая. Школа моя к содержанию никаких средств к жизни не имеет, я – бедная девица без всяких средств к жизни – нанимаю квартиру в 3–4 комнаты в деревянном домике, мерою в ширину 9 аршин, а в длину 14 аршин. В нем помещается школа и живу я сама, получаю от родителей за обучение в месяц от 2 до 4 рублей, чем и содержу себя, а дети живут при родителях на их содержании. Иногородние ученики живут у меня на моих харчах, с платою в месяц до 10 рублей; одежда и обувь от родителей. Пожертвований ни от кого ко мне не поступает; я подавала прошение господину губернатору, городскому голове, предводителю дворянства, председателю губернской земской управы, ходатайствовала о выдаче мне пособия для обзаведения школы и об отводе квартиры и в продолжение 4-х лет со дня открытия моей школы только один раз получила пособие от Тульского губернского земства 150 рублей. В губернии всего глухонемых насчитывается до 1500 человек, а у меня в школе 10 человек, другой школы в губернии нет. Если бы мне дали средства, учащихся было бы много; есть бедные родители, им платить нечем, даром учить я не беру, потому что сама не имею средств к жизни, а при помощи других, труд свой готова пожертвовать для пользы общества и воспитания бедных детей. Я обращалась о помощи ко всем местным властям, но тщетно – никто не обращает внимания на глухонемых" (Богданов-Березовский, М.В. (1901), стр. 4).

p. 116

Mlle Vosnéssensky à Toula [and others] sont des trésors d'abnégation qu'il faut non seulement encourager, mais proposer en exemple. (Moerder 1899, p. 25)

References

Basova, A.G. (1965) : *Очерки по истории сурдопедагогики в СССР*. Moscow.

Basova, A.G./ Yegorov, S.F. (1984): *Историыа Сурдопедагогики*. Moscow.

Bogdanov-Berezovsky, M.V. (1901): *Положение глухонемых в России*. St. Petersburg

Burmensky, I.A (1894): *Краткии уц ебник Русскои Грамматики*. Novocherkassk.

Burmensky, I.A (1895): *Разговорныи ыазык длыа глук онемык по вопросам и ответам*. Novocherkassk.

Burmensky, I.A (1898): *Нац ал'ныи уц ебнии словар'из области поныатий обыденной з изни*. Novocherkassk.

Derdik, K.G. (1971): F.A.Rau on the differentiated education of auditorily handicapped children; in: *Defektologiya*, 5, pp. 81-84.

D'yachkov A.I./Dobrova A.D. (1949): *Хрестоматия по истории воспитания и обучения глухонемых детей в России*,. Moscow.

Hörschelmann, C. (1903): *Übersicht über das Werk der Taubstummenbildung mit besonderer Berücksichtigung der Anstalten in Russland*. Revel' (Reval-Tallin).

Karth, J. (1902): *Das Taubstummenbildungswesen im XIX. Jahrhundert*. Breslau.

Lagovsky, N.M. (1910): *The St. Petersburg Institute for the Deaf and Dumb 1810-1910*. St. Petersburg.

[Moerder, Yvan de] (1899): *Les Sourds-Muets en Russie*. St. Petersburg.

Optical Allusions III
Some Deaf Teachers of the Deaf

Ill. 27: Sarah T. Adams (Deaf, 1871-1894) taught painting and drawing at the hearing girls' school in Waterbury, USA.

She is one of the few female Deaf teachers who left a trace... Sometimes we may find some written piece of 'second hand' information, as the one by Deaf Otto Kruse (see ill. 33 and 34, p. 125) on Deaf Margaretha Hüttmann who taught German, arithmetic and religion in the early 19th century at the school for the Deaf in Schleswig, Germany. She had a perfect command of sign language, Kruse wrote. Today there is no more trace left of Margaretha Hüttmann at 'her' school, just as for so many other (female) Deaf teachers of the Deaf.

Martha Siebke   **Friedrich Huhn**

Diese beiden Gehörlosen haben den Kindern der Israelitischen Taubstummenschule zu Berlin Schwimmunterricht erteilt und wurden von der Schulleitung auch berechtigt, über die Schwimmleistungen den Kindern Zensuren zu erteilen, d. h. gewissermaßen Lehrertätigkeit auszuüben.

Ill. 28: Martha Siebke and Friedrich Huhn (both Deaf) taught swimming at the Israelite Asylum of the Deaf in Berlin, Germany. The caption emphasizes that they were entitled to give grades.

Ill. 29: Comberry (1792-1834), Deaf founder and director of the Institute for Deaf Mutes in Lyon, France, in 1824.

Ill. 30: Jacob Beets (born in 1811 in Amsterdam, Netherlands) was the second Deaf teacher at the Institute in Groningen, Netherlands, after Derk Jan de Bie Vroom (born in 1775 in Utrecht) who taught drawing.

Ill. 31: A.J.S. Broerse (?), born in 1831 in Amsterdam, Netherlands, was the last Deaf teacher at the Institute in Groningen, until 1899; from then on until recently, there were no more Deaf teachers there.

Ill. 32: Pierre Pélissier (? - 1863) was a Deaf poet and professor at the National Institution for Deaf Mutes in Paris, France. In 1856, he published the first dictionary of signs of the Deaf to be used at school.

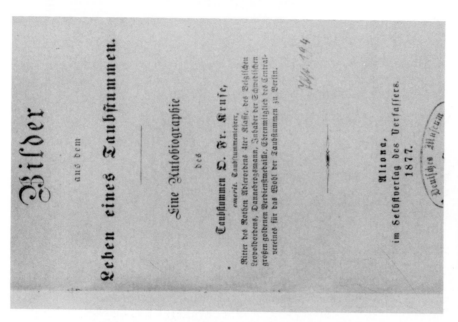

Ill. 33 and 34 : Otto Friedrich Kruse (1801-1880) was deafened at the age of 6. For about 55 years, he was a teacher of the Deaf at various schools in the north of Germany (Schleswig, Bremen, Altona b. Hamburg). The coverpage of one of his numerous works, his autobiography (1877), lists the honours he received and explicitly refers to his being a retired Deaf teacher of the Deaf.

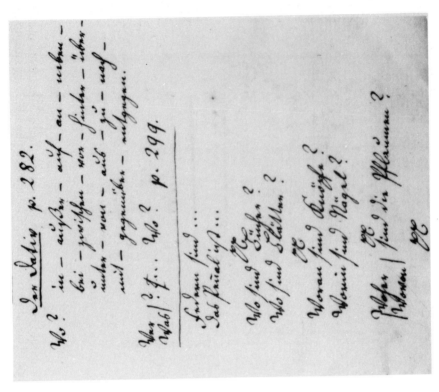

Ill. 35 and 36: Carl Wilhelm Teuscher (1803, Münster - 1835, Leipzig, Germany) was a Deaf teacher at the institute in Leipzig founded by Samuel Heinicke. He completed a comprehensive handwritten manual on the teaching of German grammar.

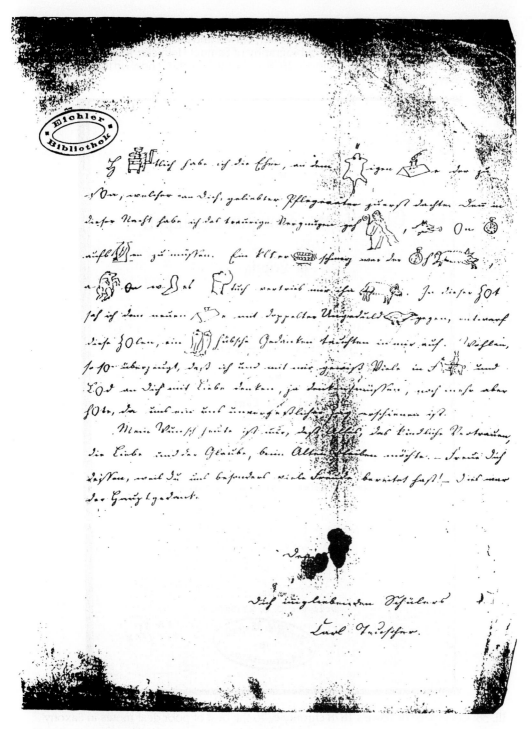

Ill. 37: An undated letter which Teuscher adressed to Carl Gottlieb Reich, his hearing teacher and director of the Leipzig school, contains rebuses some of which are based on a dialectal pronunciation of the words in question.

Carl Max Löwe (1834 - 1893) was a Deaf painter, drawer and teacher of the Deaf at the Leipzig Institute. In 1869, he published a biography of Samuel Heinicke 'founder of the first German institute for deaf mutes', and in 1878, a chronicle of the school on the occasion of its centenary.

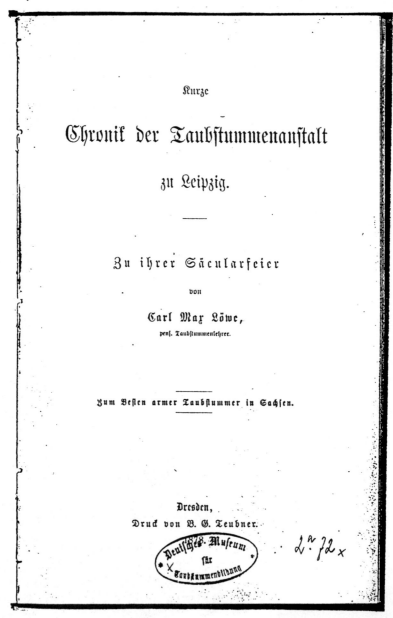

Ill. 38: Coverpage of Löwe's 1878 chronicle, 'to the best of poor deaf mutes in Saxony'.

He also left behind many unpublished works, such as a 275-page-manuscript of a grammatical 'nomenclature', and handwritten teaching material.

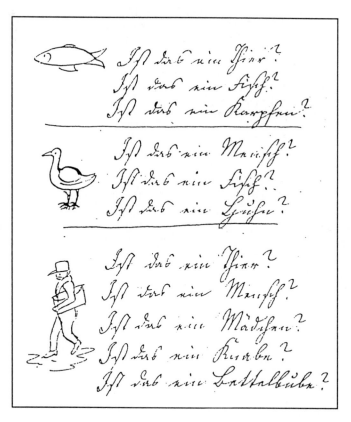

Ill. 39: A specimen of Löwe's unpublished teaching material.

Ill. 40: There is no portrait available of Carl Max Löwe – except this one showing him as a 2-year-old child.

Deaf Communities

Alexis Karacostas
Paris, France

Fragments of *Glottophagia*: Ferdinand Berthier and the Birth of the Deaf Movement in France

Summary • Résumé

This essay is a presentation of the major events which affected the Parisian Deaf community between 1822 and 1838, according to published works and manuscripts in the archives of the Institut National de Jeunes Sourds (National Institute for Young Deaf People) in Paris. It offers a description of the struggle between 'oralists' and 'gesturalists' which culminated in the birth of the first Deaf movement under the leadership of Ferdinand Berthier.

A partir de documents imprimés et de manuscrits inédits de l'Institut National de Jeunes Sourds de Paris, l'auteur présente les principaux évènements ayant concerné la communauté sourde de Paris entre 1822 et 1838, centrés sur les conflits entre 'oralistes' et partisans de la langue des signes et dont l'aboutissement fut la création, sous la houlette de Ferdinand Berthier, de la première association sourde en France.

Ill. 1: *Ferdinand Berthier*

I

In general language usage, it often happens that the two terms 'oral education' and 'oralism' become confused. This inappropriate union combines a teaching method and goal (the acquisition of spoken language) with an ideology and policy that have certain historical and social consequences.

Oralism is, in fact, a tendency which denies the value and even the existence of sign language, and which seeks to force upon the Deaf a way of expression and a life style that is patterned after that of the hearing. This tendency, which can be seen in every period and at every opportunity in the history of the Deaf, is very closely bound to the question of deafness, and is just as old as this question. Only its intensity and the areas with which it has been concerned have varied.

If sign language is the nightmare of the oralist, it is because it represented and continues to represent a main social and cultural means for self-expression in the everyday lives of deaf people. The history of sign language, in and of itself, is certainly not the only aspect of the history of the Deaf, but it surely represents an important element in understanding that history. The events that took place between 1822 and 1838 in the French Deaf community and which were connected with the Institution Nationale des Sourds-Muets[1] prove that the opposition between those who favored the rejection of Deaf identity and those who favored its recognition has determined the direction of the history of the Deaf.

Why have I chosen the Institution Nationale des Sourds-Muets in Paris? This institution exhibited interesting characteristics for the above mentioned time period. As the first public

---

1 In the past, the Paris school has had various names: Institution Nationale des Sourds-Muets, Institution Royale des Sourds-Muets, and, as it is called today, Institut National de Jeunes Sourds. Having been founded, in 1791, as a national institution, it is in fact the continuation of the abbé de L'Epée's private school.

school for the Deaf in France, it enjoyed a prominent place in the capital city, and its diplomas could open doors for the Deaf to numerous careers. Further, its size, the multiple functions that it performed, and the various groups that it accepted provide a vantage point for observing the social life of the Deaf.

Since its foundation in 1791, the institution on St. Jacques Street has lived through various, sporadically appearing, oralist trends. In order to change these trends into a real offensive, special conditions were necessary. These conditions arose simultaneously in 1830. The events described here which had never before occurred in such proportion, had considerable and unforeseen consequences, because they led to nothing less than the origin of the Deaf movement. It is also legitimate to assume that these events represent the first prelude to the general offensive of the oralists at the congress of Milan in 1880, which was played out on a much larger stage than in the school on St. Jacques Street. The effects of this latter offensive, which were catastrophic for the teaching of the Deaf, were to have completely different scope and duration.

What exactly were these crucial events?

II

The abbé Sicard died in 1822. He was 80 years old, weakened but maybe not as feeble as is generally thought, and his last years as director of the Paris school saw several violent conflicts, centered around two principal themes: on the one hand, the organization of the curriculum (specifically, the role of sign language in teaching), and on the other hand, the question of Sicard's successor at the helm of an establishment so impregnated with his personality.

Now just a word about the Deaf characters in the story. At the time, Jean Massieu, Sicard's favorite student, was still a teacher's aide. That is, he was not considered a full professor in spite of the essential role he had always played in assisting his master and the Deaf people in the school. Massieu had, after all, greatly contributed to the education of numerous Deaf students, not the least of whom was Laurent Clerc, 13 years younger than Massieu. Rather than cross the Atlantic with Thomas Hopkins Gallaudet, as Clerc did, Massieu preferred to stay in Paris and continue working with Sicard. Besides Clerc, other students of Massieu were also destined for celebrity: Alphonse Lenoir, born in 1804; Ferdinand Berthier, who was born in 1803 and arrived at the institution in 1811; and Claudius Forestier, who was born in 1810 and was only 12 years old at the time of Sicard's death. In the 1820s, these students' futures were before them. Laurent Clerc himself was only 31 when he emigrated to the United States, and, though he had thoroughly mastered French Sign Language, Berthier later related that his teaching in class was embarassingly like the so-called 'methodical signs' of the abbé de L'Epée, Sicard's predecessor.[2]

In Sicard's last years, one man undertook the reform of the school's teaching methods and tried to restore natural sign language to its proper place: Roch-Ambroise Auguste Bébian. He was born in Guadaloupe on August 4, 1789 (the same day that the privileges of the nobility were revoked in France), and as Sicard's godson, he was given the same name, Roch-Ambroise. Bébian moved to Paris, near his godfather Sicard, around 1807. He frequently visited classes at the St. Jacques school, and he made friends with Clerc, from whom

---

2 *Bébian already had an idea of the language of deaf mutes when he arrived at the Royal Institute, although he did not understand the principles of the language. Instinctively he discovered what there was about the signs used at the Institute that was wrong, insufficient, bizarre and arbitrary; he unfailingly attempted a full reform, and promised his friend Laurent Clerc success and honor if only he had the courage to initiate the reform. But Clerc feared the risk of an accusation of heresy and sacrilege if he as much as laid an innocent but daring hand on the holy ark; his veneration of the tradition of the methodical signs of the abbés de L'Epée and Sicard was so religious and profound, that Bébian decided to take things into his own hands, once he realized the futility of his efforts* (to convince Clerc). (Berthier 1839, p. 7)

Ill. 2: *Roch-Ambroise Auguste Bébian*

he learned French Sign Language (LSF). Between 1810 and 1817, Bébian began a series of serious linguistic studies of LSF. Living as closely as he did with the Deaf students and teachers, he saw the linguistic and cultural oppression they endured, and it was then that he began to understand that hearing people, even those with the best of intentions, were simply not willing to give up their privileged positions in order to grant Deaf people the power that they deserved in the field of Deaf education. Unfortunately, Bébian's stay at the school was all too short. The rivalry that developed between Bébian and the other teachers was too strong. They were jealous of his nomination to the post of pedagogical director (assistant principal), jealous of his excellent relations with the students, and jealous of his unparalleled teaching abilities. By nature an impetuous man, Bébian once struck another professor, Louis Paulmier, in the presence of Sicard. Paulmier had been trying to position himself as the successor to the old abbé. The act of striking another teacher constituted the official reason, and, of course, the pretext for the firing of Bébian in January 1821. Bébian had served as pedagogical director for less than two years. He never again held an official position in the St. Jacques school, in spite of his competence that even his worst enemies had to admit.

It is a fact that until the death of Sicard, Deaf people never held full teaching positions at the school: they served only as teacher's aides. Both oral training and teaching in sign language were practiced in the curriculum, depending on who was teaching any particular class, but the serious linguistic and pedagogical reflections on the role of sign language in education undertaken by Bébian had already begun to have an influence on the up-and-coming Deaf generation.

With the death of Sicard a long period of drifting and uncertainty began. From 1822 to 1832, a succession of directors were not able to establish enough authority to stimulate any real debate or encourage any progress in pedagogical practices at the school. The least that can be said is that these directors, all with religious backgrounds and with some understanding of education in general, were not scintillating masters in the adaptation of pedagogical methods for special students.

Nevertheless, little by little, some important changes began to appear during this period of uncertainty. The board of directors was enlarged, and the number of personnel grew as more students were admitted (120 or 130 students by the year 1830). It should be noted, however, that the growth of the staff was almost a family affair: in 1830, the administrator, the Baron de Gérando, counted his own nephew among the professors, and his niece among the teachers for the younger children; one of the professors had a brother who was a student teacher; a *surveillant*, or monitor (in the French system, a sort of extra-curricular disciplinarian), had a son who was a student teacher; another monitor had a daughter who was one of the writing teachers; the bursar had a sister who was a teacher; and the director, abbé Borel, invited a young friend and countryman to train for the post of chaplain. In other words, institutional conflicts and family affairs were most probably discussed indiscriminately both at the dinner table and in the conference room.

In addition, the school established an advisory board charged with reflecting upon and reorganizing the curriculum. But, while Bébian continued his combat outside the walls of the school by publishing linguistic essays, pedagogical manuals, newspaper and magazine articles, and anti-oralist pamphlets, the administrators of the St. Jacques school did nothing to stimulate the advisory board, and it made very little progress. The hearing teachers at the school grew older, but not wiser; classes were disorganized, and teaching methods changed frequently. But the event of the period which eventually had the greatest impact was, of course, the entrance of Deaf teachers onto the scene.

In 1829, there were two Deaf professors, Ferdinand Berthier and Alphonse Lenoir, among the six professors for the boys; no Deaf woman was among the four professors for the girls. Among the teacher's aides, there was one Deaf man for the boys, and two Deaf women for the girls. There were no Deaf people on the board of directors, none on the advisory board, none among the monitors, and none who taught vocational training. Although there were relatively few Deaf educators, there were more than there had ever been before in the establishment on St Jacques Street. Berthier, Lenoir and Forestier were already sharply aware of their situation. They **did** however, sometimes get the support of those of their hearing collegues who shared their views.

III

It is in this context of widespread uncertainty coupled with the rising generation of Deaf professors that the grand offensive of the oralists would be mounted.

Evidence of this offensive surfaced gradually in the famous 'circulars' published by the administrators of the Paris school. These circulars, four in number, date from 1827 to 1836 (*Circulaires* 1827-1836). The goals established by the administrators are outlined in the first, which is really nothing more than a publicity brochure of six pages filled with good intentions. The goals are:
- to collect as much information as possible about the education of Deaf people, nationally and internationally;
- to compare the advantages, disadvantages, and results of the different teaching methods surveyed;
- to draft practical teaching manuals;
- and finally, to ameliorate both vocational and auditory training.

Only two points concern teaching lip-reading and the age at which teaching of speech can begin in a group setting. In the first circular, then, no polemics: only good intentions.

Unfortunately, however, behind the scenes, the administrators were preparing a much more serious threat: the inauguration of the so-called 'rotation system'. Under this new system, each class of students would be taught by one and only one professor from the time the students entered school until their graduation. Since speech and lip-reading had become a mandatory part of the curriculum, Deaf professors who were not able to teach orally would necessarily be downgraded to teachers' aids working under the hearing professors. By pure chance, Berthier discovered the plot and intervened. His vehement protests to the administrators, themselves divided on the issue, caused the project of rotation to be abandoned for the time being. In fact, it was only postponed.

In the second circular, published in 1829, the administrators' principal theme was that, though it must be admitted *that sign language is the only way to enter into communication with the deaf mute (que le langage des signes est le seul moyen d'entrer en communication avec le sourd-muet)*, one should begin to eliminate the use of signing, *albeit progressively, after it has accomplished the eminent service that one expects from it* (that is, the acquisition and continual use of the French language; *pour ainsi dire progressivement, après avoir rendu le service éminent qu'on attend d'elle)*. As the Deaf student grew older, the use of gestural language would, according to the circular, constitute an obstacle to the acquisition of French. This basic theme, of course, was expounded with many more details and circumlocutions than I can go into here. Nevertheless, this pseudo-recognition of sign language, this affectation of assigning sign language an *eminent service* but of limited use in deaf education, fooled almost no one.

In any case, it did not fool the Deaf professors and students of the Paris school. By the end of 1830, a formidable Deaf movement shook the foundations of the institution. The administrators were astounded to learn that Ferdinand Berthier had the nerve to send a petition to King Louis Philippe himself. Berthier, in fact, was acting as head of a delegation of Deaf people recruited from both inside and outside the school.[3] He was even invited, with Lenoir, to a dinner with the King, who immediately asked news of Clerc and Massieu. In the petition, read to the King by his aide-de-camp, there was only one resolution, one demand: the return of Bébian to the institution. For the Deaf community, Bébian had become their beacon, their symbol, their spokesperson. In his petition Berthier evoked

> *the writings of Bébian, which have become classics and serve as the guides for teachers in France and even abroad (…). It is thanks to his teaching that we owe the power to express what we feel to Your Majesty (…). It is his method that we use to instruct our brothers in misfortune. (Adresse 1830)*

Over the years, Bébian had become the nemesis of the St. Jacques school administrators. In 1826, weary of trying to secure a post in the Paris school, Bébian established a private school in Paris on the Boulevard Montparnasse. Shortly thereafter, furious at this news, the administrators formally forbade anyone, professors or students, to have any contact with Bébian inside or even outside (!) of the school. Until 1826, Bébian was considered a nuisance: the school paid lip-service to the value of his theories and his manuals, since there were no others, but he was treated as immoral and it was considered advisable to keep a safe distance from him. With the second circular of 1829, the rupture between the administrators and Bébian became complete, and war was declared on Bébian's position on sign language. In this context, Berthier's demand that Bébian be rehired was not at all surprising. Bébian's name itself implied all identity, the rejection of paternalistic attitudes towards Deaf people, and a profound understanding of the key role that sign language played in their lives.

---

3   *Two deaf mutes, who are former pupils and are now teachers at the Institution Royale des Sourds-Muets; a third Deaf Mute who is a former pupil and teacher's aide, and who still resides at the institute; further, three or four deaf mutes, who are also former pupils of the institute but who have left it have all applied to the King,* complained the Baron de Gérando to the minister of the interior (de Gérando 1830).

Berthier's demand was vigorously denounced by the administrators, who were exasperated by the news. The students began to give the Deaf professors their full support. Insulting notes and caricatured drawings of the most despised hearing professors were seized. The ugly mood became widespread, and in a matter of days the cry: *We want Bébian!!* echoed in the corridors of the school. A delegation of sixty students wrote twice to the minister of the interior to describe the situation at the school:

> (The teachers) *do not teach in class for days at a time: one hasn't even taught in the past two years – he gives his smartest student the responsibility of making the other students practice their lessons (…). He treats us like dogs (…). We have often complained to the director and the administration. They don't believe us. While they prefer to believe the professors, it is we who are telling the truth (…). Our monitors are too old to learn our sign language, they don't understand us.* (Les élèves 1830)

The Deaf professors also reported on the school's problems to the minister:

> *Publicly, it is known only that Bébian's talents are exceptional, but we have preserved the memory of his sincere affection for deaf mutes, his constant attention to bringing out our human dignity. When he came to our institution, the unfortunate deaf mutes, victims of a prejudice that was shared by even the abbé Sicard himself, were treated as only half human and were exposed to crude treatment and vulgarities from the monitors and even from servants and staff. Mr. Bébian made all the employees feel that they were there for the students and not the other way around, a truism so obvious that one is still today tempted to overlook it. That, Mr. Minister, is what has ensured Bébian the eternal gratitude of deaf mutes.* (Berthier et al. 1830)

The administrators then initiated systematic written interrogations. They wanted to find the leaders of the protest and especially wanted to know if students were associated with the professors in the delegation that met the King. Cleverly, they spared the professors, but expelled three students as an example to the others. One of those expelled was Imbert, who would later play an important role in the Deaf community.[4] The revolt was finally checkmated by punishments, suppression of privileges, and expulsions.

The third circular appeared in 1832. Simultaneously, a new director was selected: Désiré Ordinaire, the first lay director named to the post in the entire history of the institution.

The third circular was even more explicit than the second regarding the priority of teaching speech and lip-reading. Certain teachers, like Henri-Daniel Guyot in Holland, had already protested the bias of the reports of the oralist professors of the Paris school. Comberry, the Deaf director of the school in Lyon, refused entry at his school to Miss Morel, a Paris teacher and the niece of Baron de Gérando, who wished to investigate the methods practiced in Lyon. According to contemporaries, most of the Deaf directors and teachers in France as well as abroad used the Bébian method, and were therefore summarily dismissed or criticized by the Paris administration. Laurent Clerc's work in the United States was practically ignored. Among the works about deaf education analyzed in the circular, the only ones endorsed were those by oralist authors, particularly the Germans. Bébian's most recent manual was criticized from beginning to end.

The circular saved the best, however, for last. In the appendix, it outlined the principles of the new organization of education at the Paris school: the rotation system had not only resurfaced, but had become the mandatory norm.

From 1832 to 1836, the unjust rotation system, totally rejected by Deaf students and professors alike, was shamelessly enforced at the school. It took four years of vehement protests by Berthier and his colleagues before the rotation system was abandoned: four years during which the Deaf professors lost their status as professors to serve merely as teacher's aids; four years of undisguised contempt for the cumulative experience of the Deaf professors, who were rewarded by this ultimate disgrace (not to mention the lower pay they received, in spite

---

4   The other two expelled students were Bézu and Contremoulin.

of their seniority, in comparison to their hearing colleagues). As an example, Berthier was assigned to a class of failures, students whom the system had failed miserably and from whom nothing was expected. And with Berthier, they didn't do so badly, either!

The weight of this four-year oralist offensive, sapping the energy of the Paris school, squashed all protest from the inside. It was outside the walls of the institution that the Deaf professors continued their combat. They knew it was too late to count on Bébian's being rehired at the school; he had already accepted a post as director of the Deaf school in Rouen in 1832. But serious problems forced him to abandon his post after only 14 months. In 1834 Berthier and his friends organized the first banquet honoring the abbé de L'Epée. These banquets became annual events and were used by Deaf people as a forum to publicize their demands. Bébian boarded a ship for Guadaloupe, from where he would never again return to France and where he died five years later.

But, though the labor pains were intense, the Deaf movement was born. This time, it was finally Deaf people themselves who began to take charge of their affairs. The popularity of their annual banquets and the 1836 victory over the rotation system gave them the courage they needed. In 1838 the Société Centrale d'Assistance et d'Education des Sourds-Muets (Central Society for the Assistance and the Education of Deaf Mutes) was founded, the first Deaf association in France, and, to my knowledge, in the world. The battle was won, but not the war.

In the decades that followed, there were other battles, with varying results. One example among many: the Deaf professors never had the satisfaction of seeing a Deaf person named pedagogical director. Berthier struggled unceasingly, but without success. I quote Berthier's letter of 1843 to the minister of the interior:

> *The hearing person the most accustomed to live with deaf mutes, will but understand us imperfectly; and if he is honest, he will frankly admit the undeniable superiority of his deaf colleague* (regarding his ability to communicate in signs). (Berthier 1843)[5]

For Berthier, there was no doubt: whether he was advising his superiors, his colleagues, or the families of Deaf pupils, the Deaf person alone is able to correctly evaluate what Deaf students need and he alone is capable of proposing solutions to their problems. But, in spite of the efforts of Berthier, the professor with the most seniority, the students at the Paris school would never know the joy felt by Gallaudet University students in 1988...

IV

The position adopted by the Paris school administrators illustrates perfectly that linguistic oppression plays a central role in the ultimate refusal to recognize that Deaf people have a right to be different. Faced with Deaf people who constantly demand their right to an education conducted from beginning to end in sign language, the administrators stubbornly centered their reflections on the teaching of speech and the French language. Sign language was at best for them only a stepping-stone towards integration into the world of the hearing, a temporary means to an end when nothing better can be found. According to this conception of Deaf education, French should ultimately replace sign language, should swallow it.

---

5   The answer of the members of the advisory board is written at the bottom of this letter: *The commission has charged me with informing you that such appointment is not the concern of either the commission or, as far as is known, of the ministry, and that it can only be discussed in private conversations. Monsieur de Gombert is, as am I, completely on your side, but he has heard, as have I, the insuperable objections of Messieurs Passy and Durieu, which were not directed against you, whom they greatly admire, but rather against the impossibility of giving this position, should it be created, to a deaf person, regardless of how great his other merits may be. For this reason I have let the matter rest, in fear of adding fuel to the opposition's fire by even bringing it up.*

In the articles of the oralists of the 1830s, sign language, even when it was pushed to the back, was never so completely repressed, never so completely silenced as it was after the Milan congress fifty years later. All in all, it is not difficult (even though the word was never used by the principal actors of the time) to identify the position taken by Deaf people themselves as a policy of true bilingualism facing the strict monolingualism of the hearing oralists.

Should sign language be taught? Should the acquisition of sign language take precedence over the acquisition of the national spoken language? Aren't Deaf people in the best position to teach sign language?

Deaf teachers and those, like Bébian, who supported them, asserted it without ambiguity. For them, sign language comes directly from nature:

> *Our signs do not merely name the things, they paint them, or, to speak philosophically (…) they are the veritable representation of ideas.* (Berthier 1839, p. 12)
> *The experience of 70 years is there to prove the indisputable and undisputed superiority of the system that recognizes that the education of deaf mutes depends on the language that God gave us.* (ibid., p. 41)

It is unnecessary to try to measure the validity of the arguments advanced here with the yard-stick of a linguistic theory: the true issue is human rights.

Appendix
The original French quotations:

p. 135 (footnote 2)

> En arrivant à l'Institut Royal, Bébian devinait déjà cette langue des sourds-muets dont il ignorait les principes. Son instinct lui faisait découvrir ce que les signes employés avaient de faux, de défectueux, de bizarre, d'arbitraire; et il ne cessait de provoquer une réforme complète, promettant succès et honneur à son ami s'il avait le courage de l'entreprendre. Mais Clerc eût craint d'encourir une accusation d'hérésie, de sacrilège, en essayant seulement de porter une main innocemment hardie sur l'arche sainte; sa vénération pour la tradition des signes méthodiques des abbés de L'Epée et Sicard était si religieuse, si profonde, que Bébian, convaincu de l'impuissance de ses efforts, avait pris le parti de s'en occuper lui-même. (Berthier 1839, p. 7)

p. 138

> (…) les ouvrages de Bébian, devenus classiques servent de guide aux instituteurs de France et même de l'étranger (…). C'est à ses leçons que nous devons de pouvoir exprimer à Votre Majesté ce que nous sentons (…). C'est sa méthode que nous suivons pour instruire nos frères d'infortune. (*Adresse* 1830)

p. 138 (footnote 3)

> Deux sourds-muets, anciens élèves, maintenant professeurs dans l'Institution Royale des sourds-muets, un troisième sourd-muet ancien élève aspirant et habitant encore l'institution, trois ou quatre sourds-muets anciens élèves aussi de l'institution mais qui l'ont quittée, se sont présentés, dit-on, au Roi. (de Gérando 1830)

p. 139

> [Les maîtres] ne font pas la classe pendant plusieurs jours, un d'eux ne fait pas la classe depuis deux années et il charge toujours le plus instruit de ses élèves de leur répéter ses leçons (…). Il nous traite comme des chiens (…). Nous nous sommes souvent plaints à monsieur le Directeur et à l'administration. Ils ne veulent pas nous croire, ils croient toujours plutôt nos maîtres que nous qui disons la vérité (…). Nos surveillants sont trop vieux pour apprendre le langage de nos gestes, ils ne nous comprennent pas. (Les élèves 1830)

> On ne connaît de Bébian dans le public que ses talents qui depuis longtemps l'ont mis hors de ligne, mais nous avons conservé le souvenir de son affection sincère pour les sourds-muets, de

son attention constante à relever en eux la dignité d'homme. Quand il vint dans notre institution, les malheureux sourds-muets victimes d'un préjugé qui était appuyé de l'opinion de l'abbé Sicard même étaient traités comme des demi-brutes et exposés sans protection aux mauvais traitements et aux grossièretés des surveillants et même des domestiques. M. Bébian fit sentir à tous les employés qu'ils étaient là pour les élèves et non les élèves pour eux; vérité si claire et qu'on est encore aujourd'hui bien disposé à oublier: voilà, Monsieur le Ministre, ce qui lui assure à jamais la reconnaissance éternelle des sourds-muets. (Berthier et al. 1830)

p. 140

Le parlant le mieux initié au langage mimique, le parlant le plus habitué à vivre avec les sourds-muets ne les comprendra jamais qu'imparfaitement et s'il est de bonne foi, il avouera ici franchement la supériorité réelle, incontestable de son collègue sourd-muet. (Berthier 1843)

p. 140 (footnote 5)

La commission m'a chargé de vous dire qu'il n'avait été nullement question de la création ni dans son sein ni au ministère à sa connaissance, et qu'il n'a pu en être parlé que dans des conversations privées. M. de Gombert est comme moi tout porté en votre faveur mais comme moi il a entendu les répugnances insurmontables de MM Passy et Durieu non pas contre votre personne qu'ils honorent beaucoup, mais contre l'impossibilité de donner la place si elle était créée à un sourd-muet quel que fut d'ailleurs son mérite. Et c'est toujours pour cela que j'ai laissé dormir la chose dans la crainte, en la mettant sur le tapis, de tirer les marrons du feu pour un adversaire. (answer, in Berthier 1843)

p. 141

Nos signes ne nomment pas les choses, ils les peignent ou, pour parler philosophiquement, (…) ils sont la véritable représentation des idées. (Berthier 1839, p. 12)

Une expérience de soixante-dix ans est là pour attester la supériorité incontestable et incontestée du système qui fait reposer l'enseignement des sourds-muets sur le langage que Dieu nous a donné. (ibid., p. 41)

Iconography

Ill. 1: Ferdinand Berthier
by René Hirsch, undated
Institut National de Jeunes Sourds, Paris
Photo: Studio de la Comète, Paris

Ill. 2: Roch-Ambroise Auguste Bébian
by Chassevent, undated
Institut National de Jeunes Sourds, Paris
Photo: Studio de la Comète, Paris

References

Adresse des sourds-muets au Roi (1er novembre 1830). (n.p.); in-8°, 7p.

Berthier, Ferdinand (1843): [Letter addressed to the director of the Institut Royal des Sourds-Muets in Paris, dated april 17, 1843.] Unpublished manuscript. INJS, Paris.

Berthier, Ferdinand (1839): *Notice sur la vie et les ouvrages de Auguste Bébian*. Paris.

Berthier, F./Lenoir, A./Forestier, C. (1830): [Letter adressed to the minister of the interior, dated december 18, 1830, with the seal of the Ministère de l'Intérieur.] Unpublished manuscript. Private collection.

(Première, deuxième, troisième et quatrième) Circulaire de l'Institut Royal des Sourds-Muets de Paris à toutes les Institutions de Sourds-Muets de l'Europe et de l'Amérique (1827, 1829, 1832, 1836). Paris.

de Gérando, J.-M. (1830): [Letter to the minister of the interior, dated november 16, 1830.] Unpublished manuscript. Private collection.

Les élèves de l'Institution des Sourds-Muets à Paris (1830): [Letter adressed to the minister of the interior, dated dec.12, 1830, with the seal of the Ministère de l'Intérieur.] Unpublished manuscript. Private collection.

Bernard Mottez
Paris, France

The Deaf Mute Banquets and the Birth of the Deaf Movement

Summary • Résumé

At the beginning of the 1830s the situation of deaf teachers at the Royal Institute of Deaf Mutes at Paris and the role of signing ('mimicry') were queried. In 1834 a committee of ten Deaf Mute members, presided over by Ferdinand Berthier, decided to celebrate, from then on, the anniversary of the birthday of the abbé de L'Epée with an annual banquet. Participants at these banquets were Deaf Mutes from various institutes, countries and professions. Some hearing guests were also invited to speak at every banquet, among them friends of the Deaf Mutes, journalists and outstanding personalities from the world of politics, of art and literature.

These banquets became true festivals of 'mimicry'. Signs were performed and celebrated. There even was a religious quality to the banquets: it was a religion centred on liberation and progress, the religion of a people whose pope was Ferdinand Berthier and whose messiah had been the abbé de L'Epée.For ages toasts have been proposed to the 'Spiritual Father', to the 'Saviour of the Deaf Mutes'. Before him the Deaf had been nothing, lost in darkness and ignorance; they had been pariahs. Now the Deaf are one people, one nation. It is up to them, from now on, to achieve mastery in art, literature and science and to obtain their civil rights which, although seemingly admitted, had always been threatened. The tradition of the banquets still continues but its origin has generally been forgotten.

Au début des années 1830, à l'Institution Royale des Sourds-Muets de Paris, la place des enseignants sourds et de la mimique fut mise en question. En 1834, un Comité de sourds-muets, présidé par F. Berthier, décida de fêter désormais l'anniversaire de la naissance de l'abbé de L'Epée par un banquet annuel. Participèrent à ces banquets des sourds-muets de toutes les écoles, de tous les pays, de toutes les professions. Quelques parlants – des amis des sourds-muets, des journalistes et des personnalités éminentes du monde politique, des arts et de la littérature – y étaient chaque fois invités.

Ces banquets étaient de véritables festivals de la mimique. On la vantait. On la montrait. Il y avait un aspect religieux dans ces banquets: une religion centrée sur la libération et le progrès, la religion d'un peuple ayant eu l'abbé de L'Epée pour messie et dont le pape était Berthier. Pendant des décennies on porta des toasts au 'père spirituel', au 'rédempteur' des sourds-muets. Avant lui ils étaient dans la nuit, ils n'étaient rien, ils étaient perdus, des ignorants, des parias. Maintenant ils sont un peuple, une nation. A eux de conquérir désormais la maîtrise des arts et des sciences et d'obtenir leurs droits civils toujours menacés, lors même qu'on les croit acquis. La tradition des banquets continue. Leur origine est généralement oubliée.

> *Recently there were some unkind remarks made about our fraternal association. It was said that nothing would be more disastrous for the deaf mute than to limit himself to only the company of other deaf mutes. To regroup deaf mutes into a separate nation, a special caste, would be to condemn them to a deplorable exclusion. Those who say such things have misunderstood what is in our hearts. Our spirits have never harbored such egoistic intentions of separatism. We have been rejected from the banquets of hearing-speaking people. They have wanted to suppress the language of deaf mutes: that sublime universal language given to us by Nature. And yet deaf mutes have said to their speaking brothers: 'Come among us: join us in our work and in our play; learn our language as we learn yours; let us form one people, united by indivisible ties.' My brothers, is that egoism? Is that isolation? Let our accusers with no conscience just dare again to raise their voices against us!*
> (Ferdinand Berthier, 7th banquet, 1840; in: Société Centrale 1849, p.96)

Banquets are a bit like sports. They both play an important role in the Deaf way of life. Or at least they do in France. We sometimes even joke about it. This predilection of Deaf people for sports and banquets is in fact sometimes viewed with condescension, if not outright derision, by those engaged in more 'cultural' or 'militant' activities. Banquets and sports are seen as essentially insular affairs, devoid of any attempt at reform, without any effect on society, a sort of zero level on the scale of Deaf activism.[1]

It is important for me to say first what it means to me, as a hearing person, to participate in a Deaf banquet. When I am simply invited to the house of deaf friends, I say that I am going to visit friends – and they happen to be deaf. I do not say that I am entering the 'Deaf world'. I suppose they speak of visits to our homes in the same way. But when I am invited to one of their banquets, what a difference!

Deaf people are a people without a homeland. Their Deaf Clubs are their territory. And their efforts to protect them from being taken over by hearing people are well known. Their banquets are also a kind of Deaf territory. I really feel that I am on foreign soil at a Deaf banquet. Surrounded by an exotic language which I would love to use like a native, I enjoy all the pleasure that one usually feels in a foreign country. Especially when invited as a guest, and warmly received. It is one of the rare times and places in our relationship of deaf and hearing people when it is the Deaf who do the inviting and set down the rules.

But there is more. I have always thought that Deaf people's taste for banquets constitutes a sort of turning the tables on us. For hearing people, a meal is always a good time. We enjoy mutually interrupting each other, speaking of everything and nothing in particular, and jumping from one subject to another: precisely the situation where deaf people find themselves most excluded. That they choose to invite **us** to exactly the same setting in which we normally exclude them shows, I think, grand style and only makes the invitation more precious.

In the beginning, a cry of anger

But it is of past banquets that I would like to speak – the very first banquets. I would like to share the wonder I had in discovering them. For the evidence has been preserved – everything that happened is known down to the minutest detail. The pens of scrupulous witnesses have described with great lyricism what took place. We have the texts of all the

---

1   This text is based on a lecture given at the Institut National de Jeunes Sourds de Paris during one of the monthly meetings held in preparation for the opening of the exhibition *Le pouvoir des signes. Sourds et citoyens*, which was organized on the occasion of the 200th anniversary of abbé de L'Epée's death. This lecture is partially published in the catalogue of the exhibition (Mottez 1989). It was the basis for a paper presentented at the festival *The Deaf Way* (Washington 1989).

speeches that were given, most of the toasts that were proposed, and the poems that were recited. We even have the preparatory correspondence for each banquet and the responses of renowned invited guests who wrote to excuse themselves when they could not attend (Société Centrale 1849/1864).

And in fact these early banquets, as we will see, were precisely the opposite of simply convivial insular gatherings. *Au contraire,* the date of the first banquet, November 1834, must be inscribed as one of the milestones of Deaf history. I see it, in fact, as the birthdate of the deaf mute nation.[2] It was the year when Deaf Mutes established a kind of government for themselves, which has lasted to this day.

But first, let's go back even farther in time. The abbé Sicard, abbé de L'Epée's successor, died in 1822. He left the Paris Institute in a sad state. The choice of his successor was difficult. For almost a decade, the Board of Directors insured the day-to-day running of the school. To make matters worse, the Board, obviously incompetent in matters of deaf education, made oralist choices all down the line. These choices questioned the role of sign language in the education of the pupils, and consequently, the role of deaf mute teachers. The oralist offensive takes a serious turn for the worse with the appointment of Désiré Ordinaire as Director (see the article by Alexis Karacostas, this volume, for the history of this offensive and the long battle undertaken by Ferdinand Berthier and his friends to contain it).

In mid-November 1834, Berthier and his cohorts met at his home and decided to found the Comité de Sourds-Muets (Deaf Mute Committee), which was made up of 11 members.

The first decision of this Committee – the idea seems to have come from Forestier – was to celebrate the anniversary of the birthdate of the abbé de L'Epée from then on. Two weeks later, the first of these famous banquets took place.

Who participated?
1 A deaf mute elite

> It was a curious thing to see, this banquet, with which the deaf mutes celebrated the 122nd anniversary of the birth of the abbé de L'Epée. For the first time they honoured the memory of the one who, in their poetic language so full of imagery, so evocative of the metaphoric idioms of the East, they could only call their intellectual father. At 5 o'clock, almost 60 members of this completely singular nation assembled in the salons of the restaurant on the Place Châtelet (in the heart of Paris). There were teachers, painters, engravers, various civil servants, printers, and simple laborers, who, rejected from our society by cruel Nature found the means through their intelligence to rejoin society and to win positions which allow them to live honorably (…). There were wide, high, well-constructed foreheads that would be the envy of the phrenology society; eyes sparkling with vigor; active fingers moving quicker than speech; in short, the privileged representatives of an exceptional species (...) whose existence Swift never suspected but whom his pen would have so well described had he only been aware of them. (Société Centrale 1849, p. 11)

The Deaf Mutes enjoyed boasting of the posts they had succeeded in obtaining, and congratulated each other heartily. Standard procedure, even today, to clearly publicize what

2   Faithful to the vocabulary of the period, I will often use 'deaf mute' and 'speaking person' where today we would say 'deaf' and 'hearing'. In the 19th century, they preferred to designate them by their **acts**, and by what is **visible**. Not speaking or speaking – that can be seen. It is an action. Not hearing or hearing are states, not acts, and you can't see that by looking. In most sign languages of the world, I think, the sign for 'deaf' is literally 'deaf mute' and the sign for 'hearing' is literally 'speaking'. – Deaf mutes of the 19th century often spoke lovingly of their sign language as 'mimicry'. In the banquets, they spoke often of 'deaf mute people', of 'the deaf mute nation'. Today we use the term 'Deaf community' to talk about Deaf people as more than just a collection of individuals. But there is something more in the terms 'people' and 'nation' than in the word 'community'.

Ill. 1: *Abbé de L'Epée on his death-bed, by F. Peyson, 1839.**

*   There were many artists, and especially painters, at the annual banquets. At the one in 1886, for example, which took place a few months after Berthier's death, there were, among the 63 invited Deaf Mutes, 23 painters, sculptors or others with careers having to do with the arts (etchers, lithographers, etc.). [a]
    Among them, Frédéric Peyson (1807-1877) from Montpellier was one of the most gifted painters.[b] After he spent ten years at the Paris School (1817-1827), he entered the Ecole des Beaux-Arts. He was trained in the ateliers of Gros, Hersent, Cogniet (who attended some of the banquets) and Ingres. He was one of the eleven members of the Committee of Deaf Mutes (Comité de Sourds-Muets), from which the initial idea for the banquets came (1834). At his side were two other painters, Gouin from the Paris School and Mosca from Turin.
    At the Salon of 1839 his touching painting *The abbé de L'Epée on his death-bed (Les derniers moments de l'abbé de L'Epée)* won great success, of which all Deaf Mutes were very proud. They designated it beforehand for the walls of the Paris School. Although the state was asked to bid on the painting, no offers were forthcoming. The participants of the banquet of 1842 authored a petition. Peyson finally received some bids, but he saw them as laughable and humiliating. He decided to donate the painting to the school and charged Lenoir with informing 'his brothers' at the banquet of 1844 of his decision. Naturally this announcement was received with great approval.
    The painting was exhibited at the 1880 World's Fair. In 1889 it reigned in a distinguished position in the Musée Universel des Sourds-Muets, until it landed in the attic of the school when the museum closed. After it was restored for the bicentennial celebration (Chapelle de la Sorbonne, December 1989 - January 1990), this painting, laden with history and symbols, was returned to the attic of the Institut de Jeunes Sourds in Paris.

[a]Société Universelle 1887.   [b]cf. Denis 1890.

Deaf Mutes are capable of. Which gives today's reader the right to long lists of their exemplary successes. The banquets obviously brought together an elite – only a part of those lucky enough to have been educated. Estimations of the number of Deaf Mutes in France in the middle of the 19th century vary from 20,000 to 30,000. Eugène de Montglave in 1842 estimated that only 300 had benefited from public education. Five years later, revising his figures, he estimated that there were in fact somewhat less than 1,500, though 6,000 Deaf Mutes were in a position to be able to go to school. Access to public education was in fact one of the major preoccupations of this elite.

2 An international crowd

Second observation: there were always foreign Deaf Mutes in attendance. Right from the first banquet. At the third, there were Deaf Mutes from Italy, England and Germany. They surely did not make the voyage to Paris just for the banquet, or at least certainly not the Americans. John Carlin, who painted several portraits of Laurent Clerc, immediately comes to my mind.[3] It seems to me that many of these foreign visitors, like him, were painters attracted to Paris to learn or to perfect their art, even to stay on as residents. I am sure that decades later, the Deaf American artists H. H. Moore, Douglas Tilden[4], Granville S. Redmond (friend of Charlie Chaplin), E. E. Hannan, or the painter J. A. Terry, father of the Argentinian Deaf movement, all participated in the banquets celebrating the birth of the abbé de L'Epée during their long stays in Paris.

3 Hearing guests

The chronicle of the first banquet reported that:

> *Only two* 'speaking' *people obtained the rare privilege of attending this foreign celebration: E. de Monglave (or, in sign:' moustache') himself, a friend of the deaf mutes, who speaks their language and is acquainted with the* 'customs' *of the deaf mute nation, and the second, a reporter for a major daily newspaper, an* 'incomplete man', *according to these gentlemen, a* 'wretch' *deprived of the language of mimicry, a* 'pariah' *in this society having to resort to a pencil to converse with the evening's heroes. An expression of ineffable pity could be read on their faces at his approach. The hapless one', the celebrants said, 'he won't be able to make himself understood…* '. (Société Centrale 1849, p. 12)

From the second banquet, they realized the benefits of opening the banquets up to selected hearing-speaking guests. They made a habit of inviting numerous journalists from major newspapers of the time: *Le Moniteur, le Journal des Débats, le National, le Temps, le Courrier Français, le Constitutionnel, le Droit, la Quotidienne,…* Applauded and pampered, they generally fulfilled the task expected of them: to let the public know what was going on.

There were other de Monglaves, that is, those to whom toasts in their honour declared that *they have made of themselves deaf mutes in thought and feeling (Ils se sont faits eux-mêmes sourds-muets de pensée et d'attachement).* They often served as interpreters.

Thereafter they invited, and this also became a tradition, civil servants from ministries

---

3 He made a long speech at the sixth banquet (1839), and proposed a toast at the seventh (Société Centrale 1849, pp. 87-90).

4 Douglas Tilden, friend of the deaf mute sculptor P. Choppin, was himself the master of ceremonies for one of the banquets (1891). It was one of the July banquets. These July banquets, initiated by Imbert, started in 1843. After two interruptions of several years, due to internal dissention, they continued until the end of the 19th century. They were in honour of the revolutionary law of July 21, 1791, which made the abbé de L'Epée's school a National Institution, as well as the law of June 28, 1793, never implemented, which *adopted the deaf mutes as children of France* and ordered the creation of six national schools for their education. On these banquets, see Alliance Silencieuse 1900.

that had charge of Deaf affairs, and politicians. Thus by-passing the administration of the Paris Institute, they could confidentially slip in a word or two about the harrassment at the Institute endured by Deaf Mute teachers and sign language.

Désiré Ordinaire, responsible for the tightening of the oralist line, refused to have anything to do with the banquets. With the arrival of the new director, de Lanneau (1838), who ended the oralist offensive, relations were normalized. The director(s), a large part of the staff, and even student delegations, became regular banquet-goers. The educators were there as invited guests, and usually behaved appropriately: as **guests**. Several of them, however, even there, couldn't manage to control their deplorable habit of always wanting to give advice. There were even those few who went so far as to propose a toast to spoken language!

Finally, there were the prestigious guests. At the third banquet, for example, at the opening of the doors, a wrinkled old man could be seen advancing with a somber step. It was Jean-Nicolas Bouilly, the author of *The abbé de L'Epée*, the play which revolved around the abbé's involvement in the famous Solar affair and which had a tremendous success since its creation in 1799.[5] Also applauded was John O'Connel, son of the liberator of Ireland – a clear symbol.

Scholars, theatre people, and artists, especially painters, were invited. Cogniet, in whose atelier several deaf mute painters received their training, was a regular banquet-goer.

They were not always lucky, however, with their guest stars. Since Béranger, the popular poet, could not attend, they requested a few verses about the abbé de L'Epée from him (1836). In his warm response, he revealed that it was at the house of one of his parents in Picardy where the young Solar was first taken, that same Solar whose plight had such an impact on the life of the abbé de L'Epée and for that reason his father must have known the good abbé. As for the verses, he explained that his muse had dried up and he needed more time than they had allowed him (Société Centrale 1849, pp. 39-41).

Lamartine responded (1837): *Delighted, I'm coming (Enchanté, je viens),* but had a conflicting engagement at the last minute (Société Centrale 1849, pp. 49-51).

Chateaubriand did not answer his invitation (1839), so Berthier went to his home to invite him personally, only to find him half-paralyzed, incapable even of writing to respond to Berthier's questions (Société Centrale 1849, pp. 73-76).

From A. de Vigny they managed to get a *verse to Deaf Mutes, composed on the inspiration born of the exercises at the Royal Institute (une strophe aux Sourds-Muets, composée d'inspiration à l'issue des exercices de l'Institution royale* (1840); Société Centrale 1849, pp. 93-94).

And finally (1843), Victor Hugo! Alas! He had tragically just lost his daughter and could not attend. But in expressing his regrets to Berthier, he composed these words that have been handed down to generations of Deaf Mutes: *What matters deafness of the ear, when the mind hears? The only deafness, the real deafness, the incurable deafness, is that of the intellect* (Société Centrale 1849, p. 148). Three years later, the invitation was renewed. In a rather brusque letter, Hugo answered, in essence: *Never on Sunday! (Jamais le dimanche!;* Société Centrale 1849, p. 213-214). Undiscouraged, the Deaf Mutes bided their time. And in 1850, it is Pélissier, the refined poet *of the graceful gesture (au geste souple)* who took the matter in hand. Several months before the banquet, he went to Hugo's home to persuade him. He translated one of his ballads into signs for Hugo, in order that he *experience all the luxuriousness of this picturesque language which Nature, in her compassion, has bestowed upon the poor deaf mutes* (Société Centrale 1864, pp. 22-23). The day before the banquet, Pélissier returned to remind him of the happy moment. No luck: Hugo was confined to his bed; his doctor had forbidden that he leave the house. He did, however, have

---

5 Bouilly's play, *L'abbé de L'Epée,* was translated into English (by Bouilly himself), into Dutch, German, Italian, and Spanish, and was performed in all the large theaters in Europe. This play was the stimulus for Per Aron Borg to found the first school for deaf mutes in Sweden in 1809 (Bergquist 1914). For the history of the Count de Solar and for the one of Bouilly's play, see Bernard 1941, pp. 161-177; Bézagu-Deluy 1990, pp. 189-201; Lane 1984, pp. 42-66.

some more well-turned phrases about Deaf Mutes: not wishing to treat them as the *disin-herited* (*déshérités*), he wrote, *because Nature, in depriving you of one organ, has almost always doubled your intelligence. You, Monsieur, are a noble and dazzling proof of that and you have the rare talent of being at the same time mute and eloquent!* (Société Centrale 1864, p. 30). So that was the end of that…, what a pity!

As for Eugène Süe, the popular author of *Mystères de Paris*, Berthier invited him to the 18th banquet (1845), begging him not to refuse *the opportunity to initiate himself into the mystery of the existence of deaf mutes, so little recognized or appreciate.* (Société Centrale 1849, p. 196). E. Süe did not respond. Two years later, Berthier renewed the invitation, asking him to *take on the task of revealing to the public the mysteries of a nation as strange as that of the deaf mutes* (Société Centrale 1849, p. 242). E. Süe kept silent and remained unattainable.

4 No women

But there was something really important missing at these banquets, I would say: women. True, once or twice a sensitive soul would raise a toast *to our deaf mute women! (aux sourdes-muettes, à nos femmes!)* and remind the celebrants that it was in fact through women that it all started, that they owed much to them: an allusion to the two young deaf sisters through whom the abbé de L'Epée discovered his vocation in life. But no one thought of including them in the festivities. It wasn't until 1883 that deaf women attended a banquet![6] It was quite an event.

Were these Deaf Mutes sexists? Yes, pretty sexists, I would say. But no more so than speaking people at **their** banquets, which were also for a long time men's affairs. A woman's place was in the home.

What transpired at these banquets?
1 A festival of sign language

Did the powers that be intend to attack their precious language? Well, they would see about that! They gave their speaking audience quite a show of it. It was said that the banquets were the olympics of the Deaf Mute people, *olympics four times more frequent than those of Greece, and a hundred times more exotic and appealing* (Société Centrale 1849, p. 8).

> *It seems that 60 men deprived of hearing and speech should have constituted a painful and grievous sight; but no, not in the least. The human spirit so animates their faces, most of which are truly beautiful, it so shines forth from their lively eyes, it blazes its way so rapidly to the tips of their fingers, that instead of pitying them, one is tempted to envy them. When, in the courtroom, in the pulpit, in the theatre, and in society, we so often hear words without thoughts, it is rather agreeable to see, at least once a year, thoughts without words.*
>
> *It is no exaggeration to say that none of the orators we most admire could even remotely compete with Berthier, Forestier, or Lenoir for the grace, the dignity, and the correctness of their gestures. In truth, seeing the speeches that these three young men deliver is enough, I think, to make us wish we could unlearn speech.* (Société Centrale 1849, p. 34)

And it was not only just beautiful rhetoric. Many of them courted the poetic Muse, not the least of whom was Berthier. But the enchanter, the Pindar, the delight of the banquets was Pélissier himself.

Deaf mute foreigners, in their toasts, never missed a chance to emphasize the universal nature of signs, claiming that

---

6   This was at one of the July banquets which were resumed in 1883, after an interruption of 15 years: *The female sex, whom superstition had excluded for half a century, was represented there for the first time by 28 deaf mute ladies* (Alliance Silencieuse 1900, p.6).

Ill. 2: *The annual banquett of the Deaf on november 28, 1886: a toast to the abbé de L'Epée on the occasion of his 174th birthday*

it easily wins out over all the separate limiting languages of speaking humanity, packed into a more or less limited territory. Our language encompasses all nations, the entire globe. (Société Centrale 1849, pp. 27-28)

2 A place of veneration for the abbé de L'Epée

The bust of the abbé de L'Epée, surrounded by tricolor flags, sometimes crowned with flowers, sat enthroned like an altar at the center of the u-shaped table. Obviously, most of the toasts were raised in his honour. The Deaf Mutes called him *our spiritual father, our intellectual father, our messiah, our saviour, our redeemer (notre père spirituel, notre père intellectuel, notre messie, notre sauveur, notre rédempteur)*. By 'spiritual father', they did not mean the good old dad, the family father who protects, nourishes, rewards, and punishes. It meant the 'begetter' *(géniteur)*, the original parent: 'He who led us from night to light once and for all. Now it is up to us!' The invariable theme of these toasts is: 'before him, we were nothing, we were pariahs, plunged into chaos and ingorance, marginals, and ignored, now we exist, we have been restored to society'.

It did not take long before 1834 also became a key date separating that 'before' (when we didn't exist) and and 'after'. Already at the 5th banquet (1838), Forestier, responding to the speech delivered by Master of Ceremonies Berthier, declared:

*Remember what we were only four years ago, look at what we are today (...). We were isolated in the midst of society; today we are reunited. Without support, without common bonds, each deaf mute lived for and by himself, as best he could: what a sad life, exiled in the midst of society (...). Today we have united our intellects, our efforts, our lights; today we constitute one body; all of us, active and devoted members, desire the well-being of that body; today, we who were not, **are**!* (Forestier in Société Centrale 1849, p. 65)

Thus the Deaf Mute nation was not born directly with the abbé de L'Epée, or shortly thereafter. It was born when his legacy was threatened and when Deaf Mutes themselves had to defend it.

A 'messiah', a 'before', an 'after': it is tempting to think in purely religious terms. But, in fact, it represents one of the central themes of the French Revolution; that of *regeneration* (see *Régénération* in Furet/Ozouf 1989, pp. 821-830). The theme recurs often in their toasts. It is a key to the Deaf politics of the 19th century.

3 A political forum

Banquet records of course describe the activites of the Comité de Sourds-Muets which, expanding its functions, is successively renamed the Société Centrale (1838), the Société Universelle des Sourds-Muets (1867), and then more modestly, the Société amicale des Sourds-Muets de Paris (1887) after the death of Berthier. The minutes of the banquets reveal the dreams, the plans, the struggles, the accomplishments, and the setbacks of the Deaf people beginning to reach their full potential. They also reveal the internal dissention, so very like that of today. Rival associations competed to organize the banquets, then reconciled, then again vied with one another. The tradition of the banquets spread to the provinces, then abroad.

4 Finally: A time to eat and drink. A fact that should not be forgotten

Eugène Briffault, thanks to whom we know everything about how they ate and drank in Paris in the early 19th century, devotes a few ironic pages to banquets (Briffault 1846, pp. 73-75). Banqueting reached a fever pitch. The listing of all the variations gives us an idea. First comes the patriotic banquet, then the military banquet, the philosophical banquets, the political banquets, the philanthrophic banquet (*where one eats for the poor who are starving of hunger– où l'on mange pour les pauvres qui meurent de faim),* the guild banquets, etc... *The arts have their banquets,* he wrote, *the industries have their banquets, the memorial banquets, schools and junior highs...* And he concludes with the masonic banquets *which frighten little children (qui font peur aux petits enfants).*

The food was generally very mediocre. Just reading Briffault's account of the cold dishes they served is enough to spoil our appetite. But it gets worse: he assures us that no one enjoyed it:

> *It is a chore that one submits to. The toasts that are proposed very seriously, the long speeches, and sometimes the singing of songs, complete the picture, and each banqueter has to bear his share.*

Only one kind of banquet found favour in his view: *the one which reunites childhood friends. There, sometimes the food is even bearable.*

The deaf mute banquets by definition were included in this latter category. All the evidence indicates that in taking advantage of this general mania for banquets, the Deaf Mutes raised the art to its highest level. Gastronomically, too? At the 4th banquet in 1837, they left the restaurant on the Place Châtelet for one in the Faubourg Saint-Germain. The chronicler takes pains to add that

> *for many, gastronomy counted for a lot in this solemn decision. The rich deaf mutes bow to the law of the poor. In an epoch like this one, many of them complained of a thousand trifles impossible to enumerate. The menu, awaited for 365 days, was not worthy of such long-held hopes; appetites were not satisfied; shouldn't the complaints of laborers who spend such sums once a year be sacred for the organizers of the celebration?* (Société Centrale 1849, p 45)

Ill. 3: *Menu of the banquet of 1895*

From that time on, were the meals up to the standards expected? Well, there were other changes of restaurants during the course of the century. In 1845 the banquet took place at the *Cadran Bleu,* a restaurant famous in the annals of gastronomy. In the hopes of finding the answer to this burning question through further research, we can hypothesize that at least in 1845, the meal was worthy of the occasion.

(Translated by Bill Moody)

Appendix
The original French quotations:

p. 144

Il a été fait dans une solennité récente des allusions peu bienveillantes à notre fraternelle association. Rien ne serait, a-t-on dit, plus funeste au sourd-muet que de se renfermer dans le commerce des autres sourds-muets. Former des sourds-muets une nation à part, une caste exceptionelle, ce serait les condamner à une déplorable exclusion. Non, frères, il n'en saurait être ainsi. Ils ont méconnu nos coeurs, et nos intentions, ceux qui ont tenu ce langage. Jamais l'idée d'un egoïsme étroit, d'une séquestration volontaire n'a germé dans nos esprits. On a voulu nous repousser du banquet des parlants; on a voulu proscrire de la nation des sourds-muets le langage des sourds-muets, ce langage sublime, universel, que leur a donné la nature. Et les sourds-muets ont dit à leurs frères parlants: Venez au milieu de nous! Mêlez-vous à nos travaux, à nos jeux; apprenez notre langue comme nous apprenons la vôtre; ne formons qu'un seul peuple uni par des liens indissolubles; qu'il y ait entre nous alliance perpétuelle, fusion complète à la vie, à la mort. Frères, est-ce là de l'egoïsme? Est-ce là de l'isolement? Accusateurs sans conscience, osez encore élever la voix contre nous! (Ferdinand Berthier, 7th banquet, 1840; in Société Centrale 1849, p.96)

p. 145

C'était chose curieuse à voir que ce banquet, par lequel les sourds-muets, anciens élèves de l'école de Paris, célébraient le cent vingt deuxième anniversaire de la naissance de l'abbé de L'Epée. Pour la première fois ils fêtaient le souvenir de celui que, dans leur langue si poétique, si pleine d'images, et qui semble un écho lointain des idiomes métaphoriques de l'Orient, ils n'appelèrent jamais que leur père intellectuel. A cinq heures, près de soixante membres de cette nation tout à part, étaient réunis dans les salons du restaurant de la place du Châtelet. Il y avait là des professeurs, des peintres, des graveurs, des employés de différentes administrations, des imprimeurs, de simples ouvriers, qui, rejetés par la nature marâtre du sein de notre société, ont trouvé les moyens, par leur intelligence, d'y rentrer et d'y conquérir des positions qui les font vivre honorablement (…). Il y avait des cerveaux larges, hauts et bien construits, que la société de phrénologie eût admirés; des yeux qui pétillaient de verve, des doigts actifs, rapides, qui devancent la parole, des représentants privilégiés enfin de toute une espèce exceptionelle (…) que Swift ne soupçonna pas et que sa plume aurait si bien décrite s'il l'avait connue. (Société Centrale 1849, p. 11)

p. 147

Seuls deux *'parlants'* avaient obtenu le rare privilège d'assister à cette fête étrangère: E. de Monglave [son signe était 'moustache'], ami des sourds-muets, parlant leur langue, initié aux *'us'* et *'coutumes'* de la nation et le journaliste d'un grand quotidien, *'homme incomplet'* au dire de ces messieurs, *'infortuné'* privé de la parole mimique, *'paria'* de cette société, obligé de recourir au crayon pour entrer en conversation avec les héros de la fête. Une expression d'ineffable pitié se lisait dans tous les traits à son approche. 'Le malheureux', disaient les heureux du moment, 'il ne pourra pas se faire comprendre'. (Société Centrale 1849, p. 12)

p. 148

Qu'importe la surdité de l'oreille, quand l'esprit entend? La seule surdité, la vraie surdité, la surdité incurable, c'est celle de l'intelligence. (Société Centrale 1849, p. 148)

(…) assiste à tout le luxe du langage pittoresque que, dans sa compassion, la nature a donné aux pauvres sourds-muets. (Société Centrale 1864, pp. 22-23)

p. 149

(…) car la nature, en vous retranchant l'organe, vous a presque toujours doublé l'intelligence. Vous en êtes, Monsieur, une noble éclatante preuve, et vous avez le rare talent d'être à la fois muet et éloquent. (Société Centrale 1864, p. 30)

(…) l'occasion qui se présentait à lui de s'initier au mystère de l'existence des sourds-muets, si peu connue encore et si mal appréciée. (Société Centrale 1849 , p. 196)

(…) prendre à tâche de dévoiler lui-même au public les mystères d'une nation aussi curieuse que les sourds-muets. (Société Centrale 1849, p. 242)

(…) des olympiades quatre fois plus fréquentes que celles de la Grèce, et cent fois plus curieuses, plus attachantes. (Société Centrale 1849, p. 8)

Il semblerait, que soixante hommes privés de l'ouïe et de la parole dussent former un ensemble pénible et affligeant; il n'en est rien. L'âme humaine anime tellement leurs fronts, pour la plupart fort beaux; elle se peint si vivement dans leurs yeux; elle se fraie un chemin si rapide jusqu'au bout de leurs doigts, qu'au lieu de les plaindre on serait tenté de leur porter envie. Quand au barreau, à la chaire, au théâtre, dans le monde, on entend si souvent des mots sans pensées, on n'est pas fâché de voir une fois l'an au moins, des pensées sans mots.
Ce n'est pas exagéré de dire qu'aucun des orateurs que nous admirons le plus ne pourrait lutter, même de loin, avec Berthier, Forestier ou Lenoir, pour la grâce, la dignité et la propriété du geste. En vérité, quand on voit des discours comme ceux que ces trois jeunes hommes ont prononcés, on voudrait, je crois, désapprendre la parole. (Société Centrale 1849, p. 34)

p. 149 (footnote 6)

Le sexe féminin que la superstition avait tenu à l'écart pendant un demi-siècle, a était représenté, pour la première fois, par vingt-huit dames sourdes-muettes. (Alliance Silencieuse 1900, p.6)

p. 151

(…) qu'elle [la mimique] l'emporte sur toutes les langues partielles de l'humanité parlante, parquées dans un plus ou moins grand espace. Notre langue embrasse toutes les nations, le globe entier. (Société Centrale 1849, pp. 27-28)

Souvenez-vous de ce que nous étions il y a quatre ans à peine; voyez ce que nous sommes aujourd'hui. Nous étions isolés au milieu du monde; aujourd'hui nous sommes réunis. Sans appui, sans lien commun, chacun des sourds-muets vivait pour soi et par soi-même, comme il pouvait: triste vie qui était comme une sorte d'exil au sein de la société (…). Aujourd'hui nous avons réuni nos intelligences, nos efforts, nos lumières; aujourd'hui nous formons, à nous tous, un corps, dont tous, membres actifs et dévoués, nous voulons le bien-être; aujourd'hui, nous qui n'étions pas, nous sommes! (Forestier in Société Centrale 1849, p. 65)

p. 152

Les arts ont leurs banquets, l'industrie a ses banquets, les souvenirs, les collèges et les écoles ont leurs banquets (…). (Briffault 1846)

C'est une corvée qu'on subit. Les toasts qu'on propose très sérieusement, les longs discours, et quelquefois, les chansons, achèvent l'oeuvre dont chaque convive porte le poids. (Briffault 1846)

(…) celui qui réunit les vieilles amitiés de l'enfance. Là, il arrive même que la nourriture soit supportable. (Briffault 1846)

La gastronomie entrait pour beaucoup dans cette décision solennelle. Les sourds-muets riches subissaient cette fois la loi des pauvres. A pareille époque, on avait vu ceux-ci se plaindre de mille riens impossibles à énumérer. Le menu, attendu 365 jours, n'était pas digne d'une si longue espérance; les appétits se retiraient mécontents; ces plaintes d'ouvriers qui se mettent en frais une fois l'an ne devaient-elles pas être sacrées pour les ordonnateurs de la fête? (Société Centrale 1849, p. 45)

Iconography

Ill. 1: The abbé de L'Epée on his death-bed, by Frédéric Peyson, 1839.
Institut National de Jeunes Sourds, Paris.
Photo: J.L. Charmet

Ill. 2: The annual banquet of the Deaf on november 28, 1886. A toast to the abbé de L'Epée on the occasion of his 174th birthday. Attributed to Auguste Colas, n.d.
reproduction in: *La Voix du Sourd* 165, mars 1989, p. 11.

Ill 3: Menu of the banquet of 1895
Institut National de Jeunes Sourds, Paris.
Photo: P.A. Mangolte

References

Alliance Silencieuse (1900): *Aperçu historique des banquets annuels de juillet*. Tours: Juliot.

Bergquist, J. (1914): *Schweden. Die Taubstummen-Institutionen des dritten Distriktes zu Lund*. Lund: C. Bloms Boktryckeri.

Bernard, René (1941): *Surdité, surdi-mutité et mutisme dans le théâtre français*. Paris: Rodstein.

Bézagu-Deluy, Maryse (1990): *L'abbé de L'Epée, instituteur gratuit des sourds et muets*. Paris: Seghers.

Bouilly, Jean-Nicolas (1800): *L'abbé de L'Epée. Comédie historique en cinq actes et en prose*. Paris: André.

Briffault, Eugène (1846): *Paris à table*. Paris: J. Hertzel. Reprint: 1980. Geneva, Paris: Slatkine.

Denis, T. (1890): Frédéric Peyson, peintre Sourd-muet, in: *Revue française de l'éducation des sourds-muets* 5/12 (mars 1890), pp. 261-269 and 6/1 (mai 1890), pp. 29-36.

Furet, François/Ozouf, Mona (1989): *Dictionnaire critique de la Révolution Française*. Paris.

Lane, Harlan (1984): *When the Mind Hears. A History of the Deaf*. New York: Random House.

Mottez, B. (1989): Les banquets de Sourds-Muets et la naissance du mouvement sourd; in: Couturier, L./ Karacostas, A. (eds.) (1989): *Le pouvoir des signes. Sourds et citoyens*. Catalogue de l'exposition, 13 déc. 1989 - 22 janv. 1990. Paris: Institut National de Jeunes Sourds, pp. 170-177.

Société Centrale des Sourds-Muets de Paris (1849/1864): *Banquets des Sourds-Muets réunis pour fêter les Anniversaires de la Naissance de l'Abbé de L'Epée*. Vol. 1 (1849), vol. 2 (1864). Paris: Jacques Ledoyen.

Société Universelle des Sourds-Muets (1887): *Compte-rendu du banquet du 28 novembre 1886, à l'occasion du 174ème anniversaire de la naissance de l'abbé de L' Epée*. Paris: G. Carré.

Horst Biesold
Bremen, Germany

The Fate of the Israelite Asylum for the Deaf and Dumb in Berlin

Summary • Zusammenfassung

In its first part, this article illustrates the development of the Israelite Asylum for the Deaf and Dumb (I.T.A.) in Berlin, from its foundation (1873, 1890) until the time of Hitler's rise to power. The 2nd part deals with the fate of pupils of the I.T.A. and other Jewish Deaf people under the Nazi regime.

Dieser Beitrag stellt in seinem ersten Teil die Entwicklung der Israelitischen Taubstummenanstalt (I.T.A.) in Berlin dar, von ihrer Gründung (1873 bzw. 1890) bis zur Zeit der Machtergreifung durch Hitler. Der zweite Teil geht auf das Schicksal von Schülern und Schülerinnen der I.T.A. und anderer jüdischer Gehörloser unter der Naziherrschaft ein.

146 DEAF AND DUMB JEWISH COMPATRIOTS
WERE ABDUCTED
FROM THIS HOUSE IN 1942
BY FASCIST BANDITS AND MURDERED

IN MEMORIAM OF THE DEAD
AND A WARNING TO THE LIVING

The above memorial plaque hangs on the school building, still standing, of the Israelitische Taubstummenanstalt (Israelite Asylum for the Deaf and Dumb, I. T. A.) in Berlin-Weissensee. Until recently, the former school building housed a Socialist Party headquarters of the former German Democratic Republic.

Besides the memorial plaque, there is no other reminder of this once flourishing educational, cultural and religious center for the 1000 or so Jewish Deaf in Germany in the late 19th and early 20th centuries.[1] Many significant anniversaries associated with the institution and its general sphere of influence have silently elapsed without any note being taken of them by the German Association for the Deaf, or by the field of education for the Deaf in the two former German states (FRG and GDR) in general. The 22 still surviving Jewish ex-students of the deaf school, who now live in Israel, the USA, or here in Germany, preserve the memory of the place; but they have little reason to celebrate any anniversaries. Others, however, were surely obliged to honor and commemorate this model institution and those people who accomplished so much for the Deaf, and to remember those who lived happily and joy-fully and who obtained knowledge and education there, thereby providing an example for future generations.

In the following essay we shall provide a brief historical outline of the development and influence of the Israelite Asylum for the Deaf and Dumb, asking some survivors about their fate and presenting some preliminary results of our research.

I

In the year 1857, a very gifted hearing 13-year-old Jewish boy left his home in Kolin, Bohe-mia, to go and teach children of his own age on a landed estate. Within seven years he had risen to the level of 'private tutor'. During this time, the boy in question, Markus Reich, got to know a Deaf Mute who did not fit in any way into the stereotypical picture of a Deaf Mute: this man was well educated, cultivated, well brought up, and he could speak. This meeting was to determine the further course of Reich's life. He wanted to take *deaf mutes and turn them into fully-fledged happy people!* (F. Reich 1923, p. 6). At the age of 21 (1865), he *moved to Germany, the land of science and order, the land he longed for, where he hoped to be able to learn all he needed to know to become a teacher of the Deaf and Dumb* (ibid.).

Reich studied at the Jewish Teacher Training College in Berlin. The director of the col-lege, Horwitz, recognized Reich's special gift for teaching, supported and encouraged him, and exempted him from one year of training. By working as a private tutor Reich was able to survive hunger and social hardship. From the little that he earned he was able to save enough to buy books about the Deaf and Dumb. In 1870 and 1871 he worked and studied at the Royal Asylum for the Deaf and Dumb in Berlin, where he passed the examination for teachers of the Deaf and Dumb. Later, while working at the Royal Asylum as an assistant

---

1 We have calculated this approximate figure in the following way: Deaf and dumb people in the German Reich professing to the Jewish religion (not including the states of Baden, Württemberg and the Saar) = 531 + 58 (10,91% for Baden and Württemberg) = 589 + 6 (1,10% for the Saar) = 595. A further 88 deaf schoolchildren declared their religion to be Jewish = 683. According to our esti-mates, the remaining 317 may have been made up of people very hard of hearing, people who became deaf later in life, and people with multiple handicaps.

teacher, he noticed that *children, especially Jewish children, were often turned away* (F. Reich 1923, p. 7).

Markus Reich was deeply moved by these experiences and resolved to establish a Jewish institute for the Deaf and Dumb. He was inspired by two religious motives in particular: first, by a special appeal for the support of the Deaf and Dumb in the Jewish community made by the Head Rabbi in London, Adler, in 1864 (5625 in the Jewish calendar). This appeal appeared in Adler's writing *The Morning and the Evening Sacrifice* and was supported by, among other things, a quote from Isaiah, Chapter 29, Verse 18:

> *Is it not a duty laid on us all, to take these children to us and protect them in the name of the Lord, and to teach them in such a way that, as the Prophet tells us, 'in that day the deaf shall hear the words of the book'?* (Adler 1864, pp. 13-14)

Reich's second inspiration was a passage in the Talmud: *Only the ignorant is truly poor* (Nedarin 41a).

Reich put his plans into effect and founded the Israelitische Taubstummenanstalt in 1873, in a small residential house in Fürstenwalde on the river Spree. He could now

> *give the Jewish Deaf Mutes not only normal school lessons and speech training, but also (…) (teach them) the religion of their parents (…) and plant it in their hearts.* (F. Reich 1929, p. 450)

The first years were hard and full of privations. The unknown Jewish teacher of the Deaf and Mute was poor and so were most of the 12 children in his care. In 1879 he got married and his wife Emma and his sister Anna helped untiringly with the care and teaching of the deaf children.

When the material hardship was at its most acute, Markus Reich decided to found an association for the support and relief of his 'asylum'. In 1890, with the help of the association,

Ill. 1: *In the gymnasium of the Israelite Asylum for the Deaf and Dumb, after a sports demonstration at the 25th anniversary celebration, 1933*

the Friends of the Deaf and Dumb – Jedide Ilmim, which many wealthy Jewish fellow-believers joined, Reich succeeded in moving his Institute to Weissensee, near Berlin.

From this point onwards, Markus Reich was able *to dedicate himself solely to the task of the education and upbringing of his deaf and dumb children* (F. Reich 1930, p. 43). Reich continually expanded his asylum. By 1911 there were six teachers employed there, four men and two women, teaching a total of 45 children. In the same year, alterations to the building in Weissensee were carried out, financed and supported by the Friends of the Deaf and Dumb, which by now had *thousands of members (…) and everywhere in our Father-land there was an official representative* (E. Reich 1934). But the man whose life's work the Institute was, who offered up 38 years of his life and energies, was not able to witness its end. Markus Reich died on May 23rd, 1911.

This was the death of one of the great men in the history of the Deaf in Germany, the *Pestalozzi of the Jewish deaf and dumb* (E. Reich 1934). His humanity and his educational stature is demonstrated by a quote from a contemporary of Reich's, M. Meyer, a teacher of the Deaf.

> *(…) I very often had the opportunity to listen to his masterly teaching, and in every lesson I was always amazed by the way that he was able to penetrate into the very hearts of the children. He knew exactly how to interest them, to 'grab' them, to direct them and to lead them to the objectives of the lesson without any wasting of effort (…) Markus Reich had a father's heart in his breast, he loved his deaf-and-dumb children as only a father can, and it was for this reason that he, in return, received true and genuine children's love from all his school-children. They knew themselves to be well-sheltered in his care (…).*
>
> *Reich had penetrated fully into the world and the nature of the deaf-and-dumb. He spoke the language of the deaf-and-dumb, sign language, as a hearing person only rarely can. It was even said of him that one had to be too careful not to say anything out of reach of his hearing that was not intended for his ears, because he could also lip-read! Reich could use and understand sign language and never in his life did he refrain from applying it whenever he saw fit, including during his lessons for the deaf-and-dumb (…).*
>
> *To us teachers, Markus Reich was a genuine friend and a reliable advisor. Bureaucratic pettiness was foreign to him. Once he was convinced that we took our duties seriously, he allowed us apparently free hand to teach in our own way. In the breaks, in friendly conversations, when one's heart would open and warm to him, he would pass on his pieces of advice, almost by-the-way, and would let us know how he wanted it done (…).*
>
> *The Institute was like a family, and the teachers, too, were part of that family (…).*
>
> *Markus Reich set a prime example in the way he worked for the sake of his dear deaf-and-dumb children, from the early morning till late in the night. Like a worried father, he would do another round of the dormitories late in the night, with a little night-lamp in his hand, and listen to the peaceful, deep breathing of his sleeping children. The picture of this kindly man remains fixed for all time in the hearts of his school children and his colleagues.*
>
> (Meyer cited in F. Reich 1923, p. 9sq.)

All the people involved at the I.T.A., and especially the Friends of the Deaf and Dumb, felt obliged to maintain and continue the school in the spirit of its founder. His wife Emma became the new Director of Education and took charge of the Finance Committee.

The First World War and the inflationary times that followed confronted the I.T.A. with virtually insurmountable problems. During the war, three teachers were conscripted into the military. The school continued to operate, although the number of school children dropped to 34 (cf. statistical material below).[2]

---

2 The Deputy Director at that time, Richard Höxter, *received, in December 1931, the call (…) to set up a school for the deaf-and-dumb in Jerusalem. Teaching will be given through the medium of the Hebrew language* (*Jüdische Rundschau* 26.02.1932). E. Reich confirmed this message:

Ill. 2: *Guests at the 25th anniversary celebration of the Asscociation of former pupils of the Israelite Asylum for the Deaf and Dumb, 1933*

After the end of the war, in 1919, Dr. Felix Reich, the founder's son, took over the directorship of the I.T.A. and continued its work fully in the spirit of the unforgettable man who had started it.

Having overcome the difficulties caused principally by inflation, the I.T.A. then developed in a very positive fashion. Four factors were particularly important in this development:

1. the untiring energy of the new Director, Dr. F. Reich, who knew very well how to represent the educational successes to the 'outside world', e.g. as Secretary of the Bund Deutscher Taubstummenlehrer (Association of German Teachers of Deaf Mutes, B.D.T.) and as the author of numerous publications;
2. the exemplary commitment of the Friends of the Deaf and Dumb – Jedide Ilmim;
3. the work of the Alumni Association, founded in 1908, which had a unifying effect on all concerned, and which found its visible expression in the alumni magazine, *Das Band* (The Bond), the first issue of which appeared in 1926 (E. Reich 1934);
4. the support offered by alumni by means of the Association for the Promotion of the Interests of the Israelite Deaf Mutes, to which was linked a special fund and foundation (the Bloch and Meseritz Foundation), created at F. Reich's initiative.

In the following tables, we present some data from the school's statistics, from which various positive developments can be read – restrictions have already been mentioned. The first table gives the number of students:

1873	4 children	foundation year
1889	12 children	last year of teaching in Fürstenwalde
1890	22 children	first year of teaching in Weissensee

In 1932 the founder's son-in-law was given the task of setting up an Institution for the Deaf and Dumb in Jerusalem, which he now leads (E. Reich 1934).

1911	48 children	renovation in Weissensee, death of Markus Reich
1916	34 children	wartime
1919	43 children	(28 boys and 15 girls)
1920	48 children	(31 boys and 17 girls)
1921 (no new admissions)	48 children	(31 boys and 17 girls)
1922–25	53 children	(33 boys and 20 girls)
1926 (no new admissions)	48 children	(26 boys and 22 girls)
1927	55 children	(32 boys and 23 girls)
1930	58 children	(35 boys and 23 girls)
1931/32	59 children	(36 boys and 23 girls)

The high level of education at the I.T.A. is not only evident from the various trades learned by the pupils (see below), but is also demonstrated by the fact that the Prussian state opened the first Secondary Modern School for Deaf Mutes in Germany on the basis of the ideas and arguments of the son and successor of Markus Reich (E. Reich 1934).

The I.T.A. also enjoyed a positive response from abroad, thanks to the involvement and commitment of the educational staff and the school's subsequent success. The result was an increase in the numbers of school children from foreign countries. In 1927, out of a total of 55 children attending the I.T.A., 19 were Jewish deaf children from abroad. The following table shows in detail the geographical origins of the children:

Berlin	11	Württemberg	1
East Prussia	2	The Saar	1
Pomerania	1	Lithuania	4
Thuringia	2	Poland	8
Westfalia	4	Czechoslovakia	2
Frankfurt/Main	8	Yugoslavia	1
Hesse-Nassau	2	Belgium	1
The Rhineland	2	Mexico	1
Bavaria	2	Palestine	2

The success of the teachers at this school did not remain a secret to experts in the field either. On the occasion of the 50th anniversary of the founding of the I.T.A., in October 1923, numerous addresses declared *honourable recognition of the Institution for the devoted labor given over many, many years, and the successes achieved through this labor* (Oberschulrat [chief inspector of schools] Fischer from the Provincial Schools Committee). The representative of the province of Brandenburg, Pastor Troschke, emphasized in particular the religious and spiritual considerations in the education of deaf mute children which were *rightly fostered here with such devotion*. He pointed out further that *the success of the efforts to enable the deaf-and-dumb to obtain higher school education* was awaited with great expectancy in the provincial administration (*40th-44th Annual Reports* 1927). Another authority on the education of the Deaf Mutes, the Director of the Municipal Institute for the Deaf and Dumb in Albrechtstraße, Berlin, Schorsch, attended the school's 50th anniversary celebrations in his capacity as representative of the Berlin municipal authorities and as Chairman of the B.D.T. For Schorsch,

> *these 50 years of work at the Institute for the Deaf and Dumb in Weissensee signified a tremendous current of blessings which has been released flowing to those whose ears are dead and whose mouths are mute.*

He emphasized especially the successful work of Markus Reich and his son, who *were, and still are, striving with zeal, seriousness and skill to give the mute the gift of language* (ibid.).

The efforts on the part of the educational directors and the teaching staff at the I.T.A. to *train the minds and the hands of the children in such a way that they are able to survive in life, but also, over and above this, to give the children religious feeling and spiritual values so that they may become happy persons* (ibid.) is expressed in the various kinds of occupation which past pupils entered. By October 1927, 227 pupils had attended the I.T.A. The following table shows the trades taken up by graduates of the school.

	no.	%
Tailors, cutters	24	10.57
Typesetters	14	6.17
Woodcutters, carpenters, turners	14	6.17
Mechanics, electricians, clockmakers	10	4.41
Bookbinders	10	4.41
Dental technicians	8	3.53
Shoemakers	4	1.76
Saddlers and leather-workers	4	1.76
Furriers	4	1.76
Lettering painters	4	1.76
Brushmakers	4	1.76
Gardeners, lithographers, hatters, locksmiths, tobacconists (2 each)	10	4.41
Smith, hairdresser, coachman, worker, businessman, physics student (1 each)	6	2.64
Dressmakers	31	13.66
Housekeepers	26	11.45
Milliners	5	2.20
Flower maker, gold embroiderer, embroiderer, typist (1 each)	4	1.76
No trade learnt due to mental handicap	13	5.73
No trade learnt due to eye disease	6	2.64
Changed to other schools, or left I.T.A.	26	11.45
TOTALS	227	100 %

It should also be pointed out that during the entire existence of the I.T.A. Christian children also attended the school in the Institution. This is borne out by a letter, dated December 11, 1899 and signed by Markus Reich. In this letter, Reich informed the District Council of the province of Brandenburg, amongst other things, that 4 pupils

> *are at the Institution, two of Catholic and two of Protestant faith. (…) As soon as the Protestant children have reached a suitable level of linguistic development, Pastor Dr. Krätschel gives them their Religion lessons.*

By way of summary, we should present at this point the goals of Jewish education for the Deaf in Germany with the words of its last great educator, F. Reich – and this passage also shows particularly clearly what education for the Deaf in Germany has missed.

> *In terms of methods, the teaching was hardly different from that at other institutions, at most in that a position of exaggerated rejection of sign language was never taken, and that the ultimate aim was the education of heart and mind, and not only language training.*
> *We always tried to support and encourage the children, according to their abilities, to reach an above average level in particular subjects. Children who were especially gifted received extra lessons (e.g. in arithmetic, mathematics, literature, foreign languages, drawing, writing). On the other hand, too, children who were poor in certain subjects also received special tuition. The recognition that so far nothing had been done in Germany for the gifted made the author of these lines plead for the cause of a school with more ambitions teaching aims for the deaf and dumb.*
> (F. Reich 1930, p. 43)

II

In the 1930s, the Jewish Deaf in Germany were the first group to see themselves at the mercy of a machinery of power created especially for their extermination. But at first it was not the figures in brown uniforms, known to them from daily encounters, who caused them torment and anguish – chicanery, denunciations, revilement and persecution came first from fellow sufferers, from deaf Nazis. The Nazi leaders of organizations for the Deaf began shortly after the Nazi seizure of power to force out, with brutal violence, deaf Jews of the associations. As is shown by the following report in the August 15, 1933 issue of the *Jüdische Rundschau*, they obviously did not shrink from depriving of their rights members who had done great service over the years :

> *We have received the following information: The Reichsfachschaftsleiter for the German Deaf* (Albreghs and Ballier) *have ordered that all Jewish members are to be expelled from the associations of the Deaf. Some of those affected are members who have belonged to their associations for decades, who have held leading positions in the respective managing committees and who have done great service for their associations. In Berlin, for example, 33 Jewish deaf have been expelled from the Support Association, among them a number of meritorious members of the managing committee. A large number of those expelled, who had been members for over 20 years (one deaf woman has been a member since 1876 – for 57 years), are hit particularly badly by this step, because they thereby lose their right, on the basis of their membership contributions and their advanced years, to monthly support payments.*

The pressure on the Jewish deaf people increased, now exercised by Nazis with normal hearing. The Gesetz zur Verhinderung erbkranken Nachwuchses (law for the Prevention of Offspring with Congenital diseases, GzVeN) shocked and frightened those deaf people professing the Jewish faith just as it did those 'comrades in fate' belonging to the Christian faith. The Federation of Orthodox Rabbis in Germany, with its seat in Frankfurt/Main, and the Union of Traditional Law-abiding Rabbis in Germany, based in Altona, beseeched their members to announce in their sermons that *the Jewish Religious Law does not allow sterilization* and that *no religious Jew may apply for sterilization, either for him/herself, nor for any other,* but such religious objections could do nothing to stop the racist cruelty.

We know definitely of 4 surviving Jewish deaf people who were victims of the GzVeN and were forcibly sterilized. It is not possible to provide further information about this aspect of persecution, because archives, e.g. from the I.T.A., were not obtainable anywhere, the only exception being a thin administrative file from the Brandenburg Provincial Committee.

One result of the increasing repression of Jews and their exclusion from the welfare provisions of the state was the formation, by handicapped Jews, of a Self-help Association of the Jewish Handicapped in Germany, with its seat in Berlin. The existing organizations for the Jewish Deaf – the Association for the Promotion of the Interests of the Israelite Deaf Mutes in Germany, the I.T.A. Alumni Association in Weissensee and the Branch Associations for the Promotion of the Interests of Israelite Deaf Mutes – had to reorganize themselves under the auspices of this large self-help organization for Jews (*Jüdische Rundschau* 28.09.1934).

But even in those dark days there were a very few rays of hope for the Jewish Deaf. These moments of happiness arose whenever non-Jews found the courage to take sides with them, to break a lance for them. As a shining example of this, we would like here to introduce Erwin Stemmler, a deaf man who, in spite of being personally in danger from deaf Nazi functionaries, nevertheless remained true to his Jewish friend. The newsletter of the Berlin Sports Association for the Deaf demonstrates that the Nazi functionaries in the association applied the racist ideology of those they viewed as shining examples with the same degree of harshness to all who opposed them, regardlessly. Stemmler, however, would not let himself be moved by a 'German-blooded' Jew-hater, Thomas, and brought a complaint before the Press Officer of the Association, Mehle. When Stemmler received as a reply nothing but fascist phrases instead of assistance, he tried to compel Thomas to recant. He applied for arbitration hearings, but this was not to bring any success for Stemmler, who received only hate and rejection as a 'friend of the Jews' from two Nazi-party members.

In spite of the increase in repression of every kind, Felix Reich attempted to keep up at least some semblance of teaching at the I.T.A. Some teachers had already been driven into emigration, and a few pupils managed to flee from the barbarism with their parents. But Reich held out in Weissensee. In August 1938, he tried to save eight of his youngest pupils by taking them to England. When Reich arrived in London, Hitler began the invasion of Poland. Reich's plan to get more of his deaf pupils out of Berlin-Weissensee was suddenly reduced to nothing. There was no going back. Shortly after England declared war, Reich was arrested, and later interned, because he was German and because he had been an officer at the front during the First World War. The question why the British never made any use of Reich's great educational gifts remains unanswered to this day...

For the deaf Jews who remained in Germany, there now began a terrible time of suffering which only a few would survive. Courageous commitment of a few separate German and pro-Jewish Deaf, can be documented by a short historical account of Leuner's:

> From the beginning of 1943 onwards, the deportation process was being speeded up, and besides the thousands of Jews who were victims of raids in the night, people wearing the Yellow Star were also being grabbed from their place of work. But even at this late hour there were Germans who would not admit defeat. One of them was Otto Weidt, a small man with a creased face, who had a small factory in Rosenthalerstraße in Berlin, where blind people and deaf and dumb people were employed. It has been documented that during the course of the years, he employed one hundred and sixty-five handicapped Jews, hid sixty-five of them and provided them with food, refuge and various amenities, that he was arrested by the Gestapo (and) searched a total of fifty-two times between 1940 and 1945. Weidt had the heart of a lion, and human compassion. He fought for the life of every Jew who had looked for refuge in his house or in his workshop, but only twenty-seven of his charges survived. (Leuner 1967, pp. 101-102)

Weidt kept coming up with new ideas for obtaining food for the people he was protecting. He was always in danger of his life when he was obtaining forged documents, or when he was bringing 'his' Jews from one hiding place to another. Weidt accomplished his most courageous rescue action in January of 1943. One morning, when he entered his company, he discovered that, during the night, the Gestapo had arrested all of the blind and deaf Jews employed by him. *At this time all his workers were in an assembly camp in Große Hamburgerstraße, just about to be deported. Otto Weidt, never at a loss for a way out, went to the camp* (Leuner, 1967, p.102). It has remained a secret of Weidt's how he managed to save his handicapped workers. So, in a late afternoon in January, a group of deaf, blind and otherwise handicapped Jews walked – happily! – through the streets of Berlin. Their leader was Otto Weidt. But their joy at freedom recovered did not last long, for *one after another all the Jews were removed from Weidt's company* (Leuner 1967, p. 102), among them the Jewish Deaf.

We can trace the fate of one of those deaf people who had their rights taken from them and who were unspeakably tormented . At the age of 30, Leon Milet, a deaf Jewish joiner, was taken away from the Theresienstadt ghetto in Berlin to Auschwitz concentration camp on transport *Eq–323,* on 12 December 1944. His two surviving brothers never heard from him again. Another of Leon Milet's brothers, Phillipp, was murdered in Sachsenhausen concentration camp in 1942. The names of the few surviving Jewish deaf people are often hidden stages of the deepest humiliation, of the most brutal torture and physical torment. It is simply not possible to give an account of all these terrible things – it is, as one survivor said, *indescribable, inconceivable...*

David Louis Bloch, a deaf artist from the rural districts of Floss, in the Bavarian Forest, worked his memories of the Holocaust out of his system by means of a series of haunting paintings, woodcuts and lino-cuts. Bloch survived the Dachau concentration camp, fled to Shanghai, China, lived there for nine years and then emigrated to the USA.

One other Jewish deaf person was not able to 'process' the dreadful fate he had suffered. He still suffers today from a serious case of neurasthenia caused by his persecution at that time. This illness is hardly surprising once one realizes that after his arrest (*because of my Jewish faith*), he was sent by the Vienna Gestapo to Auschwitz concentration camp in 1940, survived it, was then taken to Mühldorf, until finally being liberated in Dachau by the US army in 1945.

A further family's tragic fate from the world of the Jewish deaf need only be briefly mentioned here, since with the assistance of the author a film and documentary exhibition entitled *In der Nacht (In the Night)* have been produced in Los Angeles. Rose and Max Feld, a young married couple and both past pupils of the I.T.A., fled to France, where Max joined the Resistance, was then arrested by the Gestapo, before being deported to Auschwitz-Birkenau and there murdered. Rose and her little daughter, Esther survived a terrible time of suffering in Paris. In 1947, she emigrated to New York.

To close, we would like to tell how a deaf man from Berlin, whose mother was a Protestant Christian and father a Jew was persecuted by the Nazis. This person is of Jewish faith. His fate demonstrates for us how teachers of the Deaf who believed in racial hygiene actually dealt with Deaf people who did not fit into their scheme of things.

This persecuted man told us how he attended the I.T.A. in Berlin-Weissensee. He had to discontinue his apprenticeship after only one year, because of *dirty intrigues*. He specified later what he meant to express with the term *dirty intrigues:*

Ill. 3: *Rose and Esther Feld, 1945*

Ill. 4: *Last picture of Max Feld*

Herr Liepelt, a senior teacher of the deaf and dumb and a strong supporter of the Nazis, went to my Meister one day and told him that I was not of Aryan, but of Mosaic blood. Herr Liepelt was well known for betraying Jews, be they children, youths or adults.

Thus betrayed, he then attempted to *fight his way through*. He *always filled in employment forms incorrectly as far as religion was concerned*. However, when he had been working at one company for quite some time,

Herr Liepelt the senior teacher who at that time was working as an interpreter for the Deaf, appeared once again. He had already tracked me down several times and betrayed my religion, and this time was no different, and so I was given instant dismissal.

In this way the suffering of this deaf Jewish person was made only worse.

On account of wrongly stating my religion and because of sabotage at work (...), because I refused, due to my Jewish descent, to work in the armaments industry for Nazi war interests and Nazi desires for conquests, I landed in prison in 1940, 1941, 1943, and 1945, and there they ridiculed me, beat me and maltreated me.
I shall never be able to forget all that, it was dreadful. You can see the scars on my skull I got as a result of the treatment they gave me.

The Nazis imprisoned this deaf man for a total of 33 months, in different prisons. In addition to this, there were several short sentences.

Herr Liepelt always translated at these hearings and he always emphasized the fact that I was of Jewish descent (Blutjude [blood-Jew], as he put it). Instead of helping me, he just made things even worse.

In the following list, we detail the names and fates of Jewish Deaf people who were murdered by the Nazis. All the information was obtained either from Deaf people who were forcibly sterilized, or through our own research.

In Memoriam

Heidorn, Ilka	murdered in Bergen-Belsen
Schleidtalla, Frieda	murdered in Bergen-Belsen
Buchweiser, Käthi	School for the Deaf, Munich
Fränkel, Hans	taken away in 1943
Fränkel, Else	I.T.A. Berlin-Weissensee
Fränkel, Julius	I.T.A. Berlin-Weissensee
Bachner, Pinkus	*killed in Auschwitz concentration camp*
Kessmann, Wolfgang	
Struck, Hans	
Gutzmann, Herbert	
Kurz, Fritz	
Lawinski, Leo	*taken away from his flat in 1939*
Levin, Gerda	*Deaf School in Albrechtstr., Berlin, taken away in 1940*
Mazower, Dina	murdered in Wilna
Mazower, Leopold	murdered in Wilna
Bäcker, Louis	*family was murdered in Auschwitz*
Greveno	from Parchim in Schwerin
Isaaksohn	Special Class, Leipzig
Loew	*Frau L. was murdered in Hadamar in 1941*
Lipschitz, Hildegard	*Deaf School in Soest, taken from the school because a Jewess*
Rattner, Isidor	murdered in Minsk concentration camp
Spiegel, Lina	*I.T.A. Berlin-Weissensee, killed on way to Hungary*
Levis, Fritz	*was picked up at the Frankenthal School for the Deaf. I never saw him again.*
Hundert	*Mrs. Hundert was picked up one night. She was Jewish. We never saw her again.*
Buchholz, Hans	
Milet, Philipp	was murdered in Concentration Camp Sachsenhausen in 1942.
Milet, Leon	was murdered in 1944 when transferred by Transport *Eq–323* from the ghetto to the Auschwitz camp
Milet, Markus	*was murdered through forced labour!*
Krohner, Paul	*was a student of the I.T.A. and murdered in Auschwitz in 1941.*
Jacobson, Fredy	
Dierks	in Theresienstadt
Dierks	in Theresienstadt
Mainzer, Berta	was murdered in Auschwitz
Mainzer, Ludwig	was murdered in Auschwitz
Mainzer, Walter	was murdered in Auschwitz
Mainzer, Ruth	was murdered in Auschwitz
Sipli, Hella	Schleswig School for the Deaf
Raab, Günther	Hildesheim School for the Deaf
Jacob	Hildesheim School for the Deaf
Kahn, Philipp and wife	teachers of the Deaf at the I.T.A.
Bayer, Max	teacher of the Deaf at the I.T.A.
Schrage, Gisela	teacher at the I.T.A.
Nussbaum	was betrayed by her Catholic husband to the Nazis and murdered in the concentration camp

1 girl and 1 boy whose names were forgotten (both Jewish), Hamburg School for the Deaf

I can remember very well. I knew two Jewish girls of Worms. They were taken immediately away!

Mysterious 'disappearance' of a Jewish deaf person during the recess period in Berlin

1 boy whose name is unknown, Jewish, kidnapped, Braunschweig School for the Deaf

My first husband was a Jewish believer. He was murdered by the Nazis.

The one whose name was unknown, was killed in Auschwitz.

References

40-44th Annual Reports (1923-1927). Ed. Friends of the Deaf and Dumb – Jedide Ilmim, Berlin-Weißensee.

Adler, S. (1864): *The Morning and Evening Sacrifice*. London.

Biesold, H. (1988): *Klagende Hände. Betroffenheit und Spätfolgen in Bezug auf das Gesetz zur Verhütung erbkranken Nachwuchses, dargestellt am Beispiel der 'Taubstummen'*. Solms-Oberbiel: Jarick Oberbiel.

Goebel, J. (1983): Jüdische Gehörlosenschule in Berlin-Weissensee; in: *Sonderschule* 28, Berlin/ DDR.

Jüdische Rundschau (26.2.1932). (Berlin)

Jüdische Rundschau (15.8.1933). (Berlin)

Jüdische Rundschau (28.9.1934). (Berlin)

Leuner, H.D. (1967): *Als Mitleid ein Verbrechen war*. Wiesbaden.

Reich, E. (1934): Taubstumme entstummen! Zum 60-jährigen Bestehen der Israelitischen Taubstummenanstalt am 29. April; in: *Jüdische Rundschau,* 1st supplement, 26.4.1934. (Berlin)

Reich, F. (1923): 50 Jahre Israelitische Taubstummenanstalt und ihr Gründer Dir. M. Reich; in: *Beiträge zur Fortbildung und Unterhaltung der Taubstummen,* 30. (Schleswig)

Reich, F. (1930): Die Israelitische Taubstummenanstalt für Deutschland zu Berlin-Weissensee; in: *Taubstummenunterricht und Taubstummenfürsorge im Deutschen Reich*. Düsseldorf.

Reich, F. (1929): Der Mosaische Religionsunterricht; in: *Handbuch des Taubstummenwesens*. Osterwieck.

Gloria Pullen • Rachel Sutton-Spence
Bristol, Great Britain

The British Deaf Community during the 1939 - 1945 War

Summary

Older Deaf people in South-West England were asked to tell a Deaf researcher about their memories of the Second World War. They were asked specifically about the way they coped with rationing and air-raids. They were also asked to recount any particular events that they remember happening during that time. The stories that best capture the special experience of the Deaf community are reported here.

The Second World War was a time of trial for the people of Europe in all countries. Accounts of the lives of hearing civilians during this period abound, but there are too few accounts given by deaf people (but see, for example, Jackson, P. (1990): *Britain's Deaf Heritage*. Edinburgh: Pentland Press). The British Deaf community shared many of the common experiences of war but also have their own stories to tell of the particular experience of being Deaf during that time.

Older Deaf people living in Bristol, in South West England, have memories of those days which we have a duty to record. The younger generation knows too little about that time. Eye-witness accounts of any event are a vital contribution to history. Many elderly Deaf are uncomfortable recounting their memories in front of a video camera, and we found it best just to let them talk to a Deaf researcher who made notes on their stories. The informants then saw the final written version of the story they had told, and agreed that that was an accurate account. The following stories are selected from the many told to us. They aim to record some of the special experiences of Deaf people, and to tell of how Deaf people adapted their lives to cope with the upheaval around them. We imagine that many of these stories could come from Deaf people all over Europe. It would take a major research project to unearth the stories waiting to be told, but even the limited research carried out in Bristol has been rewarded with some very informative stories.

How the Deaf community coped with rationing

When rationing began, many Deaf people were confused by this new idea. They did not have access to many of the government's explanations about rationing, so they relied on the missioner at the Deaf club to help them. The missioner was snowed under with requests from anxious Deaf people to explain where the ration books came from and how to use their coupons. Members of the Deaf community found rationing particularly frustrating. Hearing people often heard rumours about shops which had certain foods for sale but Deaf people missed out on that. Like everyone else, a Deaf woman might be queueing from early in the morning to get what she wanted. A rumour would be running up and down the line that another shop had just received a certain food, but the Deaf woman would not be aware of this. Suddenly the queue would melt away as all the other women dashed off to another shop, leaving the Deaf woman wondering what had happened. One Deaf woman remembers *borrowing her daughter's ears*. She would take her young hearing daughter out with her and if the daughter heard a rumour she would quickly tell her mother. Another Deaf woman tells how she was queueing for some eggs and the shop-keeper ran out of eggs. He shouted out: *Sorry! No more eggs today!* and a few shoppers left, but the Deaf woman carried on queuing. When she finally got to the counter she asked for some eggs and then she was embarrassed and frustrated when she learned that she had wasted her time because there were no more eggs.

Sometimes people would help to make things less frustrating. In those days it was very important for everyone to be friendly with the shopkeepers who might do favours for their special customers, and Deaf people, too, made friends at their local shops. One shopkeeper understood the problems that a Deaf housewife was facing and always tried to help her. If he heard, for example, that the greengrocer had oranges, he would write a note to the Deaf woman telling her to go and try to get one. She gave him her shopping list before she went, and when she got back he would have tried to fill her list for her. The members of the Deaf community also helped each other. The Deaf women all tried to queue at different shops to get different things and then they would meet to pool what they had managed to buy. The Deaf club became a great centre for exchanging things. People would bring something special they had managed to get and see if they could swap it for something else. Or if someone needed a particular thing, they would ask around at the Deaf club to see if anyone had some. It was a time when the whole Deaf community worked together to help one another.

How the community coped with air raids

The special problem faced by many Deaf people was that they could not always hear the sirens warning them to take cover. The community devised many ways to overcome this problem. In many situations, of course, there was at least one hearing person who would tell everyone when there was a raid. In families where everyone was Deaf, some very useful strategies developed. At that time, nobody in Bristol locked their frontdoors in daytime, so if there was a daylight raid a neighbour or an ARP warden (Air Raid Precaution warden) could just walk into the house and warn everybody. Some people also gave a frontdoor key to a neighbour, so that if there was a raid at night, the neighbour could come in and wake them up.

Many people had faithful pets who would warn them of a raid. Some people relied on their dogs to start barking and jump up at them when the siren sounded. Other people kept their dogs in the bedroom at night to warn them. One Deaf person let the cat sleep on the bed. When the air-raid siren sounded the cat became very agitated and would wake its owner when it clawed at the bedclothes. Another couple had a budgie who would flutter its wings and shake its tail when the warning sounded. The couple took the budgie into their shelter with them too, and the budgie would let them know when the all-clear had sounded.

At night, some people used a piece of string. They tied a long piece of string around someone's toe and dangled it out of the window, down to the street below. When the siren went, the ARP warden or the missioner would tug on the string on their way to the shelter, and wake the Deaf person up. The Deaf person would wave from the window to prove that they were awake and then go and wake up the rest of the house. It was never very nice to sleep with a piece of string tied to your toe, so the members of the household used to take it in turns.

If Deaf people went to a public shelter, other people could tell them when the All-Clear had sounded, but Deaf people who had their own shelters in their homes could not hear the All-Clear siren. Many people relied on the ARP warden coming into the house to fetch them. One man remembers that he would get up when the siren went, and turn off the gas and the water. Then he would unlock his front door and go into his shelter. When the All-Clear sounded, the ARP warden would call by at the house to fetch the family out. They always gave him a cup of tea before he went on, by way of thanks. The ARP wardens were very helpful to Deaf people, and the Deaf community always tried to repay their kindness in small ways. One woman always gave her warden a piece of cake whenever he called. Another man, who didn't smoke himself, bought ten cigarettes every week to give to his warden.

Individual stories told by Deaf people

Several older people whom we interviewed offered complete stories about episodes that took place during the war. In an attempt to preserve some of the feel of the Deaf story-telling tradition, we have decided to reproduce some of these stories. Although the stories here are not exact translations of the stories told (due to the unwillingness of the informants to be filmed) we will present them as pure narratives. Some are accounts from personal experiences, and some report events that happened to others. The last three stories recount episodes experienced by the informants themselves, and for that reason we have chosen to use the first person singular in these accounts.

A Deaf man who joined the 'Blackshirts'[1]

There was a Deaf man from another town who came to Bristol. He supported Hitler, and he

---

1   The Blackshirts were members of the British Union of Fascists (BUF) led by Sir Oswald Mosely in

joined the Blackshirts. He tried to persuade the members of the Bristol Deaf club to join the British Union of Fascists (BUF). The missioner at the Deaf club warned the members against it, and they refused to become Blackshirts. One day the Deaf man brought a group of Blackshirts into the Deaf club to try to scare them into joining the BUF. They started pointing and jeering at the Deaf people and began to threaten them. They pushed chairs around to frighten people, and everyone began to worry that they might get beaten up. The missioner was in his office and called the secretary in to decide what to do for the best. In the end the missioner decided to ring for the police.

Just then a Deaf man arrived at the club. The secretary grabbed him as he went past and told him what was happening. Then the Deaf man slipped into the club room and asked three of his friends to come and join him. They all went in to the office and agreed on a plan. They went to the cleaner's cupboard and took all the broomsticks and mop-handles that they could find. Armed with the brooms and mops, they charged into the club room and really laid into the Blackshirt bully-boys. The bullies hadn't expected the Deaf people to fight back, and they turned and fled, pursued by the angry club members. They ran straight into the arms of the police who arrived at that moment, and arrested them all.

The Deaf man who had joined the Blackshirts was banned from the Deaf club. When the BUF was disbanded, he moved to Bristol, but he never mixed again with the Deaf community. He died many years later, but he never returned to the Deaf club.

The raid that disturbed the church service

Members of the Deaf community were in the Deaf club for a church service one Sunday evening. The caretaker (who was also an ARP warden) crept in and interrupted the missioner in the middle of the service. They talked for a while and then the missioner turned to the congregation and told them to walk quietly and calmly down to the cellar. Everyone filed down to the cellar, and the missioner carried on the service as though nothing unusual was happening. When the bombing began, the vibrations shook the cellar, but the missioner just carried on leading the prayers.

The caretaker came into the cellar and interrupted the missioner again. After a quick discussion the missioner chose half a dozen Deaf young men and asked them to go with the caretaker to help him. The caretaker had only recently started work at the Deaf club, and he was only part-time there because he was also the ARP warden, and he didn't know how to sign. He was worried that he would not be able to communicate with the Deaf volunteers. The missioner gave him a card which had the fingerspelling alphabet on it and told him to use that.

When they came out onto the street, everything seemed to be on fire. The men could see that the building next door was on fire so they set to work to help put it out. They didn't need the warden to use any fingerspelling to tell them what to do! He forgot all about his card and everyone used gestures that were easy to understand. The men worked very hard fighting the fires. They saw some terrible things: wounded and trapped people crying for help, dead and dying animals and many dead people. At last when there was nothing more that they could do, the missioner told everyone to go straight home. They couldn't take their usual routes home, because so many buildings were unsafe and could collapse at any time.

One of the young men arrived home at about 5a.m. He was covered in soot and dirt, and his mother shouted at him for being so late back from church and for ruining his Sunday-best suit.

---

the 1920s and 1930s. By the outbreak of the war, they were a very small party, who believed that the Fascists in Europe should not be fought unless they attacked Britain. The BUF was effectively finished in 1940 when most of its leaders were arrested.

The Deaf man whose house was bombed

My wife and I were at home when an air-raid began. We took shelter under the stairs, because that was the strongest part of the house. A bomb fell on our house and destroyed it, but the stairs did not collapse and we were not hurt. We were trapped in the ruins and had to wait for help. It was completely dark, so we could not see each other signing. Instead, we felt each other's hands while we signed. I kept my hands on the stairs above me, to try and feel any vibrations from rescue-workers moving the rubble. For a long time nobody came and we began to worry that noone would come and rescue us. We thought we might die in the ruins. Finally we were dug out.

The rescue workers were very surprised to find us there, because they had believed the house to be empty. Someone had shouted to ask if anyone was trapped and when no one had answered they had gone away. Luckily my mother had arrived at that moment, and told them to search the rubble. They had refused at first but she forced them to try to find us. If she had not called by, and been so insistent, we might never have been found.

The Deaf woman who was caught in air raids at work

I worked in Yate, just outside Bristol, in an ammunition factory, making shells. One night I was working when I suddenly noticed that the power was failing on my machine. Everything was slowing down. I looked up and the woman opposite me pointed up above her and said *Jerries above.* I knew that she meant that there was an enemy aeroplane above. I got my coat and we all started to leave the factory. Suddenly the lights went out. We all held hands and someone guided us out by calling from over by the door. It was still early in the war, and there were no air-raid shelters built yet. We were told to go and wait in a field away from the factory. We could see the railway line from there and there was a train coming along the track. The driver and fireman didn't know that a plane was following them and we were worried that they might get shot. It was very cold standing in the field. In the factory it was so hot that we often worked with just our underwear on under our overalls and that was all we were wearing while we stood in the field. In the end we all went into a cowshed to keep warm.

After a while someone came in and told us to come and look at the sight. I looked over towards Bristol and saw nothing but a sea of flames. I thought that the whole city had been destroyed. I stood there and watched the fire and cried. I was only 19.

When I finally got home, I couldn't get into the house because the front door was locked. I went round to the back and climbed over the garden wall, where the bomb shelter was because I thought maybe my parents did not know that it was safe to come out. They were not in the shelter and I began to get very worried. In the end I broke a window to get into the house. I found my parents asleep in bed. They had slept the whole night through and did not even know there had been a raid. We all looked at the piece of string tied around my mother's toe. It had snapped.

On another night the air-raid siren went, but I was working on an urgent order so I volunteered to stay at my bench for a while. When the second siren went the enemy planes were almost overhead. There was a hearing foreman there who got on very well with Deaf people, and he could communicate with me, using a special set of gestures that we had worked out between us. This foreman always worked on the same shift as I did so that he could keep an eye on me. The foreman ran up to me and said to me (in our special gestures) *Run for your life!.*

There was a wall along my route to the shelter which should have protected me, but I was in a panic, and I ran down along the wrong side of the wall where I could be seen. An aeroplane followed me, shooting at me with its machine gun. I was running as fast as I could, but I knew I had made a mistake and couldn't possibly reach the shelter before they shot me. The foreman was running down the other side of the wall and knew what was happening. As I came to a gap in the wall, he grabbed me and pulled me through to the shelter on the other side. We saw a bomb land directly on the factory and it exploded so loudly that I heard it.

When the All-Clear sounded, the foreman took me out and showed me the bullet-holes in the wall where I had been running. I was horrified to see how close they had been to me when he saved me. We went back into the factory and found that my machine had been very badly damaged. My coat had been hanging above the machine, so I had to go home without a coat.

The Deaf man who met the captured airmen

During the war, I worked as an oil-pipe layer at Avonmouth, near Bristol. One day the air-raid siren sounded and everyone went down to the shelters. I was late going down because there was something I needed to finish first. When I was ready to go to the shelter, I found I was too late and they had shut the door on me. There were some men from the Home Guard sheltering by a wall, so I went and joined them. From where we were we had a wonderful view of the planes flying overhead. They swooped down very low, trying to avoid the flak. I watched them weaving and diving around above me. It was very exciting to watch. Then one plane was hit. Fire spread through it, then it burst into flames and came crashing down. We looked up again and saw two of the crew with parachutes floating gently down through all the chaos of the air-raid. The men from the Home Guard ran off to capture them, and soon they returned with three airmen. I had not seen the third one come down. They came towards the wall with their hands behind their heads, and the rifles of the Home Guard pressed into their backs. As they came closer, I was struck by their youth. They could not have been much more than 18. They looked so frightened: three blond boys, who were prisoners of war in a foreign country. I couldn't hate them, even though I knew they were supposed to be our enemies. I just felt sorry for them. I thought, *They're only boys. Just babies really! Whatever will their parents say?*

The soldiers sat the airmen against the wall while the raid went on all around us. One soldier was left to guard them and the others went off. We all sat in a line in the shadow of the wall, with the guard separating me and the airmen. The boys looked so miserable and dejected, and I felt more and more sorry for them. No hatred; only pity. I wanted to do something for them, so I asked the guard if I could give them some cigarettes, and he agreed but he insisted that he should light them. The airmen were surprised when I leant over and offered them the cigarettes, but they took them. We all sat smoking with our palms cupped over the glowing tips and the battle still raged above us. I peeked round the soldier and caught the eye of one of the prisoners. He was looking very miserable and upset, so I gave him the thumbs up sign to try to cheer him up. He just looked at me because he didn't understand what I meant. I tried again, but this time I smiled and nodded encouragingly. Then he realised what I meant, and he smiled back, uncertainly. The guard was very suspicious – I think he thought I might be a spy or something – and told me to sit back against the wall again.

Finally the All-Clear siren sounded and we all stood up. The guard was still uncertain about me and demanded to see my identity card, but he could not find anything wrong so he told me to go back to work. He made the airmen stand up and started to lead them away. The boy who had smiled at me stopped as they passed. He patted my shoulder, smiled, and gave me the thumbs up sign. The guard made him move on, and they marched off. I never saw any of them again.

Gertrud Mally
Munich, Germany

The Long Road to Self-Confidence of the Deaf in Germany

Summary • Zusammenfassung

This article reports on how Deaf people in Munich (Germany) have searched for and found their own identity, in spite of the disastrous influences of oralism. The Deaf founder of the Kommunikationsforum took things in her own hands and attempted to counterbalance the traditional curriculum of hearing pedagogues, thus encouraging the self-confidence of the Deaf. Based on her experiences in her childhood, youth and the hearing professional world, she devised a method, developed it and tried it out. Her way is marked by a revolutionary reform which stirred up the otherwise so quiet Deaf community.

Dieser Beitrag berichtet von der Suche und dem Findungsprozeß der Münchner Gehörlosen nach Identität, angesichts des zerstörenden Einflusses des Oralismus. Die gehörlose Initiatorin des Kommunikationsforums hat aus eigenem Antrieb die Dinge selbst in die Hand genommen und ein Gegengewicht zur traditionellen Gehörlosenpädadagogik geschaffen, vor allem um das Selbstbewußtsein der Gehörlosen zu stärken. Aus den Erfahrungen ihrer Kindheit, Jugend und ihrem Arbeitsleben unter Hörenden, entwicklte sie ihre eigene Lehrmethode und probierte sie aus. Ihr Konzept hat große Unruhe und Bewegung in die sonst so stille Gehörlosengemeinschaft gebracht.

I

Until the 1970s, there was little progress for Deaf people in Germany; there was only their monotonous daily rhythm of work. The leisure-time spent in the Deaf association was the only sense of life for Deaf people. There they could build up and cultivate human relations. National and international sporting events constituted the few highlights in their life. It always struck me that there was such thirst for knowledge among the Deaf. They longed for more information and sat together until late in the night to share information. This is a typical feature of their own culture.

The result of the fully invisible and, for hearing people, unimaginable disability, is an information deficit, coupled with gaps in knowledge. Consequently, the normal spiritual and linguistic development of Deaf people suffers. Other hearing-impaired people, for example these who became deaf postlingually or the hard-of-hearing, who can acquire speech with the help of hearing aids, have better access to knowledge. They too, however, reach a certain level of knowledge, and progress no further.

After joining the community of the Deaf I noticed that the topics of their conversations were rather stereotyped. They turned around the daily problems at work and in the hearing world. There was quite a lot of gossip about acquaintances. I thought often about these topics, and wondered why the conversations always centered around them. The information which Deaf people get from hearing people is reduced to the bare necessities and there is little background information. When hearing persons talk quickly Deaf persons cannot follow – in spite of all the exercises in lip-reading. The Deaf did not know what the Hearing were talking about. Thus, this source of information was also closed to them. The little information transferred from hearing to Deaf people then was discussed in the Deaf clubs. This was a vicious circle! Still, the Deaf longed for less superficial information.

In 1972, there was an attempt to raise the underdeveloped level of education. Our Deaf friend Rudi Sailer was more knowledgeable than us because he was able to use German Sign Language with his Deaf parents. He supported the Deaf youth in Munich and tried to build up a support group for education and culture (Fördergruppe für Bildung und Kultur). Ten young Deaf people, hungry for education, immediately joined him, among them myself. Twice a year he organized weekend seminars at which teachers for the 'deaf and dumb' [1] with some knowledge of signing and Deaf pupils of the Realschule (junior high school) discussed such topics as 'to think, to learn, to forget', 'drugs, a danger for young people' and so on. These seminars were a big success. Deaf people not only from Munich but also from the surrounding areas attended them. The support group continued for two years, but then had to be dissolved because nearly all members started families and had to devote time to their professions. We returned to our everyday lives and several years passed until a historic moment in 1975.

This historic moment was the publication of the *Blue Book (Blaues Buch;* Starcke/ Maisch (eds.) 1975) the first sign-dictionary, which changed the life of German Deaf people. It was an exciting event in the history of the German Deaf. The book consisted of 3000 photographs of signs, and it was supposed to become the standard work for signed German (lautsprachbegleitende Gebärden) in the German speaking countries. With great interest we examined the photographs and reacted with extreme vehemence against those strange signs, laid down by a group of mainly hearing persons. Nevertheless, the *Blue Book* was readily accepted by the very few sign courses then existing for hearing people. I never thought that this 'wave' would one day seize me too.

---

1   In this text, the expression 'deaf and dumb' is used in connection with teachers, because the official title of the association of German teachers for Deaf children until recently has been Bund Deutscher Taubstummenlehrer, i.e. Federation of Teachers for the Deaf and Dumb.

II

Today, after 15 years of part-time jobs and honorary activities it is time to look back: my life was unexpectedly fulfilled with the many and various tasks I undertook to promote sign language, especially in Munich and the surrounding areas. These tasks molded me. There were periods of joy which gave me strong motivation, but there were also bitter disappointments which robbed me of courage and confidence. Life proceeded quickly, and involuntarily I swam in the ever growing stream of sign language. Initiative – work – new knowledge – renewed initiative, going on from one event to the next. Then at last, it became apparent! It was completely unexpected, in the light of the notions I had then.

To begin with, I would like to talk about my childhood and to introduce myself. In August 1948, I came into the world as the daughter of hearing parents, the engineer Emil Mally and his wife Hertha. My deafness was diagnosed very late because I was a very lively child, responding quickly to the natural gestures of my mother. Despite thorough examinations, the reason for my deafness remained undiscovered; I was probably born deaf. I remember quite well the communication between my parents and myself. In the beginning, the efforts to understand each other were truly desperate. My parents were unable to seek advice from experts, because at that time they did not know where the school for deaf and dumb children was located. The communication between my parents and myself developed through mutual self-help. The natural signs for 'to eat', 'to drink', 'to sleep' came spontaneously from my parents. I understood them immediately and was able to respond. As I grew older (1-5 years) I gathered much visual information and tried to process it in my head and to express my impressions. Unfortunately they did not understand me and I desperately sought for a solution. When we went to the zoo, to the cinema or shopping I pointed to certain things and used spontaneously natural gestures corresponding to my age: I imitated the puppets in the puppet show at the zoo with my hands; I put my head forward with widely opened eyes (like looking at the screen in the cinema); I simulated holding a bouquet in my hands (parsley at the greengrocer's). Thus my mother learned to understand my signed expressions, adopted them and responded with the same signs which I then immediately understood. In this way the communication was built up.

One day on a boat-trip, which I loved very much, I signed to my parents the movements of the sailor putting on his thick gloves and throwing and tightening the rope, accompanied by mimicry. Another day when I showed my mother the same signs, she shook her head negatively and I reacted with vehement obstinacy because I understood 'there will be no boat-trip'; I remember the persistent, begging questions I addressed to my father, asking him when the trip would take place. He answered by inclining his head alternatively to the left and to the right, making the sign for 'to sleep'. Then I understood that I had to wait several days.

At the age of six I entered the Taubstummenanstalt (Deaf and Dumb Institute) in Munich. Frightened and with my eyes wide open in amazement, I saw there for the first time the vivid signs of Deaf children. But soon I felt at home, although I did not understand all the signs of the children. I imitated them to show off and in order to hide my lack of comprehension. In first grade I learned to pronounce the first sounds, and then word by word the right use of my voice. However, I did not yet understand that words like 'mamma', 'papa', 'grandma', 'grandpa' had a significance. This happened only later in second grade. I remember quite well pronouncing the word 'mamma' in the presence of my mother. She embraced me with tears in her eyes, but I didn't understand why. One day I had to remain at school after the lessons because my mother had an appointment. While I was doing my homework, my classmates came rushing in to tell me that my mother was coming. But I did not understand them. Only when my mother stood in front of me, did I suddenly understand the connection: the sign for 'mamma' signed by my class-mates had the same significance as the spoken word I had learned in the pronunciation class. At that moment it became clear!

From that time on I became interested in other signs and learned to understand and to grasp the relation to the spoken words. My enthusiasm for the signed communication grew steadily. My vocabulary in sign language extended rapidly and surpassed that of spoken language. I was so happy to be able to express my thoughts to my classmates. On the other hand the spoken communication with my parents remained rather poor, and this depressed me sometimes.

In the 5th grade I realized for the first time what injustice was. My teacher, who was orally orientated and whom we all disliked, one day announced the homework for the next day. As I wanted to celebrate my name-day that evening I asked my teacher aloud, without signs, if I could do my homework at school so that I would be free at home. She agreed and one hour later I had finished. My classmates noticed this with jealousy and were angry because of this preferential treatment. Then my teacher changed her mind and freed us all from the homework. I reacted with indignation, signing 'in vain' but pronouncing badly 'unvan', as I had read it on the lips of other children. Upon hearing this the teacher attracted my attention and cried: 'What does that mean, 'unvan'?' She imitated my sign with a look full of contempt. I did not know the correct pronunciation, and I desperately looked to a hard-of-hearing school-mate and asked her to correct me. She explained to me syllable by syllable in signed German and then I pronounced the word again. 'Well, at least', the teacher replied, 'this time it was right. Remember this!' I wondered why the teacher did not tell me the right word in connection with a sign. Then I realized that she did not know the sign and furiously thought 'Why should she escape unscathed when she is not able to sign. We are always punished for not hearing and not knowing spoken words'. This event deeply imprinted itself in my heart and certainly decisively influenced the work I am doing today for the promotion of sign language.

For nine years I attended the Deaf and Dumb Institute; the Realschule (junior high school) did not exist at that time. A 3 1/2 year training course in cartography at the Bayerisches Landesvermessungsamt (Bavarian Office of Land Surveying) and at the Munich Berufsschule (school for vocational training) in lithography and cartography followed. I was naive enough to think in good faith that I would easily be able to follow the teaching in the vocational training school, since my marks in German had always been very good. What did I experience there? It was a heavy blow which shook me deeply. Suddenly I could no longer understand the spoken language. The level of speech of my hearing school-mates of the same age was much higher than I had thought. They were four or five years ahead of me. During my time at the Deaf and Dumb Institute I had become used to simplified speech. I had repeated the teacher's sentences like a parrot; the slogan of my teacher had been 'Remember! Remember!' Now I no longer understood the content of what the hearing persons said; the teachers offered no simplified explanations for me. I was allowed to copy the texts of one of my classmates but I did not understand what they meant. It was a breaking point for me. For the first time I was confronted with ordinary spoken language. I lapsed deeper and deeper, and my marks became worse and worse. Only then did I become truly aware of my handicap and my dignity was very hurt. It took a whole year to come back to myself. 'You have to work twice as much because you are handicapped', I thought to myself. I wanted to prove to hearing people that I was not as stupid as that. With an iron will and tenacity I wrote and wrote until my fingers ached. I copied all the texts in order to hold the 'optical' language with my eyes and store it in my mind. This was the most important to me, since there was nothing else I could do. It helped, and I improved. After two years of endless mechanical writing I achieved the best mark. It amuses me today to think of the examination questions. I could never be absolutely sure of the correct reply to a question because I could never understand the question quite correctly. Thus I found a trick: I wrote very long texts hoping that the right answer to the question would be hidden somewhere in my text.

Then one day, full of pride, I showed my certificate to the training chief at the Bavarian Office of Land Surveying. He looked at it unbelievingly and said that a Deaf person could never reach the best mark. He went to see my teacher at the vocational training school. Oh, how they quarreled! I watched with joy and considered it a triumphal confirmation of my regained honour!

I will never forget the special training courses for the Deaf in the Bavarian Office of Land Surveying. Our teacher wanted to prepare us for the exam, so he asked us questions to which we had to reply aloud. 'What is a negative copy?', he asked. Feeling unsure, we did not reply at all, for fear of expressing ourselves badly in German. Furiously he repeated the question, speaking very slowly and distinctly in order to facilitate lipreading. Which answer would be right and how to put it? Again, we did not react. Better to remain silent than to give a stupid answer. Otherwise a hearing person would get the impression that we were mentally disabled. Then he lost his patience. With a face as red as a beet he sharply gave us the right answer: 'A negative copy is a copy which is negative!' Puzzled we stared at his mouth to try to make sense of his answer. Again nothing! We could only repeat his sentence in order to calm the excited teacher. Only when he showed us illustrative material did we understand. During the training there were sometimes scenes of desperate attempts by the hearing persons to make themselves understood. We pitied them.... But what could we do? We were not competent enough in spoken language. We scraped through the final exam because we were excellent drawers. With this ability we were able to compensate for our gaps in theory.

About ten years later ten Deaf trainees came to our bureau to be taught. They caused great difficulties for their teacher. A Deaf employee of the bureau, the engineer Gottfried Weileder, took over the training of the Deaf students, using sign language when explaining the subjects. Thanks to him many Deaf employees have been able to become subordinate officials.

At the Bavarian Office of Land Surveying I shared a room with a hearing colleague. At first we communicated well with each other, since my pronunciation is rather good. The longer, however, I was with her and the more new experiences there were to exchange, the more I became aware that ours was a one-channel-communication, that the initiative was always mine. From the opposite direction came nothing; only the most important information: new working regulations, announcements, absences and so on. I was not told anything about a staff meeting which I had not been able to attend; there was no gossip about colleagues. Every day my office-mate was visited by other colleagues. They chattered pleasantly or discussed the latest news, but I was completely left out of the conversation. In this atmosphere I felt treated like a person who was unable to listen, unable to understand. My colleague spoke very distinctly and I could have followed her easily by reading her lips. Increasingly I longed for conversations with hearing people. It made me sick and I could not stand the lack of communication with hearing people which I constantly felt. I asked to be moved to another office when I could no longer bear the feeling that my colleagues were taking advantage of my not being able to hear.

III

One day, in 1977, a teacher for the deaf and dumb asked me whether I would be prepared to give him and his seven colleagues from the Realschule (junior high school) for the Deaf private lessons in signing. This was an extraordinary task for me, since I had been so much used to being forbidden to sign. 'And now this, especially from a teacher for the deaf and dumb!' I was naturally very puzzled, but at the same time I felt flattered to be allowed to teach signing to the instructors. Besides using the *Blue Book* I had no idea how the lessons should be structured. There was nearly no teaching material in Germany on the subject. I pondered this problem, aware of the criticisms of many Deaf people who did not accept the *Blue Book*. Thus I set to work and made for the first time drawings of the Munich signs, with a

181

view to the Munich Deaf and Dumb Institute. The texts were taken from German grammar books for foreigners. I always kept in mind the teachers' endeavour to teach the children spoken language and, therefore, stuck to spoken language. After eight lessons, summer came and the teachers gave a farewell grill party. Although they knew a few signs by this time they gaily talked to one another without signs – as if it were quite natural. I was greatly disappointed and it was very difficult not to show my inner turmoil. Only now and then did the host address me, making some signs to ask whether I would like to have another drink or a slice of bread. I felt like a dog under the table, reacting happily to the calls of his master. I came to realize that there was an unbridgeable gulf between us although they knew some signs. I asked myself if they were eager to learn signs only in order to brush up their image as teachers for the deaf and dumb, rather than to communicate with Deaf children. These lessons were over and I soon forgot this painful experience.

1 1/2 years later I received an unexpected call from the Munich Volkshochschule (School for Adults). The then director and founder of the department for the disabled, Dr. Radtke, himself confined to a wheelchair, asked me whether I would be prepared to teach a sign course at the Evening School. I had always been told that Deaf people depended upon the help of Hearing people and that they never would be able to lead an independent life. I had often heard this from my teachers, and also from my parents and other hearing people who worked with the Deaf. Besides that, I thought of the postlingually deafened person who had already been teaching for years at the Evening School and who had been asked a short time ago to initiate sign lessons for hearing persons. This is a task for well-spoken, linguistically competent, hard-of-hearing persons, able to show themselves in public; it is not a task for a Deaf person! I refused the offer of Dr. Radtke with indignation. But he insisted and called me repeatedly until I gave in. Only much later did I learn how he had come to ask

Ill. 1: *A lesson at the Munich Evening School*

me to teach the course. A teacher of the deaf and dumb to whom I had taught signs earlier had recommended me, and furthermore, many participants in the course given by the other instructor at the school were dissatisfied, because his signs, taken from the *Blue Book*, did not correspond to the signs of the Munich Deaf people.

I dug out my old teaching material and rapidly revised it. With much difficulty I improved the drawings of the hands – the method for teaching signed German was completed evening by evening, from class to class. I shall never forget the first lesson. I had my heart in my mouth when the class began. 24 hearing persons sat in front of me with great expectations, and it cost me quite some effort to talk to them. I did not know how to give an introduction to a sign course or how to deal with the participants. But soon I realized that hearing people are human beings, too, and that they were dependent on my knowledge of sign language. Then I discovered what my strengths were and I slowly gained self-confidence. This situation was so different from that with the teachers for the deaf and dumb. These students were unpretentious and from various professions.

During the following semesters the elementary course grew steadily and I learned how to handle the necessary written correspondence. Until then I had always asked my mother to correct the grammatical mistakes in my letters. But I felt uncomfortable in this dependence. I thought that my explication in spoken language in the evening classes would certainly be full of faults and that it would be in contradiction with the perfect German in my letters. Therefore I decided not to ask my mother to correct my letters and I chose to write in the style which corresponded to my personality. It is true that many hearing persons, upon seeing my mistakes, shook their heads. I ignored this and thought: 'Hearing persons should at last see reality, should see the problems of the Deaf. Our disability is invisible; our way of writing can bring the disability into the light'. This brought me to a new realization: not only signs should be taught, but also an explanation about what Deafness meant.

The correspondence I had to do increased after the beginning of the sign courses. The communication barrier receded bit by bit. When I met my hearing friends and relatives a few years later, they noticed the improvement in my spoken language and the expansion of my vocabulary. I was astonished because I myself had not been aware of this development.

At first, the beginner courses were attended especially by parents of Deaf children, by colleagues, and students of pedagogy for the Deaf. Later on, members of the training staff of the Berufsschule für Gehörlose und Schwerhörige (Vocational School for the Deaf and Hard-of-Hearing), trustees of some firms, social pedagogues, and officials of several government offices joined us. They asked me to teach them more than the basic signs. And thus the advanced course was born. Again it took me much time to revise the teaching material, this time with special terms for those who needed them in their jobs. The material I had always copied at my own expense now surpassed the limits of my low income. I therefore put together a bound brochure, *Die Sprache der Hände. Grundaufbaustufe I* (Mally 1978a), and six months later a second brochure, *Die Sprache der Hände. Grundaufbaustufe II* (Mally 1978b). I paid the printing costs for these brochures, the funds coming from my salary from the Evening School for Adults and partly from my savings. I eventually got back this sum by selling the brochures at the beginning of the courses.

From then on everything went like clockwork. Increasing numbers of participants signed up for the courses and an enlarged course for the advanced II level had to be organized. This was a result of the newly founded Stadtverband der Gehörlosen München (Munich Municipal Association for the Deaf) which functioned as a parent association for all the Deaf clubs in Munich. The chairman, Rudolf Gast, asked me to work with the groups and to teach a course for interpreters. This meant that I had to find a new way of teaching. Until then there were no interpreters in Germany. In view of the translation work, I bought a cassette recorder. My mother helped me by recording herself reading the texts I chose from several newspapers. The speech tempo accelerated gradually until it reached a normal speed.

The 'special group' thus had the possibility to practice simultaneous interpretation. A collection of these texts constituted the exercise book for *Die Sprache der Hände. Erweiterungsausbau und Übungsheft* (Mally 1980). Again I had to invest my savings in this book.

In 1981, the Munich Stadtverband could for the first time formally present a certificate to all those interpreter candidates who had attended the course for signed German.

There was a steady development after the establishment of the two advanced courses. The classes were crowded with some 30 or 40 participants each. My leisure time was cut down. I had to give up skiing, hiking, and tennis. Even on weekends and holidays I was busy because I needed much time for the preparation of the classes. Four classes a week had to be given. Work was piling up on my desk, enough to occupy my holidays.

IV

One day the *Deutsche Gehörlosen-Zeitung (German Magazine for the Deaf)* published a notice that there would be a meeting for teachers of sign courses at Büsum (city in northern Germany). This caught my attention because I had been looking for some time for such an occasion to exchange my experiences with other sign teachers. In mid-September 1982, about 25 sign teachers, invited by Herbert Feuchte, the head of the Gesellschaft zur Förderung der Hör-Sprachgeschädigten (Society for the Hearing-and-Speech-Impaired), met for the first time. We were all still very green with respect to organizing and leading classes. There were hot discussions about the *Blue Book*, which none of us liked. I still remember the naive helplessness of the sign teachers who felt patronized by the hearing persons in charge. A resolution for the promotion of sign courses in Germany was drafted by a small group of hearing persons without the assistance of the Deaf. At that time, I did not yet know the word 'resolution'. In this situation of being pushed to the side, a Deaf participant, Wolfgang Schmidt, addressed me in sign language and gave vent to his anger: 'This resolution has been made by hearing people and I don't agree with that.' I did not understand why he was so angry. He explained to me that he had been to the United States for four weeks and that the Deaf in Germany could learn a lot from that country. I still didn't quite understand the implications of his statement, because I was simply so glad that the teachers of sign courses – up to then unknown – had been called together. We all agreed that the *Blue Book* had to be revised, this time in cooperation with more Deaf people which I held to be very important.

Some months later there was a weekend seminar in the Harz, a mountainous region in Germany, with the title 'Do you know the problem?'. This event was a public relations activity introduced by Friedrich-Wilhelm Jürgens. Here I was walking on new ground. I had no idea of politics. A big assembly of mainly hearing people gathered in order to become familiar with the problem of Deafness. Several discussion groups handled topics like 'Interpreters', 'Education in the schools for the Deaf', or 'The Deaf at their workplace'. I didn't grasp much of what was going on, simply because the amount of new and strange information was too much for me. I also didn't understand a lot, because the majority of the people in the discussion groups were hearing people with little knowledge of sign language. The year following this first meeting in the Harz, the seminar for political education was moved to the Karl-Arnold-Stiftung (Karl-Arnold-Foundation) in Bad Godesberg, because of the better financial conditions there. After having participated regularly for several years, I understood bit by bit the importance of public relations work for the Deaf. I felt particularly motivated when the Deaf doctor, Dr. Inge Richter, excellently and with great success conducted the political seminar. I was very impressed by the way she led the discussions, and I told her that I would like to learn to do the same thing. Fortunately, she lived in Munich, and she promised me she would arrange this one day.

In the meantime a group of Deaf people, university pedagogues, teachers, clergymen and parents had gathered in Munich in order to put together a paper on the topic ' spoken

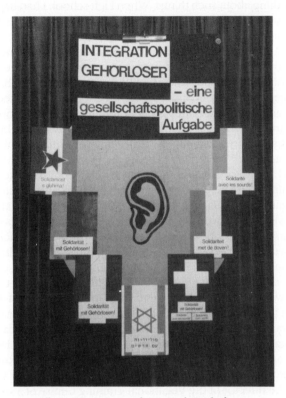

Ill. 2: *Seminarweek in Bad Godesberg*

language and signing'. On September 11th, 1982, a revised version of this paper entitled *Kommunikation mit Gehörlosen in Lautsprache und Gebärde* (Braun et al. 1982) was formally signed in the presence of Professor Braun (chair of Pedagogy for Hearing-Impaired Children, University of Munich), Peter Donath (Federal Association of Parents of Deaf Children), Wolfgang Czempin (German Federation of the Deaf), pastor Artur Keller (German Working Committee for Protestant Pastors for the Deaf), and Johannes Tigges (Federation of German Teachers for the Deaf and Dumb). In this joint statement on the 'Munich Signs', the position was that Deaf persons were to be considered as equal partners and that the gulf of communication between the Deaf and the Hearing should be bridged. Rudolf Gast (Deaf) and Peter Donath (Hearing) had cooperated in drafting this paper.

In February 1983 the leader of the Association of Parents of Deaf Children in Bavaria, Peter Donath, organized a weekend seminar which took place in the Bayerische Wald. Many parents had expressed the wish to learn signs in such a weekend seminar, because most of them were unable to undertake the long journey to attend the sign courses in Munich. This signing seminar was therefore conducted at top speed. The parents also received information about what the life of their Deaf children would be like after they had left school. I was very much impressed by the fact that many parents were astonished to meet me and other Deaf persons who managed to live quite independently. A mother told me that this was the first time she had seen Deaf adults with her own eyes, although her child was already 12 years old. She felt that she could contemplate without fear the future of her child. I was shocked by this reaction and thought of the counselling office in the School for Deaf Children. Why did they conceal this all-important information from the parents?

I could not help thinking of my own parents, because it had been just the same for them.

They also knew nothing about such things. When I left school, I had been convinced that I would always have to live with hearing people. As an apprentice in the Office of Land Surveying I met Deaf adults for the first time – ten, twenty, thirty, forty, so many of them! I couldn't believe it! At first I was astonished, and then I felt happy and relieved to be able to have conversations with Deaf colleagues during the breaks. With great enthusiasm I told my parents about my new experiences. Only then did my parents learn that there was a Deaf club, and they immediately allowed me to go there. School had educated me with a view to the hearing world and I had been oriented only to the speaking majority.

Most of the hearing persons attended my courses regularly and we became a wonderful class. We felt strong solidarity and regularly landed up in a restaurant – often until midnight – when the course was over. We exchanged news, using the signs they just had learned. Our contacts intensified and we became friends. The hearing persons learned much about Deaf culture. After the third course they realized that signed German was so artificial, and showed much interest in real sign language. I so much enjoyed their positive attitude towards our language. My beloved friends were so sad that there would be no occasion to learn it after the end of the courses. One student said that the courses should somehow continue. She and many others wished to become acquainted with other Deaf adults besides me. They wanted to learn the way that other Deaf people signed. Some kind of regular meetings should be organized. To say farewell, each of them gave me a bouquet so that I was swimming in a sea of flowers. I couldn't find enough vases in my appartment. There was no other choice: I had to put the flowers in the bathtub. For two weeks they prevented me from taking a bath, but I drank in the wonderful smell of the 'world of the Deaf', instead.

Enjoying this magnificent array of blossoms, I pondered a solution. I knew the Deaf very well. How could I attract them to a meeting with hearing persons? I knew for certain that Deaf persons would not come if they had to pay a fee. Immediately I put my plans into action. I talked to the director of the Vocational Training Centre of Munich, Ludwig Bartl, and asked him whether it would be possible to have a room – free of charge. He agreed and the first meeting between Deaf and hearing persons took place in the home for apprentices. The former participants of the courses eagerly anticipated it and the Deaf were full of curiosity. In order to avoid a stiff atmosphere, I tried to introduce 'popular' topics of conversation. I left them free to talk in sign language or with their voices. The attitude of the Deaf struck me immediately: as soon as they talked to a hearing person they automatically spoke aloud and without signs. This was due to their oral education in school. If, however, a Deaf person talked to another Deaf person they signed without speaking. They switched constantly between the two languages! I had some difficulties in convincing my Deaf friends that speaking aloud was superfluous because the hearing students had learned to sign. It took them some time to get used to the idea. The more they signed, the more the Hearing became aware of the difficulties in communication. However, they accepted not being able to understand the Deaf persons and nodded politely.

In this situation I remembered my schooltime. This acceptance was the typical attitude of my Deaf classmates; they nodded patiently even when they had not been able to understand the teacher. The mechanical nodding of the head reflected nothing but fear of exposing one's 'stupidity' or of provoking the teacher's next outburst of fury. Thus I asked the hearing students to admit honestly when they didn't understand what the Deaf partner had said. For the first time I saw them blush. 'That's it', I thought, 'I hit the mark!' I realized with astonishment that hearing people, too, try to hide the weak point in communication, the 'not-understanding'. This was very interesting to me. This is then a problem not only of Deaf people but also of hearing people. The linguistic handicap is equal! When I asked the hearing students why they didn't protest when they could not understand their Deaf conversational partners, they answered that it was a matter of tactfulness, they didn't want to interrupt Deaf people's conversation and disturb them. Then I told them what it is like for Deaf children with hearing adults.

After this exchange of experience other topics of conversation soon followed, which enriched the knowledge of both the hearing and the Deaf people present.

In June 1983, a Deaf socialworker, Wolfgang Schmidt, organized a weekend at the Kulturzentrum (cultural center) for the Deaf in Hamburg. Two Deaf experts from the United States had been invited. The topic of the workshop was 'nonverbal communication'. Burning with curiosity I travelled to Hamburg together with three hearing participants of our regular meetings. I was the only Deaf person in the group besides Schmidt, and I learned about a completely new world, shown to us by the Deaf Americans. The only means of communication were our bodies, gestures and mime. No speaking was allowed. We played group games and role-playing games, and were only allowed to pass on information to the others with 'speaking hands'. The hearing participants were extremely enthusiastic about this silent communication. For me, though, this was a completely new method, and I still couldn't understand that it could build the base for sign language. I still asked myself why the voice, the best means of communication for the hearing people, should be 'switched off' completely.

We had long discussions on this subject. Wolfgang Schmidt explained to me that visual training of the hearing could help them best to learn the 'real' sign language. The Deaf talk silently anyway! Besides this new discovery, I was greatly shaken by some new views about my own way of thinking. I had to completely change my usual attitude toward hearing persons. I should no longer consider them as occupying a 'higher rank'. A thousand questions spun through my mind, and I did not know what my mistakes had been. From that time on I began to reflect upon my disability and to examine it critically. It took weeks and years until I finally understood.

I owed this understanding also to the meetings for the publication of a new sign dictionary, which took place four times a year in Hamburg and Bonn (later in Frankfurt). After these meetings I always had time to discuss thoroughly the new self-confidence of the Deaf. Since 1984 there have been regular meetings with about 20 Deaf people fluent in sign language participating, who this time form the majority (in contrast to the *Blue Book*), and who come from several regions of Germany. Together with the editors Günter Maisch and Fritz Wisch, the group intends to publish a dictionary with seven volumes, subdivided according to subjects, with about 800 sign expressions. Many years of unpaid work on the weekends have been and will still be necessary to complete this collection. Herbert Feuchte is responsible for the financing of this publication. The general support of the Federal Ministry for Youth, Family and Health made possible the publication of the sign lexicon. Three of the seven volumes are on the market: *Basic Signs, Humans, Nature* (Maisch/Wisch (eds.) 1987ff). Others will follow in the years to come. There seems to be no end. These meetings have also led to the founding of a German Sign Language-teachers' group, which meets regularly. Thanks to Käthe George, head of the division for 'sign questions' in the German Federation of the Deaf, this group came into existence.

V

1984 was a year full of turbulence. Numerous seminars and meetings took place and the first exchanges of experience with other European countries were begun. Several sign groups were founded. In Munich many hearing people became increasingly dissatisfied with the method of signed German. Those who already had contact with Deaf adults complained about communicative difficulties using this method. They did not understand German Sign Language because it was so different from what they had learned during the courses. I became aware of this misguided development and began to think about a new teaching method. There still was no appropriate material to teach German Sign Language. I started to hunt for such material. The Landesverband Bayern der Gehörlosen (Bavarian Association of the Deaf) asked me to join the board and to supervise the promotion of German Sign Language in Bavaria.The first meeting was devoted to orientation and training of sign language teachers. Discussion seminars followed in February and May, which were organized by Dr. Inge Richter together with the managing director of the Munich Stadtverband for the Deaf, Rudi Sailer. He advocated a course for Deaf adults at the Munich Volkshochschule. Twelve Deaf people took part in the course 'How to discuss?' and learned, under the direction of a highly motivated hearing teacher, Mrs. Rieder, to express themselves. One of the exercises we had to complete was a speech before an audience, for which we chose a topic from the newspaper. We had to learn the forms and rules of a discussion. Another exercise consisted of giving our opinion about an animated film. The participants gave proof of an excellent faculty of observation. Even the teacher was astonished. This experience brought to my mind how much I had missed an exchange of opinion during my schooltime and at home. I realized that other Deaf persons also had the same difficulties in forming an opinion of their own.

In order to provide for variety in our Munich discussion circle of Deaf and hearing people I looked for an artistic occupation. For the first time we did exercises with signed songs. This was particularly difficult for the Deaf participants because they could not hear the rhythm of the music. Hearing people, however, helped in signing the songs they heard from a tape recorder. The Deaf saw this and participated with enthusiasm. These exercices created a good atmosphere of solidarity between the Deaf and the hearing people. At the end of the course we organized a big summer party at the Munich Deaf Association, at our own expense. We invited the boards of all Deaf clubs and the hearing participants of the sign language courses of the Munich Volkshochschule. The young theatre group 'Thow & Show' (Thow = **Th**eater **o**hne **W**orte, Theatre without Words) presented pantomimes and sketches from the daily life of Deaf people. The group that had learned the signed songs performed, too. It was a big success! A hearing guest described her impressions of the party in an article written for the *Deutsche Gehörlosen-Zeitung* which was entitled *Integration, the other way round (Integration umgekehrt)*. She wrote:

> *There was a cheerful and relaxed mood. The hearing guests were impressed to see that happiness, wit and humor does not depend on spoken language (...) that Deaf and hearing people laughed together – isn't this a sign of true mutual understanding?*
> (Schmitz 1984, pp. 240-241)

I was wholly satisfied with the success of our party and thought that Deaf and hearing people were finally in a position to establish contacts on their own and to build private relations. The hearing people could deepen their knowledge of sign language, something the Evening School for Adults could not offer. Then the summer vacations began.

After that I was astonished to find that neither the Deaf nor the hearing participants contented themselves with this summer party. 'It had been so nice, let us continue!', they said. Good heavens! How could I possibly arrange my already overloaded schedule to provide time for them? After short reflection I decided to continue. The conversation circle continued in September 1984 as part of the program of the Munich Volkshochschule. As before, the participants met after the classes in a restaurant. I saw how happy they were to be together. Incredible! One day we talked about the conversation circle becoming a permanent institution. It was founded on October 4th, 1984 in the apprentices' home of the vocational school. Soon we found a name for these meetings: the 'Kommunikationsforum', which seemed to be the first institution of its kind in the Federal Republic of Germany. The Munich Stadtverband of the Deaf soon accepted it as an initiative-group.

The first meetings of the Kommunikationsforum were held in German Sign Language. Deaf participants were very glad that they could understand everything and showed keen interest. Hearing participants, however, had great difficulties because they did not fully understand German Sign Language. They thought about leaving the Kommunikations-forum, and in spite of its youth, it was threatened with disintegration. I therefore introduced the total communication method as a period of transition and in order to help the hearing members to adjust to the Deaf community. This prompted them to stay, and in the course of time they acquired more and more knowledge in German Sign Language. The Kommunika-tionsforum's meetings comprise one monthly discussion meeting (we always choose a fixed topic, dealing with public relations, and follow fixed rules for the discussion) and con-versation meetings, on the other hand, that are rather free and easy and the participants choose their own topics.

VI

In 1985 the wind shifted to Hamburg where the first congress for sign language took place under the direction of the linguist Siegmund Prillwitz. This was a sensation in the German history of the Deaf. 1000 persons attended and heard for the first time: German Sign Lan-guage is an independent, fully developed linguistic system which should stand as an equal next to spoken and written German (see Prillwitz 1986). Pardon me? Unbelievable! We also learned that the promotion of sign language in Sweden was much more advanced than here, that it was recognized by law and that the training of Swedish Sign Language teachers and interpreters was subsidized. England and Denmark were also ahead of us, and espe-cially in the United States sign language was the natural means of communication for Deaf people. The situation in the field of pedagogy for the Deaf was discussed, and the negative attitudes of teachers for the deaf and dumb were laid bare. The reactions of the participants varied. I saw some hearing people, who until then had patronized the Deaf, listening to this news with horror. The Deaf waved their arms enthusiastically as a sign for 'hurrah'. They felt rescued. I myself was fascinated by this long awaited announcement, and thought of the unsatisfying teaching methods in the sign courses.

One month later, when the success of the Hamburg Sign Congress had become known, the Pfalzinsitut für Hör-Sprachbehinderte (Palatinate Institute for Children with Speech and Hearing Defects) in Frankenthal organized a counter-congress called Kongreß zum Erhalt der Lautsprach-Methode und deren Weiterentwicklung bei Gehörlosen (Congress for the Preservation of the Oral Method and its Development). Herbert Breiner, the director of the Pfalzinstitut, whom we consider as an oral fanatic and opponent of sign language invited professors from universities and directors of Deaf schools in Germany to speak. All the rep-resentatives of the pure oral method rejected the demand of the Hamburg Congress (that Deaf children should be encouraged to use sign language). They pronounced themselves firmly against the use of signs in kindergartens and in schools for the Deaf because they feared disadvantages with regard to learning the spoken language. The congress in Fran-kenthal was a closed event for experts responsible for the oral development of Deaf chil-dren. The Deaf were therefore excluded as 'incompetent speakers'. Some of them, a few functionaries of the Deutsche Gehörlosen-Bund (German Federation of the Deaf) and of the Landesverband Rheinland-Pfalz (Deaf Association of Rhenish-Palatinate), had applied to take part four weeks before, but on December 14th, 1985 they stood before closed doors. Some hearing teachers who had not registered in advance were still admitted. Robert Brück, vice-president of the German Federation of the Deaf wanted to speak on the topic 'Is the condemnation of signs proof of a hostile attitude against the hearing-impaired?'. This topic did not suit the organizers of the congress and they tried to exclude the Deaf. Robert Brück defended himself and he maintained his demand that some Deaf participants with inter-preters should be admitted. Nevertheless, the day of the congress the Deaf were refused. Only the energetic intervention of the President of the Deutsche Gehörlosen-Bund, Wolf-gang Czempin, opened the doors for them. Robert Brück started his well-prepared paper:

> *Those who contest Deaf people's use of the only means of communication they possess, namely signs, are extremely hostile to the disabled. Being Deaf, I am in a position to say with good conscience that the rejection of sign language is also a rejection and suppression of reality. The wheel of history is not to be turned back. We, the Deaf, demand a say in the question of the education of our small comrades in misfortune and we claim this right today!* (Brück cited in *Deutsche Gehörlosen-Zeitung* 1986, 1, p. 4)

These unmistakable words received much applause. Many teachers heard for the first time this day the point of view of the Deaf, and we hoped that they understood.

At the Kommunikationsforum's meeting one day somebody asked: 'Why are there so few articles about the Deaf in the newspapers?' From the discussion we came to the conclusion that the Deaf, since they had problems with the German language, rarely trusted themselves to write. Until then, the pedagogues and scientists had done it for them. And the journalists, who had little knowledge of the Deaf, provided the public with overall reports of little informative value. The specialized periodicals concentrated mainly on the problems of speaking and hearing, and how to compensate for their lack with technical aids. Too much had been written **about** the Deaf, from the point of view of the Hearing, and rarely **with** or **by** the Deaf.

The Kommunikationsforum decided to publish its own magazine. It was called *selbstbewußt werden (become self-confident)*. The first issue came out in December 1985. I also decided that Deaf authors should be allowed to write with all their mistakes in written German. Their personal opinion, their feeling of being 'socially handicapped' was more important than their mastery of German. Naturally this costs the Deaf quite some effort and they need strong self-confidence. The point of view of the Deaf is indeed different from that of hearing people who write about issues based on conversations with the Deaf. Deaf people can write about Deafness with more authority. The two groups have different experiences.

At first, I had a queer feeling when I wrote a text for publication without editing. I was afraid of having to deal with possible mockery or irony and lack of understanding. Thus I was all the more surprised by the unexpected echo. Numerous enthusiastic letters to the editor turned up in my letter-box! *This is finally the full truth we have been waiting to see for such a long time! (Das ist endlich die volle Wahrheit, worauf wir solange gewartet haben!)* Or: *Your information has done me a lot of good and I fully agree with your opinion! Do continue! (Ihre Information tat mir so gut, so daß ich Ihre Ansichten nur voll zustimmen kann. Machen Sie weiter so!)* These lines gave me a sudden incentive. At the suggestion of two hearing women, Sabine Schwarz and Andrea Schmitz, who had attended the Bad Godesberg seminary, *selbstbewußt werden* was also sent to public institutions such as charitable organizations, advisory bureaus of Deaf schools, scientific institutions with social and psycho-social sections, special-interest groups and the offices for the hearing-impaired. This was the beginning of a more intensified public relations effort, which was Andrea's particular interest. The public relations sector of the German Association of the Deaf asked her to start a collection with newspaper clippings containing reports about the Deaf in Germany. This was intended to become the basis for press releases. We are very lucky to have her here in Munich. She also told us much about the world of the hearing and established contacts with those who could open the doors to the public. Soon I noticed how valuable the publication of our magazine was. We got access to authorities or ministries, broadcasting companies or captioning services, parents' associations of the Deaf school in Munich. We learned how to write to official authorities and became aware that this work is nothing else but a political activity. Bit by bit the public began to listen to us.

A 1987 booklet of the Bavarian Ministry for Labor and Social Order (*Der Schwerbehinderte*) distributed to employers by the local Labor Offices in Bavaria, proved to be full of prejudices against the Deaf. It stated for example that language and emotion are linked and

Ill. 3: *An issue of the magazine 'selbstbewußt werden'*

that the Deaf, being linguistically poor are also emotionally poor. The Kommunikations-forum protested violently and as a consequence was asked by the Ministry to write a new chapter on Deafness. This text, written by the editorial staff of the magazine *selbstbewußt werden,* appeared in 1991.

The cooperation between five Deaf and three hearing persons editing the magazine had been excellent from the very beginning. We didn't feel any differences between us. We worked together as equals, we expressed our opinions and mutual and sincere criticism without reservation, discussed our mistakes and shared joy and sorrow. Pity? None of that! That was a foreign word for all of us! We formed the nucleus of public relations work within the Kommunikationsforum.

VII

The Hamburg Sign Congress of 1985 was followed by very stormy years and Deaf politics began to move foreward. The glamour of the highly valued ideal 'oral line' gradually van-ished. Two directions became visible: the trend toward the recognition of German Sign Language, and the continuation of the oral method. The established pedagogues, convinced of their success, clung to this method.

A Federal Association of Sign Teachers was founded in Bremen; soon afterwards the Gesellschaft für Gebärdensprache und Kommunikation Gehörloser e.V. (Society for Sign Language and Communication of the Deaf) was founded in Hamburg. In Munich, too, there was some stirring. A private group for sign language was set up; signed short stories were recorded on video tapes.

The Munich Stadtverband of the Deaf developed very well, thanks to the personal efforts of Rudi Sailer for adult education at the Volkshochschule. The interpreters, who translated these courses, even if they did not have perfect command of the language, made it possible for the Deaf to learn how to use a computer in different vocations, to expand their knowledge of politics, or to take part in art courses. Some new self-help groups such as a seniors club, a mother and child group, a theatre group and a parents group were founded. The Kommunikationsforum had its hands full with providing information to all of the groups on sign language and the identity of the Deaf.

After the *Munich Sign Paper* (Braun et al. 1982), had been published, and then disregarded by teachers at Deaf schools, the father of a Deaf child, Matthias Mala-Silbermann, filed a complaint at the Bavarian Constitutional Court. The proceedings took place on October 21, 1986. The plaintiff claimed that the Bavarian school regulations should prescribe the teaching of Deaf and hard-of-hearing children in sign language, and that the Bavarian Ministry for Cultural Affairs should issue a decree ordering the use of sign language in schools for the Deaf. He also claimed that the fact that Deaf persons were forced to use the language of hearing persons was an offense against human dignity (article no. 100 of the Bavarian Constitution) and against the right of free development of personality (article no. 101). In article 128 the right of education is granted to every citizen.[2]

The Bavarian Constitutional Court, however, ignored the action for the following reasons: the Ministry of Education is not obliged to issue an order prescribing that Deaf and hard-of-hearing children must learn sign language in the Deaf Schools. Furthermore the Court also cannot prescribe to the State which regulations it must enact, since the State is free to decide whether sign language is taught or not. The Constitutional Court is also of the opinion that the question of how important sign language may be, is not yet answered. The Ministry of Education, which is responsible for the curricula of the Deaf schools, views sign language not as an independent subject, but as a means of making the language of Hearing people easier for the Deaf and hard-of-hearing children. Learning the spoken language, therefore, should be given priority, in order to facilitate employment and professional life and contact with hearing people.

A success? Yes and no! Mr. Mala-Silbermann, the plantiff, said that it was at least a slight success, in that the judgement had not rejected the use of signs. The problem was that there was not enough proof of the importance of sign language in the classroom. The superficial view of the Court and the insufficient information and explanation in the press was also regrettable. Mr. Mala-Silbermann was very disappointed that the German Federation of the Deaf and the Bavarian Parents' Association had not supported his complaint, for fear of damaging their relations with the Ministry of Cultural Affairs. It is true that the Bavarian Federation of the Deaf had given financial help to Mr. Mala-Silbermann for legal expenses, but as plaintiff, he stood alone. From the entire episode, he concluded that the Deaf had to do their own work in actualizing the content of the judgement.

2 Art. 100: The dignity of the human personality is to be respected in the making of laws and the administration of justice.

Art. 101: Everyone has the freedom to do anything, within the bounds of the law and of good custom, that does not harm anyone else.

Art. 128: Every inhabitant of Bavaria is entitled to receive an education according to his recognizable abilities and his inner vocation.

In May 1987, the Zentrum für Deutsche Gebärdensprache und Kommunikation Gehörloser (Centre for German Sign Language and Communication of the Deaf) was founded at the University of Hamburg . With the financial help of federal ministries, they undertook research on sign language in theory and practice. The Centre also worked out a plan suitable for the whole Federal Republic for the training of interpreters and publishes a journal and book series on sign language and communication of the Deaf. Thanks to the help of Siegmund Prillwitz, some Deaf people are able to study pedagogy for the Deaf, sports, psychology etc. at the University of Hamburg. In view of the circumstances in Germany it was a great event that for the first time signing Deaf persons were included in the faculty of linguistics. Heiko Zienert, a Deaf man, was appointed lector. About 20 Deaf and another 20 Hearing people work on the Zentrum staff.

Since Deaf people had been able to reach better positions thanks to their mother tongue, a stubborn struggle arose within the German and Bavarian Federations of Teachers for the Deaf and Dumb concerning the recognition of German Sign Language as an important means of communication in the special schools for the Deaf. Many adherents of the oral method did not want to believe that German Sign Language, which they considered a primitive language with an insufficient vocabulary, could facilitate and accelerate the whole process of educating Deaf children. They held that German is a highly developed language which enables Deaf people to pursue a secondary education. In order to prevent the propagation of German Sign Language the oralists started to recommend the use of signed German, and thus to preserve at all costs the method of teaching in spoken language.

The German Federation of the Deaf, which had been a central organization without political activity for years since it was dominated by the welfare associations and the German Federation of Teachers for the Deaf and Dumb, found itself between a rock and a hard place in the struggle between the Centre for German Sign Language and most of the teachers. The political commitment still left much to be desired, and the young people's lack of interest for social politics was lamentable. There was no self-confidence at all among the Deaf citizens in Germany who should have given moral support to the Federation of the Deaf.

The 'little people' in the Deaf community caught something of the struggle in the 'higher-ranks', but they did not understand the significance and the effects of the political dispute over the recognition of German Sign Language which would contribute to the appreciation of the Deaf in our society. The opinions of the Deaf were divided. Congenitally deaf and prelingually deaf people were divided from the postlingually deafened and the hard-of-hearing. The hearing-impaired leaders with fluent speech and even those Deaf people who were 'obedient' shared the opinion of the oralists. Other Deaf people who had overcome the conflict with their disability or who were convinced that German Sign Language should be recognized banded together with the sign language teachers who had experienced the problems of teaching. The newly formed group of self-confident Deaf people was considered 'radical' by those who swore by the method of teaching in spoken language. This situation taught me to struggle for political reform.

As the appointed speaker for sign questions within the Bavarian Landesverband for the Deaf I also did my utmost to defend German Sign Language on the occasion of an information and working meeting of Bavarian sign teachers in Ingolstadt. But the majority of the Hearing-Impaired insisted on the method of signed German. Six months later I was suddenly dismissed without notice. For some time nothing was heard from the Landesverband, and gradually a schism between the North and the South of Germany developed. Whereas in the North the Deaf worked together with hearing people, discussing new directions in Deaf pedagogy and a certain success was evident, the South remained – much to my regret – behind the times. We had much difficulty with the obstinate leadership of Rudolf Gast in the Munich Stadtverband and the Bavarian Landesverband of the Deaf. He fully ignored the meetings where the evolution and research of sign language were discussed, and he did not attend the Kommunikationsforum. He ignored the information given by our magazine *selbstbewußt werden*. He stuck to the 'oral line' with signed German and maintained his contacts with the teachers for the Deaf and dumb. He spread the idea in Bavaria that sign language was primitive and out of place in the schools.

On April 4th, 1987 a symposion organized by the Stiftung zur Förderung körperbehinderter Hochbegabter (Foundation for the Sponsorship of Highly Gifted Disabled) took place in Hohenems/Vorarlberg. The *Liechtensteiner Grundsätze (Principles of Liechtenstein;* Kröhnert et al. (eds.) 1987) were drawn up stating the significance of signed speech,thus continuing to give priortity to spoken language over sign language.

In the same year the film *Children of a Lesser God* played in many cinemas in Germany. All of us, Deaf and Hearing, were struck to the core by this film. It shows what the Deaf wish: They want to learn to speak, but not at any price! In spite of this stirring film, the pedagogues remained unaffected and went obstinately on their way. Alas!

In 1988 the Bayerisches Staatsministerium für Unterricht, Kultus, Wissenschaft und Kunst (Bavarian Ministry for Education, Culture, Science and Art) revised the Richtlinien zum Einsatz manueller Kommunikationsmittel in Sonderschulen für Gehörlose (guidelines for the use of manual means of communication within the schools for the Deaf) and made some amendments. Nevertheless, the paper (Richtlinien 1988) stated that the oral method was to be retained and that signed speech was to be seen as a supportive means in the learning of spoken language. The teachers remained free to decide whether to sign with their class or not. These guidelines and the Liechtenstein paper showed that there was no progress in the South for better communication for Deaf children.

Our Deaf friend, Hans Busch, himself the father of two Deaf children, felt personally affected by the 1988 guidelines. Fed up with the stagnation in the promotion of German Sign Language in Bavaria, he decided to visit Rudolf Gast (deaf) and to talk to him. Soon he was appointed spokesperson for sign questions in the Bavarian Landesverband of the Deaf. Thus this vacancy was filled, 1 1/2 years after my dismissal.

The situation of interpreters became more and more critical in Munich. Several interpreters waited in vain for the training which had been promised by Rudolf Gast. Nothing had happened for a long time. Then Gerhard Schatzdorfer, a hearing free-lance film director at the Bavarian broadcasting company, himself one of the interpreters concerned, took the initiative to found the Landesarbeitsgemeinschaft Bayern der GebärdensprachdolmetscherInnen (Association of Sign Language Interpreters in Bavaria) on April 7th, 1989, following the example of North Rhine-Westphalia. Its aims were: the support of training and advanced training courses, the draft of a professional code, the recognition of German Sign Language interpreting as a profession, and the support of all efforts toward the recognition of German Sign Language. The Munich Evening School for Adults supported the group and offered weekend seminars for interpreters. Hans Busch, myself and other Deaf sign teachers were responsible for one advanced course.

Unfortunately even the interpreters in Bavaria were divided in two groups. One group refused to learn German Sign Language because they shared the opinion of Rudolf Gast that German Sign Language is primitive. They also did not want to accept the name 'Gebärdensprachdolmetscher' (sign language interpreter). They voted for the term 'Gehörlosendolmetscher' (interpreter for the Deaf), introduced by the Bavarian Landesverband of the Deaf because of the 'linguistic handicap' of the Deaf. The efforts of the Association were thus hindered instead of being furthered by the Landesverband, which organized its own center for interpreters, which also served as a job bank. The Bavarian Ministry for Labor and Social Order asked the Landesverband to work out a draft for the training of interpreters in cooperation with the University of Munich. Rudolf Gast himself sought out Deaf persons – without me because of my radicalism, and an advisory committee met at the University.

After the majority had recommended signed German as a topic for the courses, Hans Busch and Helga Voit convinced the members of the committee to accept sign language as a main subject. The plan was submitted to the Social Ministry and a sponsor had to be found to finance the project. In spite of the fact that Hans Busch had tried to explain the importance of sign language and bilingual education of children, the board showed no understanding. They were afraid that the teachers for the Deaf and dumb would once again close the door which had been opened at least a little bit, as soon as they heard the word 'sign language'. Irritated by this blockade of the Deaf leaders in our own ranks and by the submission to the teachers, Hans Busch published his opinion in several magazines (Busch 1990, pp. 33-35). This caused a great stir. Soon afterwards Rudolf Gast dismissed him from the Landesverband and the post was again vacant.

While the officials of the German Federation of the Deaf and the other associations and clubs continued to struggle, a ray of sun touched us in the spring of 1988. A resolution drawn up by a Regional Secretariat of the World Federation of the Deaf was adopted by the European Parliament in Strasbourg. It was decided to encourage the 12 member countries to legally recognize their sign languages, to which the Deaf had a right. It was recommended that funds be granted to each country for the promotion and development of sign language and interpreter training. The broadcasting companies were asked to provide more subtitles or interpreters and to use videotext. In the following year at the 3rd European Congress on Sign Language Research in Hamburg, the International Sign Language Association (ISLA) decided that each country should draw up a resolution according to the decision of the European Parliament and submit it to the World Federation of the Deaf.

VIII

Siegmund Prillwitz asked me to join his research center in Hamburg from October 1st, 1987 until March 31st, 1989, in order to study sign language in various German speaking regions. For this period I was exempted from my work at the Office of Land Surveying. According to his instructions I started a collection of signs in the Munich region and the Southern part of Germany. I travelled around video-taping interviews with Deaf adults born into Deaf families. I worked on the sign vocabulary and transcribed conversations. As a free lance worker I conducted my interviews mainly in Munich and travelled from time to time to Hamburg whenever consultation was necessary. During my participation in this project I learned much about linguistics, which gave me new insights. I also learned sociological and psychological aspects and scientific terminology. Aspects of word order of German Sign Language were analyzed and studied by means of the transcripts. All this was to serve as a basis for the training of sign language teachers and interpreters. Since 1990, the objective of developing and testing a course in GSL, as a basis for interpreter training, is pursued at the Hamburg Centre in cooperation with the Federal Association of Sign Language Teachers and the Sign Language Committee of the German Federation of the Deaf.

The knowledge that I acquired from that work made it clear to me why there were so many misunderstandings among the 'uninvolved' Deaf people in our country. Widespread misinformation was the reason. The functionaries with their one-sided, inflexible attitude had been too closely tied to the field of pedagogy, instead of entering the field of linguistics which could have given to them a new perspective.

At the Free University of Berlin, Horst Ebbinghaus and Jens Heßmann, together with a Deaf co-worker, Sabine Fries, had completed their two-year study of interpreting for the Deaf (Ebbinghaus/Heßmann 1989). Their next research project is being carried out in cooperation with the Hamburg Zentrum für Deutsche Gebärdensprache. The project is concerned with mouth patterns in connection with signing. A project at the University of Cologne is concerned with the training of interpreters and Deaf children's learning written

German language. And in Aachen: The Deaf researcher Horst Sieprath succeeded some time ago in getting access to the Institute of Germanic Studies, of the Aachen university. The professors were very much impressed by his report on Sign Language and decided to participate in research on the language. The project aims to develop bilingualism in schools for Deaf children.

And what about Munich? Unfortunately there was no progress here because of the very strong influence of our chairman, Alfred Braun, former chair of the Institute for Special Pedagogy (Pedagogy for the Deaf and Hard-of-Hearing) at the University of Munich. Helga Voit finally convinced him, though, that sign language should be taught to the future teachers at the Munich University. Thus in May 1990 I was appointed lecturer in German Sign Language. At the request of Alfred Braun, a course of signed German was also integrated in the curriculum in accordance with the Culture Ministry's guidelines for the employment of manual communication. This very much hinders sign language promotion. On the other hand I am very glad to have learned so much at the Hamburg Zentrum für Deutsche Gebärdensprache and thus to be able to contribute to promoting it. It is only a beginning, but I feel much more competent than before.

In October 1989 we experienced a turn of events within the German Federation of the Deaf. Ulrich Hase, who had just finished his law studies, became First President of the German Federation of the Deaf. This was a surprise and gave a new impetus to change the outdated structure of the Federation. The usual dictatorial leadership with its club fanaticism was remodeled into a modern democratic form of self-government. Several special committees were included in the plan of organization. This allowed the various experts more flexible cooperation and more scope. Ulrich Hase also organized a vote in order to find out what the delegates thought about the very much disputed recognition of German Sign Language. A large majority (74:26) voted in favour of recognition. The question whether the expression 'Gebärdensprachdolmetscher' (sign language interpreter) instead of 'Gebärdendolmetscher' (sign interpreter) or 'Gehörlosendolmetscher' (Interpreter for the Deaf) should be used was answered by a majority of 71:28 in favour of 'Gebärdensprachdolmetscher'. We were very happy about that and could finally see a more rosy future.

I was very much encouraged by this result, but on the other hand I was disappointed because of the stubborness of Bavaria and Baden-Württemberg. To the great regret of the Deaf in the southern part of Germany these federal states belonged to the minority. Again we felt a dictatorship hindering the efforts for progress. The representatives of the Association of the Deaf in Bavaria and Baden-Württemberg still disregard our claim in favor of German Sign Language.

Six years of constructive work in the Kommunikationsforum proved to be rewarding. I observed this on October 25th, 1990. Rudolf Gast, as chairman of the Munich Stadtverband of the Deaf, organized on his own a discussion about German Sign Language. Only members of the Stadtverband had been invited, no non-members, no friends. Nevertheless many came to the club center. Only the hearing adherents kept their distance. I was very astonished and happy to see suddenly so many Deaf people with self-assured behaviour on the stage. No trembling could be seen, but rather a demanding use of German Sign Language. The arguments were better than ever! Never before were there so many requests to speak. The leader of the discussion had a long waiting-list – nearly everybody wanted to speak. Unbelievable! A wonderful solidarity among the Deaf developed into a common agreement to struggle for the recognition of German Sign Language. No intimidation by the 'spoken word of authority' of the president could be seen in the eyes of the Deaf combatants.

It seems to me that I have been right with the rules I have used as a leader. I always have been a bit afraid of going in the wrong direction and compared myself with a shark or dolphin. If the leader swims in front of the pack and loses its orientation, she might mislead those behind her and strand them all. A certain sense of responsibility arose in my mind and guided me. Still more important is to criticize oneself and to recognize a mistake. That is not easy and I am now glad that my wishes have been fulfilled.

In spite of a generally positive trend in the Deaf movement, Germany still is a developing country with regard to sign language policy. There remains much to be done to reach the aim of justice for the Deaf. Sweden serves us as a model in Europe which we strive to equal. In a united effort and in solidarity we shall soon reach the aim.

As head of the Kommunikationsforum I do not want to forget to express my heartfelt thanks to the editors' group of *selbstbewußt werden* and to the loyal adherents who, in spite of the stormy and 'radical' reform, steadfastly assisted us.

(Andrea Schmitz cooperated in the English translation)

Appendix
The original German quotations:

p. 188

> Die Stimmung war gelöst und heiter. Für die Hörenden war es eindrucksvoll zu sehen, daß Fröhlichkeit, Witz und echter Humor nicht an die gesprochene Sprache gebunden sind (...) Daß Gehörlose und Hörende gemeinsam gelacht haben – ist dies nicht ein Zeichen von echtem Verstehen? (Schmitz 1984, pp. 240-241)

p. 190

> Wer aber Gehörlosen das einzige Hilfsmittel, über das sie verfügen, eben die Gebärden, streitig macht, der ist in höchstem Grad behindertenfeindlich eingestellt. Ich kann daher mit gutem Gewissen als Gehörloser sagen, daß die Absage an die Gebärde (...) auch eine Absage an die Wirklichkeit und eine Verdrängung der Realität ist. Das Rad der Geschichte läßt sich nicht zurückdrehen. Wir Gehörlosen beanspruchen in der Frage der Bildung unserer kleinen Schicksalsgenossen ein Mitspracherecht und dieses Mitspracherecht erlauben wir uns heute anzumelden. (Brück cited in *Deutsche Gehörlosen Zeitung* 1986, 1, p. 4)

p. 192 (footnote 2)

> Art. 100: Die Würde der menschlichen Persönlichkeit ist in Gesetzgebung, Verwaltung und Rechtspflege zu achten
>
> Art. 101: Jedermann hat die Freiheit, innerhalb der Schranken der Gesetze und der guten Sitten alles zu tun, was anderen nicht schadet.
>
> Art. 128: Jeder Bewohner Bayerns hat Anspruch darauf, eine seinen erkennbaren Fähigkeiten und seiner inneren Berufung entsprechende Ausbildung zu erhalten.

References

Braun, A./Donath, P./Gast, R./Keller, A./Rammel, G./Tigges, J. (1982) : *Kommunikation mit Gehörlosen in Lautsprache und Gebärde*. Bundesarbeitsgemeinschaft der Elternvertreter und Förderer Deutscher Gehörlosenschulen e.V. (n.p.) [abbreviated title: *Münchner Gebärden-Papier*].

Busch, Hans (1990): DGS - Nein Danke!; in: *Das Zeichen* 11, pp. 33-35.

Der Schwerbehinderte (1991). (Schriftenreihe des Bayerischen Staatsministeriums für Arbeit und Sozialordnung 11). München. 2nd ed. [The chapter on deafness (pp. 106-120) was written by the editors of the magazine *selbstbewußt werden*.]

Deutsche Gehörlosen-Zeitung (1/1949 sq.) Essen.

Ebbinghaus, Horst/ Heßmann, Jens (1989) : *Gehörlose, Gebärdensprache, Dolmetschen. Chancen der Integration einer sprachlichen Minderheit*. (Internationale Arbeiten zur Gebärdensprache und Kommunikation Gehörloser Bd. 7); Hamburg: Signum.

Kröhnert, O./Stiftung zur Förderung körperbehinderter Hochbegabter (Hg.) (1987): *Begabtenförderung jugendlicher und erwachsener Gehörloser im Spannungsfeld von Lautsprache und Gebärden. Bericht über das Internationale Symposium vom 2.-4.April 1987 in Hohenems*. Triesen: Frank P.van Eck.

Maisch, Günter/ Wisch, Fritz-H.(1987ff): *Gebärdenlexikon*. Hamburg: Verlag hörgeschädigte kinder, 3 vols. publ.

Mally, Gertrud (1978a): *Die Sprache der Hände. Grundaufbaustufe I*. München: Selbstverlag.

Mally, Gertrud (1978b): *Die Sprache der Hände. Grundaufbaustufe II*. München: Selbstverlag.

Mally, Gertrud (1980/revised version 1988): *Die Sprache der Hände. Erweiterungsausbau und Übungsheft*. München: Selbstverlag.

Prillwitz, Siegmund (1986): *Die Gebärde in Erziehung und Bildung Gehörloser. Internationaler Kongreß am 9. bis 10. November 1985 in Hamburg*. Hamburg: Verlag hörgeschädigte kinder.

Richtlinien für den Einsatz manueller Kommunikationsmittel in der Schule für Gehörlose (1988). Bayerisches Staatsministerium für Unterricht und Kultus, Bekanntmachung Nr. III/10-4/ 43156 vom 13.5.1988) München.

Schmitz, Andrea (1984): Integration umgekehrt. Hörende lernen die Welt der Gehörlosen kennen; in: *Deutsche Gehörlosenzeitung* 8, pp. 240-241.

selbstbewußt werden. Informationen für Gehörlose und Hörende (1/1985 sq.) München.

Starcke, H./Maisch, G. (eds.) (1975): *Die Gebärden der Gehörlosen. Ein Hand-, Lehr-, und Übungsbuch*. [called : The Blue Book.] Hamburg: Verlag hörgeschädigte kinder. 2nd ed. 1981.

Igor A. Abramov
Moscow, Russia

History of the Deaf in Russia

Myths and realities

Summary · Резйуме

For many decades it was considered that the history of the wide activities of Russian deaf people began only after 1917. However, studies of archives, historical documents and eye-witness stories show that the history of the Deaf in Russia originated, at the latest, in the first half of the 19th century, when the first educational institutions for the Deaf were founded. At the turn of the 20th century the Deaf started to widen their activities aimed at the creation of their own organizations in Moscow, St. Petersburg, Saratov and other Russian cities. At this time the Deaf took their first steps in liberating themselves from hearing people's guardianship. These activities began to influence the Deafs' upbringing, education and professional training.Deaf people's activities developed within the framework of the democratic reforms carried out by the Russian bourgeoisie at the beginning of the 20th century, but this democratic process was interrupted after the coup of October 1917. A myth began to be circulated suggesting that all the intellectual and cultural achievements that Deaf people had accomplished were only possible thanks to the new regime. Historical documents and eye-witness stories show, however, that the spiritual and cultural life of the Deaf in Russia has been strongly influenced by the rich intellectual and cultural heritage of Russian Deaf people of the beginning of the 19th century.

На протяжении многих десятилетий было принято считать, что история активной деятельности глухих в России началась после 1917 г. Однако исследования архивных и исторических документов, свидельства очевидцев доказывают, что история глухих России берет свое начало в первой половине XIX века, с момента образования первых учебных заведений для глухих. В конце XIX и начале XX веков начинается активная деятельность глухих, направленная на создание собственных организаций в Москве, Петербурге, Саратове и других городах России. В этот период начинает развиваться культура глухих: театральное творчество, творчество глухих художников, литературное творчество, среди них начали проводиться спортивные соревнования. Деятельность глухих таким образом развивалась в начале XX века в рамках демократических преобразований буржазной России. Однако, этот исторический процесс был прерван после переворота в октябре 1917 года. Создавался миф, что все интеллектуальные и культурные достижения глухих стали возможными благодаря новой власти. Фактически исторические документы свидетельствуют, что духовное и культурное вогатство глухих России находится под влиянием богатого интеллектуального и культурного наследия глухих России начала XIX века.

The situation of Deaf people has always depended on the social majority's attitude toward them. As mankind searches after knowledge, the viewpoints on the phenomenon and nature of deafness change. It is therefore impossible to study the history of the Deaf (for example, their education and training, the judicial recognition of rights, their yearning for independence and individuality) without considering mankind's universal history or the evolution of any people.

The 18th century is considered to be the century of enlightenment. It also marked the beginning of the organized education of the Deaf in Europe.

The history of the Deaf, taken as the science about their past and present, shows the historical and social trends in their development and their social status. The value of such studies lies in the fact that they allow us to analyze scientifically the contemporaneous situation of the Deaf and to try to forecast their development.

Since Russia is now suffering a fundamental breakdown of its political, social and economic system, Deaf people's concepts about their past, present and future are changing as well. Deaf people's ideas about their situation in society have developed exclusively under the influence of diverse myths, prejudices and misinterpretations. Only a few recent studies of historical documents and archives allow the truth to be established.

The forgotten 19th century

During most of the 20th century the official Soviet historiography has suggested to the Deaf the idea that their history began in 1917, i.e. at the coup d'état. The few books on pedagogy and history of the Deaf published in Russia since that time have created the myth that the Deaf were deprived of their human rights and were completely illiterate in the 19th and the beginning of the 20th centuries (*Reader on the History of Education and Training of Deaf Mute Children in Russia* 1949, p. 1). These books fabricated the myth that the education of the Deaf and judicial recognition of their capability originated in the Soviet period. It was a myth both that Russian deaf mute pedagogy was born at that time, as well as that Russian research and methods were supposedly the most advanced in the education and development of the Deaf.

The 19th century is covered by a fog of ignorance and oblivion for most of the Deaf in contemporary Russia. They ignore their history because there wasn't a single impartial work on the history of the Russian Deaf community of the 19th century published during the Soviet period. The study of historical documents and archives, however, shows that the 19th century was actually a century of enlightenment for the Russian Deaf, which was crowned with the recognition of their rights (Yenko 1903).

During the seven decades after 1917 the truth about the unprecedented activities of the St. Petersburg school for Deaf Mutes was covered up only because it was founded by the empress Maria Feodorovna, wife of the Russian emperor Paul I, in 1810 after the four year experiment of Deaf education in Pavlovsk (*The Education and Charity of the Deaf Mute in Russia* 1905, p. 200). The same fate was shared by the second largest school for Deaf Mutes in Russia, the Moscow school created in 1860, because its founder, teacher and director was Ivan Karlovich Arnold, a Deaf painter born in a noble family.

The first teachers of the Deaf in Russia were foreigners: the Polish pastor A. Sigmund and the Frenchman Jean-Baptiste Jauffret who was acquainted with the abbé Sicard, director of the Paris Institute for the Deaf (Lane 1984, p. 156). After J.B. Jauffret, the directors of the St. Petersburg school for the Deaf were the Frenchman Victor Fleury and the Turkish citizen George Gurtsev (Lagovsky 1910, p. 88). The St. Petersburg and Moscow schools for Deaf Mutes maintained close relations with similar European institutions. Thus they could adopt foreign initiatives in the education and development of the Deaf.

However, these schools had their own evolution. The activities of the St. Petersburg school were highly appreciated by the first president of the National Deaf Mute College in Washington D.C., Edward M. Gallaudet, who visited it in 1868.

Due to the positive results of their education at this school, as well as the obvious successes in their development, Deaf people were recognized as judicially capable citizens and were allowed to work as office employees on the same level as hearing people. This recognition of their capability and a series of their judicial rights were established by the provisions of the Code of Laws of the Russian Empire adopted in 1856 (*The Code of Laws* 1857). The first work on the judicial recognition of Deaf people's rights published in Russia was written in 1863 by the Deaf graduate of the St. Petersburg school, A. Sokolov (Sokolov 1863).

Time also has been unjust to the first Russian deaf teacher and the founder of the Moscow school for the Deaf Mutes, I. K. Arnold. Before he founded the school with his own means and charity donations, he studied the methods and techniques of European institutes for the Deaf (Arnold 1910). The Moscow school subsequently became one of the best educational institutions for the Deaf in Russia (*The Moscow Institution* 1906, p. 25). The school was named after I. K. Arnold when he was still alive; a rare honor even for an outstanding educator. But after 1917 his name was consigned to oblivion.

All the outstanding teachers of the Deaf and researchers of their problems were graduates of these two schools in St. Petersburg and Moscow. Both of the schools had rich libraries with thousands of books in many languages on the problems of Deaf people's education and development, their psychology and culture. The schools constantly exchanged with

Ill. 1: *Ivan Karlovich Arnold*

other European institutions information about educational problems. It would be imposssible to imagine their work without these fruitful contacts.

Their typographers published numerous books on the problems of the education and training of the Deaf. The first books, magazines and newspapers for the Deaf were edited there (Lagovsky 1910). The numerous studies of these problems as well as the schools' traditions and the experience they gained through their many activities for the Deaf in Russia served as a basis for the first national teachers' congresses in 1896 and 1903 in St. Petersburg which were dedicated to the problems of the education and training of the Deaf.

The St. Petersburg and the Moscow schools laid the foundations of the education of the Deaf in Russia and inspired the creation of similar schools in many regions. Had the development of these two schools not been interrupted in 1917, they would probably have become institutions of higher education like Gallaudet University in the United States.

At the end of the 19th century the level of education they provided allowed many of their graduates to study at the universities. These graduates later became businessmen, painters, engineers and teachers and founders of schools for the Deaf (Lagovsky 1910).

Thanks to their enlightening activities, the first organization for the Deaf in Russia was founded in St. Petersburg in 1906. A second similar organization was created in Moscow in 1912 and named after the founder of the Moscow school, I. K. Arnold. The first leaders of these organizations were graduates of the two mentioned schools.

The fact that the education of the Deaf still wasn't widespread at that time is explained in the following paragraphs about public education in Russia.

The Russian Deaf in the 20th century

By the beginning of the 20th century the level of the deaf people's social consciousness had become high enough to launch an intense fight for their unification and the creation of an All-Russian organization. There were numerous attempts to create an independent union from 1912 to 1917. This fight was crowned with the calling of the first All-Russian Congress of the Deaf in July 1917 (All-Russian Federation of the Deaf (ed.) 1985, p. 5).

However, the coup d'état of October 1917 redirected the march of history in Russia. From this moment the system of education of the Deaf, created over the course of the previous century by several generations of teachers, began to be destroyed. The achievements of the Russian Deaf Mute educators began to be underestimated and suppressed, since their work didn't coincide with the new system of moral and political viewpoints. Many Russian schools for the Deaf, including those in St. Petersburg and Moscow, owned large territories of land with large-scale farm facilities, workshops and publishing houses. They were reduced, destroyed and confiscated. No school has remained in the same facilities that it occupied before 1917. Virtually nothing has been saved of the rich libraries of the St. Petersburg and Moscow schools. The broad relations with the European educational institutions also ceased.

Originally, the education of the Deaf was grounded on the theoretical and practical legacy of the famous Russian teachers of the Deaf V. I. Fleury, A. N. Ostrogradsky, N. M. Lagovsky and S. S. Preobrazhensky. In the 1930s the only outstanding teachers of the Deaf who continued working was F. F. Rau, the director of the former Moscow Arnold school, a German by birth and pupil of Vatter. Since then there have been few outstanding teachers of the Deaf in Russia with only rare exceptions because the contact with the foreign educational institutions for the Deaf which had always played a positive part in the education of the Deaf in Russia was interrupted for decades during the communist period.

The education of the Deaf became part of the State Public Education System, notable for its uniformity of educational methods and techniques. The traditions and legacies of the best teachers of the Deaf have been ignored and forgotten.

Ill. 2: *Moscow School for the Deaf in 1906*

All of the Deaf community's attempts to create their organization were fruitless though they were ready for it. Only nine years later, in 1926, they got the opportunity from the communist goverment and managed to hold their first constitutional congress during the Soviet period. Nevertheless, from the beginning the Society of the Deaf has been under the constant control of the People's Commissariat of Social Welfare and later the Ministry of Social Welfare of Russia.This control was judicially lifted only 64 years later, in 1990, when the 14th congress of the Society approved a new charter. Thus, during all the decades of the Soviet regime, the Society was an appendage of the administrative commanding system which ruled the country. The All-Russian Society of the Deaf became virtually a structural subdivision of the State agencies of social welfare. It was not the Society but rather these agencies that determined policy toward the Deaf community. The local leaders in many towns and regions of Russia as a rule weren't elected by the Deaf, but they were picked by the authorities. More than two-thirds of all organizations of the Deaf in Russia were headed by hearing people who often had no knowledge about deaf people's problems. The main principle in assigning such bosses was their fidelity to the political and propagandistic course of the authorities.

Unfortunately, there was nobody in the country besides the All-Russian Society of the Deaf who was concerned with the Deaf people's problems. The State had declared the freedom of the Deaf and formally taken care of their problems, then virtually left them without attention. The All-Russian Society of the Deaf had therefore to take the road of self-sufficiency by creating enterprises where theDeaf could work. Their profit was used to build cultural clubs, and sport and health centers in different parts of Russia. At the same time, a part of this profit was discounted to the State budget.Thus the Society became a commercial organization where the deaf people's social problems, i.e., their education, training, the development of sign language, etc., were permanently kept in the background.

The fact that the building of the former Moscow Arnold school was occupied not by a school for the Deaf but by a district committee of the Communist Party represents a cruel twist of fate.

The Russian Deaf of the middle and second half of the 20th century know virtually no outstanding deaf persons who lived and worked before 1917. The isolation of the Russian Deaf from events in Deaf communities all over the world continued almost until the end of the 1980s. The last time the Russian press mentioned Gallaudet College was in 1913. We learned of the existence of Gallaudet University only 75 years later, on March 15, 1988, when the daily *Pravda* reported the victory of the students and staff in managing to elect a Deaf man, I.King Jordan, the University's president. This eloquent example shows the information vacuum in which the Russian Deaf found themselves in the 20th century.

The downfall of the myths and return to the legacy

We have seen how the history of the Deaf has been elaborated according to the official Soviet ideology and propaganda. When fundamental political, social and economic transformations began taking place in our country at the end of the 1980s, it was revealed that the early history of the Deaf had been abscured.

The return of their legacy and the denial of myths and distortions mean for the Russian Deaf the return of their personal dignity and self respect. The rich but unstudied heritage has great cultural and emotional importance for them. The study and spreading of the Deaf community's legacy will lead to the recognition of their cultural and spiritual world. Finally, it lays the foundation for the legal regulation of questions linked to Deaf people's lives.

Conclusions

Since the beginning of perestroika myths about the historical legacy of the Russian Deaf community have fallen apart.

It was then that the first information breakthrough took place. The Russian Deaf began avidly learning about the way of life and education of the Deaf in other countries. The news that a Deaf person became president of Gallaudet University for the first time in its history was a powerful incentive in their fight for their group-consciousness, personal dignity and their legacy.

The Russian Deaf were educated during the 20th century in submission to the authorities and suppression of personal dignity. The increasing contacts of the Russian Deaf with the Deaf communities of other countries, especially of the U.S., have allowed them to learn about many long unknown topics. Information about the numerous studies in the fields of sociology, psychology, pedagogy, culture and history of the Deaf carried out by specialists from various countries, has been a powerful stimulus for similar studies in Russia. These studies have set us on a course back to our historical, cultural and spiritual legacy.

Myths and prejudices must gradually fade away into the past. Our history must surpass the national borders and become part of mankind's universal history.

References

All-Russian Federation of the Deaf (ed.) (1985): *(History. Present. Perspectives.)* Moscow.

Arnold, I.K. (1910): *(Autobiography of the Founder of the Moscow School for the Deaf Mute Children.)* Moscow.

(The Code of Laws of the Russian Empire) (1857). St Petersburg.

(The Education and Charity Care of the Deaf Mute in Russia. An Historical Essay. Bulletin to Her Majesty, the Empress Maria Feodorovna's Board of the Guardians on the Deaf Mute People's Problems.) (1905) St. Petersburg.

Lagovsky, N.M. (1910): *The St. Petersburg School for the Deaf Mute 1810-1910. An Historical Essay.* St. Petersburg.

Lane, H. (1984): *When the Mind Hears: A History of the Deaf.* New York: Random House.

(Reader on the History of Education and Training of Deaf Mute Children in Russia.) (1949) Moscow.

Sokolov, A. (1863): *(Statute-Book about Deaf Mutes.)* St. Petersburg.

Yenko, P.D. (1903): *(A Compilation of Laws about the Deaf Mutes with an explanatory Dictionary enclosed.)* St. Petersburg.

Ill. 41: Victim of the oral method: misunderstanding and social conflict.

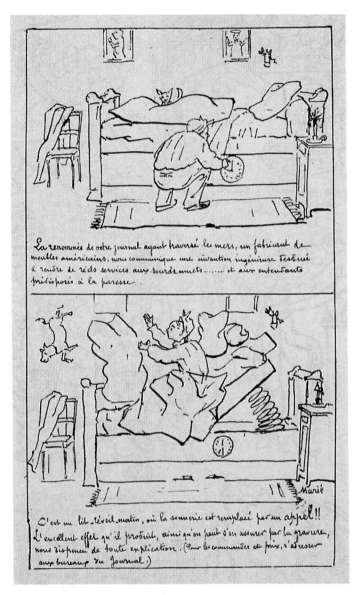

La renommée de notre journal ayant traversé les mers, un fabricant de
meubles américains, nous communique une invention ingénieure destinée
à rendre de réels services aux sourds-muets........ et aux entendants
prédisposés à la paresse.

C'est un lit-réveil-matin, où la sonnerie est remplacé par un appel !!
L'excellent effet qu'il produit, ainsi qu'on peut s'en assurer par la gravure,
nous dispense de toute explication. (Pour les commandes et prix, s'adresser
aux bureaux du Journal.)

Ill. 42: American novelty, says the French Deaf caricaturist: a piece of furniture destined to
waken up Deaf Mute and lazy hearing people...

Ill. 43: Proposing some sort of
Deaf telephone in 1932.

Sign Languages and Signed Systems

Signs of the Times

Ill. 44: Undoubtedly, this is one of the oldest representations of a non-religious gesture (in religious context): it shows a 'damned' person executing a sign probably meaning to keep away evil (early 13th century, Bamberg, Germany).

Ill. 45: Using signs at the Deaf school: 'Who did it ?' (see also ill. 46 and 47)

Ill. 46: 'Where are the scissors ?'

Ill. 47: 'Mirror'.

Ill. 48: On the occasion of a distribution of prizes, a pupil delivers a recitation in signs (about 1874, at the National Institution for Deaf Mutes in Paris, France).

Ill. 49: At a Deaf congress in France.

Ill. 50: At the swimming bath of the school for the Deaf in Paris, France, at the end of the 19th century.

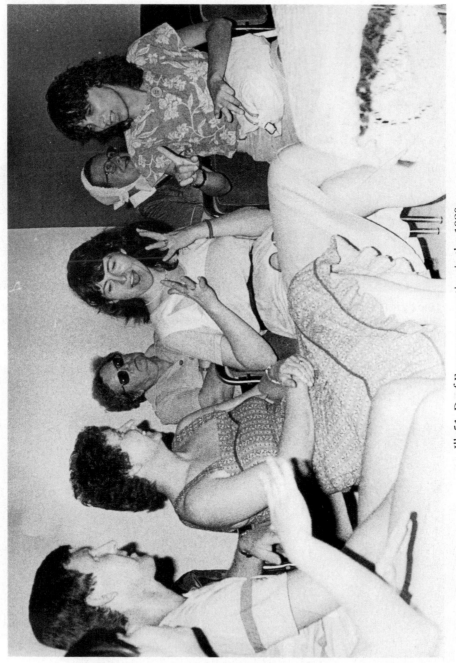

Ill. 51: Deaf Europeans meeting in the 1980s.

Ill. 52: Leipzig in1989: Minister to the Deaf Heinz Weithaas interprets the prayer for peace to the Deaf participants at one of those peace and protest assemblages which contributed to the ending of the German Democratic Republic.

Ill. 53: Deaf leaders and the press at the Gallaudet revolution in Washington, DC, USA, in March 1988.

Ill. 54: In the Deaf class at the Freinet school in Martignon, France, in 1990.

In the Dordogne at the Freinet school in Montpellier, France, in 1958.

Serena Corazza
Rome, Italy

The History of Sign Language in Italian Education of the Deaf [*]

Summary • Riassunto

The purpose of this study is to analyze the presence and use of Italian Sign Language in educational settings. In particular three historical periods are examined: from 1800 to 1880, from 1880 to 1960, and from 1960 to 1988. In each historical period, three issues are analyzed:
(a) the methods used by schools for the Deaf to respond to the needs of deaf children;
(b) attitudes in the Deaf community toward schools for the Deaf, and toward sign language;
(c) the role of Italian Sign Language in deaf education.

Questo lavoro vuole analizzare la presenza e l'uso della Lingua dei Segni Italiana nei contesti educativi. In particolare vengono identificate tre epoche: dal 1800 al 1880, dal 1880 al 1960, dal 1960 al 1988. Vengono analizzate in ogni epoca i seguenti aspetti:
(a) le risposte della Scuola nei confronti delle esigenze dei bambini sordi e le metodologie adottate,
(b) i diversi atteggiamenti della Comunità sorda nei confronti della Scuola per sordi e della Lingua dei Segni,
(c) il ruolo della LIS nell'educazione.

[*] I would like to express earnest thanks to: Anna Folchi, Jane Iverson, Paola Pinna, Elena Pizzuto, Laura Rampelli, Paolo Rossini, Virginia Volterra, as well as to my parents and the Deaf of Trieste, for their support and assistance.

A previous version of the paper has been presented at *The Deaf Way*, Gallaudet University, Washington, D.C., July 9-14, 1989.

Part of this work was supported by CNR FATMA grant for the Research Unit: *Deafness, Communication, and Stress.*

219

Introduction

The goal of this article is to explore Deaf education in order to understand the reasons that sign languages are both accepted and rejected by society.

Today, many Deaf people insist that sign languages should be used in schools, as this means of communication plays a vital role in permitting the young to pursue their academic programs. This conviction often emerges from the discussions that take place in the Deaf clubs I frequent in Italy, even if a great many Deaf individuals retain the feeling that 'school should instruct one to learn to speak and to speak well'.

In this survey, I have chosen to verify the presence of Italian Sign Language in education, without expressing a personal judgment about the methodologies used. I feel it is essential to research the problems concerning Italian Sign Language as thoroughly as possible (if it existed in schools; who used it; in what contexts). In my opinion, Deaf persons can develop a language whether it be spoken or signed, provided that they have the possibility of receiving an early and continuous 'input' in either language.

In seeking to understand the reasons behind the differing opinions expressed by Italian Deaf people and wishing to satisfy my own curiosity, I have gathered information on the education of the Deaf in Italy from 1700 to our time. For clarity I have subdivided the material into three time periods; of each period I have asked the following questions:
1. What did the institution offer?
2. Were the Deaf and the Deaf community involved in education?
3. How and when was Italian Sign Language used?

I 1800-1880: Overall picture

This first period precedes the Congress of Milan. At this time Italy was politically subdivided into many kingdoms, states, and principalities, and, naturally, many different languages were spoken. Early data concerning the education of the Deaf go back to Gerolamo Cardano (1501-1576) but he only reports information about the education of single individuals. It is only at the end of the 18th century that a school (more than one pupil gathered in one classroom) for the Deaf was created. The first Italian school for the Deaf was founded in Rome by Tommaso Silvestri (see Pinna/Rampelli/Rossini/Volterra in this vol.).

I.1 1800-1880: Schools for the Deaf

In the old texts I consulted, I discovered two types of information (see for example, Ferreri 1893):
–   data concerning residential schools for the Deaf: their location, organization, financing (see Ill. 1);
–   explanations of the teaching methods adopted.

Toward the end of the 19th century, of a total of 49 residential schools for the Deaf , 27 were co-educational, while the remainder were either exclusively male or exclusively female. In Modena, for example, there was a residential school for boys and another for girls. The number of pupils varied from school to school: some had only 34 (Modena) while others had as many as 107 (Naples).

The residential schools were financed by the state which payed for the pupils' tuition fees, by the provincial and community governments, or by funds from non-profit or charitable organizations.

According to a 1881 statistical survey all of the schools were organized as private boarding schools and only a few children could return to their homes in the evening. Together, all schools were able to accommodate a total of approximately 2,000 deaf

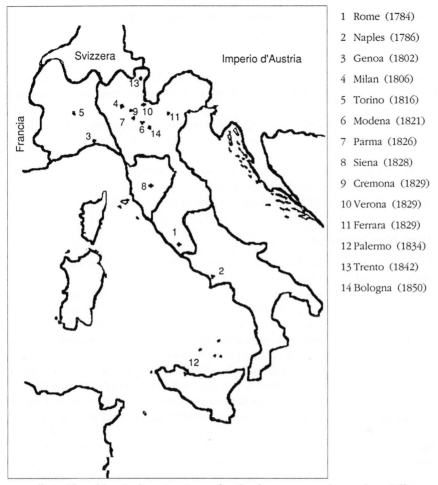

1	Rome (1784)
2	Naples (1786)
3	Genoa (1802)
4	Milan (1806)
5	Torino (1816)
6	Modena (1821)
7	Parma (1826)
8	Siena (1828)
9	Cremona (1829)
10	Verona (1829)
11	Ferrara (1829)
12	Palermo (1834)
13	Trento (1842)
14	Bologna (1850)

Ill. 1: *The oldest Italian institutes for deaf mutes were located in different states*

students. Based on the number of deaf persons who needed instruction (recorded at the time as about 4,000), Ferreri, in the aforementioned text (1893, p. 39), requested the government to construct 17 more residential schools.

In the residential schools the Deaf were given a basic education and were also taught a number of manual activities.We will discuss the methodologies employed later in relation to sign language.

I.2 1800-1880: The Deaf

As mentioned by Lane (1984), in the 19th century, there was an active debate among deaf people in France over educational methodologies and over the use of sign language, while in the Italian Deaf community these discussions were apparently non-existent. Ferreri's book, however, mentions works toward the mid-nineteenth century written by Deaf authors: Paolo Basso (1834), Giacomo Carbonieri (1858, 1870a, 1870b) and Giuseppe Minoja (1852). I therefore found it very important to retrieve these texts, and with the help of other Deaf collaborators I was able to find texts by two of the authors mentioned by Ferreri.

In his book Giacomo Carbonieri illustrates different types of deafness, characteristics of each type and their differing needs (Carbonieri 1858). Remarkably Carbonieri wrote that sign language is essential for the intellectual performance of the Deaf. Carbonieri is mentioned as a teacher at the residential school of Modena by Giuseppe Rota (1879, p. 202), but we were not able to gather more information about him.

The other Deaf author, Paolo Basso recounts the life of his friend Ottaviano Gonella who was able to understand religion thanks to the education he received at the residential school for Deaf in Genova, directed by Ottavio Assarotti and could confess and pray in sign language (Basso 1834).

We are still finding difficulties in retrieving Guiseppe Minoja's texts, but we know, from other texts (Agnelli 1964, p. 270), that he was also a teacher, and the founder of a school in Lodi (Milan).

Although these authors have been nearly forgotten, their writings testify that in the 19th century there were Deaf people who were involved in education. Unfortunately no precise mention of the methodologies has been found to date in their writings.

I.3 1800 -1880: Sign language

For the above reasons, in regard to the methodologies, I can only evaluate what the hearing educators have reported on the subject.

It is obvious from these essays that from the end of the 18th century to around 1860, the 'méthode de L'Epée' was highly respected by Italian educators (Lane 1984; Facchini 1981). For example, we have rediscovered (thanks to the late G. M. Facchini) a grammar book for deaf mutes by Marzullo, dated 1857. The book illustrates signs created intentionally to teach grammar, or, more precisely, to teach certain parts of speech (see Ill. 2).

The existence of this book clearly indicates that the so-called 'analytical' or 'methodical signs' were not only used in French schools, but also in Italian schools. It is not known whether this form of signed system (somewhat comparable to the present signed Italian adopted by bimodal education) was used exclusively for the teaching of Italian grammar or generally during in-class instruction. We do not know if in the teaching of the various subjects the educators used methodical signs or if they communicated in a true sign language. It would appear that the objective of the educators was, above all, to teach the Italian language and thereby to teach other subjects. I am inclined to call this sign system a kind of 'expanded Italian'. If one closely studies the 'Marzullo signs', one can deduce that their purpose was to inform the pupils about the type of rules of Italian to be learned and understood. These were not signs that could be used in general communication.

The author himself suggests what he considers to be the 'fairest' method to be followed by the young teachers:

> (...) The teacher must know his pupil: study his gestures, his jokes, his mimicries, in short, all the 'chironomia' of the mute language used by the student himself, which, through frequent practice, will eventually become common to both. (Marzullo 1857 p.v)

I doubt that these educational methodologies would yield even feeble results today, since we are now aware (see Supalla 1989) that the use of method signs such as signed English does not favor a normal process of successful language acquisition and development. On the other hand, these methodologies using some form of signed language might have seemed very successful at that time possibly because the Deaf easily learned the rudiments of the Italian language and then were capable of receiving effective instruction with the aid of lip reading. We should remember that at that time the illiteracy level of the hearing population was very high (in 1861, for example, 78% of the Italian population was illiterate), and that the Deaf, who received only a basic education, were more privileged than a great part of the rest of the population.

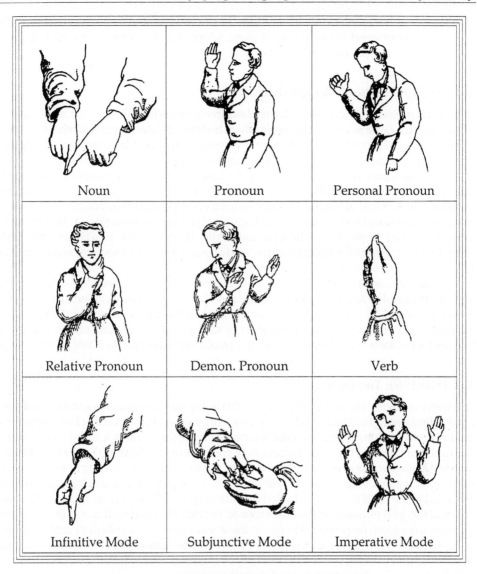

Ill. 2: *Analytical signs (segni analitici del discorso;*
from Marzullo 1857, table V)

II 1880-1960: Overall picture

At any rate, the failure or success of their methods might have influenced the educators to change their systems. As a matter of fact, after 1860, the influence of the German method became more and more pronounced, culminating in the triumph of oral language at the Milan Congress in 1880.

Traditionally, the period of 'pure oralism' began in Italy at this point and has continued to the present. Facchini (1981, 1985) very effectively described the political, religious and pedagogical reasons which resulted in this choice. I feel it is advisable to subdivide the 'pure oralism' period in Italy into two parts: first from 1880 to 1960, and second from 1960 to the present time; the first attempts to introduce deaf pupils into classes that were until then only for hearing children began in 1960.

Regarding the first phase of pure oralism, I have already stated that many educators who were 'firmly convinced' about the use of signs, adopted, to the contrary, the idea of *giving first priority to the spoken word and to lip reading* (Ferreri 1893, p. 24).

II.1 1880-1960: Schools for the Deaf

During this period, educators struggled to obtain recognition from the Italian state of the right of the Deaf to receive an education, a right which had already been granted in other countries. Ferreri (1898, p. 17) claims that the Ministry's ' passing of the buck', lasted for such a long time because of financial difficulties and difficulties on pedagogical and didactical levels.

The Italian government considered that it had accomplished enough by establishing one school for instruction of the Deaf in Milan (!). Actually, a government survey in 1887 affirmed that in certain areas of southern Italy only 4% of the Deaf were educated (!), while in other areas, no Deaf individual received any kind of formal instruction. At that time, the census counted 15,300 Deaf children and adults (Ferreri 1893, p. 41), and the 2,300 attending the residential schools are to be considered lucky even if they received instruction by the pure oral method.

Obligatory instruction for the Deaf was initiated during the period 1923-1928 with the reform instigated by Minister Gentile, who planned a non-obligatory kindergarten (for 6- to 8-year-olds) and an obligatory elementary school (for 8- to 16-year-olds). During those years, in addition to the residential schools (3 state and 80 private and religious), special classes for the Deaf were created within the public schools (Pizzuto 1986, p. 105).

II.2 1880-1960: The Deaf

It is important to mention that, in the early 1900s, lay and religious associations had been established among the Deaf in Italy; these associations were then united in 1932 to form the National Association of the Deaf (Ente Nazionale dei Sordomuti, E.N.S.). This clearly shows the need the Deaf had for a place where they could meet. The birth of these associations is probably linked to the necessity the Italian Deaf felt to communicate freely in sign language (thus sharing knowledge and especially culture), an opportunity which had been so long impeded in the residential schools. Perhaps the purpose of the strict oralist education had reached the goal pursued by the educators: to provide the Deaf with 'a complete thought process' in order to be prepared to set up these associations as symbols of autonomy and independence. It should be remembered that at that time various types of clubs, circles, and associations were being created all over Italy by classes of mostly hearing workers trying to validate their own rights by means of mutual solidarity.

I believe it is my duty to mention that the leaders of the Deaf Associations knew the spoken and written language well and often played the role of 'teacher' for the other Deaf members. What needs to be emphasized is the effort made by the more instructed Deaf to educate, or, better still, to assist those Deaf individuals who had left the academic structures with a very modest education.

The unification of the Deaf Associations marked the birth of the E.N.S., which, after the Second World War (thanks to the determination of Antonio Magarotto), organized, among other programs, professional courses for book binders, printers, etc. These programs were organized in order to demonstrate that the Deaf were capable of learning even those professions requiring a higher level of education (for example, all activities related to the press, in which a good knowledge of the written language was necessary). To qualify for these professional courses, the students often had to take supplementary courses which were also organized by the E.N.S. (the educational level of most of the participants corresponded to an elementary school diploma).

Since the objective of the courses was to combine professional competence with manual skills, sign language was not prohibited. Moreover, some of the teachers (such as Magarotto himself) were deaf. These courses were recognized by the state and were taken by students from the residential schools and by students from the special classes in regular schools where the apprenticeship of manual activities was nearly non-existent.

Later (around 1957), the E.N.S. organized secondary schools for the Deaf. These schools were in addition to the mandatory schooling prescribed by the law, and the curricula they offered did not exist within the residential schools nor as special classes. The E.N.S. wished to show that, contrary to the opinion of the educators, who merely granted the Deaf the possibility of receiving a basic education, the Deaf could continue their studies at a higher level. The aim of the Deaf was no longer just to be able to get by, but to have a higher education.

II.3 1880-1960: Sign language

It is not known if during this time signs, or say, the visual-gestural mode of communication used among the Deaf was permitted or prohibited in the residential schools. It is known, however, thanks to the testimony of some elderly Deaf persons (see Pinna et al. in this volume), that the ban on sign language began to grow more strict from 1920 on. This 'ban' could vary from one school to another; in some residential schools signs were prohibited during lesson hours, but the children could use signs to communicate with each other outside the classroom. In other residential schools, signs were totally forbidden, both in class and during recreational time. There could be differences in the same residential schools between the girls' and the boys' sections. Sometimes the nuns enforced a stronger ban with respect to the girls, while the boys enjoyed a greater liberty in gestural communication (see the interviews in Pinna et al. in this volume).

In the residential schools, outside the academic classes, students participated in courses in manual activities as apprentices in the arts and trades: shoemaker, carpenter, tailor for the boys; sewing, embroidery for the girls. Sometimes the instructors were Deaf adults who used signs, and even when the instructors were hearing, they often used gestures when teaching manual activities.

Thus it happened that even in the fortress of oralism, gestural communication retained its importance, even if it was limited to manual activities (signs also are a manual activity!). But signs were not permitted to enter the 'temple' of the academic classroom where the pupils received, in a manner of speaking, their 'true' instruction by means of the spoken word.

The institutions created by the E.N.S. also enhanced the opportunity to use sign language in education. Signing as a form of communication seems to be impossible to take away from the Deaf, in spite of all the oralist educators' efforts to do so.

III 1960-1988: Overall picture

Statistics from this time show that the academic situation of the Deaf was not the best: a national census taken in 1955 indicates an illiteracy rate among the deaf of 53%, compared to an 8.4% illiteracy rate among the Italian population in general (ISTAT 1965; Pigliacampo 1982; Pizzuto 1986). Of course, we should question the method by which the rates were determined, and also the significance of the term 'illiterate person'.

III.1 1960-1988: Schools for the Deaf

Attendance at secondary school became obligatory (for hearing as well as Deaf pupils) with the academic reform of 1962, which forced the residential schools to open higher level classes.

During the entire period following the war (1950-1970) – in spite of the fact that compulsory education of the Deaf had been extended, that new Deaf schools had been established, and that there was great involvement of the medical world and other related fields in research on deafness – the educational methodologies tended to change slowly. The teaching staff had no academic degrees or appropriate basic preparation, and very often did not manage to truly adapt new methodologies or technologies. In general, Deaf schools were not capable of keeping pace with the changes that were occurring in Italian society during that time. Deaf children still received an education of very low quality, considering their potential and their abilities.

In an attempt to provide Deaf children with better education, in 1977 law 517 was passed – a blessing, or a curse? This law declared that every handicapped child (including the Deaf) could attend the same schools as non-handicapped children (Pagliari Rampelli 1986, p. 14). By means of this resolution, Italian society wished to enhance the right of the handicapped to education by granting them complete equality, and to free them from isolation by letting them take part in society.

What did this law signify for the Deaf? With the passage of this law, families of Deaf children had, and have today, the possibility of choosing between the residential schools, the special day schools for the Deaf, and schools for the hearing. Special classes for the Deaf in regular schools were abolished. School age begins at three years with kindergarten, which is optional. Elementary school (ages 6-10) and secondary school (ages 11-13) are obligatory and equal for all. Once the academic 'itinerary' is completed, the Deaf student, like any other student, can enroll, if she or he wishes, in high school and later in a university. The state guarantees the Deaf child a teachers'-aid for several hours a week, but only for the duration of the obligatory academic period. People are beginning to discuss now the advantages of having this support in the high school as well. The elementary and secondary schools for the Deaf, public as well as private, are fewer now than before, since most families prefer to send their children to schools for the hearing. But there are three trade schools of higher education reserved for the Deaf (Torino, Padova, Rome), established by the E.N.S. and now state-owned.

III.2 1960-1988: The Deaf

During this period, the Deaf community protested law 517 of 1977, but could not do much to change it. At the same time many associations of parents of the Deaf were formed with the objective of giving decent schooling to their children but absolutely excluding sign language. To be honest, many of these children whom I have met were able to acquire considerable linguistic competence through spoken Italian; perhaps it should be pointed out, though, that it was their parents who were their first teachers. But these children even though they are Deaf like us, feel uncomfortable and are unable to communicate with other Deaf people since they do not know Italian Sign Language. It is almost as if they were 'foreigners' both with the Deaf and with the Hearing.

My personal experience with schools dates back to those years before 1977 and includes every kind of school: kindergarten with the hearing and, later, with the Deaf; elementary school in a residential school for the Deaf (two years) and then in a special class for the deaf within a school for the hearing; finally, secondary education in a school for hearing children and in an art high school for hearing students. I can testify that, at the residential school, the academic program was less challenging than the program of the special classes (I remember being very bored at the residential school), while the methods and the preparation of the teachers were nearly identical. I use Italian Sign Language inside the classrooms of the residential education, whereas in the special class, Italian Sign Language was prohibited (people there dubbed me 'monkey'). As for the elementary school and the high school with hearing students, I never encountered any difficulties with the school program except in written Italian (my oral grades, to the contrary, were good). Although I was the only Deaf student in the class, I encountered no problems at all with my fellow students; quite the contrary - I was their tutor in geometric design (for pay!).

III.3 1960-1988: Sign language

Italian Sign Language is obviously used only in schools for the Deaf (private or state-owned), even if it is not included in the didactic programs. No opportunity is granted to the Deaf to learn Italian Sign Language, or especially to know other Deaf persons, while they attend the hearing school. It is not my intention to discuss the results of this educational system, since they have already been reported by teachers, doctors, speech therapists, audiologists, parents, and by the Deaf themselves in recent meetings and conferences (*Atti* 1988, for example).

If the teaching personnel were all intelligent and all Deaf children were prodigies, law 517 could theoretically realize its full potential. I am in favor of children attending a normal school because it gives them the opportunity to remain at home, but the family circle requires communication. This communication will usually be vocal, as vocal as the communication required by teachers and fellow-students in school. This means that the deaf child is 'condemned' to use vocal communication with non-deaf people throughout the entire day. This is a true condemnation since Italian Sign Language is very important for the development of linguistic competence and for the acquisition of a true identity, as linguistic, psychological and sociological research carried out in various countries, and recently in Italy, has demonstrated. Research accomplished at the Institute of Psychology of the National Research Council (Consiglio Nazionale delle Ricerche, C.N.R.), for example, in the last few years (Pagliari Rampelli 1986; Caselli/Pagliari Rampelli 1989, p. 53), shows that today Deaf children attending special schools or mainstreamed in normal schools acquire a linguistic competence in both Italian and Italian Sign Language inferior to linguistic competence in Italian of hearing schoolmates of their own age (although, there should be further investigation about Italian Sign Language competence). This shortcoming, which could have serious consequences for intellect and personality, was completely foreseeable. Among all children, Deaf or hearing, there always has been and always will be a kind of competitiveness, a need to confront themselves, to challenge their own ability and competence. Deaf children cannot satisfy this need in today's mainstreaming.

In evaluating the effectiveness of a Deaf child's education, several factors must be considered such as, the participation and involvement of the family, and the preparation of class teachers and teacher's-aids.

Conclusion

What I have related up until now is the product of my personal experience and of research using historical documents, as well as testimonies gathered from Italian Deaf persons. I hope that it will serve as a stimulus for debate and informational exchanges on the topic of Deaf education.

It is clear that, in order for Deaf children to receive a good education, there must be close collaboration between family, teachers, and Deaf individuals.

Linguistic ability can develop for both comprehension and production only when there is spontaneous exposure to a natural language. By natural language I mean, for example, the Italian language (auditory-vocal modality) or the Italian Sign Language (visual-gestural modality). I do not consider natural language (for instance) signed Italian, a signed system that follows the grammatical order of the Italian language and which I prefer to call 'expanded Italian'. For further information about this concept, I recommend the account by Supalla 1989 who treats this problem of 'false language' in greater detail.

As I said earlier, even among the Deaf there are two divergent opinions: some insist that Italian Sign Language is indispensable in Deaf children's education in order to develop their optimum potential and intelligence; others believe that the school should teach the child to speak well because the student must know written and spoken Italian perfectly in order to receive an education.

It should be kept in mind that the Deaf who greatly insist upon the importance of 'speaking well' are the so-called 'speaking Deaf'; they are better educated, and were usually not born deaf but became so later in life. The time of life when one becomes deaf is critical as it is closely linked to the development of linguistic competence: the later one becomes deaf, the easier oral education will be. If someone becomes deaf after 4 or 5 years of age, it means that she or he will have already acquired a certain linguistic competence. In this case the task of the educators consists of 're-education' (*reeducazione dei bambini sordi* denoting the teaching of spoken language vocally and in writing). The word 're-education', so dear to educators, is totally inappropriate if used with respect to children born or having become deaf before two years of age. If they have not received a linguistic 'input', it will not be a question of 're-education' but only of 'education' – of providing them with the linguistic competence they could not develop. Unfortunately, this information was not well known until recently and, as a result, many deaf children living in the country, far from urban centers, only began their 're-education' at the age of six or later.

The Deaf who are in favor of Italian Sign Language are usually born deaf or are aware that they have gained more knowledge through Italian Sign Language. They think it is important to know sign language well before learning spoken and written language.

So I have found differing opinions expressed by Italian Deaf people regarding education: some are in favor of the use of sign language in educating deaf children while some feel that schools should continue the traditional oral method of instructing Deaf children to speak. My impression is that Deaf people are strongly influenced by their personal experiences. Despite these differences, it seems to me that both sides are pursuing the same goal: to provide Deaf children with a better education and more academic opportunities.

Appendix
The complete original Italian quotation:

p. 222

> Quegli poi che animo gli educatori italiani ad abbandonare la mimica e a dare nell'istruzione dei sordomuti il primo posto alla parola orale e letta dal labbro fu l'ab. Serafino Balestra il quale viaggiando nel 1867 in Svizzera, Belgio, Olanda e Francia si persuase che la parola pot-era darsi in generale a tutti i sordomuti. (Ferreri 1893, p. 24)

References

Agnelli, G. (1964): *Lodi ed il suo territorio, nella sua storia, nella geografia e nell'arte*. Milano: Edizione Pierre.

Atti del Convegno: Il problema dei Sordi e la Scuola. (1988). Bologna: Istituto Gualandi.

Basso, P. (1834): *Cenni su la vita e l'avventurata morte del giovane sordo-muto Ottaviano Gonella*. Torino: Per Giacinto Marietti

Carbonieri, G. (1858): *Osservazioni sopra l'opinione del signor Giovanni Gandolfi, prof. di medicina legale nella R. Università di Modena, intorno ai sordo-muti*. Modena: Tipografia di Carlo Vincenzi.

Carbonieri, G. (1870a): *Due parole a giustificazione di offesa personalità*. Modena: Coi tipi di Carlo Vincenzi.

Carbonieri, B. (1870b): *Risposta alle conclusioni dell'avv. prof. Cavagnari*. Modena.

Cardano, G. (1663): *Opera Omnia*. Lione.

Caselli, M.C. / Pagliari Rampelli, L. (1989): Il bambino sordo nella scuola materna: interazione e competenza linguistica; in: *Età evolutiva*, 34, pp. 51-62.

Facchini, G.M. (1981): Riflessioni storiche sul metodo orale e il linguaggio dei segni in Italia; in: V. Volterra (ed.): *I segni come parole*. Torino: Boringhieri.

Facchini, G.M. (1985): An Historical Reconstruction of Events Leading to the Congress of Milan in 1880; in: Stokoe, W./Volterra, V. (eds.): *SLR '83*. Proceedings *of the IIIrd International Symposium on Sign Language Research*. Silver Spring: Linstok Press and Rome: I.P. CNR, pp. 356-362.

Ferreri, G. (1893): *L'educazione dei sordomuti in Italia*. Siena: Tip. Edit. S. Bernardino.

Ferreri, G. (1898): I Sordomuti e l'istruzione obbligatoria; in: *Estratto dagli atti del primo congresso di beneficenza dei sordomuti*. Milano: Tipografia Pulzato & Giani, pp. 1-23.

I.S.T.A.T. (Istituto Centrale di Statistica)(1965): *Annuario statistico dell'istruzione italiana*. vols. 15 and 16.

Lane, H. (1984): *When the Mind Hears. A History of the Deaf*. New York: Random House.

Marzullo, C. (1857): *La grammatica dei sordo-muti*. Palermo: Tipografia di Michele Amenta.

Minoja, G. (1852): *L'integrazione possibile. Una ricerca sull'inserimento dei disabili sensoriali*. Milano: I.R.R.S.A.E. Lombardia.

Pagliari Rampelli, L. (1986): *Il bambino sordo a scuola: interazione e didattica*. Rapporto Tecnico, Roma: Istituto di Psicologia - CNR.

Pigliacampo, R. (1982): *Indagine medico-socio-culturale su soggetti affetti da sordomutismo e sitazione dell'inserimento dei sordi gravi nella scuola ordinaria*. Recanati: USL 14.

Pizzuto, E. (1986): Italy. In: J. Van Cleve (ed.), *Gallaudet Encyclopedia of Deaf People and Deafness*. New York: McGraw-Hill Books, pp.105-109.

Rota, G. (1879): *L'emancipazione dei sordo-muti*. Trieste: Tipografia e Calcografia di G. Balestra & C.

Selva, L. (1973): *Scuole e metodi nella pedagogia degli anacusici*. Bologna: Scuola Professionale Tipografia Sordomuti.

Supalla, S. (1989): Equality in Educational Opportunities: The Deaf Version. Paper presented at *The Deaf Way*, Gallaudet University, Washington D.C., July 9-14, 1989.

Odd-Inge Schröder
Oslo, Norway

Introduction to the History of Norwegian Sign Language

Summary • Sammendrag

Through a brief review of the older part of the history of Norwegian Sign Language (NSL) we discover that there is still very little we know about what this language really looked like. We read of the conflict between the natural desire of Deaf people to use sign language and the desire of hearing schoolmasters to 'normalize' the Deaf, i.e. to teach the Deaf to speak. It is possible that the emphasis on oralism was strong in Norway, seen in relation to other Nordic countries, since there was an early movement towards signed Norwegian. Throughout this paper there is one important problem which emerges. How reliable are the written sources? Is it possible to rely solely upon an oral tradition based upon doubt, pride and self-hate? How is one to research a language when the only available descriptions of it are in another language, namely written Norwegian? In essence: This paper is **about** NSL, not a diachronic description of NSL because of the lack of materials.

Gjennom skisseringen over den eldste del av historien til norsk tegnsprog (NTS) oppdager vi at det fortsatt er lite vi vet om hvordan dette sproget så ut. Vi leser om konflikten mellom døves naturlige trang til å bruke tegnsprog og de hørende skolemestres ønske om normalisering av døve, dvs bli talende døve. Kanskje vektleggingen av det orale ble sterkt i Norge sammenlignet med andre nordiske land med tidlig strev mot tegn og tale. Gjennom skisseringen oppstår det et problem: Hvor pålitelig er de skriftlige kildene? Kan man stole på den muntlige tradisjon som er preget av tvil, stolthet og selvforakt? Hvordan skal man forske i et sprog (NTS) når det bare finnes beskrivelser av det på et annet sprog, nemlig norsk skriftsprog? Kort og godt: Denne artikkelen er **om** NTS, og ikke en historisk beskrivelse, fordi vi mangler materiell.

I Brief historical review

I.1

The oldest documented indication that a sign language was used in Norway is from the year 1815. The first deaf person in any of the Nordic countries who taught the Deaf was Andreas Christian Møller (1794-1874). He taught four adult Deaf people in Trondheim using sign language as a medium of instruction. This happened ten years before he, together with his father and brother, founded the first school for the Deaf in Norway in 1825. Møller had attended a school for the Deaf in Copenhagen, where the founder, the Norwegian-born physician Peter Atke Castberg (1779-1823), wanted Møller to become a teacher there. Castberg founded his school in 1807, after a visit to the school founded by de L'Epée in Paris.

In the first reader for the deaf mutes (*Første Læsebog for Døvstumme;* 1825) written by P.A.Castberg, we can read the following passage: *Some people cannot hear, they are deaf. I cannot hear. I am deaf. ... years ago I was mute and deaf/ a deaf mute. Now I am not deaf mute, now I am deaf* (Castberg 1825, p. 129).

How ought we to interpret this? Mutism implies a lack of expressive language. If one can write, use the manual alphabet or sign, then one is consequently not 'mute' any more.

Ill. 1: *Andreas Christian Møller*

I.2

During the first period of the Trondheim school for the Deaf there was no speech training for the students. The language of instruction was sign language, as well as written language and the manual alphabet (the same as was used in Copenhagen, but which in time obtained its own local variants).

This was at a time when Denmark had recently given up Norway, which thus had become a nation, although it was still in union with Sweden. It is a fair assumption though, that the sign language of this period was closely related to the Danish sign language, as the written language of Norway at this time was practically the same as Danish. There were Norwegians who dreamed of having their own written language, distinct from Danish. This drive towards independence led in time to Norway obtaining the two official written languages which the country has today: bokmål (literally: the language of books) and nynorsk (New Norwegian). This says something of how much Norwegians focus on the Norwegian language.

The fact that Andreas Møller was able to establish contact with four Deaf adults and to educate them indicates that all these persons had some prior knowledge of one another, and it also points to the possibility of there having been some form or other of visual communication in existence in Trondheim before 1815. There were two other Deaf people who also worked as teachers at the school for the Deaf in Trondheim – one of these was Johan Julius Dircks and the other the Swedish Pehr Pehrson (? - 1870).

A nominal sign which is still in use in Norway, PER (Peter) [closed 3-hand], and another one, the sign SVERIGE (Sweden) [closed 5-hand], are in fact a minimal pair: these signs are identical with respect to placement and movement, but not in hand form. The Trondheim sign HVIT (white) is practically the same as the Danish sign HVID (white), and the now obsolete sign SPEBARN (infant) was the same as the Danish sign for the same thing. A sign such as DÅRLIG (bad) reminds us strongly of the Swedish sign DÅLIGT (bad). With some degree of impunity we can claim that Norwegian Sign Language is much closer to the Danish sign language than it is to the Swedish, as long as we base our claims solely on manual parts of the signs. Møller was educated in Danish Sign Language. What we lack here are thorough comparative studies of the Nordic sign languages. Word-pictures (visual representations on the lips of words) most probably did not occur during the earliest periods, but nonetheless we can assume that NSL signs had, like other sign languages do, oral components. Sign language teaching first occurred during the second half of the last century, and the influence of spoken language on sign language is thus from bokmål and not from nynorsk.

I.3

The first oralist school for the deaf in the Nordic countries was founded in 1848 in Christiania (today Oslo) by a hearing teacher: Fredrik Glad Balchen (1815 -1899). After having studied the education of the deaf in Trondheim, Stockholm and Germany he founded his school. Traditionally, he is said to have been influenced by the Danish and Germanic sign languages. He was not strictly oralist however, since he used some signing in the primary level classes. Natural signs were, however, not only tolerated, but used by the teachers, as they put it themselves: in order to promote the pupils' understanding and to facilitate lip reading. We can read in a report written by principal Lars Smith that translations were made from the language of gestures to written language at the Trondheim school as early as in 1848. This 'could' have been the beginnings of true bilingual education for the deaf. Niels Waage (1831-1892) who was principal at the Bergen school wrote:

<table>
</table>

Ill. 2:	Ill. 3:	Ill. 4:
Lars A. Havstad	*Erik O. Strangestad*	*Frederik G. Balchen*

The instructional situation includes both the vocal and the written languages, of which two, the first-mentioned is mainly utilized as a means of communication. Natural sign language is used as a teaching aid, artificial sign language or the manual alphabet is not used in the instructional situation; although most of the pupils learn the normal manual alphabet in the due course of time. (cited in Sander 1980)

Balchen had a former Deaf pupil employed as teacher: Erik Strangestad (1837-1893). This person was engaged to teach the academically weaker pupils. It is fairly typical that Deaf teachers traditionally have been used to teach the weakest or most difficult pupils – this is stigmatization, but at the same time it also provides us with evidence that it is Deaf people who are the most skilled in communication with other Deaf people. This is a potential that has not been properly utilized or recognized. Nonetheless, Strangestad clearly became a language model for his pupils. He also taught sign language to the first minister for the Deaf in Norway, Conrad Svendsen (1862-1942). About 25% of the school's pupils were hard of hearing children who used some form of signed Norwegian, this is still in use today – *tegn & tale* (sign and speech). This school had also some hearing-impaired pupils for a shorter period, namely a royal prince and princess who were taught lip reading. Two of the school's pupils became the first Deaf students in the Nordic countries (Halvard Aschehoug, 1851-1880 and Lars A. Havstad, 1851-1913). This meant there was a certain degree of focus upon, and pride expressed about, what the oral method had been able to achieve (Schröder 1978).

The three schools in the southern part of Norway emphasized spoken language in their instructional programs. Professor V. Uchermann showed for example in his great survey of Deaf people conducted in1888, that 64,5% of the Deaf population in Bergen used spoken language when communicating with hearing people. Deaf children who did not show clear progress in their speech skills were sent to the Trondheim school. This was in effect a serious stigmatization of Deaf sign language users. What in fact was concealed behind the practice of streaming deaf students into A-, B- and C-classes was selection, not on the basis of academic skills, but on the basis of skills in spoken Norwegian. In this way the general attitude was created that it was best to use as much spoken language as possible in one's sign language (Sander 1980).

Ragnhild Kaata (1873-1947) was the first deaf-blind person in Norway to receive speech-training. This was provided by Elias Hofgaard (Havstad's brother in law) in 1888 at Hamar School for the Deaf. She learned how to 'lip-read' by putting her fingers on people's mouths. This inspired a visiting American lady, Mrs. Lansom, who studied Hofgaard's method, and subsequently Helen Keller was given speech-training. It was said at the Hamar school that one should use the oral method also with those having limited abilities, but if the student proved too slow to learn, then supporting signs should be used, (Hammer 1954).

I.4

By 1900 the number of uneducated deaf people amounted to 300 of a total population comprising about 2 million. These people were referred to as deaf mutes, that is to say deaf and unable to speak, while the term '(the) deaf' was often used for deafened adults. Educated Deaf persons wished however to be called deaf, so the authorities implemented a name change from the term 'deaf mute' to 'deaf' in all schools and churches for the Deaf as early as in the 1890s. This was well before any of the other Nordic countries did the same thing. Again, there was a focus on Deaf people being able to speak. By the time of the First World War there were practically no Deaf persons who had had an education without being taught to speak (according to tradition, about five or six elderly persons still lived at that time who were educated without being able to speak).

In 1881 Norway, like other countries in Europe, introduced a law which provided compulsory education for all Deaf people. In the regulations for this system of education it was stated that there must not be a mixing of methods at any one school. Each school was to choose either the oral or the manual method. The Trondheim school for the Deaf for instance wanted to use the speech method, but waited do do this until all the Deaf teachers had retired.

When the new system of schooling for the Deaf was introduced at the Balchen school in 1887, Erik Olsen Strangestad was pensioned off. This represented a death sentence for any official recognition of sign language within Deaf education. Oralism means that deaf people become unusable as teachers!

The next Deaf teacher of the Deaf was a woman: Margarethe Hauberg (1869-1954) who never worked in Norway, but emigrated to the USA and received her education at Gallaudet University. She worked there as a teacher for the Deaf from 1904. Since then, only some few Deaf people have functioned as teachers of woodwork and tailoring at schools for the Deaf. The next Deaf teacher of the Deaf with an education did not appear until 1975.

I.5

Conrad Svendsen, a former teacher of the Deaf, subsequently became Minister for the Deaf – the first person in the world with this type of full-time position. He was employed and paid to begin with by the Oslo Deaf Association – quite a unique situation – until the Norwegian state took over the responsibility for his position. He came to defend the use of sign language among Deaf people, in spite of the fact that he was a keen supporter of the oral method from a pedagogical point of view. Conrad Svendsen came thus to carry on a signing tradition first initiated by pupils at the Balchen school for the Deaf – sign supported speech. The clergy for the Deaf, as well as a hearing minister from the North (Sigvald Skavlan), came thus to be defenders of sign language use in the course of the long period during which sign language was banned from schools for the Deaf right up until the early 1970s. If one was, as a minister, to reach into the hearts of the Deaf people during prayers, then one was obliged to use signs during the services, said Conrad Svendsen (1889). Far into the 1960s the clergy for the Deaf were told that their use of signing was tearing down the fine work being done by teachers of the Deaf among their pupils. Use of signs continued unabated in all four

Ill. 5: *Conrad Svendsen*   Ill. 6: *Conrad Bonnevie-Svendsen*

churches of the Deaf and in all the local Deaf associations throughout the country. Conrad Svendsen sought out Deaf Mutes who had never received an education and brought them forward for Confirmation, after having first taught and prepared them. The Deaf Axel Fleischer functioned as teaching assistant during such preparation for Confirmation.

I.6

In the northern part of Norway, a single-handed manual alphabet was used, this being a derivation of the Danish manual alphabet, which dates from 1807. In 1899 a Christmas gathering was held at the local Deaf association in Trondheim. Here the twenty minute principal speech was given by a Deaf woman using only the manual alphabet.

In the South of Norway the manual alphabet was not used at all in educational settings. However, many Deaf people learned a two-handed alphabet outside of school or after school hours from hearing people, either from seamen or from Scouts (since there was a presentation of this alphabet in older editions of *The Scout's Manual*). New Norwegian words were presented by means of careful, explicit pronounciation, the index finger being directed towards the mouth – so this was a question of using borrowed elements from Norwegian, generally presented in an unmodified form. At a later stage these would be amalgamated into the sign as a regular constituent. This seems to be a phenomenon which is found in a number of European sign languages (Ebbinghaus/Hessmann 1990; Pimiä 1990; Padden 1990). Also 'riddle-signs' or purely mnemonic signs were constructed which later became the basis for conventional signs; for example: KONGRESS (congress) is signed KONG + GRESS (king + grass) and the sign SUPPE (soup) with a little change of movement is used to mean SUPER (super).

I.7

At the first Nordic Congress for the Deaf Mute (Nordiske døvstummekongress) in Copenhagen in 1907 a Norwegian representative wanted the assembly to introduce the use of the term 'deaf' instead of 'deaf mute' in Nordic contexts, since the Deaf had received speech-training. Discussion however, centered on the situation of those Deaf people who had not received this kind of training, and as a result a majority of the Nordic delegates declared that they were satisfied with the use of the general term 'deaf mute'. The archaic Norwegian sign DØVSTUM (deaf mute) has been more or less completely superceded by the more recent sign DØV (deaf). Otherwise, Anders Rendedahl stood forward at the congress as an exponent for the right to sign language, declaring this to be an irreplaceable means of communication for deaf mutes. He pointed out that even hearing infants used natural signs before they were able to express themselves in words, and he said he considered that adult deaf mutes ought to be allowed to influence the implementation of teaching methods in schools for the Deaf. A Deaf Finn, Hirn, wanted a Nordic sign language with a common manual alphabet. The congress then appointed a committee, where Hagbert de Falsen (brother-in-law of C. Holmsen), Anders Rendedahl and Conrad Svendsen were chosen as members from Norway.

Around 1914, at Norway's oldest local Deaf association (established in Oslo in 1878) a committee was set up by Martin Skollerud. The mandate of this committee was apparently to remove 'bad' signs from NSL. We do not however, know much about what was meant by this (Schröder 1978). Nonetheless, this illustrates the interest that was shown for sign language, which has, as far back as sources can tell us, been referred to as the mother tongue of the Deaf in spite of the fact that most Deaf people have hearing parents. This says something of the relationship that most Deaf people have to sign language.

I.8

At the first national assembly held by the Norwegian Association of the Deaf (NAD) in Bergen in 1920, a sign language debate immediately materialized. There were as many as three resolutions proposed, so the whole thing ended with a compromise. Local Deaf associations were to work toward the use by their members of what was characterized as a *beautiful sign language*, with a common set of signs throughout the whole country. What the concept 'beautiful' was meant to imply seems open to free individual interpretation. This resolution was repeated at the next national assembly held in Trondheim in 1924, concurrently with the third Nordic Congress of the Deaf. Demands were made here for the development of a sign language dictionary, and for the use of sign language in the education of Deaf children in schools for the Deaf. As it turned out, the greatest resistance to these demands came from hearing participants. A teacher of the Deaf Johannes Berge (1870-1959), himself a hearing person and at the time chairman of the NAD, complained afterwards:

> *When deaf people from all parts of the country came together at a national assembly, one of the first demands which materialized was for a common sign language, a common national language of signs. But even this completely neutral demand it was* **hearing people** *who would confound.* (cited in Sander 1980)

At the national assembly in 1930 in Bergen, there was again a demand that sign language be used as an aid to teaching, and here the expression *mother tongue of the deaf* was again used. It would appear that in this case it was more a question of signs used in support of speech. Pastor Conrad Bonnevie-Svendsen had provided novice teachers of the Deaf with some instruction, but complained that this was too little. Deaf people pointed out that if teachers were to become accomplished signers, then they would have to mingle extensively with adult Deaf people. The only school which used sign language to any extent before the Second World War was the college of further education in Bergen, but this was not widespread knowledge, since attitudes among teachers towards sign language and sign systems were extremely negative. Some teachers of the Deaf were even against the use of the Danish mouth-hand system, since they considered that it would lead to poorer lip reading skills. With such a dominant emphasis on spoken language in education of the deaf it is obvious that transmission of knowledge came second in line.

The national assembly in 1924 decided that Oslo was to have responsibility for the development of a signing handbook. In 1944 the first dictionary was published as a serial supplement to the magazine *Tegn og Tale* (Sign and Speech), which today has become *Døves Tidsskrift* (Journal of the Deaf). It was Axel Fleischer who must be honoured for its completion, together with two other Deaf people: C.R. Helgesen, Egmont Nørregaard (who had attended the 1907 congress) and Conrad Bonnevie-Svendsen. In the preface it was mentioned that several of the signs were similar to the Danish and the German equivalents since the Norwegian Deaf schools had their origins in these countries.

> *Our sign system is of German origin. The deceased school principal Balchen completed namely his studies at the deaf schools in Germany and brought back home the signs that were used there. That they have not deviated much from their origins, has been established by many deaf people over the years during their visits there previously. Similarly, the deviations from Danish sign language are not particularly great. (...) There is amongst other things a widespread opinion that there exists an international sign language, but this is unfortunately not the case. Norwegian and Swedish deaf people do not understand one another through sign language alone, but must use lip reading as an aid.* (Fleischer et al. 1944)

Balchen was later called the father of Norwegian Sign Language, but this is certainly an exaggeration, since sign language existed in Norway long before his time. But even today we can note that the sign JA (yes) is the same in Norway, Denmark, Netherlands, Flemish Belgium, and Germany. Here is also a field where there is a need for contrastive research in order to find out to what degree these languages are related to one another.

What then was this sign dictionary like? It contained, first, one sheet showing 30 different hand forms. Then came a list of Norwegian words presented in alphabetic order, with a description of the position and movements in corresponding signs, related to the handforms presented on the sheet. All in all there are mentioned 1629 signs. Many of these signs are still in use today. We should also examine more closely the extent to which signs were constructed for specific occasions. Signs demonstrated by elderly Deaf people should be recorded on video, since one can in this way reconstruct the way the signs may have been produced. In the aforementioned sign dictionary there is not one single illustration of what a sign looks like. The first time signs were shown in print in Norway was in 1950! This was a full-page sheet showing common Nordic signs.

I.9

A new sign NORGE (Norway) [N-hand tracing the contours of the mountains] was established and ratified by the national assembly of the Norwegian Association of the Deaf in 1950, in Bergen. Some previously used signs for Norway were: HER (here), SIRKEL (circle) or KYST (coast), using the right hand to trace the southern part of Norway. These days, practically all Deaf people in Norway use the new NORGE sign.

In 1948 the clergy for the deaf requested the Department of Education to introduce sign language as a school subject. The ministers mentioned in their request that there had previously been natural signing used within Deaf education, and that this had led to the development of a cultivated sign language among Deaf people.

> *Since sign language was forbidden in education, teachers of the deaf have not had any influence upon the students' sign language. Net result: The Sign Language has declined! This is something one can begin to rectify at the college of higher education in Bergen.* (cited in Sander 1979)

We can see that this is in fact a theme which regularly reappears throughout the whole century. On the one hand, sign language is in decline and on the other hand, it is the teachers of the Deaf who are to 'improve' the students' sign language. In section II.1 this issue will be examined more closely.

As a result of collaboration between all the Nordic countries, an attempt was made to establish a Nordic sign language; this being an old demand, dating back to the first Nordic Congress of the Deaf in 1907. The dictionary, under the leadership of Danish Ole Munk Plum, was finished in 1967 and included about 2000 signs. This dictionary was criticized for being much too Danish-orientated, but then on the other hand, the delegates from the other Nordic countries had not taken a particularly active role in this collaboration. Only very few of the signs shown in this dictionary are in fact used by Deaf people in Norway today.

I.10

We shall end this brief historical review by quickly mentioning what took place between 1950 and today – since 1950 the choice between signed Norwegian and NSL has become a question of sign language politics. As long as schools for the Deaf maintained an exclusively oralist policy, one had to struggle for the introduction of sign language into education tactically by championing sign supported speech. The Norwegian Association of the Deaf appointed a sign language expert body under the leadership of the energetic Deaf Thorbjørn Sander (born in 1928), for many years editor of the NAD magazine *Døves Tidsskrift*. The older system of sign supported speech was chosen, but extended to a system with one sign for each word, since this was considered to facilitate a better understanding of Norwegian for the Deaf. In 1974 the Norwegian Association of the Deaf adopted a Total Communication philosophy.

'Sign language'- courses were begun all over the country. The course materials were Norwegian texts which the students were supposed to learn to sign word for word. Criticism against the NAD sign language materials at this time had to do with the fact that they were based on the assumption that Norwegian first and foremost is a written language, while it is in fact a spoken language (Slethei 1979). This also says something of how Deaf people in fact experience Norwegian not so much as a spoken but as a written medium. The authors of these materials meant well, but they still ended up by perpetuating further repression of the Deaf, since many Deaf people joined sign language courses with the hope of becoming better at Norwegian by using 'the new signing'.

Many thousands of hearing people learnt this form of signing over the years these materials and courses were offered. They quickly discovered, however, that having taken part in a sign language course was not sufficient for understanding Deaf people's normal everyday sign language communication. It was explained that the Deaf were lackadaisical signers or used 'bad' signs, or that they were not good enough at Norwegian with signs. Nonetheless, the most important thing was that hearing people learned to try and communicate with Deaf people. Hearing people discovered as time went on that there was another exciting, natural sign language. That was the good thing about this particular 'reform'.

However, as a further result of this 'reform', there were many Deaf people who had confirmed their own perception of their sign language as something bad. The older sign for mother was for instance replaced by the Danish sign MOR (mother), a new number-sign for 9 was constructed with a bent littlefinger (something which is physiologically rather uncomfortable to perform), the American sign THREE was introduced on the presupposition that the older Norwegian signs were bad or meaningless (Sander 1979). The following principle was adhered to: every word should have a sign, and some signs were also constructed to visualize the grammatical and morphological structures of Norwegian, for instance past tense was given its own sign, but not present tense. The syntax of the signs corresponded to the written form of Norwegian.

So if other sign language researchers were to use the Norwegian sign language dictionary in order to find examples of signs from Norwegian Sign Language, then this would be, to put it mildly, somewhat unrepresentative. From this particular point of view, the 'reform' must be said to have represented a raping of Norwegian Sign Language, since large numbers of lexical signs were ignored and sign language syntax and grammar were considered to be inferior.

A change came in 1979 when the normalizing process slowed down more or less to a stop. Opinions regarding the form and function of the sign language dictionary were so different and so highly and hotly debated within the consulting body on sign language, that the NAD decided to suspend the body for two years. Later, in 1989, the NAD established an independent foundation for promoting research into Norwegian Sign Language – the Sign Language Institute in Oslo with the author of this article as the director.

The Deaf Irene Greftegreff (born in 1959), a native signer as her parents are Deaf, has written the first phonological description of NSL, a doctoral thesis at the University of Trondheim in August 1991. Also in 1991, the hearing great grand-daughter of Pastor Conrad Svendsen, Marit Vogt-Svendsen (born in 1949) will defend her doctoral thesis at the University of Trondheim, which is an investigation into various aspects of interrogative sentences in NSL. A full circle has thus been turned.

II An analysis of articles by Skavlan and Havstad

II.1

Sigvald Skavlan (1839-?) was principal at the Trondheim school for the Deaf; later he became a minister and worked with other, non-Deaf congregations. As minister he continued his contact with Deaf people and also maintained his sign language skills. In 1875, he wrote an article entitled 'Tegnsproget' (The Language of Signs) as a contribution to a celebratory publication in conjunction with the 50th anniversary of the school for the Deaf in Trondheim. This is the oldest written account of Norwegian Sign Language. The article is however mainly about the nature and usefulness of sign language, rather than being a detailed description of how individual signs were built up. The author was fully aware of the necessity of using either extensive written explanations or preferably lithographic illustrations and woodcuts to adequately represent signs. He described some signs for the days of the week several of which are still in use today (those for Tuesday, Friday, Saturday, and Sunday).

He pointed out that hearing children also use gestures. This is something which every mother becomes quickly aware of. This is sign language at a basic level. On the basis of the expressions and gestures the Deaf child sees in other people, and by imitation of these, it develops and gradually builds up its own sign language – in exactly the same way in which the hearing and speaking child acquires its spoken language.

There is, wrote Skavlan, a pointless controversy which has raged, as to which of the two, the sign or the word, is the mother tongue or natural language of the deaf mute. It is strange to read that Skavlan finds it necessary to explain that there is a difference between 'sign language' and 'finger language' – this is a distinction which is still unclear for the majority of today's journalists.[1]

Skavlan categorizes signs in the following ways:

---

1 While Skavlan quite rightly pointed out that it is not possible for a deaf person to lip read everything that someone says (1875), the oralist Hedevig Rosing (1827-1913), founder of what later became the Holmestrand school for the deaf, maintained that a gifted deaf person could, from their window, read the lips of people walking in the street! This she wrote in her booklet

1. natural signs (demonstrative, configurative, operative, expressive, relative);[2]
2. transcendental or metaphysical signs; and
3. methodical signs.

When the pupils found out a person's proper name they performed an illustrative sign, while at the same time using the manual alphabet to show the first letter of the name – this is a method which Skavlan claims dates back to de L'Epée's time. The signs he presents in his article seem to be the same as today's – a bird being characterized by the flapping wings, a shivering movement characterizing winter. The signs for days of the week are more or less the same as today. The sign for TUESDAY is for instance really the sign for CODFISH, which is what the students were given to eat on that particular day of the week.

Skavlan thinks that de L'Epée had assumed that the world of abstraction was totally inaccessible for deaf people. The hearing teacher had therefore to think for the deaf mute and then transmit the impression of this thought to him. Skavlan did not agree with this for it is

> (…) a grave underestimation of the deaf mute's natural abilities and the general process of human development. It would seem this one great underestimation of the deaf mute in himself we believe has led to another, equally great, underestimation of the Sign Language of the Deaf. One has denied this language the ability or the right to express anything that lies beyond the limits of simple observed exteriors. This is greatly unfair. Deaf Mutes certainly need no special education, no teacher's influence in order to find mimetic expressions for metaphysical concepts such as, for instance: think, forget, industry, sin, yesterday, today etc. (Skavlan 1875)

Skavlan emphasized also the importance of a language community: The less developed deaf people are, the more strange they are in their forms and gestures; but they enrich each other's signs and mutually hone down one another's gestures. For this reason he opposed the textbooks about the *Døvstummevæsenet* (The Institution of Deaf Mutism) which demanded

> (…) that the teacher must educate and purify the deaf mute's signs. We believe that this is both in itself unnecessary and in fact fairly useless. The deaf mutes have – since sign is their element – by and large a particular refinement and graciousness, by which they understand to perform their signs, which the hearing person with difficulty can attain, even though he might be their master. (Skavlan 1875)

Skavlan thought that methodical signs had little significance for life in general. Why for instance use the left hand over the right to indicate an adjective, throw the hand backwards over the shoulder to indicate the past, or indicate conjunctions by two crossed fingers – a system developed by de L'Epée and Sicard? Some of these things reappeared in Signed Norwegian in the 1960s and 1970s as sign markers of past tense and genitives. Skavlan was of the opinion that such signs were unnecessary in order for Deaf people to learn the written language.

It is easy to see that Skavlan had read both French and German literature. He mentions that the basic requirements for good signing are decisiveness, clarity and brevity – just like in any good composition. Otherwise he mentions disposition, placement (localization) and action. On the basis of localization, wrote Skavlan, *the silent language* knows therefore no

---

which was sold to finance the formation of the first national association: De norske døvstummes forening i Christiania (Association of Norwegian Deaf Mutes in Christiania; Rosing 1878).

2 By relative signs he means signs for relationships between two or more objects, which can be expressed by the use of two hands. An example of relative signs might be the comparative sign for FØLGE SAMMEN (move along together) where both objects are moving in the same direction, or adversatives (e.g. the sign for MØTE (meet) or GÅ-FRA-HVERANDRE (leave one another)) where they move in opposite directions.

conjunctions, which indicate the expressions' logical relationships to one another Sign language simply follows the order of time.

He emphasized that sign is a direct expression of thought, not a translation of spoken language, since each language has a syntax, and sign language also has one of its own. As an example he provided the sentence: *My black hat is hanging on the wall.* In sign language this would be expressed as: WALL ON HAT BLACK MY HANG.

Nonetheless, Skavlan claimed that sign language was at such a primitive state of development, similar to those barbarian languages spoken amongst heathens, being so bereft of all expression beyond that which is at the level of the senses, that missionaries have had great problems in conveying the spirit of Christianity in the tongues of heathens. What really was at issue is the question of a certain type of education and cultural development and not the structural possibilities inherent in the language. He considered Norwegian Sign Language to lack elements for nouns, adjectives, verbs and adverbs; in fact it also lacked articles, passive voice, copulas and most conjunctions. Instead of morphological processes signs had to be modified by additional signs: 'mannens' (the man's) = MANN+TILHØRER (man+belong to); menn (men) = MANN+NOEN/MANGE (man+some/many).

He stressed that there is one important weakness with sign language, it is unclear, unprecise and quickly forgotten. Therefore written language is the most ideal. But he forgot to compare sign language with spoken language, since this also can be unclear, unprecise and easily forgotten. It was furthermore strenuous to use this language, since one had to set manual work aside while speaking it, whereas on the other hand, with speech, one could continue working unaffected. He was also against sectarianism – i.e. those who swore by the one or the other method – either signing or speech. The truth lies as usual somewhere in the middle:

> *And thanks to this controversy, we have now, in our opinion, by and large been left with a relative acceptance of both languages' usefulness and necessity for the deaf mute and his education.*

Thus, we can read in his article a program for bilingualism for Deaf people, but he was not willing to treat sign language as an educational tool, only as a technical aid; he would only describe sign language as it was used in the community associated with the school for the deaf in Trondheim.

He would not accept either, that sign language might be a universal language, only to the extent that music and art might be said to be similar, since the discrepancies of sign languages were too great. Signs do not characterize words, but concepts and ideas. He referred to Chinese and Egyptian writing in order to demonstrate something similar. This he did instead of making the most obvious comparison: words do not illustrate signs either, but rather represent concepts and ideas. He looked into the nature of hieroglyphics and reached the following conclusion: Hieroglyphic writing compares quite closely to the sign language of the deaf mute; hieratical writing to the language of sound, which may be represented either as articulation, writing or the manual alphabet.

He explained that deaf mutes themselves preferred sign language amongst themselves, since it is strenuous to first find words and expressions, and thereafter through the appropriate mouth shapes pronounce and communicate clearly, because so much concentrated attention and so much effort is required in order to perform the mechanical skill which lip reading is. The deaf felt the contempt hearing people displayed for the inadequacy of this language. The deaf mutes who can speak look with similar contempt upon their equals who do not speak, but either exclusively, or preferentially, gesticulate. He claimed that the deaf mute (with education) turns immediately to the spoken or written language whenever there is something which cannot effectively be conveyed by sign language.

The blind see with their fingers, the Deaf hear with their eyes and the mute speak with their hands.

II.2

Lars A. Havstad (1851-1913) wrote an article in 1892 in the *American Annals of the Deaf: How the Deaf Converse with each other in Norway* (Havstad 1892). He had become deaf himself at the age of five; later he went on to become the first Deaf student and was for a time editor of a political weekly. It seems clear from his article that he considered a signed system which followed the syntax of the spoken language to be the ideal. It is obvious that he ignored the way in which Deaf people at large conversed. On the other hand, there are some articles by him which demonstrate that this 'ideal' did not in fact prevail amongst the Norwegian Deaf community.

He claimed that Norwegian Sign Language was markedly different from the Swedish and Danish sign languages. This he interpreted as if: *it marks an advanced stage of progress and lies nearer to the language of the future* (Havstad 1892).

In 1881 and 1882 the pure oral method, first used by Arnold, was introduced into all the Norwegian schools for the deaf except the school at Trondheim. But this change is yet of recent date, wrote Havstad, and it has still not affected Deaf people's sign language. Here we can mention as an aside that this is still the case today.

He said there was little contact between deaf mute sign users and deaf sign users – between Oslo and Trondheim. This statement should be taken with a grain of salt. It is presumably orally oriented deaf/ hard of hearing persons who allow their sign language to lie closer to the syntax of Norwegian, whilst Deaf people in general have their sign language use much more closely associated with the genuine language. It is possible that the differences were to do with the so-called visual elements. Havstad said that the signs in Trondheim were much more elaborate and that the manual alphabet was used there. A seasoned principal at the Trondheim school for the Deaf could not even understand the children's use of the manual alphabet.

> *The spoken word now can be said to be the real basis of the language of the average deaf. Signs are chiefly used as a means of facilitating lip reading.* (Havstad 1892)

Here he pointed out that there were a number of signs which coincided due to lipreading. These were the following signs: DAME (lady), PIKE (girl), KONE (wife), KVINNE (woman). These signs have become more differentiated today. He also warned against excessive use of sign language, since the idea was that Deaf people should take part in society as a whole:

> *The language of signs is certainly very much favored by the deaf and facilitates their conversation between themselves, but it is not indispensable and inevitable as the basis of the language of the deaf (…) the teaching of speech will make signs the servants, and by degrees deferential ones too, and not the masters of the language of the deaf.* (Havstad 1892)

He told of the efficacy of the oral method with reference to Ragnhild Kaata. She had been deaf-blind since the age of three. She used only spoken language. Her fellow pupils used neither signs nor the manual alphabet. But what happened as a result? The majority of Deaf people thought it was unpleasant to have her hands inserted into their mouths so that she could interpret what was said from their lip movements. She resorted therefore to using signs with Deaf people and they replied to her by use of signs and making the motions of writing in her palm:

> *(…) deaf are inclined to express their thoughts by signs, and they can do so in most cases, except when the delicacy or subtlety of the idea requires a more precise and detailed form of language. But the great defect of the sign-language, as admitted by all, is that its grammar is different from that of any other language used by mankind. Without depriving the deaf of the use of signs, it by degrees substitutes the grammar of*

spoken words for that of the sign language. But there can be no doubt that the transition of the language of the deaf from signs will be much retarded in places where there are large gatherings of the deaf using signs only. The small minority must speak as the large majority do. There lies, in a nutshell, the chief cause of the opposition on the part of the deaf to the oral method. (Havstad 1883)

Havstad reacted to what he characterized as deaf people's clannishness. He was for instance, against Conrad Svendsen confirming Deaf youngsters in the Deaf Church; this he wrote in the leading cultural organ of the time: *Dagbladet.* He wrote amongst other things that audible speech is neglected and therefore becomes less and less understandable as time goes on. This effect appears as peculiarities in behaviour and language and ways of thinking, and indeed, makes its mark upon the whole physiognomy of the individual. He claimed in fact that Deaf people would start to look 'deaf-like' through using sign language.

It is well-known that the intellectual standing of the deaf mute is to no small degree independent of his ability to use spoken language according to the rules of grammar, something which everyone who knows how to communicate with such persons will have experienced. That gestures however, will come to play a by no means modest role in conversations between deaf mutes, should this be conducted either by means of the finger-language or by mutually reading one another's lips, I must allow to be definitive. (Havstad 1883)

He was aware that a number of deaf people would be unable to master spoken Norwegian:

The deaf taught by signs or the manual alphabet, therefore, are like people who are every day obliged to speak with two different tongues. Perhaps a few gifted deaf are capable of mastering both languages alike. But are the large majority? (Havstad 1880)

However, according to the obituaries in the newspapers at Havstad's death, it was said that he had almost unintelligible speech. It was thus rather a paradox that he fought so defiantly for the efficacy of speech, but this tells something of the psychological pressure which oralism exerted on this otherwise so enthusiastic exponent of sign supported speech (Schröder 1978).

III Other sources

III.1

A third source of our knowledge of the history of NSL is the first magazine for the Deaf in Norway – *Journal for døve* 1890-94 – published by deaf people themselves, later appropriated by the clergy for the Deaf (and still existing as *De døves blad*). There are several articles of interest on sign language and about Deaf people in other countries. In the very first number there are pieces taken from the German Deaf press mentioning that most German Deaf people support signing.

Axel Fleischer wrote that educated Deaf people used pure spoken language without voice and with supporting signs. This was a program which he in his more mature years did not follow. An article with the signature P.-r. claimed that sign language was obviously in decline, and the author hoped that there would develop a common Nordic sign language. But these claims were rejected in later numbers, on the grounds that sign language had advanced so that it approached more closely the spoken language. Discussion between exponents for these two points of view has repeated itself continuously in the Norwegian deaf community right up to the present day. But the article by P.-r. had some common traits with what was also claimed in France and Sweden at that time – sign language was in decline because it was banned as a language of instruction. It was being reduced to mere conversational use. The stationer Charles Leisner – one of the editors of the *Journal for døve* – claimed: The deaf ought not use 'shortened expressions' – meaning signs which can not have a concurrent visualization on the lips of a Norwegian word (word-picture), but which must have their own unique oral components (Vogt-Svendsen 1984; Schröder 1985). He was himself hard of hearing, but he pointed out the need for a school where there was systematic education in sign language in order to refine the language. This type of school has still not come into existence. The closest we have to this today is the sign language teacher training course at the NAD's people's academy at Ål, run by the NAD. A consistent contributor was Ragnar Ziener who emphasized how important it was for Deaf people to be allowed to use sign language amongst themselves. This was promoted with great zeal: *Tegnsproget vil aldrig dø, så lenge der er døve (Sign Language will never die as long as there are deaf people)*.

III.2

Other written sources are protocols, annual reports, letters, a vanished diary of Pehr Pehrson's which there is some hope of recovering, hand-written lecture notes aimed at teachers of the Deaf written by ministers of the Deaf C. Svendsen and C. Bonnevie-Svendsen from around 1920-30. All these materials have still not been analyzed. In the novel *Ikke som de andre (Not like the others)* by Arve Fjørtoft (1944), one of the teachers exclaims that it seems to be unnatural to teach the Deaf to speak and use language to some degree of correctness:

> *Sign language is really their proper language anyway! — It is namely, even though you may not be acquainted with the fact, much more difficult being a pupil, than it is being a teacher, at a school for the deaf!* (Fjørtoft 1944)

Most of the sources of information on Norwegian Sign Language have been written by teachers of the Deaf and by Deaf people who, for the most part, have adopted hearing people's attitudes. On the one hand they say that sign language is the mother tongue of the deaf, on the other they say that it must be refined and improved because it is impoverished. As Caramore (1990) has already pointed out, a great deal of the available literature has originated from teachers of the Deaf who often have had a particular ideological attitude to sign language.

What can we conclude from all this? This has been primarily a preliminary investigation of some of the available written sources. We have not attempted to make a systematic search through everything that has been written but which still is unpublished. For instance, the signs which were described in the list of signs of 1944 ought to be presented live and recorded on video so that a subsequent analysis can be made.

III.3

We have only sporadically touched upon some examples from the oral tradition. Some things which were still common during the 1950s and right up until the present day might be mentioned here: Constant apologies made because one does not know enough words. That sign language always functioned as a stigma for deafness. That sign language should not be used out on the street, in cafés or on the tram because hearing people would stare at us. Discussions between Deaf people which would be interrupted through use of the argument that hearing people have said so – so there!

At the other extreme, we have the kind of statements made by a Deaf man, Harald M., who commiserated with poor hearing people who were obliged to use spoken language. There is only a tiny crack of a mouth opening and shutting. Look how lively and powerful sign language is!

It is the first time that the examples cited below are in print. We ought to collect oral tradition through video recordings and transcribe them. The local section of the Norwegian Society of Deaf History in Oslo has a working group making video-recordings of older deaf people's recollections, stories etc.

A person who moved from Trondheim to Oslo in 1926 was reprimanded for using Trondheim signs at the Oslo association meetings. One was nonetheless aware of norms in sign language use. The chairman of the Oslo association was refused permission to use sign language in public by his board, since his signing movements were so awkward (Schröder 1978). Dialectal differences were in fact minimal, and there is less difference today than there was 70 years ago. The main differences had mostly to do with the relative intensity of the signing; with signing in Trondheim being generally more dynamic, and using the signing space to a greater degree, than the Oslo variant, which generally was more heavily influenced by Norwegian.

The oldest Deaf people in Norway still-living are now about ninety years of age. They ought to be interviewed copiously and recorded on video tape. One must almost certainly allow for a certain amount of haziness of memories and embellishments of the truth. For instance, a Deaf person, Nils H., was interviewed by a weekly magazine and maintained that he was given a hiding because he had used signs at an oralist school, when the truth of the matter was that he considered himself both hard of hearing and an oralist during his youth.

One approach might be to ask Deaf people directly what their opinion of sign language is. Another approach might be to get Deaf people to tell stories about how good it was to be able to use sign language. A third approach is to have Deaf people tell about the repression of sign langauge, and possibly have them say something about how good or bad they consider Norwegian to be in relation to sign language.

From the early 1950s there are a number of films which were made at ceremonial occasions such as congresses and national assemblies. These might provide some indication of what was considered to be 'proper' sign language from the podium, and what was characterized as nice and refined. This seems to be markedly different from the 'everyday' sign language used by Deaf people in their normal social interaction, which is characterized by being easy to understand, entertaining and pleasing to watch.

Since the advent of video technology there are to be found extensive materials, admittedly of varying quality, but these will be of value as investigatory sources, on the basis of which one will be able to arrive at a more complete description of Norwegian Sign Language.

This research must be initiated as soon as possible, since the oldest informants will not continue to get much older. As Caramore pointed out: *A wide field of research continues to go to unexplored, and so far there is no deeply rooted awareness of the importance of such research, neither among Deaf nor among hearing people* (Caramore 1990, p. 23). (Translated by Patrick J. Coppock)

Appendix
The original Norwegian quotations:

p. 234

> Undervisningen omfatter saavel lyd- som skriftsproget, av hvilke først-nevnte overveiende anvendes som meddelelsesmiddel. Det naturlige tegnsprog anvendes som hjelpemiddel, kunstigt tegnsprog eller fingersprog benyttes ikke ved undervisningen; dog lærer de fleste elever det alminnelige fingeralfabet underhaanden. (cited in Sander 1980)

p. 237

> Da landsdelenes døve samledes i en enhet for det hele land, var et av de første krav som meldte seg dette: å få et felles tegnsprog, et felles riksmål i tegn. Men selv dette helt neutrale krav var det hørende som skulle forpurre. (cited in Sander 1980)

p. 238

> Vårt tegnsystem er av tysk opprinnelse. Avdøde skolebestyrer Balchen avsluttet nemlig sine studier ved døveskolene i Tyskland og tok de der brukte tegn med seg hjem. At de ikke har avveket svært fra sin opprinnelse, har mange norske kunnet konstatere i årenes løp ved sine besøk der nede i tidligere år. Likeledes er avvikelsene fra det danske tegnspråk ikke svært store. (...) Det er blant utenforstående en utbredt oppfatning at det eksisterer et internasjonalt tegnspråk, men det er dessverre ikke tilfelle. Norske og svenske døve forstår ikke hverandre med tegnspråket alene, men må ta munnavlesningen til hjelp. (Fleischer et al. 1944)

p. 238/ p. 239

> Efterat tegnsproget ble forbudt i undervisningen har ikke døvelærerne fått noen innflydelse på elevenes tegnsprog. Resultat: Tegnsproget har forfalt! Dette kan en begynne å rette på ved yrkesskolen i Bergen. (cited in Sander 1979)

p. 241

> En stor Miskjendelse af den Døvstummes naturlige Evner og almen-menneskelige utviklings-gang. Det er imidlertid denne ene Miskjendelse af den Døvstumme selv, der, tro vi, har ført til en anden ligesaa stor Miskjendelse af den Døvstummes Tegnsprog. Man har frakjendt dette Evnen eller Berettigelsen til at udtrykke Noget, der ligger udenfor den simple udvortes Ans-kuelse. Tilvisse med stor Uret. De døvstumme behøve sikkerlig ingen speciel Undervisning, ingen Lærerens indflydelse for at finde mimiske Udtryk for metaphysiske Begreper som f.eks. tenke, glemme, flid, synd, igår, idag osv. (Skavlan 1875)

> at Læreren har at uddanne og rense de Døvstummes Tegn, tro vi, at dette er baade i og for sig unødvendigt og ganske utjenligt. De døvstumme have – just fordi Tegnet er deres Element – i Almindelighed en særegen Finhed og Gratie, hvormed de forstaa at udføre sine Tegn, som den Hørende vanskelig tilegner sig, endsige at han deri skulde være deres Mester. (Skavlan 1875)

p. 242

> Og takket være Striden, er man nu, mene vi, i Almindelighed bleven staarende ved en relativ Anerkjendelse af begge Sprogs Brugbarhed og Nødvendighet for den Døvstumme og hans Opdragelse.

Iconography

Ill. 1: Andreas Christian Møller
   Skjølber, T. (1898): *Andreas Christian Møller*. Bergen: Døves Forlag A.s, p. 8.

Ill. 2, 3 and 4:
   L.A. Havstad , E.O. Strangestad, F.G. Balchen
   Schröder, O.I. (1978): *Døve Foreningen 1879-1978*. Oslo: H. Aschehoug.

Ill. 5 and 6:
   C. Svendsen, C.Bonnevie-Svendsen
   Dahl, H. (1928): *De Døve Forening 1878-1928*. Oslo: Lie, p. 31.

References

Anderson, Per (1969): *Hovedlinjer i døveundervisningens historiske utvikling.* Oslo.

Becker, C. (1909): *Beretning om den første nordiske døvstummekongress i København 1907.* Copenhagen.

Caramore, Benno (1990): Sign Language in the Education of the Deaf in 19th Century Switzerland; in: Prillwitz, S./Vollhaber, T. (eds.): *Current Trends in European Sign Language Research.* Hamburg: Signum, pp. 23-34.

Castberg, P.A. (1825): *Første Læsebog for Døvstumme,* Trondheim.

Ebbinghaus, Horst/Hessmann, Jens (1990): German Words in German Sign Language; in: Prillwitz, S./Vollhaber, T. (eds.): *Current Trends in European Sign Language Research.* Hamburg: Signum, pp. 97-114.

Fjørtoft, Arve (1944): *Ikke som andre.* Oslo.

Fjørtoft, J.A. (1887): *Talemethoden contra skriftmethoden.* Kristiania.

Fleischer, Axel et al. (1944): *Det norske Tegnspråk.* Oslo.

Hammer, Ragnvald (1954): *Ragnhild Kåta.* Bergen.

Havstad, Lars A. (1883): *Rejse-Beretning vedkommende døvstumme-sagen.* Kristiania.

Havstad, Lars A. (1880): *Vore skoler for døvstumme. Et tilbageblik.* Kristiania.

Havstad, Lars A. (1892): How the Deaf Converse with each other in Norway; in: *American Annals of the Deaf. Journal for døve* 1890-1894

Padden, Carol A. (1990): Rethinking fingerspelling; in: *Sign Post* 4., pp. 2-4.

Pimiä, Päivi (1990): Semantic Features of Some Mouth Patterns in Finnish Sign Language; in: Prillwitz, S./Vollhaber, T. (eds.) *Current Trends in European Sign Language Research.* Hamburg: Signum, pp. 115-118.

Rosing, Hedevig (1878): *Nogle Ord om de Døvstumme.*Kristiania.

Sander, Thorbjørn J. (1979): *Konferanse om tegnspråk-arbeidet.* Ål.

Sander, Thorbjørn J. (1980): *Med landets døve gjennom hundre år. Bergen Døveforening 1880-1980.* Bergen.

Schröder, Odd-Inge (1978): *Døveforeningen 1878 - 1978.* Oslo.

Schröder, Odd-Inge (1985): A Problem in Phonological Description; in: Stokoe, W./Volterra, V.: *SLR '83.* Silver Spring, MD - Rome.

Skavlan, Sigvald (1875): *Tegnsproget.* Trondhjem.

Slethei, Kolbjørn (1979): Tegn i tiden. Et innlegg til konferansen på Ål. (unpubl.)

Svendsen, Conrad (1889): *Om døvstummes undervisning. En reiseberetning.* Kristiania.

Vogt-Svendsen, Marit (1984): *Word-pictures in Norwegian sign language (NSL) - a preliminary analysis.* Trondheim.

Vogt-Svendsen, Marit (1987): *Tegnspråk og norsk og blandingsformer av de to språkene.* Oslo.

María Angeles Rodríguez-González
Barcelona, Spain

Francisco Fernández Villabrille (1811-1864) and 'el lenguaje de signos'

Summary · Resumen

Francisco Fernández Villabrille was a teacher at the Deaf Mutes School in Madrid. He wrote several books in which he makes clear the situation of Deaf education in Spain during the years prior to the Milan congress.

'Sign language' appeared in all programmes for Deaf teaching as the main tool to understand the Spanish. Villabrille was aware of the importance of 'sign language', and in 1851 he published a dictionary with 1547 descriptions about the way of articulating signs.

Villabrille classifies the signs as 'indicatives', 'descriptives' and 'relatives', and points out some highly important current remarks, e.g. the limited number of elements comprised in a sign, the main condition of the right hand in making a sign.

His discussion of 'mimography', a possible system for writing signs, is of special interest. Villabrille gives advice to future teachers of the Deaf about the use of 'sign language'.

The author's work we have consulted has been published by the printing house of the Deaf Mutes Royal School in Madrid and can be found in the Madrid National library.

Don Francisco Fernández Villabrille, profesor del Colegio de Sordomudos de Madrid, escribió varias obras en las que pone de manifiesto la situación de la educación del sordo en España, en los años anteriores al Congreso de Milán.

En todos los programas de enseñanza de sordos, el 'lenguaje de signos' figuraba como instrumento principal para comprender el idioma. Francisco Fernández Villabrille, consciente de la importancia del 'lenguaje de signos', publica, en 1851, un Diccionario con mil quinientas cuarenta y siete descripciones sobre la forma de articular los signos.

Fernández Villabrille clasifica los signos en 'indicativos', 'descriptivos' y 'relativos', y apunta observaciones de gran actualidad; por ejemplo, sus referencias al número limitado de elementos que comprende un signo, a la condición principal de la mano derecha en la realización de un signo, ponen de relieve una reflexión profunda del autor sobre el lenguaje de signos. De especial interés son sus apreciaciones acerca de lo que denomina 'mimografía' o sistema posible para escribir los signos. Asimismo, Francisco Fernández Villabrille ofrece una serie de consejos a los futuros maestros de sordos sobre la utilización del 'lenguaje de signos' en la enseñanza.

Los trabajos del autor que hemos consultado están editados por la imprenta del Colegio Real de Sordomudos de Madrid, y proceden de la Biblioteca Nacional de Madrid.

Francisco Fernández Villabrille was a teacher at the Colegio Real de Sordomudos of Madrid from 1836 to his death in 1864. He published several papers about Deaf education and founded a review with Juan Manuel Ballesteros, the school's director, for discussing the teaching of the deaf and blind. From 1856, he was senior professor of this school. In 1857, he was in charge of elaborating the teaching programme of a special three month course of studies for the students of the training college's last year of studies. This special course taught basics of Deaf education.

In 1858, Villabrille was sent to visit, during six months, the more important Deaf schools in France, Belgium and Germany. A report about his observations was published in 1862.

In the writings of Fernández Villabrille, we can see the importance of *'el lenguaje de signos' (sign language)* for Deaf education in Spain.[1]

> In all the deaf mute schools sign language is allowed in order to give knowledge of the Spanish language, because writing and pronunciation alone are not enough to acquire it. (1845, p. 70)

Villabrille distinguishes two aspects in teaching the Deaf: one, formal, mechanical, is used generally, to give shape and representation to the speech, including dactylology or hand alphabet, lip reading and pronunciation. The other aspect is qualified as 'philosophical'. It consists in giving intelligibility to Spanish. For that purpose, two means are proposed: drawing and 'sign language' (1845, p. 11).

We can find the same distinction in the later works. In 1858, he writes: *the second part is more philosophical, more interesting and impressive* (1858, p. 31). This second part includes essential means for linking the signed expression to the meaning of Spanish words, and *associated with the method of the first part, they are useful to the deaf mute in performing the complete thinking translation of thought and to get intellectual culture as great as possible* (1858, p. 32).

In the aforementioned report published in 1862, he says again that the basic methods of communication in Deaf education are *writing, the hand alphabet, the lip alphabet, pronunciation, drawing and sign language* (1862, p. 107). And he also says that all these things *must be put together and combined to complete the teaching* (1862, p. 109).

The special education of the Deaf child begins when he or she is eight years old and lasts until the age of fourteen, that is to say, six years. Villabrille was aware of the importance of the preschool period for the child's learning development. He writes in 1858 that it is necessary to get in contact with and communicate with the very young child:

> This communication between the child and mother develops early. The first signs point only to objects and material needs, but this language of action gets enriched little by little and, at last, expresses all his desires. (1858, p. 11)

He advises parents to prepare their children for the education they will receive in the school through sign communication, *keeping in mind that nature is the true guide in the selection of mimic signs* (1858, p. 12).

Francisco Fernández Villabrille is in favour of the Deaf child attending the kindergarten. In this way, the teacher will encourage the child to make signs about objects and pictures. *These signs, learned by the teacher, will be the means of expression the ideas and of communication* (1858, p. 21).

Some of Fernández Villabrille's comments on el lenguaje de signos are quite remarkable. For instance, he points out the dominant character of the right hand in performing signs: *The signs are projected in the air by the arm movements, in which the right hand is more active* (1845, p. 68): Likewise, he notices the cognitive effects of 'sign language':

---

1 In this paper, no discussion of the status of Villabrille's 'sign language' is given (i.e., to what extent it was a signed system rather than an authentic sign language of the Deaf).

> *When a deaf mute child starts school, his language is poor, because he has not prac-*
> *tised and his intelligence has not developed by means of instruction. Suddenly he is*
> *among other schoolmates who know and practice the mimic language. The great*
> *amount of knowledge he acquires in a short time is remarkable.* (1845, p. 68)

In his report, we find the following remarks about the evolution of signs, up to arbitrariness
in sign creation:

> *His tireless temperament and his skill to devise signs based on analogy, and to reduce*
> *them to convention when no satisfactory expressions could be found in nature, are*
> *what improves this language day by day.* (1845, p. 68)
> *These signs, based on nature on the one hand and on convention on the other, are the*
> *true language of the deaf mute who has a tireless genius to reduce it to explicit or tacit*
> *convention.* (1858, p. 43)
> *Each shape and gesture of the hand and body can receive an arbitrary value, by*
> *means of specific conventions between the teacher and the student or only among the*
> *pupils, to communicate their ideas.* (1858, p. 44)

Fernández Villabrille classified signs in three groups:
1) **Indicative** signs, for pointing to present objects.
2) **Descriptive** signs, referring to absent things, form the basis of sign language.
Fernández Villabrille analyses several ways of designating (concerning beings, acts, professions, etc.by the way of selecting imitative aspects; 1845, pp. 77-87).
3) **Relative** signs, which resemble the methodical signs invented by de L'Epée and Sicard.
Fernández Villabrille says that these relative signs are necessary in order to complete *el lenguaje de signos* and to be able to analyse written Spanish sentences. He offers some examples and points out that the teacher can modify them (1845, pp. 87-90).

In 1851, Fernández Villabrille published a *Diccionario usual de mímica y dactilogía*.
It was presented as an improvement on the method of de L'Epée and Sicard. This book
offered descriptions of signs for 1547 words, in alphabetical order:

> **Easy** . *The thumb touches the tip of the forefinger and moves a little. One performs the*
> *sign of 'difficult' followed by a sign of negation.*
> **False** . *The right forefinger designs on the right cheek, but without touching it, repeated*
> *diagonals, from the ear to the corner of the mouth.* (1851, p. 61)

Compound signs are frequent in el *lenguaje de signos*, e.g.:

> **Room** . *This sign preceded by the sign for 'eating' means 'dining room', with 'sleep',*
> *'bedroom', with 'teach', 'classroom', and so on.* (1858, pp. 45-46)

Another of Villabrille's interesting observations is about the possibility of expressing so-
called abstract ideas and a tendency to make the effect stand for the cause and the part for
the whole in several signs, that is, a metonymic trend (1858, p. 46).

Even more interesting is Fernández Villabrille's appraisal of the so-called *mimografía*
or system for writing signs. He recognizes the great importance of fixing signs and transmit-
ting them to other schools. He also knows of the difficulties of putting signs and facial
expressions onto paper. But he says that this could be possible because *this astonishing*
wealth of signs stems from a small number of elements, and these can be fixed and classi-
fied (1845, p. 93). Fernández Villabrille does not study these elements, he was a teacher,
not a researcher.

Villabrille lists some characters for writing the positions of the hand and its different
movements, also some for representing physiognomy. But he recognizes that they are so
complicated that it is impossible to keep them in memory (1845, p. 94).

The specialized course on the education for deaf mutes worked out by Fernández Villa-brille in 1857 is intended for the preparation of future teachers. Out of fifty subjects, four were dedicated to sign or *el lenguaje de signos*. This programme (published in 1858) is meant for the teacher in primary school. In 1862, Villabrille demanded more rigourous education to train special teachers for deaf mute and blind children, through the creation of a 'Normal School', and he accepted some younger teachers with the title of aspiring or 'assistant professor'. *This has an advantage,* he says. *To place these future teachers amidst the deaf children will make them more familiar with sign language and other communication methods* (1862, p. 95).

He points out some rules of 'sign language' use for the teacher:

1. *The teacher must acquire of the signs his pupil uses, as valuable material to begin the educational process.*
2. *Through these signs, he puts himself in direct communication with the pupil in order to study his capability and character.*
3. *He should correct and straighten these signs without changing their nature.*
4. *He must put the signs together to perform descriptive scenes.*
5. *He should create new and elementary signs in order to enrich the language.*
6. *The new signs must be natural and easily understandable for everybody.*
7. *The signs with faulty and insufficient analogy for expressing their meaning must be abandoned.*
8. *The use of sign language must be abandoned when the child knows the value of the word. It must not be used in the last phase of education.* (1845, pp. 90-91)

About the progressive abandoning of sign language he writes in 1858:

> *When the deaf child knows the value of the expressions of our language, and we must try to make him familiar with them, we must restrict the use of sign language.* (p. 44)

In the writings of Francisco Fernández Villabrille we can see, therefore, not only the preoccupation of a hearing teacher of the Deaf with his work, but also the importance assigned to el *lenguaje de signos* in Deaf education in Spain prior to the Milan congress.

Appendix
The original Spanish quotations:

p. 250

> En todos los establecimientos de sordomudos está admitido el uso del lenguaje mímico para darles conocimiento de su idioma patrio, porque la escritura y la pronunciación no sirven por sí solas para ejecutarlo. (1845, p. 70)
>
> (…) la segunda parte del arte es más filosófica, más interesante y grandiosa. (1858, p. 31)
>
> (…) asociados con los medios de la primera parte, sirven al sordomudo para la entera traducción del pensamiento y para obtener la cultura de sus facultades intelectuales en el mayor grado posible. (1858, p. 32)
>
> (…) la escritura, el alfabeto manual, el alfabeto labial, la pronunciación, el dibujo y el lenguaje de signos. (1862, p. 107)
>
> (…) deben reunirse y combinarse para que la enseñanza sea completa. (1862, p. 109)

(...) esta comunicación pronto se establece entre el niño y la madre: los primeros signos se referirán tan sólo a las cosas y a las necesidades materiales, mas este lenguaje de acción se va enriqueciendo poco a poco y sirve para expresar todos los deseos. (1858, p. 11)

(...) teniendo presente que la naturaleza es el verdadero guía en la elección de los signos mímicos. (1858, p. 12)

(...) estos signos, de que se apoderará el profesor, serán la expresión de las ideas y el medio de conversación. (1858, p. 21)

Los signos se proyectan en el aire con los movimientos de los brazos, de los que la mano derecha desempeña la parte más principal. (1845, p. 68)

p. 251

Cuando un sordomudo entra en el colegio, su lenguaje es pobre, porque no ha tenido ocasión de ejercitarlo y porque su inteligencia no se ha desarrollado por medio de la instrucción; pero se halla de repente en medio de otros compañeros de desgracia, verdaderos depositarios del lenguaje mímico y del caudal de ideas que se perpetúa en el colegio por tradición, y entonces es curioso observar la extensión considerable que adquiere el nuevo discípulo, sometiéndose a una mejora incalculable. (1845, p. 68)

Su genio infatigable y su habilidad para inventar signos fundados en la analogía y para reducirlos a convenciones cuando no hallan en la naturaleza expresiones ni caracteres que les satisfagan, son los que perfeccionan de día en día este lenguaje. (1845, p. 68)

Estos signos, fundados parte en la naturaleza y parte en la convención, forman el verdadero lenguaje del sordo-mudo, que tiene un genio infatigable para reducirlo a convenciones expresas o tácitas. (1858, p. 43)

Toda postura y además de las manos y del cuerpo puede recibir un valor arbitrario por una convención expresa entre maestro y discípulos o sólo entre estos últimos para comunicarse mutuamente sus ideas. (1858, p. 44)

Fácil. Se pone el dedo pulgar en la extremidad del dedo índice y se mueven un poco. Se hace el signo 'difícil' seguido de un signo negativo.
Falso. El índice de la mano derecha traza, sobre el carrillo derecho pero sin rozar con él, repetidas diagonales, desde la oreja a la extremidad de la boca. (1851, p. 61)

Sala. Su signo presedido del de *comer*, significa el *comedor*. Del de *dormir*, el *dormitorio*. Del de *enseñar*, la *clase*, y así sucesivamente. (1858, pp. 45-46)

(...) esta asombrosa multitud de signos mímicos proviene de un corto número de elementos que se pueden determinar y clasificar de algún modo. (1845, p. 93)

p. 252

Este medio tiene una ventaja y es que fijando a los futuros maestros en medio de los discípulos, los familiariza con el lenguaje de signos y otros medios de comunicación. (1862, p. 95)

1. El profesor debe apoderarse de los signos que ya ejecuta su discípulo, como de unos materiales preciosos para dar principio a la instrucción.
2. Por medio de estos signos entrar en comunicación directa con el discípulo para estudiar su capacidad y su carácter.
3. Corregir y rectificar estos signos sin alterar su naturaleza.
4. Irlos agrupando para formar escenas descriptivas, según las explicaciones.
5. Formar signos nuevos y elementales para ir enriqueciendo el lenguaje.
6. Los signos que se formen nuevamente deben ser naturales y comprendidos por todo el mundo.
7. Los signos en que la anaogía sea imperfecta e insuficiente para expresar la cosa significada deben abandonarse.
8. Se ha de abandonar el uso de los signos luego que por ellos sea conocido el valor de las palabras, usando muy poco el lenguaje mímico en los últimos periodos de la instrucción. (1845, pp. 90-91)

Cuando el niño sordo conozca el valor de las expresiones de nuestra lengua y se trate de hacérsela familiar, se debe restringir el uso de los signos. (1858, p. 44)

References

Villabrille, Francisco Fernández
- (1845): *Curso elemental de instrucción de sordomudos.* En colaboración con Ballesteros, Juan Manuel. Madrid: Imprenta del Colegio de Sordo-Mudos y Ciegos.
- (1851): *Diccionario usual de mímica y dactilología.* Madrid: Imprenta del Colegio de Sordo-Mudos y Ciegos.
- (1857): *Discurso de inauguración de la Escuela Normal.* Madrid: Imprenta del Colegio de Sordo-Mudos y Ciegos.
- (1858): *Instrucción popular para uso de los padres, maestros y amigos de los sordo-mudos.* Madrid: Imprenta del Colegio de Sordo-Mudos y Ciegos.
- (1862): *Memoria sobre el estado actual y organización de la enseñanza de sordo-mudos y de ciegos.* Madrid: Imprenta del Colegio de Sordo-Mudos y Ciegos.

Patrick McDonnell • *Helena Saunders*
Dublin, Ireland

Sit on your Hands

Strategies to prevent signing

Summary

When schools for the Deaf changed to oral methods they tried to eliminate signing among the pupils. A wide variety of strategies were used. Some strategies aimed to influence the pupils themselves. Other strategies were directed at those adults who were most closely associated with pupils, especially parents and teachers. Since Deaf pupils had no other realistic way to communicate with each other, they acquired Sign Language or developed some other sign system. Signing became an underground activity. Conflict between the communication needs of pupils and the language policies of schools was a central feature of Deaf pupils' experience.

Introduction

This paper explores a neglected area in Deaf education. In particular it describes the strategies used by one school in Ireland in its attempt to suppress signing among the pupils. It also describes the school experience of one Deaf person and shows how Deaf pupils maintained a signing community in a hostile environment.

All the quotations (in italics) in this paper come from a number of interviews with a former pupil of a school for Deaf girls. She attended this school – one of the largest in Ireland – during the late 1950s and early 1960s and was there in the crucial period when oralism was introduced on an extensive basis. The interviews were carried out early in 1990. They were conducted through sign language and English and were recorded in written English.

The change to oral methods

In schools for the Deaf in Ireland the change from sign to oral methods took place during the 1950s. Oral schooling was introduced gradually and by 1960 pupils in oral programmes were segregated from pupils in programmes that used signs. The oralist approach dominated teacher training and audio equipment dominated the classroom. All forms of signing – whether sign language or signed English – were marginalised to non-mainstream classes.

The introduction of oral methods brought a radical change in the lives of Deaf pupils. The oralist ideology included a very strong anti-signing bias. It was believed that the use of signs would impede the development of speech and speechreading (Ireland, Department of Education 1972, chap. 6). Every effort was made to eradicate signing among the pupils.

> *The school authorities were very strict especially after the changeover to oralism. If we were caught signing we were slapped on the hands with a leather strap. We were deprived of meals or sent to bed early. Sometimes we were sent to work in the kitchens...*

The pupils now found themselves in an impossible dilemma. They had neither grammatical nor communicative competence in spoken language. They needed to sign to be able to communicate with each other. Their communication needs therefore came into direct conflict with the linguistic aims of the school (McDonnell 1983). As a result, the pupils secretly acquired signs from peers or from other signers in the school environment.

> *We learned signs from other deaf children. We met adult deaf workers in the laundry and learned signs from them. We made up our own signs too, related to events in our lives. For example, our sign for Easter was the same as our sign for April.*

The pupils had no choice even though they knew it was against school rules and would be severely punished. *In school everybody signed. No matter how we tried not to sign with our friends, it was impossible. We had to communicate, there was no other way.*

Researches have described a wide variety of communicaton systems existing in schools for the deaf (Bochner/Albertini 1988; Moores 1974; Schlesinger/Namir 1978; Tervoort 1978; Wilbur 1976, 1979). Sign systems have been observed even in schools which pursue strict anti-signing policies (Cicourel/Boese 1972; Moores 1974). The pupils then, had the potential to construct or recreate a signing community. The school authorities recognised this potential and therefore devised a range of strategies to suppress signs and promote oralism.

Internal strategies against signing

There were two main kinds of strategies, internal and external. Internal strategies operated within the school. They were directed at the pupils. At one level, internal strategies tried to eradicate any form of body movement that was seen as signing. Pupils who were caught signing were punished in a variety of ways; they were slapped, deprived of meals or privileges or humiliated in some way.

Sometimes we were put out of the classroom. If the principal saw you standing outside the door you would be slapped. But if you were caught very often she would say, 'You're always signing, go away'.

Pupils came under constant surveillance and since the staff was outnumbered, older pupils were encouraged to report incidents of signing to the school authorities. *We were not really afraid of the older pupils. They might tell us to stop signing but they didn't report us. Anyway they themselves signed too.*

The suppression of signing affected every part of school life – how pupils lived, how they played, how they learned and most of all, how they communicated. Even ordinary gestures and natural physical movements during communication were subject to strict control. *Sometimes we were made to sit on our hands or keep them behind our backs.*

However the pupils could not be completely immobilised. So minimal body movements took on linguistic meaning. Pupils communicated through body posture, facial expression or eye movement.

We were very vigilant when we signed. We always had to be ready for someone to come along. We had a particular posture which meant 'Be careful!'. There were eye movements which said, 'Stop signing, someone is coming!' Every movement became a sign.

On another level, there were internal strategies which were meant to convince pupils that signing was wrong and harmful. These strategies were designed to influence the belief, attitudes and values of the pupils since it was impossible for the staff to monitor and control the children in every situation.

We signed in private but we were always on the lookout for staff. We used to sign in the toilets. In the dormitory we could open the curtains to let in a little light. We used to sign away for hours.

The school therefore developed strategies aimed at those situations where pupils could not be directly supervised. Firstly, anti-signing attitudes and values were inculcated.

Our teachers told us that if we signed, our speech would deteriorate and we would never learn anything. We believed them when they said that signing was bad and that it was stupid.

Secondly, positive attitudes towards speech were promoted.

The teachers kept telling us our speech was very good. I believed speech was very important and I did my best but when I went home nobody could understand me.

Speech was connected to moral behaviour; signing was related to disobedience and sin.

We had to go to confession every two weeks. But if we were caught signing we had to go in between times and confess that we had been signing. We were asked to give up signing for Lent. It was like giving up smoking and promising to be good.

The strategies against signing had a powerful effect on the pupils' attitudes and values.

We were influenced by what we were told. Friendships were lost over signing. Some pupils dropped their friends because they signed.

Language and identity

The language that people use and the way in which they use it helps individuals to establish and sustain an identity. Even very young children are aware of this function of language and several researchers have shown how much children influence each other's language (Labov 1972; Saville-Troike 1982). One of the most important strategies in the school for the deaf aimed at establishing a separate identity for pupils in oral programmes. Signing pupils were segregated from pupils in oral programmes.

> *The signing pupils were hidden away where no one could see them. They had their own refectory and dormitory. They played in an enclosed yard and we never met them.*

Elitist attitudes were fostered among oral pupils while signing pupils were labelled in a negative way.

> *If we were caught signing the staff threatened to send us to the signing school. We learned to look down on them and to think they were inferior. We had a sign for being sent to the manual school. It was like the sign for* THROW, *like being thrown out or being thrown into a rubbish bin.*

On important religious occasions in the children's lives, such as First Communion Day, signing pupils were '*put at the back of the church*'.The effects of these strategies lasted long after the pupils had left.

> *Many years after I left school I behaved as if I was still being supervised. My school experience affected my relationship with my own children who are hearing. For example, I was afraid to sign to them. I was worried it would harm their linguistic development. It took a long time to overcome this.*

After the conflict experienced in school it was difficult to establish a clear identity.
> *When I left school I met adult signers and I could not understand them. I had poor speech so hearing people could not understand me. I was neither hearing nor Deaf.*

The learning needs of the pupils

In the classroom there was conflict between the learning needs of the pupils and the oral policy of the school.

> *Understanding did not come first. No teacher used signs. Lip reading was very tiring. I tried to understand the words that were said but in the end I had no story. I could not understand long sentences.*

Oral schooling meant that the form of communication was more important than the content. It emphasised **how** the pupils communicated and not **what** they communicated. This emphasis contradicted the way language normally works – where primacy is more often given to what people say rather than to how they say it (Brennan 1975; Brown 1973).

> *At school knowledge and understanding of any subject came second. All that mattered was speech. We were made to imitate what was said even though we did not understand it. I remember one poem…*
>
> > Up the airy mountain,
> > Down the rushy glen,
> > We daren't go a-hunting
> > For fear of little men;

> *Wee folk, good folk,*
> *Trooping all together,*
> *Green jacket, red cap,*
> *And white owl's feather.*
> I learned it but I had no notion of what it meant.

When a better balance in communication was restored, pupils really began to learn.

> *When I was in secondary school I experienced education for the first time. It was with a teacher who did nothing with speech, and didn't know any signs. But he used gestures and a lot of writing and he made sure we understood what we were learning.*

External strategies against signing

External anti-signing strategies were directed in a general way at the public. Successful oral students received public recognition for their achievements. *Oral classes had much higher status than signing classes. They followed mainstream courses and sat for public examinations. Pupils in signing classes did not.*

Signing had no place in the public perception of what went on in the school. *At the end of term we put on shows and did plays for parents and the visiting public. It was mostly speech, movement and dance. There was no place for signing.* Visitors were given the impression that pupils in oral programmes did not sign.

> *When visitors were expected in the classroom we were warned not to sign. Parents or other visitors were taken into selected classrooms where some pupils would be picked out to demonstrate their oral skills.*

External strategies were directed in a particular way at those who were most closely associated with the pupils. Parents especially, were exhorted to promote the language policies of the school, including the ban on signs. *Our parents were told, 'Don't let them sign at home. It makes them look mental'.*

Teachers were the key personnel in the school. They had to implement the day to day language policy and enforce the anti-signing strategies of the school. It was important therefore, that teachers should learn to accept these practices. Training for teachers of the Deaf was built around oral methodology; methods which included the use of signs had little or no part in this course. (Ireland, Department of Education 1972, chap. 9) Teachers were clearly influenced by their training.

> *The teachers never signed in the classroom. They were more strict than the after school care staff. The care staff often took no notice when they saw pupils signing.*

Even employers were incorporated into the anti-signing strategy:

> *After I left school I went to work in a large department store. The principal of the school told the manager that I was not allowed to sign and he circulated a letter to the staff telling them that they should neither sign to me nor accept signs from me. The following year a second deaf school leaver got a job in the store. The manager told me he would take her on provided she and I would never meet during break times.*

The social context of the school was transferred to the workplace and the two workers coped as they had done in school.

> *We made all kinds of secret arrangements. We met wherever and whenever we could. Supervisors caught us once or twice but we said we were only passing by.*

Conclusion

The school experiences of the deaf pupil quoted in this paper are not unique to Ireland. As a rule, schools for the Deaf have overlooked the need of pupils for a medium of communication **for themselves**. Both theorists and teachers have focused mainly on communication between hearing adults and deaf children. In fact most interaction – perhaps the most important interaction – occurs among the pupils themselves (McDonnell 1992). And this interaction among the pupils themselves has been seen only as a threat and an offence. It had to be controlled because it presented opportunities for signing.

Strategies to suppress signing created conflicts between the school and its pupils. The conflicts were expressed in several areas – in communication, in values, in identity and in learning. The strategies directed attention away from the real language needs of the pupils – to communicate ideas, to express emotion, to interact socially, to understand and control reality, to assert personal and social identity and to develop cognitive skills.

The more extreme anti-signing strategies may have now disappeared. Some, but not all schools for the Deaf have introduced modest sign language programmes into their mainstream curricula. However, in many areas associated with the eduation of the Deaf, signing is still regarded with fear and suspicion. Sign language as a medium of instruction remains very much a second class option for pupils and there is still a long way to go before the wishes of the Deaf themselves are realised.

The dream and hope of the Deaf is that signing be given the same status as oral language; that signing should mean signing in our language; that information on Deaf culture and the history of Deaf people and Deaf experience be part of the school curriculum ; that books written by the Deaf, about the Deaf or about growing up as a Deaf person be in the school library.

References

Bochner, J. H. /Albertini, J.A. (1988): Language varieties in the deaf population and their acquisition by children and adults; in: M. Strong (ed.): *Language Learning and Deafness*. Cambridge: University Press.

Brennan, M. (1975): Can deaf children acquire a language? *American Annals of the Deaf,* 120, pp. 463-479.

Brown, R. (1973): *A First Language*. Harmondsworth: Penguin Books.

Cicourel, A. V. /Boese, R. J. (1972): Sign language acquisition and the teaching of deaf children. *American Annals of the Deaf,* 117 (Feb.), pp. 27-33, (June), pp.403-411.

Ireland, Department of Education (1972): *The Education of Children Who Are Handicapped by Impaired Hearing*. Dublin: Stationery Office.

Labov, W. (1972): *Sociolinguistic Patterns*. Philadelphia: University of Pennsylvania Press.

McDonnell, P. (1983): Social context and language usage: Implications for deaf children; in: Mac Mathúna, L./ Singleton, D. (eds.): *Language across Cultures. Irish Association for Applied Linguistics. Proceedings of a symposium, St. Patrick's College, Drumcondra, Dublin, 8-9 July*, pp. 141-153.

McDonnell, P. (1992): *Patterns of Communication among Deaf Pupils*. Sociological Association of Ireland in association with The National Rehabilitation Board. Dublin.

Moores, D.F. (1974): Non-vocal systems of verbal behaviour; in: Schiefelbusch, R.L./Lloyd, L.L. (eds.): *Language Perspectives: Acquisition, Retardation and Intervention*. London: Macmillan, pp. 377-417.

Saville-Troike, M. (1982): *The Ethnography of Communication*. Oxford: Basil Blackwell.

Schlesinger, L.M./Namir, L. (eds.) (1978) : *Sign Language of the Deaf*. London: Academic Press.

Tervoort, B. (1978): Bilingual interference; in: Schlesinger, L.M./Namir, L. (eds.). pp.169-240.

Wilbur, R. (1976): The linguistics of manual languages and manual systems; in: Lloyd L.L. (ed.): *Communication Assessment and Intervention Strategies*. Baltimore: University Park Press, pp. 424-491.

Wilbur , R. (1979): *American Sign Language and Sign Systems*. Baltimore: University Park Press.

Hand Alphabets

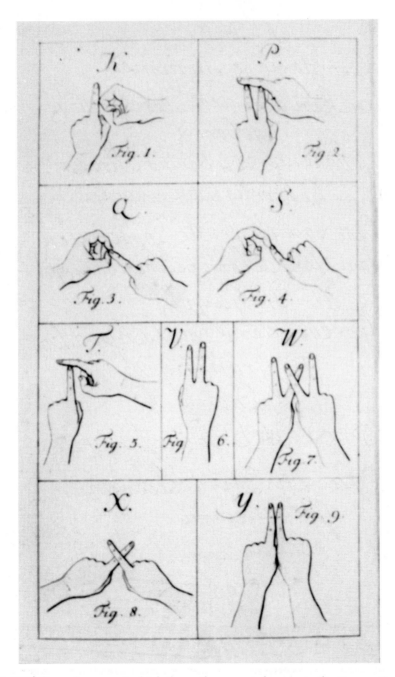

Ill. 55: A 1796 'finger language' which the author says is known in the Franconian region (around Nürnberg, Germany) and supposed to serve 'pitiable people who have had an accident'.

Het Alphabet Manuel
of het
A. B. C.
Voor dove & Stommen
Geteken door den doof & stom
geboren
Johannes Lubertus Morser
Geboortig van Groenloo,
Een van de Eerste Discipelen
van den Alom bekenden Onderwyser
H: D: Guyot,
Gerenomeerd waalsch predikant
te Groningen
En
Door L: W: E: beneffens de
Heeren Directeuren
Goedgekeurd
in den jaar
1795

Ill. 56: Coverpage for a handwritten hand alphabet by Johannes L. Morser (Deaf), published in 1795 in Groningen, Netherlands (see also ill. 57, p. 263).

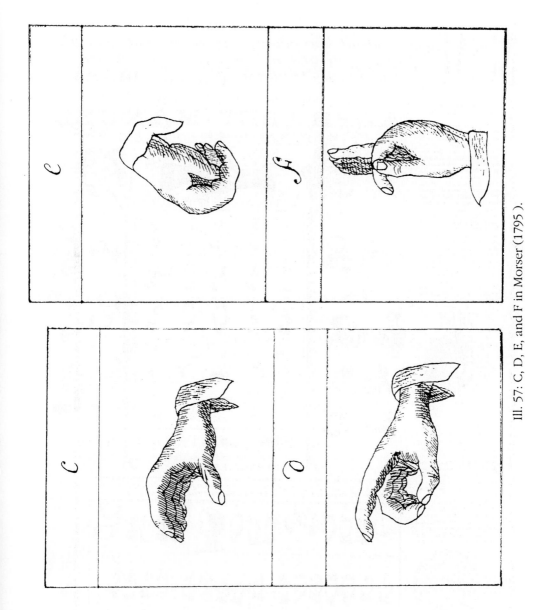

Ill. 57: C, D, E, and F in Morser (1795).

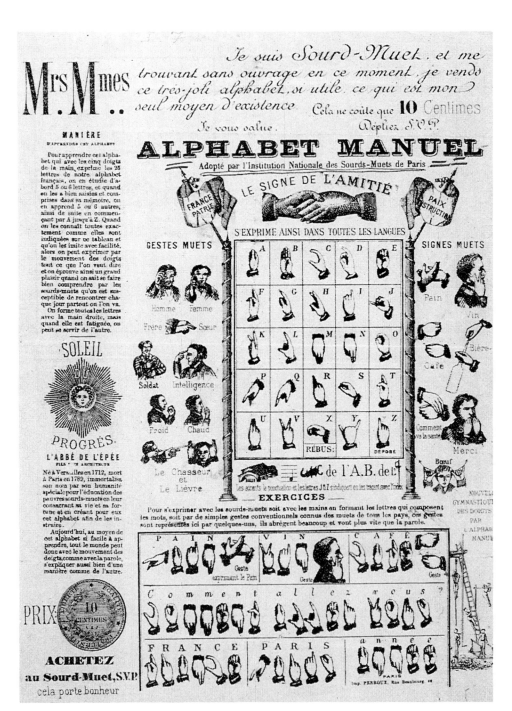

Ill. 58: An anonymous undated flyer showing the hand alphabet 'adopted by the National Institution for Deaf Mutes in Paris', of the kind that were distributed by Deaf beggars in the 19th century.

264

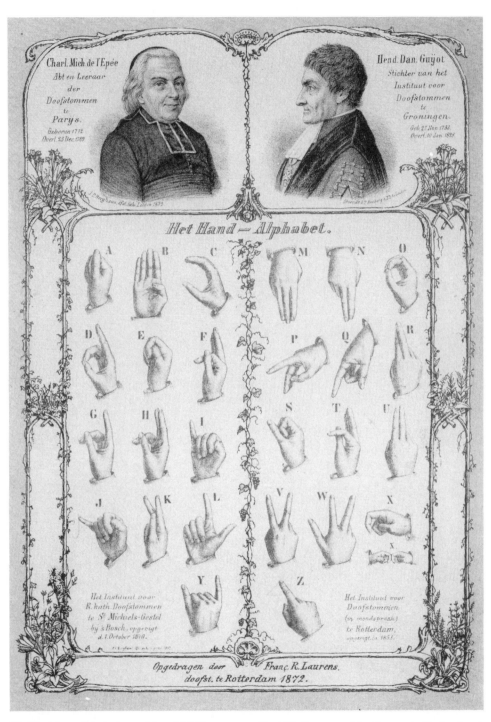

Ill. 59: A hand alphabet table of 1872, executed by F.R. Laurens, 'deaf mute in Rotterdam',
Netherlands. This table was re-issued as a poster on the occasion of the bicentenary of the
Institute for the Deaf in Groningen/Haren in 1990.

Deaf Education in the
Context of Oralism

Joachim Winkler
Leipzig, Germany

Anna Catharina Elisabeth Heinicke (1757-1840)

First female principal of a German school for the Deaf

Summary • Zusammenfassung

Anna Catharina Elisabeth Heinicke was the first German woman to be head of a school for the Deaf, namely the Deaf Mute Institute founded in Leipzig by Samuel Heinicke.

In short, her life might be summed up in the following data: she was sister to two Deaf brothers, widowed for the second time at the age of 32 after Samuel Heinicke's death; her first husband died when she was barely nineteen. She was director of the Deaf Mute Institute in Leipzig for 38 years, gave birth to three children, was grandmother to numerous grandchildren, moved seven times, and, in 1813, had to flee the Napoleonic forces with her Institute.

In the year before her retirement, she received municipal and royal honours for 50 years of service.

Anna Catharina Elisabeth Heinicke war die erste Frau in Deutschland, die als Direktorin eine Gehörlosenschule leitete, nämlich das von Samuel Heinicke in Leipzig gegründete Taubstummeninstitut.

In Kurzfassung läßt sich ihr Leben in folgenden Fakten umreißen: Sie war die Schwester zweier taubstummer Brüder, zum zweiten Mal mit 32 Jahren nach Samuel Heinickes Tod verwitwet; ihr erster Mann starb, als sie gerade erst 19 Jahre alt war. Sie leitete 38 Jahre lang das Taubstummeninstitut in Leipzig. Sie hatte drei Kinder geboren, war Großmutter zahlreicher Enkel, bewältigte sieben Umzüge und mußte 1813 mit ihrem Institut vor den napoleonischen Truppen fliehen.

Im Jahre vor ihrer Pensionierung erfuhr sie mit 50 Dienstjahren städtische und königliche Ehrungen.

Ill. 1: *Anna Catharina Elisabeth Heinicke*

I

In the late 18th century, Anna Catharina Elisabeth Heinicke was the first German woman to be head of a school for the Deaf, namely the Deaf Mute Institute founded in Leipzig by Samuel Heinicke, her husband. She held this post for almost four decades.

We know of her work of many years and great merit through a multitude of official letters and partly through her own handwritten letters kept in the archives of the Samuel Heinicke School and the University of Leipzig.

Her life was filled with decades of responsible activity. Just turned twenty, Anna Catharina Elisabeth, widowed Morin, née Kludt, married Samuel Heinicke 1778 in Hamburg. He was her senior by thirty years. In taking this step, she undertook a considerable responsibility, since she suddenly had to care for four stepchildren from age eight to eighteen, and some ten Deaf pupils. She did not appear before the public with pedagogical tracts of her own, like her husband, nor did she develop new teaching methods. But she strove with never tiring diligence and remarkable commitment not only to maintain the Institute in her husband's spirit, but also to develop, enlarge and improve it. Having lived to the age of 83, she outlived Samuel Heinicke by exactly half a century.

Anna Catharina Elisabeth Heinicke came from the North of Germany. She was born hearing on November 9th, 1757 in Jüthorn near Wandsbek. Her father, Simon Kludt, was in the employ of the Baron von Schimmelmann, Samuel Heinicke's generous patron during his stay in Altona, Eppendorf and Hamburg in the years 1758-1778. She was still a very young woman when her two deaf brothers Carl and Friedrich were taught to speak, read and write by Samuel Heinicke in his little school house in Eppendorf. The elder of the two was confirmed in April 1776. Heinicke's first wife was already dead at that time. And at the very same time, Anna Catharina Elisabeth was experiencing a single year of marital bliss with her first husband, only to be followed by months of deep grief.

Around the time of her twentieth birthday, it came to pass that fifty-year-old Heinicke described his difficult situation to her, disclosed his innermost thoughts and dreams, and asked her to marry him and be a mother to his four children. In the previous October, Samuel Heinicke had moved his institute from Eppendorf to Hamburg. The wedding was held there on January 8th, 1778.

On the day before the wedding, the ruling Prince of Saxony, Elector Friedrich August III, sent a letter to the University of Leipzig, asking that the university assist the teacher, much esteemed for his excellent skill in teaching deaf mute pupils, in his desire to found a school for them in Leipzig where the Elector previously had appointed Heinicke in September 1777.

The new family went through a cold and snowy winter in Hamburg and did not move to Leipzig until the spring. On April 13th, 1778, Samuel Heinicke arrived in Leipzig with his young wife, four children and nine Deaf pupils. The following day, he opened the new Churfürstlich-Sächsisches Institut für Stumme und andere mit Sprachgebrechen behaftete Personen (Electoral Saxonian Institute for the Mute and other Persons with Speech Disorders) at the Roßplatz.

Samuel Heinicke was director of the Institute for twelve years. Anna Catharina Heinicke remained at his side through all highs and lows, especially through his disappointment that his dreams and expectations did not come true in the degree he had hoped. He had intended to establish a large and much noted institute in the universally known city of the fairs.

On December 30th of the year of the family's move to Leipzig, daughter Wilhelmine Rosina was born.

In 1782, the Institute moved from Roßplatz into Klostergasse in the center of the city, close to the Thomaskirche. The institution was legally subordinated to the University. From the reports of this superintending Board of Education, we learn details of the domestic life at the Institute, for which 'Pflegemutter Heinicke' (foster-mother Heinicke) was mainly responsible. The Institute did not have a private building at its disposal at that time (and not until many years later). As a rule, they moved into one floor of a private block of flats and set up a school with a family atmosphere. Two reports from 1783 give a glimpse of the Institute's daily routine: 13 people of different ranks and ages are living in several rooms, some of which are comfortable and spacious, whereas others are quite cramped. Two women are in charge of the cleaning. All of the pupils eat at the same table with the director and his family. They eat what he eats. They are under his and his family's constant supervision. Out of class, they occupy themselves with writing, reading, drawing or playing parlour games. The girls are taught female accomplishments as well. Moreover, they often go for walks, safely escorted, and thus get the necessary air and exercise (cited in G. and P. Schumann 1909, pp. 28-29).

In the new Klostergasse lodgings, the second daughter, Amalie Regina, affectionately called Malchen by her mother, was born in May 1783. She was to go down in the history of Deaf education as the wife of the school's second headmaster, C.G. Reich, and foster-mother to Deaf pupils.

In 1785, there was another move, this time to Neuer Kirchhof, opposite the Matthäi-Kirche. Son Samuel Anton was born there in June 1788. At that time, a 22-year-old student named Eschke frequented the family's house. He was interested in working with deaf pupils, and fell in love with Heinicke's eldest daughter, Juliane Caroline Tugendreich, whom he married the same year. She followed him to Berlin, where Ernst Adolf Eschke (1766-1811) founded the first Prussian Deaf Mute Institute in 1788.

Heinicke's state of health had deteriorated increasingly during the last years. He suffered from gout and depression. Concern about his family weighed heavily upon him, since he had not been able to save any money over the years. He reached his 63rd birthday on April 10th, 1790, and died a few days later, on April 30. There was great sorrow and despair in the Heinicke household. The deceased left his young widow impoverished – the widow's pension applied for in 1782 had not been granted.[1] The children were small and not yet of age, the youngest not even two years old. Frau Heinicke did not have the money to buy mourning clothes, so she had to borrow them from a teaching assistant, the student of theology, Petschke.

II

And the Institute? What was to become of that? How were they to go on? The appointment and yearly pension of 400 Taler had been granted to headmaster Heinicke in person. Everything would have to be applied for anew – and Anna Catharina Elisabeth Heinicke was a woman.

To begin with, she advertised the death of her husband in several Leipzig and Halle newspapers. There was an advertisement in a Hamburg newspaper as well:

> *Instead of the usual mourning notes, I hereby notify my out-of-town relatives, friends and patrons of the death of my beloved husband, Samuel Heinicke, director of the Electoral Institute for the Deaf and Mute in Leipzig, in the morning of April 30th, in his 64th year, of a stroke (…).* (cited in G. and P. Schumann 1909, p. 45)

In these notices she assured the public that the teaching would not be interrupted, and that people interested in the Institute should retain their honoured confidence in it.

Of course she also notified the elector, namely on May 2nd, and added that she was equipped with firm knowledge and abilities in the teaching of deaf mutes. Not only had she been introduced to the methods of teaching by her husband, but she had herself taught deaf pupils under his supervision and instruction. This precaution had been taken in the event of her husband's death, so that she should be able to provide for herself. At the close of her letter, she asked the elector to allow her to continue teaching under the previous conditions, together with the teaching assistant August Fr. Petschke (1759-1822), who had been employed at the Institute since 1788 (A1, 6-9).

During 1790 an active correspondence developed between the applicants for appointment or continuation of employment and the electoral chancellery. Petschke sent a petition in the same spirit as Frau Heinicke's to Dresden on 4. May, and even E.A. Eschke from Berlin addressed himself to the elector on 20. May and asked to be considered for appointment as the new headmaster in Leipzig, since he had learned the deaf mute teaching method from Samuel Heinicke himself.

In a *Gehorsamstes Pro Memoria (most obedient memorandum)* of 18. May 1790, Frau Heinicke explained in detail, apart from her basic qualification for deaf mute teaching, why she needed a second teacher, and a male one at that, for the Institute. She often had to teach

---

1   At that time, Samuel Heinicke had written to the elector: *If your Electoral Highness granted me an allowance of 200 Taler on top of my present pension, and, in case of my decease, a widow's pension of 200 Taler to my wife, I will endeavour to teach my method to two or three (…) persons allotted to me for that purpose every year* (cited in G. and P. Schumann 1909, p. 27).

downright uncultured persons between the ages of 20 and 30 (oft 20 bis 30jährige, durchaus sehr uncultivirte Menschen), spoilt by their parents, used to a vagrant life, slow to comprehend, with whom it was necessary at first to apply *coercive means and punishment* (*Zwangsmittel und Strafen; A2, 15-16*). Moreover, she needed much time for the organization of the Institute, time that would have to be taken away from the all-important teaching. The students must not lose a minute, however, since it was necessary for them to receive nine to ten hours of fixed classes every day. Therefore she needed the student of theology Petschke as teacher. They could share duties – in the letter's words:

> *(...) neither of us can preside over the teaching without the other; he because of discipline and the necessity of keeping good order, supervision and teaching, myself to supervise the teaching in the spirit of my late husband, and to fix the pupils' language, so that they will not forget either speech or writing. Moreover, I am concerned with the domestic duties, and teaching the children, especially those of the female sex, other suitable accomplishments. We have agreed to retain the teaching method introduced by my late husband and to support and help each other. (A2, 15-16)*

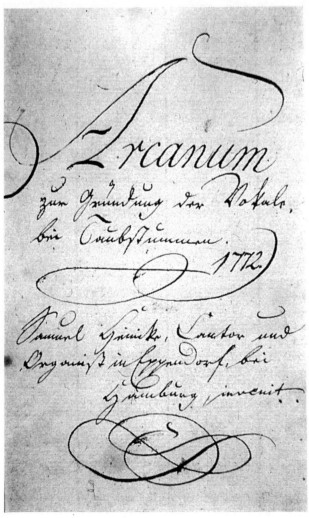

Ill. 2: *Samuel Heinicke's Arcanum (frontispiece), Eppendorf 1772*

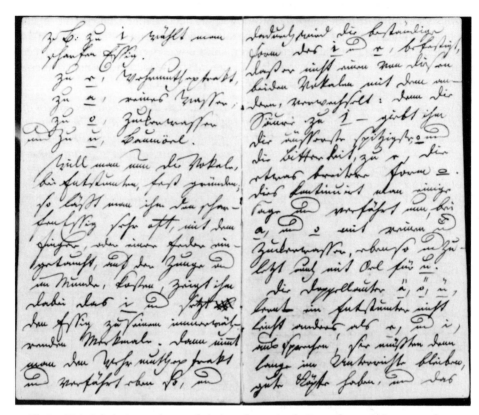

Ill. 3: *Heinicke's Arcanum explaining the articulation of vowels by way of taste*

The unison of the content of Petschke's and Frau Heinicke's letters, and the assertion that one could not very well work in the Institute without the other, may have had a deeper reason. A.C.E Heinicke was a 32 year old widow; Petschke was two years younger. Heinicke scholar Paul Schumann tells of courting attempts on the part of Petschke and eventually a marriage proposal, which was rejected. (G. and P. Schumann 1909, p. 52)

On July 10th, 1790, a reassuring promise arrived in Leipzig: Frau Heinicke was to receive her husband's salary, so as not to interrupt the work of the Institute (G. and P. Schumann 1909, p. 50), and on October 30th, the Leipzig applicants were appointed by a decree to joint management of the Institute. Therein, the elector obliged them to the full use of Heinicke's method for teaching the deaf, including the supposed secret of fixing the language (G. and P. Schumann 1909, p. 50).

The greater part of the following years' correspondence was concerned with this peculiar 'secret of language fixation'. The 'secret' in question is the famous *Arcanum*, that short eight-page paper of Heinicke's that formulates his very personal teaching method and his 'invention' for fixing articulated sounds for the Deaf and making them permanent by means of the sense of taste. Samuel Heinicke had sealed this tract and put it with the most important family documents, probably to provide for his wife and family in the event of his early death. Initially, he thought he might be able to sell it for a considerable sum, but he never managed to do so. Ordered by the elector to reveal the secret in October 1790, Frau Heinicke declared to him on December 8th:

(..) but a sacred oath is barring me (from disclosing the secret), *which I had to give my dying husband, not to part with the secret of the Arcanum even to my step-children, but to keep it for my son, or, if he should not live, not to give it away until upon my death-bed.* (G. and P. Schumann 1909, p. 50)

At the same time, she asked the elector's forgiveness: it was neither mistrust nor disobedience to his gracious order, but she could not release herself from the oath she had taken. The elector might allow her to keep the Arcanum for her son, or until her death.

One year later, the elector directed the University to make further inquiries into the meaning of the Arcanum. These were carried out until April 1791. In the course of the inquiries, marked doubts about the value of Heinicke's secret remedy were expressed by the University members, namely that:

(...) this alleged secret, which has never been mentioned by a deaf mute teacher, and most probably relates to the late Heinicke's pet theory, that the Deaf had to learn to taste the sounds of speech since they could not hear them, (...) is nothing but a singularly improbable, wholly imaginary claim, (...). (cited in G. and P. Schumann 1909, p. 51)

Moreover, a Leipzig University 'Reskript' to Frau Heinicke of November 25th, 1791 obliged her to pass on the teaching method to other teachers, according to the appointment decree of 1777, and stated that Samuel Heinicke could not by rights have demanded such an oath from his wife.

On May 18th, 1792, there was a new turn regarding the Arcanum. Frau Heinicke designated Petschke and another teacher, Magister Stein from Leipzig, who had been employed in the meantime by the Institute, as persons suitable to learn the secret, provided they would not use it to the widow's disadvantage. On September 12th, of the same year, she gave her pledge to the University to initiate both teachers fully into the secret, and this initiation was carried out accordingly.

By and by the Arcanum was forgotten because of its insignificance. In 1805 it is once more mentioned in detail – probably for the last time – by the teacher Junghannß. There had been a considerable controversy between him and Director Heinicke, which we will recount later. So much for the events concerning the Arcanum. Back to the year 1791.

In 1791 the school moved to Neue Straße, outside of the Hallische Pförtchen in the North of the city, where the Deaf Mute Institute would remain for eight years. The joint directorship of A. C. E. Heinicke and A.F. Petschke had not proved successful in the long run. There emerged more and more nerve-racking arguments, perhaps caused in part by Frau Heinicke's reserved attitude towards Petschke. Owing to these quarrels, there were lengthy settlement proceedings presided over by the University commission, and finally a mediation of the controversy. In consequence, Frau Heinicke was appointed to sole directorship of the Institute by an electoral decree in 1792, shortly before her 35th birthday, while the candidate of theology, Petschke, was appointed head teacher, with a yearly salary of 150 Taler.

Frau Heinicke and the superintending University board were eager to reorganize the Institute. Since the training period for Deaf people had been only three to four years up to then, A.C. E. Heinicke asked the elector for an extension of that period for able and talented students. She also asked for the opportunity to rid the school of the mentally retarded, *half-witted (blödsinnige)* students who were not deaf or mute. In consequence, the number of pupils sank temporarily, so that only five were listed in her handwritten roll in 1795.

Because of rising prices in the city, the Institute was to be transferred from Leipzig to a smaller town in order to save money. But Frau Heinicke was strictly opposed to this idea, since Leipzig , as a large city, so she argued, was best suited for developing deaf people's ideas, because of the city's diversity. Moreover, the busy tourist traffic, owing to the Fair, commerce and the University, brought numerous visitors to their house, and with them donations for the poorer students' linen and clothing (A3, 170-171). A visitor's book started in 1795 lists callers from almost all of Europe.

In the past, Frau Heinicke had spared no expense in the matter of publications and advertisements for her Institute, but she was of the opinion that, above all, it should be the government's duty to make the Institute better known to the public. She also thought about ways of improving and securing the Institute's financial situation, and performed very precise calculations to this purpose. Thus in 1796 she proposed a state collection, calculating a total amount of 83,333 Taler if every citizen of Saxony were to give one Groschen ($^1/_{10}$ of a Taler). 75,000 Taler might be permanently invested, and the interest of 2,625 Taler be used to pay for the Institute's regular expenses, while a new private school building could be bought with the remaining 8,333 Taler, since the number of pupils had grown and more space was needed (A3, 171R-172).

Ill. 4: *A.C.E. Heinicke's register of their first pupils*

In 1798, there were eleven pupils, six boys and five girls, and the lodgings on Neue Straße were too small for this number. The flat consisted of four rooms: a parlor with two windows, used as living, dining, and classroom, one room next to this one for the *Frau Directorin* and her three children, a small entrance-hall, a kitchen, a larger chamber as bedroom for seven pupils and two maids and, finally, a small, windowless *closet resembling a cow-shed more than a room fit to live in (Behältnis, das eher einem Kuhstall als einem Wohnraum* [glich]); four pupils slept in there (Schlenkrich 1928, p. 61). For that reason, Frau Heinicke applied to the superior University commission with a request for the acquisition of a suitable house as Institute building, *because landlords refuse to accept a school, especially a deaf mute institute, into a larger flat (da Hausbesitzer sich weigern, eine Schule, besonders aber ein Taubstummen-Institut in eine größere Mietwohnung zu nehmen);* Schlenkrich 1928, p. 61). For over a year, another pressing reason for buying a house had been the gratifyingly large number of provisional enrollments of new pupils. There had been 15 to 20 applications from Saxony and some more from Denmark, but they had had to be rejected for reasons of space. The wish for an independent school building was to remain unfulfilled for many years to come.

Apart from the need to improve their housing conditions, Frau Heinicke was also concerned about her pupils' future lives, their occupational training and placement opportunities to enable their certain integration into industry and craft. She developed many ideas and made proposals to this end. For two years, she had been proposing the foundation of an industrial school, and in 1798 she thought of a printing office:

> One could establish a printing office next to the Institute, if the printers' union allowed it, or a coloured paper and wallpaper factory, or a factory for playing cards, all of which would be arrangements, as it seems to me, that might assure the Mutes' future livelihood after their leaving school. (A4, 220R)

In 1800, the poet Johann Wolfgang von Goethe stayed in Leipzig, where he also visited the Deaf Mute Institute. Frau Heinicke presented the visitor's book to him where he inscribed his name.

In December 1800, improved living and working conditions were finally provided for the Institute by a move to Neugasse. Now they had six living rooms, three cabinets, two kitchens and additional rooms at their disposal. The elector granted an additional 100 Taler for the move, the higher rent and numerous new acquisitions. More pupils than ever could now be accepted. In 1801, there were 17 students, in 1805 there were 20.

Several expert opinions in these years credit the director with excellent management in several respects: pupils of both sexes learned according to Samuel Heinicke's method, including the secret of language fixation. Out of class, they acquired skills in suitable and useful handicraft. The male pupils drew, the female pupils did needlework. The food was flawless, order and the utmost neatness prevailed everywhere (Schlenkrich 1928, p. 63).

Notwithstanding the improved accommodations, the examining Oberkonsistorialpräsident von Gärtner called for a private house once more in 1801, with an infirmary, a courtyard and a sunny garden. He proposed building a suitable house on the premises of the Leipziger Pleißenburg's unused bastion, and laying out a garden (Schlenkrich 1928, p. 63). But von Gärtner's plan could not be put into practice owing to a too high estimate and the outbreak of the Napoleonic wars in the following years.

Among the medical-technical innovations of the time was galvanism. Frau Heinicke, who was advised by the Institute physician Prof. Dr. Rosenmüller, applied at once for the purchase of a galvanic healing machine. Her request was supported by the University Senate and granted by the elector, but the actual treatment given to pupils did not bring about the results that had been hoped for.

The year 1805 brought hard times for Frau Heinicke, with her existence threatened, she bore the brunt of disappointments and personal insults. In the previous year, the elector had demanded the revelation of the speech sounds-fixation secret or else she would lose her financial support. Thus, renewed difficulties were created by the Arcanum. On top of this, the teacher Junghannß, employed since 1799, fell out with Frau Heinicke over a salary raise, and as a result sent pages and pages of letters to the elector, with malicious denunciations and libel about the inner and outer situation of the Institute. With regard to the 'secret', he wrote, for example:

> *As everybody knows, Madame Heinicke makes all sort of fuss about the so-called Arcanum, which she has from time to time and now once again been ordered to reveal to some subjects of this state, and she acts as if it was the ultimate invention, the secret of secrets, without which teaching the deaf would not be possible at all.* (A5, 31R)

Frau Heinicke protested sharply against all these attacks, and introduced her defence with the following words:

> *It is humiliating and depressing for me to have to defend myself, because of Herr Junghannß' formal denunciation of 12. February of this year, against such things as have been said therein about the Institute, so graciously entrusted to myself, and the method used there (...).* (A6, 33)

In October of the same year, the difficulties seemed to have been overcome. About the passing on of her husband's method to younger persons Frau Heinicke declared in another *Gehorsamstes Pro Memoria*:

> *I have several times (…) stated my willingness to give young people the opportunity to learn the method of teaching the deaf,which I have proved with Prof. Stein (Magister Stein), now employed as a teacher at the graues Kloster in Berlin, as the enclosed attestation may show, and am proving now with the Magister Ludwig August Rosenmüller (...).* (A7, 65)

Handwritten testimonies of the truth of this statement by both persons mentioned were enclosed. That Frau Heinicke came out of the Junghannß disagreement unscathed is confirmed by a letter of October 1805, in which she writes: *I am flattered by the good esteem in which I have the luck to be held by my high and highest superiors (…; A8, 66).*

The year 1806 brought hard times to the city of Leipzig due to the war and the resulting defeat of Prussia by Napoleon. The realization of all plans and schemes dependent on financial means stagnated in consequence. Nevertheless, Frau Heinicke did not stop putting many proposals and petitions to the University and the elector. She was supported by the two directors of the University, professors Tittmann and Rosenmüller.

On May 1st, 1810, the Institute was able to employ Magister Carl Gottlob Reich (1782-1852) as an assistant teacher, which was to prove an important gain for the Institute's future. Likewise in 1810, Friedrich August, who in the meantime had become King of Saxony[2], granted Frau Heinicke a raise in her income by 200 Taler.

Meanwhile, the Saxonian treasury had been gradually filling again, so that an application for a premium dating from 1806, now renewed, was granted in 1811 and decreed as a royal Generale. It said that every master who took on a deaf mute as an apprentice was to receive a non-recurring premium of 50 Taler out of the royal premium treasury. Initially, the Generale restricted the granting of such premiums to a period of six years. Every deaf mute was to be allowed to practice his acquired profession or craft, after having passed his examination, without having to obtain masters' or guild rights first (A12, 155-156R).

In 1812, a confidential message, unofficial as yet, gave rise to a great hope for the Institute. Frau Heinicke was visiting her former homeland at the time. A letter from her daughter Amalie, of 18. July, reached her in Hamburg, containing this piece of news:

---

2   The elector Friedrich August III reigned as King Friedrich August I after 1806.

A sickly rich old lady has included the Deaf Mute Institute in her will! Reich has talked to one of his lawyer acquaintances who revealed it to him in strict confidence, and he told me (...). (cited in Schlenkrich 1928, p. 69)

More could not be learned; three years were to go by before the beneficial secret was to be known. But before that, there came a very hard year for Frau Heinicke in 1813. She received a terrible blow in February. Her daughter Wilhelmine Rosina, married for but three years in Hamburg, died at the age of 35. Just a few years earlier, Frau Heinicke had mourned her father, who had died in Jüthorn in 1810, and her 'step-son-in-law' E. A. Eschke who died in Berlin in 1811. Her efforts for improvements in the Institute went on nevertheless.

In September, she addressed herself to the king once more in the matter of a house, recounting the gratifying growth of the number of pupils to 24, and the resulting necessity of renting a larger building. She would need an additional sum of 150-200 Taler. Furthermore, she asked for a salary raise, because the exchange rate had fallen. Both applications failed, however, because the Völkerschlacht (battle of the nations) raged in Leipzig one month later. Since the Institute was situated outside the city gates, facing the Grimmaische Tor, Frau Heinicke fled with her charges to the city center, and found shelter with Prof. Rosenmüller and, after a few days, with his father in the superintendency.

Typhus soon spread in the city, and also afflicted one of the pupils. To avoid further infection, Frau Heinicke moved with her pupils to Volkmarsdorf near Leipzig for a time. Life in the city was growing back to normal, and a new opportunity in her permanent search for a house suited to the new number of pupils offered itself in the middle of June 1814. Frau Heinicke wrote of this in a letter to her daughter Amalie:

I went into town yesterday, meaning to take the Schreiters' house, out of necessity. It was to cost 300 Taler. Before that, I went to Reichel's, since I had announced my visit to him; I did not hope to find anything there, but found lodgings spacious and pretty beyond all expectation, with 15 large and small rooms. It is the corner of the Thomaspförtchen (...). (cited in Schlenkrich 1928, p. 68)

The flat cost a rent of 400 Taler. Frau Heinicke applied for an extra rent allowance of 200 Taler in Dresden and moved into the new lodgings immediately. Some weeks later, the rent allowance was granted.

Years of joy and relief followed. Hopes inspired by daughter Amalie's news, in 1812, of a possible benefactor were fulfilled to an exceedingly liberal degree. After the death of that *sickly rich old lady*, one widowed Frau Luise Carl in 1815, the Institute inherited a sum of 40,000 Taler in 1815 that was to be held in trust by the University pension office. Now the Institute was freed from its financial predicaments and its future was secured. Petschke, who had suffered from gout since 1812, was pensioned with an annuity of 150 Taler the same year. Likewise in 1815, Heinicke's youngest son Samuel Anton, for whom the Arcanum was to have been kept initially, got married. The following year, another joyful celebration took place: Carl Gottlob Reich, who had been teaching at the Institute with much commitment, pedagogical skill, psychological knowledge and great talent since 1810, married daughter Amalie in March 1816, and became the director's son in law. She had in him an eager collaborator full of ideas, whose initiative had, for example, led to the foundation of a Sunday School in 1818. Deaf adults could meet there, develop their knowledge, keep up social contacts and thus find a way out of their isolation.

In all the years of her contact with deaf people – from her childhood onwards – Anna Heinicke collected much experience and developed a sensitive way of thinking about them and treating them. Apart from her ability as organizer and manager, Frau Heinicke had also, little by little, gained practical pedagogical and psychological knowledge, which showed partly in her yearly appraisals of her pupils, but mostly in several official documents written by her.

In 1815/16 she suggested an entrance examination for future pupils, to investigate their *ability of understanding and ability of being taught (Verstandes- und Unterrichtsfähigkeit),* and recommended a number of concrete examination criteria in the form of several questions:

> *One should ask the parents if the child is fit for domestic work suited to his age and strength, whether he plays with other children – whether he can find his way back to his parents' house when he is so far away from it that the child cannot see it anymore – if he can carry out little shopping assignments with small change (...).* (A14, 261R)

and, with regard to the same subject, in another letter:

> *(...) whether he can count, can tell how many chairs, tables, people are in a room and, if some of them are taken away, how many are left and how many are missing (...). Also, what he occupies himself with, whether he shows an inclination for work or remains idly inactive for several hours.* (A13, 205R)

Frau Heinicke particularly insisted on suitable persons for the giving of such examinations, and her fine instinct and her skillful approach are evident when she demands:

> *Such an examination must of course be carried out by such persons as are known to the child, and perhaps be repeated several times, until the child has learned to trust the examiner. It takes the utmost caution not to pass sentence upon such an unfortunate creature too soon. Preachers and school teachers are suited best for this humane examination, since there is nothing in their dwelling that might deter the unhappy deaf mute. A loving approach will gain his trust in them. This is not so when they enter a council office, where the child's mind is frightened – he does not know what the gentlemen want of him, he retracts into himself (...).* (A15, 262)

In a much earlier document, A. C. E. Heinicke concerned herself with the language acquisition of the Deaf and the necessary number of school years for its achievement. It was very difficult to give an exact number, she said, because one could never foretell with absolute certainty when a pupil might be ready to be released from school with good results. In this context, she reflected on the complexity of language, and wrote:

> *Whoever has thought a little about the difficulties we encounter in learning a foreign language, although we are in possession of all our five senses, will easily be able to imagine those the deaf mute has to overcome. Give me for example, just one rule of our language for choosing the article, or forming the plural of the nouns, or declining them in the first place. If there is any language that has a lot of anomalies, it must surely be ours. And that is leaving aside pronunciation. How many obstacles does syntax provide, the inner life of a language, the turns of speech: a thought may often be expressed in more than one way, and still there may be only one expression right or best for a particular passage.*
> *It cannot be overlooked, therefore, that the deaf mute who is wrenched from the classroom too soon will probably come off the path he had been led onto, because of all these obstacles, and fall back into his previous condition if he is not naturally eager to learn, because he will not, or cannot, practice enough for lack of time, since he will be occupied with other things. To prevent this, he must be taught in his lessons how to overcome the obstacles, and be led on the way to helping himself.* (A9, 108)

Frau Heinicke compared the language acquisition process of hearing infants to that of deaf ones, and observed the differences:

> *I cannot very well leave unobserved the fact that a hearing child starts receiving instruction soon after his birth. He learns to listen to the voice of his parents and those*

around him, to tell them from each other, and once he has received the art of speech sounds, he instructs himself continually. How different is the case with the poor child born deaf. He does receive impressions from outside, just as the other does, but the involuntary instruction that the other is receiving every moment is lost to him because he cannot hear, and must be replaced by a sign language, which, however, only serves to indicate his material needs. Such a child remains with his parents, who have been disheartened by the inconvenience of talking to him, until his 11th or 12th year (…). (A10, 109)

In her school practice, Frau Heinicke permanently saw pupils enrolled in or brought to the Institute much too late, often at the age of 15 or 20, and sometimes even older. In the letter cited above, she referred to two deaf students a little older and a little younger than 14 years of age, *Of course they are in their early manhood, when with regard to their knowledge they have not even reached boyhood* (*Freilich sind sie in dem Jünglingsalter, da sie ihren Kenntnissen nach erst und da noch nicht einmal im Knabenalter stehen*). Linguistically, Frau Heinicke put them *much behind a two- or three-year-old child* (*ungleich weiter hinter dem 2 oder 3jährigen Kinde*).

Are not such children unfortunate? Of course, only one who is concerned solely with them can see the sadness of their situation, the restriction of their brains, their more than childish simplicity in the first stages of teaching. (A11, 109)

These two examples are meant to illustrate Frau Heinicke's concern with the substantial professional side of her field.

The search for a private house was finally brought to a happy conclusion in 1821. Frau Heinicke bought a suitable house and plot of land on Klitzschergasse, close to the

Ill. 5: *Deaf Mute Institute of Leipzig (Klitzschergasse)*

Pleißenburg, for 12,000 Taler out of the Carl donation fund. After the necessary alterations for school and boarding purposes had been completed, the Institute was able to move there on April 12th, 1822. Thus, a long-cherished dream finally came true, after the Leipzig Deaf Mute Institute had been in existence for 44 years. Independent of landlords, financially secure, and furnished with much larger capacity, the new Institute already accommodated 38 pupils in 1823. They were taught in four forms and had 40 hours of lessons per week. These lessons were spread from Monday to Saturday, and usually held from 8-12 in the morning and 2-5 in the afternoon. This can be seen from an 1822 schedule (A16, 230R-231).

III

An important anniversary was gradually approaching: in 1828, the Institute looked back on 50 years of existence, and A.C.E.Heinicke celebrated 50 years of service. The ceremonies were to take place in a setting worthy of the occasion and had to be well prepared. To this purpose, several decrees were issued by the authorities. The new King Anton had been reigning in Dresden since the death of King Friedrich August I in 1827. He had paid a visit to the Institute in the very first year of his reign. He decreed an adequate tribute for the director (70 years old by now) to be celebrated. At her age, it was understandable that she expressed the wish to hand over the management of the Institute and retire after so many years of work and responsibility. It was with this request that she addressed the superintending University board on January 1st, 1828. She wrote in her letter that the Institute for Deaf Mutes had now been in existence for 50 years. She also praised her husband's work and that of the succeeding teachers Petschke and Reich. But most of all she pointed out Magister Carl Gottlob Reich's meritorious work for the benefit of the Deaf, that he

> *(...) has made a study of the way to teach these unfortunate people, has delved into their sad condition so deeply that he succeeded in bringing them further in the development of their mental powers than has ever happened before, nor been thought possible, with the difficulties that stand in the way of this kind of teaching. Magister Reich has worked night and day in this undertaking and will not tire in coming nearer to his set goal. One of his achievements was and still is that he trained the pupil Teuscher to be a teacher, who, born completely deaf, has never heard a sound. His work is acknowledged, by our honoured authorities, by headmasters and teachers of similar institutions elsewhere.* (A17, 95-95R)

It was her most urgent wish, therefore, that C.G.Reich should be appointed as future director, and this in time for the foundation's anniversary on April 13th, if possible. Further, she asked for continuation of her previous salary of 400 Taler for herself, and the same sum for Reich in the future. The presidents of the University board, professors Tittmann and Beck, passed her request on to Dresden, and received the order to arrange the anniversary *with due ceremony (mit angemessener Feierlichkeit;* A18, 99-99R).

A letter from King Anton himself was sent to the University, in which, among other things, the following was written:

> *In answer to your most subservient report of the 19th of this month, regarding the celebration of the Leipzig Deaf Mute Institute's foundation 50 years ago, and the useful activity demonstrated for the same span of years by the widow Heinicke, We have decided to give a diamond ring to said Heinicke on the occasion of the planned festivities, in order to demonstrate Our contentment with her previous achievements and with the present condition of the Institute directed by her (...).* (A19, 100)

She did not, however, obtain consent to her request to be released from the directorship and to hand over the leadership to her son-in-law Reich, at least not for the present year. The celebrations were held in due pomp and lasted two days. The deaf chronicler C. M. Löwe writes about them:

> *On the first day of the jubilee, the 'jubilee mother', being in her 71st year, was surprised with a morning serenade. During the forenoon many presents, some of them precious, were given to her. She also received several letters, poems and presents from former pupils and friends of the Institute. Several of them had travelled to Leipzig in order to take part in the festivities in person. (...) Early on the second day of the jubilee, the day of the principal celebration, the classroom where the public examination of the pupils was to take place was festively decorated with garlands and wreaths.* (Löwe 1878, pp. 60-61)

Löwe goes on to recount that the University's deputies, Oberhofgerichtspräsident von Ende, the two directors of the Institute and other officials and patrons arrived at about nine o'clock. After the *jubilee mother* and the gentlemen had taken their seats in the first row, Oberhofgerichtspräsident von Ende made a ceremonious speech and presented the precious diamond ring on behalf of the king, as a sign of recognition. Then Magister Reich opened the pupils' examination with a speech to the assembled persons. After the three-hour examination, all of the approximately 80 people present went to a banquet. The celebrations continued until dinner.

In his biography of Samuel Heinicke written in 1828, C. G. Reich also remembered Frau Heinicke *who with acknowledged loyalty and truly motherly care has now been living for her profession for 50 years ((...) welche mit anerkannter Treue und wahrhaft mütterlicher Sorgfalt nun 50 Jahre ihrem Berufe gelebt hat;* Reich 1828, p. 106).

She continued to hold the Institute's directorship until the end of that year. On 1. January 1829 she was allowed to retire by a royal decree *in most gracious acknowledgement of the merit gained in the many years of the Institute's directorship* with an *allowance of three hundred Taler per year ((...) in gnädigster Anerkennung der während der langjährigen Direction des Instituts um dasselbe sich erworbenen Verdienste (...)* (mit einem) *Gnadengehalt von Drey Hundert Thalern jährlich;* A20, 180).

C. G. Reich succeeded her. A. C. E. Heinicke was able to devote almost 12 years to private matters and enjoy her well earned retirement. Naturally, she continued living in the Institute and helped wherever she was needed, after her usual fashion. We learn from a multitude of letters that she was a very kind, modest, and universally loved mother, grandmother and 'foster mother' (Heinicke, A.C.E. AII/1).

During her last years, she wrote a short chronicle of the Heinicke and Kludt families on 17 pages of a small copy-book titled *Familien-Nachrichten (family news)*. It is a concise listing of all relevant family members with the dates of their birth and death, as well as their places of birth and later dwelling places, and it extends as far as her grandchildren and great-grandchildren.

Towards the end of her life, there was an accumulation of deaths in her family once again. Four grandchildren died, in addition to her son Samuel Anton, her brother Wolfgang, stepson Carl A. Dietrich and, finally, her mother. Thus, time and time again, she had to carry much personal grief in her later life, apart from all the problems and worries concerning her Institute.

The last year of her life, however, brought joy once more, and the fulfillment of a long-cherished dream. By order of the Saxonian government, a municipal building was planned for the Deaf Mute Institute, located on a suitable plot beyond the Windmühlentor; the foundation-stone was laid on 4. September 1839. Frau Heinicke was able to see the raising of this handsome building in good health, but not, unfortunately, its opening on October 27th/28th, 1840.

She died on August 6th, 1840. Carl Gottlob Reich had the following notice printed in the *Leipziger Tageblatt* of August 8th:

Today, during the 12th hour, our beloved and honoured mother and grandmother Frau Anna Katharina Heinicke passed away, without pain and without a presentiment of death, in her 83rd year.
As wife of the local Deaf Mute Institute's founder, our unforgettable father Samuel Heinicke, and as directress of this Institute after his early death in 1790, she has performed the duties of her profession with motherly loyalty, through manifold worries and partly bitter experiences, and has thus earned a full right to the lasting gratefulness of her deaf mute foster children and the high esteem of all who were witnesses of her meritorious work. Those who have known the rich goodness of her heart, and her affectionate love for her people, will not deny us the quiet sympathy that we would herewith like to ask from her friends and our dear friends.
6.August 1840   *The Reich Family*
(cited in Schlenkrich 1928, p. 74)

Her work and merits in the field of deaf education were remembered in a three-page appreciation in the *Neuer Nekrolog der Deutschen* of 1840, by way of listing particular stations of her life. She was *loved by all near and far members of her family, highly esteemed by dear friends, gratefully honoured by her deaf mute foster children* (geliebt von allen nahen und fernen Gliedern ihrer Familie, hochgeachtet von lieben Freunden dankbar geehrt von ihren taubstummen Pflegekindern; anon. 1840, p. 875).

(Translated by Trixi Flügel)

Appendix
The original German quotations:

p. 272

> Meinen auswärtigen Anverwandten, Freunden u. Gönnern, zeige hiermit statt der gewöhnlichen Trauerbriefe an, daß mein geliebter Ehemann, Samuel Heinicke, Dir.d.Ch.I.f. Tbste. i.L. d. 30.Ap.a.c. früh an einem Steck- u. Schlagfluß im 64sten Jahre seines Alters verstorben (…). (cited in G. and P. Schumann 1909, p. 45)

p. 272 (footnote 1)

> Wenn mir eine Zulage von 200 Thlrn. zu meiner gegenwärtigen Pension, u. auf den Fall meines Absterbens, meiner Frau ein Witwengehalt, von 200 Thlrn., von Ew.Churftl.Durchl. zugesichert wird, mache ich mich anheischig meine Lehrmethode, jährl. zween od. dreyen (…) dazu mir angewiesenen Subjekten bey zu bringen. (cited in G. and P. Schumann 1909, p. 27)

p. 273

> (…) daß keines von beiden allein ohne das andere dem Unterrichte vorstehen kann; er wegen der Disziplin und sonst zu erhaltenden guten Ordnung, Aufsicht und Ertheilung des Unterrichts, und ich sowohl um den ganzen Unterricht nach dem Geiste meines seel. Mannes zu leiten und die Sprache der Schüler endlich zu fixiren, damit sie Ton- und Schriftsprache nicht wieder vergessen, als auch um die häuslichen Angelegenheiten zu besorgen und die Kinder, besonders die so weiblichen Geschlechts, in den für sie schicklichen Arbeiten noch außerdem zu unterrichten, und wir haben uns darinnen mit einander einverstanden, die Unterrichtsmethode, so wie solche von meinem seel. Manne ist eingeführt worden, künftig zu behalten und uns einander zur gegenseitigen Hülfe zu dienen. (A2, 15-16)

p. 275

(…) allein ein heiliger Eid, den ich meinem sterbenden Manne habe leisten müssen, das Geheimnis des Arcanums nicht aus den Händen, auch nicht einmal meinen Stief-Kindern zu geben, sondern es für meinen Sohn aufzubewahren und im Falle er nicht am Leben bleiben sollte, es erst auf dem Sterbebette auszuhändigen, hindert mich daran. (cited in G. and P. Schumann 1909, p. 50)

(…) dieses vorgegebene noch nie von einem Lehrer der Taubstummen erwähnte u. allem Vermuten nach sich auf des verstorb. H. Lieblings-Hypothese, daß die Tauben die Sprach-töne müßten schmecken lernen, da sie selbige nicht hören könnten, beziehende Geheimnis (…) nichts als eine bloß in der Einbildung bestehende höchst unwahrscheinliche Behaup-tung zu sein scheint, (…). (cited in G. and P. Schumann 1909, p. 51)

p. 277

Man könnte bei dem Institute eine Buchdruckerei anlegen, wenn es die Gesellschaft der Buchdrucker duldete, oder eine bunte Papier- und Tapetenfabrik, oder eine Spielkartenfa-brik, welches, wie es mir scheinet, alles Dinge wären, wo die Stummen, nach ihrem Austritte aus der Schule, wegen ihres künftigen Unterhaltes gedekt wären. (A4, 220R)

p. 278

Mit dem sogenanten Arcanum, welches die M.H. von Zeit zu Zeit einigen Landeskindern bekant zu machen neuerdings wieder angewiesen worden ist, macht sie bekantl. erstaunend viel Umstände, und thut damit, als wäre es das non plus ultra von Erfindung, und das Geheim-nis aller Geheimnisse, ohne welches gar kein Unterricht der Taubstumen möglich sei. (A5, 31R)

Es ist kränkend und niederschlagend für mich, daß ich durch eine unterm 12ten Februar d.J. von H.Junghannß eingereichte förmliche Anklage in die Nothwendigkeit versetzt werde, mich gegen solche Dinge, als in derselben von der mir gnädigst anvertrauten Anstalt und der darin gebräuchlichen Methode gesagt worden, vertheidigen zu müssen, (…). (A6, 33)

Ich habe schon mehrmals geäussert und mich (…) willig bezeugt, jungen Leuten Gelegenheit zu geben, die Methode Taubstumme zu unterrichten zu lehren, wie ich auch an den jetzt in Berlin am grauen Kloster als Lehrer angestellten Prof: Stein bewiesen habe, welches beigeleg-tes Zeugniß zu erkennen giebt, und nun durch den Herrn Mag: Ludwig August Rosenmüller (…) beweise (…). (A7, 65)

Ich schmeichle mir den guten Ruf, in dem ich bei meinen höchsten und hohen Vorgesetzten zu stehen das Glück habe, (…). (A8, 66)

p. 279

Eine reiche alte kränkliche Dame hat das Taubstummen-Institut in ihrem Testament bedacht! Reich, der mit einem Juristen seiner Bekanntschaft gesprochen hat und der es ihm im Ver-trauen entdeckt hat, hat es mir erzählt (…). (cited in Schlenrich 1928, p. 69)

Gestern gieng ich in der Absicht in die Stadt, das Schreitersche Haus auf der Windmühlengaße aus Noth zu nehmen, es sollte 300 thlr. kosten. Vorher ging ich zu Reichel, weil ich es ihm hatte sagen laßen, ich glaubte bei ihm nichts zu finden und fand ein über alle Erwartung gro-ßes und hübsches Lokal, welches 15 große und kleine Zimmer hat, es ist die Ecke vom Tho-maspförtchen (…). (cited in Schlenrich 1928, p. 68)

p. 280

Man frage die Eltern, ob das Kind zu häuslichen, seinem Alter und Kräften angemessenen Ver-richtungen zu gebrauchen ist – ob es mit andern Kindern spielt – ob es sich wieder nach seiner Eltern Haus finden kan, wenn es so weit davon entfernt ist, daß das Kind es nicht mehr sieht - ob es Kleinigkeiten für kleine Münze holen (…). (A14, 216R)

(…) ob er zählen kann, ob er bemerken kan wie viel Stühle, Tische, Personen in der Stube sind und wen einiges davon weggenomen, wie viel noch übrig u wie viel fehlet (…). Auch womit er sich beschäftigt, ob er Lust zur Arbeit zeiget oder ob er unbeschäftigt mehrere Stunden in Unthätigkeit bleibet. (A13, 205R)

Eine solche Prüfung muß freilich von solchen Personen, die dem Kinde bekant sind angestellt und vielleicht öfter wiederholt werden bis das Kind erst Zutraun zu dem Fragenden bekömt. Es ist dabei die äußerste Behutsamkeit nöthig um nicht zu bald über ein solch unglückliches

Wesen abzustimen. Die hl. Prediger u. Schullehrer eignen sich am besten zu dieser menschenfreundlichen Untersuchung, den bei ihnen und in ihrer Behausung ist nichts was den unglücklichen Taubstumen zurück schreckt. Ein liebevolles Annähern wird ihnen sein Zutraun erwerben. Nicht so ist es, wen sie in eine Amtsstube treten, da wird das Gemüth eines solchen Kindes beängstiget, es weiß nicht was die Herren von ihm wollen, es tritt schon in sich zurück (...). (A15, 262)

Wer nur einigermaßen über die Schwierigkeiten nachgedacht hat, die sich uns bei der Erlernung einer fremden Sprache in den Weg stellen, ob wir gleich unsre 5 Sinne haben, der wird wohl leicht die sich vorstellen können, die der Taubstumme zu überwinden hat. Man gebe mir nur z.B. für unsre Sprache eine bestimte Regel an, nach welcher ich den Artikel setzen oder den Plural der Nennwörter machen oder diese überhaupt deklinieren soll. Giebt es eine Sprache, die viele Anomalien hat, so ist es gewiß die unsrige. Der AusSprache noch gar nicht zu gedenken. Wie viele Hindernisse hat nicht wieder die Syntax, das Innre der Sprache, die Wendungen, da sich ein Gedanke öfters auf mehr als eine Art ausdrücken läßt, und wo doch nur ein Ausdruck gerade an der gegenwärtigen Stelle der rechte oder der beste ist.

Es läßt sich daher nicht übersehen, daß der Taubstumme wenn er zu früh dem Unterrichte entrissen wird, wenn er nicht von Natur lernbegierig ist, in Betreff dieser Schwierigkeiten nicht wieder von dem Wege abgeht, auf den er gebracht worden und just in seinen vorigen Zustand wieder verfällt, weil er sich nicht hinreichend übt und, aus Mangel an Zeit, da ihn andre Dinge beschäftigen, nicht üben kann. Diesem also vorzubeugen muß er während seines Unterrichts gelehrt werden, die Hindernisse zu übersteigen und auf den Weg gebracht werden, sich selbst fortzuhelfen. (A9, 108)

p. 280 / p. 281

Nun kann ich nicht unbemerkt laßen, daß ein hörendes K. bald nach seiner Geburt schon anfängt Unterricht zu empfangen, es lernt auf die Stimme seiner Aeltern und der es Umgebenden zu merken, sie von einander zu unterscheiden und bekomt es erst die Kunst der Ton Sprache, so unterrichtet es sich unaufhörlich; wie geht es aber dagegen dem armen taubgebornen. Er empfängt zwar wohl auch Eindrücke von außen, so gut wie jenes, der unwillkürliche Unterricht aber, den jenes jeden Augenblick erhält, geht aus Mangel des Gehörs für ihn verloren, und soll durch eine Zeichensprache, die aber durchaus nur die sinnlichen Bedürfnisse bei ihm anzeigt, ersetzt werden. Dieß Kind bleibt bei seinen Eltern, die die Unbequemlichkeit sich mit ihm zu unterhalten, muthlos gemacht bis in sein 11tes 12tes Jahr, (...). (A10, 109)

p. 281

Wie unglücklich sind daher nicht solche Kinder? Das Traurige dieser Lage, das Eingeschränkte ihres Verstandes, ihre mehr als kindische Einfalt bei dem Anfange des Unterrichts sieht aber nur freilich der, der sich mit ihnen ausschließend beschäftigt. (A11, 109)

p. 282

(...) der Art des Unterrichts dieser Unglücklichen nachgeforscht, sich ganz in ihren traurigen Zustande hinein gedacht, daß es ihm gelungen ist in der Entwicklung ihrer Geisteskräfte sie weiter zu bringen denn jemals geschehen, noch für möglich gehalten worden ist, bei den Schwierigkeiten, welche sich diesem Unterrichte entgegen stellen. M. Reich hat Tag und Nacht an dem Werke gearbeitet und ruht noch nicht dem vorgesetzten Ziele näher zu komen. Eine seiner Leistungen war und ist noch die Ausbildung des Zöglings Teuscher zum Lehrer welcher, ganz taub geboren, niemals einen Laut vernomen hat. Anerkant ist was er leistet, von unsern verehrten Behörden, von Vorstehern und Lehrern auswärtiger ähnlichen Anstalten. (A17, 95-95R)

Wir haben auf euren unterthänigsten Bericht vom 19n vorigen Monats in Betreff der Feier der vor fünfzig Jahren erfolgten Gründung der Taubstummen-Anstalt in Leipzig und der seit eben so langer Zeit von der dermaligen Vorsteherin derselben, der verwittweten Heinicke bei ihr bewiesenen nützlichen Wirksamkeit, beschlossen, der genannten Heinicke zur Bezeigung Unsrer Zufriedenheit mit den bisherigen Leistungen und dem dermaligen Zustande des von ihr dirigirten Instituts bei Gelegenheit der obgedachten Feier, einen Brillant-Ring aushändigen (...) zu lassen. (A19, 100)

p. 283

Am ersten Jubeltage wurde die im 71. Jahre ihres Lebens stehende Jubelmutter von einem Morgenständchen überrascht. Im Laufe des Vormittags wurden ihr viele, zum Theile kostbare

Geschenke dargebracht. Verschiedene Briefe, Gedichte und Geschenke wurden ihr auch von ehemaligen Zöglingen und Freunden des Instituts übersandt. Mehrere von jenen waren nach Leipzig hergereist, um an der Feier persönlichen Theil zu nehmen. (...) – Am zweiten Jubeltage, dem Hauptfesttage, früh wurde der Schulsaal, wo die öffentliche Prüfung der Zöglinge gehalten werden sollte, mit Guirlanden und Kränzen festlich geschmückt. (Löwe 1878, pp. 60-61)

p. 284

Heute in der 12. Stunde Mittags entschlief ohne Schmerz und Todesahnung unsere geliebte und ehrwürdige Mutter und Großmutter Frau Anna Katharina Elisabeth Heinicke im 83. Jahre ihres Lebens.
Als Gattin des Stifters des hiesigen Taubstummen-Instituts, unseres unvergeßlichen Vaters: Samuel Heinicke, und nach dessen schon im Jahre 1790 erfolgten Tode, Vorsteherin dieser Anstalt, hat sie unter mancherlei Sorgen und zum Theil bitteren Erfahrungen Fünfzig Jahre hindurch die Pflichten ihres Berufs mit mütterlicher Treue geübt und sich dadurch ein schönes Recht auf den bleibenden Dank ihrer taubstummen Pflegekinder und auf die hohe Achtung aller, welche Zeugen ihres verdienstlichen Wirkens waren, erworben. Uns aber wird, wer ihres Herzens reiche Güte und ihre innige Liebe zu den Ihrigen kannte, in unserer Wehmuth die stille Theilnahme nicht versagen, um welche wir ihre und unsere lieben Freunde hiermit bitten wollen.
Am 6. August 1840   Die Familie Reich
(cited in Schlenkrich 1928, p. 74)

Iconography

Ill. 1: A.C.E. Heinicke
etching by Bernhard Thomas
Bibliothek des Hör- und Sprachgeschädigtenwesens, Leipzig
Photo: Hans Ballschuh
Ill. 2: S. Heinicke: Arcanum zur Gründung der Vokale, bei Taubstummen. Eppendorf 1772
(manuscript), Leipzig
Samuel-Heinicke-Schule, Leipzig (AIV/4, Bl.1)
Photo: Joachim Winkler
Ill. 3: id.
Photo: Hans Ballschuh
Ill. 4: A.C.E. Heinicke: register of the first pupils of the Samuel Heinicke School, Leipzig
unnumbered page, information about her deaf brother J.F. Kludt
Photo: Hans Ballschuh
Ill. 5: Deaf Mute Institute of Leipzig (Klitzschergasse)
In: *Königliche Taubstummen-Anstalt zu Leipzig.Festgabe zur Weihefeier am 7. September 1915.* (n.d.) Leipzig, p. 9

References

unpublished
1. from the archives of the Samuel-Heinicke-Schule Leipzig
Heinicke, S. (1772): Arcanum zur Gründung der Vokale, bei Taubstummen. Eppendorf. – A IV/4.
Heinicke, A.C.E.(n.d.): Familien-Nachrichten. Leipzig. – A IV/16.
Heinicke, A. C. E.(1800 sq.): 49 Briefe aus den Jahren 1800-1829. – AII/1.
ACTA. Das allhier befindliche Institut für taubstumme betreffend.

A1:   Brief der A.C.E.Heinicke an den Kurfürsten Friedrich August III. vom 2.5.1790 (zeitgenöss. Abschrift von fremder Hand). – A I/3, Bl.6-9R.

A2:   Gehorsamstes Pro Memoria der A.C.E.Heinicke an die Universität Leipzig vom 18.5.1790. – A I/3, Bl.15-16.

ACTA. Das Institut der Taubstummen, und derer darinnen aufgenommenen Personen Behandlung von dem Directore Herrn Samuel Heinicke betr..

A3:   Ergebenstes Pro Memoria der A.C.E.Heinicke an die Universität Leipzig vom 22.6.1796.
        – A I/2, Bl.170-173R.

A4:   Ergebenstes Pro Memoria der A.C.E.Heinicke an die Universität Leipzig vom 18.4.1798.
        – A I/2, Bl.217-221.

ACTA. Das allhier befindliche Institut für taubstumme betreffend.

A5:   Brief des C.B.Junghannß an unbekannt vom 12.2.1805. – A I/4b, Bl.18-32R.

A6:   Brief der A.C.E.Heinicke, vermutl. an die Universität Leipzig, vom 14.3.1805 (zeitgenöss. Abschrift von fremder Hand). – A I/4b, Bl.33-42R.

A7-A8: Gehorsamstes Pro Memoria der A.C.E.Heinicke an die Universität Leipzig vom 3.10.1805 (zeitgenöss. Abschrift von fremder Hand). – A I/4b, Bl.65-68.

A9-A11: Gehorsamstes Pro Memoria (handschr. Entwurf) der A.C.E.Heinicke, vermutl. an die Universität Leipzig, vom 27.8.1801. – A I/5, Bl.108-109.

A12:   Generale des Königs Friedrich August I. von Sachsen vom 27.7.1811 (gedruckt). – A I/5, Bl.155-156R.

A13:   Brief der A.C.E.Heinicke (handschr. Entwurf) (o.Dat.) – A I/5, Bl.205-206.

A14-A15: Brief der A.C.E.Heinicke (handschr. Entwurf) (o.Dat.) an die königl.-preuß. Regierung zu Merseburg. – A I/5, Bl.261-263.

2. from the archives of the University of Leipzig

ACTA. Das Taubstummen-Institut betreffend. Repert.II/I E 13.

A16:   Lections-Plan für das Jahr 1822. – Bl.230R-231.

A17:   Gehorsamstes Promemoria der A.C.E.Heinicke an die Universität Leipzig vom 28.1.1828. – Bl.95-96R.

A18:   Schreiben des Conferenz-Ministers u. Geheimen Rathes v. Nostitz u. Zänkendorf vom 12.4.1828. – Bl.98-99R.

A19:   Schreiben des Königs Anton von Sachsen an die Universität Leipzig vom 14.4.1828.
        – Bl.100-101R.

A20:   Schreiben des Königs Anton von Sachsen an die Universität Leipzig vom 23.1.1829.
        – Bl.178-180R.

published

(anon.) (1840): Anna Katharine Elisabeth Heinicke, geborne Kludt, Direktorin des Taubstummeninstituts zu Leipzig; in: *Neuer Nekrolog der Deutschen* 18, pp. 872-875.

Löwe, C. M. (1878): *Kurze Chronik der Taubstummen-Anstalt zu Leipzig*. Dresden.

Reich, C. G. (1828): *Samuel Heinicke - Direktor des Taubstummen-Instituts zu Leipzig*. Leipzig.

Schlenkrich, J. (1928): Zur Geschichte der Leipziger Taubstummen-Anstalt, in: *Die staatliche Taubstummen-Anstalt zu Leipzig (1778-1928). Festschrift zum 150jährigen Bestehen der staatlichen Taubstummen-Anstalt*. Leipzig, pp. 54-99.

Schumann, G./ Schumann, P. (1909): *Neue Beiträge zur Kenntnis Samuel Heinickes*. Leipzig.

Samuel Heinicke

Ill. 60: Samuel Heinicke (1727, Nautschütz - 1790, Leipzig).

Ill. 61: St. Johannis-Eppendorf, Hamburg, Germany, where Heinicke worked as an organist, among others, from 1768 to 1778. At that time, there was a little school house, too, where Heinicke taught some Deaf children.

Ill. 62: In 1778, Heinicke opened the first German school for the Deaf in Leipzig, Germany. The illustration shows a contemporary view of the center of Leipzig.

Ueber die

Denkart

der

Taubstummen,

und

die Mißhandlungen,

welchen sie

durch unsinnige Kuren und Lehrarten

ausgesetzt sind.

Ein Fragment

von Samuel Heinicke,

Director des churfürstl. sächsis. Instituts für Stumme
in Leipzig.

~~~~~~~~~~~~~~~~~~~~~~~~~~~~~~

Leipzig,

bey Christian Gottlieb Hilscher,

1 7 8 0.

Ill. 63: Heinicke published, among other works, a 'fragment' on 'the way of thinking of the deaf mutes' and on 'the ill-treatment they are exposed to because of senseless cures and ways of teaching' (1780).

Ill. 64: 'The creation of the fish and the birds.' This hand coloured etching is contained in an undated version of Samuel Heinicke's 'Biblical History' which, in 1775, was to become the first printed manual for Deaf children.

292

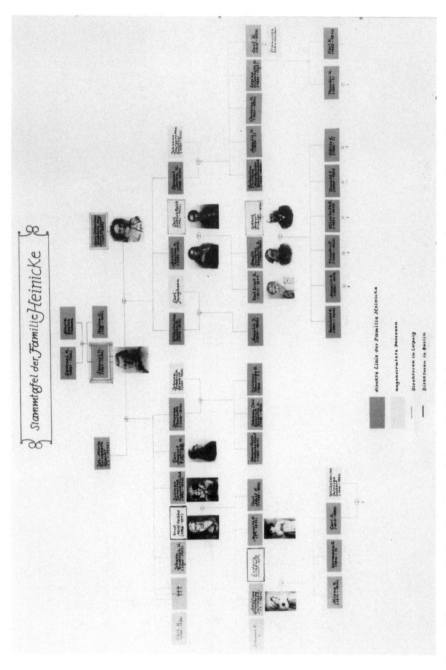

Ill. 65: Genealogy of the Heinicke family. Son Carl August Dietrich founded a private school for the Deaf in Krefeld; daughter Juliane married Ernst Adolf Eschke, founder of a school for the Deaf in Berlin; daughter Amalie married Carl Gottlob Reich, successor of Samuel and Anna C. E. Heinicke at the Leipzig Institute.

Howard G. Williams • *Polina Fyodorova*
Weston-super-Mare, Great Britain • St. Petersburg, Russia

The Origins of the St. Petersburg Institute for the Deaf

Summary • Резюме

The formal beginnings of education of the Deaf in Russia stem from the development of an experimental school established at Pavlovsk in 1806. Drawing upon the memoirs of one of its first pupils, and other information, data are provided about this foundation which later grew into the St. Petersburg Institute for the Deaf, the largest school of its kind in all of Imperial Russia. The philanthropic contribution of the Dowager Empress Maria Feodorovna is described.

Формальное образование глухих в России началось с развитием экспериментальной школы, открытой в Павловске в 1806 году. Используя воспоминания одного из ее первых учеников и другие сведения, приводятся данные об этом учреждении, которое в дальнейшем выросло в Санкт-Петербурский институт глухих, крупнейшее учебное заведение подобного типа во всей Российской империи. Описывается филантропический вклад вдовствующей императрицы Марии Федоровны.

Ill. 1: *St. Petersburg Institute for the Deaf and Dumb*

I

The St. Petersburg Institute was the first school for the Deaf to be formally set up in Imperial Russia. Some isolated teaching of Deaf persons had been carried on earlier[1], but the opening of the Institute at the beginning of the 19th century really marks the beginning of such educational work. Two memoirs written by Aleksandr Meller, the first pupil chosen to be taught there, constitute remarkable testimony to the Institute's origins.

The first of Meller's documents is a letter, dated 1872, written to P.I. Stepanov, then Director at the St. Petersburg Institute, in reply to an inquiry that Stepanov had dispatched to him on the February 15th of that year. This letter (reproduced in Lagovsky 1910, pp. 9-13) gives details of a chance meeting between himself and the Dowager Empress Maria Feodorovna in the gardens of Pavlovsk Palace near St. Petersburg in the summer of 1806, which prompted her to set up and endow a school for Meller and other Deaf children. Meller's second testimony can be found in a few pages of *Pavlovsk: ocherki istorii i opisanie (1777-1877)* that was produced by order of His Imperial Highness the Grand Duke Konstantin Nikolaevich on the centennial of the foundation of the palace and gardens at Pavlovsk (Nikolaevich 1877, pp. 252-255). There is a note appended to Meller's information saying that he *personally testified* (to the author of this 1877 work) *to all written here about him.* While these two memoirs largely overlap and corroborate each other, the 1872 letter also provides details about Meller's later life as a Deaf man employed in the Civil Service of the Imperial Court at St. Petersburg.

The 1872 letter is actually incorporated in an introductory section to N.M. Lagovsky's monumental work *S.-Peterburgskoe Uchilishche Glukhonemykh (1810-1910)*, which was published at the Institute's own printing works at Gorokhovaya ulitsa 18, in 1910. Lagovsky precedes his main and extremely detailed text with this material because, as he maintains,

---

1   These developments were in the more advanced Western or Baltic provinces of Imperial Russia: for instance at Pernau in Livonia (Pärnu, Estonia), where a Jakob Wilde taught as early as 1709. There were also small private schools extant in Riga in Latvia in 1802 and 1809, and at Vilnius in Lithuania about 1805 (Basova 1965).

Opytnago Uchilishcha glukhonemykhi v Pavlovske (the Experimental School for the deaf and dumb in Pavlovsk; Lagovsky 1910, p. 5). provided *est' koren', iz kotorago vyroslo Uchihshche S.-Peterburgskoe (the very beginning, the root of the St. Petersburg Institute;* ibid.). This establishment was to grow until it became the largest school for the deaf in the whole of Imperial Russia. The initial pages of Lagovsky's work also include the full text of a letter sent in 1808 by the Dowager Empress to the abbé Sicard in Paris asking for help in opening up a larger school than the experimental one originally sited at Pavlovsk.

It is of interest to note that certain Soviet commentaries covering this period are available, but, in line with the ideology of the period in which they were written, they read tendentiously and are aligned toward presenting a political case that usually denigrates pre-revolutionary developments, especially any of Tsarist foundation.[2]

II

To summarise the events leading to the foundation of the school: Aleksandr Meller was a Deaf boy, son of a Major-General, and in the summer of 1806 was staying at Pavlovsk with the family of Lieutenant-General Akhverdov, who was tutor to the Grand Dukes Nikolai and Mikhail Pavlovich, sons of the Dowager Empress Maria; Akhverdov's wife was Aleksandr's aunt. One day while walking with her nephew in the park, Ekaterina Borisovna Akhverdova met the Empress, who started a conversation with her. On learning that Aleksandr was Deaf and that there were two other sons and a daughter similarly Deaf amongst the six children of the paternal family, Maria Feodorovna

> *became thoughtful and, as was natural to her compassion, said: 'In other countries the governments have long been aware of such children; special institutions have been set up there for their education; but we have not, unfortunately, done anything yet in this respect'.* (Meller in Nikolaevich 1877, pp. 252-253)

Meller continues almost identically in both the memoirs at this point. He writes that

> *as she talked, the Empress patted my cheek and gave me a few of the sweets that she always carried with her on her usual walks for distribution to children. (She loved children, allowed them to come to her and, every afternoon in the village* (of Pavlovsk nearby), *she gave children a breakfast consisting of milk, butter, cream and so on. Continuing to speak to my aunt, she suggested that my parents could be asked to send me abroad to her brother, the Duke of Württemberg, to study at the Institute* (there) *for the deaf; but my relatives did not want to part with me and, after expressing their gratitude, declined Her Majesty's generous offer. The matter ended there. The next day I was again walking with my aunt in the garden and happened to meet the Empress. She called to my aunt and spoke the following significant words: 'I could not sleep last night because of this boy; I was thinking till morning about his fate and of other children like him, and today, immediately after dressing, I sent for my secretary Villanov and ordered him to engage one of the most well-known professors from abroad to set up a school for deaf mutes in St. Petersburg, where the first students will be the children of your brother.' After relating these happy words to me, my aunt, moved to tears by such generosity, started to thank the Empress and kissed her hand. Very soon Father Sicard–Sigmund[3] arrived from Poland and the first school for the deaf and dumb was founded by him in the fortress of Pavlovsk.* (Meller in Lagovsky 1910, p. 10)[4]

---

2   Basova 1940 is particularly dismissive, and her later publications of 1965 and of 1984 (with S.F. Yegerov) also skate around the actual historical situation. In D'yachkov 1957, there is a reference to Meller's 1872 memoir in the bibliography (p. 342) but, for some reason, its publication is attributed to a Moscow venue and there is minimal comment upon it in the body of the book itself.

3   In the 1910 text, Lagovsky introduces a query at this point because it appears that Meller has been slightly confused and has hyphenated Sicard's name to that of Father Sigmund.

Ill. 2: *The fortress of Marienthal, or Pavlovsk, in 1991*

The fortress of Marienthal, or Pavlovsk, stood in the grounds of Pavlovsk Palace but is currently in ruins, having been destroyed in World War II when the area was occupied by forces of Fascist regimes. Unlike most of the rest of Pavlovsk Palace, Park and Gardens, it has not been restored, though there are said to be plans to do so.

According to Meller's testimonies, he and his elder brother were the first to go to this experimental school

> *in 1806 or 1807. Soon two more boys and five girls began to study with us. There were only nine pupils in all. Father Sigmund, through his hard work and knowledgeable pedagogic experience, began to fulfill the Empress's wishes. The Empress herself continually looked after our progress and when, after a short time, I began to read and write and pronounce some words, Her Majesty was very pleased, and in 1809 sent me a gold watch through the secretary Villanov. Later in 1810, the school was moved to St. Petersburg and transferred to the Widow's Home on Vyborgskaya side* (of the Neva) *which is now the Mikhailovsky Artillery School.* (Meller in Lagovsky 1910, pp. 11-12)[5]

The Institute was later set up in its own larger premises on Gorokhovaya ulitsa, near Krasnyi Bridge, where it became known as the St. Petersburg Institute for the Deaf and Dumb. The establishment was to continue on that site until the late 1960's, when it was transferred to buildings near Engels Prospekt in the north of Leningrad, where the Leningrad School for the Deaf No.1 still exists as the Institute's linear successor. The original premises on Gorokhovaya, which was renamed Dzerzhinskaya after the Revolution, are now largely vacant,

---

4   This long quotation is taken from the 1872 letter which identifies the site of the first school as being in the fortress of Pavlovsk; in the 1877 memoir, this citadel is called *the fortress of Marienthal* (Nikolaevich 1877, p. 253).

5   This quotation also taken from the 1872 letter identifies the first site of the Institute in St. Petersburg as the Widow's Home on Vyborgskaya, which later became the Mikhailovsky Artillery School. It is mentioned in Lane (1988) *as a large house on the right bank of the Neva.* The building still exists as an Artillery School but (at the time of writing in August 1991) was named after M.I. Kalinin, a former President of the Soviet Union. The classical outlines of the exterior are little changed from its original appearance except for a set of Soviet arms above the portico and a few other armorial embellishments devoted to Lenin.

although, in October 1990, part of the building was occupied by the Library of the Herzen Pedagogical Institute's Faculty of Defectology, which trains teachers of the deaf inter alia.[6]

III

The letter recorded in Lagovsky's book continues with additional autobiographical details about Meller. Meller relates that, in 1810, Father Sigmund *to everyone's sorrow (Kobsh-chemu nashemu sozhaleniyu;* Lagovsky 1910, p. 12) returned to Poland and was replaced by Professor Jauffret from Paris,

> *(...) and I, because my parents wished it, together with my brother, was taken from the school in 1812, and continued my lessons with the then well-known Professor Haüy.*[7] *I lived with my aunt in my family where there were many military people preparing for the campaign of defending the Motherland* (against invasion by Napoleon). *I wanted to set out together with them and asked if I could join the Life Guards where my brother was serving, but I was not allowed. Then suddenly I got the chance to join the Civil Service. I lived in Mikhailovsky Palace near the Summer Gardens. Once I was walking with my aunt and met Her Imperial Majesty. She recognized me, called me to her and said: 'You have forgotten me, Aleksandr. I have not seen you for a long time and have not gotten any drawings from you as it used to be.' These words touched my soul deeply. I looked up to the sky and, with the help of my dear aunt, tried to explain to my beloved Empress that if I ever forgot her, then God should forget me. Then I asked Her Majesty to help me with suitable employment so that I could prove my love for my Motherland. 'I will be happy to do what he wants; he can write well so I shall put him in My Office; he will work with the papers', and she soon did so. So I began to work in Her Majesty's Office from September 20th, 1817. Later H.M. Office was renamed the IVth Department of Her Imperial Majesty's Private Office, and I worked there from February 16th, 1829 as an official; then I was an assistant to a senior official from January 13th, 1845 until January 31st, 1856. I left that work because I was ill; I received a pension plus two years' salary for my 39 years of service.* (Meller in Lagovski 1910, pp. 12-13)

IV

Meller's letter of 1872 ends at this point but both Nikolaevich 1877 and Lagovsky 1910 provide additional information about the development of the first *experimental school*. The Dowager Empress had instructed that the project should go ahead with all due speed and a specialized teacher of the Deaf was soon found in Father Sigmund who came from Wilno (Vilnius). The initial plans for the school were actually approved by Maria Feodorovna at Gatchina (another palace near Pavlovsk) on October 14th, 1806, which was her birthday; Prince Dimitri M. Volkonsky, confidant to Maria's son Tsar Alexander I, quickly organised the school at Pavlovsk, utilizing the sum of 700 roubles given by the Empress herself. Within six weeks of the initial idea, Volkonsky had set up accommodation at Marienthal and on December 2nd, 1806 was able to inform Maria Feodorovna that

---

6   It should be noted that the Herzen P.I. has been renamed as the Russian State Pedagogical University, and that Dzerzhinskaya has been reverted to Gorokhovaya (as of 1991).

7   Valentin Haüy (1745–1822) was invited to St. Petersburg by Tsar Alexander I after the Institute for the Blind in Paris had been closed by Napoleon. He arrived in 1806 and agreed to organise a school for the blind there. Though he originally planned only to stay for a year, Haüy remained in Russia for 11 years and, though he was more concerned with the education of the blind, he did tutor individual deaf pupils from wealthy families, having been trained to some extent at de L'Epée's Paris Institute. While studying in Paris he had also become closely acquainted with the works of Sicard. Basova (1940, p. 33) argues that Haüy was influential in bringing Sicard's work to the attention of officials in the Department of the Dowager Empress Maria Feodorovna and even suggests that Jauffret's arrival was due to Haüy's prompting (see also Skrebitsky 1886).

In accordance with Your Imperial Majesty's expressed wish of October 14th, about establishing a school in the town of Pavlovsk, this experimental school for the deaf-and-dumb is open. I wish to submit to Your Imperial Majesty the list of pupils at this school.[8]

No	When admitted and from where	Male	Age	When admitted and from where	Female	Age
1	From Professor Anselm Sigmund	Polish native Ivan Raetski	11	From Mr Korsberg, the Administrative Manager of Krasnosel'skaya province, Member of the City Council of Pavlovsk	Daughter of peasant of Krasnosel'skaya province Nikita Krashenninikov, Anna Nikitina	13
2				From Private Counsellor, Honorary Trustee and Cavalier Alexei Grigor'evich Teplov	Ul'yana Nikolaevna from educational home under No 666 Born in 1791	15
3				From Warden of Gatcjina rural educational home Nikitin	Dar'ya Nikitina under No 368 Born in 1794	12

Volkonsky's list of children admitted to the Experimental School for the Deaf in 1806

This list[9] indicates that the Pavlovsk school opened with four deaf pupils (three girls and a boy) aged 11 to 15 years and that the Meller brothers were not initially present (presumably joining later).

According to the initial plan of 14th October, the school was to provide for up to twelve children of both sexes – six boys and six girls. Every year expenses of 4500 roubles were to be provided for the school's maintenance from the Empress's own funds: the sum of 2660 roubles was allocated for the salaries of teacher and helpers and 1840 roubles for the provision of all food and clothing for the pupils. Paragraph 2 of the plan for the school noted that this latter allocation took into account that the twelve pupils on roll were to come *from educational homes, from families from amongst the lower social classes, people who were working in public service and 'raznochinsti'* (of mixed social status). Paragraph 3 allowed for a certain sum to be drawn from extraordinary expenses and added to the regular fixed expenditure for the maintenance of possible boarders from the nobility. Such pupils would be provided with different food, clothing and accommodation – for instance, Paragraph 5 indicated that five extra kopecks a day would be allowed for their food and that additionally these boarders were entitled to special separate bedrooms. The degree of social stratification was such that even amongst the nobility two kinds of boarders were envisaged– those of the highest rank who would study at the school and only have food and bed there, and those lesser, who would also be supplied with clothes and bed-linen by the school.[10]

8   Information (including Volkonsky's list) appended to Meller's letter (in Lagovsky 1910, pp. 13–14).

9   This list is also reproduced in Basova (1940, p. 30) with some typographical errors relating to the names of two of the girls and sponsor Korsberg; the age of pupil Raetski is also wrongly given. The *educational homes* from which Ul'yana Nikolaeva and Dar'ya Nikitina came (under files reference No. 666 and No. 368) could be considered somewhat equivalent to an orphanage. Anna Nikitina was the daughter of a peasant-bondsman.

10   Basova 1940 tends to fulminate against such differential treatment and goes so far as to denigrate much of the school's work, even saying that Meller's letter was *historically not credible*. She further stigmatises the venture at Pavlovsk as being *a private boarding school for pupils from the upper classes and a shelter for pupils from the educational homes*. In denying the value of the spirit of charity and philanthropy that informed the school's foundation, she preferred to see it all as *only a cover for attracting pupils from the families of the landlords and rich merchants* (while) *attracting funds from private philanthropists for the maintenance of a few pupils from the lower classes* (p. 31).

Ill. 3: *Dowager Empress Maria Feodorovna*

As well as appointing Father Sigmund to the school to be in charge of the education and upbringing of the pupils, there was a supervisor in attendance who (with his wife) looked after the domestic side of affairs.

V

In addition to the information supplied by Meller, there is some correspondence available from the Empress about the early stages of the school's work: a letter of December 4th, 1808 is of particular importance. This letter was written to the abbé Sicard in Paris and, after its receipt and attention, was left in the archives of the National Institute of Paris until 1876 when its text was published (Landes 1876, pp. 5-7).[11] The letter was written in French and asked Sicard specifically for help to enable the pupils at Pavlovsk to be taught more about God and religion. Father Sigmund (though not named) is described as an honest Polish ecclesiastic who had been trained in Vienna and who was very competent as a teacher but, as the Empress writes: *Il n'en est pas encore avec eux aux idées de la Divinité et du Culte (He has*

---

11 Copy provided by Alexis Karacostas, archivist at the Institut National de Jeunes Sourds, Paris. There is a long footnote and commentary by Landes to this letter (p.14) which analyses the style of the Dowager Empress's script, remarks upon the quality and water-mark of the paper used, and which even, with a certain gallant Gallic nuance, touches upon *the faint scent* that still clung to the correspondence!

not yet introduced them to the ideas of God and Religion) to which she says to give much importance (the Empress in Landes 1876, pp. 5-6; also in Lagovsky 1910, pp. 17-18). The Empress had received a book written by Sicard about the methods used in Paris to educate the Deaf and, in her letter to him, she said further that she would like *connoître plus particulièrement la manière dont vous êtes vous pris pour les communiquer à vos élèves (to know more particularly the way you teach these* (subjects) *to your pupils;* ibid.). She continued:

> For that reason I want to send someone to Paris who knows the Russian language very well and who has the preliminary understanding that you would judge necessary, who would be able not only under your supervision to observe the instruction of the deaf but would be able also to apply your method in the mother tongue. If you approve of this idea, (…) I will be pleased if you could indicate what he should know, so that he will be able to profit from your instruction. (The Empress in Landes 1876, p. 6; also in Lagovsky 1910, p. 18)

Sicard's response was to send the Empress a copy of his recent book *Théorie des signes* (Sicard 1808), which hardly appertained to the matters she had raised about religious training and the concomitant instruction of a Russian as teacher of the Deaf. The abbé also wrote proposing that Jean-Baptiste Jauffret, head of a secondary school in Paris, should be the new director of the school for the Deaf that would soon be in St. Petersburg after transfer from Pavlovsk.

There was also some mention that Laurent Clerc should accompany Jauffret because the latter knew little of the Deaf or sign language.[12] In any event the Dowager Empress, while agreeing to Sicard's proposition about a new director at St. Petersburg, only provided enough funds for one person to travel to Russia to help the school's development. Jauffret was to build on the work of Father Sigmund, about whose contribution the Empress appeared to have been so distinctly dissatisfied.

VI

Where Father Sigmund himself is concerned, very little seems to be known about his life other than that he was trained at the Vienna School under the abbé Storck, but the fact that the St. Petersburg school continued to function for four years under his leadership is evidence of his due energy, resource and commitment (see Bogdanov-Berezovsky 1901, p. 74). Though he was a foreigner, he tried to teach his pupils Russian according to the provincial school's program and curriculum of 1804, adding some German and exercises in calligraphy. Judging by the books that the school used, the teaching included elements of natural science and the Code of Conduct in ordinary life; religious studies were also pursued. The children were able to acquire their general education through the application of de L'Epée's mimic method which used visual supports in the teaching process. But Sigmund, following the practice of the Vienna School, also taught some articulation, as Aleksandr Meller corroborated. From the list of books used in the class, and detailed by the Honorary Trustee Davydov, it would appear that Sigmund was influenced not only by his training in Vienna but also knew of the works of Pestalozzi and used them in his work, as well as dictionaries and visual aids. There might well have been official suspicion of the apparent worldliness of some of the subjects like natural science and languages that were prominent features in Sigmund's teaching approach, and this suspicion is reflected in the Dowager Empress's misgivings in

---

12 See Lane 1988, p. 156. It is an intriguing thought that, if Laurent Clerc had gone to Russia, probably like Jauffret to remain there for a considerable time, then the history of the education of the Deaf in the United States of America might well have been significantly different from what it has become…

her letter to Sicard where she expresses regret that the knowledge of religion and the divine power remain inaccessible to the students. The displeasure with Sigmund might also have been prompted by nationalistic motives: he was Polish and a Catholic priest, and this background was not in keeping with the general tendency in Russia to prefer trained Russian teachers or to invite well-known foreign specialists (like Haüy or Jauffret) to teach there.

Whatever the circumstances, on January 26th, 1810 the experimental school was transferred from Pavlovsk to St. Petersburg, where it passed into the authority of the Trustees' Council that also had responsibility for two educational homes. There is a comment in Bogdanov-Berezovsky that

> *Russian society was not initially sympathetic towards the school: for a long time the new venture was watched incredulously, and this attitude had its effect on the number of pupils admitted, and on the financial support offered to the school.* (1901, p. 80)

The fact of the transfer and the transformation of the Pavlovsk venture into a school under the authority of the St. Petersburg Trustees' Council was a positive step, however, in securing the establishment's future existence – for it meant that financial support could be gained from the Trustees in addition to the Empress's personal participation.

Despite this support, there were financial problems which necessitated the introduction of school fees, buttressed by the strict social division between wealthy noble and poorer pupils. Fees for the first category were charged at 400 roubles, for the second, 250 roubles. In 1816 the fees were raised to 650 and 450 roubles respectively, and from 1835 the total fees reached 800 roubles for both categories. Little money came from philanthropic support and the school authorities looked after themselves by raising income from selling fruit from the school garden and making nets for fishing. Before 1835 the school remained small – in 1810, it had 12 pupils, in 1815 34, in 1820 40, and only by 1835 did it become viable with 100 pupils. (Basova 1940, derived from: Bogdanov-Berezovsky 1901)

With the transfer to St. Petersburg, the content of the educational program changed, with a distinct division being made between that available for the more privileged pupils and for the others. Those from privileged background were introduced to French, arithmetic and the basics of geometry, history and drawing on an individual basis, and received as well gymnastics and dancing lessons. For the pupils from educational homes and belonging to other social groups, lessons were given in etching, turnery, book-binding, carpentry and tailoring to provide professional or vocational training; the girls had lessons in those household crafts that were considered to be appropriate to them. From the beginning

> *it was expected that paying boarders would leave the school after the completion of the six-year period of studies, and pupils studying at Government expense would remain at the school, boys until the age of 21 years and girls until the age of 18. After that, the school authorities and administrators of the Trustees' Council were expected to find suitable placements for them.* (Bogdanov-Berezovsky 1901, p. 80)

It was early expected then that the education of the Deaf pupils would be closely connected with their vocational training, and this feature can still be seen in the Russian educational system for the Deaf that had its beginnings at Pavlovsk almost 200 years ago.

(Thanks must be expressed to Anton Mazhuren for assistance in securing the recent photograph of buildings in St. Petersburg. Acknowledgement is also made to Ms. Suzanne Massie at Harvard Russian Research Center for details about Nikolaevich 1877.)

Appendix
The original quotations:

p. 297

(…)zadumalas' i s svoístvennymeí sostkadanien skazala: 'Za granitseyu na uchast' podob-
nykh deteí davno uzhe obrashcheno vnimanie pravitel'stva; tam, dlya obrazovaniya ikh, uch-
rezhdeny spetsial'nye instituty; a u nas, K sozhaleniyu, v etom otnoshenii nichego eshche ne
sdelano'. (Meller in Nikolaevich 1877, pp. 252-253)

Pri etom IMPERATRISTA, potrepav menya po shcheke dala mne neskolko konfekt, kotoryya
Ona vo vremya obychnykh progulok vsegda imela pri Sebe dlya razdachi detyam. (Ona las-
kala, balovala ikh i predostavlyala im k Sebe svobodnyí dostup; kroine togo, v polden' ezhed-
nevo na ferme Eya podavalsya detyam sel'skii zavtrak, sostoyavshii iz moloka, slivok, masla,
tvorogu i prostokvashi). Prodolzhaya razgovarivat' s moeyu tetkoyu, IMPERATRITSA predlo-
zhila cherez nee moim rodnym otpravit' meny vmeste s Eya bratom gertsogom Virtembergs-
kim zagranitsu dlya postupleniya v institut; no moi rodnye ne reshilis' razstat'sya so mnoyu i,
vyraziv blagodarnost', otkazalis' prinyat' Eya velikodushnoe predlozhenie. Etim delo i kon-
chilos'. Na sleduyushchii den' ya, opyat' progulivayac' v sadu c tetkoyu, imel schast'e vstretit'
IMPERATRITSU. Ona izvolila podozvat' k Sebe moyu tetku i skazala eí sledyushchiya zna-
menatel'nyya slova: 'Vash plemyannik ne dal mne tseluyu noch' usnut'; Ya do utra dumala ob
uchasti ego i podobnikh emu detei, i segodnya, lish' tol'ko odelac', poslala za sekretarem Vil-
lamovym i poruchila emu vypisat' iz zagranitsy odnogo iz bolee izvestnykh professorov,
chtoby uchredit' v Peterburge uchilishche glukhonemykh, v kotoroe i budut pervymi
pomeshcheny deti vashego brata'. Tronutaya do slez vyrazheniem takoi milosti, tetka moya,
peredav mne etu radost', brosilas' blagodarit'i tselovat' ruku IMPERATRITSY. Volya EYA VEL-
ICHESTVA byla neobyknovenno skoro ispolnena. Pater Sikard (?) Sigmund ne zamedlil pri-
byt' iz Pol'shi i pervonachal'noe uchilishche glukhonemykh bylo im ustroeno v Pavlovskoi
kreposti. (Meller in Lagovsky 1910, p. 10)

p. 298

(…) v 1806 ili v 1807 godu; vskore k nam prisoedinilis' eshche dva mal'chika i pyat' devochek;
vsego nas bulo togda devyat' chelovek. Pochin v organizatsii etogo uchrezhdeniya prinad-
lezhit' pateru Sigmundu, Kotoryí trudami svoimi, znaniem dela i pedagogicheskoyu opyt-
nost'yu sumel vpolne opravdat' ozhidaniya IMPERATRITSY, postoyanno sledivshei za uspek-
hami vospitannikov, i kogda v dovol'no kopotkoe vremya ya uspel vychit'sya chitat' i pisat',
dazhe proiznocit' nekotoryya slova, EYA VELICHESTVO izvolila obratit' osoboe vnimanie na
moi uspekhi i v nagradu prislala mne v 1809 godu cherez sekretarya Villamova zolotue chasy.
Vposledstvii v 1810 godu uchilishche glukhonemykh perevedeno v S.-Peterburg i pomesh-
cheno na Vyborgskoi storone, v byvshem vdov'em dome, chto nyme Mikhailovskoe artille-
riiskoe uchilishche. (Meller in Lagovsky 1910, pp. 11-12)

p. 299

(…) a ya, mezhdu tem, po zhelaniyu rodnykh, vzyat byl vmeste s bratom moim iz uchilishcha
v 1812 godu i dlya prodolzheniya zanyatií pol'zovalsya chastnymi urokami u izvestnago v to
vremya professora Gayu. (Meller in Lagovsky 1910, pp. 12-13. Because the rest of the quotation does not deal directly with the circumstances of the St. Petersburg Institute, only the relevant Russian sentence about Meller's education is offered here.)

p. 300

Vo ispolnenie Vysochaishago VASHEGO IMPERATORSKOGO VELICHESTVA poveleniya ot
14 minuvshago oktyabrya vosposledovavshago o uchrezhdenii v g. Pavlovske opytnago
uchilishcha glukho-nemykh; onoe uchilishche sego dekabrya 2 dnya otkryto. O chem VAS-
HEMU IMPERATORSKOMU VELICHESTVU vsepoddaneishe donesya, imeyu shchastie
predstavit' pri sem spirsok o postupivshikh v to uchilishche detyakh
Knyaz' Dmitrii Volkonskii
Dekabrya 3 dnya 1806 goda.

p. 302

Je désirerois par cette raison envoyer quelqu'un à Paris, qui sachant parfaitement la langue
russe, et ayant les connaissances préliminaires que vous jugeriez necessaires, put non seulement se former sous vos yeux pour l'instruction des sourds-muets, mais appliquer aussi votre

méthode à sa langue maternelle. Si vous approuvez cette idée, (…) vous me feriez plaisir en m'indiquant les connaissances qu'il doit avoir pour profiter de vos leçons. (The Empress in Landes 1876, p. 6 and Lagovsky 1910, p. 18)

References

Basova, A.G. (1940): *Istoriya Obucheniya Glukhonemykh*. Moscow.

Basova, A.G. (1965): *Ocherki po Istorii Surdopedagogiki*. Moscow

Basova, A.G./ Yegerov, S.F. (1984): *Istoriya Surdopedagogiki*. Moscow.

Bogdanov-Berezovsky, M.V. (1901): *Polozhenie glukhonemykh v Rossii*. St. Petersburg.

D'yachkov, A.I. (1957): *Vospitanie i obuchenie glukhonemykh detei*. Moscow.

Lagovsky, N.M. (1910): *S.-Peterburgskoe Uchilishche Glukhonemykh (1810-1910)*. St. Petersburg.

Landes, M.J. (1876): *Une Lettre de l'Impératrice Marie Théodorowna de Russie à l'abbé Sicard (…)*. Sarlat: Imprimerie Michelet, Hôtel de la Mairie.

Lane, Harlan (1988): *When the Mind hears. A History of the Deaf*. London: Penguin Ed.

Massie, Suzanne (1990): *Pavlovsk: The Life of a Russian Palace*. London: Hodder and Stoughton.

Nikolaevich, Konstantin (1877): *Ocherki istorii i opisanie (1777-1877)*. St. Petersburg.

Sicard, R.-A.-C. (1808): *Théorie des signes (…)*. Paris. 2 vols.

Skrebitsky, A. (1886): *Sozdatel' metodov obucheniya slepykh V. Gayui*. St. Petersburg.

Graciela Alisedo • *Carlos Skliar*
Buenos Aires, Argentina

The Influence of Italian Oralism in Argentina

Summary • Resumen

This work describes the influence of the Italian pedagogy that developed from the Congress of Milan on Argentine teachers for the Deaf. The first documents that make reference to the education of Deaf children in Argentina allow us to state that there has been a real preoccupation with this subject since 1857. In answer to special cases, people like Karl Keil (a German teacher living in Argentina) or José Facio (an Argentinian medical doctor, father of a Deaf child), resolved the problem by creating places of instruction for those children. Historians agree in that the period between 1862 and 1880 was one of major changes in economic and social structures in Argentina; the objective of politicians and intellectuals of the time was to modernize political life and to improve education. In light of these objectives, the First Pedagogical Congress was convened in 1882 order to organize the educational process. A project entitled' Argentine Deaf Mute, his Instruction and his Education', by the lawyer and eminent politician J.A. Terry, was the most significant factor, allowing the application of real scholarship to Deaf children's education, according to the models that Terry had personally appraised at the Italian institutes of Milan and Siena. The conclusions of the First Pedagogical Congress point out the ideological route of Deaf childrens' education: *the articulated labial system must be preferred to the mimic system.* Canon Balestra (a controversial figure) and Luis Molfino, both of them Italian, were successively engaged by the Argentinian government to organize education and to train the first teachers of deaf children, according to the theoretical guidelines that all Italian institutes of the time embraced. The influence of the Italian model that only admits one methodological frame – oralization – subsists in Argentinian public and private schools up to our time.

Los primeros documentos que hacen referencia a la educación del niño sordo en Argentina permiten comprobar la existencia de una preocupacion real desde 1857. En respuesta a casos precisos, personas como K. Keil (maestro aleman, residente en Argentina) o J. Facio (médico argentino, padre de un niño sordo) intentaron resolver el problema creando sitios de instruccion para estos niños. En el marco del Primer Congreso Pedagógico de 1882, cuyo objetivo central era el de organizar el sistema educativo del país, el abogado y eminente hombre político, J. A. Terry, presentó un proyecto llamado: 'El sordomudo argentino, su instrucción y educacion'. Este trabajo propone los lineamientos filosóficos, pedagógicos y terapéuticos de la educación del niño sordo, que Terry había apreciado personalmente en los Institutos de Milán y Siena. Las conclusiones de este Congreso marcan ya el rumbo ideológico en la educación del niño sordo: *se debe preferir al sistema mímico, el articulado labial*. El canonigo S. Balestra, una controvertida personalidad, y L. Molfino, ambos italianos, son contratados sucesivamente por el gobierno argentino para organizar la educación y formar a los primeros maestros de niños sordos, segun la concepción oralista. La influencia de este modelo oralista perdura hasta nuestros días en las escuelas públicas y privadas de Argentina.

Private initiatives in the beginning of the education of Argentinian Deaf

The first educational organization for the benefit of the Deaf was begun in Argentina by a philanthropic society in Buenos Aires. It was called Regeneración, and its main purpose was *to shelter, to protect and to educate the Deaf Mute (amparar, proteger y educar al sordo-mudo;* Correa-Luna 1925, pp. 171-172; Meyer-Arana 1911, pp. 86-89).

In 1857, the first school in Buenos Aires, under the direction of the German teacher Karl Keil, was founded. As is the case with other aspects of Argentinian history, not much information has survived the passing of the years. There are no concrete details about the number of children who attended the school, or about its schedule, much less about the methodology used in this inaugural attempt.

In 1871, an epidemic of yellow fever struck Buenos Aires. The Deaf school closed its doors after the death of Keil, one of the many victims of the fatal disease. In the following years, a new educational initiative was launched by José Facio, a medical doctor and father of a Deaf child. After the disappearance of Keil's school, Facio intuitively made up a program for the education of his son, and soon his house was crowded with Deaf children. He started giving classes with scarce economical resources and no subsidy from the government. His task soon required the organization of a real school.

In February 1873, Facio asked the government for the necessary resources to establish a Deaf school, and for an official subsidy for its support. He finally received the subsidy, thanks to a decree. It is worth wondering what the educational project and the methodology used at Facio's school were like. Did Keil and Facio use different systems? This is not an easy question to answer. Quiros (1966 p. 242) is of the opinion that: *He used a combination of French and German methods.* Nevertheless, it can be said, that the disciples of Italian educators (Robles 1889, p. 12 e.g.; Solá 1894b) refer to Facio's methodology as outdated and of little prestige, two ways of describing the gesture method at that time. It is possible, then, to imagine that Facio tolerated and may have included the use of gestures in his school. Anyway, it does not seem as if Facio showed too much resistance to the education reforms proposed by a commission that analyzed his work in 1883, for after a short interruption in his function as principal of the National Institute, he held this position again in 1886, when the regulations of the institute required the application of the pure oral method.

During the presidency of Nicolás Avellaneda (1874-1880), the National Congress sanctioned a law that federalized the city of Buenos Aires, which consequently became the capital of the Republic of Argentina. Thus, all elementary schools in Buenos Aires, including the institute for the Deaf directed by Facio, came under new jurisdiction and became national schools.

However, the theoretical and practical beginning of a real educational policy for the Deaf was in 1882, not with the efforts of Facio ten years earlier, and even less with Keil's pioneering work. The First International Pedagogic Congress, organized by the National Council of Education in April 1882, was a good opportunity for discussion about special education for the Deaf in Argentina and Latin America.

Education as a state's priority

The period between 1862 and 1880, according to most historians, is decisive in the history of Argentina. Changes in social and economic structures affected all aspects of Argentinians' lives.

In the beginning of the 1880s, Argentina experienced an economic expansion, especially in agriculture. The objectives of politicians and intellectuals who constituted the so-called 80s' generation were precise: modernization of the economic structure of the country, organization of the political system into constitutional forms, encouragement of immigration, foreign policy aimed especially at European countries, and the development, in depth, of national education (Ferrari/Gallo (eds.) 1982).

The ideals of the 80s' generation reflected their confidence in scientific, technical and cultural progress. The function of the church in public education was reduced by the state, and primary education was organized on a solid, democratic basis. School was considered, then, to be a liberating institution, for it rescued the citizens of the nation from ignorance, and thereby from moral and political misery.

In November 1881, the recently created National Council of Education started to gather educators and qualified people to discuss, in conferences and pedagogical debates, teaching and popular education, with the intention of encouraging and improving it.

The notice convening the First Pedagogical Congress was clear: it was necessary to organize education. This congress was attended by educators not only from different Argentinian provinces but also from Uruguay, Paraguay, Brazil, Bolivia, the United States of America and countries of Central America. The Pedagogical Congress was inaugurated in Buenos Aires on April 10th, 1882. During its fourth session, Dr. Navarro Viola, in his lecture about the *resources to contribute to the stability, improvement and expansion of common education (medios de contribuir a la estabilidad, mejora y ensanche de la educación común;* in *Actas del Congreso Pedagogico* 1882, p. XXIII) made the first reference to the necessity of creating special schools for *beggars, deaf mutes, blind children and idiots (mendigos, sordo-mudos, ciegos e idiotas).* The proposal that really started the organization of the education of Argentinian Deaf, however was not read until a week later. On April 22nd, a lecture was held on *The Argentinian Deaf Mute, his Instruction and Education (El sordo-mudo argentino, su instruccion y educacion),* an essay sent from Naples, Italy, by Dr. José Antonio Terry, at that moment traveling around Europe (Terry 1882). This subject immediately interested the Minister of Public Instruction, Dr. Eduardo Wilde.

The author, the Argentinian lawyer José Antonio Terry, was an eminent statesman. His multiple political activities – journalist, deputy, senator, Minister of Finance and Foreign Affairs, and Plenipotentiary in Chile – were complemented by his preoccupation with the most unsheltered sectors of society. For a number of years he acted as lawyer for the Charity Society of Buenos Aires, whose presidency was later occupied by his wife, Leonor Quirno Costa de Terry. He also initiated the commission of Childhood Patronage.

For a better understanding of Terry's interest in special education, it is necessary to state that in March 1878, the Terrys had their first son, José Antonio,[1] who, like his sisters Leonor (born in Buenos Aires 1880) and Sotera (born in Naples, 1882), was Deaf. His own children were the principal reason for his concern about the education of other Deaf children. Moreover, he had the necessary means and political connections to travel frequently to Europe and to have access to the European institutions for the education of the Deaf Mutes.

When reading Terry's article, one notices that his work is a meticulous program that clearly follows the ones written for years by the Germans and their Italian disciples.

With his work, Terry was not only the first in Argentina to publicly declare the *inhuman, unfortunate and dangerous (inhumana, desgraciada y peligrosa)* nature of the uneducated Deaf Mute (Terry 1882, p. 7), but also the first to impose an idea of the methodology to use and, finally, to determine the practical patterns to follow, which coincided with the ones he had just learned at the Italian institutes.

Terry's project stated that if the obligation of educating hearing children exists, it *is even more sacred to educate the Deaf Mute (más sagrado aún es el de instruir y educar a los sordo-mudos;* Terry 1882, p. 7). Likewise, if elementary instruction for hearing children is

---

1 José Antonio Terry, jr. became a famous painter. Mottez (1989, p.171) shows another aspect of his personality; he was the *father of the Argentine Deaf movement (père du mouvement sourd argentin).*

Ill. 1: *José Antonio Terry, sr.*

obligatory and free, *with more reason it should be the same for the Deaf Mutes (otro tanto y con mayor razon debiera ser para los sordo-mudos).*

But what is, then, the definition Terry gave of Argentinian Deaf Mutes? His description embraced all possible topics, for instance, anthropological: *they may be compared, without offending, to these irrational beings that accompany man at work or at home;* social: *they grow to be good sons and useful citizens for the country instead of these unfortunate beings, resigned to a purely animal life;* intellectual: *a gloomy intellectual darkness prevails around them, damned to live in an endless night;* linguistic: *foreigners in their own land;* and existential: *they find themselves impotent, sunk under the weight of their miserable existence* (Terry 1882, p. 9). Terry even proposed some features of deafness that had never before been acknowledged in Argentina, though they had been discussed in Europe: *their chests and lungs are less developed and more inclined to tuberculous diseases* (ibid.). Notice that this idea had its origin with Itard (1821) and was later developed in Italy by Ferreri (1888).

The purpose of Terry's paper is to call the congress's attention to the urgent necessity and the obligation of protecting these *unfortunate people that afflict the Argentinian society in great number (desgraciados que en gran numero afligen a la sociedad argentina;* Terry 1882, p. 11). In fact, the figures that resulted from the 1869 National Census showed that, in proportion to the population, Argentina had more Deaf than any other 'civilized' country:

> *By the census of 1869 Argentina counted with 1,877,490 inhabitants and 6,626 deaf mutes; so it results that in our country there exist 35 deaf mutes for each 10,000 inhabitants, i.e., eleven more than Belgium, France, England and the United States of America.* (Terry 1882, pp. 11-12)

Terry alleged that Deaf Mute education was *an obligation of nations and governments, whose nonfulfillment would be a real crime. It is a necessity because an uneducated Deaf Mute may be dangerous;* Terry 1882, p. 11).

The organization of this task was urgent, and Terry did not believe it worthwhile to waste time in searching for a methodology or a group of strategies particularly related to the Argentinian situation. According to Terry, *Argentinian government and educators would not invent anything new. The path is already well known, hundreds of European and American institutes would be useful as patterns* (Terry 1882, p. 24). Terry's proposal was well defined:

> Out of all institutes, I would propose the Milan Institute; first, because it is considered one of the best institutes of Europe; second, because of the Italian institutes it is the one where the oral method is most used; and third because of language reasons. (Terry 1882, p. 25)

In relation to the last statement it is possible that Terry was referring to the prospect of training Argentinian teachers by means of Italian books and documentation. In fact, it is possible that the 80s' generation was able to read the Italian language effortlessly due to the important Italian immigration at this time, and this would have meant an important economy of effort.

However, Terry's intention was not only to bring written solutions from Europe, but also to bring an actual educator, in view of the *commanding necessity of establishing a school as soon as possible. A European teacher and one of our doctors would be enough to direct this school* (Terry 1882, p. 27). When Terry spoke of a European teacher, his preference seems to have been for an Italian educator, as the facts would confirm years later.

The wording of his 1882 report reflects a remarkable influence of the respective Italian vocabulary of the times. Terry chose expressions identical to the ones which appeared in the famous acts of the Milan Congress of 1880: e.g., the *living word* and *long life to the pure word.* But the similarity does not end there; his expressions are similar to those used in less known Italian documents. For instance, he defines the methodology to be used as *maternal and reflexive.* This expression has its origin in a declaration signed by the principal and the educational corps of the Royal Institute of Milan, addressed to the committee promoter of the First Congress of Italian Educators of Deaf Mutes that was held in Siena in 1873 (Tosti (ed.) 1972, p. 37).

During his travels around Europe, and especially around the north of Italy, Terry rapidly learned the ideological foundations of the most suitable special pedagogy for Argentinian Deaf. He presented this pedagogy as an *example to all nations around the world that pride themselves on being fairly civilized, and as the one able to instruct, educate and regenerate the Argentinian Deaf Mute, until now completely forgotten* (Terry 1882, p. 16).

The tacit approval of Thomas Pendola, at that time principal of the Siena Institute, gave him enough confidence to state that *the practice of this system* (making reference to the phonic system) *generalized today all around the world, has been perfected to the point of producing real miracles that astonish the curious people* (Terry 1882, p. 16). This is followed by a complete description of the principles and stages of the process.

> It is started with breathing exercises. These exercises develop the lungs and spare the youngster from serious dangers in the future. At the same time, the gift of imitation is developed in the deaf-mute and his vocal organs are submitted to gymnastic exercises, without articulating any sound. This exercise binds the child to attention and meditation, prepares him for the easy lip reading and gives the vocal organs the necessary flexibility for the articulation of the words. (Terry 1882, p. 16)

With this advice, the basis for the therapeutic education of the Argentinian Deaf was established, because, as is indicated in Terry's project, *it is the educator's obligation not only to attain the social regeneration of the deaf mute by means of instruction, but also to remove the causes that originated this serious disease.* To fulfill this difficult task *the teacher has to pay special attention to pronunciation mistakes. He has to declare war to the death on pronunciation mistakes, without forgiveness* (Terry 1882, p. 16).

311

In the final statements of the Pedagogical Congress, within the chapter concerning Deaf education (in Terry 1882, pp. 31-32), one can read that the labial articulated system must be preferred to the mimic system as the one most suitable for social life.

Terry's message had a significant echo, for the Argentinian government became now seriously interested in the fate of the Deaf. A few months later, in September 1882, the Minister of Public Instruction, E. Wilde, nominated an examining commission, consisting of Terry, G. Rawson, E. Goñi, L. Meléndez and A. Gandolfo (all hearing), that was in charge of reviewing the programs, teaching methods and educational reforms to be applied at Facio's school.

The commission stated in its report the necessity of introducing in the Institute the reforms that had been imposed by special pedagogy in Europe (Quiros 1966, p. 345). It also advised the use of the pure oral method and the creation of a school for the preparation of special teachers and suggested the hiring of experienced European teachers. In September 1883, the National Congress brought in a draft of law, signed by President Roca and the Minister of Public Instruction, in which the necessity of establishing a public institute for the education of the Deaf is stated.

In 1884, Emilio Goñi, a member of the examining commission, traveled to Europe with two precise destinations in the same country: Italy. The chosen institutes were the ones of Siena and Milan. Remembering what was happening in Italy at the time (Facchini 1981), it may be understood that this choice was not accidental. Milan and Siena, as well as Como, constituted the bastions of Italian oralism with influence in France, and from that moment on in Argentina as well. On September 19th, 1885, the National Congress sanctioned the law number 1666 that created the National Institute of the Deaf Mutes, the first oralist institute in Latin America. This is an important date for the history of Deaf education and the Deaf community of Argentina, which adopted it as *the day of the Deaf* (Manzanedo 1973). The new National Institute of the Deaf Mutes started to function in April 1886 under the direction of a newcomer, unknown in Argentina: the Italian Serafino Balestra.

Serafino Balestra in Buenos Aires

Serafino Balestra arrived in Buenos Aires in May 1885, under contract to the Argentinian government. He was 56 years old. Scientific organizations and many countries had presented him with many awards in recognition of his continuous and fervent work for the education of Deaf people. Among these awards we may mention the great medal of the French Archaeological Society, the silver medal given by Napoleon III, the gold medal of the Agricultural Society of Lombardy, the silver medal of the Society for Public Instruction of Como, the copper medal of the French Society responsible for teaching the Deaf. Balestra was besides a member of the Legion of Honour, a Cavalier of St. Mauricio with the right to use the cross, a member of the Academy of Fine Arts of Milan, an official of the Academy of France and a member of the Institute of France. In Italy, King Victor Emmanuel named him a member of his commission in charge of the project for the rules and regulations for the Italian Institutes of Public Instruction. We found no comments of Deaf people about Balestra.

He had many other activities, such as teacher of physics and mathematics at several Italian universities, teacher of architecture at the Diocesan seminary and director of the Deaf Mute Institute for Girls, both in Como. He took part in many Italian and European congresses of archaeology, architecture, geography, geology and pedagogy. At the Congress of Milan in 1880, he was one of the most important orators.[2]

---

2 On this occasion, Melchor Rinino honored him as 'an apostle of the word'. The president abbé Tarra proposed *an applause and a vote in honour of the sacred fire that burns in our friend Balestra, who, after having visited all the schools of Europe, comes to spark the flame in favour of the word to the Deaf Mute of our kingdom and France* (Comitato in Milano 1897, p. 53).

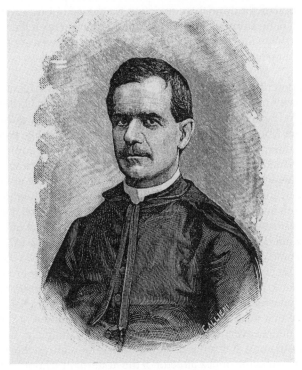

Ill. 2: *Serafino Balestra*

Undoubtedly, the Argentinian examining commission took all these antecedents into account when they chose Balestra to organize the education of the Deaf in Argentina. But who was Serafino Balestra really?

Pereire's biographer, La Rochelle (cited in Lane 1984, p. 382), called him *one of the most passionate apostles of speech;* Drouot said: *He was an ardent propagandist but he lacked science and patience.* Arnold (cited in Lane 1984, pp. 392-393) comment upon Ballestra:

> *His gestures, his expressions, his fiery zeal with his vigorous Italian, made one first suspect the presence or absence of something that disturbed his mental balance. But we erred. The man was perfectly sane, but possessed of a soul whose sympathy was with deaf mutes. This was his ambition, his mission, and on it he lavished all his genius and affection.*

Another Frenchman, Théophile Denis, who presumed to be a close friend, introduced him saying that

> *His part, in the memorable battle of the methods, has been to be the most noble champion of the word. In this field, he was an angry fighter, with the immoderation of one deluded and with imperfect equilibrium, though deeply honest and generous to the point of forgetting his own welfare. In a word, he was capable of supreme sacrifice because of his devotion to an idea.* (Denis 1895, chap. VI)

Balestra promoted the pure oral method in ministries and institutes for Deaf people. He was against immobility as his ample movements showed. Though his oralist colleagues objected to the fact that he couldn't struggle against sign language while making so many gestures himself, he explained to them that *as an apostle of a new method I'll always make gestures, not signs. Even when I lie in the grave and you hear noises you will say: 'It's Canon*

313

Balestra who is still making gestures' (cited in Ferreri 1893, p. 96). He was convinced of adopting the pure oral method and this conviction was based upon a mystic fervor. During the Congress of Milan, he affirmed: *The minister of Christ must open the mouth of the deaf. I will add that for a catholic priest mutes must speak, for we have confession and in the countryside the priest would misunderstand what the deaf mute tells him in sign* (cited in Lane 1984, p. 393).

It is not easy to describe Balestra's itinerary, before his arrival in Argentina, from the geographical as well as ideological point of view. He was interested in abolishing signs in the schools and struggled against all evidence of signs in Deaf children. Was this the attitude of a convert? There was a different ideological support in his initial training. Balestra was Italian, and it is necessary to remember that in Italy the education of Deaf people was closely connected with the sign method or French method. The director of the first school for Deaf children founded in 1784 was the abbé Tomas Silvestri, a disciple of the abbé de L'Epée. The second was founded in Naples by the abbé Cozzolino in 1788. The third Italian school, located in Genoa and inaugurated in 1800 was directed by O. Assaroti, a direct follower of the abbé Sicard. Besides we must remember that the leader of Deaf Italian education, T. Pendola, recommended the use of signs (e.g. Pendola 1896, pp. 12-13).

According to some data provided by Harlan Lane (1984, pp. 385-393), Balestra, like many other Italian directors, was not initially in disagreement with the French method. Lane says that in a letter dated May 1879 addressed to the Home Office Minister of the French government, Le Père, Balestra acknowledged that his change began in 1867, when he was 38. Since September of that year, he studied comparatively the different methods and their results, and visited almost every school for the Deaf in Italy, Belgium, France, Spain, Holland, Germany, Austria and Switzerland. Nevertheless, he realized the 'superiority of the oral method' when he met the oralist director of the Rotterdam school, David Hirsh. In that school, he discovered the 'miracle of the word as a gift'. At this point, his conversion began. From then on he tried to convince everybody and was determined to make everybody hear him. When he introduced the oralist method in Italy, he began by changing the Deaf school of Como. Balestra admitted that he encountered the opposition of the Institute of Milan, but in 1860 he was able to organize a class with the exclusive use of the pure oral method. Results could be judged two months later, Balestra said and he received the visits of the principals of other institutes.

In 1869, the principal of the Royal Milan Institute, abbé Giulio Tarra, adopted the new methodology. The year of 1871 marked the conversion of Pendola to the new way of teaching. As principal of the Siena Institute Pendola had had nearly fifty years of different experience. If the example of the Como and Milan institutes led to the reform of all Lombardy and Venice schools, then the changes of the school of Siena accelerated the transformation of other institutes in central and southern Italy. Balestra took pride in the fact that by the end of 1871, the articulation method was practiced from Turin to Venice, from Bologne to Rome and from Naples to Palermo.

The abbés Balestra, Pendola and Tarra, responsible for the change of methodology and pedagogy in Italy, founded, with other assistants, the magazine *L'Educazione del sordomuto*, which first appeared in January 1872. Therein, they exposed all they wanted to about the pure oral method, and they triumphed in discussion against some imaginary litigants.

However, Balestra was not satisfied with the conversion to the oralist theory within the Italian frontiers alone. His missionary duty led him to attempt a universal reform:

So, by the end of 1871 (as Balestra stated in his report to the French minister) *Turin, Venice, Bologna, Rome, Naples, Palermo were all teaching in the Italian language. Now with Austria, Switzerland, Belgium, Holland, Norway, and Italy using oral methods, 'the world is waiting for France (...). It will be your glory, M. le Ministre, to instigate*

the reform by appointing me to the Paris institiution.' Give me only two months, Bales-
tra begged, and you shall speak with your deaf pupils. (Lane 1984, p. 385)

The answer he received was prudent. Although the French institutes were not opposed to
innovations, they preferred to work on solid ground and resented any quick transformation
of teaching in public institutes; but this did not trouble Balestra, who wrote a project of reor-
ganization for French institutes of the Deaf to be presented to the Home Office Minister of
the French government:[3]

> *Taking into consideration that the word is the usual and desired way Providence gave*
> *to men to communicate ideas between themselves, that the sign language and the dac-*
> *tylology are not understood by the majority of men and that Deaf Mutes who only*
> *havethese ways to express themselves remain isolated from society; taking into conside-*
> *ration the unquestionable advantage that results from instruction by way of the word*
> *for the physical and moral health of the Deaf, all the Deaf Mutes, including those by*
> *birth, of lip reading and of their being able to talk themselves, the minister decrees*
> *because of these reasons:*
> *1. The suppression of dactylology in Deaf Mute teaching. From now on, dactylology*
> *must not be used either by the pupils or the teachers, neither during class nor out of it.*
> *2. Signs are only tolerated to begin the instruction, as a way of relating to the pupils, but*
> *never as a teaching method. Signs are forbidden in the higher grades.*
> *3. The articulation method, that is, the teaching of the word by the word, is obligatory*
> *in all public schools.* (cited in Facchini, in press)

The French minister prudently discarded the text of the decree by Balestra and organized a
commission in the Ministry to judge Balestra's procedures when teaching the word to deaf
children.

> *The abbé* (Balestra) *appeared as requested and gave the commissioners a lecture on*
> *the order of teaching the sounds of French. Then he had some pupils blow out candles.*
> *The commission concluded, naturally, that it had too slender a basis to reach any con-*
> *clusion and recommended an extension of the experimental class, provided it was*
> *short. Balestra asked for a fortnight but at the end of that time he asked for four months.*
> (Lane 1984, p. 385)

Balestra asked for more time and got another fifteen days, that eventually became two
months, because French minister Le Père decided that the temporary mission given to Balestra must take a little more time. From Rome, Balestra enthusiastically accepted the extra time.

His mission in the institute founded by the abbé de L'Epée made him give up the Deaf Mute
Institute in Rome (a vacancy due to the death of its former principal) and he went back to Paris.

Meanwhile, the Home Office Minister of France decided that some of his public officials
must visit the most important European institutions for the Deaf to observe the pure oral
method for teaching the Deaf. After visiting the main institutes in Belgium, Holland, Germany and Switzerland, the report of those officials advised the adoption of the oral method.
In March 1880, the Inspector General, O. Claveau, was sent by Le Père to examine Balestra's
pupils. The result was mediocre: it was pointed out in the report that the organization was
not entirely satisfactory because

> *the pure oral method pupils were not apart from those who were educated with sign lan-*
> *guage, they were not in separate classes and during the hours without class they passed*
> *the time with their companions. They lacked reading material, pictures and several*
> *objects to use during the articulation class.* (Facchini, in press)

3   The following considerations are still valid for the teaching practice in special schools for Deaf
    children in Argentina, as well as for the basic philosophy in teacher training.

Ill. 3: *Serafino Balestra with a Deaf pupil*

In consequence of the efforts Balestra took in Paris, the pure oral method started to be used systematically after October 1879 (Cuxac 1983, p. 153). The new methodology was officially introduced in public institutes in France with the Home Office Minister's approbation; the Bordeaux Institute was the first to apply this decision.

The results of the experiment were good enough, and the national administration did not seem to need more proof of the method's effectiveness. It was not interested in going on with Balestra's essays after that. The canon went back to Italy to occupy his place as headmaster of the Como Deaf Institute, where he remained until his departure for Buenos Aires in 1885. A year later, in April 1886, the Deaf National Institute of Buenos Aires opened its doors with the Canon Serafino Balestra as its principal.

Four months later several confused circumstances disrupted the normal conduct of the institute, and an Argentinian government decree dismissed Balestra from his place as principal. The reasons for his dismissal are not very clear; a report of those days merely lists: *lack of discipline, untidiness, and the neglect of the institute (por indisciplina, por lamentable desaseo y abandono del Instituto;* Robles 1889).

316

Balestra fell ill; he was morally broken. The medical doctors advised him to breathe pure country air, and he moved to a nearby place, lodging in the priest's house. His health grew worse and he returned to Buenos Aires to seek help in the Italian Hospital. One night, thinking that he was dying, he wrote his own epitaph: *Here lies Canon Serafino Balestra. He lived propagating the word and died without having anybody with whom to interchange it* (cited in Ferreri 1893, p. 84).

He died on October 26th, 1886, in such poverty that the funeral costs and the removal to the cemetery had to be paid by his friends. Dr. J.M. Estrada, Catholic Association President, ex-vice-president of the 1882 First Pedagogic Congress and defender of Argentine Catholic education took part in the funeral. It is very strange to see that neither the men of the Buenos Aires Deaf Mute Institute nor the people who had proposed Balestra for principal appear in the newspapers' funeral participation lists of the time.[4]

4 Ten years later, in 1896, the providential travel of Melchor Rinino, Italian delegate to the Italian Exposition Buenos Aires, allowed Italian friends and colleagues of Balestra to replevy him publicly. A positive answer of Argentinians gave rise to a great ceremony. Apparently, the only person present who had been involved in the hiring of the abbé in 1885 was the old Minister of Finance José A. Terry. Neither Robles nor Solá are mentioned among the Argentinians quoted in Comitato in Milano 1897.

The splendid ceremony, solemn and impressive, which took place in Buenos Aires in June of the last year for the erection of a monument to abbé Ballestra who championed a voice for Deaf Mutes, had fairly modest beginnings. – A few days before my (Rinino) departure for the Argentine Republic, the distinguished prof. Luigi Casanova, abbé Tarra's successor and a friend of Balestra (…), and I, taking advantage of the opportunity, went to place a wreath on his tomb (…). (Comitato in Milano 1897, p.1)
One would have thought that locating the tomb of a man like Balestra would be relatively simple. However, even this part of the task presented us with a fair number of difficulties. At the Italian Hospital I (Rinino) was only able to learn that he was admitted on Oct. 6th 1886 and died on the 26th of the same month, aged 55, and that he had been buried on the 27th in the Cemetery of the Recoleta. – There I learned only one thing; that he was buried in the chapel reserved for clerics. I then continued my investigation at the Pantheon but none of my enquiries met with any success (…). I concluded that Balestra's coffin must have been mixed up amongst those we had seen in the chapel vaults, we could not suppose that it was on one of the higher levels, without an inscription and marked only with a number (…). Quite by fortune we later discovered from the Recoleta parish registers that the coffin was in the recess marked number 36. Having verified this, we then turned our minds to thinking of a suitable comemmoration. – (…) One of the principal prominent men of Buenos Aires, Dr. Francisco Ayersa, a lawyer who had closely and courageously defended our apostle of the word when he was a victim of the most terrible and bloody accusations that led him to death before it was time. Dr. Ayersa was the real deliverer of the name of the poor Balestra (…). His generosity is at the origin of the great salute that took place on June 11th, (…). In his bureau (…) was born the idea (…) of rebuilding the Pantheon and transporting the body of Balestra to a central recess, of putting (…) a brass crown in the name of Italians and Argentinians, of preparing finally an inscription that related the gratitude and admiration of the whole world. (Comitato in Milano 1897, pp. 7-10)
On the gravestone was engraved this inscription:

SERAFINO BALESTRÆ
INFANTES UTRIUSQUE MUNDI
QUIBUS
APOSTOLICA PIETATE
VERBUM QUO CARUERE INFLAVIT
INGENTIS BENEFICII MEMORES
AD PERPETUAM GLORIAM
DICANT
MDCCCXCVI

Dr. Ayersa offered a brass crown with the following words: *To the canon Serafino Balestra – The Deaf Mutes Argentinians and Italians (Al canónigo Serafino Balestra – Los sordomudos argentinos y italianos;* Comitato in Milano 1897, p. 36).

After Balestra was dismissed from the Institute, the doctors Garaño and Facio took over his position. It was necessary to reorganize the school and, once again, an Italian teacher was engaged: Luigi Molfino, a teacher at the Siena Deaf Institute who arrived in Argentina in 1892. As the Institute principal, Molfino laid out a definite pattern for the teaching of the Deaf and for the Normal School added to the Institute, where the first Argentinian teachers (all hearing) were trained in that speciality.

Once Molfino had reorganized the Institute and prepared some teachers, he decided to go back to Italy. In September 1894, he wrote a letter to the Council Board justifying his departure:

> *Taking into consideration that Argentina now has the necessary teachers to meet the demand for the development of teaching in the country, and considering that among them there are two distinguished normal teachers graduated in this capital, I have thought that my presence in the Institute is not indispensable. That is why I ask, in consequence, the cancellation of the contract. I leave with the satisfaction of having done something for the regeneration of the Argentinian Deaf Mute, I am ready to return to the Institute in better times if the Council thinks it convenient.* (cited in Quiros 1966, P. 364)

The Public Instruction Minister named Bartolome Ayrolo, one of Molfino's disciples and vice-principal of the Institute, as principal of the Institute. The position of Principal of the National Institute would always thereafter be occupied by Argentinian teachers, all hearing people.

Balestra's image, however, was not quickly forgotten. The force of his temperament, his conviction and charisma led him to form two disciples, Robles and Solá, who dedicated their lives to propagating the teacher's word and attempting to neutralize opposing opinions. With respect to this, Robles (1889, p. 6) said:

> *This clever teacher was not satisfied with the fact that Mutes were able to talk, he wanted to make them enjoy the pleasures of music as well. He said it and he did it; but some people considered it ridiculous for Mutes to play the violin and sing in harmony, considering them ignorant people in these matters and underrating the value of such great experiments. Some of his disciples, perhaps overtaxed by such great experiments, did not succeed in being completely possessed by doctrine, and since they were not yet marked as incompetent, they made fun of such fine education. They attended the Institute not as people who attend class to receive lessons from the teacher, but like those who go to a championship to see fabulous spectacles. We have shown proof, but we only received a kind of recognition as if we were using diabolic arts to attain our goal.[5]*

We remember that the Deaf Mute National Institute of Argentina was born in the context of the 1882 First Pedagogical Congress, and that it was involved in Common Education Law 1420, passed in 1884. This law established the basics of education in Argentina, and was also generated by the cultural freedom existing in the First Pedagogical Congress. Its principles were those of universality, equality, free and obligatory education, refusal of dogmatism, popular participation in the government of education, functional and financial autonomy, the dignity of the teacher, massive diffusion of culture, etc. (Bravo (ed.) 1985). On the other hand, the influence of a determined philosophy on Deaf education, represented by the Ital-

---

5 In this context, we must emphasize the intense polemic that was created by Balestra's systematic use of electricity as a therapeutic method for Argentinian Deaf people. The extensive chapter his disciple Robles wrote, titled *Electricity, galvanism, animal magnetism and hypnotism combined to teach the deaf (La electricidad, el galvanismo, el magnetismo animal y la hipnosis en relacion a la educacion del sordo;* Robles 1889, pp. 64-68) is a testimony of this circumstance. Some references to this therapeutic method can also be found in Ferreri 1888, pp. 9-11, 18-19.

ian teachers Balestra and Molfino, remains strongly related to the education of Argentinian Deaf people[6] and constitutes a philosophic paradigm. The result is an education that, in public or private schools, from its official beginnings and, lamentably, up to the present day with a few exceptions,[7] accepts only one methodological option: Oralism.

Appendix
The original quotations:

p. 310

bien pueden ser comparados, sin ofender, a esos seres irracionales que acompañan al hombre en el trabajo y en el hogar (…). – (…) se formen en lo sucesivo buenos hijos de familia y útiles cuidadanos para la patria en lugar de esos seres desgraciados, sometidos a una vida puramente animal (…). – (…) extranjeros en su propia patria (…). – (…) una tenebrosa oscuridad intelectual reina a su alrededor, condenados a vivir en perpetua noche (…). – (…) se encuentran impotentes, hundidos siempre bajo el peso de su mísera existencia (…). – (…) su pecho y sus pulmones se encuentran menos dessarrollados y más predispuestos a las enfermedades tuberculosas (…). (Terry 1882, p. 9)

Por el censo de 1869 la República Argentina contaba con 1.877.490 habitantes y 6.626 sordo-mudos, de donde resulta que en nuestro pais existen, término medio, 35 sordo-mudos por cada 10.000 habitantes, es decir 11 mas en cada 10.000 que la Suiza, y 28,29,30 y 31 mas que la Bélgica, la Francia, la Inglaterra y los Estados-Unidos. (Terry 1882, pp. 11-12)

(…) un deber de pueblos y gobiernos. Su inobservacion comportaria un verdadero crimen. Es una necesidad publica por que el sordomudo no educado puede ser un peligro. (Terry 1882, p. 11)

p. 311

El gobierno y los educadores argentinos nada tendrian que inventar. El camino es conocido y en Europa y Estados Unidos, cientos de institutos podran servirnos de modelo. (Terry 1882, p. 24)

De todos los institutos propondria el Real Instituto de Milán; primero por que es considerado uno de los mejores de Europa; segundo, por que de los de Italia es el que más ha practicado el metodo oral; y, tercero, por razones de idioma. (Terry 1882, p. 25)

(…) es de imperiosa necesidad establecer lo más pronto una Escuela Normal. Un maestro europeo y uno de nuestros médicos bastarían para regentear esta escuela. (Terry 1882, p. 27)

(…) ejemplo de todas las naciones del mundo que se precien de ser civilizadas y como aquella capaz de instruir, educar y regenerar al sordomudo argentino, hasta hoy completamente olvidado. (Terry 1882, p. 16)

---

6 Priest Provolo, founder of the Verona School in 1830, also represents a specific influence in Argentine Deaf education. The school in Buenos Aires that bears his name has reached more than 75 years of service guided by the motto: *To give the word to a child is to praise God.* Ferreri (1893, p. 83) affirms that: *If the educators of the deaf mutes had seconded Provolo's efforts the reputation of which was spread in the whole of Italy, we would have applied the oral method since 1840, and it would today have reached the perfection that is yet wanting.*

7 Nowadays, since the 2nd Deaf Latin American Conference, Buenos Aires, November 1985, the bilingual pedagogical proposition (sign language/spoken language) goes ahead as quickly as possible with Deaf adults participating in the education of Deaf children, and the constitution of teams made up of teachers, linguists and Deaf people for the compilation of dictionaries of LSA (Lengua de Signos Argentina – Argentinian Sign Language).

(...) la práctica de este sistema (...) hoy generalizado en todo el mundo, se ha perfeccionado hasta el caso de producir verdaderos milagros que asombran al curioso. (Terry 1882, p. 16)

(...) se principia por ejercitar la respiración. Este ejercicio desarrolla los pulmones y libera al joven de serios peligros para el futuro. Simultáneamante se desarrolla en el sordomudo el don de imitación y se somete a ejercicios gimnásticos su órgano vocal, sin articular sonido alguno; este ejercicio obliga al niño a la atención y a la meditación, lo prepara a la fácil lectura en los labios y da al órgano vocal la flexibilidad necesaria para la articulación de la palabra. (Terry 1882, p. 16)

(...) es deber del educador no solo atender a la regeneracion social del sordomudo por medio de la instrucción, sino también a la remoción de las causas que originan esta grave enfermedad. – (...) el maestro debe atender muy especialmente a los defectos de articulación. No perdonarlos y declararles una guerra a muerte. (Terry 1882, p.16)

p. 312 (footnote 2)

(...) un aplauso y un voto en homenaje al fuego sagrado que inflamar a nuestro buen amigo Balestra, el cual despues de haber visitado todas las escuelas de Europa, viene a encender la llama en favor de la palabra a los sordomudos de nuestro Reino y Francia.(Comitato in Milano 1897, p. 53)

p. 313

Son rôle, dans la mémorable bataille des méthodes, a été celui du plus chevaleresque champion de la parole. Sur ce terrain, ce fut un lutteur fougueux et résolu; avec l'immodération de l'halluciné, je le veux bien; avec des imperfections d'équilibre, d'accord; mais profondément honnête, et désintéressé jusqu'à l'oubli même du pain quotidien; en un mot, passionné pour son idée jusqu'au sacrifice suprême. (Denis 1895, chap. VI)

p. 317

Qui giace il canonigo Serafino Balestra. Ha vissuto a favore della parola, ha morto senza avere col chi intercambiarla). (cited in Ferreri 1893, p. 84)

p. 317 (footnote 4)

La splendida, solenne, imponente cerimonia che seguiva nel giugno dello scorso anno in America, a Buenos Aires, per l'erezione di un ricordo all'abate Balestro, l'apostolo della parola pei sordo-muti, ebbe qui un'origine modestissima. – Pochi giorni prima della mia partenza per la Repubblica Argentina, il successore dell'abate Tarra, l'egregio sac. prof. Luigi Casanova, quale direttore dell' Istituto dei sordomuti poveri di campagna e membro del Comitato promotore dell' istruzione dei sordomuti, ed io, quale amico del Balestra, rilevavamo la convenienza di cogliere la favorevole occasione per compiere un dovere, deponendo una corona sulla sua tomba; (...). (Comitato in Milano 1897, p. 1)

Il rintracciare la tomba di un uomo come il Balestra, (...) si sarebbe detto cosa assai facile. Anche questa parte dell'impegno assunto doveva invece presentare non poche difficoltà (...). All'Ospedale italiano, (...) appresi soltanto che vi era entrato il 6 ottobre del 1886 e morto il 26 dello stesso mese a 55 anni di 'stenosi mitrale'; e che era stato sepolto il giorno 27 nel Cimitero della Recoleta. Alla Recoleta poi una sola informazione, (...) che la salma del povero Balestra era stata collocata nella Cappella riservata agli ecclesiastici. (...) incominciai tosto la mia ispezione al Pantheon (...); ma ogni indagine riusci vana (...) concludendo che la bara del Balestra doveva essere confusa fra le molte che avevamo veduto nel sotterraneo della Cappella, non potendo supporre che fosse in una delle nicchie superiori, senza iscrizione e segnate con un semplice numero. (...) per buona sorte, si giunse a scoprire dai registri della parrocchia della Recoleta (...) che la salma si trovava in una nicchia portante il numero 36. Ciò constatato, urgeva pensare ad una degna commemorazione. – (...) una delle principali notabilità di Buenos Aires, nel dott. Francisco Ayersa, l'illustre avvocato che aveva strenuamente e coraggiosamente difeso il nostro apostolo della parola, quando era fatto segno alle più atroci, alle più sanguinose accuse, a quelle accuse che dovevano aprirgli anzitempo la tomba. Il dott. Ayersa fu il vero rivendicatore del nome del povero Balestra (...). Dalla sua generosità l'origine della grande dimostrazione che doveva aver luogo l'11 giugno. (...) nel suo studio (...) nacque l'idea di (...) restaurare (...) il Pantheon, e per trasportare la salma del Balestra in una nicchiia centrale; di deporre (...) una (...) corona (...) di bronzo, a nome degli italiani e degli argentini; di preparare infine una iscrizione che attestasse la gratitudine e l'ammirazione del mondo intero. (Comitato in Milano 1897, pp. 7-10)

p. 318

Teniendo en cuenta que la Argentina posee ahora un número de maestros superior a las exigencias del desenvolvimiento de esta enseñanza en el país y considerando que entre ellos se encuentran dos distinguidos profesores normales, graduados en esta capital, he creído llegado el momento de hacer presente a la Honorable Comisión Directiva que mi presencia al frente del Instituto no es indispensable actualmente dadas las consideraciones expuestas, por lo que me permite pedir, en consecuencia, la rescisión del contrato. Parto con la satisfaccion de haber hecho algo en el sentido de la regeneracion del sordomudo argentino, dispuesto a volver al frente del Instituto cuando la Comisión, en tiempos mejores para los pobres sordos, lo creyera conveniente. (cited in Quirós 1966, P. 364)

Este sabio maestro, no se contentó con que los mudos hablasen; quiso también hacerles disfrutar de las delicias de la música; así lo dijo y lo hizo y sin embargo después de oir ejecutar escalas a los mudos tanto en el violín como de viva voz, no faltó quien tomara ésto por una ridiculez, despreciando, como ignorantes en la materia, tan grandes experimentos. Algunos de sus discípulos, abismados tal vez por tan grandes resultados, no lograban posesionarse de la doctrina y por no recibir el título de incompetentes se reían más bien de los resultados de tan sublime ensenanza y asistian al instituto, no como quien asiste al aula para recibir las lecciones del maestro, sino como quien va a un torneo a ver grandiosos espectáculos (…). A pesar de las numerosas pruebas que hemos dado, no hemos recibido hasta hoy mas que desprecios como si usáramos de artes diabólicas para conseguir nuestro intento. (Robles 1889, p. 6)

p. 319 (footnote 6)

Se gli educatori dei sordomuti avessero allora secondato gli sforzi del Provolo che la fama divulgava in tutta Italia, il metodo orale sarebbe stato applicato da noi gia fino das 1840 ed oggi avrebbe forse raggiunto quella perfezione che tuttora si ricerca.

Iconography

Ill. 1: José Antonio Terry, sr.
Comitato in Milano per diffondere l'educazione de' sordomuti (1897): *La dimostrazione italo-americana in onore dell'abate Serafino Balestra*. Milano: Cogliati.

Ill. 2: Serafino Balestra
Comitato in Milano per diffondere l'educazione de' sordomuti (1897): *La dimostrazione italo-americana in onore dell'abate Serafino Balestra*. Milano: Cogliati.

Ill. 3: Serafino Balestra with a Deaf pupil
Robles, J. (1889): *El auxiliar del maestro para la enseñanza de los sordomudos segun el sistema de la palabra pura*, Paris: Imprimerie Veuve Chantriaux.
Institut National de Jeunes Sourds, Paris.
Photo: P.A. Mangolte

References

Alisedo, G. (1984): Quelle articulation entre l'intégration scolaire et l'école spécialisée?; in: *Réadaptation* 309 (= *Actes du congrès 'L'intégration scolaire des enfants et adolescents sourds'*, Ministère d'Education Nationale, Paris), pp. 24-25.

Alisedo, G. (1985): Parler par écrit; in: *Santé Mentale* 85.

Alisedo, G. (1987): Fundamentos semiológicos para una pedagogía de la lectura y la escritura en el niño sordo; in: *Lectura y vida*, pp. 15-21.

Alisedo, G./ Alvarez, A./ Famularo, R./ Skliar, C. (1989): Una esperienza bilingua nell'educazione dei bambini sordi in Argentina, Istituto di Psicologia del CNR, Roma, Italia.

Alisedo, G./ Bernard, M./ Leclerc, G.(1987): *De la surdité*, Rapport pour le Ministère des Affaires Sociaux et de la Solidarité. IRESCO, Paris.

Alisedo, G. /Gremaud, G. (1988): Les troubles de l'audition; in: Rondal/ Pierart (eds.): *Psychopédagogie de l'éducation spécialisée. Aperçu théorique, recherche et perspectives.* Bruxelles: Labor. vol. 3, pp. 7-74.

Alisedo, G./Lorente, E.(in press): Sociolinguística de la sordera: el caso de la comunidad sorda argentina, *V. Encontro Nacional da Anpoll, Recife, Brasil, 25-27 Agosto 1990.*

Bravo, H. (ed.) (1985): *A cien años de la Ley 1420.* Buenos Aires: Centro Editor de America Latina.

Comitato in Milano per diffondere l'educazione de' sordomuti (1897): *La dimostrazione italo-americana in onore dell'abate Serafino Balestra.* Milano: Cogliati.

Correa-Luna, C. (1925): *Historia de la Sociedad de Beneficencia.* Buenos Aires: Sociedad de Beneficencia de la Capital.

Cuxac, C. (1983): *Le langage des sourds.* Paris: Payot.

Denis, T. (1895): *Etudes variées concernant les sourds-muets.* Paris.

Facchini, M. (1981): Riflessioni storiche sul metodo orale e il linguaggio dei segni in Italia; in: Volterra, V. (ed.): *I segni come parole.* Torino: Boringhieri pp. 15-27.

Facchini, M. (in press): *Contesto storico del Congresso di Milano in 1880.* Roma: CNR.

Ferrari, G./ Gallo, E. (eds.) (1982): *La Argentina del 80 al Centenario.* Buenos Aires: Ed. Sudamericana.

Ferreri, G. (1888): *L'otoogia e le scuole dei sordomuti.* Siena: Tip. San Bernardino.

Ferreri, G. (1893): *L'educazione dei sordomuti in Italia.* Siena: Tip. San Bernardino.

Itard, J. (1821): *Traité des maladies de l'oreille et de l'audition.* Paris: Mequinon-Marvis.

Lane, H. (1984): *When the Mind hears. A History of the Deaf.* New York: Random House.

Manzanedo, T. (1973): La gran historia de los sordomudos; in: *Ad Verbum* (organo oficial de la Confederation Argentina de Sordos). Año 4, num. 15, febrero-marzo-abril, pp. 13-17.

Meyer-Arana, A. (1911): *La caridad en Buenos Aires.* Buenos Aires.

Mottez, B. (1989): Les banquets des sourds-muets et la naissance du mouvement sourd; in: Couturier, L./ Karacostas, A. (eds.): *Le pouvoir des signes. Sourds et citoyens.* Paris: INJS.

Pendola, T. (1896): *Curso de lecciones de pedagogia especial.* La Plata: Talleres Sola.

Quirós, J. (1966): *La comunicación humana y su patológia.* (Series del Centro Médico de Investigaciones foniátricas y audiológicas) Buenos Aires.

Robles, J. (1889): *El auxiliar del maestro para la enseñanza de los sordomudos según el sistema de la palabra pura.* Paris: Imprimerie Veuve Chantriaux.

Skliar, C. (1987): Investigaciones sobre comunicación e inteligencia en niños sordos. Tesis Doctoral, Universidad del Museo Social Argentino, Buenos Aires.

Skliar, C. (1990): Il problema della relazione pensiero – linguaggio nei bambini sord. Una metodologia di valutazione dei contesti comunicativi in: *Le ipocusie in età pediatrica;* Roma: Ed. Latina, pp. 235-252.

Solá, J. (1894a): *Nociones de aritmética para sordomudos,* La Plata.

Solá, J. (1894b): *Método de lectura para sordomudos.* La Plata.

Terry, J. (1882): El sordomudo argentino, su instrucción y educación, Memoria presentada en el Congreso Pedagógico Internacional de 1882. Biblioteca del Ministerio de Educación, Buenos Aires.

Tosti, O. (ed.) (1972): *Atti del primo congresso degli insegnanti italiani dei sordomuti.* Siena: Scuola Tipografica Sordomuti.

Optical Allusions VIII
Articulation
Speech training – the postcard version

Ill. 66: Pronunciation.

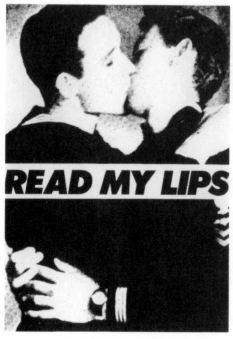

Ill. 67: Lip reading.

Ill. 68: Hearing-aids.

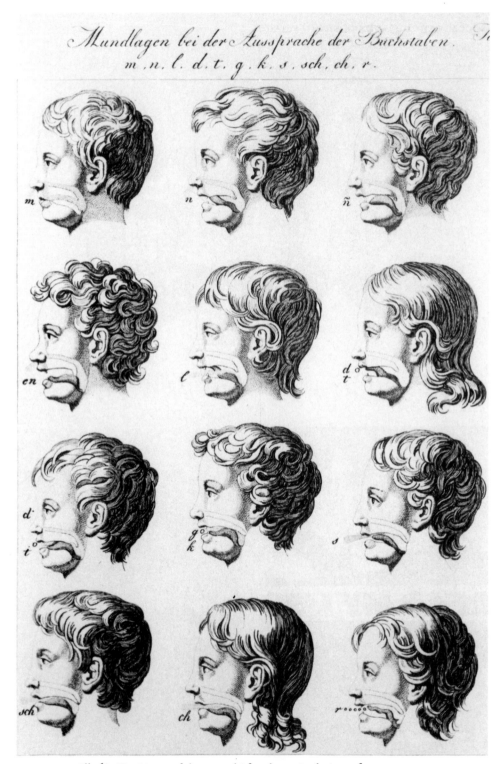

Ill. 69: 'Positions of the mouth' for the articulation of consonants.

Ill. 70: Articulating 'o'.

Immobile hands

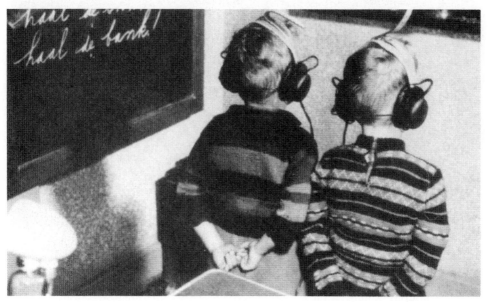

Ill. 71

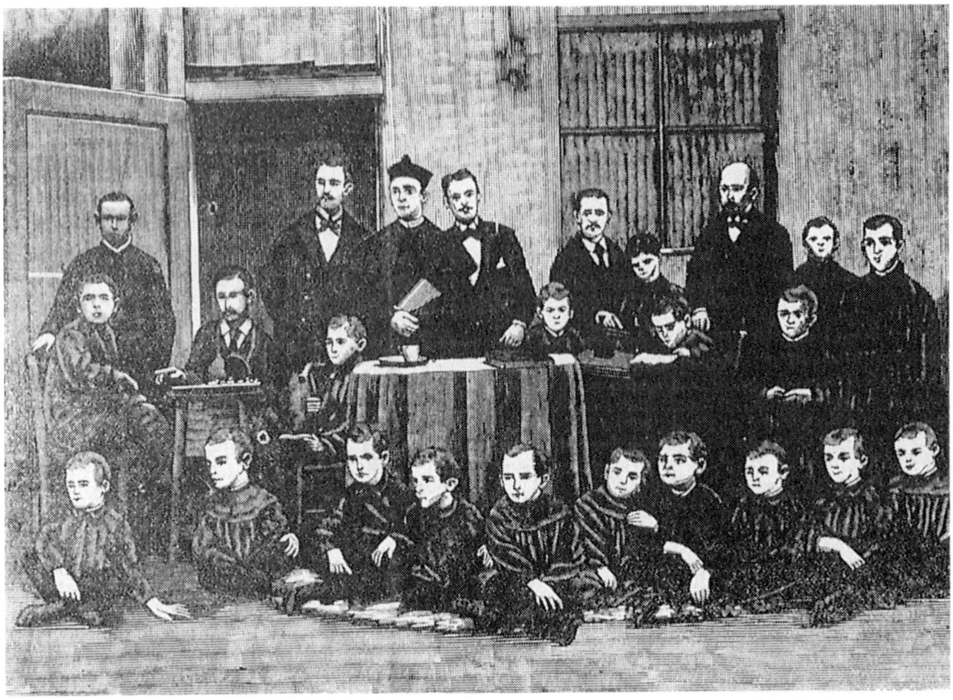

Ill. 72: Institute of the Deaf Mutes P. Luigi Ajello in Naples, Italy.

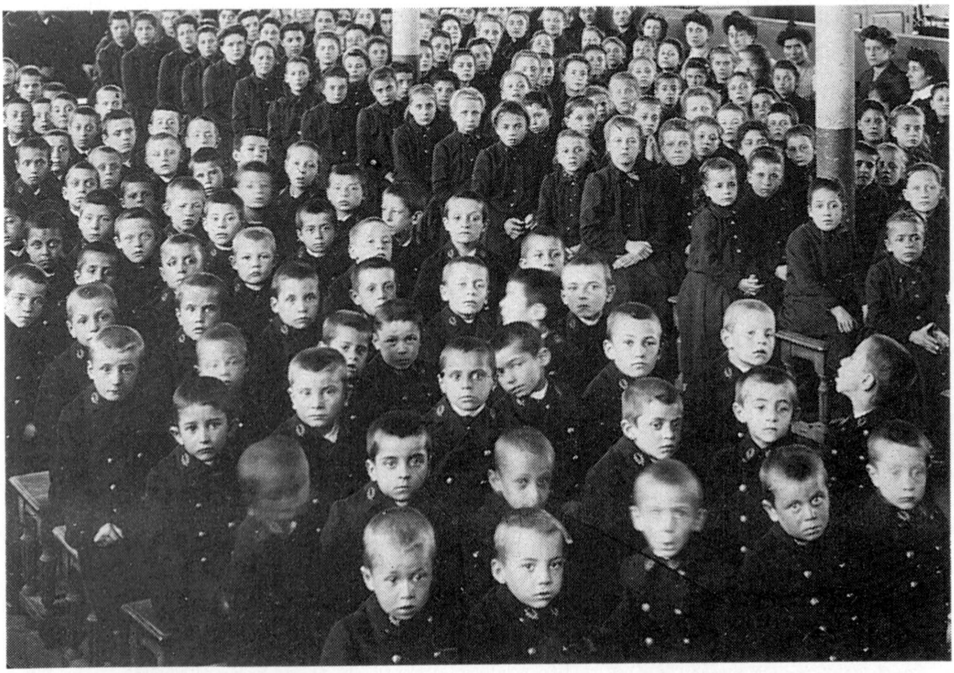

Ill. 73: Deaf pupils waiting for the President's arrival, at the Department's Institute for Deaf Mutes at Asnières, France.

Ill. 74: At the Institute for the Deaf in Groningen, Netherlands.

Ill. 75: J.R. Pereire and his pupil Marie Marois in 18th century Paris, France.

Ill. 76: A speech lesson as depicted in a manual from Vienna, Austria, in 1836.

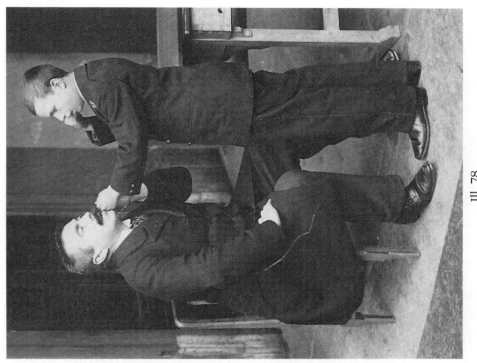

Ill. 78

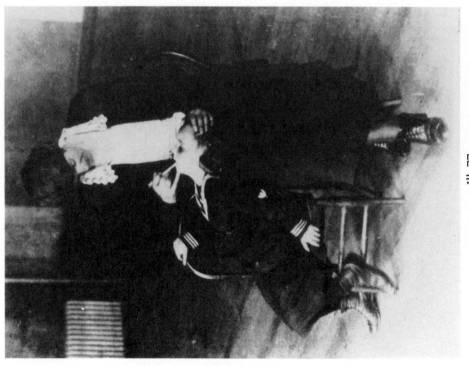

Ill. 77

329

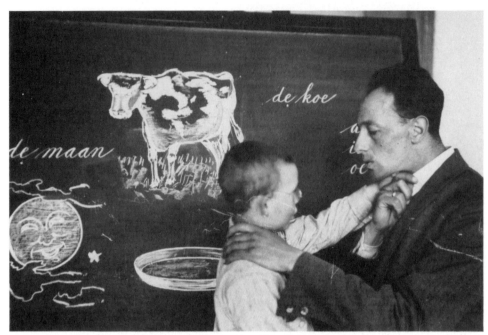

Ill. 79: At the Institute for the Deaf in Groningen, Netherlands.

Ill. 80: At the Institute for the Deaf in Groningen, Netherlands, in 1909.

The mirror scene

Ill. 81: At the National Institution for Deaf Mutes in Paris, France.

Ill. 82: At the Institute for the Deaf in Groningen, Netherlands.

Ill. 83: At the School for the Deaf in Wildeshausen, Germany.

Ill. 84: At the School for the Deaf in Ankara, Turkey, in 1971.

John Vickrey Van Cleve

Washington, USA

The Academic Integration of Deaf Children

A historical perspective

Summary

Attempts to educate deaf children in public schools rather than in separate facilities began in Europe soon after deaf education became a government responsibility. They gained their first American stronghold in the state of Wisconsin in the late 19th century and gained acceptance slowly thereafter. Today, academic integration of deaf children is ubiquitous and represents the single most important movement within deaf education. Ironically, coeducation of deaf and hearing children has proliferated despite evidence of its failure and despite the opposition of the adult Deaf community. This article reviews the historical roots of academic integration and offers suggestions for understanding its appeal and persistence.

Theoretically considered, Alexander Graham Bell wrote in 1905, *the best school for a deaf child, is a school with only one deaf child in it (...) one deaf child with an environment of hearing children* (Alexander Graham Bell to F.H. Haserot). Bell was not alone in this belief. Attempts to separate deaf children from each other and integrate them with hearing children during their school years have formed a consistent theme in the history of deaf education. Within 50 years of the first public attempts to educate deaf children, schools in various German-speaking European states were endeavoring to educate together deaf and hearing children (Gordon 1885, p. 123).

By the end of the 20th century, support for academic integration – termed 'mainstreaming' in the United States – was nearly ubiquitous.[1] In 1990 almost three-fourths of all deaf school children in the United States, for example, attended classes in an integrated setting (Schools and Classes 1990, p. 135). The numbers for the state of Illinois are illustrative: in 1990, 1200 deaf students were enrolled in Chicago's public schools, but only 270 attended the state residential institution (Schools and Classes 1990, pp. 99-100). Even American state-supported residential schools, such as Illinois', however, are so overwhelmed by the ideological and political imperatives of deaf-hearing coeducation that nearly all offer mainstreaming programs for their students.[2] Yet, ironically, the benefits of academic integration have been and remain a chimera.

The first major study of such attempts made this point unequivocally. Joseph C. Gordon, a professor at the National Deaf-Mute College (today's Gallaudet University) and later superintendent of the Illinois School for the Deaf, carefully reviewed the literature related to German, French, and English endeavors to co-educate deaf and hearing children. In 1884 and 1885 he reported his findings. European parents, educators, philanthropists, and government officials in the early 19th century all *advocated the education of the deaf in more or less intimate connection with the public schools*, Gordon discovered. Almost no one defended residential institutions that segregated deaf from hearing students (Gordon 1885, p. 123). Nevertheless, Gordon concluded, *disappointment and failure* of coeducation programs were so uniform that *systematic and organized efforts in this direction* (were) *abandoned* in Europe by the mid-1880s (Gordon 1885, pp. 141-142).

Gordon's study was well-known within the United States. He presented it orally at an unusual session of the national convention of the National Educational Association (NEA) in 1884. The following year he published an extended version in the *American Annals of the Deaf*, at that time an authoritative and widely-read journal. Gordon, moreover, was an intimate of Bell, the most articulate and forceful American proponent of academic integration. Bell was at the NEA convention; yet neither he nor anyone else ever tried to refute Gordon's findings directly, choosing to ignore European experience and the conclusions Gordon drew from it. There is no evidence that Deaf people themselves have advocated coeducation with hearing children, either. To the contrary, those who have articulated a position have nearly always supported separate educational facilities for deaf children.[3]

The following account places this seemingly paradoxical situation – the unremitting pursuit of the academic integration of deaf and hearing children despite abundant evidence of its failure as an educational model – into historical perspective by examining closely the early record of American efforts at deaf-hearing coeducation.

---

1   See *La Integracion en el mundo* 1985, pp. 35-37 for a review of recent European movements toward the academic integraton of deaf children.

2   In 1990, residential schools in only three states – Missouri, New Jersey and West Virginia – did not report having mainstream options. (Schools and Classes 1990, pp. 88-134)

3   For a good review of the perspective of many contemporary Deaf Americans, see Malzkuhn 1988.

Private schools

The overriding ideological goal of most of these efforts has been to accustom deaf children to the mores and communication methods of persons who hear and thus to prevent them from developing a culture apart from the hearing community. The complexity and frustrations inherent in this objective, however, have led to a plethora of schemes in both the United States and Europe. These have ranged from totally coeducational experiences, where students at all ages and all grade levels were integrated in the same classrooms, to various efforts to place self-contained deaf classes in the same building with hearing children. Some programs integrated young hearing and deaf children and then sent the older deaf ones on to deaf residential schools; others commenced deaf children's education in segregated schools and then transferred them to integrated public schools for advanced studies.[4] One remarkable American school, however, had an entirely different objective than the others: David Bartlett's Family School sought to acculturate hearing children to those who were deaf.

Bartlett operated a small, integrated primary school at various locations in New York and Connecticut from 1852 until 1861. His ostensible objective was to extend education to very young deaf children who had not yet reached the age of legal admission to residential institutions, usually 10 or 12. Yet his school in fact pioneered revolutionary ideas. It challenged two important ideological presumptions: first, that Deaf people must become as similar to hearing people as possible if they are to be happy or successful, and second, that a weak minority – in this case Deaf people – must always adapt their culture to meet the cultural preference of the stronger majority.

Bartlett suggested that hearing families could adapt to their deaf children, rather than vice versa, and he placed deaf and hearing pupils on a truly equal footing. He encouraged his deaf pupils to be joined in the school by their hearing siblings, so that the latter could acquire the language of signs and assist their deaf brothers and sisters in communicating with members of their families (Fay 1893, p. 4). Deaf alumnus Henry Winter Syle wrote that at Bartlett's *there was perfect equality in every respect* between the deaf and hearing pupils; prayers were conducted in signs, and in class, Syle emphasized, **all** *recited manually* (quoted in Fay 1893, p. 6).

Bartlett's model for an integrated education for deaf and hearing children was unique. A former and future teacher in residential schools, Bartlett was comfortable with sign language. He recognized its importance to deaf students, and he believed that it could form the basis for shared experiences among deaf and hearing people. Rather than force his deaf charges to try to imitate their hearing fellows by communicating with speech and speechreading – which would necessarily put the deaf children at a social and educational disadvantage – Bartlett expected the hearing students to conform to the communication requirements of those who could not hear, which put no one at a relative disadvantage. Fingerspelling and signs (apparently in English word order) were used throughout his school (see the Comments of George Wing in Fay 1893, p. 7).

Financially, Bartlett's, like most small private schools, was a failure, but educationally his approach apparently was successful. Educated Deaf contemporaries commented on the academic and social skills of the school's alumni, who included not only Syle, the first Deaf Episcopal priest in the United States, but also Gideon Moore, the first Deaf American to earn a doctoral degree (Gannon 1981, p. 7). Other 19th century private schools that integrated deaf and hearing children, however, followed a completely different course, attempting to force the Deaf minority to accommodate to the hearing majority and rejecting the idea that a manual language could be shared by Deaf and hearing people.

---

4   Both were tried in mid-19th century France; the latter has been more common in the United States and is practiced by many residential schools today. For France, see Gordon 1885, pp. 123-124, pp. 128-129.

Alexander Graham Bell's experimental school in Washington, D.C., and F. Knapp's Institute in Baltimore, Maryland, both attempted to achieve integration by encouraging their deaf pupils to adapt to the communication methods used by hearing people. Knapp's, a large bilingual private school offering German and English instruction for the children of German immigrants, began admitting a few deaf students in the 1870s. Their education commenced in a 'Deaf Department', where they were taught speech and speechreading. When the deaf children *attained sufficient command of articulate speech and facility in reading the lips* they were dispersed into regular classes with hearing pupils (Knapp 1893, p. 4). The rationale for this approach was the founder's belief, in his son's words, that *the more the deaf commingled with the hearing, the less would they notice their defect.* (Knapp 1893, p. 11) Sign language and fingerspelling were absolutely forbidden. Hearing children who motioned or gestured to a deaf child were sent out of the classroom, and both deaf and hearing children who used *signs or the manual alphabet* were gloved, as *evidence of stupidity and punishment* (Knapp 1893, pp. 11-12).

Bell did not encounter such problems in his tiny school. A maximum of four deaf students were enrolled at one time; all were very young; and Bell was careful to admit only children who had never learned formal signs (AGB to Miss Littlefield). The Bell school's integration efforts differed somewhat from Knapp's, in that the deaf and hearing children were kept in separate classes within the same building but only mingled during playtime and for certain other activities (Hitz Burton, p. 10). Bell's underlying assumptions and motivations, though, were the same as Knapp's. He planned to open the school, in his words, because *the best plan that has yet been devised* to educate deaf children was **the method of bringing together deaf children in small numbers in the midst of hearing children in large numbers**. (AGB to Mary True) Furthermore, the school would present Bell with an opportunity to *prove empirically that all deaf children can be taught to speak – and understand speech by the eye* (AGB to Edward J. Herman). A failure, the school closed after two difficult years, but its experience did not dim the enthusiasm of Bell or other theorists of academic integration.

Public schools

As the 19th century progressed, American advocates of deaf-hearing coeducation focused their efforts on public schools. Large scale academic integration of American deaf students could never result from the efforts of private schools such as Bartlett's, Knapp's, or Bell's. Only governments have been able to provide consistently the financial resources necessary to educate deaf children. Thus state and local governments (and in the late 20th century the United States federal government) have become the loci for academic integration efforts. The state legislature of Wisconsin, in particular, provided the arena in which deaf-hearing public coeducation received its first and most important impetus in the United States.

Wisconsin's importance to deaf education resulted primarily from the state's ethnic characteristics, the working of the state's political system, and the convincing presence of Alexander Graham Bell at crucial moments. An attempt to secure public funding for a private school for the deaf children of Milwaukee's many German immigrants became, eventually, the key to a wide-ranging experiment in state support for a particular kind of academic integration.

In 1878, recent German immigrants in Milwaukee opened the Milwaukee Day School for their deaf children. Like German parents in cities such as Detroit, Baltimore, and New York, who also supported private schools, they wished their deaf children to preserve German cultural traditions and envisioned private schooling as a means to that end. Consequently, they employed a German teacher who followed German educational methods, using speech and speechreading rather than sign language as the basis for communication.

Overseen by a charitable foundation called the Wisconsin Phonological Institute, which sought donations to support the endeavor, the Milwaukee Day School nevertheless soon ran short of money and asked the state for assistance (Spencer 1898, pp. 3-6).

The Wisconsin legislature, however, balked. An initial deaf education bill, proposed in 1881, would have granted support only to the Milwaukee school. This was seen as narrow, self-interested legislation, lacking any broader purpose than relieving a group of German-American parents of private school tuition. To gain more support, it was rewritten to extend state financial aid to any municipality that might wish to establish its own school for deaf children. In 1881 and 1883, however, the legislature still refused to approve the bill.[5] Taxpayers already supported the Wisconsin School for the Deaf, a residential institution at Delavan, and most lawmakers saw no reason to support other educational options for deaf children. They changed their minds, though, after Bell twice visited Madison and explained the practical and ideological underpinnings of academic integration.

Bell became involved with Wisconsin at the request of Robert C. Spencer, the first English-speaking head of the Wisconsin Phonological Institute and the proprietor of a Milwaukee business college (Robert Closson Spencer 1967, p. 11). Desperate to secure state support for the Milwaukee Day School, he wrote to Bell, whose ideas about academic integration were already known, and asked for the famous inventor's assistance (AGB to Robert C. Spencer). Fortuitously, in 1884 the NEA planned to hold its national meeting in Madison, Wisconsin. At Spencer's urging, Bell arranged with the NEA's president to schedule a special session addressing the issue of *Deaf-Mute Instruction in Relation to the Work of the Public Schools* (Robert C. Spencer to AGB 1883; Robert C. Spencer to AGB 1884) In the summer of 1884, the NEA's unusual session was held in the Wisconsin State Senate Chamber in Madison. Governor Jeremiah Rusk was in attendance to hear Bell talk about the importance of educating deaf children within the context of a hearing environment. (Winnie 1912, p. 11) Here Gordon also first presented his study of deaf-hearing coeducation's failure in European schools (This meeting is discussed in The National Educational Association 1884, p. 339). But it was not Gordon that Governor Rusk heard.

At the opening of the Wisconsin state legislature in 1885, Rusk recommended the passage of a law to provide state support for 'day schools' in Wisconsin's cities and towns. He used information provided by Bell to support this request, arguing that locally operated day schools would prepare deaf children *to enter the common schools and receive the same education as other children* (*Journal of Proceedings of the Thirty-Seventh Session of the Wisconsin Legislature* 1885, p. 14). He also asked Bell to visit Madison again and to speak directly to the education committees of the state legislature about the need for day schools. Bell had privately made this suggestion to Rusk and readily accepted the public offer (AGB to Jeremiah Rusk; Mabel Hubbard Bell's Journal). Thus the stage was set for a clear and unambiguous statement of the ideology of academic integration of deaf children.

Bell presented his argument to the state legislators in terms that they could understand and appreciate. Day schools, he argued, would reach deaf students who were not attending the state residential school because of their parents' desire to keep them at home. Without education, he warned, they would grow up in ignorance and possibly be a threat to the community. The day school option would please parents, he continued, for they would be able to keep their children under their daily tutelage and supervision, and yet the children would still receive the education they needed. Furthermore, day schools would be cheaper than a new or expanded state residential institution, and Wisconsin would benefit by showing itself a pioneer in an important new philanthropic endeavor.

---

5 *Journal of Proceedings of the Thirty-Fourth Annual Session of the Wisconsin Legislature* 1881, pp. 454-455, 550, 578, 656, 686, 693, 744. *Journal of Proceedings of the Thirty-Sixth Session of the Wisconson Legislature* (n.d.), pp. 71, 595-596.

The heart of the academic integration position, however, was more subtle. Day schools, Bell told the lawmakers, embodied *a principle of dealing with the deaf and dumb that has long been seen to be advisable from a theoretical point of view (...). The principle involved may be tersely described as the policy of decentralization, – the policy of keeping deaf-mutes separated from one another as much as possible* (AGB *Open Letter*). Bell was particularly emphatic in his desire to achieve *decentralization* because of his eugenic concerns, but the continuing appeal of academic integration lies elsewhere.[6] Genetic knowledge and the 20th century horrors perpetrated in the name of eugenics have largely discredited that aspect of the academic integrationist position (Kevles 1985 is the best study of this issue).

What has not been discredited is the belief Bell also articulated that both individual Deaf people and the nation as a whole benefit when deaf children are placed in an environment of coeducation with their hearing peers, in which the dominant language is that of the hearing majority. Bell told Wisconsin legislators that *every means that will bring the deaf child into closer association and affiliation with hearing children of his own age will promote his happiness and success in adult life* (AGB Open Letter). In other words, Deaf people's road to life satisfaction was that followed by hearing people as well. Bell, a hearing man, believed that he knew what was best for those who were Deaf, and what was best for them was to conform to the ways of the hearing community. Although not everyone would agree with this conclusion – as will be discussed below – Wisconsin legislators did and enacted day school legislation in April of 1885.

Wisconsin's experiment in academic integration provided cities or towns with $100 for each deaf pupil they placed into their own day school (*Laws of Wisconsin* 1885, Chapter. 315, pp. 293-295). Later, the level of state funding increased several times; eventually the state even paid for the costs of boarding non-resident pupils with local families so that they might attend day schools.[7] Within a few years, 18 Wisconsin cities, many of them quite small, had created day schools for deaf children, and an approximately equal number of students were enrolled in day schools and the Wisconsin School for the Deaf.[8] Subsequently the number of students in day schools steadily increased, while the number in the residential school fluctuated but never exceeded the total present in 1885, when the first day school bill was enacted. By 1920, more than twice as many deaf children attended day schools as attended the residential institution at Delavan, and a new trend had begun in America's education of her deaf children (A. B. Cook to T. Emery Bray).

Following the Wisconsin victory, Bell and his integrationist supporters extended their success to other states. Bell personally became involved in legislative discussions of hearing-deaf coeducation in Illinois, Ohio, Michigan, and Minnesota, while closely observing the situation in California.[9] Soon each of these states and Missouri as well followed Wisconsin's example of voting state government support for day schools (Parker 1902, p. 19; Howard 1916). Integrationist zealots tried to prevent Deaf teachers from employment in day schools, and, in Wisconsin at least, also attempted to have the residential institution closed.[10]

The day schools resulting from this flurry of activity were not uniform in every respect, but each followed a pattern designed to facilitate integration of deaf and hearing children

6   Bell's most emphatic statement of his eugenic beliefs is in *Memoir Upon the Creation of a Deaf Variety of the Human Race.* For a review of Bell and eugenics see Winefield 1987, esp. pp. 82-96.

7   *Laws of Wisconsin* 1893, pp. 498-499; *Laws of Wisconsin* 1909, p. 203; *Laws of Wisconsin* 1917, p. 598; *Laws of Wisconsin* 1919, p. 583.

8   Parker 1902, pp. 7, 14, 21-22. Schools opened and closed with some regularity. Thus precise numbers of either students or cities have little significance.

9   AGB to Mabel Hubbard Bell; Jeannie Bright Holden to AGB; W.C. Martindale to AGB; AGB to Andrew W. Smith; Adolph O. Eberhart to AGB.

10 Robert C. Spencer to AGB 1896; Elmer W. Walker to Annie E. Scheffer ; Draft of Assembly bill #412, A; Elmer W. Walker to A.J. Winnie; A.J. Winnie to Elmer W. Walker; Elmer W. Walker to M.C. Potter. For a variety of reasons, Bell refused to support attempts to close residential institutions.

without burdening the latter. They all copied the integrationist model of F. Knapp's Institute and Bell's private school, rejecting the Bartlett school's attempt at integration through modifying the behavior of hearing students.

Although in contemporary terminology these experiments in deaf-hearing coeducation were called 'day schools', most today would be characterized 'day classes', rather than 'schools', for they usually consisted of a single classroom for deaf children within a public school (Parker 1902, p. 15). A hearing teacher, female and trained at a normal school connected with a large urban day school, taught all the deaf students by means of speech and speechreading (Parker 1902, pp. 18, 41-42. See Elizabeth Van Adestine to AGB for the situation in Michigan). The children were placed into classes with hearing pupils for activities such as art and physical education where precise communication was assumed to be unnecessary. Another important assumption was that the day school experience, with gradually increasing integration of educational activities, would prepare the brighter deaf children to take their place in completely integrated classrooms with hearing children. This could happen at any time, but was expected to occur no later than the completion of eighth grade (Spencer 1898, p. 1056; Winnie 1912, p. 30).

Legislation creating day schools in various states carefully avoided comments about sign language or communication. To raise this issue, Bell argued, would create unnecessary complications in the attempt to establish coeducation (AGB to Andrew W. Smith). *The promoters of this bill*, he told Wisconsin legislators, *have wisely abstained from restricting in any way the methods of instruction to be used in the schools (...). The State may rest assured, that, when the interests of their afflicted children are at stake, the parents will be apt to make a careful choice* (AGB Open Letter). Bell surmised that hearing parents, isolated from the adult Deaf community and vulnerable to the promises of oralism, would support education by speech and speechreading only. And his surmise was correct: sign language was not used by the teachers or students.

Indeed, attempts were made in the day schools, as in Bell's experimental school in Washington, to prevent students familiar with sign from enrolling (Robert C. Spencer to Fred C. Larsen).

One of the most compelling arguments of integrationists, then and now, was that placing deaf children in local public schools kept them under beneficial parental influence. Ironically, however, by the turn of the century nearly 40 percent of Wisconsin's day school students outside of Milwaukee did not live at home but boarded with strangers in day school towns. Twenty years later the proportion had risen to almost one-half (Parker 1902, p. 24; A.B. Cook to Emery Bray). The low incidence of deafness and its intermittent character should have made the need for boarding obvious. Furthermore, experience with day classes in hearing schools in densely populated London, England – organized before those in Wisconsin – demonstrated the necessity for boarding deaf day school students, even under optimum conditions (Buxton 1885, pp. 76-77).

Integration criticized

The unpleasant reality of boarding provided one basis for criticism of day schools. Boarded deaf children lived away from their parents while school was in session, as did students at the residential schools. But boarders, unlike their residential school counterparts, were not in a closely supervised environment surrounded by other deaf children and both hearing and deaf adults; rather, they lived with a hearing family that agreed to provide the deaf child with food and sleeping accommodations in exchange for a fee paid by the state. Strong parental bonds that might have helped to lessen the inevitable communication difficulty between hearing adults and a deaf child were absent in the boarding relationship, which was, at its core, a pecuniary one between the state and the individuals providing the boarding service. For older children, particularly those entering adolescence, the boarding arrangement raised a host of problems. These were especially acute for deaf females boarded outside of their homes and often unable to communicate easily and accurately with adult women in the household or in the school.[11]

As day schools spread in the United States, other objections mounted. Frequently these challenged the practical realities of academic integration; less frequently they attacked its fundamental ideological basis. The strongest critics tended to be residential school administrators and Deaf adults, neither of whom had been invited to address the Wisconsin State Legislature as it discussed the future of the state's deaf children.

School administrators and Deaf adults raised the practical objection that day schools or classes precluded grouping deaf students by grade or skill level (Hanson 1901; Elmer W. Walker to H.C. Buell). The number of deaf students in each town or city with a public school was insufficient for such classification, which was one of the reasons why residential schools were believed necessary in the early 19th century. Outside of Milwaukee, the average enrollment in a Wisconsin day school in 1901, for example, was less than nine deaf students in all age groups combined (Parker 1902, pp. 7, 14). Even in a metropolis like London, England, similar problems had emerged when deaf students were put in day classes of public schools. There were not sufficient numbers in each age category to allow each teacher to instruct simultaneously more than one or two pupils (Gordon 1885, pp. 139-140). Without classification according to age and ability, academic progress beyond the most elementary level was impossible. Teachers were spread too thinly and could do no more than try to familiarize students with basic, common skills, which most frequently meant focusing on oral work – speech and speechreading – to the exclusion of academic subjects.

Similarly, specialized vocational training was not practical in an integrated academic setting. This issue was of particular concern to Deaf adults as they contemplated America's rapidly changing and more competitive industrial climate of the late 19th century.[12] Residential schools for deaf children had been ahead of public schools in developing vocational training and making it a significant part of their curriculum, usually encompassing half of each day's school activities. School administrators believed that skilled trades offered the best employment possibilities for Deaf persons. In the 19th and early 20th centuries, Deaf adults accepted this rationale for vocational education and were loath to see an employment advantage lost if deaf children attended public schools (Hanson 1901).

Deaf adults and residential school administrators also believed that coeducation with hearing students hampered the academic achievement of deaf children. The primary reason for this, deaf people argued, was that deaf pupils could not accommodate themselves to the communication method used by hearing children, which was, and is, the model of academic integration followed by American public schools. In an official publication of the National Association of the Deaf, Olof Hanson – Deaf architect, Gallaudet College graduate, teacher, and Episcopal priest – insisted in 1901 that deaf students would fall behind academically in any situation where they had to rely on speech and speechreading, rather than sign language, to communicate with their teachers or with each other. In an oral environment, he wrote, deaf children took so long to acquire *a fair command of language* that they did not have the time or the ability to learn other subjects (Hanson 1901).

Residential school administrators provided anecdotal evidence to support this charge. In 1896 the superintendents of the Michigan and Illinois residential schools toured the day schools of Wisconsin, testing students as they went along. They reported that they were

---

11   For the comments of a woman day school supervisor in Wisconsin who evidently was worried about molestation of Deaf girls in boarding households, see L.H. Lowell to Elmer W. Walker.

12   See Van Cleve/ Crouch 1989, pp. 155-163 for a more thorough discussion of employment concerns during this period. The advent of vocational programs in public schools is discussed in Hogan 1985.

appalled by the students' unfamiliarity with the most elementary subjects. Furthermore, they were struck by the students' inability to speak intelligibly or to speechread their instructors, although this seemed to be the major focus of teachers' efforts (S.T. Walker to J.W. Swiler; Francis D. Clarke to J.W. Swiler).

A 1902 report on Wisconsin's day schools, conducted by a coeducation advocate, provided support for the belief that academic integration was not meeting the needs of many deaf students. Warren Downs Parker, the report's author and the state inspector of day schools, stated that only 109 of the 208 day school pupils he examined could *read lips*; and yet this was the primary basis for communication from teacher to student, since all formal signs were prohibited (Parker 1902, p. 24).

Elmer Walker, for many years superintendent of the Wisconsin School for the Deaf at Delavan, summarized the situation well. He reported that of 118 pupils who had transferred to his school from integrated settings none was *able to keep up grade for grade with those who had been in our school for the same length of time* (Elmer W. Walker to E. L. Michaelson). *As it is now*, he wrote in 1905, *most of the children who go through the day schools are left stranded. They are given no industrial training and they are not taken far enough in their academic work either to provide what could be called a fair education or to fit them for college* (Elmer W. Walker to G.D. Jones).

Such objections, however, have never addressed the wider ideological context of academic integration. As Bell argued to the Wisconsin legislature, the purpose of educating deaf children in an environment dominated by hearing people was to acculturate them. For integrationists the cultural imperative was more important than academic achievement or occupational success, although they seemed to believe that one necessarily would follow the other. Socialization to the hearing world would be accomplished in the home, Bell said, where hearing parents would ensure that their deaf children adapted to the ways of their hearing families, and in the schools, where the presence of overwhelming numbers of hearing children and hearing adults would force deaf students to speak, to speechread, and to become – figuratively – hearing persons. The *tendency of educational progress in regard to* (disabled children), Bell insisted in 1898, *is to keep to the normal environment of the child as closely as possible* (AGB 1883, pp. 1058-1059). If this were not done, if deaf children instead were allowed to grow up among their deaf peers and in the presence of signing Deaf adults, the president of the NEA argued in 1911, *they would become social outcasts, freaks* (Pearse 1912, pp. 2-3). Both society and Deaf individuals, academic integrationists insisted, ultimately would profit from the coeducation of deaf children, preferably in their local schools.

Some critics argued, however, that appeals to the value of parental influence and the family home rested on a weak foundation and demonstrated ignorance of the typical family situation confronting deaf children. Beginning with Edward Allen Fay, a number of people in the 19th and early 20th century challenged Bell's sentimentalization and idealization of the home environment. Fay, vice president of Gallaudet College, contemptuously argued in 1882 that for deaf children the home provided *no beneficial influences whatever*. Friends and relatives of deaf children, Fay went on, *cannot or will not – certainly, in most cases, do not – learn to converse with them except. (...) by rude and elementary gestures* (Fay 1882a, p. 185). The WSD's Walker argued that deaf children with hearing parents have *no family existence* as hearing people understand it (Elmer W. Walker to H.C. Buell). The deaf child *may be loved and fed and clothed and sheltered but he is not part of the intellectual life of the home* (Elmer W. Walker to M.C. Potter).

Whether academically integrated deaf children became part of the intellectual or social life of the local schools they attended is questionable as well. Hearing children were not encouraged to sign to their deaf classmates; on the contrary, except in Bartlett's school the rule in integrated settings has been that the deaf children must conform to the needs of spoken English, even if it is a communication medium for which they are physically unsuited.

Reports from various sources indicated that true integration, in the sense of equal social intercourse among hearing and deaf children, did not occur in day school settings. A Wisconsin mother wrote that during the integrated recesses of her local day school the deaf children stood around and watched the hearing children play. *They simply have a recess with no pleasure in it*, she concluded, and sent her deaf daughter to the residential school. (G.H. Jones to Elmer W. Walker) William Stainer, who organized eight London day schools and was strongly committed to the belief that Deaf people must be socialized to the hearing world, noticed the same phenomenon. On the playground, he wrote, deaf children *seem to mix, but they are not assimilated* with their hearing schoolmates (quoted in Gordon 1885, p. 139).

The strongest condemnation of academic integration came from Deaf people who experienced it themselves. George Wing and Elizabeth Fitzgerald were particularly articulate critics of the coeducation of deaf and hearing children, at a time when the system had just begun to evolve in the United States. Both were hard-of-hearing, with easily understood speech and, by their own measure, excellent speechreading abilities. Both had begun their education in integrated settings; both were skillful in written and spoken English, and yet both found academic integration a humiliating and destructive experience. Wing wrote in an 1886 article that the placement of deaf children in a classroom with hearing children – as he had been placed – was a *cruel* experiment sure to be *barren of good results*. (Wing 1886) Fitzgerald said in a 1905 speech, published in 1906, that day schools *believe it a good plan to place their pupils (...) in schools for the hearing. That is the way I was educated and I would give a great deal had it not been so*. She described her experience in an integrated academic setting as one of social isolation, embarrassment, and lack of enthusiasm for subjects that depended on class discussions she could not follow (Fitzgerald 1906).

Yet supporters of coeducation in the United States did not solicit the views of Deaf people or even listen to them when offered, either by individuals or by organized groups such as the National Association of the Deaf. To have done so, perhaps, would have been to recognize the autonomy of Deaf culture and to surrender the superiority hearing people felt toward those who were Deaf. Walker, the enlightened and compassionate Wisconsin superintendent, wrote to a Minnesota correspondent that the latter should heed what Deaf people in his state had to say about academic integration. *I suggest*, Walker stated in a sentence truly remarkable for its time, *that the educated deaf, themselves, are more familiar with what is best for them and their kind than are the educated hearing* (Elmer W. Walker to M.C. Potter). More typical, however, was the attitude of the Chicago Board of Education.

In 1904 that body refused even to permit a group of Deaf adults to address them about the city's day schools. The Deaf petitioners were hardly unqualified to speak to a school board: they included a Methodist minister, a chemist, and a newspaper publisher. All were college graduates in an era when high school diplomas were not common among hearing people. The Chicago Board of Education, while advocating academic integration as a eugenic measure to prevent Deaf intermarriage and the production of deaf offspring, nevertheless (and apparently without irony) told the Deaf adults that their testimony about education of deaf children would have no relevance because they were not themselves parents of deaf children (Hasenstab et al. 1904).

The Chicago Board of Education was typical of the many states and local governments that have gone ahead, followed the advice of integrationists, and ignored other voices. Indeed, by 1975 even the United States federal government had given its legal and financial support to academic integration with the passage of the Education of All Handicapped Children Act, which made no clear distinctions among children with various kinds of disabilities, instead mandating mainstreaming *to the maximum extent appropriate* for all disabled school children.[13] A lobbyist and frequent advocate for Deaf rights rhapsodized in 1983 that

---

13 For a discussion of this law see Geer 1987, pp. 380-383. For Deaf peoples' role in its enactment, see Malzkuhn 1988.

this law *precipitated great improvements in the education for the handicapped. Millions of handicapped children have been brought into the schools or given new special programs* since its enactment (Tweedie 1983, p. 48). Reviewing the effects of the Education for All Handicapped Children Act, two American scholars concluded in 1987 that *few other pieces of social legislation affecting children have conferred so many benefits on a needy group and done so without unintended negative consequences* (Singer/Butler 1987, p. 125).

The continuing appeal

Why has the academic integration of deaf children grown from its weak roots in Wisconsin's public schools to become the most significant factor in deaf education today, not only in the United States but throughout much of the world? The historical record in the United States does not yet provide easy answers. Part of the difficulty lies in the decentralized structure of American education. Local school boards, state legislatures, and today the federal government, all are participants in defining the school experience for both deaf and hearing children. Archival research needs to examine closely individual instances of legislative discussions of this issue. As a review of Wisconsin's experience demonstrates, the drive to integrate deaf and hearing children there actually began from an unrelated issue, that is, an attempt to secure state support for a private school. Furthermore, decisions by legislative bodies (including school boards) are often compromises, supported by different groups for a plethora of sometimes unrelated reasons, frequently poorly articulated and documented. Despite these limitations, however, tentative suggestions can be made.

Certainly one consistent factor in encouraging the academic integration of deaf children has been cost. Joseph Gordon reported the relevance of this for European efforts at coeducation in the first decades of the 19th century. German states in particular, he wrote, were impoverished by efforts to defeat Napoleon, and consequently turned to academic integration as one small cost-cutting step in public expenditures (Gordon1885, p. 125). As early as 1881, a publication of the United States Bureau of Education urged public schools to enroll more deaf children in order to reduce the expenses associated with the segregated residential institutions. (Fay 1882b, pp. 123-124).

Individuals who wished other states to copy Wisconsin's day school experiment emphasized its financial benefit. The Wisconsin Phonological Institute's Robert Spencer, for instance, claimed that day schools saved the state over $100,000 in their first ten years (Spencer 1898, p. 1057). A state-funded study in 1902 supported this claim, reporting that the average cost per pupil per year at the Wisconsin School for the Deaf was $180, but it was only $134 at the day schools (Parker 1902, p. 21; for similar data for Massachusetts, see Adams 1910, pp. 354-357). These numbers surely impressed lawmakers.

Economic incentives, however, cannot be the whole explanation. Legislative bodies work within an intellectual framework, a system of beliefs, that defines the boundaries of their actions. If legislators had thought – or think today – that academic integration was destructive of their values or contrary to the wishes of articulate constituents, they would not have supported it, whatever its financial advantages. Bell and other savvy advocates of coeducation understood this point. They carefully stressed the ideological aspects of their preferred method of educating Deaf people.

Academic integrationists made, and continue to make, at least three significant arguments that have resonance within modern society. One is that the nation functions most smoothly and to the benefit of the greatest number of individuals when it is not torn by cultural conflicts, when it is culturally homogenous. This argument was particularly appealing in the United States at the turn of the century when large numbers of immigrants were arriving, bringing unfamiliar languages, religions, and cultures to American shores. Bell emphasized it again and again. Unless Deaf people were educated with hearing people, and socialized to use their language, he said, they would become a class apart and therefore threaten social harmony (this idea is developed most strongly in Bell 1883). One might suggest that this argument also is appealing in the late 20th century as the United States and other nations try to resolve problems related to ethnic tensions, and one way of doing so is simply to deny minorities the right to use their own language, which almost inevitably results from academic integration.

A second powerful argument is that daily parental care and supervision provides all children, including those who are deaf, with advantages not available in a boarding school. In the 19th century some people publicly challenged this position, arguing that non-signing, hearing family members and friends could not provide the communication richness and social interaction deaf children needed to mature, whereas the residential institutions could. In the late 20th century, however, with the continued sentimentalization of children and the unquestioned acceptance of the value of child rearing within nuclear families, this issue seems muted. Both in law and in public feeling, a child is nearly always presumed to be better off in the hands of his or her parents than in an institution. Educational integration of deaf children with those who hear provides a means to keep the former out of residential institutions and with their biological families.

Finally, integrationists argue that deaf children raised among hearing peers will be figuratively if not actually 'normal'. The appeal of this promise has been recognized for decades: parents fervently desire 'normality' for their children. As a group of Deaf adults wrote in 1904, hearing parents wish *to get as far away as possible from the fact that their children are grievously afflicted*. Thus the parents *become easy victims to almost any suggestion (...) that seems to hold out the possibility of their children attaining to an equality with the hearing* (Hasenstab et al. 1904). Few would argue that *equality with the hearing* is not a laudable goal for parents and educators and friends of deaf children.

Historians might ask, however, *What is 'normal' for Deaf people?* Nora Groce has suggested in *Everyone Here Spoke Sign Language* that sign language-using Deaf people on Martha's Vineyard were considered 'normal' until the 20th century, although, when given the opportunity, they chose segregated education among other deaf children (Groce 1985). Further, when residential schools were founded in the United States, Thomas Gallaudet, Laurent Clerc, and others believed that segregating deaf children and educating them by means of signs was 'normal'. Deaf minister Philip Hasenstab and his Deaf cohorts argued in 1904 that nothing could be more 'normal' for Deaf adults than to wish to segregate themselves from those who hear, in order to feel comfortable and not be exposed to ridicule and the difficulty of communicating with non-signers (Hasenstab et al. 1904). If the definition of 'normal' has changed historically, then, it is a socially-determined label, not one defined by biology.

Historians can add perspective to discussions of academic integration by looking at change through time, examining what has been meant by 'normal' and how that has affected the ways that Deaf people have lived, have viewed themselves, have been viewed by non-Deaf people, and have been educated. They also can examine and discuss historical alternatives to current models of academic integration, such as that proposed and briefly carried through by David Bartlett. Such studies, together with detailed examinations of the immediate causes and long-term results of academic integration, may provide useful data to those who question the value and direction of this seemingly ubiquitous and ideologically appealing policy.

Abbreviations

AGB	Alexander Graham Bell
AGBFP	Alexander Graham Bell Family Papers, Manuscript Division, Library of Congress, Washington D.C.
Annals	*American Annals of the Deaf*
PIBHC, WSD	Public Instruction, Bureau for Handicapped Childred, Wisconsin School for the Deaf, Archives of the State Historical Society of Wisconsin, Madison, Wisconsin.

References
unpublished

Elizabeth van Adestine to AGB (11/19/1903); in: AGBFP, cont. 178.

Bell, Alexander Graham (2/18/1885):Open letter to Committees on Education of the Senate and Assembly of the Legislature of Wisconsin; in: AGBFP, cont. 179.

Bell, Alexander Graham

to Mabel Hubbard Bell (2/14/1886); in: ABGFP, cont . 38.
to F.H. Haserot (5/6/1905); in: AGBF, cont. 178.
to Edward J. Herman (11/2/1883); in: AGBFP, cont. 173.
to Miss Littlefield, (10/11/1884): Journal of Private School for Deaf Children; in: AGBFP, cont. 191.
to Jeremiah Rusk (11/26/1884); in: AGBFP, cont. 178.
to Andrew A. Smith (1/10/1906); in: AGBF, cont. 178.
to Robert C. Spencer (9/28/1883); in: AGBF, cont. 171.
to Mary True (1/11/1883); in: AGBFP, cont.191.

Mabel Hubbard Bell's Journal (2/7/1885); in: AGBFP, cont. 34.

Francis D. Clarke to John W. Swiler (5/8/1896); PIBHC, WSD.

A.B. Cook to T. Emery Bray (12/6/1920); PIBHC, WSD.

Adolph O. Eberhart to AGB (1/20/1914); in: AGBFP, cont. 178.

Jeannie Bright Holden to AGB (3/11/1903); in: AGBFP, cont. 178.

G.H. Jones to Elmer W. Walker (3/17/1905); PIBHC, WSD.

Hasenstab, P.J./ Dougherty, G.T./ O'Donnell, W./ Regensburg, O.H. / Codman, C.C. (11/15/1904): Petition to the Board of Education of the City of Chicago; PIBHC, WSD.

Hitz Burton, Gertrude: Dr. A. Graham Bell's Private School: Line Writing and Kindergarten. Pamphlet available in: AGBFP, cont. 191.

L. H. Lowell to Elmer W. Walker, PIBHC, WSD.

Malzkuhn, Mary C. (1988): Listening to the Deaf: An In-depth Case study and Policy Analysis of Board of Education V. Rowley. University of Maryland College Park.

W.C. Martindale to AGB (6/14/1905); in: AGBFP, cont. 178.

Spencer, Robert C.

to AGB (12/29/1883); in: AGBFP, cont. 179.
to AGB (4/28/1884); in: AGBFP, cont. 171.
to AGB (3/5/1896); in: AGBFP, cont. 198.
to Fred C. Larsen (2/14/1907); PIBHC, WSD.

To the Legislature of Wisconsin in Session Assembled (7/15/1914), a petition by 'present and former deaf citizens of Wisconsin', PIBHC, WSD.

Walker, Elmer W.

to H.C. Buell (5/5/1903); PIBHC, WSD
to G. D. Jones (3/18/1905); PIBHC, WSD.
to E. L. Michaelson (10/28/1913); PIBHC, WSD.
to M. C. Potter (8/12/1913); PIBHC, WSD.
to Annie E. Scheffer (4/15/1903); PIBHC, WSD.
to A. J. Winnie (3/4/1909); PIBHC, WSD.

S. T. Walker to J. W. Swiler (5/7/1896); PIBHC, WSD.

A. J. Winnie to Elmer W. Walker (2/25/1909); PIBHC, WSD.

published

(anon.) (1967): Robert Closson Spencer; in: *The National Cyclopedia of American Biography* . (Reprint) Ann Arbor: University Microfilms. Vol. 8, p.11.

(anon.) (1990): Schools and Classes for the Deaf in the United State; in: *Annals* 135. pp. 88-134.

(anon.) (1884): The National Educational Association; in: *Annals* 29, p. 339.

Adams, Mabel Ellery (1910): Day Schools and Institutional; in: *Volta Review 12.* pp. 354-357.

Bell, Alexander Graham: Closing Adress; in: *Proceedings:* National Educational Association

Bell, Alexander Graham (1883): *Memoir Upon The Creation of a Deaf Variety of the Human Race, presented to the National Academy of Sciences at New Haven, Connecticut (Nov., 13, 1883);* (reprinted 1969: AGB Association for the Deaf, Washington D.C.).

Buxton, David (1885): Day Schools; in: *Annals* 30, pp. 76-77.

Fay, Edward Allen (1882a): Day Schools Compared with Institution; in: *Annals* 27, p.185.

Fay, Edward Allen (1882b): Notices of Publications; in: *Annals.,* pp. 123-124.

Fay, Edward Allen (1893): Mr. Bartlett's Family School; in: Fay, E.A. (ed.): *Histories of American Schools for the Deaf, 1817 - 1893.* Washington D.C.: Volta Bureau, vol. 3.

Fitzgerald, Elizabeth (1906): Echoes of the Mortganton Convention; in: *Annals* 51. pp. 167-169.

Gannon, Jack R. (1981): *Deaf Heritage: A Narrative History of Deaf America.* Silver Spring, MD.

Geer, Sarah S. (1987): Education of the Handicapped Act; in: Van Cleve, J.V. (ed.): *Gallaudet Encyclopedia of Deaf People and Deafness.* New York: McGraw-Hill. Vol. 1, pp. 380-383.

Groce, Nora (1985): *Everyone Here Spoke Sign Language: Hereditary Deafness On Martha's Vineyard.* Cambridge: Harvard University Press.

Gordon, Joseph C. (1885): Deaf-Mutes and the Public Schools from 1815 to the Present Day; in: *Annals* 30, pp. 121-143.

Hanson, Olof (1901): Day Schools for the Deaf; in: *Circular of Information.* National Association of the Deaf.

Hogan, David John (1985): *Class and Reform: School and Society in Chicago, 1880 - 1930.* Philadelphia: University of Pennsylvania Press.

Howard, Jay C. (1916): The Minnesota Plan of Educating the Deaf; in: *Companion,* Nov. 15.

Journal of Proceedings of the Thirty-Fourth Annual Session of the Wisconsin Legislature (1881). Madison: David Atwood.

Journal of Proceedings of the Thirty-Sixth Annual Session of the Wisconsin Legislature. (n.d.) Madison: Democrat Printing Co.

Journal of Proceedings of the Thirty-Seventh Session of the Wisconsin Legislature (1885). Madison: Democrat Printing Co.

Kevles, Daniel J. (1985): *In The Name of Eugenics: Genetics and the Uses of Human Heredity.* New York: Alfred A. Knopf.

Knapp, William A. (1893): The Department for the Deaf of F. Knapp's Institute; in: Fay, E.A. (ed.): *Histories of American Schools for the Deaf, 1817 - 1893.* Washington D.C.: Volta Bureau, vol. 3.

La integracion en el mundo (1985); in: *PROAS: Promocion y Asistenca a Sordos 105,* pp. 35-37.

Parker, Warren Downs (1902): *First Annual Report of the Inspector of Schools for the Deaf.* Madison: Democrat Printing Co.

Pearse, Carrol G. (1912): The Oral Teaching of the Deaf; in: *Nebraska Journal* 40, pp. 2-3.

Singer, Judith / Butler, John (1987): The Education for All Handicapped Children Act: Schools as Agents of Social Reform; in: *Harvard Educational Review* 57. pp 125-152.

Spencer, Robert C. (1893): The Wisconsin System of Public Day Schools for Deaf Mutes; in: Fay, E.A. (ed.): *Histories of American Schools for the Deaf, 1817 - 1893.* Washington D.C.: Volta Bureau vol. 3.

Spencer Robert C. (1898): The Wisconsin Public Day Schools for the Deaf; in: *Journal of Addresses and Proceedings of the Thirty-Seventh Annual Meeting.* National Educational Association, Chicago: University of Chicago Press.

Tweedie, Jack (1983): The Politics of Legalization in Special Education Reforms; in: Chambers, J.C./ Hartman, W.T. (eds.): *Special Education Policies:Their History; Implementation and Finance.* Philadelphia: Temple University Press, pp. 48-71.

Van Cleve, John Vickrey / Crouch, Barry A. (1989): *A Place of Their Own: Creating the Deaf Community in America.* Washington D.C.: Gallaudet University Press.

Wing, George (1886): The Associate Feature in the Education af the Deaf; in: *Annals 31.* pp. 22-35

Winefield, Richard (1987): *Never The Twain Shall Meet: Bell, Gallaudet and the Communication Debate.* Washington D.C.: Gallaudet University Press.

Winnie, A.J. (1912): *Compiler: History and Handbook of Day Schools for the Deaf and Blind.* Madison: Democrat Printing Co.

Paola Pinna • Laura Pagliari Rampelli
Paolo Rossini • Virginia Volterra
Rome, Italy

Written and Unwritten Records from a Residential School for the Deaf in Rome[*]

Summary • Riassunto

This study reports information on the first school for the Deaf founded in 1784 in Rome by a disciple of de L'Epée, the abbé Tommaso Silvestri.

We have reconstructed the history of the school in two ways:

-through writings by the founder and his successors which still exist in the library and in the archive of the school;

-through the remembrances collected from Deaf people who attended the school at different periods, in particular through the history of three generations from the same family who all attended the school.

A comparison between 'official' written history and 'collective memories' of the older generations of Deaf people is given.

Questo studio fornisce informazioni sulla prima scuola fondata a Roma da un allievo del de L'Epée, l'abate Tommaso Silvestri, nel 1784. Abbiamo ricostruito la storia della scuola in due modi:
- attraverso gli scritti del fondatore e dei suoi successori, ancora conservati nella biblioteca e nell'archivio della scuola;
- attraverso le memorie raccolte dalle persone sorde che hanno frequentato la scuola in epoche diverse, in particolare attraverso la storia de tre generazioni della stessa famiglia tutti frequentanti la scuola.
Viene proposto un confronto tra storia scritta 'ufficiale' e la 'memoria collettiva' dei sordi anziani.

* We would like to thank Serena Corazza for her suggestions and criticism, Elizabeth Bates, Elena Pizzuto and William Stokoe for their great help with the English version and all the people interviewed for their collaboration and patience. A previous version of this paper was presented at *The Deaf Way*, Gallaudet University, Washington D.C. July 9-14, 1989 and has been published in *Sign Language Studies* 67, 1990. Part of this work was supported by CNR FATMA grant for the Research Unit: *Deafness, Communication, and Stress*.

I Introduction

The present chapter is a first contribution on the history and the culture of Deaf people from our country and in particular from our city: Rome. One way to learn about the history of the Roman Deaf was to reconstruct the history of the earliest residential school for the Deaf; a place where Deaf people, especially in the past, spent many years of their childhood and adolescence, far from their families, a place where many of them had the first opportunity to meet other Deaf like themselves, where they learned sign language and received an education, where they started friendships and relationships that would last all their lives.

In Rome there were, and still are, many schools for the Deaf, each with different traditions, each located in a different part of the city and often very distant from one another. We choose to reconstruct the history of the oldest school: the State Residential School of the Deaf of 'Via Nomentana'. The actual building in Via Nomentana was erected in 1889, but the original school was founded near the end of the 18th century by the abbé Tommaso Silvestri, a disciple of abbé de L'Epée, and it has been described as the first and oldest school for the Deaf in Italy. All four of the authors of this paper have been or are connected with this school. Paolo Rossini, like his Deaf father and his Deaf grandfather, was a student in the school and today with Paola Pinna is member of the S.I.L.I.S. (Study and Information on Italian Sign Language), a group which contributes to an experiment in bilingual teaching that has been begun with the children who attend the school at the present time; Laura Rampelli has been a teacher at the school for many years; Virginia Volterra coordinates a research unit of the Italian National Research Council (Consiglio Nazionale delle Ricerche, C.N.R.) within the school.

In reconstructing the history of the school we followed two paths. First, we collected all the written records (books, papers, journal articles, etc.) we could find about the school from the end of the 18th century until today. These written records were often very detailed, but were always written by hearing people, for official purposes and in a formal style. They report no information about the everyday life, thoughts, or feelings of Deaf children attending the school. In order to collect this second type of information, we decided to interview Deaf people who had attended the school from the beginning of this century until the present.

Our final goal was to compare the 'official' history with personal accounts, histories that were perhaps more informal but no less relevant for a complete reconstruction of the history of

---

- Silvestri, T. (1785): *Maniera di far parlare e di istruire speditamente i sordi e muti di nascita*. Unpublished Manuscript.
- Donnino, A.G. (1889): *L'arte di far parlare i sordomuti dalla nascita e l'Abbate Tommaso Silvestri-Memorie*. Roma: con i Tipi di Mario Armani nell'Orfanotrofio Comunale.

  Ferreri, G. (1893): *L'educazione dei sordomuti in Italia*. Siena: Tip. Edit. S.Bernardino.
- Lazzerotti, C. (1927): *Disegno storico del Regio Istituto dei Sordomuti in Roma*. Off. Tip. nel R. Ist. Sordomuti.

  Boggi-Bosi, G. (1939): *Il R. Istituto per i sordomuti – Dall'ospizio di Termini alla sede di via Nomentana (1838-1939)*. Roma: Tipografia del Gianicolo.

  Leproux, A. (1941): *Studio sulla vita onirica dei sordomuti*. Rapporto dell'Istituto di Psicologia del C.N.R.
- Scala, M. (1965/1966): *L'evoluzione storica dell'Istituto statale dei sordomuti di Roma*. Estratto da Udito-Voce-Parola. Fasc. 4 e 1,2 e 3. Padova : La Garangola.

  Facchini, M. (1981): Riflessioni storiche sul metodo orale e il linguaggio dei segni in Italia; in: V. Volterra (ed.): *I segni come parole*. Torino: Boringhieri, pp. 15-27.

  Facchini, M. (1983): *Commenti al Congresso di Milano del 1880*. Unpublished Manuscript.

  Lane, H. (1984) : *When the mind hears. A history of the deaf*. New York: Random House.

Table 1: *Written materials used for the history of the Nomentana School* the school. We wanted to insure, above all, that the precious memories of Deaf people from this century were not lost as the collective memory of previous generations of students has been.

II Method

We found most of the pertinent written materials within the school, and we thank the director of the school who kindly made them available to us. Other written information came from the C.N.R. library located in the school. A complete list by date of the material consulted is reported in Table 1. We have made use of reports of various teachers and directors (indicated with •) of the school as well as old and modern writings on the history of Deaf education.

To obtain the oral histories we began with an outline of questions to ask the interviewees in a format that would facilitate their recall (see Table 2).

Our goal was to obtain comparable information from Deaf people who had attended the school at different times, in the eighty year period from 1900 until the present. To date

- Which year did you enter the Institution? How old were you?
- Which year did you leave? And how old were you?
- Were you a boarder or a day-pupil?
- What was your sign-name?
- Which classes did you attend?
- How many years did you spend in the school?
- How was the school organized?
- Who were your teachers?
- What were their names? Did they have sign-names?
- What was the daily schedule ?
- What did you do after lunch?
- What time did you get up? And what time did you go to sleep?
- How and where did you do homework?
- How and where did you play?
- What did you do on Sunday? Where did you go?
- Who were your schoolmates?
- Do you remember a particular day or a particular year?
- Is there any special event that you remember?
- How many children were there in the school in your classroom?
- Where was your classroom located?
- How did you communicate among yourselves?
- How did the teachers communicate with you?
- What trade did you learn in the school?
- Who were the teachers in the workshops?
- Who were the assistants? How did they communicate with you?
- How did you feel in the school?
- Did you have theater performances or special parties?
- Where, what and with whom did you eat?
- Who was the director? When did you see him?
- Where did you go when you went out? With whom?
- How did you communicate outside the school?
- Did you go to church?
- Did you have articulatory exercises? What kind?
- Did you use a hearing aid or other devices?
- Where you happy or sorry when you left the school?

Table 2: *Questions we asked former pupils of the Nomentana School*

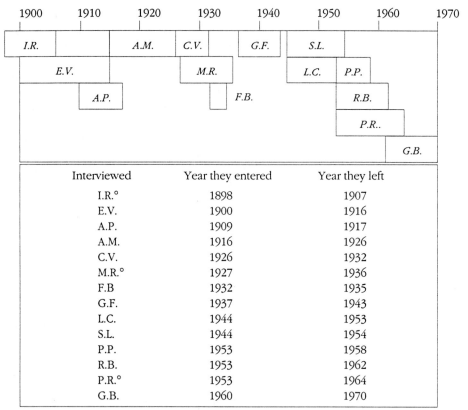

1900	1910	1920	1930	1940	1950	1960	1970

Interviewed	Year they entered	Year they left
I.R.°	1898	1907
E.V.	1900	1916
A.P.	1909	1917
A.M.	1916	1926
C.V.	1926	1932
M.R.°	1927	1936
F.B	1932	1935
G.F.	1937	1943
L.C.	1944	1953
S.L.	1944	1954
P.P.	1953	1958
R.B.	1953	1962
P.R.°	1953	1964
G.B.	1960	1970

Table 3: *Former pupils of the Nomentana School*

we have collected 14 personal histories with these questions. The dates of attendance at the Via Nomentana School for each person (11 males and 3 females) are reported in Table 3.

In the table the symbol ° indicates three generations from the same family. Three of the interviews were conducted with the children (one Deaf, and two hearing who are both LIS interpreters) of deceased former students: these records are essentially second hand. All the interviews were conducted in Italian Sign Language (LIS). Half of them were videotaped and then transcribed into Italian. The others were edited from detailed notes taken during the interview. All the original transcriptions are available in Italian for those who are interested. In the present article eight interviews translated in English are reported in the Appendix.

Finally, we also asked all the people interviewed to bring us any family records they could find (diaries, schoolbooks, photographs). Although many did bring photographs, none of the families kept diaries or written material from the school.

III Results
III.1 Written records

From the written records, we could reconstruct quite precisely the history of the school with regard to its foundation, its founder and his successors, their methods of teaching and administrative and organizational aspects of the school. As expected, the history of the school appears strictly related to and influenced by the historical events (in education of the Deaf and the world at large) of the various periods of its existence.

The founder

About 1782, a rich Roman lawyer named Pasquale Di Pietro, 'well known for his charity', decided that he wanted to help Deaf people in his city. At that time the Roman Deaf received no form of public education. To remedy this situation, Di Pietro sent the abbé Tommaso Silvestri to Paris to learn from the abbé de L'Epée his method of instructing the Deaf. After six months in Paris Tommaso Silvestri came back to Rome, and at the beginning of 1784 opened a school with eight Deaf pupils in the house of his patron Di Pietro. His enterprise met with great success; various disciples came from other cities (Naples, Malta, Modena) to learn his method. Silvestri continued his teaching for five years until his death in 1789.

The method of teaching

Silvestri had described his method in a work entitled *Maniera di far parlare e d'istruire speditamente i sordi e muti di nascita (A quick method for teaching speech and instructing those who are deaf and mute from birth)*. But only part of this manuscript has been found (see ill. 1).

Ill. 1: *One page of the manuscript by Tommaso Silvestri still kept in the school*

On one of the pages, Silvestri clearly states that he had adopted the method he learned from de L'Epée: to teach the Deaf through the use of 'methodical signs'. From his writings it appears that he also taught his pupils articulation and lip-reading with remarkable success, but he always kept signs as the main form of communication. As he states:

> *Our aim in Rome is not only to give back speech to these poor people, but also to improve their most interesting quality that is their intelligence. Towards this end I use very simple natural means that do not violate the natural strength of the deaf mute, but rather favor that very same manner of communication with which he is well acquainted, derived from the very nature of this terrible infirmity, rendering him agile and at ease. By the means of signs every deaf mute fully expresses his wishes and needs; these signs have thus been adopted by the school for his education, with certain systematic corrections. They are systematically subjected to grammatical ordering, giving verbs their correct tenses, moods, persons, numbers, etc. To nouns in turn, we add cases and genders where convenient. Signs are distinguished according to their qualities as substantives, adjectives, and other aspects of their character, energy and meaning; in short, to clarify the activity and use of each part of speech, exposing its spirit and feeling, arriving step by step at the ability to compose. And in order, finally, to restore him completely to society, the school does not neglect to instruct him also in the understanding of movements of the lips and the thoughts behind them, permitting him to give the right answers immediately, with no help other than the living voice.* (Silvestri 1785, pp. 53-54)

The successors

After Silvestri died, Pasquale Di Pietro entrusted the abbé Mariani with the direction of the school. Mariani had no experience in instructing the Deaf, and learned the method of his predecessor by reading his writings and by asking the Deaf pupils themselves about the way they had been taught before. He kept teaching in the school for 42 years, until 1832, which seems to show that he must have learned quite well. All Mariani's successors continued to use the same method of teaching until about the time of the Milan congress (1880), when the official educational policy of the school changed and the oral method was adopted. Interestingly, however, it seems that the school was not too actively involved in the spreading of the oralist philosophy since, for example, the school teachers from Rome are not mentioned in the proceedings of the oralist meetings before and after Milan. But from 1880 on all the directors and others who wrote about the school tended to present Silvestri as a pioneer of the oral method, describing his inclination for teaching the Deaf to speak and conveniently forgetting that he taught Italian by the use of methodical signs (Donnino 1889; Lazzerotti 1927; Scala 1965/1966).

At the beginning of the present century another important change occurred: the direction of the school, managed until then by religious orders, passed into secular hands. Only the women's section remained under the control of nuns. Below in Table 4 are listed the directors of the school and the dates they were in charge (inc = director-in-charge).

An asterisk (*) indicates directors who belonged to religious orders. One of the most recent directors, Decio Scuri, was a phoniatrician, an indication of the progressive 'medicalization' of education for the Deaf. Scuri, not surprisingly, was also one of the directors who strongly advocated the primacy of the oral method. What this actually meant in terms of educational policy and sign language status inside the school will appear more clearly from our interviews.

Organizational aspects

As we mentioned earlier, the school was founded by the Di Pietro family, who continued to provide most of its funding until 1827, when it became an 'Opera Pia' or charitable institution under the administrative control of the Papal States. Pope Gregorio XVI

*	Silvestri	1784 - 1789
*	Mariani	1789 - 1832
*	Gioazzini	1832 - 1849
*	Ralli	1849
*	Morani	1849 - 1865
*	Muti	1865 - 1879
*	Sironi	1879 - ?
*	Procida	?
*	Donnino	? - 1901
*	Tamburrini	1901 - 1904
	Maggioni	1904 - 1905
*	Fabbri (inc)	1905 - 1910
	Lazzerotti	1910 - 1936
	Scala (inc)	1936 - 1939
	Gaddi	1939 - 1952
	Scuri	1952 - 1970
	Cifariello	1971 - 1991
	Francese	1991 - present

Table 4: *Directors of the Nomentana School from its founding*

transformed the school into a residential institution (boarding school) in 1838. For special occasions, the school presented highly celebrated public demonstrations following the example of similar institutions. Many cardinals and important prelates, often including the Pope, attended these demonstrations.

Apart from a brief break during the Roman Republic (1849), the school continued to be financed by the Papal State until 1870, when the various states were unified and Rome became capital of the Kingdom of Italy. As a 'Royal Institution', the school fell under the control of the Ministry of Public Instruction, and the boarding of the students was financed by the local administration (Provincia). During this period the protection of the school was undertaken by the Royal Family of Savoy, and on different occasions the Queen herself and other dignitaries visited the school. After the Second World War, all Royal Institutions became State Institutions, but the administrative organization remained more or less the same.

In these two hundred years in the life of the school, the number of its students varied considerably, from the 8 pupils of Silvestri to more than 200 in 1965, and on to 20 in 1988 and to only 8 today. This decrease is due to the 1977 law according to which Deaf children can be mainstreamed with hearing peers. Table 5 shows the number of boys and girls attending the school at different periods. After its foundation, the school changed location many times, until it was finally established in 1889 in the present building in the Via Nomentana. In Ill. 2 we show a map of Rome with the various locations of the school.

III.2 Unwritten records

From our interviews with Deaf people, we were able to gather a great deal of information of a different kind. After some initial hesitation, they were very happy to answer our questions, and they provided many useful anecdotes. Only a direct viewing of the videotapes or close reading of the transcripts can give a faithful and complete report of all the information gathered (in the Appendix some of the interviews are reported).

Below we have tried to summarize some important facts about life as led by the children in the Institution, about the way they communicated with other children and adults, and about their personal feelings and memories.

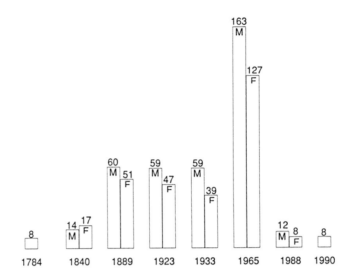

Table 5: *Number of boys (M) and girls (F) attending the school at different periods*

Life in the boarding school

From 1900 until 1950, children entered the school between 6 and 8 years of age, and they remained there for about ten years. They were between 17 and 20 years old when they left. They went home only during summer holidays, but some of them never returned home at all because they attended summer camps. Relatives could visit them for Christmas and Easter, and on Sunday morning if they lived in or near Rome. In a few circumstances children could go out with relatives, but they had to come back to the school before evening.

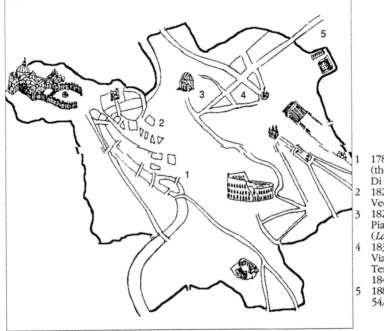

1 1784 Via dei Barbieri (the house of the lawyer Di Pietro)
2 1822 Via del Governo Vecchio 44
3 1827 Corso Rinascimento/ Piazza della Minerva (*La Sapienza* University)
4 1838 Via Cernaia/ Via Pastrengo (1838 Termini's Workhouse) 1844 Locale Calanca
5 1889 Via Nomentana 54/56

Ill. 2: *Map of Rome with the 5 locations of the school*

Life was strictly regimented: wake-up at seven, breakfast and classes between 8:30 and 12, lunch until 1, then playtime, and in the afternoon from 3 to 6 the younger children played and did homework, while the older learned a trade in the workshops. At 7 was dinner, then about one hour for chatting and off to bed at 9 in the large dormitories.

Girls, strictly separated from boys, attended Mass every morning and said the Rosary every evening. On Sunday everyone went to Church; some received visits from their relatives, and in the afternoon everyone went for a walk.

In the boarding school children were looked after by assistants: laymen for boys, and nuns for girls. All of these caretakers were hearing.

This regimen changed partially only after 1950, when the nursery school was officially opened and children were admitted at the age of four. A few pupils were allowed to attend the school as day-boarders, from 8 in the morning to 7 in the evening. On Sunday, children could go to the cinema, and many more than before began to return home during holidays, unless their families lived far from Rome.

The school

In the morning boys were in the classrooms at 8:30, the girls at 9. The boys had lay teachers, both men and women, but the girls received their education entirely from nuns. After the foundation of the nursery school in 1950, nuns cared for the smaller boys and girls together.

Although the pupils remained many years in the school (about ten years) they went no further than the fourth elementary grade, and at most they were able to obtain only an elementary school diploma upon leaving. (Only after 1970 did the school experiment for a short time with secondary education.)

All of the former students remember beginning with exercises in articulation, followed by the teaching of writing, mathematics, history, etc. Many of those interviewed comment that *they forced us to study verbs a lot.* When the pupils made mistakes, some of the stricter teachers struck their hands with a stick or pulled their ears. Of course, we must not forget that such educational practices were quite common at that time.

Even after fifty years, the teachers' names (both Italian and sign names) are still remembered, as is their temperament: strict or patient. The Deaf students can still judge clearly whether their teachers were bad or good, and above all, whether the teachers were lazy or attentive to their work. Some of the teachers started as assistants in the same school; but in every case, classroom teachers for academic subjects were hearing.

In the afternoon the students went to workshops with different teachers (expert crafts-people) and learned useful trades: for the boys shoemaking, tailoring, bookbinding, carpentry (and in some periods also printing and upholstery). The girls learned dress-making, embroidery, mending and knitting. Both hearing and deaf persons taught these manual arts. The interviews attest to at least four Deaf teachers: two taught drawing, one shoemaking, one knitting. Two of them (the shoemaker and the knitting instructor) had been students in the same school years before. All of those interviewed expressed pleasure and pride in having learned a trade, but they are much less sure of their academic education.

Re-education with earphones had been tried with some of the pupils, but only for a short time; with very few exceptions, these efforts apparently had negative results.

Means of communication

All the children communicated among themselves with signs, a form of communication that most of them learned after entering the school. Even the children with Deaf parents who signed fluently at home learned to use the particular signs of 'Via Nomentana', signs which were different in many cases from those used at home.

For example, P.R. and his brother attended two different Deaf schools in Rome (Via Nomentana and Gualandi); he remembers very clearly the different signs that he and his brother used, signs that in turn differed from the ones they both used at home with their parents. Examples include signs for numbers, the signs for PAPA (daddy), DONNA (woman), LAVORO (work), VECCHIO (old man), BAMBINA (girl), COME-SI-CHIAMA (what is your name?).

Some of these signs are still used by the Deaf children attending the school today, but former pupils no longer use them outside because they look 'old fashioned'. Examples of these 'old-fashioned' signs include the signs for MILANO (Milan), ZIO (uncle), ESAME (exam), UOMO (man)

All the pupils had sign names. These were usually created inside the Institute by the assistants, the nuns or schoolmates: for example, A.P.'s name sign was the sign for monkey, because he was extraordinary quick at climbing. Even when the child already had a name sign (coming from a Deaf family), another name was often given in school: for example, P.R. was given the sign name of a cousin who was just leaving the school when he entered.

The teachers, the assistants, the nuns and the director each had a name sign which remained the same, passing from one generation of pupils to another.

In the classroom pupils were forced to communicate orally, but when something was not clear, they were permitted recourse to signs; outside the classroom, during playtime, in the workshops and in the dormitory life, gesturing was not forbidden, and the children could sign freely. The adults all had at least some skill in some form of gestural communication, and some assistants and nuns were particularly adept. It is clear that the instructors in the workshops signed a great deal of the time; some of them of course were deaf.

Sign communication was accepted and tolerated in the Via Nomentana much more then in other institutions, according to several of those we interviewed who compared their situation in school with that of friends or relatives attending different schools. P.P., who moved to Via Nomentana from a school for the Deaf in Milan, confirmed that signs were used much less in the Tarra school. Of all the Nomentana directors, only the phoniatrician Scuri is remembered as openly hostile to sign *(he was very strict, he wanted everyone to speak)*.

During playtime or in the evening before going to bed, the older children told younger ones about events that they had seen or heard about from others. Usually the assistants studied while children played dominoes, draughts or chess. Sometimes a schoolmate would tell the story of a movie (for example *Tom the cowboy* or *Tex*), while others invented stories.

One man interviewed, a dayboarder and child of Deaf parents, remembered school friends around him asking about news from the 'outside', information he may have gathered from his father or friends.

One woman interviewed reported about *a nun who told us what the radio was saying or the story of San Francesco; she spoke and signed together.*

Individual memories

It is difficult to choose among the various anecdotes provided by our Deaf informants, some of them amusing, some rather sad, but all still vivid in their minds.
– The long wait for King Vittorio Emanuele, who never did arrive, sending in his place a representative who gave every child a box of chocolates.
– The first student protest, for better food and heating, with good results.
– The screening of a film lent by the House of Savoy, with boys and girls trying to arrange dates and exchange tickets around a barrier between the sexes formed by a curtain and a long line of nuns.
– The first theatrical recital, with comic scenes, before the whole school and guests invited from outside.

- Long walks toward Montesacro, now a busy quarter but countryside in the early 1900s.
- Fist fights with schoolmates and arguments with the director, who called a Deaf adult to serve as referee.
- Tales, part reality and part imagination, of escapes from the dormitory and pirate raids into the giant attic.

In general, those interviewed showed a great sense of liberation when they finished school but also a profound sadness at leaving behind Deaf schoolmates.

IV Conclusion

We do not consider this historical research concluded; more work remains to be done, but we can underscore a few interesting points that have emerged from both the written and the oral records, and especially, from a comparison between the two.

In many respects, the two sources concur: the importance of getting instruction in situations that were particularly difficult or disagreeable at the beginning, the opportunity to learn a manual skill or trade, the rigid separation between male and female pupils, and so on. In other matters the two sources are complementary. Above all, we hear about signs, used so conscientiously by the founder of the school, Silvestri, based on his experience in France, used continuously and with official acceptance through the 1800s to teach the Deaf reading, writing and lip-reading. Obviously with those students who were so predisposed, articulation was taught as well. It was only after the congress of Milan that the 'oral method' was imposed by various directors of the school. Despite these official positions, gestures (actually sign language) continued to play an important role, indeed, a crucial role in the students' lives and in their education.

In contrast with other institutions, signs were never really banned in Via Nomentana. Children signed in the courtyards, in the dormitories, in the workshops, less in the classroom even though here as well they were permitted recourse to sign to clarify anything that had not been understood. Some signed more, some less, but everyone knew sign: the students, the teachers, the assistants. None of this is mentioned in the written records; the 'official' account does not correspond in this case to the real facts. Furthermore, the signs of Via Nomentana have a character of their own that has been passed on from one generation of pupils to another.

These facts force us to confront the current situation: even though the teachers and their methods have remained virtually unchanged in the last forty years, the number of students has decreased sharply and their scholastic level has decreased as well. The present teachers and educators are discouraged, attributing the decline to the mainstreaming of the great majority of Deaf children with hearing children, leaving the Institute with only those children who are 'most difficult' or 'less gifted'. We think instead that something else is missing today: with fewer than 10 children, what is missing now is the system of communication and transmission of culture that children formerly gained through signing within a much larger Deaf community. The rich stimulation provided by the Deaf linguistic community, which included both Deaf children and Deaf and hearing adults, favored the children's cognitive and linguistic development and facilitated the academic process even though this contribution was never recognized explicitly after the Congress of Milan.

It is no accident that, in the last few years, one begins to hear of the need for a 'gestural method', a 'bilingual education' or a 'bimodal method'. In Via Nomentana, as in other institutions, the bilingual community used to exist in full force, albeit without official recognition. Given all we know today, there is of course no way to justify a return to the structures that separated children from their families and from the rest of society for many years. But the Institute at Via Nomentana is now moving in new directions that may remedy the loss of community suffered by Deaf students in the last 10 years. On the one hand, the school is experimenting with a project that brings mainstreamed Deaf children back to Via Nomentana for special training in the use of new computer technologies. On the other hand, small groups of Deaf adults have begun to organize activities and sign language classes within the school, using the Institute as a meeting place also for chess and theater groups. These efforts may result in the re-creation of a bilingual community that can maintain and transmit the language, culture and traditions of the Deaf, facilitating the educational process for which this school was founded more than 200 years ago.

Appendix

Interview with M.R. about his father I.R.

My father was born in 1890. He was admitted to the Institute in 1898 at the age of eight and came out in 1907 at the age of 17. He was a boarder. He was there at the same time as both V. and P. *(see interview about A.P.)* and they remained friendly even after they left. Also my mother went to Via Nomentana but I don't know whether they met at school or outside as boys and girls were kept completely separated at the time.

He learned to speak, read and write very well. For his whole life, up to the age of eighty he went on reading the newspaper every day. At the Institute he had learned bookbinding, a trade that he continued for the rest of his life. He also learned to play chess at the Institute and later taught both me and my son P. *(see interview with P.R.).*

One of his teachers was Fabbri, and when I attended the Institute he always used to tell how my father had been one of his pupils.

At the Institute he also learned signs, which he didn't know before he went. His life as a boarder was much the same as mine.

He had fond memories of the Institute.

(see below for the interview concerning M.R. himself)

Interview with A.M. P.[1] about his father A.P.

I don't know much as my father talked very little about the school, while my mother was much more expansive about it.

She was a better pupil while my father nearly got expelled, and perhaps actually was.

He only went as far as the 4th elementary grade. He boarded. For me he was the most wonderful, kindest father.

He was born in 1903 and joined the school at the age of 5 or 6, or perhaps even later.

He was delighted to to go to the Institute because there he was sure to get three meals a day, clean sheets, and a bath every week. There was nothing like this in his native village, Vivaro Romano, only dire poverty.

Among other things his father had migrated to America when he was at the Institute, coming back after he had left it (with what he had earned he was able to buy the house).

There were five children – three boys and two girls – and he was the second, the first boy. He was the only deaf member of the family, and became so at the age of two after an attack of meningitis. He had in fact been operated on, probably only a short time afterwards, and has

---

1 A.M.P. is currently an LIS interpreter.

a large scar on the back of his neck (although the reason for the operation is not known). He must certainly have had good residual hearing, because even when he was elderly he could always hear something and also had good voice intonation.

He always used to say that if his hearing had been normal he would have been a lawyer.

He was a good speaker, and he very much liked reading (especially history, about the ancient Romans, wars, etc.). He had trouble writing in Italian, but was good at math.

At Via Nomentana he learned tailoring, a trade he continued to ply after he left, first at other tailor's shops and then in a shop he opened himself at San Lorenzo in the '40s.

It appears that he was expelled from the Institute because he had instigated a kind of revolution to protest against a sudden decline in the quality of the food. He used to speak quite proudly of this 'feat'.

He used to speak of a certain Professor Francocci, whom he was very fond of, but who did not stay very long as he had to go to the war. He was accustomed to living in the country and everything he learned, he learned at school: speaking, reading, writing, his trade, sign language.

His sign name 'monkey' (which I inherited) was given to him because he was very good at rope climbing during gym, probably because he had learned to climb trees in the country. He was very good at gym.

He had probably never met any other Deaf persons in his village (while in my mother's village there was another Deaf girl who never went to school). He was very fond of the Institute because things were so hard at home in his village.

On Sundays they used to go on long walks. He can remember Via Nomentana when it was only countryside. Some Sundays his sisters would visit him and bring him some fruit.

As far as the Institute is concerned he never mentioned beatings but can remember people being caned.

Interview with A.M. (80 years old)

My name is A. M. and I was born in Naples in 1909. I am now 80.

At the age of 2 I lost my hearing as the result of an accident. I went to the Naples School for the Deaf until the age of 9. I left it to go to the Via Nomentana school in 1919, which I left in 1926 at the age of 17. I went as far as the 4th grade.

A typical day at the School was as follows: get up at 7-7.30 in the morning, breakfast at 8 and lessons until 12. Lunch from 12.30 until 1.30. Then there was recreation, when we played with a ball or cards, chess or dominos. At 3 o'clock we went to learn a trade: the boys did carpentry, tailoring, shoemaking or bookbinding. There was no kindergarten. That started later, but I can't remember when.

I learned dressmaking. When I left the school I went on learning the same trade and then set up on my own.

My parents paid for me to be a boarder because they lived in Naples and came to see me once a week, on Sundays.

The school was on the second floor. There were 8 of us in the class, but I can't remember all their names, just a few, as we often meet as we go to the same ENS section Deaf club *(Ente Nazionale dei Sordomuti, E.N.S., Italian National Association of the Deaf)*. At school we learned articulation, verbs, sign language wasn't used. The teachers and assistants knew sign language quite well, although not all the signs, just a few gestures to make themselves understood well enough. I didn't like going to school and actually didn't learn to speak very well.

The headmaster was Gaddi. On Sundays we used to go out on long walks, to Montesacro, Villa Borghese, the zoo, or to play football in another field. There were never any plays or parties, only the visit of the representative of the King of Italy who brought us bags of sweets.

There were prayers morning and evening. Mass was said only on Sundays by a priest from the 'Gualandi' (a religious institution for the Deaf). We used to do voice exercises such as 'a', 'o', 'u', etc., with a stick in our mouth for the 'r'. There were no hearing aids or other appliances; later on there were, but only for the hard of hearing.

Some of the assistants were nice and others less nice. I didn't like any of them much. I remember a quarrel with the deputy headmaster Scala. I have forgotten the exact reason, but I remember we came to blows and I was expelled from the boarding school. Luckily it was my last year.

I was always successful but I don't remember the school with pleasure. I didn't like going there and the food wasn't any good. It was a relief to leave the Institute because I had a hard time there. I haven't kept any photos or exercise books.

Interview with M. R. (70 years old)

I started going to Via Nomentana in 1927 at the age of 8 and came out in 1936 at the age of 17. I went as far as the 5th grade.

At the beginning I wasn't very happy. I didn't want to stay at the Institute. I was a bit confused. They took me and showed me where I was to sleep. Then, the next day, I started school, in first class. In class they taught me how to pronounce 'a', 'o', 'u'. When lessons were over we had lunch from midday till one o'clock, then we played football until five.

The food wasn't much good. The first dish was overcooked pasta, followed by meat or cooked ham. The evening meal was light – tasteless soup, cheese. There was no wine, only water. I used to feel hungry.

The first teacher was Fabbri. He was a priest and had also taught my father. My next master was Trafico, who always taught the same way (for example, in math, adding, subtracting) but he wasn't a good teacher. This changed when Gaddi came. He was a good teacher but used the cane. Never on the body, only on the hands. But he was a good teacher.

In the junior classes they didn't teach very much. Then we got Leso in the fourth grade. He discovered they hadn't done any Italian and got very annoyed. He taught Italian. He was the teacher in 4th and 5th grades.

Leso was the headmaster and Scala the deputy headmaster.

The classroom was on the second floor of the boys' wing. We had our meals downstairs. There were a lot of people at table. There was also B. F., but he was older and sat at another table. Some of the other boys of that time now live in Rome, others live outside.

We used to play in the courtyard in the boys' section. On Sundays we always played football or went for a walk. We used to go as far as Montesacro.

I never saw the theatre, even though there was one on the nuns' side. But in 1934 B. F. *(his interview is not reported here)* set up the cinema. When he came a lot of things changed. They also put in central heating and the food improved. Then they also started showing films. Unfortunately I left two years later.

There were never any parties. Once King Vittorio Emanuele was supposed to come and we were all looking forward to it. Instead his representative came bringing each of us a box of sweets.

Some teachers insisted on articulation, particularly Fabbri, Gaddi and Leso were good teachers. Trafico didn't do anything. In any case I never used either a hearing aid or an earphone.

At the age of 10 I started learning the bookbinder's trade. Lessons were from 2 p.m. until 6 p.m., four hours every day. We sometimes worked until midday on half holidays. Only the best boys were selected. The teacher, Remo, didn't want too many boys, only 4 or 5. He taught us how to set up, saw and sew, and then to cut and paste. He was a good teacher. I did this until the age of 12 or 13, and then I started leather binding. Remo was a good teacher and knew sign language very well.

One day we were going out to do an exam in Via Pio X, on the Tuscolana. Remo had picked the best and we had to do a job of binding and then hand it in with our name on it, in order to be assessed. I was with Greggi and a lot of other hearing people. I didn't know how to use gilt. I hadn't been taught. But I was good at the rest.

I did a very good job and came in third. I even got a diploma. Afterwards Remo gave me some money on the sly and I was very happy.

The assistants usually studied while the children were playing dominos, checkers or chess. Sometimes one of the boys would talk about a film (Tom the cowboy, for example, or Tex). The others would make up stories or the deaf boarders would tell the story of films and other things.

One of the assistants was called Spinosi. He was good at sign language. Yes, I understood him very well. He used to work in the Vatican.

We were usually well behaved. Sometimes we would have a fight or swear at each other, mostly for fun. In cases like these the assistant would punish us by putting us in the corner.

I lost my copy books when I moved but I still have some photos.

Interview with G.F. (58 years old)

I started boarding in 1937 at the age of 6 and left in 1943 at the age of 12. I wasn't born deaf. I probably became deaf at the age of nine months after attacks of convulsions I had had also at an earlier stage (three and six months). My mother used to call me and I didn't answer so they took me to the doctor at the 'Bambin Gesu' Hospital. He discovered I was deaf and my mother fainted.

When I started boarding I was very sad. I cried a lot because I was separated from mummy and daddy. Even as I got older I always used to think of my mother and father. Then I slowly got used to it and began to spend more time with my school companions.

I was a full boarder and used to go home only in June because my parents were poor and couldn't afford travel expenses.

At school we used to get up at seven o'clock, make our beds and then go to mass at eight o'clock every day. At 8.30 we had breakfast and had lessons from 9 until 12. In the afternoon I can't remember exactly what we did but I think we stayed at school from 3 p.m. until 5 p.m. and then there was embroidery and recreation. We then went to church and said the rosary. After supper we had more recreation until 9 o'clock and then we went to bed.

The teachers were good. I had a different mistress each year. The first one was Sister Carmela for voice training, and in the second year Elsa. Then I had Sister Patrizia and Sister Placida. Then I left school.

I had also gone to nursery school when they taught articulation 'pa po pu' and 'a o u'. You were allowed to sign. Gestures were not prohibited. There were a lot of toys, even instructive toys.

At the age of 7 in first class with Sister Carmela I did some more articulation. There were six or seven children and the nun was very patient and taught us all in turn.

At recreation we went out and played hide and seek if it was fine. If it rained we stayed inside. We were free to chatter in sign language while we were walking in the courtyard.

The nuns taught us to knit. My mother brought me some wool to knit pullovers for my brothers. I knitted them with sleeves longer than their arms. We also did embroidery, and sewed and mended the linen. I have never used a knitting machine, although some other girls did. They also learned dressmaking.

On Sunday mornings we used to draw. In the afternoon we went for a walk in Villa Borghese or visited churches. Sometimes they had a party at the boarding school, or they showed a film or we went to the St. Joseph's parish cinema.

A nun often used to tell us what she heard on the radio or the story of St. Francis. She spoke and signed at the same time.

At table we ate our meals at a long table. The food was good and I liked everything. Some other children didn't like the food and used to give it to me. There was a girl whose parents used to bring her sweets. She didn't like them so I used to eat them.

I can't remember my school companions very well. They had given me a sign name. It used to belong to another girl who had left and had the same name as me. It was a sign that was handed down to those who had the same name.

There were holidays every now and then. At Epiphany we used to play bingo. There were lots of prizes. At the end of the year people came from outside to see the play or gym exhibition. I was happy to leave although I missed a friend of mine.

I don't think I can remember a story or event which happened at the Institute as I was small, naive and not at all curious.

There were about 80 of us girls and the assistants were all nuns. Some of the girls were very clever. Unfortunately, after all these years, I no longer have any books or copy books. I lost them all when I moved.

Interview with P.P. (48 years old)

I was born in Rome but spent my school days in Milan, at the Tarra school in Viale Zara: it's a state school for deaf mutes and the hard of hearing, but there are no boarders, it's just a day school. I was there from 1945 to 1953.

Then my family moved to Rome because there was no more work in Milan, and I began to attend the Institute in via Nomentana. I was 12 years old in 1953 and I didn't like the boarding school, I wasn't happy there; I'd been accustomed to going back and forth between home and day school, and I was out of my element; the teaching was good in Milan but not here – things were quite different. In the morning there was school, and that was fine, but we played in the afternoon, studied little, slouched about a bit, and some had little will to do anything at all. We learnt trades (tailoring or carpentry) and nothing else – unlike Milan, where I spent the afternoons studying at home.

There were a lot of deaf mutes at the via Nomentana school; 98 boys, about 30-40 in the kindergarten, and I was told there were about 70-80 in the girls' section. The classes were full but the separation of boys and girls was too rigid; there was a wall between us. There was not much culture because we were cut off from the world. It would have been better if the boys and girls had been together – it would have been more normal and there would have been more mixing, but there was no real warmth. It was right to have separate dormitories, but we could have been together during school hours.

The boys were with the assistants, who allowed them more freedom, but the girls were with the nuns, who kept them under very strict surveillance.

My teacher was Lucia, who is now director; I've forgotten her sign name – perhaps it was L in dactylology. She used few signs in class, talking most of the time, but her lip movements were very clear and there was no difficulty in following her. I don't remember how long she was my teacher; I had another one afterwards who subsequently retired. In 1953 I was in 3rd grade: I had been in the 4th in Milan but they put me back because there was a difference in the levels between the two schools. I got confused with both the spoken and written language; in Milan there was more spoken language and it was clearer, while sign language was used more in Rome.

I went to school in the morning, then about 12.30 we ate and then played until 2 p.m. Then I went to learn tailoring until 6. p.m., with a break for a snack; when the weather was bad we stayed in the hall from 7. to 8. p.m., playing and, some at any rate, studying. If the weather was good we played together in the yard. Before supper we went to church with the assistants for prayers (we also had ten minutes' prayers before school in the morning), and then ate at 7.30. This was followed by an hour's recreation and at about 9. we would go to bed.

In the tailor's workshop my instructor, Dante, was a very good signer; his father had taught tailoring for many years too, then Dante took over from him.

Then there were the other assistants, each with his own particular duty. I remember one from Genoa, although I've forgotten his name: he was stout, bald, strict, exacting but good-natured; he liked to go for long walks on Sunday – 3 or 4 kilometers to Villa Borghese on foot all the way, and all the way back too, and he would spur us on, but we were tired because we'd already been playing football in the morning. Every now and then my aunt would come to fetch me and take me home with her.

Sometimes we would ask to go to the cinema. The assistant asked permission of the director, Scuri, who would think about it for a bit and then agree, and we were happy.

There was a projector in the Institute itself; the girls were on one side, the boys on the other, with the nuns in a line in the middle forming a sort of barrier, although the assistants didn't seem to care. We wanted to date the girls but the nuns hemmed them in and we couldn't arrange anything. One May, at the end of the school year, there was a coach trip to Pompey, but the boys and girls travelled separately in two different coaches. We had our trip and came back in the evening; there was always a trip at the end of the school year.

We used to put on plays in the Institute with a tall, sturdy assistant called Daniele who came from Sicily, I think, and another assistant called Pasquale Pelosi, who was practically in charge of everything. The deaf and dumb girls were invited to the performances too, so all the boarders were there, all the deaf boys and girls. We put on a sketch with doctors in an operating theatre: I played the doctor operating on a fat patient and pretended to pull out his intestines and throw them to an imaginary cat, which I also imitated. The audience all looked for the cat, but it wasn't there. I squirted water from a rubber bulb, arousing the curiosity of the deaf audience who wanted to know where the water came from.

During the performance we used sign mostly; after 30 years, I can't remember if we used any words but it's unlikely because they couldn't be understood very well from a distance, while gestures and miming were clear.

The Director did not come to see the performances, but the teachers did. They had never gone in for acting before I went to the Institute – I was the first to do it, although the idea came from the assistant Daniele.

After my arrival there they started re-education with earphones; the first to try it was a boy who was hard of hearing. I tried together with the others but, apart from a small minority, the results were negative. Lucia Cifariello organized these experiments, and the equipment was kept in the former printshop on the ground floor.

They didn't give us much work to do at school and we all followed our own inclinations, some doing quite a lot, some very little; there was little teaching and we were very lazy. The food wasn't good, although it got a bit better on Sundays. Later on, around 1957, the meals improved, but that was when I left the Institute.

When I left, at the end of the 5th elementary grade, they didn't give me a certificate – I don't know why: in Milan they gave you a certificate every year just like the council schools. After boarding school I attended the ENS training Institute, in the press room, and got a certificate every year.

In the via Nomentana Institute we played football every day and never tired of playing; everyone took part, even the ones that were no good at football. When it rained we played in the dormitory with a paper ball. Once one of the boys kicked the ball right up in the air and broke a window. The Director, Scuri, got very angry and confiscated our ball. We often broke windows, which is why they began to play basketball in 1958-59, but I was no longer there. Scuri was very keen on basketball, but he couldn't stand football.

Scuri used to talk to us; he was very strict, and wanted all of us to speak. He would come to supervise the running of the Institute, always very busy and never still for a moment. Once when Scuri was in charge the food at lunch was bad; I told him it was bad but he didn't believe it. So I gave him a taste of it and he said I was right; he told off the nuns through the hatch, and the food got better after that.

I heard of some boys running away from the boarding school and going back to their families without any notice; they ran away because they couldn't get on with the others, and this made them sad. These were the ones who were always in the Institute and never went home except in the summer. I was lucky because I had my aunt and uncle who used to fetch me on Sunday and take me home with them, although the vice-director Scala didn't want them to.

I never failed the year, but I remember finding this a bit absurd: with very few exceptions everyone passed. I started at the via Nomentana Institute in 1953 and left in 1957. I spent 4 years in Rome and 8 in Milan.

Interview with P.R. (39 years old)

I started attending this school in '53 and left in '64. I began with kindergarten at the age of four and went on through to the 5th level, when I finished at the age of 15.

To the day I left the director was always the same, Scuri (in fingerspelling); he also had a sign name but I don't know who gave it to him – it was already his name when I joined the school.

I too immediately received a sign name – the same name as a cousin of mine who was on his way out when I arrived at the boarding school. In practice, his name was passed on to me. I told the children I had a different sign name (the one my parents used at home), but they insisted and so I agreed to it.

I remember that the kindergarten was run by nuns, including sister Brini who immediately taught us to use our voices; then she taught us to write and encouraged us to play with construction sets, among other games. In the first year of elementary school there was Ms. Gasparri, who taught me history, geography and various other subjects as well as writing. Then I had Laura Rampelli in the 3rd and 4th elementary levels, I think. The last teacher I had was Da Barp (in fingerspelling), who is dead now. I left with the 5th elementary grade certificate.

I never tried any aids – just the earphones in the 2nd elementary level, I think, when I was 7 or 8: I would sit behind a glass screen and speak into a microphone. Then I gave it up.

The nuns used mostly to speak, as did Ms. Gasparri – although she knew sign because she had two deaf children. Laura talked and used sign. Da Barp used sign mostly, in a sort of very precise Italian. His signs were very different from ours, but we understood him all the same.

Some – especially some assistants – had a very good command of sign: Pelosi, De Piccoli, Matteo.

The general practice was to use voice plus sign; to ask the teacher a question you used your voice but often she didn't understand, so you would help yourself to communicate with sign. Gestures were never prohibited, and you were free to use sign when you wanted to. Both teachers and assistants all had sign names, and when Laura arrived as the new teacher we immediately gave her one (L like her initial).

When I was little my mother used to take me and I would go up to the kindergarten on the second floor of the girls' section. At 12.30 we went down to lunch; I didn't eat because I didn't like it, but later on I ate at home. When they made me eat I would hide the meat and then my mother would find it in my pinafore pockets.

At 1 o'clock we went out into the yard to play ball, ring-a-ring of roses, etc. until 2. Then we went up to the classroom to play, draw and build things. At 5. my mother came to fetch me.

Then I went up to the elementary classes in the boys' section. It was organized along more or less the same lines, but when you reached a certain age you started to learn a trade.

In the morning we had school from 8.15 to 12.30; then there was lunch until 1 o'clock, after which we played until 2.30 and then went to learn a trade until 6.: book-binding, tailoring, carpentry, cobbling. At six o'clock I went back home.

I did book-binding under the instruction of a hearing person, Remo, who also knew sign, however; my father had been a pupil of his too. Three times a week I went for typing and drawing lessons. The teachers came from outside and the typing teacher explained things to me vocally but I didn't understand anything – only when and where I had to hit the keys. On the other hand Santoro, the drawing teacher, was deaf and I understood everything.

To sum it all up, we had normal school with hearing teachers in the morning, and in the afternoon we had deaf instructors and hearing instructors who knew sign; shoemaking was taught by a deaf instructor, book-binding by an instructor who knew sign, as also carpentry; tailoring I don't know, because I never saw the instructor. The shoemaker was an old pupil of the school who still lives in Rome.

As I said, I was on half-board; I went home in the evening, and so I was able to bring my school fellows news from outside – news from the club and my father's other deaf friends, and about films, spors and television (there was no television here at that time). In the morning or afternoon or during playtime we would gather round in a circle and I would tell them my news. We also used to break off from work in the workshop for a chat, although we got told off by the instructor. Generally it was we day boys who did the talking because the boarders had little news; they only went home on Saturday and Sunday – some only at Easter and Christmas.

Sometimes the boarders would tell us what had happened in the evening: a fight might have broken out between a boy and one of the assistants because the assistant had made fun of the boy, for example, and the boy had retaliated with a punch. This resulted in cuts and bruises and they were summoned before the director in the presence of F. B., who acted as go-between because the director didn't understand sign. Or someone might have stolen something from the attic used to store furniture and other articles, but only useless, worthless things were stolen.

Sometimes they would recount past events: arguments between the director and some of the bigger boys, the changes F. B. had brought about in the Institute (radiators, better food). My father described some of these things to me, too. When certain assistants became proper teachers new assistants arrived and the boarders gave each his name, which they would then tell me. Sometimes they were bad names; for example, one assistant had an aquiline nose and so his name was 'big nose'.

However, this teacher with the bad sign name was the kindest. All the assistants were hearing persons, but the kitchen and cleaning staff included some deaf people. For example, there were six deaf women in the girls' section. I didn't know them personally; the boys' and girls' sections were separate.

On the whole I didn't like the Institute; all I wanted to do was go out and enjoy myself because I was a day boy. Looking back now, however, I have the impression that we were taught little and wasted our time playing and chattering; the teacher would often leave us to our own devices. I've learnt a lot from my parents and my aunt, who insisted on teaching me. Later I made up for the time wasted.

When I finished school I was pleased as Punch; I couldn't wait to change my life and see new things in the outside world.

Interview with G. B. (23 age years old)

I was born in Ponza; I first went to the Institute in 1960 at the age of 8 and left at 18, in 1970, with the secondary school 3rd level certificate. I became deaf at the age of 6 and went to an Institute but I no longer have a clear memory of it; I saw children using sign and understood nothing. I was used to speaking, although in Neapolitan dialect. Little by little I learnt the signs. When I arrived in this school I had to begin the first elementary level from scratch once again, having forgotten everything on account of my illness. The teachers were all nuns: sister Eugenia, sister Elisa, sister Emerenziana, sister Eufemia – in the elementary school they were all nuns too.

Sister Elisa taught only verbs; first we had to study the verbs, then gathered all around her we had to have prompt answers for the questions the teacher asked, and anyone that took some time to answer got a rap across the palm of the hand, while children who didn't know their verbs were locked in the bathroom for punishment. In my opinion this method was right because you learn to speak and communicate properly; I owe my ability to speak to this and, thanks also to this method, I can make myself understood.

The nuns taught with voice and sign, never just sign.

With the other girls I had to use sign. The nuns used to get angry; it was forbidden in school but not always outside – they got tired of telling us it was forbidden because we went on regardless.

I was a boarder for 10 years; the food was all right – not like home cooking, of course, but not too bad. It wasn't compulsory to attend Mass on weekdays. If you wanted to go you said so.

During the recreation time we would make up games like imitating actors, for example, or play hide-and-seek, etc. We were like prisoners in the boarding school.

I didn't like working; in fact, I'm lazy, and I always looked for some excuse to avoid work. There was a deaf hosier called Benedetta – a really fine person – and I was very fond of her company. She told me about what went on outside the boarding school; I was very curious and wanted to know a lot of things, and so I was already prepared for the life outside when I left the boarding school.

My sign name was quite offensive: it was given me by a nun and represented a duck's bill, because I had this mania about wanting to know everything that was said or happened both inside the boarding school and out. I was also friends with some day girls but I never dreamt of asking them anything.

My secondary school teachers were Lucia Cifariello, Cervo and a French woman whose name I forget. The French teacher didn't know sign; she taught with lip-reading but I understood nothing – just the written language, word for word. Lucia Cifariello only used sign when she was about to explain something I didn't understand. I was deputy head girl. School was from 8 to 12, and then from 6. p.m. to 7. p.m. I tried the hearing aid but it was no use because I couldn't hear anything.

At School

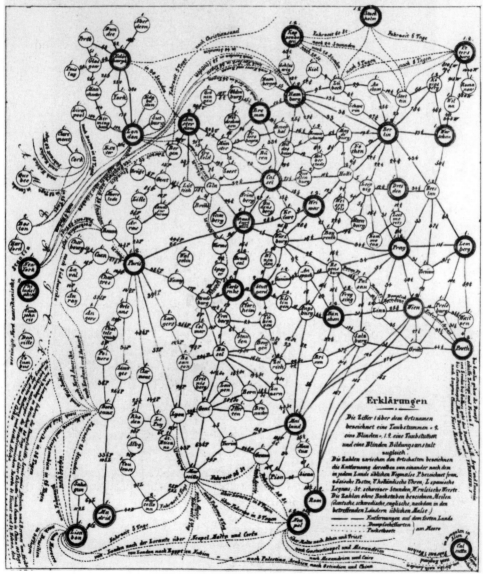

Ill.85: International map showing existent and past institutes for the Deaf and/or for the Blind up to 1837.

Scholastica von Gottes gnaden Edtilchinne des freien Wettlichen Stifte Gherenrode
und Frochin geporne Forstin zu Inhatt Graffinne zu Aschanien

Ill. 86: The abbess Scholastica is reported to have instructed a young Deaf woman using signs in the 15th century, at Gernrode. This is the first instruction of a Deaf person in Germany we know of.

Ill. 87: A lesson at the institute in Groningen, Netherlands, about 1810. Fictitious representation.

Ill. 88: Public exercises at the National Institution of Deaf Mutes in Paris in the early 19th century.

Ill. 89: Undated advertising for the Institution of the Deaf and Dumb and of the Blind at Lübeck, Germany.

Ill. 90: Anthropometry of Deaf pupils at the Provincial Institute of the Deaf and Dumb and of the Blind in Berchem, Belgium.

Ill. 91: Learning spoken language by way of pictures: 'punishment', after Moritz Hill (1805-1874).

Ill. 92: Jam and the gourmand: a lesson at the deaf mute section of the Provincial Institute of the Deaf and Dumb and of the Blind in Berchem, Belgium.

Ill. 93: German Wehrmacht troops having fled their camp in the girls' house of the Institute for the Deaf H.D. Guyot in Groningen, Netherlands, in 1945.

Ill. 94: 'M. Laveau and his dear deaf mutes': The director of the Institute for the Deaf and Dumb in Orléans, France, Abbé Laveau (? - 1869), in 1864.

Ich und meine Artikulationsklasse.

Ill. 95: 'Me and my class of articulation': Johannes Vatter (1842-1916), father of the 'pure oral method'.

Issues Concerning Medicalization, Sociology, and Philosophy

Aude de Saint-Loup
Paris, France

Images of the Deaf in Medieval Western Europe

Summary • Résumé

Despite long held beliefs, the Middle Ages were in many respects an eventful period in the history of the Deaf. Reactions towards Deaf people were diverse: both rejection and integration existed simultaneously. These contradictory reactions resulted from ignorance on one hand and a will to understand and meet on the other. Have those behaviors really changed since? However, that long period of time (5th - 15th century) is remarkable for several reasons. Since the centralized state did not yet exist and the Church, in spite of its considerable influence, could not control everything, the organization of society was left largely to local initiative. As a consequence there was no official standpoint towards the Deaf. Everything was possible, the better as well as the worse. Besides, the great majority of people were illiterate and manual laborers. Therefore the deaf person was better adjusted to society than nowadays. Finally, even though speech was considered very important, gestures and pictures were widespread; the Deaf benefited from this specific situation, as using gestures and learning from pictures was a generally accepted principle. Whether these codes were not always available to the Deaf is a different matter. Through the different ways of representing the Deaf in the Middle Ages and taking into account characteristics of that civilization, it appears that in spite of their difference the Deaf were less disadvantaged in the Middle Ages than other handicapped people and certainly less than they are today.

Pour l'Histoire des sourd(e)s et contrairement à ce que l'on a cru longtemps, le Moyen Age se révèle très riche. Les réactions vis-à-vis des sourd(e)s sont variées: rejet et intégration coexistent.Ce sont les conséquences d'un état d'ignorance ou au contraire, d'une volonté de compréhension et de rencontre. Ces comportements ont-ils beaucoup changé? Cependant, cette longue période (Vème - XVème siècles) est originale à plusieurs titres. Son organisation laisse une grande part aux initiatives locales: l'Etat centralisateur n'a pas encore de réalité et l'Eglise ne peut pas tout contrôler même si son influence est importante. Il n'y a donc pas de prise de position officielle à l'égard des sourd(e)s. Tout est possible, le meilleur comme le pire. D'autre part, la grande majorité de la population est illettrée et travaille manuellement: les personnes sourdes sont donc moins inadaptées qu' à notre époque. Enfin, même si l'on reconnaît à la parole une grande importance, les gestes et les images sont également très développés: cela ne pouvait nuire aux sourd(e)s puisque le principe même d'utiliser des gestes et d'apprendre par les images était admis. Que les codes ne leur aient pas toujours été accessibles, est une autre question. Au travers des diverses représentations des sourd(e)s au Moyen Age et compte tenu des caractères propres à cette civilisation, il ressort que les personnes sourdes, certes différentes, étaient peut-être moins pénalisées que d'autres handicapés, et certainement moins pénalisées qu'aujourd'hui.

Historiography

Up to now, except for a few works by German historians (Schmalz 1830, Walter 1882 and especially Schumann 1940), the history of the Deaf and the Dumb in the Middle Ages has been, to say the least, very neglected. At the worst, discussions about that long millenium disposed of it with one sentence, judging the period to be so hostile toward the Deaf that it is not even worth dwelling on.

Why such a blank? Probably because prejudices about medieval obscurantism die hard. What could those 'barbarians' have had to say about the Deaf?

In fact, deafness is seldom directly dealt with in medieval sources, even where it might be expected. In those sources, Deaf persons are portrayed in two ways as living on the fringe of society. They belong to an informal group of recognized outcasts: beggars, wanderers, invalids, thieves and unemployed mercenaries: exceptionally a few Deaf people appear in this group. Very often they are stray or needy children[1] like so many of the others. In this constellation, deafness only aggravates their misfortune but does not justify their situation.

As the deaf person does not fit into any clear-cut category, information about all the Deaf is dispersed but existent. Because they can neither hear nor speak, they are called 'disabled', as is the leper, the blind person or the crippie. But as the Deaf remain physically autonomous, they can share in manual work, which is people's main occupation. Consequently they appear less and less in documents that deal with the 'true' disabled, those who are physically dependent on others and can't support themselves.

We may wonder if this apparent succinctness in medieval Western Europe concerning the Deaf person isn't just a logical consequence of complex factors of integration. The Deaf person was more easily subsumed into medieval societies than heor she is in ours. It is therefore necessary to find how this was possible.

Let's get back to the sources: where are the Deaf quoted?

Sources

Some series of documents are more enlightening than others. The stories of saints' lives (hagiographies), for example, are fairly informative. Religious communities flourished during the whole period and competed against each other to attract pilgrims (and their donations!). The best propaganda was the purported healing power of holy relics (bodies or parts of persons recognized as saints, or items that belonged to them) held by the individual churches. Deaf and dumb people appear in these more or less stereotyped ways of understanding the handicap and its consequences. Often the writers' more personal reactions show us that they had actually been in contact with Deaf people.

Medical treatises also dedicate chapters to the description of the ear and attempt to understand auditory function by means of the various defects that occur. The suggestions for curing ear problems are plentiful, but their efficacy remains questionable.

Other sources are literary as well as legal (or customary, as the law changed from one area to another), rhetorical and theological. Each of these sources is enlightening, but I will privilege one particular source here: iconography.

The picture acts differently than the text, even if the picture is often associated with the text in a rich interplay of interpretation (for instance, the words may be composed in such a

---

1 Polilia, a young deaf and dumb girl, begged in Rocamadour (Albe 1907, p. 138); Ermenfridus, deaf and dumb, begged at the door of St. Bertin's monastery by shaking a hand-rattle (St. Bertin's Miracles, col.130); another begged with a 'professional' from sanctuary to sanctuary (St. *Rema-*cle's Miracles, col. 698); a 12-year-old dumb boy was cruelly burnt in his mouth in St. Michael's abbey: he had been suspected of simulating (Lesort 1909, p. 25).

way that they literally draw figures or fit into the picture itself). The picture conveys a message or suggests an interpretation that doesn't come through the text. There is another advantage to pictures: it is much easier to control and censor a text than a picture, especially in the Middle Ages. In other words, even when the orders for pictures were precise or direct, and in spite of warnings that appeared from time to time against those productions, medieval iconography remained partially independent: while the picture illustrates a theme (generally religious), it reveals the artist's special sensitivity, influenced by his or her region and time.

Iconographic samples about the Deaf are still too scarce to reach any final conclusions. Those pictures that are available to us reach us as the remains of a history lacking many elements. An excellent reason to continue research!

Medical treatises

There are very few illustrations to be found in medical treatises before the 14th century, and on the theme of deafness even fewer, unsurprisingly. It is therefore interesting to note three or four pictures that follow the evolution of medicine.

Towards the middle of the 13th century, in Avicenna's Canon (Avicenna was an Arabian doctor, 987-1037) translated by a Spanish doctor, Gerard of Cremona, an illuminator illustrates an anatomical chapter on ears. Inserted in the text is a modest miniature, an ornamental letter, illustrating *Auris* (ears).

Ill. 1: *The academic lesson: a doctor explains the anatomy of the ear*

A person is shown in full-face: his hands spread his outer ears so that they can be clearly seen. He is the subject-object of the study. Identifiable by his headdress, the doctor solemnly stands at his side in three-quarters view: he is not the center of attention, but indicates the first person with his open and outstretched left hand. Thus he pedagogically orients the attention on the object of his lesson. His upward-pointed forefinger indicates that he is declaiming a speech. Except for an exchange of gaze, there is no contact between the two men. The doctor is a university professor or a scholar who cites theoretical knowledge based on the 'authorities' (recognized learned writers of the past). Learning can be done by observing at a distance, but reading remains the most appropriate way to become a doctor.[2] Practice is left to the 'surgeons', manual technicians...

In a 14th century treatise, a seated doctor observes the auditory duct of a man leaning on him. He maintains the patient's head in position by holding his chin, while with the other hand he delicately pulls the outer ear to display the duct. It is an observation with the naked eye, though the practice of using a speculum (a little mirror) was known at the time. The patient's free hand, with the palm half-opened, makes a gesture that could be interpreted as fear, but is more likely a sign of submission. He came to consult a doctor and has to rely on him, on his knowledge and on his ability; he can't judge for himself or follow the doctor's gestures with his eyes. Though uneasy, his only alternative is to trust and submit.

Ill. 2: *Observation and medical act*

2 Since the beginning of the Middle Ages, monastical schools were founded and some of them became centers of theoretical and practical medicine, more or less developed. Early, great progress was made in the South of Europe (Italy and Spain) thanks to the meetings of Byzantines, Arabs, Jews and various Europeans, that never stopped even during conflicts. Slowly, those contributions spread on the continent and, finally medical art was admitted as a universitary science.

Another 14th century version of Avicenna's Canon offers less accomplished drawings. In the chapter concerning 'blocked ears', another seated doctor examines the ear of a man standing, obviously ill at ease, open mouthed, and pointing to his ear with his finger (Avicenna's Canon, fol. 113). The doctor holds a long instrument; is it used for observation or for an operation?

Observation existed before the 14th century, but from that period on it became a pattern of investigation fit to follow. Permission to dissect bodies, until then forbidden by the Church, largely contributed to its progress. The embalmers (those who treated dead bodies in order to preserve them), often doctors themselves, had already the opportunity to make close examinations of the body. The ear is particularly complex and only the external part up to the eardrum was known, as was the auditory nerve, which was mentioned by Claudius Galen (130-200 AD), a Greek doctor. Anatomical and consequently physiological knowledge were both restricted. From Aristotle, who had observed the Eustachian tube, doctors revived the idea that sound is perceived when internal air is put in motion by the outer air, and from Galien they took the notion of circulating vital spirits manufactured in the heart, transformed into animal spirits in the brain and then distributed to the sensory and motor nerves. From these two theories, Avicenna reached the conclusion that profound deafness results from obstruction of the Eustachian tube and the auditory nerve (see, for example, Segal/ Willemot (eds.) 1981).

What are the causes of these obstructions? Various traumas, parasites or foreign bodies introduced by mistake, unstable fluids, effects of climate or food, and age (repeatedly frequent otitises for the young and progressive deafness for the elderly).

What are the cures? None when deafness has lasted for more than two years: the doctors were honest and declared it incurable. Otherwise, they used the basic treatments for all diseases: purgatives, emetics, the inevitable bloodletting and diets which were prescribed until the 19th century. More or less long and varied cures included plasters, fumigations, instillations, lozenges and potions. Sometimes rather quaint advice slips in: to get the worm out of the ear, a piece of apple should be applied against the outer ear, and the worm can't resist it; in the case of a stray spider, a flea will work likewise (Le Tresor de Maistre Arnault de Ville Nove, A XII). Surgical operations were carried out, but fortunately only on a limited basis: the outer ear was incised to free the auditory duct, and tumours were removed by various techniques. In case of some discharges, the liquids were sucked up with a cannula, or the extremity was heated to induce evaporation (Bernard de Gordon 1550, p. 297). Music therapy and acoustical trumpets complete the list of treatments, but they were less developed.

The limits of medical knowledge are particularly obvious in the case of muteness. The subject never appears in the chapters on ears and deafness, but rather in the chapters dealing with the vocal organs. To 'untie' the tongue, the 'bit', the ligaments that link the tongue to the lower jaw, is cut. If the mute couldn't speak after the operation, blessed are those who got away without a hemorrhage!

Common sense also advised against excessive treatment and limited medical care to the relief of pain, achieved thanks to the anesthetic properties of certain well-known plant extracts like almond oil. At last, aware of their incompetence regarding long-lasting deafnesses doctors took a basic and necessary step and accepted the handicap.

But what is deafness?

A 1412 medical and surgical treatise conveys a more explicit idea of deafness with the picture rather than the text. The folio (manuscript page) that interests us here appears in three parts: a large anatomical model with instruments fills the center and, above it, the doctor's hand holds a thread, ready to stitch the wounds of another reclining body. Undoubtedly

Ill. 3: *What is deafness, in fact?*

observation and the medical act are the focus. It is not necessary to represent the doctor in full size: his saving hand is almighty (for the patient's recovery), like God's hand in other circumstances. The text follows the lines of the central figures and lists a series of medical prescriptions. This constellation emphasizes the importance of the figure, and by an optical trick, the model's elbows look as if they are actually pushing the text off the page. Is it possible to better demonstrate that the cures that depend on medical knowledge rely for the most part on observation and practice? Finally there are figures cast on the edge of the drawings and surrounding the text. Their presence is more or less narrative. The sick and crippled are placed facing the texts dealing with their respective ailments.

Each prescription is related to a figure, except in the case of deafness, where two figures are necessary to perform a small animated act. Deafness represented with only one person was no novelty; such illustrations portrayed a deaf man pointing to his ears and his mouth (see Ill. 4). Did the illuminator of the afore mentioned text want to show that deafness is not an ill in itself but only in relation to others? That it becomes a handicap only when the deaf person comes in contact with those who hear and speak?

Ill. 4: *A deaf person presents himself to the crowd*

The deaf person in that illustration (Ill. 3) shows composure; with one hand he spreads his outer ear and points the forefinger of his other hand towards the prescription *contra sur-ditatem*. The second figure faces him with his back to the text, and therefore can't see it. With his mouth wide open he shouts at the deaf man, and the effort he makes to amplify his voice is reproduced comically: his legs move restlessly while he throws his body towards the deaf person. There is a very clear constrast between the excitement of the character unable to make himself understood and the calmness of the other unable to hear but apparently saying: 'Don't strain yourself, I am deaf, look behind you'.

Here the comical character is not the deaf person but rather the hearing person who strives to communicate in the only way he knows and yet remains powerless. This illustration gives us a foretaste of the comic strip dialogues between Professor Calculus and Captain Haddock, with one difference: Calculus speaks but misses the point in his answers, thus making himself comical, while here the deaf person simply points out that he has no access to that type of communication.

This simple draft in the margin of a medical text gets much credit for raising an essential and ever-present aspect of the deaf person's problem: the misappreciation of the handicap by a hearer. If unidentified, the deaf persons scarcely have a chance to live their relationship with others in a positive way.

To digress: as a teacher of young Deaf people for a few years, I collect errors made repeatedly by otherwise open-minded hearing people, but who have obviously never had contact with deaf people. Spontaneously they ask me if I use the Braille alphabet or if I teach at the Institute for the Young Blind. Twice I have found in the works of art historians that Zachary, a Biblical character, was blind, whereas the Bible depicts him as dumb. Such confusions are timeless and reveal how difficult it is, even today, to imagine deafness and dumbness.

Because of this ignorance, there is always a loser in every attempt at communication between a hearing and a deaf person. In Ill. 3 the character persisting pig-headedly in trying to make himself heard appears ridiculous, but the reverse situation also exists. In a few medieval documents I happened to find deaf people laughed at because they didn't understand what was said to them, either in spoken language or with signs (Radulphus Ardens, Col. 2037; St. Majolus's Miracles, col. 967). Their families feel more shame than pain (St. Remacle's Miracles, col. 698-702), and secret abandonments were sometimes encouraged. Deaf children's parents would leave them in abbeys granted special donations to take care of them (Schumann 1940, p. 21).

Yet, in spite of what may be thought, such references are not so frequent and the Deaf are not subject to so much mockery. It is interesting to notice that in farces and fabliaux (tales) the blind appear more often, because they can be made visual comics. The 'hard of hearing' person *(surdastrus)* is sometimes used for verbal misunderstandings but he can also act as an imitator who actually mocks his counterpart (Ouy 1984, verses 32-79). The speechless profoundly deaf person never appears since he has no visible physical defect. As a result he is not belittled in the first and most important evaluation: the other's perception. He can move about normally, doesn't stumble, and will not be visually deceived or even laughed at for his wrong answers since he is unable to speak. His absence of reaction and his silence to questions are ambiguous. In *Le chaudronnier* (Tissier 1984, p.71), a farce in which a couple in the middle of a domestic row falls silent, a visitor cries out: *Is she deaf? Is she stupid? Hey, Master, are you deaf, dumb or stupid?* In the absence of communication, three hypotheses are offered: deafness? dumbness? or stupidity? It is unfortunately probable that necessary distinctions have not always been made.

Silence can be felt as an aggression or an aggressive threat. Hearers are often provoked while reaching out for deaf persons unaware of their disability and misunderstanding it. In such a situation silence seems to be a refusal. Because there is no apparent warning about the handicap, the deaf person's silence is therefore interpreted, at first, as a will not to speak or even as an innate incapacity. It arouses confusion and anxiety. In *Le chevalier au lion* (Chrétien de Troyes 1923, p. 177), Calogrenant, the hero, meets a villain that *does not utter a word, no more than a beast* and fears that *he does not know how to speak and has lost his reason.* To add to Calogrenant's uneasiness, the villain is stout and his features are coarse. He has in particular *moss-grown ears as big as an elephant's.* And to crown it all he remains motionless. So the word will establish contact (it 'breaks the ice' as one says today) and reassures Calogrenant. When this 'monster' finally answers, his first words are revealing: *I am a man.* The physical aspect is not important anymore: by speaking the villain has given proof he was not a monster.

Silence is disturbing, but an ill-controlled voice is possibly even more so. It upsets the hearer and evokes a feeling of animality or monstrosity. One text tells of a deaf person who wanted to participate in a religious service and tried to imitate the others singing psalms. But he *roared*, said the author, with an *unusual and horrible* sound during the periods of silence and forced the service to be interrupted (St. Bertin's Miracles, col. 130).

Values attributed to audition and speech

These episodes clearly demonstrate the assumption of an intimate link between the faculty of speech and human nature, as well as with reason, separating humans from animals. They also express the doubt cast on the humanity of a being with the physical appearance of a human, but lacking the ability to speak or with a speech impediment. The strength of this belief is depicted in certain pictures of the Creation. When God created Adam, the first man, he molded his body in clay and then he blew the Spirit into him. This divine breath is the vital breath that gives life and even more. The animals, who are also God's creatures, were not

Ill. 5: *God blows the Spirit to Adam*

granted this privilege. Illuminators chose that particular moment in preference to others, since this is the instant at which human are distinguished from animals. Adam either lies on the ground, sits or stands. God blows on his face or more precisely, towards his mouth. The breath is shown by a series of parallel lines, like the wind. Some artists add a dove carried by the breath and pointing its beak towards Adam's mouth. The dove is the Holy Spirit, the messenger between God and humans, a specialist in linguistics and communication.

An illustration of the Creation in Barthélémy l'Anglais' famous work Des Propriétés des Choses (fol 22) displays a more distinctive concept since there is neither breath nor dove. It shows with more accuracy that the awakening to life and the 'humanizing' of man are seem to be simultaneous with the gift of speech. Adam lies on the ground with his eyes closed and

Ill. 6: *Creation of man*

a nearly cadaveric rigidity. God is standing nearby with his hand stretched over Adam's head in a gesture of blessing. Looking at the illustration closely, it is possible to notice that a faint red mark runs from God's fingers. The axis of this mark corresponds to Adam's tongue, which discreetly emerges from his mouth. Since the original sin had not yet been committed, this line cannot represent the blood of salvation. Instead it represents the act of bringing to life, based on speech.

In the Garden of Eden where the first man and the first woman were free of work and pain, Adam received one task: God asked him to name the animals. The scene chosen by the artist to illustrate the original sin is not always linked to gathering or eating the forbidden fruit, but often is the moment when Eve is tempted by the diabolical snake's speech: the

Ill. 7: *Eve is tempted by the diabolical snake's speech: the fatal kiss*

words are finalized by a fatal kiss of the snake's forked tongue on the woman's lips. After the fall from grace, human kind's only remaining bond with God is the faculty of speech and of

Ill. 8: *God's Word is to be devoured*

hearing the Divine Word. The Bible is God's Word of Revelation, and Christ the Incarnation of the Word.

The Word made flesh: a rather difficult concept to understand. Yet some artists didn't hesitate in depicting it straightforwardly. *Verbum* is the Word of God. First the Word creates Light. Light shines. Light beams and breath intermingle. Thus the Word gives a meaning to reality and illuminates human reason. It warms the heart, and gives life, as is represented by the lion in Bestiaries when it revives still-born lion cubs by blowing on them. The Word is to be eaten, even devoured according to certain prophets (see Ill. 8). It feeds the body and fuels the soul. It is a treat like honey, assert the spiritual gourmets. And it generates.

Another concept very difficult to apprehend is the immaculate conception of Christ. The Annunciation (the moment of conception) has been extensively illustrated. The setting of the scene varies and some pictures put more emphasis than others on the process of *conceptio per aurem* (conception by the ear). In the pictures illustrating the *conceptio per aurem*, the angel Gabriel touches the Virgin Mary's ear with his hand, or the Holy Spirit as a dove puts his beak on the Virgin's ear, or beams shining from a celestial cloud reinforce Gabriel's words. But the artist responsible for the tympanum of the Marienkapelle portal in Würzburg was the boldest of all. In the lower part of the tympanum, Gabriel and Mary kneel facing each other; the angel spreads a phylactery (handwritten banner) on which the words of the Annunciation are written in Latin: *Hail Mary, full of grace....*In the upper part God sits on a throne and holds a kind of thread that connects his mouth to Mary's ear. A little child slides along the thread and near Mary's ear there is a dove, representing the Holy Spirit.

Ill. 9: *Conceived through Mary's ear, the Word is made flesh*

This visual boldness is echoed in secular writings like the Bestiaries, where a weasel conceives by the ear and gives birth through the mouth. It becomes openly licentious in Rabelais (n.d., p. 46) when Gargamelle gives birth to Gargantua through the ear, thus reversing the game. Françoise Dolto remarked about this passage: *born from the word his mother heard.*

Distorted or not, these religious themes appear in secular literature and are extensively present in all medieval minds. The medieval Western European person apart from the Christian cultural basis remains a riddle. Keeping the Church in mind is essential in outlining the Deaf person's place in society.

The Annunciation contains the ancient concept of the efficency of faith. Mary gave birth because she believed what she heard. But faith also comes from what one hears. The terrible *fides ex auditu* (faith through listening), when it was interpreted to the letter, excluded the Deaf from the Church and its sacraments. In the 5th century St. Jerome warned against such a radical standpoint and claimed that the Deaf can understand the Gospel with signs, since hearing is also a perception from the heart (St. Jerome, col. 349). In a few miraculous stories Deaf Mute people prayed in their hearts. Little by little the Christian church accepted the Deaf, granting them the sacraments of baptism in the 5th, matrimony in the 11th, penance in the 13th and the possibility to pronounce monastic vows in the 16th century.[3] In each of these instances the persons involved can sign if they cannot speak.

Negative views of deafness

Nevertheless deafness remained a major obstacle to conversion. In religious commentaries some pictures combine deafness with resistance to conversion. The texts could explain the comparison by specifying the allegory,[4] but in the picture the allegory doesn't work : deaf people, Jews, heretics, pagans, all end up in the same mold.

Ill. 10: *The Church and the Synagogue*

3 See Vacant (and success., eds.) 1909 ff/ Tables générales, entries "Muets" and "Surdité. Sourds"; Pontal 1971, p. 289; Naz 1965, article 'Surdité'.
4 Beda the Venerable, Homilia XIX, lib. II; Haymo from Alberstat, Homilia CXXIV, col. 664-669; Werner, from St. Blaise, col. 1108-1109; Radolphus Ardens, Homilia XXVII, col. 2036-2039.

In an 11th century Crucifixion scene, two characters are standing on either side of the Cross. The figure on the right symbolizes the Church and on the left the Synagogue. Everything between them is in opposition. On the reader's left, that is on the right side of the cross, the place for the chosen, upright, and well balanced, the man is crowned and wears beautiful, harmoniously pleated gowns. His head is turned upward in contemplation of Christ; his features are serene. He opens his arms in a sign of adoration. On the reader's right and on Christ's left, where the damned are to be found in scenes of the Last Judgement, a man with a tormented face, his body distorted, is wearing shapeless creased rags. Parts of his body are naked, including his feet. Covering his dishevelled red hair, a turban hides his ears and muzzles his mouth. To make his handicap more obvious, he himself points his index finger toward his hidden ear. Strangely enough, at the place where his ear would be, there is a red mark on the headband; it runs to the edge of the almond-shaped frame. The man cannot hear because his ears have been wounded. We will soon see why. A bent branch grows from the Cross as a reminder of the tree where the original sin occurred, and sets him off balance. The branch corresponds to the sickle he holds in his left hand: after the Fall, humans were condemned to work. To prevent himself from staggering or because he limps, the character leans on a stick. The branch also refers to the Jews, who were considered responsible for Christ's death on the Cross and who, refusing to recognize him, persisted in their mistake.

In another picture this same interpretation appears again, but here deafness does not suggest the Jew's mistake, but the actual image of the Jew gives origin to the idea of deafness. According to the only partially detailed text, from the Gospel of Mark, 7:31, the picture illustrates a healing miracle performed by Christ on a deaf mute (or deaf stammerer in modern translations). This illumination is from the 14th century and is English.

Ill. 11: *The deaf and dumb's miraculous healing by Christ (14th century)*

Located in the center of the picture, the deaf person is the smallest of all the characters present. He has a hooked nose like a caricatured Jew, a shaven head and wears a simple beltless tunic. His legs and feet are bare. He is shown in profile, a position representing inferiority in the medieval iconographic code. This perspective reveals both his physical and moral pain. With clasped hands he reaches toward Christ in a gesture of entire submission. Christ indicates the handicap by pointing to the deaf man's ear with his right forefinger and to his mouth with his left one.

Allegorically, the recovery of audition is to the deaf person what conversion is to the Jew. Whatever their natures, evangelical miracles are signs sent to humans to acknowledge divine omnipotence. Diseases and human suffering are signs of the original sin, though also a condition for Salvation. But this theory was not convincing to all. Many people thought disease and disability were an element of disorder. There was a suspicion that the sick or handicapped persons had earned their affliction as a punishment. Folk tradition advised to distrust people who had lost their physical integrity, a visible sign of a moral and spiritual flaw. These restricted judgements find echo in certain customs: because Deaf Mutes don't understand what is said to them and can't express themselves, they could not take oath. To various extents and according to areas, they were denied some of the rights a healthy person could claim.[5]

However, if only these negative instances were taken into consideration here, this would falsify the richer and more complex reality. Difference is difficult to live with but there are always unabashed persons, aware of and curious about differences and what they can bring to human knowledge when an effort is made to understand and admit them. As for all patterns of societies those differences are elements of evolution.

Medieval Western European Christendom defines itself as the gathering of various human communities in gestation: persons who adapted themselves to Christianity as much as they adapted it to themselves. Contemporaries said the Bible had a 'wax nose', e.g. that according to circumstances, the interpretations of the sacred texts could be so unlimited as to end up in contradiction. Anthropomorphic and proselytic characteristics of Christianity favoured those various interpretations, so that limited by its ignorance and its fears, Christendom unsurprisingly created negative representations of the Deaf and in the meantime encouraged their integration in the community.The first step towards integration is relatively simple: to recognize the Deaf person as a human being and to show it.

Another deafness

Though based on the same passage from Mark illustrated by the previous English illumination (Ill. 11), six other pictures shed a very different light on the story. They show the variety of reactions towards deafness and confirm that, in spite of the particulars, the text common to the series of pictures doesn't impose only one standpoint. Let's take three examples.

One of the oldest known illustrations is a 9th century fresco in the German church of Saint John in Münster. Neither the Deaf person's looks nor his clothes distinguish him from the other characters present, the crowd on one side and the disciples of Christ on the other. In fact, a small point of detail could only be but a coincidence: the Deaf person wears a white tunic with a red cloak like the disciples, whereas the man in the first row of the crowd wears a dark blue one. Does this color symbolize that the Deaf person is more like the disciples because in advancing toward Christ he showed faith in him? Unambiguous is the figure of Christ; his height and aureole, in accordance with the iconographic code, make him unmistakable. The facial features of all the figures though, are all alike, showing that they all belong to the same family: humankind. Christ himself became human; his aureole is the only reminder of his divinity.

---

5 Customs varied from place to place: the Deaf could be deprived of the right to inherit in Wales, to make their will in the North of France for instance, but these limitations were not systematic.

Ill. 12: *The deaf and dumb's miraculous healing by Christ (9th century)*

One last detail to note in this fresco: Christ and the Deaf person both put their index fingers on the mute mouth. There is no indication about the ear. Muteness and the recovery of speech appear more important than deafness, perhaps muteness was understood to imply deafness as well. Both hypotheses are legitimate and concur with the widespread practice in the texts of calling someone simply 'dumb' who was also Deaf.

In an 11th century illumination, also German, distinctions appear between the Deaf person and the others. He wears a modest tunic and is bent forward. He seems so unsteady on his legs, that someone in the crowd props him up from behind. Were it nor for the stick that he carries, this gesture could be interpreted as encouragement to go toward Christ. Besides, the reason for the stick is unclear, as if it had been added after the completion of the drawing. The Deaf person's hand does not grasp it at all, and simple graphical clumsiness as an explanation for this ambiguity is unsatisfactory. I finally had the opportunity to see the original in Spain, and noticed a detail curiously missing in the reproductions: the Deaf person's left eye is closed. The picture looks altered, as if the first or second illuminator found it necessary to add visible disabilities to an invisible handicap. So Mark's Deaf Mute becomes hunchbacked, crippled and one-eyed: a collection of afflictions! However, in this illumination it is difficult to find a pejorative connotation like that of the English illumination: even with an eye shut, the Deaf person's face looks like any other. Unhappy he is, but nobody would hold him responsible for it. On the contrary, the attitude of those around him suggest sympathy. All this is in clear contrast with the chilliness expressed by the English illumination, and it reverses the interpretation. The gestures of Christ are especially revealing: the hand lifting up the Deaf person's head rests along the cheek and under the chin, while his thumb gently touches his lips . With the back of the other hand he lightly strokes him toward the ear. These are healing and loving gestures. Nevertheless there are still ambiguities. The left index finger presumably moving toward the ear is near the open eye. The artist might just as well be understood as showing the healing of blindness if it were not for the text around the illumination and the inscription in the upper part. But let's let it keep some mystery...

Ill. 13: *The deaf and dumb's miraculous healing by Christ (12th century)*

The third and last example is a 12th century illumination, again German, illustrating Hildegard of Bingen's prayer-book. She is one of the most remarkable medieval feminine figures. In this illustration there is no witness to the miracle. As he does in Mark's text, Christ accomplishes healing away from the crowd. The intimacy makes the relationship between Christ and the Deaf man more intense. Both faces are stunningly alike. There is nothing to belittle the Deaf person, except for his tunic being shorter on his left side.

This illumination is a snapshot of the precise moment when conversion and healing meet. Conversion is to be understood as a transposition or change of position. Christ's legs indicate that he moves toward the Deaf person, who is at the same time changing position from three-quarters back in relation to Christ: he is directing his right foot and turning his head like someone calling. The healing process occurs by an exchange of looks more than by a manual operation, though one can admire the position of the hands. The Deaf man himself indicates his disability by pointing his left index finger to his ear (whence comes the evil). Christ points his right index finger (whence comes the good) toward the Deaf man's mouth. Due to the inclination of the head, their respective fingers draw a horizontal line illustrating the link between deafness and dumbness.

This very simple picture is meaningful and harmonious. Though self-explanatory, it is accompanied by an inscription: *Spirit, from this possessed deaf and dumb man, be gone!,* partially expressed as well in the phylactery held by Christ: *Spirit, from this deaf and dumb man, be gone!* That Christ orders out a spirit makes it clear that the Deaf man is possessed. This fact is not in Mark's text, but may represent a slight confusion with the possessed dumb (Matthew 9:32) and with other evangelical mentions of Christ's exorcisms. In order to strengthen the spiritual meaning of conversion, the original *ephphata* (open yourself) is changed: the person seeking God is relieved from all physical and spiritual disorders.

Of course these miracles are to be understood literally. A disabled person has been healed miraculously. His disability is more or less visible for the others to notice. But a second glance can go further: the healing process is contained in Christ's gestures toward the other person, as well as in the will to recognize and understand his trouble and to manifest compassion, not in the sense of pity, but rather of sharing (compassion) for the handicapped person. Wouldn't recovering hearing also mean introducing a communication until then considered to be impossible?

The texts describing miracles performed by the Virgin Mary or by saints in the Middle Ages lack subtlety even when they use a symbolic code in reference to the Bible. The miracles are generally rather spectacular, with a hemorrhage of the ear and/or the mouth immediately preceding the recovery of hearing and speech. A few more interesting stories though deserve special attention for what they reveal about the comprehension of the handicap. Common among them is a healing process that occurs in two stages: hearing first and speech later. The authors innocently justify the necessity of two miracles with the fact that originally there were two disabilites, and thus set apart deafness and dumbness. In the stories, the period between miracles is a time of learning. Beda the Venerable gives an account interesting for its ambiguity about the dumb man's miracle performed by Bishop John of Hexham in the 8th century (Beda the Venerable 1882, pp. 228-230). The bishop traces the sign of the cross on the dumb man's tongue, and calls on divine intervention. The rest of the procedure looks more like accelerated coaching in speech therapie. John has the deaf man pronounce each letter of the alphabet, then syllables, words, and in the end, sentences.

Communication

No hint is ever made of specialized training for the Deaf, either with written or spoken language or with the use of signs, but now and then Deaf people appear to have used lipreading or signs to communicate with people around them. So it seems there were individual spontaneous more or less successful efforts. These instances appear in family contexts or in shared activities (a Deaf woman with a hearing daughter, the Deaf person working in the field with other villagers, the Deaf child apprenticed to a tailor, a Deaf lay brother or doorkeeper in a religious community, Deaf children of noble extraction with their governess, etc.).[6]

Communal and individual relationships (family, village, convents) play very important roles: the Deaf person has a place in those structures where she or he can be useful. Besides, the methods of communication developed in medieval society also promoted the integration of the Deaf. To begin with, deaf persons were not handicapped just because they could not read or write, since the majority of the population was illiterate. For that reason the Church never strictly censored images in Western Europe during that period: it acknowledged their pedagogical function.

In each scene of the Ten Commandments sculpted on a 15th century tombstone in Frankfurt, a hand indicates the corresponding number. Even simple figures are avoided

6 Nicolas de Cues 1986, p. 83; St. Theodoricus Miracles col. 627; St. Mary from Laon's Miracles col. 968-069; Jacques de Voragine 1967, vol. 1, p. 155; *Robert Le Diable* 1981, pp. 62-63.
   In one of two beautiful miracles in the Cantigas de Santa Maria where pictures and texts complete themselves well, we learn about Deaf and Dumb Pedro de Solarana. He went with his brother, a monk, to Toledo: *He didn't speak and hear, but he understood things very well by signs (...). Whatever they asked him, he did it; there was nobody else like him.* (Cantigas tol I. 1, fol 101 v.- 102v.). And see Ill. 4 for another example of communication in the Cantigas.

Ill. 14: *The Ten Commandments*

(Roman and Arabic numerals only came into widespread use in the last centuries of the Middle Ages). The learned people themselves kept the habit of numbering their paragraphs with little hands drawn in the margins.

For daily use there were also signalling systems. For instance, the words *Aqua-ductus* (aqueduct) on a boundary-stone were framed with two hands pointing towards the ground and meaning: *Watch your step, there is a water channel beneath your feet!*

Visual education encouraged the development of signs and symbols. Characters are recognized by their clothes, coats of arms were the identification for nobles, craftsmen's corporations and townsmen. Colors, their associations, each element of Creation and body language had their own meaning. Hands especially formed complex signs in carved and painted images. Countless dialogues are set in manuscripts by means of hand gestures and depicted body movements. At this point, historians are trying to decipher the codes to understand the signs. Scattered texts provide detailed explanations of the finger and the body symbolism, and also for certain gestures, but we don't have all the clues yet.

The Benedictine monks, who observed the rule of silence, had put together sign dictionaries in a very specific field from the 11th century.[7] Is extra proof needed? Clearly the Middle Ages distrusted gestures less than words. Accepting them in a sacred context was the best way to make them worthy. However, just as there were warnings about speech, there were warnings about the use of these gestures (Casagrande/Vecchio 1987). According to one source in England, monks had gone so far with signs as to become gesticulating chatterboxes (Rijnberk 1953). Ethical and esthetic principles rejected those histrionics, jugglers and other buffoons and with them all movement that can distort the body or the face. These warnings are reminders that measure is necessary in all things.

Gestures mark the daily routine in secular as well as religious ceremonies. In a 15th century illustration of homage (see ill. 15), a vassal needed not less than five arms to express:
1. that he swore to his lord to be 'his man' (index finger in the mouth),
2. that he will serve him loyally in exchange for his protection (he places both his clasped hands in his lord's),
3. that in the name of that bond, he will receive a fief, an estate (he indicates sheaves of corn). He binds himself in gestures and in speech before witnesses.

More than one article indeed, a book would be needed to list the various uses of the hand and the gesture in the Middle Ages. The hand is also a mnemonic device used to learn the alphabet or the numbers (Alexandre-Bidon 1989, pp. 977-979). Complex calculations,

7 Rijnberk 1953; Davril 1980; see Schmitt 1990 for further bibliographic information.

Ill. 15: *A homage: a complete binding agreement*

Ill. 16: *"Loquela digitorum" or finger language for calculating the dates of unfixed religious holidays*

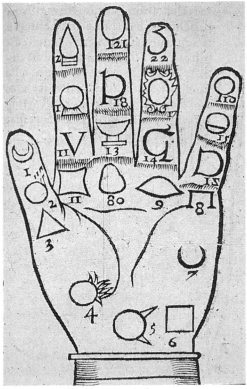

Ill. 17: *A coded sermon*

for unfixed religious holidays for instance, were made with the help of hands (see Ill. 16). Traveling preachers (their number grew steadily from the 13th century) used symbols written on their hand to outline the different parts of their speech. They often added gestures to their sermons in order to be more persuasive. Sometimes their gesticulating became excessive, as one Italian witness asserts. The congregation couldn't focus its attention on the content of the sermon but rather on whether or not the preacher would fall from the pulpit (Baxandall 1985, p. 102). There were also musical hands (letters with the value of musical notes written on the hand) and astrological hands still used by palmists today. The hand not only conveys meaning, it also performs an action: it protects. Even the Church, so reluctant to accept magic, grants to the sign of the cross the power to operate miracles. White and black magic use gestures to cast spells.

It would be interesting to follow the specific history of certain gestures that have never fallen out of use, but whose meanings may have changed. One such symbol is the 'fig': a closed fist, with the thumb tucked between the index and the second finger, its end showing. It clearly symbolizes the female sex, and according to circumstances, the meaning can be either positive or negative. In the Cantigas of Santa Maria (13th century), two men have been punished for making this gesture toward the sky; it was a blasphemy against Mary (see Ill. 18). In a Last Supper painted by Cranach, Judas the traitor makes this sign with his left hand behind his back, which is turned. In a more positive sense, Corsican women still wear little fists as a fertility charm. Moldings of goodluck hands were hung on houses and among them appears the fig. A few specimens, from the 17th century have managed to reach us (see Ill. 19).

Ill. 18: *A gesture called the "fig" in French; here, a blasphemous version*

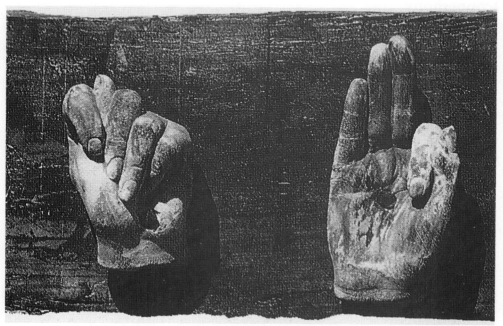

Ill. 19: *Plaster casts of hands for protecting the houses and their dwellers*

Conclusion

Gestures have always been part of language and of people's deeds. Depending on the era they have been more or less accepted or developed. I hope I have given enough proof that the Middle Ages were a flourishing period for them. Gestures are not equivalent to speech and vice versa, just as the picture works differently than the written word. But gestures and pictures can associate with spoken and written words, give strength to them and complete the message. Why then does society privilege words? This is a debate for linguists, anthropologists, ethnologists, historians and others.

For the Middle Ages historical factors were important in the predominance of gesture: the disintegration of the Roman Empire, the confrontation of very different languages (reappearance of native languages, infiltration and invasion of people coming from the North and the East, the transformation of Latin, the emergence of Romance and Germanic languages), the eclipse of the written word, the remoteness of areas, even of villages, the near disappearance of many cities, the isolation of intellectual knowledge in monasteries, etc. Let's stop here, otherwise the list would be too long. But let's recognize that the situation was not bad for signs and gestures spontaneously used by the Deaf, even if the conventions set up by those who could speak and hear were not always accessible to them.

The Deaf and hearing people have a common heritage. The desire to meet can only benefit both groups. Each one has much to learn from the other about what they are, about what we all are: people of flesh, of feelings, of reason and language. History changes the angles of view and offers wide ranges of behaviours that we have partly forgotten. It is good to get back to them to make progress in understanding ourselves and others as well as to correct overly restrictive judgements.

Undoubtedly the Middle Ages is to the history of the Deaf what they are to history in general – a marvellous laboratory.

Iconography

Ill. 1: The academic lesson: a doctor explains the anatomy of the ear.
Avicenna's Canon, translated by Gerard of Cremona, mid-13th century; bibliothèque Municipale Besançon, ms 457, fol 158v.

Ill. 2: Observation and medical act.
Treatise on medicine, 14th century.

Ill. 3: What is deafness, in fact?
Medical and surgical Art, 1412. Royal Library, Stockholm.

Ill. 4: A deaf person presents himself to the crowd.
Cantigas de Santa Maria, 13th century. San Lorenzo del Escorial, ms T I.1, fol 146.

Ill. 5: God blows the Spirit to Adam.
Bible of the Pantheon, 11th century, Vatican Library, ms Lat. 12958, fol 4v.

Ill. 6: Creation of man; in: Bartholémy l'Anglais: Livre des Propriétés des choses. Fundación Lázaro Galdiano, Biblioteca, Madrid, ms 37/10, fol 22.

Ill. 7: Eve is tempted by the diabolical snake's speech: the fatal kiss.
Bible of the Pantheon, 11th century, Vatican Library, ms Lat. 12958, fol 4v.

Ill. 8: God's Word is to be devoured.
The prophet Ezekiel in a latin Bible. Bibliothèque Nationale, Paris, ms Lat, 16744, fol 81.

Ill. 9: Conceived through Mary's ear, the Word is made flesh.
North portal of the Marienkapelle, 1420. Würzburg.

Ill. 10: The Church and the Synagogue. The Jew is a man unable to hear and speak, branded by the original sin and persisting in his mistake.
Crucifixion scene in the Pericopes by Uta of Niedermünster, early 11th century. Bayerische Staatsbibliothek, Munich, Clm 13601 fol. 3v.

Ill. 11: The deaf and dumb's miraculous healing by Christ.
English Bible, 14th century. Bodleian Library, Oxford.

Ill. 12: The deaf and dumb's miraculous healing by Christ.
Fresco, 9th century, St. John's church, Münster.

Ill. 13: The deaf and dumb's miraculous healing by Christ.
Prayer book by Hildegard of Bingen, late 12th century. Bayerische Staatsbibliothek, Munich, Clm 935, fol 30v.

Ill. 14: The Ten Commandments.
Tombstone, 1468. Historisches Museum, Frankfurt am Main.

Ill. 15: A homage: a complete binding agreement.
Saxon Mirror, 14th century. Universitätsbibliothek, Heidelberg.

Ill. 16: "Loquela digitorum" or finger language for calculating the dates of unfixed religious holidays.
De Computo vel loquela digitorum by Beda the Venerable, 14th century. Bibliothèque Nationale, Paris, Lat. 7418, fol 5.

Ill. 17: A coded sermon, early 17th century.
BN Lyon, 813182.

Ill. 18: A gesture called the " fig" in French; here, a blasphemous version.
Cantigas de Santa Maria, XIIIth century. San Lorenzo del Escorial, ms T I.1, fol. 608, fol 219.

Ill. 19: Plaster casts of hands for protecting the houses and their dwellers, 17th century.

References
unpublished

Avicenna's Canon. Biblioteca Nacional, Madrid, ms 928.

Barthélémy l'Anglais: Des Propriétés des choses. Fundación Lázaro Galdiano, Biblioteca, Madrid, ms 37/10.

Cantigas de Santa Maria, XIIIᵉˢ, Codice Rico de Alfonso X, ms. T I-1, Biblioteca de San Lorenzo del Escorial.

Le trésor de Maistre Arnault de Ville Nove. Bibliothèque de l'Arsenal, Paris, ms 2889.

published

Albe, E. (1907): *Les miracles de Notre Dame de Rocamadour*. Paris.

Alexandre-Bidon, D. (1989): La lettre volée. Apprendre à lire à l'enfant au Moyen-Age; in: *Annales ESC* 4, Juillet-Août 1989, pp. 953-992.

Baxandall, M. (1985): *L'Oeil du Quattrocento*. Paris.

Beda the Venerable: *Historia Ecclesiastica Gentis Anglorum*. Edition 1882 by A. Holder. Freiburg, Tübingen.

Beda the Venerable: Homiliae; in: *Patrologiae Latinae* 94, col. 234-290.

Bernard de Gordon: *Lilium Medicinae*. Edition 1550 by G. Roville. Lyon.

Bolland, J. (and succ., eds.) (1643-1940): *Acta Sanctorum quotquot toto orbe coluntur*. Anvers, Bruxelles.

Casagrande, C./ Vecchio, S. (1987): *I peccati della lingua*. Rome.

Chrétien de Troyes: *Le chevalier au lion*. Edition 1923 by A. Mary. Paris.

Davril, A. (1980): Un catalogue des signes de l'abbaye de Fleury; in: *Sous la règle de S. Benoît*. (Les Hautes Etudes Médiévales et Modernes 47) Paris, pp. 51-74.

Haymo from Alberstat: Homiliae; in: *Patrologiae Latinae* 118.

Jacques de Voragine: *La légende dorée*. Edition 1967, transl. J.B.M. Roze. Paris. 2 vols.

Lesort, A. (1909): Chroniques et chartes de l'abbaye de S. Mihiel; in: *Mettensia* VI.

Mabillon, J. (ed.) (1668-1701): *Acta Sanctorum Ordini Sancti Benedicti* [OSB]. Paris

Migne, J.P. (ed.) (1844ff): *Patrologiae cursus completus. Patres (...) ecclesiae latinae* [Patrologiae Latinae] Paris, 221 vols.

Naz, E. (1965): *Dictionnaire de droit canonique*. Paris.

Nicolas de Cues: *Le tableau ou la vision de Dieu*. Edition 1986, transl. A. Minazzoli. Paris.

Ouy, G. (1984): *Le miracle des trois pèlerins de St. Jacques*. Paris.

Pontal, O. (1971): Les statuts synodaux français au XIIIème siècle; in: *Documents inédits de l'histoire de France*. Paris. vol. 9,2.

Rabelais: *Gargantua et Pantagruel*. Transl. G. Bechtel. (n.d.; n.p.)

Radulphus Ardens: Homiliae; in: *Patrologiae Latinae* 155.

Rijnberk, G.V. (1953): *Le langage par signes chez les moines*. Amsterdam.

Robert Le Diable et autres récits. Edition 1981, pres. L. Andries. Paris.

Schmalz, K. (1830): *Geschichte und Statistik der Taubstummenanstalten*. Dresden.

Schmitt, J. C. (1990): *La raison des gestes dans l'occident médiéval*. Paris.

Schumann, P. (1940): *Geschichte des Taubstummenwesens*. Frankfurt.

Segal, A. /Willemot, J. (eds.) (1981): *Naissance et développement de l'ORL dans l'histoire de la médecine*. = *Acta ORL Belgica*, vol. V, suppl. II.

(St. Bertin's Miracles); in: *Acta Sanctorum (…)* OSB III.

St. Jerome: (Commentaire de l'Epître aux Galates); in: *Patrologiae Latinae* 138.

(St. Majolus's Miracles); in: *Acta Sanctorum (…)*, mai II.

(St. Mary from Laon's Miracles); in: *Patrologiae Latinae* 156.

(St. Remacle's Miracles); in: *Acta Sanctorum (…)*, septembre I.

(St. Theodoricus's Miracles); in: *Acta Sanctorum (…)* OSB I.

Tissier, A. (1984): *Farces du Moyen-Age*. Paris.

Vacant, A. (and success., eds.) (1909 ff): *Dictionnaire de théologie catholique contenant l'exposé des doctrines de la théologie catholique. Leurs preuves et leur histoire*. Paris. 15 vols; Tables générales (1972 ff), 3 vols.

Walter, E. (1882): *Geschichte des Taubstummenbildungswesens*. Bielefeld, Leipzig.

Werner from St. Blaise: Libri deflorationum sive excerptionum; in: *Patrologiae Latinae* 157.

Avraham Zwiebel
Ramat-Gan, Israel

The Status of the Deaf in the Light of Jewish Sources[*]

A comparison with the state of the art

Summary • סיכום

This article reports on a comprehensive study of Jewish sources concerning deafness. Sources studied include the Mishnah, the Talmud and the Responsa and Psika literature. The findings concern such aspects as the legal status of the hearing-impaired in the light of their inclusion in the legal category of the deaf, the retarded and minors; the status of various sub-groups within the general population of the hearing-impaired; the philosophy underlying the legal decisions; ways of assessing cognitive and communicative development; and the status of the deaf in Jewish society. The findings are compared with the current state-of-the-art, pointing out the existence of a large number of schools of thought concerning the level and thinking processes of deaf people both in Jewish sources and in the scientific community, with the controversy regarding the connection between language and cognition at its core. The position taken by Jewish sources throughout the ages is shown to be in accordance with modern views. A humanistic, rehabilitative attitude as well as the existence of education of deaf people in Jewish society from early times on is demonstrated.

במאמר זה, מובא מחקר השוואתי של מקרורות היהדות הנוגעים
לחרשות. החקורות שנחקרו כוללים את המשנה, התלמוד, ספרות
השו"ת וספרות ההלכה והפסיקה. המימצאים מובאים תחת כותרות
המשנה הבאות: המעמד המשפטי של החרשים לאור הכללתם בקבוצה
ה"חרש, השוטה והקטן". המעמד של תת-קבוצות החרשים (כבדי
שמיעה, מחרשים וכו'), הפילוסופיה העומדת מאחורי ההחלטות
לגבי המעמד החוקי של החרשים. דרכים להערכת רמתם
הקומוניקטיבית והקוגניטיבית של החרשים ומעמד החרשים בחברה
היהודית במהלך ההסטוריה. המימצאים מושווים למימצאים

[*] This paper was supported by the Eliezer Stern Institute for Research and Advancement in Religious Education of the Bar Ilan University, School of Education.

מדעיים עדכניים ומוכיחים קיומן של אסכולות שונות בדבר
רמת החשיבה של אנשים חרשים הן בקהילה המדעית והן במקורות
היהודיים הקדומים כשגרעין המחלוקת טמון במהות הקשר בין
שפה לבין חשיבה. מוכח, שעמדת המקורות היהודיים זהה לגישה
המודרנית הטוענת שחרשות כזאת אינה סיבה לנחיתות
אינטלקטואלית כמו־כן מוכחת במאמר גישה ההומניסטית
והשיקומית של החברה היהודית כלפי החרשים כבר בזמנים קדומים.

Introduction

Jewish traditional attitudes toward deafness have been reviewed by authors (Dicarlo 1964; Mann 1983) at best as ambivalent. Mann described this attitude as characterized by a sense of charity. The Book of Leviticus contains an admonition against cursing the Deaf, and the Mishnah and the Talmud include the Deaf in the same category as the retarded (*shote*)[1] and as minors. This has led Mann to maintain that in terms of legal rights, Deaf people were originally treated as helpless and retarded individuals. Even laws against harassing, abusing and robbing the Deaf have been interpreted as historical proof that people were actually acting in such ways against the Deaf. In Moores's opinion, there is no evidence of any attempt to educate the Deaf, *although the Talmud did modify some of the more negative beliefs about the inability of deaf persons to reason* (Moores 1982, p. 30).

The inclusion of the Deaf in the same category as the retarded and minors seemed to these researchers to prove that the philosophy underlying this categorization was that the cognitive and emotional 'levels' attained by the Deaf are lower than those attained by hearing individuals. Such a philosophy would explain the restriction of legal rights which had, in their opinion, been imposed upon the Deaf in Jewish society.

Including the Deaf in a limiting legal category seems to be in direct contrast to the present day situation. But it also seems to be in contrast to the past when Deaf people achieved important standing in Jewish communities. The aim of this paper is to shed light on this apparent contradiction. It will also discuss the legal status of the Deaf throughout Jewish history up to the present days and attempt to establish a better definition of the term 'the deaf, the retarded and minors' which has served as proof of the inferior status of the Deaf. In addition an attempt will be made to establish to whom the category 'Deaf' is applied, of the whole range of the hearing-impaired population, and to discuss whether this is indeed to be seen as a limiting category.

A clarification of the legal status of the Deaf will enable us to examine the claim that the philosophy underlying the legal term regards the cognitive level of the Deaf as low. Such a philosophy would clearly contradict both the facts and the principles of Jewish heritage. These legal points are important since it is clear that legal definitions have always influenced – and still do – the general attitudes of people towards the Deaf. It is interesting, while dwelling on the topic of cognition, to compare the stand Judaism takes on this issue with the positions prevalent within the scientific community at large, both past and present in relation to Deaf people. These positions are complex, especially in light of the intricate theoretical question of the connection between language and cognition. Regarding this topic, contemporary Jewish positions will be compared with recent developments of the past decade.

An attempt will therefore be made to characterize the attitude of Jewish sources towards the Deaf as a humane one dating from ancient times and evidence will be given, both direct and circumstantial, that Jewish society provided Deaf education throughout the ages.

---

1 A literal translation of the word *shote* would be 'fool', which is interpreted as meaning 'emotionally disturbed'. However, most sources use the translation 'retarded' and this paper will do it likewise.

Researching into Jewish sources regarding the deaf is important for a number of reasons. First, Jewish culture is an ancient culture, which has existed from the dawn of history to our days, and the Jewish religion has influenced the religions and cultures of large parts of the world (mainly the Christian world and the Moslem world as well). Secondly, it must be remembered that Jewish society is considered a scholarly society. It is spread throughout the world, both influencing and being influenced by other cultures. Findings about the status of the Deaf in different periods of Jewish history might therefore give us information about the status of the Deaf in various countries. Thirdly, the laws which defined the legal status of the Deaf were valid throughout Jewish history. Even today, Family law in Israel is still conducted according to Halachic law, so that in important areas Halachic law is extremely important for the Deaf.

The sources which were collected and analysed include all sources in the Bible, the Mishna, the Tosefta, the Talmud Bavli and Talmud Yerushalmi, the Responsa from the Geonim period, the Middle Ages and the Modern Era, as well as psikot of law courts and poskim in our times. In addition, bibliographical collections of articles in Jewish studies were consulted. For studying the Responsa, a computerized project at Bar Ilan University was used. This project includes 250 volumes, constituting a sample of the main collections of Responsa, distributed according to period and geographical location.

In this article, the summarized findings of this study and its conclusions will be presented under four headings: the legal status of the hearing-impaired and its various types; the philosophy and basic attitude to deafness underlying legal decisions; assement of cognitive and communicative development; the social, economical and educational status of the Deaf in Jewish society.

The legal status of the hearing-impaired

The Deaf are included in the legal category of 'the deaf, the retarded and minors' in the Mishna and the Talmud, and as a result throughout Halachic literature. This category includes people who are not considered as possessing full cognitive competence. Their legal responsibility concerning money and possessions is therefore invalidated, they are not obliged to observe religious commands and their responsibility for any action requiring sense, thought, purpose or hearing and speaking aloud is negated. On the other hand, they have full one-sided protection; that is, any person who hurts them is culpable whereas if they harm anyone they are considered blameless.

Those sources which define the term 'deaf' restrict the definition to a Deaf person who does not talk at all, that is, a Deaf Mute (Mishnah Trumot A,2). This means that Deaf people who talk are considered as persons with equal rights and responsibilities, like anyone else. Where speech is mentioned, this does not mean only perfect but also partial command of speech. As far as non-talking Deaf are concerned, the ruling is that marriage and divorce are legally binding for them (in contrast to the retarded and minors, for whom they are not binding). In addition, a system was arranged for diagnosing the existence of a minimal non-oral communicative ability enabling the Deaf to receive full equality in legal categories where property is concerned (except for real estate).

Three schools are discernible in the Mishnah regarding the smaller population of Deaf Mutes. The first (which is the one which has become Halacha) is the one mentioned above saying that the Deaf Mutes do not possess full cognitive competence and need all the laws passed for them in order to maintain a personal and possessory status. This is the position taken by some of the Tanaim (Mishnah Trumot A,1). A second opinion held by the Tanaim is that of Rabbi Yehudah, who claims that even Deaf Mutes possess full cognitive competence (Tosefta Trumot A,1). A third opinion is that of Rabbi Eliezer (ibid.), who does not totally negate the cognitive abilities of the Deaf, and whose opinion is interpreted as meaning that there are areas or times at which the Deaf person might be functioning at the same cognitive level, as a hearing person.

The large number of opinions and the debates in Jewish sources as to the cognitive level attainable by the Deaf, concentrating as they do on a small group of Deaf people who do not talk at all and who have no other communicative ability, can thus be seen to be fairly advanced in comparison with most contemporary civilizations in antiquity as described by Moores (1987), such as for example Hellenistic and Roman civilizations. The Justinian Code, which parallels the stricter opinion in Judaism, was legislated only in the 6th century AD, and the truth is that even this position was greatly eroded in large areas of Europe. For example, the Deaf were denied the right to participate in several Christian religious rituals throughout the Middle Ages, even their full right to marry being limited.

The various sub-groups of hearing-impaired individuals are accorded differential treatment by Jewish sources. The first group as to which there are doubts is that of people deafened at a later period in life rather than being deaf from birth, but who nevertheless do not talk at all. Here too three different views are discernible. The first one excludes this group of Deaf Mutes from the group of people who have no cognitive competence, and states that although they may not be communicating in the present, they are considered normal individuals (Raban Shimon ben Gamliel in Talmud Yerushalmi Trumot 1, A and Gittin 7, A). The second view claims that persons who have lost their hearing and who have in addition lost their communicative ability are considered as the deaf who are not fully cognitively competent and cannot be held responsible for their actions (Mishnah Yevamot 14, A; Talmud Yevamot 14, A; Rabbi Meir, in Talmud Yerushalmi Trumot 1, A and Gittin 7, A; Maimonides as interpreted by *Melechet Cheresh* 1864). The third view claims that these individuals are questionably cognitively competent (*Peri Megadim* 1954).

The second group are the hard of hearing who have no language and no communication with their surroundings. All opinions indicate that the hard of hearing who do not talk are considered as normal human beings as far as legal rights are concerned (Maimonides Mechira 29, 2; *Peri Megadim* 1954; *Rosh* Responsa 1954; *Halakhot Ketanot* 1897; *Ginat Veradim* 1970; *Maharsham* 1962; *Shevut Yaakov* 1972; *Igrot Moshe* 1981). With the development of hearing aids in the last generations, hearing-impaired persons with even minimal vestiges of hearing ability, who were considered deaf in the past and whose aural receptive abilities can nowadays be amplified, are considered as normal, even if they do not talk. They are however free from observing commandments requiring hearing and talking, according to a number of Poskim (*Igrot Moshe* 1964).

The third group consists of learned Deaf Mutes, who have proven the existence of a considerable cognitive level which has helped them acquire knowlege and skills. There is evidence of discussions concerning this group, mainly in the last few centuries, with the development of educational institutions in society. There is a divergence of categorization concerning this group as well. Some include them in the normal category of normals (*Heichal Yitzchak* 1960; *Halakhot Ketanot* 1897; *Maharsham* 1962; *Shevet Sofer* 1899) and some include them in the group of Deaf people, claiming that it is impossible to take exceptions into account, and preferring to see the Deaf as a homogeneous group (Talmud Gittin 71, B; Rabbi Chayim Halberstein, in *Melechet Cheresh* 1864). In addition there are a number of scholars who do not reach any conclusion regarding this question (*Minchat Yitzchak* 1955).

The philosophy and basic attitude to Deaf people underlying legal decisions

A study of the reasoning and the argumentation between the supporters of various views reveals their beliefs concerning the emotional and cognitive level of different groups of Deaf people.

As far as emotional aspects are concerned, no source casts any doubt on the emotional maturity of even Deaf Mutes who lack communicative ability. In any case, this cannot be a reason for their being included in the group of non-reasoning persons, among whom we find the emotionally disturbed, who exhibit signs of insanity. Rabbi Moshe Sofer (*Chatam Sofer* 1972) explicitly states that the Deaf are not included in the category of 'emotionally disturbed' (*shote*) of the Mishnah and the Talmud, which therefore casts no doubt on their emotional maturity.

Regarding the cognitive level of the Deaf we find doubts throughout. All authorities state that it is clear that a Deaf person who has communicative abilities (be they partial and imperfect as they may) must have a cognitive level. Even Maimonides, who presents a minority view, does not attribute any mental retardation to the Deaf either (Maimonides Mechira 29:2). There are, however, doubts about Deaf persons who do not have these communicative abilities, and therefore are seen to lack the means for cognitive development and environmental enrichment. The school which accords a restricted legal status to the Deaf claims that they can not understand things in depth. The second opinion, which maintains that the Deaf are cognitively competent, relies however on facts. In the Mishnah, in the 1st century AD, Rabbi Yehuda calls to attention a number of well known personages of his time, who were Deaf Mutes but who nevertheless held highly responsible positions which demanded great learning and understanding in the Temple in Jerusalem. These were the sons of Rabbi Yochanan ben Gudgoda, who were in charge of purification. As time goes by, the reasons given for seeing the Deaf as possessing a cognitive level like the one of hearing people are based also on cases of professionals who proved through their deeds that they possessed high reasoning powers. The school which regards the Deaf as mentally handicapped does not generalize from these positive examples but maintains that even in cases where it is clear that Deaf persons are intelligent in spite of their total deafness and inability to talk, they are to be included in the legal category of 'deaf'. This is so that no mistakes should be made concerning Deaf people who have no reasoning powers and that they should not be accorded normal status as far as rights are concerned and be required to fulfill all duties even if they are unable to (the Halachic concept of *lo plug*). As stated above, the sages holding this opinion legislated laws which actually give these people the opportunity to hold a legal status almost like a hearing person and yet receive protection.

The treatment of these four sub-types – [i.e., the hard of hearing; people who can hear partly with a hearing aid; Deaf people who talk; Deaf people who can communicate with signs (meaning almost minimal pantomime and not proper sign language] indicates that Jewish sources (including the most ancient ones) do not see deafness in itself as a cause of poor cognitive achievement of Deaf people who cannot talk; rather, it is held that an inability to communicate causes this. A clear example is the following 17th century quote by Rabbi Yaakov Yisrael Hagiz: *For as is commonly known, the deaf lacks nothing but his sense of hearing. And it is because he hears not that he learns not from other humans* (*Halakhot Ketanot* Part II, Paragraph 38).

The doubts arising about learned Deaf people who talk do not contradict this. The opinions according to which such persons belong to a legally restricting category are relying on a legal rule which does not recognize differences, distinctions and exceptions (*lo plug*). Nowadays there is a great deal of debate on this point since there is almost no Deaf person today who is uneducated. Legal rulings, however, are still divided on this subject. The majority's opinion regards the legal status of such individuals as normal. Rabbi Yisrael Waldenberg (*Tzitz Eliezer* 1983) says that almost all poskim hold that the Deaf are to be treated exactly as hearing people are, if it is proven that they possess communicative skills and are able to read.

Assessment of cognitive and communicative development

A comparison of the view Jewish sources take as to the cognitive level of the Deaf on the one hand with the state of the art on the other shows that doubts, deliberations and debates existed also in certain periods in the past, in which researchers claimed that the Deaf possess an inferior cognitive ability because of their inferiority in spoken language (see reviews in Moores 1987; Myklebust 1964).

In the history of deaf studies, it is clear that the theoretical question of the connection between language and cognition has a great influence on the discussion of the cognitive level of the Deaf. The school claiming a strong connection between verbal language (spoken language) and cognition (e.g. Watson 1929; Vygotsky 1962; Luria 1960; Deese 1965) may not hold a unanimous theoretical position, yet claims that the lack of (spoken) language experienced by the Deaf, whose language is not considered equivalent to that of hearing individuals, must perforce result in a reduced cognitive level. This theoretical stand was extremely popular in the past and was indeed almost universally accepted. However, another school of researchers insisted on the separate existence of language and cognitive processes, a position which leads one to believe the Deaf person as such is not inferior to a hearing individual (Piaget 1962; Inhelder/Sinclair 1969). The inferiority of Deaf people in comparative studies is held by this school to be the result of circumstantial communicative inferiority, or of the mistaken use of verbal (spoken language) intelligence tests, which cannot be fair to the Deaf (Furth 1971).

The study of the cognitive development of the Deaf has gone through a number of stages in the last decades. Comparative studies of the IQs of Deaf subjects and those of hearing subjects were conducted at the time of the development of IQ tests in the first decades of the 20th century. The findings usually indicated inferiority on the part of the Deaf. Then theories were developed postulating a more concrete type of thinking on the part of the Deaf, which is not necessarily lower (Myklebust's Organismic Shift Hypothesis, 1964). The development of advanced test sets and the higher sophistication of the scientific endeavor in the last decade indicate equality between Deaf and hearing individuals (Conrad/Weisenkrantz 1981; Kusche et al. 1983; Sisco/Anderson 1980; Zwiebel/Milgram 1982; Zwiebel 1986). More recent scientific developments, however, hypothesize the existence of a different cognitive structure for the Deaf, and present evidence that their cognitive development is not totally identical to that of hearing individuals. Research techniques are based on methods such as factor analysis attempting to analyse processes of thought. For example, it has been concluded that the Deaf possess a type of thought related to vision rather than audition (Zwiebel/Mertens 1985; Zwiebel 1992).

These developments indicate that there are still some strong doubts as to the cognitive development of the Deaf, and that this complex subject has not yet been treated in a fully satisfactory way.

The views expressed in Jewish sources always referred to environmental deprivation rather than deafness as such. The importance of the aural and oral element has been seen to lie not in any connection between language and thought but in their connection to environmental deprivation. This view is in accordance with the second school discussed above, that of Furth and his colleagues, as regards the cognitive development of the Deaf, as well as with studies proving equality between Deaf individuals and hearing individuals. In addition, it is important to note that the doubts and deliberations existing to this very day in Jewish sources are not far removed from those shown by the scientific community when dealing with this complex issue.

As said before, Jewish sources deal with communicative abilities as well. Quite a few refer to the way in which evaluations were carried out to find out whether the Deaf were able to understand property purchase, marriage and divorce. It has been mentioned above that the Rabbis found various ways to ensure that the Deaf could lead everyday lives like everybody. However, doubts did sometimes arise about those Deaf people who were mute and lacked communicative abilities, and the sages had to validate the parting of families, with the financial ramifications for the entire family, or to validate a will or a property deed. In the Mishnah and the Talmud a number of ways are mentioned of checking the cognitive achievements of even Deaf individuals lacking any way of communicating (Mishnah Gittin 5,7; Mishnah Yevamont 14,1; Talmud Gittin 59 A; Maimonides Mechira 29,2). The sages communicated at various levels through pantomime in order to ensure that the Deaf person did indeed understand the legal action which was to be made valid. A description of a divorce proceeding can be found in *Melechet Cheresh* (1864). The Deaf man must be checked three times. Through pantomime, he is asked *Should we write a divorce bill for your wife?* and he is to answer, again in signs, in the affirmative. Then he is to be asked, *And for your sister?*, to which he should answer in the negative. Then he is asked again – *And your wife?*, to which he should signal *Yes*. In addition, he is to be asked questions which are not connected with the divorce bill, to make sure that he is indeed capable of understanding what is being communicated to him.

The status of the Deaf in Jewish society

A study of historical sources proves that Deaf people were able to attain a high social status. Throughout the literature one finds that Deaf individuals who do talk, as well as individuals who are hard of hearing are not even called 'deaf'. As far as the Deaf Mutes are concerned, there are lively discussions of their legal status (54 sources in the Mishnah and 333 sources in the Talmud). The plurality of schools and their debatings helped to form a social view of Deaf individuals which was not automatically a low one. The Mishnah mentions cases where Deaf individuals married hearing individuals (Mishnah Yevamot 14,4). The Mishnah also mentions the Deaf sons of Rabbi Yochanan ben Gudgoda, who was considered a Righteous person and a Levite who had a special status in the Temple. They received a position which demanded studying and theoretical knowledge. The Talmud mentions the case of Rabbi Malchio, who lived in the 4th century and was one of the prominent personages of his age, who looked after a Deaf person who lived nearby, married him to a wise and praiseworthy wife, supported him financially so that the match would work, and helped him to become self-supporting (Talmud Yevamot 113, A). This is an example of how to help those Deaf individuals who cannot attain a normal status on their own.

There is evidence of Deaf people who wrote Torah scrolls, Tefillin and Mezuzoth in 17th century Moravia (*Shivat Zion* 1966). These are skills demanding practical training as well as theoretical understanding. There is also evidence of Deaf tailors who were considered learned in Eretz Yisrael of the 17th century (*Halakhot Ketanot* 1897), and three cases of Jewish Polish merchants in the 17th century, who were considered well educated, used to conduct business negotiations in mime and signs and were financially well off (*Maharsham* 1962; *Tzemah Tzedek* 1769) These cases prove the existence of individual education already in the 1st century AD as well as in later periods. There is an interesting story about an associative teaching method, dating from Eretz Yisrael of the 17th century (*Halakhot Ketanot* 1897). Rabbi Yaakov Hagiz tells about a Deaf man who was well educated and literate. He would be brought an object, shown all the letters of the alphabet, and have to point out the letters making up the word for it. In this way he learned to read and write. There is also evidence of sending Jewish Deaf children to study in general schools in Hungary of the 18th century (*Chatam Sofer* 1972). As far as Deaf schools are concerned, the first known source concerns Vienna of the early 19th century. In the Responsa where the Jewish Deaf school is mentioned (*Shevet Sofer* 1899), the writer says he was invited to visit the school and to examine its educational policies and methods closely. He was pleasantly surprised by the knowledge the students displayed and instructed the school to buy them ritual objects and treat them as hearing individuals. *Melechet Cheresh,* a book in which all rulings concerning the deaf were collected, was published in 1864. The author claimed that he wrote this book after seeing how a Jewish school in Vienna had succeeded in making deaf students as cognitively competent as their hearing colleagues.

It seems then that in spite of all the complexity and the deliberation in Jewish sources regarding the legal status of the Deaf, a deliberation which continues to our very days and is not disconnected from the scientific controversy, the facts indicate a humane attitude of respect towards the Deaf in Jewish society. The legal definition of 'deaf' greatly limited the number of 'Deaf' people in the population of the hearing-impaired. There is evidence of the existence of Deaf individuals with a high socio-economic status already from the 1st century AD, furthermore of educational openings for the Deaf, both within Jewish frameworks and individually. Legal thought was also far in advance of its time. With the advances of technology, the majority seems to maintain that the status of educated Deaf people has now reached equality with that of hearing individuals.

References

Chatam Sofer [Rabbi Moshe Sofer, Hungary, 18th and 19th centuries]. Edition 1972. Jerusalem: Machon Chatum Sofer.

Conrad, R. / Weisenkrantz, B.C. (1981): On the cognitive ability of deaf children with deaf parents; in: *American Annals of the Deaf,* 126, pp. 995-1003.

Deese, J. (1965): *The Structure of Associations in Language and Thought.* Baltimore: Johns Hopkins University Press.

Dicarlo, L.M. (1964): *The Deaf.* Englewood Cliffs: Prentice-Hall.

Furth, H.G. (1962): Research with the Deaf: Implications for language and cognition; in: *Psychological Bulletin,* 64, pp. 145-164.

Furth, H. G. (1971): Linguistic deficiency and thinking research with deaf children, 1964-1969; in: *Psychological Bulletin,* 76, pp. 58-72.

Ginat Veradim [Rabbi Avraham ben Mordechai Halevi, Egypt, 17 and 18th centuries]. Edition 1970. Jerusalem.

Halakhot Ketanot [Rabbi Yaakov Yisrael Hagiz, Israel, 17. century]. Edition 1897. Krakow: Horowitz.

Heichal Yitzhak [Rabbi Yitzhak Izik Halevi Herzog, Ireland and Israel, 20. century]. Edition 1967. Jerusalem.

Holy Scriptures. Edition 1917. Philadelphia: Jewish Publication Society. 2 vols.

Igrot Moshe [Rabbi Moshe Feinstein, Lithuania and U.S.A., 20th century]. Edition 1964. New York: Balshan.

Inhelder, B. / Sinclair, H. (1969): Learning cognitive structures; in: Mussen, J.L. / Cavington, M. (eds.): *Trends and Issues in Developmental Psychology.* New York: Holt, Reinhart and Winston.

Kusche, C.A../ Greenberg, M.T. /Garfield, T. S. (1988): Non-verbal intelligence and verbal achievement in deaf adolescents: An examination of heredity and environment; in: *American Annals of the Deaf,* 127, pp. 458-466.

Luria, A. R. (1960): The role of speech in the regulation of normal and abnormal behavior. Seminar on the mental health of the abnormal child. Bethesda, Maryland: Dept. of Health, Education and Welfare.

Maharsham [Rabbi Shalom Shvadron, Poland 19th and 20th centuries] Edition 1962. New York: Grossman Publishing House.

Maimonides, M. [12th century]: *Mishneh Torah.* Edition 1962. New York. M.P. Press. 6 vols.

Mann, L. (1983): *History of Childhood Exceptionality and Special Education.* Baltimore, University Park Press.

Melechet Cheresh [Rabbi Yehudah Leibush ben Rabbi Chayim]. Edition 1864. Vienna: Selbstverlag.

Minchat Yitzhak [Rabbi Yitzchak Yaakow Weiss, England and Israel, 20th century] . Edition 1962. London: Hachinuch.

Mishnah. Edition 1964. Jerusalem: Mif'al Lehotzaat Mishnaiot.

Moores, D. F. (1982): *Educating the Deaf*. (2nd ed.) Boston: Houghton Mifflin.

Moores, D. F. (1987): *Educating the Deaf*. (3rd ed.) Boston: Houghton Mifflin.

Myklebust, H. R. (1964): *The Psychology of Deafness*. New York: Grune and Stratton.

Peri Chadash [Hezkiah ben Davin da Silva, Israel, 17th and 18th centuries]. Edition 1954; in: *Shulchan Aruch*, New York: Grossman Publishing House.

Peri Megadim [Rabbi Yoseph ben Meir Teomim, Galicia 18th century]. Edition 1954; in: *Shulchan Aruch*, New York: Grossman Publishing House.

Piaget, J. (1962): Comments; in: Vygotsky, L. S.: *Thought and Language*. Cambridge, Mass.: M.I.T. Press.

Rosenstein, J. (1961): Perception, cognition and language in deaf children; in: *Exceptional Children* 27, pp. 276-284.

Rosh [Rabbi Asher ben Yechiel, Germany and Spain, 13th century]. Edition 1954. New York.

Shevet Sofer [Rabbi Simcha Bunim Sofer, Hungary 19th century]. Edition 1899. Budapest, Vienna.

Shevut Yaakov [Rabbi Yaakov Reisha, Poland and Germany, 17th and 18th century]. Edition 1972. Jerusalem

Shivat Zion [Rabbi Shmuel ben Yechezkel Landa, Moravia 18th and 19th centruries]. Edition 1966. New York.

Sisco, F. H.. / Anderson, R. J. (1980): Deaf children' s performance on the WISC-R relative to hearing status of parents and child-rearing experiences; in: *American Annals of the Deaf*, 125, pp. 923-930.

Talmud. Ed. I. Epstein, 1961. London: Soncino Press. 18 vols.

Talmud Yerushalmi. Edition 1899. Jerusalem: Lunz.

Tosefta. Ed. Zukermandel, 1938. Jerusalem: Baberger and Wahrmann.

Tzemah Tzedek [Rabbi Menachem of Mikolshberg]. Edition 1769. Poland.

Tzitz Eliezer [Rabbi Yisrael J. Waldenberg]. Edition 1983; in: *Responsa*. Jerusalem.

Vernon, M. (1968): Fifty years of research on the intelligence of the deaf and hard of hearing children; in: *Journal of Rehabilitation of the Deaf*, 113, pp. 1-12.

Vygotsky, L. S. (1962): *Thought and Language*. Cambridge, Mass.: M.I. T. Press.

Watson, J. B. (1929): *Psychology from a Standpoint of a Behaviorist*. Philadelphia: Lippincott Company.

Zwiebel, A. (1986): More on the effects of early manual communication on the cognitive development of deaf children; in: *American Annals of the Deaf*, 133, pp. 16-20.

Zwiebel, A. (1992): Intellectual structure of hearing-impaired children and adolescents: A follow-up study; in: Martin, S. M. (ed.): *Cognition, Education and Deafness: Directions for Research and Instruction*. Washington, D. C.: Gallaudet University Press.

Zwiebel, A. / Mertens, D. M. (1985): A comparison of intellectual structure in deaf and hearing children; in: *American Annals of the Deaf*, 130, pp. 27-32.

Zwiebel, A. / Milgram, N. (1982): (Cognitive and communicative development in deaf children); in: *Israel Journal of Behavior Sciences*, 26, pp. 115-130 (Hebrew).

Jean-René Presneau
Clermont-Ferrand, France

The Scholars, the Deaf, and the Language of Signs in France in the 18th Century

Summary • Résumé

During the 18th century, reflections on Deaf people played a large part in the development of scientific and philosophical ideas on humankind and on the origin and nature of language.

This paper calls attention to the role of Deaf people, particularly pupils (who are often unidentified) of famous teachers of the Deaf.

Au XVIIIème siècle, les sourd(e)s ont contribué au développement des idées scientifiques et philosophiques sur l'Homme, ainsi que sur les questions de l'origine et la nature des langues.

L'auteur essaie, ici, de restituer la part qui revient aux sourd(e)s, en particulier aux élèves, souvent méconnu(e)s, de précepteurs célèbres.

413

I

In 18th century Paris, where many foreigners and provincials worked and lived, languages were numerous. When a person from the center of France wanted to communicate with another from the West (an Auvergnat with a Vendeen, for example), they were reduced to rudimentary French completed by gestural signs, which could not be considered as a true sign language, but only as means to show something to someone: the way, a direction, something to be done.

The sign language of the Deaf was different, with its own vocabulary and grammar. So the scholars of that time took a special interest in it, as we will see in the pages that follow.

The upper classes did not appreciate the language of signs. They thought it obscure and unseemly. They also considered that only 'savages' make signs and use a gestural language, not 'civilized' persons. Yet, on certain occasions, they took a pleasure in using gestures as well.

When the French priest, the abbé de L'Epée, decided in the 1760s to use signs for the education of the Deaf, many people agreed with him. Philosophers, like Condillac, thought that the practice might be useful for young hearing children as well: *The language of action* (signs) *has many advantages over the articulated sounds of (...) our teachers* (Condillac 1775). In fact, the gestural language could have been very effective for teaching French and other things to hearing children.

The Deaf people used what could, at the time, be considered a language to which hearing people were unaccustomed. Those who believed this had read St. Augustine or Descartes, who said that it was possible to learn the language of the Deaf, but that it was difficult (St. Augustine about 400; Descartes 1637). The Deaf also seemed odd and suspicious in the eyes of those who could hear. The language of signs puzzled the scholars, who reflected upon it with perseverance, but their approaches nevertheless remained superficial.

These scholars (philosophers like Diderot, Condillac, grammarians like Court de Gébelin, Copineau) compared this language with the spoken ones with a view to elucidating the origins of human languages. They wondered if those languages were natural, conventional (created by humans) or divine (created by God, with or without the help of Adam, the first man according to the Bible). Other unsolved questions included: is the language of signs universal? Did the first men and women use it?

For cultured people, a Deaf person was a peculiar, incomprehensible human being: *he lives like an animal or a machine,* wrote Fontenelle (1703), a member of the Royal Academy of Sciences; *he is like a child,* replied the empiricist philosopher Condillac (1746). The Deaf persons' minds were considered primitive, particularly dependent on the senses of sight or touch. They did not seem able to have abstract ideas. A Deaf person was often considered a falsifier (anon. 1734).

Buffon, the famous scientist, a member of the French Royal Academy of Sciences, wrote: *A deaf person is inevitably mute and can have no knowledge of abstract and general ideas,* and further on : *the deaf and dumb are the most ignorant of all men* (Buffon 1751). It was a fact that the majority of the Deaf (just like hearing people) did not know how to read and write; they counted on their fingers. And if they wrote, hearing scholars said that their writings were unreadable and incomprehensible.

> *There is a (...) deaf mute in Effiat (...). He knows how to write (...) but he cannot write a coherent account of anything and what he writes is almost incomprehensible; hence I believe that it is intellectually impossible for someone born deaf to make a speech that has any sense. I don't conceive of his even speaking.* (anon. 1734)

As for speaking it was widely thought impossible for Deaf people, although some scholars like a Jesuit (anon. 1701) or La Mettrie (1747) who had read Amman's book *Dissertatio de loquela* (1700) thought otherwise.

What did scientists say about the cause of deafness? Deafness was an impediment to hearing, and of course to speaking. The physicians supposed that deafness and muteness resulted either from the paralysis of nerves (the lingual nerve and the acoustic nerve) or from the obstruction of the auditory canal by 'depraved humours' (now we say 'purulent otitis'). The physicians also distinguished deafness from birth, deafness from childhood (illnesses were numerous and often serious during infancy), or caused by an accident (children could pierce their eardrum with a pencil, or an insect could lay eggs in the auditory canal, which was frequent in the country, etc.). A significant cause of deafness during the 18th century was old age; some of the most famous scholars were deaf: Fontenelle, Lesage, Voltaire etc. The physicians noticed that, when children became deaf, they stopped speaking, they became dumb; so doctors thought increasingly that deafness was the cause of dumbness. But they also thought that deafness was incurable, despite the many charlatans who sold quack remedies that were more or less dangerous. So the Deaf did their best to avoid those remedies and so-called magic potions. Near Nantes (a town in the West of France) during the French Revolution, every Deaf person knew that a bogus scientist used electricity to treat deafness. When he appeared in the neighbourhood, they hid or they warned their families not to listen to him. This man named Le Bouvyer-Desmortiers tried to cure a young girl who was Deaf: he only managed to hurt her and aggravate her deafness (Le Bouvyer-Desmortiers 1800). He was not alone in this business.

The Deaf claimed that they could live just as well as hearing people, and they could communicate with the help of their signs, even with those who were not Deaf, provided that the signs were simple and not ambiguous. It was possible, because, as we have said, many hearing people used gestures and knew the manual alphabet, too.

In the upper classes, people used signs during masked balls, for fear of being recognized by their voices and getting a forfeit (having to do something difficult or unpleasant in front of all the participants). People of all classes liked attending the mime shows – for example, the Commedia dell'arte. Desloges who became deaf at the age of seven, wrote in his book (1779) that he learned the language of signs from the Deaf servant of an actor of the Commedia dell'arte. Other gestural languages, not employed in everyday life, were known to scholars and were compared with the sign language of the Deaf; for example, the sign language of the monks and that of the mutes of the seraglio. As a matter of fact, many Deaf children of the upper classes were educated in monasteries and convents (to which they were relegated, kept out of sight, by their families). That education was given with the help of signs, as in the case of the Deaf architect and teacher, Etienne de Fay who lived in the abbey of St. Jean in Amiens. Deaf people could receive an education in Benedictine monasteries. In those places silence was the rule, and the monks had to be silent during the services, during the reading of the Holy texts, at meal times and at bedtime. The rule of silence could only be circumvented by the use of discreet signs. A language evolved from these practices during the Middle Ages, and it was possible to carry on a conversation using these signs (Gougard 1929). Two sorts of signs were admitted; single signs, for example BOOK (holding out one's hand and moving it as if turning the pages), and sign sequences, for example HONEY expressed by the sign for BEE followed by that for MILD. The monks could make sentences by combining several signs: *Where do you fish for salmon?* was signed WHERE-YOU-TO FISH- SALMON. The language of the mutes of the seraglio was similar, but it was despised because used by terrifying men. The seraglio was the place where the numerous wives of the Sultan lived, as was permitted by the Moslem religion, but nobody was allowed to speak to them. In the Ottoman Empire, the mutes were in charge, at the Sultan's court, of strangling the undesirable male children (who stood in the way of the heir apparent). The order to kill the children was passed on with signs. The murder was committed out of sight, without words (Grosrichard 1979, p. 175). The existance of a sign language of the seraglio was only known in Europe to the readers of travel books, but its use in the seraglio was a pretext for saying that this language was a bad one, for saying, too, that those who made signs were beasts.

In olden days there was another way of communicating in silence or secretly – namely, with manual alphabets. The oldest one was a computing method used for commercial transactions, but it could be changed into a secret language: raising the little finger [1] for A, raising the little finger and the ring finger [2] to form B, raising these fingers plus the middle one [3] to form C, and so on. To say 'danger', sign 4-1-14-7-5-18. Hearing French and English pupils used a two handed alphabet during the 18th century with which they imitated the letters. Another alphabet from Italy consisted in showing a part of the face or body: nose for N, lip for L etc. In Spain and in the Franciscan religious order, a hand alphabet created by St. Bonaventure in the 13th century was practiced to confess and to assist dying people (Ivars 1920). The knowledge of this alphabet was also advantageous for confessors in order to communicate with very deaf penitents who knew this hand alphabet. In this way, the confessor could respond to what the deaf penitents said without the danger of having to shout during confession. The secrecy of confession could be respected even if the penitent was very deaf. Many religious people knew this alphabet, which was not different from the one used by the Deaf community today. This alphabet from St. Bonaventure and the Franciscans was used by the first teachers of the Spanish Deaf during the 16th century (Pedro Ponce de Leon first, then Ramirez de Carrión) to teach the Deaf children of the Spanish court to read, write and speak (Chaves/Soler 1974). The manual alphabet Ramirez de Carrión used in order to communicate with the Deaf would be introduced in France during the 18th century by Pereire (to educate deaf children of the upper classes), and then by the abbé de L'Epée in preference to the two-handed alphabet of the ordinary school children. Yet the abbé de L'Epée thought that sign language was better than the manual alphabet in order to teach the Deaf, because signs were the natural and native 'tongue' of the Deaf.

II

The language of signs of the Deaf in the 18th century is largely unknown to us. But we have some indications from the Deaf themselves (Pierre Desloges) and from some hearing persons who associated with them, like Diderot, the abbé de L'Epée or Baron de Gérando (de Gérando was a member of the Conseil d'Administration of the Institute for the Deaf in Paris about 1820).

Diderot, a French philosopher, writes about how he communicated, by way of gestural signs, with a Deaf man who can be identified, I think, as Saboureux de Fontenay, the most famous pupil of Pereire (Diderot 1751). Near the end of a game of chess, when Diderot was losing the game, Saboureux signed that it is easy to win *with the help of two kibitzers and everyone else who comes through*. Diderot narrated:

> *But pointing at all the spectators one by one, and making at the same time a little movement with his lips, to which he added a great gesture of his two arms indicating the door and the tables, he answered me that it was a thing of little worth to be got out of a fix with the help of two kibitzers and everyone else who comes through.*
> (Diderot 1751/1969, p. 529)

This last phrase was idiomatic; everybody around Diderot and Saboureux understood what the latter wished to say. Saboureux was speaking, writing and reading, but he was also able to use signs, because he was deaf from birth, as he said in a letter published in *Le Journal de Verdun* (1765); yet, he had no contact with the Deaf community in his childhood.

The Deaf author Pierre Desloges, cited earlier, who became deaf through illness at the age of seven and who later became a member of the Parisian Deaf community, described the sign language of the Deaf Parisians. He wrote: *when a deaf and mute person meets another one who is more educated, he learns to combine and to perfect his signs, which were without order and connection before* (Desloges 1779). And he cited some examples: to name a person known, two or three signs were enough – a gender sign (hand at the hat for masculine, at the breast for feminine) plus the most particular sign for characterizing this person. Another example is the sign for

> MERCHANT: *we take a piece of our clothes between the thumb and forefinger, like a merchant who sells his merchandise, then we sign the action of counting money in our hand and we fold our arms like someone who is taking a rest.* (Desloges 1779, p. 48)

Desloges distinguished between three kinds of signs: the ordinary or original signs (natural signs which were common to all Deaf and hearing people alike, but the Deaf using them *on good grounds (en connaissance de cause)*), the reflexive signs (natural signs the usage of which demands *some reflexion*), and the analytical signs (similar to the 'methodical signs' of the abbé de L'Epée).

De Gérando in 1827 described some signs of Deaf pupils. Signs of Deaf children without any instruction (spontaneous signs): CHILD – sign for SMALL plus action of suckling or of rocking a baby, or of someone who is carrying a baby in his or her arms. Signs that all the Deaf had in common: JOINER – imitation of a person who is sawing. But some differences between girls and boys could be noticed: girls had signs of affection, of emotional life in common, boys signs of labour. The Deaf community was similar to the hearing community: men went to work, women stayed home with the children. Signs collected in the Institute of Paris: FISH – the hand is held out horizontally, moving like a snake (Deaf pupils from Paris), or imitation of fishing (Deaf pupils from the provinces). It might be noted that the Parisians seemed to use 'descriptive' signs (they looked at things) and that provincials talked in active signs (they knew how to use things). Last but not least, the pupils used signs created by those who lived with the abbé de L'Epée, and transmitted year by year by the Deaf. The great variety of signs (which did not disturb the Deaf) would be a pretext (among others) for prohibiting signs in schools in the second part of the 19th century.

III

The Deaf do not hear, hence they do not speak. They use visual signs. About 1750, the question was: are visual signs linguistic ones or are they not? A sign was considered, in general, as a representation of an idea. A visual sign has a similar value: it *paints* an idea *immediately* (Copineau 1779). To the Enlightenment philosophers (Diderot, Condillac, Rousseau) the sign language of the Deaf was a language, but they allowed some degrees, some differences between that language and the spoken one, as well as between different sorts of spoken and sign languages. As a matter of fact, the scholars distinguished between several languages, according to their conception of deafness and also according to their representation of Deaf persons. Some other philosophers wrote that sign language was not a language, not at all, just gesticulation. Gestural signs are only imitations of things or of emotions: they seemed to prove that the Deaf lived like animals, fearing neither God nor humans, *they only have their feelings for guides* (*Ils n'ont que leurs passions pour guide;* Deschamps 1779, p. 12). That was the major pretext for imposing the learning of spoken language on the Deaf: humans speak, animals do not. Many philosophers, and most of the scholars thought that sign language was a sort of pre-language, a primitive language. There were several conceptions of this original language, but the most important conceptions regarded this language as either that of primitive people, in very ancient times, or of little children.

Those who wished to give some education to the Deaf wanted to help them, but each of them had a different point of view. Some, like Amman or the abbé Deschamps, wished to teach them how to speak with the help of lip reading or writing without making any gestural signs; others, like Pereire, wished to teach them how to read with the help of the manual alphabet. As for the abbé de L'Epée, he expected to save their souls and to teach them the catechism by the use of written French and gestural signs. Finally, but not often, a few people passed on knowledge with the help of gestural signs, like the Deaf Etienne de Fay.

Scholars and other persons reflected on those practices and expressed their opinions:

On Etienne de Fay, first. A member of the Academy of Sciences visited him in 1733 and noted that Etienne de Fay wrote acceptable French and that he understood when one asked him a written question. We know that Etienne de Fay taught mathematics and other things with the help of signs to some pupils. That was reported by some journalists. Bruhier d'Ablaincourt wrote that Deaf children could easily learn mathematics (1740).

On Amman, second. The most well known teacher before Pereire and de L'Epée was Amman; a Jesuit (anon. 1701) and La Mettrie (1747) gave a review of his book *Dissertatio de loquela* (1700). Amman (1669-1724) was a physician who considered humans as machines (as Descartes professed), so he thought that it was easy to show the Deaf and mute how to speak. The Deaf persons whose vocal organs are intact must be attentive to the movements of the teacher's lips and to the vibrations of the throat. The vocal machine should be started again by way of imitation and self observation, particularly in a mirror. But Amman was strongly opposed to sign language: the use of gestural signs is a feeble resource, limited to some people familiar with the Deaf. The abbé Deschamps, who was a follower of Amman about 1780, had a similar opinion of the signs of the Deaf; he added that God has given humans the faculty of speech, not of making signs. For Deschamps, the abbé de L'Epée's 'methodical signs' were bad ones and harmful to the Deaf. Desloges, who was Deaf, as we said, criticized the abbé Deschamps' method of teaching the Deaf: this method was difficult for the Deaf and not useful for teaching them how to write, to convey one's feelings and to obtain new knowledge. Desloges preferred the abbé de L'Epée's method.

On Pereire, third. About 1750, the most famous teacher of the deaf was Pereire (1715-1780). Pereire used a similar method to that of Amman, whose book he had read, as well as the commentaries by a Jesuit (who stated in 1701 that Amman's method was praiseworthy and useful for eavesdropping on the pupils by reading their lips at a distance). Pronunciation was taught after a thorough knowledge of the vocal tract and of the vocal cords. Pereire also used the sense of touch, to make the deaf child feel the resonance of voice. He also used a manual alphabet, the Spanish one, which was completed by manual signs for syllables and consonant clusters peculiar to French, which made it easier for the pupils to learn how to read and speak. Saboureux de Fontenay called this special alphabet 'dactylology' (language of the fingers). The dactylological sign signalled sound and letters: as a matter of fact, Pereire's method was a method better suited to written than to spoken French. It is known that Saboureux used a writing slate to communicate with hearing persons and that he wrote in perfect French. Pereire said that sign language was not a true language because every word, every thing had a sign, and it was very difficult to know and remember all the signs, which are too numerous (similar to hieroglyphics), also because signs have no connection to abstract ideas etc. (La Rochelle 1882, p. 338).

Scholars like Buffon (the famous naturalist) and Lecat (famous physician) became keen on Pereire because he was teaching the Deaf how to speak, read and write. Lecat, for example wrote that Pereire's pupils became *orators and scholars* who had been *restored to society* (Lecat 1767, p. 545). Rousseau wrote about 1760:

> *Pereire and those who teach mutes, as he does, not only how to speak but also to know what they are saying, are obliged to teach them another language first (...) with the help of which they can lead them to understand* (French). (Rousseau 1760/1970, p. 37)

Now the issue raised by Rousseau is very important because it touches upon the Deaf child's mother tongue. A careful reading of tables published by Perrolle (1782), which give the names and characteristics of some of de L'Epée's male pupils, shows that all those listed could hear to some degree by bone conduction – the ticking of a pocket watch when pressed against the skull. Biographies of Pereire (e.g., La Rochelle 1882) indicate that his pupils, too, had residual hearing. Thus some of these pupils may have acquired some knowledge of French as a mother tongue in the usual way (this would definitely be true of any late-deafened pupils), and from de L'Epée and Pereire they may have learned artificial systems, 'methodical signs' and 'dactylology' (Presneau 1988).

On the abbé de L'Epée, fourth. The abbé de L'Epée thought that the most important thing was not knowing how to speak but how to have ideas, how to obtain new ideas and how to convey those ideas. He used a special device to teach the Deaf French written language and the catholic catechism: he called it 'signes méthodiques' (de L'Epée 1776). The system of 'methodical signs' was built up from the supposedly natural language of the Deaf themselves, but well-ordered and completed with artificial signs created by the abbé. For example: TO LOVE – *look at a thing and put one's right hand on the mouth while the left one is upon the heart* (de L'Epée 1776, p. 72); for LOVELY the same sign, adding the sign for ADVERB etc. This system was very elaborate and involved, in part, a reflection of the grammar of French. The scholars who went to the house of the abbé de L'Epée saw this spectacle; the lesson went off as follows: the teacher (de L'Epée himself or a disciple) read a text aloud (the Bible for instance) and translated it into 'methodical signs'; the pupils read the signer's hands, translated in the reverse order and wrote the sentence down on a sheet of paper. To tell the truth, the pupils only repeated what the teacher signed without understanding the real meaning of the sentences. Much of their real education came from mutual instruction, no doubt. The scholar Copineau was a supporter of de L'Epée's method, he advocated the use of signs in the education of all children, even those who were hearing. He wrote (in Desloges 1779) that sign language is *a constant definition of the ideas* which are in the mind; so this language might be useful to teach children the meaning of words, because ideas are represented to perfection by gestural signs.

IV

Thus the Deaf played a great part in the intellectual history of the 18th century, in reflections on the origins and nature of language and in the foundations of special education. They contributed to the development of methods to come, for teaching not only Deaf children but also all children who have difficulty in learning to communicate. Do not forget this: behind the hearing teacher (Pereire, de L'Epée, Sicard, …) there was always a Deaf person (Saboureux de Fontenay, Adelaïde Bernard, Jean Massieu, …) fighting in silence against the whole hearing world for her or his emancipation.

Appendix
The original French quotations:

p. 414

> Le langage d'action possède des avantages sur les sons articulés de nos gouvernantes et de nos précepteurs. (Condillac 1775)

> Un sourd est nécessairement muet. Il ne doit avoir aucune connaissance des idées abstraites et générales. (…) Les sourds et muets sont les plus ignorants de tous les hommes. (Buffon 1751)

Il y a un (…) sourd et muet à Effiat (…), il sait écrire (…) mais il ne peut faire un discours suivi et l'on ne comprend presque rien à ce qu'il écrit, aussi crois-je qu'il est moralement impossible à un sourd de naissance de faire un discours qui ait du sens. Je n'imagine pas même qu'il puisse parler. (anon. 1734)

p. 416

Mais lui, me montrant du doigt tous les spectateurs les uns après les autres, et faisant en même temps un petit mouvement des lèvres qu'il accompagna d'un grand mouvement de ses deux bras qui allaient et venaient dans la direction de la porte et des tables, me répondit qu'il y avait peu de mérite à être sorti du mauvais pas où j'étais, avec le conseil *du tiers, du quart et des passants*. (Diderot 1751/1969, p. 529)

p. 417

Marchand: nous prenons avec le pouce et l'index un bout de nos vêtements ou tout autre objet que nous présentons comme un marchand qui offre sa marchandise; nous faisons ensuite l'action de compter de l'argent dans notre main et sur le champ nous croisons les bras comme quelqu'un qui se repose. (Desloges 1779, p. 48)

p. 418

Il était réservé à M.Pereire de transformer un sourd et muet de naissance en Orateur et en Savant, de rendre à la société une partie de notre espèce, qui paraissait condamnée par la nature à faire une classe mitoyenne entre la brute et nous. (Lecat 1767, p. 545)

Le sieur Pereire et ceux qui comme lui apprennent aux muets non seulement à parler, mais à savoir ce qu'ils disent sont bien forcés de leur apprendre auparavant une autre langue non moins compliquée, à l'aide de laquelle ils puissent leur faire entendre celle-là. (Rousseau 1760/1970, p. 37)

p. 419

[le verbe AIMER] s'exécute en regardant l'objet dont il s'agit, et mettant fortement sa main droite sur la bouche pendant que la gauche est sur le cœur (…). (de L'Epée 1776, p. 72)

References

(anon). (1701): Review of Amman's 'Traité de la parole'; in: *Mémoires pour l'histoire des sciences et des beaux-arts (Mémoires de Trévoux)*. Trévoux, p. 85.

(anon). (1734): Au rédacteur du Journal de Verdun. *Journal historique sur le matières du temps (Journal de Verdun)*, mai, p. 329.

Amman, J.C. (1700/1779): *Dissertatio de loquela*. Amsterdam: Wolters. French translation: *Dissertation sur la parole*; in: Deschamps, C.F. (1779): *Cours élémentaire d'éducation des sourds et muets*. Paris: Debure, pp. 225 sq.

Bruhier d'Ablaincourt, J.J. (1740): Lettre sur les sourds et muets. *Journal de Verdun*, pp. 406-411.

Buffon, G.L. de (1751): (Art.); in: *Mercure de France,* mars.

Chaves, T.L. / Soler, I.L. (1974): Pedro Ponce de Leon, First Teacher of the Deaf. *Sign Language Studies*, 5, pp. 48-63.

Condillac, E.B. de (1746/1947): *Essai sur l'origine des connaissances humaines*. Amsterdam: Mortier. Reprinted 1947: O*euvres philosophiques*. Texte établi et présenté par G. Le Roy. Paris: Presses Universitaires de France, vol. 1, pp. 1-118.

Condillac, E.B. de (1775/1947): *Grammaire*. Reprinted 1947: *Oeuvres philosophiques*. Texte établi et présenté par G. Le Roy. Paris: Presses Universitaires de France, vol. 1, pp. 425-513.

Copineau, [?] (1779): Notes; in: Desloges, P.: *Observations d'un sourd et muet (…)*. Paris: Morin.

Descartes, R. (1637/1930): *Discours de la méthode (…)*. Paris. Reprinted 1930.

Deschamps, C.F. (1779): *Cours élémentaire d'éducation des sourds et muets*. Paris: Debure.

Desloges, P. (1779): *Observations d'un sourd et muet (…)*. Paris: Morin.

Diderot, D. (1751/1969): *Lettre sur les sourds et muets*. Reprinted 1969: *Oeuvres complètes*. Paris: Club Français du Livre, vol. 2.

Fontenelle, B. (1703/1739): *Histoire de l'Académie Royale des Sciences*. Reprinted 1739, Paris: Imprimerie Royale.

Gérando, J.M. de (1827): *De l'éducation des sourds et muets de naissance*. Paris: Méquignon.

Gougard, L. (1929): Le langage des silencieux. *Revue Mabillon*, 19, pp. 93-100.

Grosrichard, A. (1979): *Structure du sérail*. Paris: Seuil.

Ivars, P.A. (1920): Cuestionaro histórico. *Archivo Iberamericano*, 12, pp. 385-396.

La Mettrie, J.O. de (1747): *Histoire naturelle de l'âme*. Paris.

La Rochelle, E. (1882): *Jacob Rodrigues Pereire (…)*. Paris: Dupont.

Le Bouvyer-Desmortiers, U.R.T. (1800): *Mémoire ou considérations sur les sourds-muets de naissance*. Paris: Buisson.

Lecat, J.B. (1767): *Traité des sensations*. Paris: Volat la Chapelle.

L'Epée, C.M. de (1776): *Institution des sourds et muets de naissance (…)*. Paris: Nyon.

Perrolle, M. (1782): *Dissertation anatomico-acoustique*. Paris: Méquignon.

Presneau, J.R. (1988): Le sourd et muet au XVIIIème siècle. Entre le fou et l'homme civilisé. *Revue Synapse*, 49, pp. 64-70.

Rousseau, J.-J. (1760/1970): *Essai sur l'origine des langues*. Reprinted Bordeaux, 1970.

Saboureux de Fontenay, [?] (1765): Lettre de M. Saboureux de Fontenay, sourd et muet de naissance (…). *Journal de Verdun*, 98, pp. 284-298, 361-372.

St. Augustin (388, 389, 420/1948): *Dialogues philosophiques*. French translation. Reprinted Bruges, 1948.

ILLVSTRIS VIRI
GODOFR, GVILIELMI
LEIBNITII
COLLECTANEA
ETYMOLOGICA,
ILLVSTRATIONI LINGVARVM,
VETERIS CELTICÆ, GERMANICÆ
GALLICÆ, ALIARVMQVE
INSERVIENTIA.
CVM
PRÆFATIONE
JO. GEORGII ECCARDI.
CONTENTA SEQVENS PAGINA INDICAT.

HANOVERÆ,
Sumptibus NICOLAI FOERSTERI,
M DCC XVII.

Ill. 96: Gottfried W. Leibniz's 1717 book contains descriptions (no illustrations) of gestures of Cistercian monks, e.g. of the abbey of Loccum in Northern Germany.

L'ARTE DE' CENNI

CON LA QVALE FORMANDOSI FAVELLA VISIBILE,

SI TRATTA DELLA MVTA ELOQVENZA, CHE NON E' ALTRO CHE VN FACONDO SILENTIO.

DIVISA IN DVE PARTI.

Nella prima si tratta de i cenni, che da noi con le membra del nostro corpo sono fatti, scoprendo la loro significatione, e quella con l'autorità di famosi Autori confirmando.

Nella seconda si dimostra come di questa cognitione tutte l'arti liberali, e mecaniche si preuagliano.

Materia nuoua à tutti gli huomini pertinente, e massimamente à Prencipi, che per loro dignità, più con cenni, che con parole si fanno intendere.

DI GIOVANNI BONIFACCIO
Giureconsulto, & Assessore.

L'OPPORTVNO ACADEMICO FILARMONICO.

IN VICENZA, MDCXVI.

Appresso Francesco Grossi. *Con licenza de' Superiori.*

Ill. 97: Bonifaccio (1616) on 'mute eloquence', containing, among others, considerations on the status of (rhetorical) gestures and descriptions of gestures (no illustrations).

Ill. 99: Aquapendente (1600) on vision, voicing and hearing.

Ill. 98: Portrait of Hieronymus Fabricius ab Aquapendente (1537-1619).

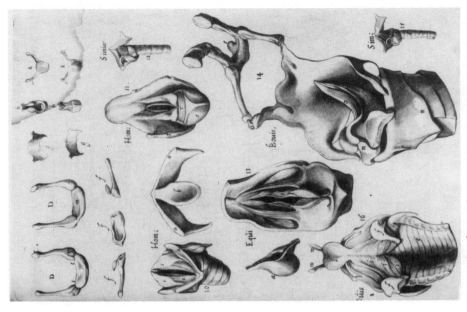

Ill. 101: Dissection of apes, horses, bovines and humans for inspection of their larynxes, in Aquapendente (1600).

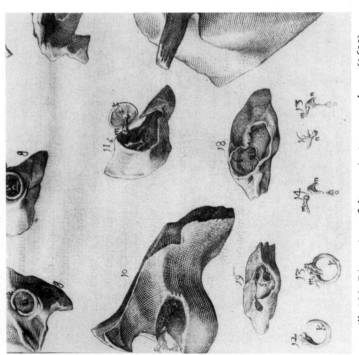

Ill. 100: Dissection of the ear in Aquapendente (1600).

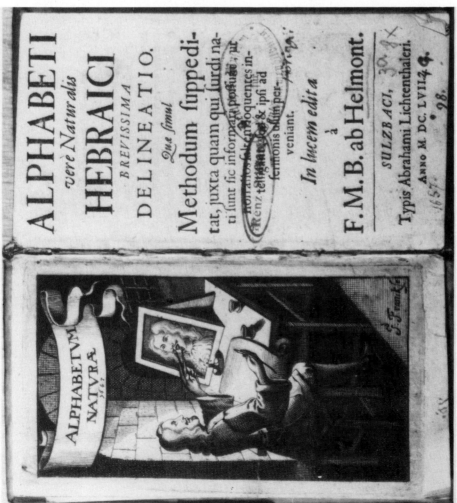

Ill. 102: van Helmont (1657) on the 'natural' Hebraic alphabet, considered valid for learning to articulate all spoken languages.

Renate Fischer
Hamburg, Germany

Language of Action

Summary • Zusammenfassung • Résumé

This contribution outlines some basic theoretical issues developed in the 18th century about Deaf people and their sign languages. The main concern is with Condillac's positions in theory of language and epistemology, and with the different ways in which these were taken up by prominent representatives of the Paris School for the Deaf before and after 1800.

A short version of this article in international signs may be obtained from the author.

Der Beitrag zeigt für die Auseinandersetzung um Gehörlose und ihre Gebärdensprachen im 18. Jahrhundert einige grundsätzliche theoretische Bezüge auf. Im wesentlichen geht es um sprach- und erkenntnistheoretische Positionen Condillacs und um die Unterschiede, mit denen diese durch herausragende Vertreter der Pariser Gehörlosenschule vor und nach 1800 aufgegriffen wurden.

Eine Kurzversion dieses Beitrags in internationalen Gebärden kann bei der Verfasserin angefordert werden.

L'article présente quelques aspects théoriques fondamentaux de la discussion concernant les sourd(e)s et leurs langues des signes au XVIIIème siècle. Il s'agit pour l'essentiel de positions proposées par Condillac dans le domaine de l'épistémologie et de la théorie du langage, et des divergences avec lesquelles ces positions condillaciennes ont été utilisées par d'importants représentants de l'institution de Paris avant et après 1800.

Vous pouvez obtenir un abrégé de cet article en signes internationaux sur demande adressée à l'auteur de l'article.

I Introduction

1.

The debate on the sign languages of Deaf communities which reflects a power struggle, is carried on with the help of arguments taken from various theoretical fields. Philosophy of language and linguistics are two of those fields. These theories which are almost entirely the work of hearing people, always have a large indirect influence on the Deaf when situations of dependence on hearing people are maintained. In a history of the Deaf it seems necessary to me, therefore, to consider the history of ideas of hearing people as well.

The example I have chosen for such interweavings of linguistic theory and education of the Deaf concerns the epistemology and philosophy of language of Etienne Bonnot de Condillac (1715-1780) in 18th century France. I intend to demonstrate how this theory was used for the treatment of signs and sign language at the newly founded Paris School for the Deaf. I will consider the school's founder, Charles-Michel de L'Epée (1712-1789), his successor Roch-Ambroise-Cucurron Sicard (1742-1822), and Roch-Ambroise Auguste Bébian (1789-1839), who taught at the school.

My question is: Can works about signs at the Paris School in the late 18th and early 19th century be connected to the most famous French epistemology and theory of language of the time? If so, to what extent does this connection explain common features or differences in the positions taken up in the matter of sign language by three important hearing personages of the first great gestural school for the Deaf – de L'Epée, who with his *signes méthodiques* (methodical signs) made the gestural method famous; Sicard, who, by his own account, further developed de L'Epée's method and was a theorist of grammar; Bébian, who pleaded for the sign language of the Deaf and had a good command of it, unlike most of the other hearing teachers.

2.

To be answered within the given frame, however, this question must be spelled out in more than one respect:

a) My emphasis is on aspects of theory of language. Any influence of Condillac's which might be found in other fields, e.g. that of psychology of learning, will not be considered.

b) In the field of language, the focus is on Condillac's statements on a signed form of language which he calls *langage d'action* (language of action).

c) The assessments presented here can by no means be applied to the respective method (of de L'Epée, Sicard, Bébian) **as a whole** without further scrutiny. – With 18th century authors, there seems to be a surprising mixture of principles and individual ideas that are generally considered to be completely opposed to each other, and thus by rights not compatible. This applies especially to elements from rationalist vs. sensualist theories, the two major philosophical movements of the 17th and 18th centuries. Even the main exponents of sensualist philosophy, like Condillac, are no longer presented, in some more recent publications, as having been free from any rationalist influence. The importance of this merging of philosophical positions for the discussion about Deaf people and their sign languages, and its practical consequences has not yet been investigated.

3.

The expression *langage d'action* is hardly common or even known today, in contrast to earlier centuries. In the 19th century, for example, it was one of the terms used by French Deaf people to designate their sign language, along with other expressions such as *la mimique* (mimicry), *langue/langage des gestes* (language of gestures), *langue/langage des signes* (language of signs) or *les signes* (signs), *les gestes* (gestures). Ferdinand Berthier, for example, says, with regard to the criteria for choosing a teacher of the Deaf:

(…) among the qualifications he has to possess, none is more important for this kind of sacred office than a perfect command of, and long practice in, the language of action. (Berthier 1840, p.61)

Another example: In 1858, Augustin Grosselin (hearing) and Pierre Pélissier (Deaf) wanted to contribute to the propagation of the sign language of the Deaf by publishing special language learning cards, because

(…) their language of action, which is so rich and expressive, is unknown to speaking persons to such an extent that a deaf mute rarely has anyone in his family who is able to converse with him. (Grosselin/Pélissier 1858, prospectus)

Condillac is repeatedly represented as the creator of this term in works concerned with philosophy of language. The use of *langage d'action* in learned literature of the 18th and 19th century is clearly linked to the massive influence of Condillac's works; in this connection, *langage d'action* appears even in the first known book by a Deaf person (Desloges 1779/1985-1986, II p. 12). However, Condillac cannot be seen as the inventor of the expression *langage d'action*; it is, in all likelihood, only the *success of the expression* ((la) *fortune de l'expression*) that is due to Condillac's *Essai* of 1746, as Robinet (1978, p. 223 n.4) proposes. Indeed, the expression can already be found in a French translation of parts of a work by William Warburton, which Condillac (1746) quotes at length.[1] A detailed comparison of the passages shows that the translator repeatedly uses *langage d'action*, although Warburton employs different expressions in the English original. In the chapter subdivision established especially for the 1744 edition of the French version, *langage d'action* is used consistently, and it is, moreover, only in the French version that it appears in the index. Possibly the translator goes back to an expression already coined but not established in learned contexts; and in contrast to the English original, he lends an almost technical character to the term *langage d'action*. The learned employment of the term in a narrower sense could then be said to start with its integration into Condillac's sensualist system.

It is typical both for the earlier sign discussion and for that influenced by Condillac that it made no distinction between the sign languages of the Deaf and diverse forms of communication by gestures (pantomime, dance, rhetorical gestures, etc.).

II Etienne Bonnot de Condillac

1.

In the 18th century, Condillac presented the first consistent epistemology and theory of language within the then revolutionary frame of sensualism. In contrast to other theories, sensualism does not suppose that language and reasoning were given to humans by God (that they are innate), but rather that humankind had continually developed its reasoning and language abilities, from the very simplest of forms, on the basis of the senses or sensory perceptions, and driven by various needs (hunger, need for protection, mutual help etc.). Language and reasoning are developed in a kind of spiral according to this theory (Tort 1976), they are interdependent. Both were strongly linked to the senses or sensory perceptions at first and could be developed ('perfected') to high degrees of abstraction. Prerequisite for this development were a natural ability (as a physical disposition) for the acquisition of reasoning and language on the one hand; and the presence or development of so-called operations of the mind like attention, memory, etc. on the other (Condillac 1746/1947).

---

1 The work in question is: W. Warburton, *The divine legation of Moses*, 1737ff. The partial translation into French used by Condillac (W. Warburton, *Essai sur les hiéroglyphes*, 1744) was carried out by L. des Malpeines according to Robinet (1978, p. 223 n.4).

As the two basic principles allowing for the development of language and reasoning, Condillac names *analogie* and *analyse* (1775/1947, pp. 429ff): the first signs had a sort of representational relationship to the objects perceived by the senses. Sign formation by analogy also played an important part in the further development. The second principle is that of analysis. Condillac sees a progression in the further analysis of linguistic expressions and of the sensory perceptions contained in them (*décomposition*), and in the increasing differentiation of aspects of meaning. To give an example: initially, human beings perhaps developed a word for 'tree' – as it presented itself to them as a whole. By analysis and because of circumstances and needs, they then differentiated more and more parts and named them: 'branch, root, trunk', etc.

Both principles have strongly influenced many works on Deaf people and signs. In the following, I will go into the principle of analysis in more detail.

2.

In Condillac's theory, the *langage d'action* is the first form of language that animals, including human beings, create for themselves. It is not at all simple, however, to describe this *langage d'action* in Condillac's system, since he has presented it twice, in very different ways.

In an early work (the *Essai* of 1746), Condillac says that the *langage d'action* was a language initially suited to the low intelligence of its users. Rather concisely, he states that the *langage d'action* probably consisted *of contortions and violent agitations* (*en contorsions et en agitations violentes*), supplemented by the *cries of emotion* (*cris des passions*), i.e. a vocal element (1746/1947, p. 61). The vocal element, the *articulated sounds* (*sons articulés*), however, underwent a more intense development, and after a phase of coexistence, *speech* (*la parole*) or *the use of articulated sounds* (*l'usage des sons articulés*; 1746/1947, pp. 62-63) predominated and was then developed as language and became almost completely responsible for the further development of intelligence. Consequently, deaf people, lacking language, are considered unable to pass into the realms of intelligence, and are seen as primitive humans (1746/1947, pp. 43ff).

In a later work (the *Grammaire* of 1775), Condillac no longer restricts the *langage d'action* to the earliest phases of reasoning and language. This is also the work in which he gives an enthusiastic account of his visit to de L'Epée's school and of the *signes méthodiques*.

How is the *langage d'action* represented by Condillac thirty years after his first work? He starts by giving a detailed description of all the elements that, to his mind, make up the *langage d'action* (1775/1947, p. 428): the foundation are signs, meaning movements of the arms, head and the whole body;[2] they are able to express *all the sentiments of the soul* (*tous les sentimens de l'âme*). But the *elegance of this language* (*élégance de ce langage*) is in the facial movements and particularly the expression of the eyes: these round off the *tableau* begun by the gestures with fine shadings. In the third place, Condillac names a vocal element (*des cris*), which, however, is least efficient; it serves mainly for gaining attention.

It is important to note that Condillac distinguishes two kinds of *langage d'action* here (1775/1947, p. 429): a first one, called 'natural', which is a direct expression of the as yet not well developed abilities of reasoning, and whose signs are very 'analogous' to the designated objects. This early *langage d'action*, however, exists only for a short time, because humankind soon starts to form additional signs and to differentiate things by way of analogy and analysis. Such a *langage d'action* is not a 'natural' one anymore, but, like spoken lan-

---

2 In view of the prevailing concentration on the manual level, even in sign language linguistics (cf., for example, various notation systems), this different emphasis in Condillac seems remarkable to me.

guage, 'artificial' (because it has been worked upon), and as such, this *langage d'action* could *be extended sufficiently to render all the ideas of the human mind* (*être assez étendu pour rendre toutes les conceptions de l'esprit humain*) – i.e., for Condillac (in the *Grammaire* of 1775), the *langage d'action* is **not** limited in its efficiency just because it employs gestures rather than sounds. At this point, he inserts the remark on de L'Epée and his *signes méthodiques*. He emphasizes that deaf people taught in this way received from de L'Epée *more exact and precise ideas than those which are usually acquired with the help of the ear* (*des idées plus exactes et plus précises que celles qu'on acquiert communément avec le secours de l'ouïe;* 1775/1947, pp. 429-430 n.1). For the main method employed by de L'Epée was, after all, analysis (i.e., analysis manifested in signs), and such an analysis was provided far less obviously in spoken language.[3]

This revolutionary view about the independence of language efficiency from its medium expressed by Condillac in 1775 (with which he strongly modifies his views of 1746), does not, however, become a dominant pillar of his further argument. On the contrary, he does not even try to justify the, in view of the *langage d'action*'s efficiency, inexplicable switch of humankind to spoken language. His work is centered on spoken language for all that. It must further be stressed that he does not speak of the communication among the Deaf in de L'Epée's school, but only of de L'Epée's artificial system, which he admires – corresponding to his own theory – for its analytical character.

I would like to add that this change in Condillac's view of the *langage d'action* in his *Grammaire* is hardly noticed even in modern research (philosophy, philology, linguistics); the *langage d'action* in Condillac's *Grammaire* is almost consistently linked to a form of reasoning and language seen as primitive. In contrast to this, Ferdinand Berthier, Deaf teacher at the Paris school, previously pointed out Condillac's change of view (Berthier 1840, p. 74; see also Aléa 1824, pp. 115-116). Among the different factors which may be decisive for the one-sided reception of the *Grammaire*, it must surely be stated that, even today, there prevails a restricted view in favour of spoken language in the above-mentioned fields of research.

III Charles-Michel de L'Epée

1.
What was de L'Epée's system of signs like, which fascinated Condillac as the realization of an ideal *langage d'action* ?

It is often said that de L'Epée's *signes méthodiques* had been a sort of signed French (*français signé*), because in them he connected lexical and grammatical elements in signs according to the rules of French. In my opinion, this comparison misses an important point: the *signes méthodiques* were a heterogeneous system, which contained, among other things, an analytical treatment of lexical elements. With *je crois* (I believe), for example, de L'Epée proceeded in a way that is very similar to Condillac's analysis of 'complex' ideas into 'simple' ones:

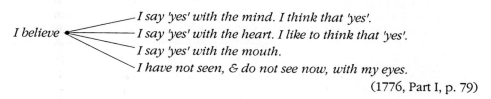

I believe
- *I say 'yes' with the mind. I think that 'yes'.*
- *I say 'yes' with the heart. I like to think that 'yes'.*
- *I say 'yes' with the mouth.*
- *I have not seen, & do not see now, with my eyes.*

(1776, Part I, p. 79)

---

3 José Aléa , who employed de L'Epée's method in Spain, proposed consequently to teach not only deaf but also hearing children with *signes méthodiques* in elementary school (Aléa 1824).

In his work of 1776 de L'Epée characterizes his procedure as follows (without calling it analysis here):

> *(…) there is no thing which cannot be signified by one or more words. (…) if one utters them and they are not understood, one explains them with other words in speaking (…). With the deaf mutes, one performs exactly the same operation in writing, until one has arrived at words which have been understood in signs hundreds of times (…).* (1776, Part I, pp. 77-78)

A 'word' that is thought to be very difficult to understand, like *je crois*, is written onto the blackboard and connected with lines to its *explication* (which has four parts in this case), in order to show that all this is contained (*renfermé;* 1776, Part I, p. 79) in it. For de L'Epée, it is not a matter of simply rewording or paraphrasing the original expression. The example *je crois* shows that a 'word' is seen as a possible, but not imperative, expression of a certain 'complex' meaning. If this meaning, this 'word', cannot be understood, one 'explains' by dividing the 'complex' meaning into different expressions which name individual aspects: the 'complex' meaning, expressed in one word, appears as an addition or synthesis of different constitutive parts which may be named individually.[4]

Eight years later, de L'Epée again gives some comments on the same example (1784, pp. 126ff), which differ from the 1776 version (although a large part is a word by word repetition)[5] in that de L'Epée designates this procedure, with regard to the scholars, as *analyse* (1784, p. 127). After some comments on derivations, he finally says that all this shows *the use of analysis joined with the signes méthodiques* (*l'usage de l'analyse joint à celui des Signes méthodiques*), and de L'Epée (1784, pp. 132ff) quotes the passage from Condillac's *Grammaire*, mentioning him by name, that praises his *signes méthodiques*.[6]

The *analyse* of French words for the purpose of rendering them in sequences of natural signs appeared previously in the *Lettre II* (1772) as one of the dominant aspects of the *signes méthodiques* (de L'Epée 1776, Part II, p. 34 and repeatedly):

> *(…) if the idea which recalls a verb does not offer a sign to our mind which would be proper and would make it sensible at once, then we fall back on analysis; and with this device, we regain the range of natural signs.* (1776, Part II, p. 36)

---

4 The sign sequence corresponding to the written *explication*, i.e. the *signes méthodiques*, is the following: *(…) first, I make the sign for the first person singular by pointing towards myself with the index finger of my right hand, its point directed towards my breast. Then I put my finger on my forehead, the domed part of which is supposed to encompass my mind, that is, my intelligence, and make the sign for 'yes'. Then I make the same sign for 'yes' by putting my finger on that part which is usually considered to be the seat of what we call our heart, in the spiritual sense, i.e. our ability to love (…). Subsequently, I make the same sign for 'yes' on my mouth, moving my lips. Finally, I put my hand over my eyes, and show, while making the sign for 'no' at the same time, that I do not see anything. Now I only have to make the sign for 'present tense', and one writes 'I believe'; (…).* (1776, Part I, pp. 80-81)

5 The *explication* in four parts is likewise almost identical to the earlier version (1784, p. 129).

6 In this context, I can only briefly point out that between these two publications of de L'Epée's, there is the one by the Deaf Pierre Desloges of 1779. Apart from postulating a category of *signes analytiques* (analytical signs) for the sign language of his Parisian Deaf community, he quotes the above-mentioned passage from Condillac's *Grammaire* about de L'Epée's *langage d'action* being characterized by analysis, roughly five years before de L'Epée did so (Desloges 1779/1985-1986, II p.12). Desloges says of the *signes analytiques* that they are *(…) those that have been made natural by analysis. These signs are meant to render those ideas which – having, strictly speaking, no natural sign – have been brought to expression in sign language through the means of analysis. It is mostly these signs, and those of the preceding class, which M. l'Abbé de L'Epée has subjected to methodical rules (…).* (1779/1985-1986, II p. 9)

The *specific meaning of each term (signification particulaire de chaque terme)* is understood as a synthesis of the components of the concept represented by the term (or of the 'object' in itself, but that is still another problem…). This specific meaning is broken down into its components and is made **visible**, in the truest sense of the word, to the Deaf pupils[7] by way of *natural signs, or those made natural by analysis (signes naturels, ou rendus naturels par l'analyse;* 1776, Part II, p. 38), so that they can learn the (French) word. In this respect, signs invented by de L'Epée himself constitute a relatively large share of the developing of the method as such (1776, Part II, pp. 45ff).

Ill. 1: *Abbé de L'Epée in his school*

Although *analyse* functions repeatedly as the central term for the treatment of the meanings of (French) words with *signes méthodiques*, it seems that de L'Epée wants to make some distinctions. While *analyse* means comparable things in Condillac and de L'Epée, de L'Epée obviously (but not consistently) separates *décomposition* from *analyse*, in contrast to Condillac. He makes the following distinction between *analyse* and *décomposition* as two of probably four ways of 'explaining' words:

---

7 *The most metaphysical ideas must be put, by way of signs, on the same level as those objects which can easily be portrayed visibly, and thus the meaning of the words which express them* (the metaphysical ideas) *enter the mind through the organ of the eye.* (de L'Epée 1776, Part I, p.181)

*We perform the **analysis** of a simplex whose meaning is complex, e.g. 'croire* (to believe), *adorer* (to adore)' *&c. (...). We **decompose** the words which contain one or more prepositions with a verb, such as 'emprisonner* (to imprison), *désemprisonner* (to release from prison)' *or nouns (...) with a verb, such as 'pétrifier* (to turn into stone) *(...)' or adverbs with a verb, like 'satisfaire* (to satisfy), *introduire* (to introduce)'. (1776, Part I, pp. 88-89; emphasis mine)

2.

One might ask whether Condillac and his philosophical system influenced de L'Epée's system. Previous answers to this question have been controversial (in so far as the intellectual background of de L'Epée's work has been treated at all). It seems difficult to find an answer even for the issue of analysis.

As a source of inspiration, the *Grammaire* published in 1775 is, of course, out of the question. It had, however, been finished, or in draft form, for many years prior to publication (see below) and might have circulated – surely of no small interest to de L'Epée in that it was a part of Condillac's *Cours d'étude* for the Prince of Parma. If there is any noteworthy influence from Condillac, it must in any case have started before de L'Epée's *Lettre II* of 1772, because analysis is a basic feature of de L'Epée's system even then.

However, de L'Epée was not at all dependent on Condillac for the idea of analyzing meanings. Instead of theoretical references, he himself points out the common procedure in everyday language for difficulties of comprehension (see above). There is a possibility that de L'Epée took over analytical traits from sign language. A further aspect is linked to de L'Epée's intention – which often remains unnoted – to sketch a universal language project in his work of 1776. One of the first universal language projects seems to have been put forward by George Dalgarno in 1661. It contains symbols for 'complex concepts', which are a combination of likewise symbolized 'simple notions'. To express a 'complex idea' like 'palace', one would have to combine the symbols for the following 'simple notions': 'house', 'king', 'belonging to' (Large 1985, pp. 31-32). Dalgarno is known to have had contact with Deaf people. In any case, this analysis is also similar to the one cited by Pierre Desloges for certain classes of signs used by the Deaf (see above).

Summing up, it may be said that the question of Condillac's influence on de L'Epée's sign system seems to be difficult to settle in detail. Despite obvious proximity, there are several reasons for not seeing Condillac as the one who was originally determining for the analysis aspect of the *signes méthodiques*.

3.

In view of the change I have sketched in Condillac's opinion of signs, one might ask as well whether de L'Epée had any influence on Condillac. There was, after all, no Paris School for the Deaf in 1746; it was founded between 1760 and 1770, the earliest published program of de L'Epée's demonstrations of Deaf education dates from 1771. It was in 1775 that Condillac published the *Grammaire* with the crucial change in the conception of the *langage d'action*.

It may be helpful in answering this question to go back to a version of the *Grammaire* already completed by 1768, which differs greatly from the one worked out, presumably, by 1774 and published in 1775.[8] A comparison of the two versions shows that the early *Grammaire* already features a conception of the *langage d'action* which differs crucially from the one presented in the *Essai* of 1746, and is already similar to the one published in 1775. The two *Grammaire* versions are, however, considerably different as well. In particular, the version which was worked out later has been expanded by important details; only here

---

8   The earlier version was not published until 1782; on the chronology of the different versions of the *Grammaire* cf. Ricken 1986.

do we find the distinction between a *langage d'action naturel* (natural language of action) and a *langage d'action artificiel* (artificial language of action). The differentiations which are implied in the early *Grammaire* version are thus made more explicit and conceptually settled. Furthermore, only the later version contains a second passage about the functional comparability of the *langage d'action* with spoken language, which provides the basis for the detailed reference to de L'Epée.

It seems likely, therefore, that Condillac came to advance and sharpen a change in his theoretical conception of the *langage d'action*, which had already begun to emerge earlier, thanks to his knowledge of the Paris School for the Deaf and the *signes méthodiques*. Even if the knowledge of the *signes méthodiques* was probably not the impetus for the basic change of conception, it has nevertheless obviously functioned as confirmation and stimulus for the theory of the *langage d'action*.

This connection (de L'Epée – Condillac – analysis) was highly influential on further positions taken at the Paris school with respect to Deaf people and signs.

IV Roch-Ambroise-Cucurron Sicard

1.

Sicard, de L'Epée's successor, is of the opinion that he has elaborated *a complete system, a theory whose principles are now invariable* (*un système complet, une théorie dont les principes sont aujourd'hui invariables;* 1799-1800, p. xxviij) from de L'Epée's beginnings; this he has achieved *enlightened by the beacon of an infallible metaphysics* (*éclairé du flambeau d'une métaphysique sûre;* 1799-1800, p. xxv), which he does not specify by name. In this view (which proves to be influenced by Condillac),[9] the deaf man[10] is a *child of nature* (*l'homme de la nature;* 1799-1800, p. xxvij), a creature that does not know the simplest of linguistic expressions for its first perceptions (1799-1800, pp. xxxiij, x).[11] This creature will learn *to become human* (*à devenir homme;* 1799-1800, p. 5): a creature of nature (similar to primitive humans) grows into a part of society.

For Sicard, the deaf are initially separated from their fellow men not by a fundamental difference – they have the same kind of *organisation* (physical structure) – but by a consequence of their deafness: the deaf person cannot hear, and consequently cannot acquire spoken language, nor communicate, nor learn to record perceptions with the help of signs, to elaborate reasoning and language successively (1808, vol. 1, p. vij). The question still hotly debated in the 18th century, whether the deaf could be educated at all, is thus without doubt to be answered positively for Sicard (1799-1800, pp. iff). The subject of his reflections is the 'uneducated' deaf person (1799-1800, pp. xiv-xv), whose education constitutes a kind of metaphysical experiment according to the editor (1799-1800, p. x).

9　I have already pointed out in the introduction that other influences must be taken into account as well if one wants to judge the method **as a whole**.

10　I take over the gender specific wording of most of the works considered, which seems to apply to the male pupil exclusively. – Ferdinand Neumann (1827, pp. 42-43) made the following observation in 1822, on the occasion of public exercises at the Paris School for the Deaf : *At 12 o'clock, about 15 to 20 boys were brought in by a teacher and took their seats on the estrade. They were followed by Abbé Salvan. Not one of the institution's female pupils appeared, and the audience had to be content with the assurance implied in one of the afore-mentioned oil paintings, which showed two deaf mute girls among Sicard's pupils, that girls were taught here as well. – It is remarkable with what cloister-like severity the female pupils are watched over here. However often I expressed my wish to Salvan to be told about the organization of the girls' house and the branches of activity introduced there, he always knew how to guide my attention to some other subject immediately and – I never reached my aim.*

11　In another context, however, Sicard emphasizes the fact, as de L'Epée had done before him, that the deaf pupil had signs at his disposal even when starting school (1808, vol. 1, pp.8-9).

Ill. 2: *Abbé Sicard with some Deaf pupils, and Jean Massieu*

Although Sicard therefore objects to a conception of the deaf as *machines* etc. (1799-1800, pp. ij-iij), he does not hesitate to describe the uneducated deaf person as *living automaton* (*automate vivant*), as *a kind of walking machine* (*une sorte de machine ambulante;* 1799-1800, pp. vj and ix respectively; cf. also p. 6), who must be denied almost any emotions other than mere object and self-related ones (1799-1800, p. 20). The uneducated deaf person also appears as *empty vessel* (*vase pur;* 1799-1800, p. xxj) or as *newly come to earth* (*nouveau venu sur la terre;* 1799-1800, p. 20) – true to the sensualist view that almost no ideas can exist before the development of reasoning by language development, and that until then the world cannot be understood. The teacher of the deaf is accordingly called upon to fill this void with whatever seems relevant to him (1799-1800, p. xxj), and the teaching of the deaf is portrayed as the meritorious act of creating a human being:

> *The entire course of their education must aim at turning them into human beings. It is not a matter of teaching a language but of animating a kind of clay, illuminating a mind, awakening a soul, helping an intellectual being to thought.* (1808, vol. 1, p. 16) (…) *Massieu became human, he began to be communicative … and he owed this dawn of good fortune to me!* (1799-1800, p. 12)

With special regard to his pupil Massieu, with whom he largely implemented this teaching concept (perhaps the only case), Sicard says, *that he had never seen other people than his parents, who had not even taken the trouble to convey purely physical ideas to him. (...) MASSIEU was a creature of the woods who knew only purely animal habits and was astonished and frightened by everything.* (1799-1800, pp. 4-5)

In contrast to this, Massieu gives the following account of his 'uneducated' self (i.e. until shortly before his 14th birthday):

I expressed my ideas with manual signs or gestures. The signs which I used then in order to express my ideas to my parents, and my brothers and sisters (his siblings were Deaf, like himself), *were very different from those of the educated deaf mutes. Strangers never understood us when we expressed our ideas to them through signs, but our neighbours did.* (Massieu cited in Sicard 1808, vol. 2, p. 634)

Before my education, when I was a child, I could neither write nor read. I wanted so much to read and write. (...) I asked my father for permission to go to school with tears in my eyes; (...) but my father refused the permission I asked him for, by making signs which gave me to understand that I could never learn anything because I was deaf mute. – At this, I cried out very loudly. (...) I ran from my father's house and went to the school, without telling my father: I presented myself to the teacher. He rejected me harshly and drove me out of the school. This made me cry very much, but it did not discourage me. I often thought of reading and writing; I was twelve years old then: I tried to form characters with a pen all by myself. (Massieu cited in Sicard 1808, vol. 2, pp. 634-635)

2.

If the ontogenesis of language and reasoning is, in the case of deaf people, seen as corresponding to the phylogenesis of humankind, the general plan of teaching is clearly evident. On no account can it be the same procedure as for hearing children in Sicard's opinion (1799-1800, pp. xvff). Instead, one must create conditions that enable and encourage the ontogenetic development of the deaf person, repeating the phylogenetic development of humankind, both of which are especially dependent on the mutual differentiation of language and reasoning.

Imitate nature, let them (the uneducated deaf persons) *travel through the tableau of all the ideas which can be within the reach of the most untrained mind, in the order of their generation. From the 'sensible' ideas, which are the first and perhaps the only effort of which the solitary human being, lacking all means of communication, is capable; up to the most abstract ideas, which are all pure creations of our mind: If you thus travel through all the links of the chain of thinking with the deaf mutes, you will see how the ideas must necessarily have preceded the invention of signs, and how the signs must in turn have served to enlarge the store of ideas by encouraging diverse combinations; (...).* (1808, vol. 1, p. 23)

This cannot be accomplished by offering something to the deaf person which is ahead of his state of development: the deaf person is unable to connect the same ideas with the respective words as someone who has grown up with spoken language (1799-1800, p. xix). It is not a matter of simply teaching him a language (i.e. of conveying fully differentiated concepts); but of *creating souls* ((des) *âmes à faire;* 1799-1800, p. xxxij).

To reach this aim, Sicard first of all wants to convey to his pupil that there exists such a relation as 'sign for'. First, he does this with the help of *analogie*, namely with drawings of the respective objects; the written versions of the corresponding French words are then introduced successively (not necessarily in their orthographically correct form; 1799-1800, p. 19) and thus, a sign relation without analogy is conveyed (1799-1800, pp. 6ff). This enables the construction of a *nomenclature*, and his pupil now wants *to name everything, to write everything* (*tout nommer, tout écrire;* 1799-1800, p. 20). In this process, a mutual exchange of linguistic signs takes place: the teacher's French written signs for the deaf person's gestural signs for the same object (1799-1800, p. 20 and repeatedly).

The expansion of the naming ability is carried out by the naming and the 'analyzing' of all visible objects in the immediate vicinity. Then, the teacher follows his pupil everywhere and even takes him on excursions, e.g. to the country (1799-1800, pp. 26ff).

These beginnings[12] are very strongly characterized by analysis and *décomposition*, the teacher's task being the creation of favourable conditions (1808, vol. 1, p. 9 and repeatedly). The pupil will find his own way to analysis out of curiosity (1799-1800, pp. 12-13), but he can also be guided by the teacher, who explains the basic principle, *that every part, like the whole, has a name which distinguishes it from another part* (*que chaque partie, comme le tout, a un nom qui la distingue d'une autre partie;* 1799-1800, p. 21), which results in a multitude of signs and differentiations of objects for the pupil. In this, the linguistic development is closely linked to the intellectual:

> *Massieu saw, in this instant, that there could be no being, no thing in nature which could not be analyzed in the way his body had just been analyzed. He saw so many names to be learned as parts could be contained in every object. Therefore, he paid more attention to finding out everything which might have a special function in any body; and this research, resulting from his curiosity, made him a better observer.* (1799-1800, p. 25)

The analytic-synthetic principle of decomposing a whole into parts and of recomposing these parts into a whole, is demonstrated graphically as well: *(...) all these parts form particular 'wholes', all these 'wholes' form a general whole which is embraced by a great bracket (...)* (1799-1800, p. 24).

3.

Does the uneducated deaf person possess language according to Sicard ? It is not easy to answer this question, since Sicard gives contradictory statements. For Sicard, any language has two essential ingredients: the *list of words which form the dictionary* (of the language); *and the relative value of the words which constitutes the language's phrasing and syntax* ((la) *nomenclature des mots qui en forment le dictionnaire; et la valeur relative des mots, ce qui constitue la phrase et la syntaxe de la langue;* 1799-1800, p. xxxvj). A language with *nomenclature* only does not possess the *liaison* that is important for intellectual development. It may be that this is the view which Sicard holds of uneducated deaf persons and their *langage d'action: beings who have nothing but manual signs for the manifestation of their ideas* (*des êtres qui, pour la manifestation de leurs idées, n'ont que des signes manuels;* 1799-1800, p. 1). There are other statements, however, which deny **any** command of linguistic signs for the deaf: *not a single sign for recording and combining his ideas* (*aucun signe pour fixer ses idées et pour les combiner;* 1799-1800, p. ix). The above-mentioned conception of the uneducated deaf person as automaton is based on this. For his theoretical system, on the other hand, Sicard needs the assumption that the deaf person possesses a few linguistic signs at least: else, communication between teacher and pupil, and thus the deaf person's ascension to *'speaking' humans' dignity* (*dignité des hommes 'parlans';* 1799-1800, p. 26) would not be possible.

Corresponding to his view of the deaf person as similar to primitive man, Sicard rates sign language as the means of communication suited to the primitive stage of development. This *langage d'action* is seen as natural (*langue de la nature,* 1799-1800, p. lj), because its signs possess *a real value* (*une valeur réelle*), whereas the words of spoken language have a value *by convention* (*par convention;* 1799-1800, p. lij). The *langage*

---

12 On the further development, see 1799-1800, pp. 36ff.

d'action is a sort of pantomime, of an imitative character, which might render it suitable as a universal language (1799-1800, pp. xlvij-xlviij). The use of such signs in teaching is absolutely necessary, because only the 'natural' signs available to both teacher and pupil enable them to establish communication. Therefore, the teacher must learn his pupil's signs just as the pupil learns the words. Apparently the teacher/Sicard even gives some explanations in signs (invented, but preferably learned and taken over from the deaf pupil; 1799-1800, pp. 15-16, 18 and repeatedly). The use of gestural signs is not motivated sociopsychologically, but results from the assumption that progress can only be made possible by signs suited to the deaf pupil's stage of development. This is why the teacher should not invent signs but rather leave this to his pupil (1799-1800, pp. xlvij, 21 and repeatedly).

If the *langage d'action* is seen as inferior to spoken language here, Sicard emphasizes elsewhere that this language is, on the contrary, superior to spoken language in some ways (*more true, more rich, more faithfully imitating* ; *plus vraie, plus riche, plus fidèlement imitative;* 1799-1800, p. liij – this is not a mainly aesthetic argument, but motivated by epistemology). Sicard even takes over Condillac's view of 1775, that the *langage d'action* could be developed to such a degree that it could equal spoken language in functionality, or even surpass it, in all language-related areas (1799-1800, pp. xlixff). This was not a reality, however, because the deaf grew up scattered and isolated instead of forming a *people* (*peuple;* 1799-1800, pp. xxiij, xxiv), as he put forward.

It is clear from what has been said that Sicard was extremely committed theoretically, both with regard to the deaf pupil's person and to sign language. Signs are here located within a theoretical system which could accommodate the consideration of a sign language, but which is not used in such a manner by Sicard. Instead, the *langage d'action* seems to be something conducive to the transition to a 'proper human being', and expendable after having fulfilled this function. Sicard never took it seriously as a linguistic medium in itself anyway: he refrains, with remarkable consistency, from anything of the kind, although the Parisian Deaf community might have taught him otherwise, and he depicts the deaf individual as an isolated being in a hearing environment, who lacks any potential for communal development and conventionalization of his sign language.

4.

The *Théorie de signes* of 1808 goes into more detail about the gestures to be used in the initial phases of teaching.

The acquisition of (French) spoken language is the aim,[13] and it is only to this end that gestures are employed at all. According to the sensualist theory which is taken as basis, the French used at the time is the result of centuries of development of language and reasoning. The 'primitive' deaf pupil, therefore, must be guided there on a roundabout way suited to his abilities: one must start with single symbols for 'isolated ideas', for which gestural signs are to be used. The teaching then goes on to more and more complex, 'composed' ideas and their symbols.

> *Every word is therefore enacted, so to speak, and it will be seen that I always designate as many persons as are needed for showing its use, instead of defining the word. The explanation of any word that expresses an intellectual or moral idea is thus rendered in a pantomime or in 'mimic scenes', which define the meaning and use of the word by demonstrating its employment.* (1808, vol. 1, p. lvj)
>
> *These little scenes, in which the pantomime of several actors always serves so well to explain each of the words, are carefully enacted with the aim both of allowing the pupil to grasp an unknown word and of displaying its meaning.* (1808, vol. 1, p. lvij)

---

13 In this article, I use the term of 'spoken language' to refer to non-signed natural languages, irrespective of whether they are taught as speech or in writing.

As Sicard saw it, without the temporary use of this phylo- and ontogenetically advisable aid for the acquisition of spoken language and the meanings put down therein, the as yet uneducated deaf pupils would be hopelessly overtaxed:

> *(...) they are absolute savages still! One would present them incessantly with words of a language which has been improved continuously by the experience of many centuries, without taking into consideration that, for them, the world is still in its cradle.* (1808, vol. 1, pp. 15-16)

This aspect of the use of signs is so important to Sicard that he adds a subtitle to later editions of his *Théorie des signes* (1814 and 1823): *wherein the meaning of words, instead of being defined, is put into action (où le sens des mots, au lieu d'être défini, est mis en action).*

The teacher, from his supposedly advanced stage of development, has the following duties:
– to analyse all words (*décomposition*),
– to make out 'simple' words for 'simple' ideas; these are to be used as a starting point in teaching,
– to guide the pupil from 'simple' ideas and symbols (i.e. words and signs) by way of *composition* towards more and more 'complex' ideas and symbols. In this, he has to make sure that his pupil, and not the teacher himself, invents sign sequences.

In order to record this progression in instruction and make it available to others, Sicard offers a two-volume dictionary in 1808, which contains, under French headwords, representations of sign sequences which are meant to fit the French words' *décomposition*. This *Théorie des signes* is arranged as follows:

> *(...) all parts that make up his being, his needs, everything that surrounds him, his house, his furniture, his fields, types of rocks, plants, animals, his town and all ranks of society, customs, manners, government, religion, the church and its ministers, finally, everything that is visible and can be distinguished by functions and the manner of clothing indicating this, all physical qualities of man, his diseases, his virtues, his faults, his acts – all this forms the FIRST VOLUME. All human intellectual or moral acts, together with the signs of the grammatical part, form the SECOND VOLUME.* (1808, vol. 1, pp. ix-x)

The descriptions of individual sign sequences given by Sicard vary in character and length. Most of the sequences are subdivided into three parts; but there can be one or five just as well. In some cases, the last remark serves to identify the part of speech of the French word (as in de L'Epée). Sicard originally planned to leave out the signs considered as natural, but short allusions to them can be found – e.g., that one has to perform pointing gestures in order to name the parts of the body with which the teaching is supposed to begin (1808, vol. 1, p. 26). In contrast to this, the French word *pain* (bread) is to be analyzed and signed as follows:

> *The sign for BREAD consists of first enacting the way of making it, for which one pretends to stir flour into water as the bakers do; one performs the action of putting the dough, which one has seemingly formed like a loaf of bread, onto the shovel; one imitates the person who puts it into the oven; one pretends to take the bread out again, to cut it up and nourish oneself with it. (...) The signs for the different parts of the bread are contributed by the deaf mutes themselves, on simply inspecting every part, like the 'crusts', one on top, one below, which the deaf mute compares to the skin that covers the bones of his hand.* (1808, vol. 1, pp. 27-28)

Or consider the *expression d'admiration*:

> *AH! OH! 1. Enact a person who stands in front of the COLONNADE OF THE LOUVRE, or the APOLLON BELVEDERE, or the painting of the TRANSFIGURATION, by RAPHAEL or*

the one of the CORONATION, by Monsieur DAVID, member of the Institut de France; or any other masterpiece. 2. Represent this person as standing, with the head not moving, the mouth half-opened, as he contemplates these wonderful works of architecture, sculpture or painting for a long time, without letting himself be disturbed. 3. Sign for interjection. (1808, vol. 2, p. 619)

The use of supposedly primitive signs indeed allows the visual decomposition of meaning contained in words, acted out by several persons instead of being uttered by one!

There are several cases of sign sequences where the execution of single numbered sections calls for plenty of signs instead of a single one – which, strictly speaking, runs counter to the idea of *décomposition*, but can still be united with the thesis that *scènes mimiques* may provide the deaf pupil with an understanding of the meaning of words.

Sicard apparently takes this through to the sign language of the Deaf, and moves away from wholly theoretically motivated sign sequences although he points out that the sign sequences described by him are not those usually used by the Deaf themselves:

(…) with the deaf mutes especially, very many ellipses are customary, and the manner of language, which in the beginning is very long, is shortened by and by to a smaller number of signs. (1808, vol. 1, p. lvij)

Clearly, he thinks that the sign sequences of his dictionary, invented by the deaf pupils (as he repeatedly emphasizes), are compatible with a sign language used by the Deaf because the full sequences are only necessary for a first understanding; after the sign formation (connecting a sign sequence, the French word and the analyzed meaning), the extensive sign may be reduced to a *sign of recall* (*signe de rappel*): *(…) the principal action, or two or three actions, are sufficient for serving as sign of recall ((…) il suffira de l'action principale, ou de deux, ou de trois actions, pour servir de signe de rappel;* 1808, vol. 1, pp. 30-31).

He talks of his *desire to make the language of the mutes uniform* (*désir de rendre uniforme le langage des Muets;* 1808, vol. 1, p. 7), and says that his work is a dictionary *which is to record and fix the language of this new people* (*qui doit fixer la langue de ce nouveau peuple;* 1808 , vol. 1, dedication; cf. also p. xl). This raises the question, however, whether these two aspects (dictionary for the sign language of the Deaf – sensualistically dominated theory of language and reasoning) are easily compatible. We may conclude that they are not. Sicard's original intention was to facilitate the **teacher's** work with his dictionary. Sensualistically speaking, such a dictionary is wrong for the pupil, since Sicard emphasizes repeatedly that every pupil, in his individual development, must find out the relation of meaning and sign sequence for himself (*work up to the pupils' finding it out for themselves, so to speak; Travailler à les faire imaginer, en quelque sorte, à ses élèves;* 1808, vol. 1, p. 3). A sign language dictionary in the proper sense requires cooperation with the Deaf concerned, as well as acceptance and usage of the existing sign language, irrespective of theoretical concepts. Neither condition is met in Sicard's case, if one considers the Parisian Deaf community of his time. From Sicard's own viewpoint, however, which sees the Deaf as primitive humans, the *peuple* of the Deaf might be a group characterized by its supposed 'primitivity', with a language to match. To write a dictionary for this language would then represent the 'metaphysical' act of working out the inventory of symbols of humankind's first language; i.e. the Deaf and their sign languages would simply be used for the philosophical exertions of hearing people. Such an interpretation of the classification as dictionary is not least supported by Sicard's statement in a letter to Henri Guyot, a Dutch instructor of Deaf children, dated 1792:

(…) this new language (which he was working out) *is no translation of any other language. It is a primitive language of which, on the contrary, the others are translations.*

It is not surprising, therefore, that the Deaf Berthier's judgement on Sicard's signs is exceedingly negative: the *Théorie des signes* was *a long sequence of clumsy paraphrases, which are capable of confusing and deterring even the strongest will* (Berthier 1836, p. 12). Bébian, on the other hand, had the merit of having *freed the teaching from this learned obscurity, from these pretentious subtleties, with which a superficial philosophy had undertaken to envelop it* (Berthier 1836, p. 14).

V Roch-Ambroise Auguste Bébian

1.

Bébian's starting point differs from Condillac's or Sicard's in a crucial way. He knows the sign language of the Deaf:

> *The ties of friendship I had formed to some of your pupils, and particularly to L. Clerc, (…) had made me familiar with the language of gestures which no one teaches them. (…) I was astonished at the resources of this language; (…).* (1817, dedication to Sicard)

He devotes himself to the problem of the catastrophic educational conditions of the majority of the Deaf – even that small group who do receive a school education:

> *(…) among twenty pupils who leave the institution every year, there is hardly one who has been sufficiently instructed to use a dictionary. Their teacher is the only dictionary they have.* (1825, p. 37)

The allusion to the teacher as dictionary is aimed at methods of controlling the development of the Deaf pupils' language and reasoning in the manner of Sicard (and of de L'Epée who considered himself to be a *living dictionary* for his pupils (*dictionnaire vivant;* de L'Epée 1784, p. 146)). Bébian realizes that the Deaf pupils must be put into a position of being able to learn on their own in order to improve their situation – for him, that implies a central role of their sign language, the *langage d'action*, in the classroom.

2.

The *langage d'action* is not specific to the Deaf alone for Bébian. He thinks, with Condillac, that every animal species, including human beings, has its own specific *langage d'action* (1817, pp. 82ff). Humankind's *langage d'action* preceded spoken language in phylogenesis (1817, p. 97); it is the same for all humans irrespective of time and place and may be observed in a great variety of situations:

> *There is a language which exists everywhere and at all times, which is of the same type everywhere, because it is an expression of our physical structure which does not change; a language which has preceded all other languages and has largely determined their foundation; which, in its general forms, is equally understood in the Huron's hut and the Arab's tent; under a thatched roof as under a gilt panelled ceiling. Our forefathers spoke it, and it will be understood by our last descendants. – Due to this language, man is never stranger to man anywhere. (…) Through this language a traveller who has lost his way far from home knows how to ask for shelter to rest his head, for food to regain his strength. (…) – admirable result of the union of body and soul, spirit and matter: everything that goes on within us is reflected in our facial expression and gestures. – Through this double door open to our ideas, a language as rich as it is expressive, mimicry, emerges. It is the language of those that have none; it is the language of the deaf mutes, or rather, it is the proper language of the human species.* (1825, pp. 1-2)

The fact that this language is the same for all people is linked to the 'naturalness' of the signs:

The signs which have a direct and natural connection to the ideas and recall these out of themselves, without having been conventionalized first, may be called 'natural signs' (...). – If we take this expression in its strictest sense, we can give the name 'natural sign' only to those signs which not only immediately recall the idea but are furthermore inspired by nature alone, and are produced without study and without artifice. (1817, pp. 1-2)

Thus, the *langage d'action* can be said to function as a universal language among the Deaf, too:

(...) they all understand each other (...). Clerc and Massieu (...) have often been called by the authorities to serve as interpreters for the deaf mute vagabonds arrested in the streets of Paris. Clerc was like another guardian angel to all his uninstructed fellows: it was him they turned to to ask for work or help. (1817, p. 114)

Nevertheless, Bébian points out differences between various *langages d'action*. In the case of hearing people, their *langage d'action* is due, for example, to the fact that they are not used to expressing their ideas without words because they have become accustomed to spoken language (1817, p. 117). The *langage d'action* in the case of the Deaf is, by the same token, the result of particular conditions, i.e., a skill in gestural communication brought about by deafness (1825, p. 2). Moreover, it is hardly possible to express every imaginable idea in a simple, universally intelligible sign (1827, p.118). 'Natural signs' with the same referent may further differ from each other because they give linguistic representations for different aspects of a given object (1817, pp. 66ff). A last important aspect is that the *langage d'action* of the Deaf changes under the influence of spoken language – to its disadvantage, and resulting in an impediment to easy communication (1817, pp. 27, 47-48).

In spite of the references to a universal *langage d'action*, Bébian already starts to designate differences; this is a prerequisite for the later view of the Deaf as linguistic minority.

3.

What role is the *langage d'action* supposed to play in the education of the Deaf?

In order to answer this question, Bébian goes back to some of Condillac's views about the relation between language and reasoning.

The *langage d'action*, in the form observed, is an expression of the mental development of the Deaf: *one can easily imagine that one will find many traces of their ignorance and inexperience (on pense bien que l'on doit y trouver les traces fréquentes de leur ignorance et de leur inexpérience;* 1825, p. 5). This should not, however, lead to the conventional conclusion that one must switch over to spoken language; on the contrary, it is necessary to develop the *langage d'action* itself:

Admittedly, the perfection of the linguistic signs has a great influence on the formation of ideas, and even on the development of intelligence: and one does not assume too much about them when one says that a well-ordered system of signs, based on nature and the analogy of ideas, cuts down to half the teacher's task and the pupil's work. One cannot accord too much attention to this so important part of the art of instructing the deaf mutes, therefore. (1825, p. 5)

For the Deaf individual, the development of language and reasoning occurs in and with the help of his language, the *langage d'action;* and it is only on this basis that the pupil can be made to understand the 'analyses' effected by the spoken languages:

The thought necessarily precedes any sign that is meant to express it in the mind; the word does not have any connection to the idea in and of itself, it cannot produce the idea, nor render it, it rather serves to recall it, after a previous conventionalization has linked it to this already well-grasped idea. In order to establish this convention with the deaf mutes one has to be able to talk with them; before one wants to teach them to express an idea through a word, one has to make sure that they have control of this idea in a very clear and precise manner; and if they do not possess it as yet, one must develop it in their minds. We cannot penetrate their minds and see what goes on there; but they can let us know, and they do this with an admirable facility, with the help of signs which they have invented themselves, and which we understand easily, since they are taken from the very nature of the idea. These signs which come from the pupils are carefully collected by the teacher, and serve to recall the idea. From that point, as from a mutual starting point, the teacher will proceed and develop new ideas; these will call forth new signs in turn, which one only has to replace then with the corresponding words in the language which is to be taught to them. (1817, pp. 23-24; cf. also 1825, pp. 26ff)

The acquisition of French is one of the goals, but the realization of this aim is only possible by way of the *langage d'action*. The *langage d'action*'s signs themselves must be differentiated through *décomposition*, so that in the end, the knowledge recorded in signs only has to be **translated** into French words. The actual acquisition of knowledge occurs in sign language. This process of developing suitable signs is most important and not at all easy to accomplish:

If this sign is right, if it is a faithful expression of the idea, it will be adopted in all the schools. If it is inexact, it will provoke a discussion, which may enlighten the minds and lead to a correction. The language will grow more perfect, will settle itself, it will be the same in all the schools; and these improvements, going beyond our borders, will reestablish the uniformity of natural language for the deaf mutes, in the midst of the diversity of languages which divides the peoples of the world. (1825, pp. 6-7)

4.

How can this be achieved?

By way of the already familiar device of *décomposition*, for one thing. Bébian explicitly relinquishes the spoken language orientation here: he does not aim at duplication of analyses dubiously recorded in spoken language through *scènes mimiques* or similar things (as in Sicard), but rather at something that aspires to Condillac's ideal of a 'perfect language': *All signs will be the result of analytical operations, and will recall an equal number of clear and precise ideas (Tous les signes seront le produit d'opérations analytiques, et rappelleront autant d'idées claires et précises;* Bébian 1817, p. 68).

Bébian wants to employ a process that is similar to those in which the technical terms of natural sciences are created (1817, pp. 68-69) – in this, he evidently has Condillac's conception of an ideal language in view. To Condillac, not just any spoken language is a perfect language, even if it is true that *each language is an analytical method, and each analytical method is a language (toute langue est une méthode analytique, et toute méthode analytique est une langue;* Condillac 1798/1981, p. 1). The degree of perfection depends on the precision of the analyses or the obtrusiveness of the influence of *l'usage;* as an example of a perfect language, Condillac names algebra (1798/1981, pp. 1ff). Not wanting to duplicate the development of spoken language, Bébian does not, for example, dictate the differentiation of parts of speech demonstrated phylogenetically by Condillac for spoken language (Bébian says repeatedly that these differentiations probably do not exist in the *langage d'action*). Bébian accepts the differences and follows the pattern worked out by Condillac for the construction of any 'perfect language'. Doubtless, this implies the danger of patronizing the language users, as does the belief in progress with respect to the 'modern sciences' (Bébian 1817, p. 63 and repeatedly).[14] But this is done out of an attitude

---

14 On the problematic nature of the ideal of science, in the context of the discussion about the Deaf, as early as Diderot, see Fischer 1990.

that patronizes all those who do not possess a certain knowledge, not the Deaf specifically.

Bébian apparently wants to lessen the massive modifications of the *langage d'action* which must be expected in attempting to construct a 'perfect' language, by emphasizing that the *langage d'action*, as it stands, is a serious object of study in itself. Thus, he wants to take the signs used by the Deaf *for guides* (*pour guides*) in his kind of language planning project of sign formation, instead of signs which are strictly bound to scientific methods (1817, p. 70). Bébian also praises the *langage d'action* in its existing form as an interesting research subject in its entirety (1825, p. 4), i.e. including, for example, syntax, which had been completely neglected until then. And finally, his writing system for the *langage d'action* is based on the signs used among the Deaf.

In modern terms, the *langage d'action* seems to be applied as both medium and subject in Bébian's conception. The latter occurs, for example, when the pupils start to learn how to write their *langages d'action*. Bébian emphasizes the importance of group instruction in sign language rather than spoken language:

> *The invaluable advantage which the reunion of the deaf mutes offers, and which cannot be connected to their instruction by spoken language, is the enrichment of everyone with the ideas of all the others; it is the awakening of their intelligence by stimulating their attention; it is the compulsion to give a clear and precise form to all their ideas, which enables them to be transmitted by gestures.* (1817, p. 16)

The *langage d'action* plays an important part because it enables the Deaf pupil to work independently: it improves and deepens the process of learning (1825, pp. 36-37 and repeatedly). The acquisition of spoken language is promoted as well, because the pupil can, for example, write down a sign next to a word, and repetition, revision, etc. are made possible for the first time in this way: *(...) he could, without the risk of errors, reread and study the teacher's lesson, and even go beyond it. ((...) il pourrait, sans risque de se tromper, revoir, étudier la leçon du maître, et même la devancer;* 1825, p. 37). Ideally, the pupil could be provided with a dictionary in two languages, based on *décomposition* (1817, pp. 42-43).

5.

In order to enable the pupil to work in this fashion and to allow the sign language research as outlined, it must be possible to record the language in writing. Bébian proposes a suitable sign writing system: his 'Mimographie', which probably represents the first sign language notation (even if it was not the first sign notation). The writing system is based on the signs used by the Deaf; it is *based entirely on facts (tout entier appuyé sur des faits;* 1825, p. 10), and not on signs invented in the spirit of perfecting the language (i.e, it is free from *speculations which are always contestable* (*spéculations toujours contestables;* 1825, p. 10)). Furthermore, it is kept so simple that it does not overtax even the youngest pupils (1825, pp. 8-9).

Apart from these practical advantages, this writing system is also meant to further intellectual development by way of making the user analyze the **signs** instead of the **words**, as usual. The 'Mimographie' is planned in such a way that *(...) it clearly shows, without destroying the unity of the sign, all the elements which must be noticed if one wants to apply the words that are to translate them* (1825, p. 29).

Background to these reflections is the observation that often more than one word must be used to represent a sign, i.e., that there are different kinds and degrees of 'analysis' in sign and spoken language. This must be difficult to grasp for the pupils, however, until they realize, by 'analyzing' their signs through writing them, that the comprehensive single gesture also contains the different parts of the whole. The 'Mimographie' amounts to breaking down the signs into their various ingredients: *If we add the accent 'diminutive' to the sign expressing an eye that is closing, we have written the sign for winking (...);* (1825, p. 22).

447

In this way, intellectual and linguistic development are combined for the pupils in their natural language; they can advance their intellectual and linguistic development in and with this language, and learn something about the structure of this *langage d'action* at the same time. I must pass over the question here, how far the analysis through 'Mimographie' already leads away from an analysis in the sensualist sense to one in a structural and linguistic sense. The 'Mimographie' seems to contain the beginnings of a classification that amounts to an analysis of linguistic duality of patterning (double articulation). Bébian can thus be said to represent not only the start of acknowledgement of the sign languages of the Deaf for the purposes of teaching, but also, despite all contact with the language - reasoning - discussion of the 18th century, the start of an exploration of sign language as a language as such. Bébian's departure from earlier artificial sign systems is born out by a statement of Berthier's:

> (…) *since the entrance of M.Bébian, the methodical signs, which bowed to the forms of our conventional languages* (spoken languages), *have been banished from the Royal Institution.* (1836, p. 16)

Ill. 3: *Untitled engraving by F. Berthier*

It is surely justified to see a central force for the emergence of the Deaf movement(s) in 19th century France in Bébian's work. In 1839, for example, it was possible for Berthier to sign his lecture at the congress of the Institut Historique, and to have the contributions to the ensuing discussion translated for him:

During the entire discussion, in the midst of all those speeches, (...) M. Eugène de Mon-
glave constantly transmitted in signs everything which was said on the rostrum to M.
Ferdinand Berthier, who was sitting near him at the desk. (Congrès 1840, p. 134)

Referring to the philosopher Laromiguière, who was influenced by Condillac, Berthier
comes full circle back to Condillac's view of the *langage d'action*: it *might be able to*
receive and render all the feelings in the human heart and all thoughts in his mind, just
like a spoken language (Laromiguière cited in *Congrès* 1840, p. 140). In 1839, however,
64 years after Condillac's original hypothesis, it is stated at the congress that such a promising language is **in actuality** observable in *countless deaf mutes* (*une foule de sourds-*
muets; Laromiguière cited in *Congrès* 1840, p. 140).

VI Questions

In this article, I have tried to work out some aspects of an early phase in the debate about the
sign languages of the Deaf.[15] Among the questions which might ensue are the following:

– How was the discussion about sign language carried out by the Deaf themselves, e.g. in
  the Deaf movement which emerged at the Paris School in the first third of the 19th century? Which conceptions did the Deaf use in order to promote their sign language?
– The works I have presented are dominated by the view that the sign language of the
  Deaf has characteristics which make it suitable as a universal language, among other
  things. Beginning when, with what arguments and by whom is the contrasting view put
  forward, namely that the sign languages of the Deaf are specific and must be separated
  from other gestural forms of communication as well as spoken language? Which factors
  in society, science, and politics favour this development?
– Closely linked to this complex is the question, when was the argument that the Deaf are
  a linguistic minority explicitly developed, in relation to the above mentioned language
  specificity and with appropriate language and education policies.

In closing, I would like to go into one of the results of this study in particular, albeit briefly.
The four authors considered share theoretical references, and yet they basically relate differently to the sign language of the Deaf. This can surely be explained in part by the influence of
the prevailing zeitgeist, which can be felt, even in unconventional positions, as a unifying
factor in some form or other. The extensive development of the Deaf community in and
around the Paris School for the Deaf doubtlessly also weighs heavily. Beyond that, the differences which can be demonstrated between Bébian and Sicard, despite their partly identical
theoretical foundations, point towards conflicting interests which have been shown to be a
general problem of scientific activity by feminist and ecological criticism of science or by sociology of science: the way in which a particular theory is shaped and taken up, and to what
aims it is employed in social confrontations, is largely dependent on factors that have little to
do with the respective theory, but a lot to do with the scientists' personalities, their being
enmeshed in social contexts, etc. Non-theoretical motivations for scientific activity are not
made explicit generally, and rarely discussed; nevertheless, these often are the decisive
motivations for the defending of a certain point of view, rather than theoretical aspects in the

15 In describing Condillac's influence on the faculty of the Paris School for the Deaf, I have not differentiated, in the scope of this article, between direct influence through reception of Condillac's works and secondary influence through knowledge of works and personalities that might
be termed critically supportive of Condillac. Although we know of several connections of this
kind (some conflict-ridden, some beneficial), especially to so-called Ideologists, their importance and relation to the school's development has not yet been sufficiently explored.

proper sense. The difference between the positions taken up by Sicard and Bébian may perhaps be seen as an historical example of this. We can see in every modern attempt at interpretation of history how difficult it is to shed light on such latent constellations of interests, and how firmly most of us remain in well-tried frames of argument – this also applies to me as author of this article, and perhaps to you, dear reader, when you discuss language...?

(Trixi Flügel cooperated in the English translation)

Appendix
The original quotations:

p. 431

(...) des conditions qu'il doit réunir, il n'en est aucune qui importe plus à cette espèce de sacerdoce qu'une parfaite connaissance et une longue pratique du langage d'action. (Berthier 1840, p. 61)

(...) leur langage d'action, si abondant et si expressif, est à ce point ignoré des parlants, qu'à peine un sourd-muet rencontre-t-il dans sa propre famille quelqu'un qui puisse converser avec lui. (Grosselin/Pélissier 1858, prospectus)

p. 433

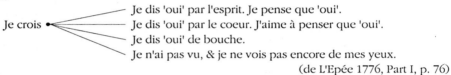

Je crois
— Je dis 'oui' par l'esprit. Je pense que 'oui'.
— Je dis 'oui' par le coeur. J'aime à penser que 'oui'.
— Je dis 'oui' de bouche.
— Je n'ai pas vu, & je ne vois pas encore de mes yeux.

(de L'Epée 1776, Part I, p. 76)

p. 434

(...) il n'est point de chose qui ne puisse être signifiée par un ou plusieurs mots. (...) Lorsqu'on les dit, & qu'ils ne sont pas entendus, c'est-à-dire, compris, on les explique de vive voix par d'autres mots (...). Avec les Sourds & Muets, c'est précisément la même opération qui se fait par écrit, jusqu'à ce qu'on soit parvenu à des mots qui ont été cent & cent fois compris par signes (...). (de L'Epée 1776, Part I, pp. 77-78)

(...) lorsque l'idée qu'un verbe rappelle, ne présente à notre esprit aucun signe qui lui soit propre, & qui puisse sur le champ la rendre sensible, nous recourons à l'analyse; & par son moyen, nous rentrons dans l'ordre des signes naturels. (de L'Epée 1776, Part II, p. 36)

p. 434 (footnote 4)

(...) je fais d'abord le signe de la première personne du singulier en me montrant moi-même avec l'index de ma main droite, dont le bout est tourné vers ma poitrine. Je mets ensuite mon doigt sur mon front, dont la partie concave est censée renfermer mon esprit, c'est-à-dire, ma faculté de penser, & je fais le signe de 'oui'. Après cela je fais le même signe de 'oui' en mettant mon doigt sur la partie de moi-même, qu'on regarde ordinairement comme le siège de ce que nous appellons notre coeur dans l'ordre spirituel, c'est-à-dire, de notre faculté d'aimer (...). Je fais ensuite le même signe de 'oui' sur ma bouche en remuant mes lèvres. Enfin je mets ma main sur mes yeux; & en faisant le geste de 'non', je montre que je ne vois pas. Il ne me reste plus que le signe du présent à faire, & on écrit 'je crois'; (...). (de L'Epée 1776, Part I, pp. 80-81)

p. 434 (footnote 6)

(...) ceux qui sont rendus naturèls par l'analyse. Ces signes sont destinés à représenter des idées qui n'ayant point, à proprement parler, de signe naturèl, sont ramenés à l'expression du langage des signes par le moyen de l'analyse. Ce sont ces signes surtout, & ceux de la classe précédante que M. l'Abbé de l'Epée a assujetis à des règles méthodiques (...). (Desloges 1789/1985-1986 II, p. 9)

p. 435 (footnote 7)

Il faut que les idées les plus métaphysiques (…) viennent s'enchaîner sous la dépendance des signes dans la classe des objets qu'il est très-possible de peindre à la vue, en faisant entrer dans l'esprit par l'organe des yeux la signification des mots qui les expriment. (de L'Epée 1776, Part I, p. 181)

p. 436

Nous faisons l'analyse d'un mot simple dont la signification est composée, comme 'croire, adorer' &c. (…) Nous décomposons les mots qui renferment une ou plusieurs prépositions avec un verbe, comme 'emprisonner, désemprisonner' ou des noms (…) avec un verbe, tels que 'pétrifier (…)' ou des adverbes avec un verbe, comme 'satisfaire, introduire'. (de L'Epée 1776, Part I, pp. 88-89)

p. 437 (footnote 10)

Um 12 Uhr wurden etwa 15 bis 20 Knaben von einem Lehrer hereingeführt und nahmen auf der Estrade Platz, ihnen folgte Abbé Salvan. Von den weiblichen Zöglingen der Anstalt kam keine einzige zum Vorschein und das Publikum mußte sich mit der aus einem der vorbezeichneten Ölgemälde, auf welchem auch 2 taubstumme Mädchen unter Sicards Schülern abgebildet waren, hervorgehenden Zusicherung, dass hier auch Mädchen unterrichtet würden, begnügen. – Es ist auffallend, mit welcher klösterlichen Strenge hier die weiblichen Zöglinge gehütet werden. So oft ich auch Salvan meinen Wunsch zu erkennen gab, von der Einrichtung des Mädchenhauses und den dort eingeführten Beschäftigungszweigen unterrichtet zu seyn, so wusste er meine Aufmerksamkeit immer augenblicklich auf einen andern Gegenstand zu lenken und – ich kam nie zum Ziele. (Neumann 1827, pp. 42-43)

p. 438

Tout le cours de leur instruction doit avoir pour objet d'en faire des hommes. Il ne s'agit pas d'enseigner une langue; c'est une sorte d'argile à animer, une intelligence à éclairer, une âme à réveiller, un être intellectuel à faire penser. (Sicard 1808, vol. 1, p. 16)

(…) Massieu alloit devenir homme; il commençoit à être communicatif … et il me devoit cette aurore de bonheur! (Sicard 1799-1800, p. 12)

p. 439

(…) qu'il n'avoit jamais vu d'autres individus que ses parens, qui même n'avoient pas pris la peine de lui communiquer des idées purement physiques. (…) MASSIEU étoit l'homme des bois, ne connoissant encore que des habitudes purement animales, s'étonnant et s'effrayant de tout. (Sicard 1799-1800, pp. 4-5)

J'exprimois mes idées par les signes manuels ou le geste. Les signes dont je me servois alors, pour exprimer mes idées à mes parens, et à mes frères et soeurs, étoient bien différens de ceux des Sourds-Muets instruits. Les étrangers ne nous comprenoient jamais quand nous leur exprimions, par signes, nos idées; mais les voisins nous comprenoient. (Massieu cited in Sicard 1808, vol. 2, p. 634)

Avant mon éducation, lorsque j'étois un enfant, je ne savois ni écrire ni lire; je désirois écrire et lire. (…) Je demandois à mon père, les larmes aux yeux, la permission d'aller à l'école; (…) mais mon père me refusoit la permission que je lui demandois, en me faisant signe que je ne pourrois jamais rien apprendre, parce que j'étois sourd-muet. – Alors je criai très-haut. (…) je sortis de la maison paternelle, et j'allais à l'école, sans le dire à mon père: je me présentai au maître, (…). Il me refusa durement, et me chassa de l'école. Cela me fit beaucoup pleurer, mais ne me rébuta pas. Je pensois souvent à écrire et à lire; alors j'avois douze ans: j'essayois tout seul à former, avec une plume, des signes d'écriture. (Sicard 1808, vol. 2, pp. 634-635)

Imitez la nature, faites parcourir, dans l'ordre même de leur génération, le tableau de toutes les idées qui peuvent être du domaine de l'intelligence la moins exercée, depuis les idées 'sensibles', qui sont le premier, et peut-être le seul effort dont soit capable l'homme solitaire et privé de tout moyen de communication, jusqu'aux idées les plus abstraites, qui sont toutes de pures créations de notre esprit. En parcourant, avec le Sourd-Muet, tous les anneaux de la chaîne de la pensée, vous verrez comment les idées ont dû nécessairement précéder l'invention des signes, et comment les signes, à leur tour, ont dû servir à augmenter la provision des idées, en favorisant leurs diverses combinaisons; (…). (Sicard 1808, vol. 1, p. 23) p.440

Massieu vit, à l'instant, qu'il ne pouvoit y avoir dans la nature, ni Etre, ni Chose qui, comme son corps venoit de l'être, ne pût être décomposé. Il vit donc devant lui autant de noms à apprendre que chaque objet pouvoit renfermer de parties. Il en devint plus attentif à rechercher tout ce qui, dans chaque corps, avoit des fonctions particulières; et cette recherche, effet de sa curiosité, le rendit plus observateur. (Sicard 1799-1800, p. 25)

(...) toutes ces parties formant des 'touts' particuliers, tous ces 'touts' formant un tout général, renfermé dans une grande accolade (...). (Sicard 1799-1800, p. 24)

p. 441

Aussi chaque mot est-il mis en scène, en quelque sorte, et l'on verra qu'au lieu de le définir, je suppose toujours autant de personnes qu'il en faut pour en faire l'emploi. L'explication de chaque mot exprimant une idée intellectuelle ou morale, est donc donnée dans une pantomime, ou 'scène mimique', qui, en déterminant l'emploi, en fixe la signification et l'usage. (Sicard 1808, vol. 1, p. lvj)

C'est autant pour donner aux élèves l'intelligence d'un mot inconnu, que pour en exprimer la signification, que sont ménagées ces petites scènes où la pantomime de plusieurs acteurs a toujours si heureusement servi à l'explication de chacun de ces mots. (Sicard 1808, vol. 1, p. lvij)

p. 442

(...) ils sont encore absolument sauvages! On leur présenteroit sans cesse les mots d'une langue que l'expérience d'un grand nombre de siècles n'a cessé de perfectionner, sans songer que pour eux le monde est encore à son berceau. (Sicard 1808, vol. 1, pp. 15-16)

(...) toutes les parties qui composent son être, ses besoins, tout ce qui l'entoure, sa maison, ses meubles, ses champs, les minéraux, les végétaux, les animaux, sa ville, et tous les états de la société, les usages, les moeurs, le gouvernement, la religion, le culte et ses ministres, enfin tout ce qui est visible et distingué par des fonctions et par des costumes qui les annoncent; toutes les qualités physiques de l'homme, ses maladies, ses vertus, ses défauts, ses actions, tout cela forme le PREMIER VOLUME. Toutes les actions de l'homme intellectuel ou moral, avec les signes de la partie grammaticale, forment le SECOND VOLUME. (Sicard 1808, vol. 1, pp. ix-x)

Le signe du PAIN consiste à figurer d'abord la manière de le faire, et pour cela, on fait comme si on détrempoit de la farine avec de l'eau, à la manière des boulangers; on figure l'action de mettre sur une pelle la pâte à laquelle on semble avoir donné la forme du pain; on imite celui qui la met dans le four; on a l'air d'en retirer le pain, de le couper et de s'en nourrir. (...) Les signes des parties du pain seront donnés, par les Sourds-Muets eux-mêmes, à la seule inspection de chaque partie, comme la 'croûte'; celle de dessus, celle de dessous, que le Sourd-Muet compare à la peau qui couvre les os de la main. (Sicard 1808, vol. 1, pp. 27-28)

p. 442 / p. 443

AH! OH! 1°. Figurer une personne placée en face de la COLONNADE DU LOUVRE, ou de l'APOLLON DU BELVÉDÈRE, ou du tableau de la TRANSFIGURATION, par RAPHAEL, ou de celui du COURONNEMENT, par M. DAVID, membre de l'Institut de France; ou de tout autre chef-d'oeuvre. 2°. Représenter cette personne debout, la tête fixe, la bouche à demi-ouverte, et regardant longtemps, sans pouvoir en être distraite, ces merveilleuses productions de l'architecture, de la sculpture et de la peinture. 3°. Signe d'interjection. (Sicard 1808, vol. 2, p. 619)

p. 443

(...) c'est surtout chez les Sourds-Muets qu'il se fait le plus d'ellipses, et que le langage qui est d'abord le plus long, se réduit, peu à peu, à un plus petit nombre de signes. (Sicard 1808, vol. 1, p. lvij)

(...) cette nouvelle langue n'est pas une traduction d'une autre langue. c'est une langue primitive dont les autres sont plutôt les traductions. (Sicard 1792)

p. 444

(...) une longue suite de lourdes périphrases, capables d'égarer et de rebuter la volonté même la plus forte. (Berthier 1836, p. 12)

(...) dépouillé l'enseignement de cette obscurité savante, de ces subtilités prétentieuses dont une philosophie superficielle avait pris à tâche de l'envelopper. (Berthier 1836, p. 14)

Les liaisons d'amitié que j'avais formées avec quelques-uns de vos élèves, et particulièrement L. Clerc, (...) m'avaient familiarisé avec le langage des gestes que personne ne leur apprend (...). Je fus frappé des ressources de ce langage; (...). (Bébian 1817, dedication to Sicard)

(...) sur vingt élèves qui sortent chaque année de l'institution, il s'en trouve à peine un qui soit assez instruit pour faire usage d'un dictionnaire. Leur seul dictionnaire, c'est leur professeur. (Bébian 1825, p. 37)

Il y a un langage qui est de tous les lieux et de tous les temps, dont le type est partout le même, parce qu'il est l'expression de notre organisation qui ne varie pas; un langage qui a précédé toutes les langues, et qui a présidé à leur formation; qui, dans ses formes générales, est également compris sous la hutte du Huron et sous la tente de l'Arabe; sous le chaume, comme sous les lambris dorés. Nos premiers pères l'ont parlé, et il sera entendu de nos derniers neveux. – Par ce langage, l'homme n'est nulle part étranger à l'homme. (...) Par lui le voyageur, égaré loin de sa patrie, sait demander un abri pour reposer sa tête, des alimens pour réparer ses forces.(...) – Admirable effet de l'union de l'âme et du corps, de l'esprit et de la matière: tout ce qui se passe au dedans de nous se réfléchit et dans notre physionomie et dans nos gestes. – De cette double porte ouverte à nos idées sort un langage aussi riche qu'expressif, le langage mimique. C'est la langue de ceux qui n'en ont point; c'est celle des sourds-muets; ou plutôt, c'est le langage propre de l'espèce humaine. (Bébian 1825, pp. 1-2)

p. 445

Les signes qui ont un rapport direct et naturel aux idées, et les rappellent par eux-mêmes, sans convention préliminaire, peuvent être appelés 'signes naturels' (...). – Si on veut prendre cette expression dans le sens le plus rigoureux, on ne donnera le nom de 'signes naturels' qu'à ceux qui, non seulement rappellent immédiatement l'idée, mais sont encore inspirés par la nature même et produits sans étude et sans art (...). (Bébian 1817, pp. 1-2)

(...) ils s'entendent tous entr'eux (...). Clerc et Massieu (...) ont été fréquemment appelés par l'autorité pour servir d'interprètes aux sourds-muets vagabonds qu'on arrête dans les rues de Paris. Clerc était comme une autre providence pour tous ses camarades non instruits: c'était à lui qu'ils s'adressaient pour solliciter du travail ou des secours (...). (Bébian 1817, p. 114)

Il est reconnu que la perfection des signes du langage exerce la plus grande influence sur la formation des idées, et même sur le développement de l'intelligence: et ce n'est pas trop en présumer, que de dire qu'un système régulier de signes établis sur la nature et sur l'analogie des idées, allégerait de moitié la tâche de l'instituteur et le travail des élèves. On ne saurait donc accorder une trop sérieuse attention à cette partie si importante de l'art d'instruire les sourds-muets. (Bébian 1825, p. 5)

p. 445 / p. 446

La pensée précède nécessairement dans l'esprit les signes quelconques destinés à l'exprimer; le mot n'a en lui-même aucun rapport avec l'idée; il ne peut faire naître l'idée, ni la donner, mais il sert à la rappeler quand une convention préliminaire l'a lié à cette idée antérieurement bien saisie. Pour établir cette convention avec les sourds-muets, il faut avant tout qu'on sache s'entendre avec eux; avant de vouloir leur apprendre à exprimer une idée par un mot, il faut s'assurer qu'ils possèdent cette idée d'une manière claire et précise; et s'ils ne l'ont pas encore, il faut la développer dans leur esprit. Nous ne pouvons pénétrer dans leur intelligence et examiner ce qui s'y passe; mais ils peuvent nous en instruire, et ils le font avec une merveilleuse facilité, à l'aide de signes qu'ils trouvent eux-mêmes, et que nous entendons sans peine, parce qu'ils sont pris dans la nature même de l'idée. Ces signes donnés par l'élève, sont recueillis soigneusement par le maître, et lui servent à rappeler cette idée; de là, comme d'un point de départ commun à tous deux, il va marcher en avant, et développer de nouvelles idées; celles-ci provoqueront de nouveaux signes, auxquels il ne faudra plus que substituer les mots correspondans dans la langue qu'on veut leur enseigner. (Bébian 1817, pp. 23-24)

p. 446

Si ce signe est juste, s'il est l'expression fidèle de l'idée, il sera adopté dans toutes les écoles. S'il est inexact, il provoquera une discussion, qui éclairera les esprits et amènera une correction. Le langage se perfectionnera, se fixera, il sera le même dans toutes les écoles; et ces améliorations, franchissant nos frontières, rétabliront, pour les sourds-muets, l'uniformité du langage naturel, au milieu de la diversité des langues, qui divise les peuples. (Bébian 1825, pp. 6-7)

p. 447

L'avantage inappréciable qu'offre la réunion des sourds-muets, et qui ne peut s'allier avec leur instruction par la parole, c'est d'enrichir chacun des idées de tous les autres; c'est de réveiller leur intelligence en stimulant leur attention; c'est de les forcer à donner à toutes leurs conceptions une forme claire et précise, qui les rende susceptibles d'être transmises par le geste. (Bébian 1817, p. 16)

(...) sans détruire l'unité du signe, elle laisse voir distinctement tous les élémens, qu'il est indispensable d'y reconnaître pour y appliquer les mots qui doivent les traduire. (Bébian 1825, p. 29)

Si dans le signe qui exprime l'oeil qui se ferme, nous ajoutons, sur le caractère du mouvement, l'accent 'diminutif', nous aurons écrit le signe de cligner (...). (Bébian 1825, p. 22)

p. 448

(...) depuis l'entrée de M. Bébian les signes méthodiques qui se plient aux formes de nos langues conventionnelles ont été bannis de l'institution royale. (Berthier 1836, p. 16)

p. 449

Pendant toute cette discussion, au milieu de ces discours, (…) M. Eugène de Monglave n'a cessé de transmettre par signes à M. Ferdinand Berthier, placé près de lui au bureau, tout ce qui se disait à la tribune . (*Congrès* 1840, p. 134)

(…) elle [la langue d'action] pourrait, aussi bien qu'une langue parlée, recevoir et rendre tous les sentiments qui sont dans le coeur de l'homme, toutes les idées qui sont dans son esprit. (Laromiguière cited in *Congrès* 1840, p. 140)

Iconography

Ill. 1: Abbé de L'Epée in his school. Lithograph by E. Signol, undated.
    Collection Institut National de Jeunes Sourds, Paris.
    Photo: Studio de la Comète, Paris.
Ill. 2: Abbé Sicard with some Deaf pupils, and Jean Massieu. Painting by J. Langlois, 1806 (before its restauration).
    Collection Institut National de Jeunes Sourds, Paris.
    Photo: J.L. Charmet.
Ill. 3: Untitled engraving by F.Berthier, undated.
    Collection Institut National de Jeunes Sourds, Paris.
    Photo: Studio de la Comète, Paris.

References

Aléa, J.M. (1824): *Eloge de l'abbé de l'Epée, ou Essai sur les avantages du système des signes méthodiques, appliqué à l'instruction générale élémentaire. (…)* Paris.

Bébian, R.-A. A. (1817): *Essai sur les sourds-muets et sur le langage naturel, ou Introduction à une classification naturelle des idées avec leurs signes propres.* Paris.

Bébian, R.-A. A. (1825): *Mimographie, ou Essai d'écriture mimique, propre à régulariser le langage des sourds-muets.* Paris.

Berthier, F. (1836): *Histoire et statistique de l'éducation des sourds-muets.* Paris.

Berthier, F. (1840): *Les sourds-muets avant et depuis l'Abbé de l'Epée. (…)* Paris.

Condillac, E.B. de (1746/1947): *Essai sur l'origine des connaissances humaines;* in: *Oeuvres philosophiques de Condillac,* ed. G. Le Roy. Paris. vol. 1, pp. 1-118.

Condillac, E.B. de (1775/1947): *Grammaire;* in: *Oeuvres philosophiques de Condillac,* ed. G. Le Roy. Paris. vol. 1, pp. 425-513.

Condillac, E.B. de (1782): *Grammaire;* in: id., *Cours d'étude pour l'instruction du Prince de Parme* (...). Aux Deux-Ponts. vol. 1, pp. 129ff.

Condillac, E.B. de (1798/1981): *La langue des calculs.* Ed. critique par S. Auroux et A.M. Chouillet. Lille.

Congrès historique, réuni à Paris au siège de l'Institut historique, sept.-oct. 1839 (1840). Paris.

Desloges, P. (1779/1985-1986): *Observations d'un sourd et muèt, sur un cours élémentaire d'éducation des sourds et muèts, publié en 1779 par M. l'Abbé Deschamps, chapelain de l'église d'Orléans.* Amsterdam, Paris. Republished in: *Coup d'oeil* 43, suppl. 3 (=I) and *Coup d'oeil* 44, suppl. 2 (=II).

Fischer, R. (1990): Sign language and French enlightenment. Diderot's "Lettre sur les sourds et muets"; in: Prillwitz, S./Vollhaber, T. (eds.): *Current trends in European sign language research.* Hamburg, pp. 35-58.

Grosselin, A./Pélissier, P. (1858): Cartes mimo-mnémoniques pour l'étude des langues (...). Paris.

Large, Andrew (1985): *The artificial language movement.* Oxford etc.

L'Epée, C.M. de (1776): *Institution des sourds et muets, par la voie des signes méthodiques; Ouvrage qui contient le projet d'une langue universelle, par l'entremise des signes naturels assujettis à une méthode.* Paris.

L'Epée, C.M. de (1784): *La véritable manière d'instruire les sourds et muets, confirmée par une longue expérience.* Paris.

Neumann, F. (1827): *Die Taubstummen-Anstalt zu Paris im Jahre 1822* (...). Königsberg.

Ricken, U. (1986): Les deux "Grammaires" de Condillac; in: *Histoire - Epistémologie - Langage* 8, pp. 71-90.

Robinet, A. (1978): *Le langage à l'âge classique.* Paris.

Sicard, R.-A.-C. (1792): [unpublished letter to H.D. Guyot, dated july 17, 1792]. Archive of the Koninklijk Instituut voor Doven "H.D. Guyot", Haren.

Sicard, R.-A.-C. (1799-1800; an VIII): *Cours d'instruction d'un sourd-muet de naissance, pour servir à l'éducation des sourds-muets, et qui peut être utile à celle de ceux qui entendent et qui parlent.* Paris.

Sicard, R.-A.-C. (1808): *Théorie des signes pour l'instruction des sourds-muets,* dédiée à S.M. l'Empereur et Roi. Suivie d'une notice sur l'enfance de Massieu. Paris. 2 vols.

Tort, P. (1976): Dialectique des signes chez Condillac; in: Parret, H. (ed.): *History of linguistic thought and contemporary linguistics.* Berlin, etc., pp. 488-502.

Jonna Widell
Copenhagen, Denmark

The Danish Deaf Culture in European and Western Society

Summary • Sammenfatning

Since the start of the first Deaf club, the Deaf culture has passed through different historical periods. The adaptation of the Deaf culture to these historical periods has formed the special characteristics of what I have called *historical phases of Deaf culture*.

Studies of marginal groups in society reveal deep unequality mechanisms in society, often wrapped up and defended by rationalism and logic. These mechanisms are for the benefit of some people at the expense of others.

So, while studying Deaf culture in a greater social context, a lot can be learned about Deaf culture specifically, and, at the same time, about society, its way of thinking and its values.

Siden de første døveforening startede, har døvekulturen gået gennem forskellige historiske perioder. Døvekulturens tilpasning til disse historiske perioder har formet nogle særlige, karakteristiske træk, som kommer til udtryk i hvad jeg har kaldt *døvekulturens historiske faser*.

Studier af samfundets marginalgrupper afslører dybe ulighedsmekanismer i samfundet ofte indhyllet i og forsvaret af rationalisme og logik. Disse mekanismer fungerer til fordel for nogle, på bekostning af andre.

Når man således studerer døvekulturen i en større samfundsmæssig sammenhæng, kan man lære meget om selve døvekulturen og samtidig om samfundet, dets måde at tænke på og dets værdier.

Introduction

My dissertation in sociology from the University of Copenhagen was completed in 1983. It was published in 1988 in Danish with the title *Den Danske Døvekultur* (The Danish Deaf Culture).[1] The book covers a wide area, as it analyzes and describes the dynamic interaction between the educational system, the labour market and deaf culture.

Doing a major study of the Danish Deaf Culture has certainly had a wider aim for me. It has been to learn more about the deep structures of society at large – in this case the European and Western society.

My aim has been very much as Freud stated; that his studies of the hysterics helped him to see engrossed patterns difficult to discern in people in general. Following this, studying the Deaf culture situated at the outskirts of society would clearly reveal problematic and not easily perceived patterns in Western society as a whole. My study of the Danish Deaf culture has also been of personal interest as I am Danish and have been brought up in a Deaf family.

In this article, I have chosen to focus on what I call the three historical phases of the Deaf culture. This is followed by a schematic overview of the major trends from 1750 and up to today. The time around 1850 is especially important because in this period the first Deaf associations were established which manifested the establishment of a Deaf culture. This fundamental description (Part I) is followed by some comments on various areas of the cultural story that widen up the whole perspective (Part II).

Part I

The opening phase from 1866 – 1893

In 1866 a group of Deaf craftsmen established an association called *The Deaf Mute Association of 1866* in Copenhagen, Denmark. A deaf Norwegian travelling craftsman had enthusiastically told of an association for Deaf people in Berlin, which the Deaf community in Denmark found very interesting. At that time there was a boom of new associations amongst the hearing workers in Copenhagen, as in Berlin, supported by journeymen especially.

The purpose of these workman associations was primarily social because of the low living standards in the 19th century. The principal initiator and the first chairman of the Deaf Mute Association, Ole Jørgensen, had previously been in contact with a workman association. The goal of these associations was for the members to support each other in case of disease, death and unemployment. In addition to this, the associations were to provide information and stimulation through lectures and relevant entertainment.

The majority of the Deaf community consisted of skilled workers and it was characteristic of the period that the goal of the Deaf association was similar to the goal of the workman associations. The Deaf community also wished to unify to help each other in emergencies while mingling socially and sharing information. Within a few years the Deaf community had established an emergency fund, an insurance fund and a burial club. Furthermore, they aimed at finding work for the unemployed.

A photograph of the founders shows a group of proud Copenhagen citizens, and rightly so. They were all skilled workers with roots in a professional tradition. And they belonged to the first group of Deaf people who had received school education at all – an education which used sign language and the hand alphabet. Only half a century before, Deaf people

---

1 Available at: Danske Døves Landsforbund, Fensmarkgade 1, 2200 Copenhagen N, Denmark. Bibliographical references can be found in this book.

had ranked at the bottom of society without status. Contrary to this, Deaf people now had a respectable education which meant that they were often able to read and write the Danish language in a satisfactory way.

Ill. 1: *Ole Jørgensen, Deaf himself and workshop leader at the Deaf Mute Institute, was the main initiator of the establishment of the first Deaf association in Denmark. He became the first chairman of the association and for this he received public honour. At that time the attitude of society was sympathetic towards Deaf people.*

Naturally, sign language and fingerspelling were used both in the Deaf association and in the families. The majority of Deaf men had married Deaf women whom they had met at school and together they had children. Most of their children were hearing which was very convenient, as they could help with interpretation and, as such, be a link to the hearing society. In this way, Deaf people lived their lives for better or for worse and in the Deaf association they were fortunate to have friends to console and encourage them in the ups and downs of life.

Hearing workers from the countryside had migrated in thousands to Copenhagen where they constituted a poorly educated and highly exploited part of the labour force for the growing industry. Usually, these proletarian families lived in poverty and under miserable conditions. Compared to these, the skilled workers of the Deaf community lived a considerably better life, although modest. Furthermore, the attitude of bourgeois society to Deaf people and other 'deserving poor' was positive and open.

According to the standards of that time the hearing teachers at the Deaf Mute Institute were well-educated and some of them had good connections to the leaders of society. They encouraged Deaf adults to become teachers at the school. The school also stayed in touch with former students, for example by having the meetings of the Deaf association take place

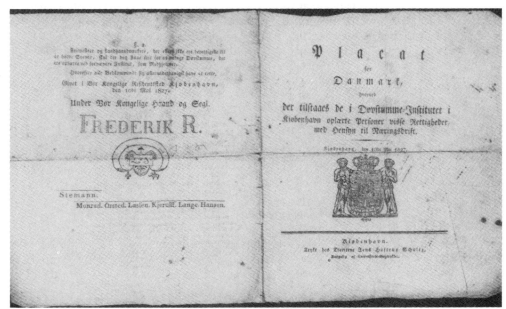

Ill. 2: *Shortly after Deaf education had been initiated in 1807, Danish Deaf craftsmen were given royal authority to work as independent master artisans and employ hearing journeymen.*

on the premises of the school. Several of the teachers participated in these meetings and they were often lecturers. Moreover, the school contributed to a great extent to the integration of the Deaf community in the labour market.

On the basis of all this Deaf people were open to society. A positive relationship between the deaf community and society was formed. The Deaf Mute Association was even favoured by the royal family and at the 25th anniversary of the Association in 1891 the deaf founder, Ole Jørgensen, was honoured with the Silver Cross of the Order of Dannebrog. But change was soon to come.

Explanations

A society in transition – here between the feudal system and the new industrial capitalistic system – allows more freedom of thought and action, which also applies to education. It is no coincidence that the sign method, which was positively disposed toward Deaf people, first appeared in France in the period just before the French Revolution. But with the establishment of the industrial society around 1880 societal thinking became bound to new and 'rigid' forms, including educational forms and methods.

Human thinking – or to be more explicit: the thoughts we accept as our own without hesitation or question and as that which is right – is in the highest degree bound by societal frames. For the Deaf community these new thought-forms at the end of the 19th century had the effect that oralism – that is the oral method as the only proper teaching method for Deaf people – made its breakthrough in Deaf education all over the Western world.

It is exceedingly important to focus on teaching methods in relation to Deaf culture, because the educational system functions as the extended arm of society. The educational system reflects the attitude of society. This is therefore a very important factor if we are to understand the development and nature of Deaf culture.

Already in 1880 it was decided at the international congress of teachers of the Deaf in Milan that the oral method should be given the status of the only proper teaching method for Deaf people. At the same time the sign method was rejected as it was claimed that signs destroyed the children's speaking capability. The argument for this was that 'as everybody knows children are lazy', and therefore, whenever possible, the children would change from the difficult oral language to sign language.

On this questionable basis oralism as a philosophy/ideology spread and Deaf teachers of the Deaf were forced to leave the schools for the Deaf, some were even fired immediately. Almost a century would pass until Deaf people were again allowed to work as teachers of the deaf.

Through close reading of the congress addresses and seen from a sociological perspective, it is quite clear that the oral method did not prevail because of the superiority of the method. The oral method became a dominant ideology because it was especially suited to the new historical period. How did it fit in?

1. The Theory of Evolution formulated by the famous Charles Darwin in the field of zoology was generalized and used in the social sciences. As monkeys were considered to be at a low evolutionary stage and human beings at a high stage, so, too, other cultures were considered lower than the Western civilization. Following the same line of thought, sign language was considered to be at a lower stage and irrevocably had to be abandoned for the benefit of the higher stage – the oral language.

2. The new period involved another type of social control. In all societies a necessary system of common rules and sanctions exists in order to ensure the unity of society. Religion and show trials were important features of the old feudal power system, but from the 19th century onwards the Power of the Norm became dominant.

   The Power of the Norm manifested itself in the strict discipline of the big institutions (including the schools for the Deaf) and in a quantitative attitude toward deviance: It is normal to be a hearing person. In principle we can all hear, although a person hard of hearing does not hear so well and a Deaf person hears very poorly. So a Deaf person is a poorly functioning hearing person = deviant.

3. In the society in transition an individual was regarded as a mobile, contributing citizen in relation to society. The creators of the sign method had seen the Deaf child and the language which the Deaf child had created and shaped Deaf education accordingly. At a later stage industrial production was given priority at the expense of the individual's achievement. This was reflected psychologically in learning theories in which human beings were considered 'empty vessels to be filled', and at work the labour force merely had to adapt to a slowly changeable production. Within Deaf education the Deaf child was only 'seen' and given value to a small extent and oralism was to give speech to Deaf children. The children were taught the most common standard pronunciations and with this level of restricted language the school accomplishment was considered acceptable, as the requirements of industry for oral communication were limited to a few short messages and technical instructions. All for society!

Oralism was thus well suited for society, but how did the attitudes hidden in this teaching method fit the Deaf culture? Would the Deaf culture one-sidedly adapt to the requirements of society?

The isolation phase from 1893 – 1980

The answer to this is no. But even if the Milan congress and the opening of the first State Speech Training School for the Deaf in Fredericia took place already in 1880-1881 the Deaf culture's first real serious breach with society did not take place until 1893. From then on a new attitude was to prevail.

Society's attitude towards the Deaf community was gradually changing. In some areas of society changes happened fast and in others slowly. In the beginning society was still open towards Deaf people which was shown, for example, in the form of concrete support from leading hearing citizens to the building of the Deaf Mute Association's own house in Brohusgade, Copenhagen, in 1889. The house formed the setting for the activities of the association and, in addition to this, provided accommodations for elderly Deaf people.

But in the area of education new and strict demands were soon to be made. Deaf people had to learn to speak, they must adapt to 'a higher development' and give up sign language. Georg Jørgensen, hearing teacher at the school for the Deaf in Copenhagen, was a capable signer and a leading hearing person in the association work of the Deaf community. Paradoxically, from 1881 he was also principal of the first Speech Training School in Fredericia where he held very firmly to the new demands.

Georg Jørgensen was an excellent personification of the paradoxical shift in the attitudes of society. While he was still a member of the board of the Deaf Mute Association, he prevented two Deaf sisters from having contact with each other. One of the sisters had been trained in sign language in Copenhagen and she was not to be allowed to destroy her sister's ability to speak. The latter had been trained in Fredericia. Later Georg Jørgensen even succeeded in stopping a travelling church service for Deaf people. Through the ministry he had an injunction issued against Reverend Heiberg who, *as a hand-alphabet preacher, should not be allowed to preach for Deaf people who had learned to speak.*

An event of vital importance for the breach marking this isolation phase was the situation around the establishment of the association *Effata*. On the 25th of July 1893 the largest Danish newspaper, *Berlingske Tidende*, wrote that the teachers for the speech–trained part of the Deaf community at the schools in Fredericia and Nyborg had formed an association for the students from these schools. The object was to get the Deaf community out of the isolation and to create a link to the surrounding world – without sign language. At the same time they applied for public support for this work!

To the members of the Deaf Mute Association this was too much. *Effata* attempted to split up the Deaf community by turning Deaf people in Denmark against one another. Furthermore, *Effata* tried to make it much more difficult for the old Deaf association to receive public support and contributions for the Deaf community. The breach with the dominating influences and attitudes in society took place as follows:

At the Deaf Mute Association general assembly in 1893 Georg Jørgensen was appointed to honorary member, primarily because polite, older members of the Deaf community wanted to show their gratitude for his previous services. However, on the same occasion the association decided on a new goal: The main task of the future would be the preservation of sign language.

The fact that society set up limits did not cause a stagnation of the Deaf culture. The self-confidence and strength which had been acquired during the opening phase were preserved in the Deaf culture and were passed on through contact between succeeding generations.

This self-confidence and strength within the Deaf community was now being used for internal expansion and stabilization. Local branches of the Deaf Mute Association were established around the country in the form of Deaf clubs. The association in Copenhagen got its own house and the congregation its own church. Participants were sent to international meetings and congresses and as a result of the new goal new sign language dictionaries were published in 1907 and 1926.

There was plenty of work to do. The Deaf community also participated in the public debate about education, signs and speech – usually through the magazine *Papers for the Deaf Mute Community*. But Deaf people were now being pushed to the outskirts of society and were isolated there and society did not want to listen to them.

Ill. 3: *While society previously had been sympathetic towards Deaf people they were being rejected during the isolation phase. But the activities of the Deaf community did not stop. Instead the Deaf community expanded internally – nationally as well as internationally. The strength originated from the opening phase. New Deaf clubs mushroomed across the country. In 1907 a Scandinavian Deaf Mute Congress was held in Copenhagen. The picture shows the many participants on a visit to Tivoli Gardens.*

The isolation phase lasted for almost a century which is a long period to live under pressure and lack of responsiveness and acceptance. Hearing professionals working with Deaf people would often say: 'Deaf people want to isolate themselves. They do not want to speak and become integrated!' In the eyes of the hearing society Deaf people changed from being 'physical deviants' to being 'social deviants' with the resulting negative sanctions against them as a just consequence. To make fun of Deaf people and tell spiteful jokes were considered fully legitimate. Unfortunately, many of these distortions of the actual situation have been allowed to survive for too long.

Explanations

The fact is that Deaf people were pushed out and isolated by the hearing society or environments because Deaf people insisted on maintaining sign language which made it easy for them to communicate on all matters with each other. That the Deaf community insisted so strongly on maintaining sign language could be due to a deep respect for an inner creative power of a human and social nature. This creative power had made it possible for the Deaf community to develop a good and practically functioning language – sign language – which facilitated their development despite all odds. A topic in the societal debate today in the 1990s is how to unite with nature, how to make friends with nature again. The Deaf community's maintenance of sign language can be seen as an example of such a friendship. It was the hearing environment which in conformity with the spirit of the time alienated itself from Deaf people's natural ability to create a language best suited for their situation.

This rejection of the life nerve of the Deaf culture and the demand that Deaf children should learn to speak the Danish language in a manner which was unnatural and unreasonably difficult for them, namely through the spoken word, eventually began to leave its marks on the personality of Deaf individuals. Especially through schooling Deaf children experienced a feeling of 'I cannot, I am no good, to be a hearing person is good, to be deaf is bad', and this often repeated experience has left its deep marks.

Fortunately for the Deaf individual, the Deaf community had united in a favourable period which I have called the opening phase. The strength which had grown from the belief in their own power and confidence in life and which was developed in this period - among other things through the comprehensibility and thereby humaneness of the sign method - is still 'built into' the Deaf culture as an experience from one generation to the next.

The isolation phase weakened the Deaf community, but the rich experience and the strength from the opening phase made the Danish deaf culture close itself offensively without the extreme and degrading submissiveness which have been seen among Deaf people in some other countries. This offensive reaction provided the Danish Deaf community with power to build up a strong organization internally in order to secure the needs of the Deaf community. Their many associations and self-initiated institutions testify to this. Here social life is often lively, but also serious.

One could say that in the Deaf clubs a socialization has taken place. Socialization means: to learn about social life in the family, at school, at work, among friends, in a shop, in a cinema. This socialization process has literally protected the life of the Deaf community from failure. 'Primary socialization' in the family was mostly sadly difficult in a society where the parents were given no help. In addition to this, 'secondary socialization' in the school was alarmingly incomplete – both psychologically and in relation to learning – and on certain points even sadly damaging. The school system distinguished itself by providing the children with a simple level of speech and the necessary discipline, so they could be absorbed into the labour market. But it was due to the tertiary socialization in the Deaf clubs that Deaf people have learnt how to succeed socially in a job and stay in it. It was in the Deaf clubs that Deaf people talked about and found solutions to problems concerning hearing ridicule, labour unions etc.

On the basis of these understanding and adaptation mechanisms the concept of 'Deaf workplaces' emerged. This refers to companies which had good experiences with Deaf workers and therefore wished to continue hiring Deaf people and Deaf apprentices as well. As a result of Deaf (people's) integration in the labour market there was very little unemployment among Deaf people for many years.

The last part of the isolation phase leading up to the next phase (1960 – 1980)

In the 1960s conditions changed, first and foremost in the labour market and consequently in the education sector and then in Danish Deaf culture as well. The Deaf culture was still in the isolation phase, but changes were happening that enabled the Deaf community to prepare to get out of the isolation.

The increase in productivity in the 1960s which formed the basis of the welfare society demanded more manpower. The marginal groups of the labour market, particularly women, joined the labour force and so did people who had been kept out because of disease or disability. The Rehabilitation Act of 1960 ensured rehabilitation for the latter groups. This made it possible for Deaf people to receive interpreter services. The use of sign language interpreters in education was now introduced.

Education for the larger community became an important element. Young people from working class families got the opportunity to get the General Certificate of Education as well as advanced education. It was a new trend for so many to receive higher education and for young Deaf people to choose theoretical education. Deaf people graduated from comprehensive school, senior school and technical school and became engineers, draftspeople, social workers, teachers, pedagogues, accountants etc. At the same time, vocational education changed from being mainly practical training into an education with fifty percent theoretical studies.

The prerequisite of the 'success' of oralism began thus to disintegrate. The labour market where brief routine messages were adequate did not exist anymore. Such abilities as writing, understanding written language, thinking at an abstract level and understanding and discussing complex matters were now required.

In 1979 Dr. R. Conrad in Oxford, England, published an analysis of the results of oralism which documented that British oralism had only in few exceptional cases been able to live up to its own goals. In fact, it was far from reaching its goals. Such an evaluation could, of course, have been made 50 years before, and it was, indeed, yet the labour market/society did not support such disclosures, on the contrary.

Young Deaf people wished to educate themselves with the use of sign language interpreters, and on this basis their parents supported the attempt of the Deaf culture to introduce sign language in primary schools. Parents and the Deaf community together exerted heavy pressure. The oral teaching at the schools for the Deaf disintegrated and total communication projects gained a footing in the schools.

Total communication is a concept first used by the anthropologist Margaret Mead. The idea is that when encountering another culture any means available are used in order to exchange ideas and understand each other to the best possible extent. The concept of total communication or rather the philosophy has today spread to the countries where oralism has not been able to keep its status and the concept has become more and more popular.

Total communication is a humane philosophy, but it is not a teaching method and, as such, it is not suitable for Deaf education. It is, however, used as a teaching method, and therefore the total communication projects within Deaf education can be characterized as a humane 'ad hoc method': 'Perhaps this time we shall succeed!'

But the labour market is constantly changing. The lack of manpower and increased competition from other countries in combination with the wish for higher productivity pave the way for the introduction of new and advanced machinery, automation and new technology. One of the first sectors to be affected was the textile sector, where new industries make the ordinary tailor redundant.

The tailoring trades originally belonged to a special group of professions where many skilled Deaf people used to work. These trades were: shoemakers, joiners, tailors and needlewomen. Now deaf tailors were facing the disintegration of their craft and they were instead given jobs as semi-skilled workers. This became the destiny of several other crafts as well.

This trend along with new educational opportunities has had the effect that Deaf people are more scattered over a variety of jobs. At the same time the old boarding school system disappears and Deaf children are sent to different types of schools – schools for the Deaf, integrated schools and public schools as mainstreamed individuals. The Deaf community has thus changed from being a relatively 'homogeneous group' of people with a highly similar background to being a 'heterogeneous group' of people with different backgrounds, education and working environments.

The new mobility especially within the white-collar jobs and higher education activates the dynamic powers of minority groups. In the Deaf community this is shown through a renewed involvement aimed at making society accept the attitudes and wishes of the Deaf culture. In 1980 the Danish Deaf Association arranged a school conference in Fredericia where the association made it very clear to the invited educators that from now on the Deaf community assumes responsibility for the schooling and future of Deaf children – not as children, but as **Deaf** children. Only Deaf adults are experts on what it means to live a complete life as a Deaf person in a hearing society! With this manifesto the Deaf culture entered a new phase.

The manifestation phase since 1980

This phase is characterized by changes. Some of the baggage of negative self-awareness carried on from the isolation phase is cleaned up under the label 'Deaf Awareness' and the attitude 'Deaf people cannot' is reworded into 'Deaf people can'. There is an inner dynamic that makes things happen. In addition to this, society is undergoing rapid changes as a transition into the so-called information society. Society is also opening up to the opinions of the minority groups, but nothing comes easy – every single step forward takes a struggle.

With renewed self-confidence the Deaf community started fighting for political key issues like videos and text telephones for all Deaf people, a folk high school[2] for Deaf people and sign language as a subject in schools. These four goals have been reached and are a reality today in 1991. In the action programme of the Danish Deaf Association further areas are described that need to be worked on, so there is still plenty of work to be done.

A bilingual teaching method for Deaf people is today given top priority in Deaf education. This way of teaching requires the introduction of sign language as an independent school subject. Sign language must be the basic language as it is the only language suited for all Deaf children. When the children have learned this the Danish language will be taught as a foreign language.

2   Folk high schools are a strong Danish and Scandinavian phenomenon. They originated from the ideas of the Danish priest and writer N. F. S. Grundtvig (1783-1872) and were established in order to give peasants access to ecucation. Today there are many folk high schools scattered all over Denmark. Adults of all ages, educational backgrounds and professions, can participate and do courses or studies for a period of three months to a year. There are no exams. The folk high schools have more liberal attitudes and a freer dialogue than is found in the traditional educational system.

Ill. 4: *In the last century the board of the Deaf Association of 1866 consisted of men only. In conformity with our times the chairperson today is a woman, Lene Ravn. She is seen here in relaxed conversation with a female minister (former Minister of Cultural Affairs, Mimi Stilling Jacobsen). Society today shows renewed openness towards the Deaf community. Deaf people still have to fight for their key issues, but today it is possible to break through the barriers and succeed.*

In order to develop an actual teaching method the following is necessary: that sign language can be maintained as a 'written language', either via sign writing which has been developed and is used in Denmark and the United States or via a computer screen; that the teachers of the Deaf are trained in sign language; that approximately half the teachers of the schools are Deaf themselves; and that a series of new teaching materials are developed.

The twin school model – two independent schools, one for hearing children and one for Deaf children, cooperating within the same institution – will be the best type of school for all children who need both sign language and Danish – i.e. Deaf children and the large group of hearing-impaired children. This will offer the best two-cultural education, as the Deaf culture will have a strong position as opposed to the hearing culture – and the children need both.

Furthermore, it is important to find out how the Deaf community can benefit from the new information technology which will be dominating in the information society. It is important to be aware of the fact that information technology covers many levels of society and therefore a complex and wide spectrum of knowledge is required. The latter also applies to other sectors where new ways of thinking are predominant – theatre life, residential homes and institutions, youth centers for Deaf children etc.

To start creating concrete innovations in society which are suitable for as many as possible is always complicated, but it is also very exciting.

A major and important area to be decided on is the future activities and functions of the Deaf clubs. The Deaf community today consists of people with different backgrounds. Do they understand each other? Are some being pushed out and isolated because of a lack of ability to analyse a given situation? Is there a lack of tolerance towards the Deaf individuals who have been integrated in the public schools? When is a person considered 'arrogant and clever', when just having a different line of thought? And what about the group of multi-handicapped Deaf people? How do they fit in?

EUROPE

Transition Society 1850 ⟶ 1880 Industrial Society ⟶

Varying degrees of   Breakthrough of
industrialization   industrialization

DK: Minor trade industries (Cph.)
      Deaf people allowed to run
      independent business.

France: Sign method.
Germany: Oral method.

1880: in Milan the
congress of teachers of the Deaf
decides that the oral method is
the only true method/oralism.

The Theory of Evolution -
sign language is placed at a
lower stage of development
than oral language.

Social integration
and view of man

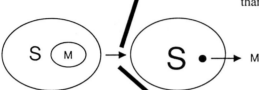

THE DANISH

The Opening Phase 1866-1893

The establishment of the Deaf Association
inspired by workmen associations and
Berlin's Deaf Association. The founders
are all skilled deaf workers

Deaf People / Society:
Openness towards society (trust).

School: The sign method. Signs and
HA are accepted. More Deaf teachers.

Work: Workmen. Special professions:
Shoemaker, joiner, tailor, needlewoman.
(Great social distance to the poor proletariat -
workmen pride).

Mental Features: Strong.
Deaf people can!

Goal: Social Support.
Group Education at Boarding Schools
Joint social responsibility. Group solidarity.

The Isolation Phase 1893-1980

The Deaf community maintains sign
language and is isolated. Internal
expansion (new Deaf clubs, s.l.dict.).
Intern. co-operation among deaf people.

Deaf People / Society: *Deaf people do not*
want to speak. They isolate themselves.

School: Oralism. In DK 'mild' oral
method, MHS, a few signs. Deaf
teachers of the deaf disappear.
Work: Stable labour. Well integrated on
the labour market. Often connected to
to certain companies, several workers
at the same workplace (tertiary socialization in the Deaf clubs - Deaf adults to
the younger generation).
Mental Features: Weak (and strong
from the Opening Phase).
Deaf people cannot! Weak features are
gradually enhanced (through oral
education and society's attitude).
Goal: Preservation of sign language

Homogenous Group ⟶

Table 1:

EUROPE

1960 ──────────→ 1980 Transition to Information Society

Changed labour market structure

Labour is intensified.
Labour force reserve is taken in
(women and handicapped people).

DK: The Rehabilitation Act
(Deaf people are educated
with an interpreter).

Demands for abstract thinking.
Oralism is questioned.
Total Communication.

New technology

Crisis / unemployment. Major change in
the labour market (demands for flexibility
and retraining).

DEAF CULTURE

'Passive' opening outwards (not a
change of phases). The Nordic
common sign dictionary is published.

Deaf people become deviants. *The poor
blind man, the stubborn deaf old brute!*

School: Total communication -
ad hoc method. Less oppostition to S.L.
A few Deaf teachers.

Work: Deaf people become qualified
(➚ theoretical education) and
dequalified (➘ semi-skilled workers).

The Manifestation Phase 1980 -

An offensive opening towards society.
Sign dictionaries, sign language
research and education.

Deaf People / Society: The Deaf
community manifests its attitudes towards
society
School: Bilingualism on an experimental
basis in some schools. More Deaf teachers
and pedagogues.

Work: Unemployment - young people
and middle-aged workers.

Mental Features: Deaf awareness.
The weak features are diminished.

Goal: To create open activity centres based
on sign language

Boarding schools disappear ──────→ Individual Education
Responsibility for yourself only (day-, integrated schools, individual mainstreaming).
──→ Heterogeneous Group   Cultural Crisis

Schematic overview of the phases

469

And what about the young and unemployed? Are the many non-employed members given sufficient opportunities during the daytime? The rejection of Deaf people from the labour market is a great problem in the present transitional society. If we are going to have cultural centers for the Deaf instead of the old fashioned houses for the Deaf, how are they to be managed? How do we enhance the engagement of the members? Do management and members have sufficient knowledge of the development in society today? Do they realize that each Deaf individual will have to change his or her thoughts and attitudes before the Deaf culture can change to become a well-functioning, up-to-date community? And how is it possible to change from being an 'onlooker' to being a 'participant' in one's own life?

On the management training courses of the Danish Deaf Association we try to shed light on these questions. They are not traditional management training courses. Every Deaf individual can participate as the main issue is group co-operation. It is the common initiative and joint responsibility that results in goal-oriented management and action on a joint basis. These 'flat' group based structures will play an important part in the society of the future.

It is of utmost importance that the Deaf community obtain knowledge of the areas which are today referred to as 'alternative' (wholistic philosophy, therapy, medicine, etc.). We must remember that much of that which is alternative today will be the main currents of tomorrow – and this is especially true in a society in transition.

Finally it should be stressed that a Deaf person in Denmark belongs to two cultures – the Deaf culture and the Danish culture. Many Deaf people think that the Danish culture is simply a 'hearing' culture and therefore not suited for them. This is an unfortunate and wrong conclusion. It is only a small part of the Danish culture in which deaf people cannot or can only with difficulty take part.

Deaf people live in two cultures, but are also in a double-situation in another way. The Deaf community is both a handicap group and a cultural minority as regards language. The more the members of Deaf community and the Deaf community as a whole are able to manage their own lives, the more they become a minority group and the less a handicap group. This process, this challenge is more emphasized in what I call the manifestation phase – if Deaf people want it to be so! The reward, it seems to me, will be an open and equal interplay with the hearing community – if Deaf people dare! The final reward will eventually be – entering the equality phase!

Part II

The cultural concept in brief

It is important to view cultures on the basis of a practical point of view. Only then can a culture be understood and only then will an obvious acceptance of the culture take place.

Culture means the way in which a given group solves its problems of existence. When such solutions are organized and practised for a long time, social habits are expressed and these allow us to identify a culture.

When a culture – and in the case of the Deaf community a sub-culture/minority culture – is not deeply understood in its own necessity by the majority of society the situation will continuously fluctuate between tolerance and intolerance. The minority culture will then always have to fight for respect, understanding and equality.

If a culture is constantly forced to fight for the matters which the group regards/defines as fundamental and absolutely necessary problems to be solved, then the group will have difficulty finding the strength needed to express its potential cultural richness.

From this it follows that when the dominant majority of society prevents minority cultures from expressing themselves, then this majority is also excluding itself from gaining a considerable enrichment.

How to use this model in other countries

The most important thing is to identify the main tendencies common to all Deaf cultures. The next step is to identify factors that will either strengthen or weaken or modify these main tendencies. I will give some examples later.

When industrial society had more or less found its form around 1880 all Western deaf cultures became subject to a certain set of thought-forms – the popularisation of the Theory of Evolution and the Power of the Norm – and the concrete actions and attitudes in society derived from these underlying thought-forms.

In industrial society there was a lot of suppression of 'deviants'. At the same time many material advancements were made and positive, humane organizing was established (e.g. the labour movement), creating opposing forces working towards a better distribution of power in society. But the so-called 'deviants' lost their power and have to recapture it today in the Manifestation Phase.

The important question is: How much power did they lose? It has been easier for Deaf cultures to make their ideas manifest at the present time if some power (if they had some) had been stored in the Deaf culture during the 100 years of the isolation phase.

Therefore, when we look at a Deaf culture we need to consider whether there actually was an opening phase in the period of the transitional society where strength could be built up, not only in the individual but also in the Deaf culture as a whole. Only a Deaf organization – a well defined and structured group covering three or more generations of people – can keep this power alive during such a long period.

If a Deaf culture was organized in a country where industrial society was very early established (e.g. England around 1850) this is a weakening factor. If the transitional society was prolonged and Deaf people themselves took action to organize themselves (e.g. Denmark in 1866) then this is a strengthening factor. The results of these differences have been that in Denmark Deaf people have run their own clubs. Hearing people have helped them, but basically Deaf people have always been the ones in charge. In England hearing people have been in charge and strongly paternalistic and disempowering forces have weakened the Deaf culture there.

There are other factors such as:
* Were the founders of the Deaf clubs oralists or not?
* How were Deaf people integrated on the labour market? Were they mainly craftspeople or unskilled factory workers? As craftspeople, they would bear with them pride and power from a craftspeople tradition with roots in feudal society (as e.g. in Denmark). As unskilled factory workers, they would share the more dehumanizing influences operating on this group at the beginning of industrialization. Strong self-organizing amongst the workers could be a strengthening influence.
* The success of oral education is dependent on an authoritarian and strict educational system. Therefore, nonauthoritarian influences on the educational system will weaken the oral and disempowering forces. (In Denmark the influence of the folk high school movement from last century turned oral education into what I have called 'a mild oralism'.)

What is important to remember is: The major suppressing and disempowering influences from industrial society are the unavoidable main rule. But different societal patterns in the individual countries can modify the common pattern. So, in spite of this common factor, each Deaf culture is unique.

Each society has its own dominating thought-forms

What I call thought-forms are the underlying determining ideas in a given society. There are basic thought-forms dealing with economic relations, cultural relations, the individual's relation to society, ideas of development etc. In fact, there are only a few basic thought-forms and they are important to understand.

To use a metaphor, thought-forms are like the operating system in a computer. It determines the possibilities and limitations of any software programme for this computer. This means that any programme that does not fit into the operating system will not function.

Similarly, during the era of industrial society it was impossible for Deaf people to come through in society with their demands for cultural acceptance and respect for sign language. Deaf people's demands did not correspond with the dominating cultural thought-form – the Theory of Evolution.

Darwin's impressive theory, developed in the field of natural science, was improperly 'borrowed' by the social sciences and was used to favour unjust cultural thinking in society and politics of unequality. In this way Darwin's theory was popularized into social Darwinism.

The 'Power of the Norm' as described by the French social philosopher Michel Foucault is another dominating thought-form. The function of the norm is to use the ideal of equality from the bourgeois French Revolution to legitimate the advantages of one social group and the disadvantages of another social group. In this way the ideal of equality was vulgarized.

The 'Power of the Norm' functions as a social controlling factor to fix all people to the same ideal: 'We are all alike, but some are less alike than the rest. They will have to learn to be like us!' The function of this thought-form is thus to create a sort of binding unity in society out of differences and opposites. Oralism belongs to this thought-form.

Today many people recognize this way of thinking as distorted. But it did function and permeated the thinking of most citizens during the last one hundred years, even bright and well-meaning people. Today society is in a 'transition phase' where people are breaking up old forms and old ideas to move along with new impulses. Only because we are at this point in time and development, it is possible to distinguish these old forms and ideas and change them.

Cultural concepts and their correlation with teaching methods

Each historical period has its own view on minority cultures. Moreover, this cultural perception is linked to a certain 'view of human kind', to a school of psychological theories and, in the end, to a teaching philosophy and method. Following this, any historical period contains a specific pattern different from that of another period.

Table 2 shows a schematic overview of compensatory educational models and, as a part of this, methods used in Deaf education. The different compensatory methods are here connected with concepts of development and models of cultural concepts.

The preformation model and the sign method

According to this model, cultural differences are preformed and determined by inner constellations. Development derives from inner dynamics and there is focus on the immanent, i.e. what is inside the person as in the case of the French sign method. This method implicates an observation of the inner dynamics of the deaf child as it expresses itself in a unique, self-created language. Deaf education was based on this capacity. The result was a societal integration of Deaf people who would grow into responsible citizens with an ability to understand their social context.

The sign method is named after the country where it originated, i.e. France. Basically it is connected with the period of transition into industrial society, and certainly with the spark-

Model of Understanding	View on Development	Development Theories	Pedagogical Models	Deaf Education
Preformation Development	Development seen as primarily determined from inside	*Endogenetic Development* e.g. Psychoanalysis	*Development pedagogy* e.g. growth theories, anti-authoritarian pedagogy	*French Sign Method* DK: 1807 to 1880
The Cultural Deficiency Model	Development seen as primarily determinded from outside	*Exogenic theories* e.g. the social learning theory, behaviourism	*Communication Models* directional learning educational technology	*Oral Method* speech-training DK: 1880 to 1971 a mild oralism
The Cultural Difference Model as Hidden Deficiency Model	Development seen as determined by inner as well as outer conditions	*Dialectic Theories* e.g. development oriented cognitive theory, Piaget, Furth	*Dialogue Pedagogical Model* e.g. Swedish dialogue pedagogy	*Total Communication* speech and signs in mixed forms, cued speech, mouth-hand-system DK: 1971
The Cultural Difference Model as Equal Cultural Model	Development seen as determined by inner as well as outer conditions	*Materialistic & dialectic theories* e.g. cultural historical school	*Emancipating pedagogy* e.g. Negt, Freire	*Bilingual Education* DK: 1980 In Scandinavia various bilingual projects; Denmark: 1991 sign language as a school subject.

Table 2: *Compensatory Education Models*

ling new ideals erupting with the deep stirring changes in European societies of which the French Revolution is the clearest expression. The essence of the sign method can be expressed as follows:

> You cannot hear, but you speak with your hands. Teach me your signs then I will teach you the hand alphabet. These two combined will enableyou to learn the French language – to read and write it in order to express yourself.

The cultural deficiency model and the oral method

'Lack' is the central theme in this model. A culture or person is seen as either lacking something important and/or there is a lack of attention on the part of the educational system. In this model it is not considered important to focus on inner needs and necessities as they cannot be observed directly.

In contrast with the previous model, development is here determined by outer factors. So with the right stimulation a certain behaviour can be changed or modified into a normal behaviour or response. The psychological theories involved here are behaviouristic stimulus-response theories.

Symbolically the pupil is seen as an empty blackboard that the teacher can write upon and define. The blackboard can also be seen as a black hole that the teacher is filling up with 'imprints', with what he thinks all Deaf people should have (the educational system as an important ideological function of the state).

The child's own experiences are not valued in these educational programmes. The theoretical, educational approach is strict and it is believed that by using a punishment/reward method the teacher can mould the child into almost anything.

The oral method obviously belongs to this category. The deficiency model is closely connected with the pathological model and functions as a socio-pathological model. Therefore the wide use of concepts as sick, lacking, pathologic, deviant, underdeveloped countries, cultures and persons. At the other end of the scale is the ideal normal behaviour. The essence of the oral method can be expressed as follows:

> You cannot hear. Your gestures are certainly not a real language. I will teach you my language, the spoken word that all people use. Of course, it is difficult for you, but I am patient. With the use of hearing aids you can learn to listen and speak (formerly: lip read and speak). Do not use signs and then you will no longer be deaf, you will be hearing-impaired. Listen, look at my mouth and repeat what I say, repeat, repeat, repeat. I know that it is difficult, but it is necessary. No signs, many words, the same words over and over. When you are able to speak you are one of us.

The cultural difference model as a hidden deficiency model and total communication

Cultural differences are accepted in this model, but not in depth. There are still remnants from the previous model below a positive humanistic surface.

The implication of this is that the distinctive cultural characteristics of a group are accepted, but with some distortion. This could be idyllization or positive discrimination. It could also be real love of the 'colour' or characteristics of a certain group, but with a lack of understanding of the underlying necessities and deeper essence of the group. According to this view, the central needs of the group are not being met and therefore integration in society will still serve the functioning of the Power of the Norm and therefore serve inequality.

The pupil is accepted as is with his or her lack of hearing and with sign language or whatever means of commuciation he or she commands. There is a larger degree of acceptance, but the pupil's essence is not consciously and effectively supported. There is not a full and complete acceptance and thus the integration process becomes distorted, because true integration demands that each individual part of the process is equally and fully accepted and supported.

If we look at total communication programmes in any country it is obvious that sign language as deaf people use it is neglected, considered unimportant or plays a minor role. A whole range of visually supporting efforts are being put to use - only not sign language which is of the highest importance to Deaf people! The Danish Total Communication Centre in Copenhagen has been very aware of this neglect and therefore has worked to promote sign language in Danish society as an essential part of the total communication model.

Furthermore, total communication projects have not been functioning as true educational models. They seem to be positive philosophies combined with different ad hoc practices functioning as an escape from oralism.

Hans Furth is known as a controversial theorist in Deaf education and has supported this escape from oralism. He has written a book called *Thinking Without Language* and based his work on the ideas of Piaget. Furth has most certainly been able to avoid the deeper language issue and as such he is not radical enough to penetrate into the next state. But, at the same time, I want to emphasize that Furth and total communication have been necessary steps away from the intolerable polarization of sign versus speech and thus a step in the direction of bilingualism.

The hidden deficiency model functions likewise as a pathway away from the deficiency model and towards the true cultural difference model. The essence of total communication can be expressed in this way:

> You are deaf. I know that you have extraordinary visual needs. Therefore I will try the best I can to visualize what I want to teach you, including spoken language. I know that it is still difficult for you to learn to speak my language. But this method is more convenient and less exhausting for both of us than the oral method.

The cultural difference model and the bilingual teaching method

The acknowledgement here is that we are different and both have a fundamental reason to be so and, in this respect, have equal rights to have what we need.

The best way to understand development is through materialistic and dialectic theories. These theories focus on the interplay between inner and outer factors and, at the same time, are positively and negatively critical towards society's means of socializing and adapting its members. These theories are also aware of the distribution of power in society and put the following questions: If one part has taken more power who has then given away their power? And is this okay if the aim is equality?

Through education Oscar Negt and Paolo Freire certainly have worked on making the powerless regain their power in order to be equal. The bilingual method works clearly towards the same goal: To make Deaf people fully regain their language, their identity and a renewed openness towards the rest of society. The essence of the bilingual teaching method can be expressed like this:

> You are Deaf. You have together invented and developed sign language. Teach me your language well. My language is difficult and foreign to you, but when we communicate well together in your language I can help you translate into my language. You can never learn my language in an easy and natural way. This you can do with sign language and with that as a basis you can certainly learn my and society's language as a foreign language.

How to develop a bilingual teaching method

There are a lot of obstacles to be overcome because it demands much effort, organization and imagination to build up a thorough bilingual teaching method.
The following issues need to be dealt with:

- Sign language has to be studied and described properly. Teaching methods and materials must be developed. It will be necessary to establish school libraries with a variety of combined video/text materials. Some videos will be in sign language while others will be interpreted into sign language by the teacher while watching the video. The important thing is that the children get a bilingual input – in sign language as well as in written language.

- Sign language must be made visible in such a way that it can be maintained as a 'written language'. This can be done through the use of sign writing or interactive video. Both techniques involve the use of modern computer technology.

- Teachers of the Deaf must all go through formal language education to be fluent users of sign language. In order to practise bilingual education you have to be skilled in both languages. This goes for hearing as well as Deaf teachers.

There also have to be developed sign language training programmes for all groups of professionals who work with Deaf people, i.e. clerks, counselors, social workers, psychologists, etc. It is important that everybody in the entire school system and Deaf community is capable of using sign language in order to create a true sign language environment.

- Deaf teachers of the Deaf are very important. In fact, half the teaching staff should be Deaf themselves to maintain a cultural balance. It will also be a natural thing that Deaf teachers are the ones who teach the subject 'sign language'.

Moreover, Deaf teachers will be a natural source of cultural insight and language development for the Deaf pupils as well as the hearing teachers.

Furthermore, the Deaf culture will get a deeper knowledge of the hearing culture through the Deaf teachers' communication in sign language with their fluent hearing colleagues. So, while Deaf teachers will teach the children about the Deaf culture and how to integrate in society, the hearing teachers will teach about the majority culture and other aspects of integration.

- Courage, integrity and commitment are important qualities to maintain for all experimenting teachers. They will, undoubtedly, be met with a lot of critical questions and comments from long-time oralists and a lack of commitment from people who are focussed on total communication. Often the oralists will demand scientific proof and most people want security before anything else. But there is no such security in experimenting.

Experiments should, of course, be founded on reason and logic, but also on a clear vision and trust in the process towards the goal. Developing a bilingual teaching method is a great step away from old and outgrown teaching methods and is certainly a long-term goal. Too many people are focussed on security and they want definite proofs before they start any experiment, but it often takes 15 - 20 years of experimenting before these proofs can be given. Remember that in a complex society experimenting often involves various groups and 'systems', and it takes time to bring them to work together towards the same goal.

In Scandinavia the bilingual experiments and projects have so far resulted in great improvements in Deaf education and have thus laid the foundation for going on towards fully developed bilingual education.

- It is important to bear clearly in mind that the bilingual teaching method means teaching based on a fully developed command of sign language by all participants. On this foundation the spoken language can be taught. Signed Danish/English can be used positively to visualize the spoken language. It has no other function in bilingual education.

Socially we may see young Deaf people having a proper language foundation who are not confused, but feel good about using signed Danish/English in private communication with hearing or hearing-impaired people who are not so skilled in sign language.

- The last thing is the most fundamental: Deaf children and their families must learn sign language as early as possible. This means that parents should begin as soon as they know that their child is Deaf.

Moreover, group integration of the deaf child with other signing Deaf peers will be very important during pre-school time. Only in this way, will the majority of Deaf children be able to catch up with their hearing peers in conceptual knowledge, fundamental language skills, emotional expression and group consciousness. In this way, the deaf children will be well prepared for starting their bilingual school education.

The time has come when the 'unnatural law' that Deaf people must always be behind comes to an end. Human beings are more equal than we believe – if we allow differences!

A comment on cultures and acceptance of language

With the many writings and discussions about cultural identity, language and European integration into the Single Market in 1992 that has been taking place, it should be obvious to most European people today that cultural and personal identity is closely tied to acceptance of language. Many people all over the world find no problem in mastering languages other than their own. Groups of people who are not accepted to their own satisfaction, i.e. who feel oppressed, tend to separate and withdraw to maintain their identity.

Groups of people who feel accepted personally and politically and have a clear identity tend to mingle openly with the rest of the human family. They know they are special, but they also know that they have a lot in common with all other people. That is the basis of true societal integration.

Today and the future

Most Deaf cultures today stand at the line between the isolation phase and the manifestation phase. Some Deaf cultures have crossed the line and the sign of this breakthrough is mainly widespread use of interpreters. Others have stepped even further into the manifestation phase – for instance the Scandinavian Deaf cultures.

The greater societal changes play a fundamental role in the development of each national Deaf culture, but there are also national and cultural differences. Some Deaf cultures have been able to develop under more fortunate societal circumstances and therefore have reached more of their goals than other less fortunate Deaf cultures have. The more fortunate Deaf cultures become the ones who hold the vision and through the international deaf network they are able to support the less fortunate Deaf cultures in reaching their goals.

These efforts will be especially important in the next decade. The basic question in relation to society is: What image of themselves do Deaf people want to project out into society and make manifest through a wide range of projects that show what Deaf people can do?

In the isolation phase Deaf people were 'invisible' to society and society 'invented' a Deaf figure – some people would say a misfit. Now in the manifestation phase Deaf people must define themselves and prove what they want to be. The guiding rule derived from this is simple: Say no to projects, thoughts and behaviour that represent the old image and 'yes' to those that move towards the new and better image. With every new effort and manifestation the Deaf culture will eventually but surely enter the equality phase.

I will not try to project future developments, although there are elements of future traits and main features already distinguishable in present society. Awareness of one's own history together with a better understanding of society enhances the self-knowledge of a group and makes it easier to set up clear long-term as well as short-term goals for a given group.

As such, history is not just interesting stories, but much more meaningful if it goes down to the roots of societal patterning. Thus it can influence the future in a true humanistic direction. The choice is: Do we want to be objects in history or do we want to be the acting subject?

The acting subject is not a victim, not a mere complainer or demander, but someone who feels responsible for putting things into motion with or without the help of the official authorities. This is 'The Human Model' and it is necessary for Deaf cultures and their members to identify with this model in order to do well in the manifestation phase. There are various political areas in Deaf policy that need to be dealt with:

- Pre-school
- Education
- Vocational training
- Interpretation services

- The labour market
- Unemployment
- Media
- Technology
- Theater and other cultural activities.

When the short-term strategies within each area reach the long-term goals, when Deaf people feel satisfied in respect to equality and when the societal image of Deaf people has been totally transformed - then the time has come to enter the equality phase. It is not easy to get there, but it is certainly within reach.

Harlan Lane
Boston, USA

The Medicalization
of Cultural Deafness
in Historical Perspective

Summary

Surgical implantation of cochlear prostheses in early-deafened children is becoming more widespread in the United States since its approval by the Food and Drug Administration in June of 1990. Although implantation requires general anesthesia, protracted surgery, severe structural damage to the middle and inner ear, and extended rehabilitation, there has been no comprehensive evaluation of the long-term risks and benefits of the procedure. The use of experimental medical and surgical procedures of unproven therapeutic value on Deaf children has a long history. It is underpinned by practitioners' belief in the severe infirmity of the members of Deaf communities.

I

On June 27, 1990, the United States Food and Drug Administration approved the proposal of the Cochlear Corporation to market a 'bionic ear' for surgical insertion in Deaf children over the age of two. More properly called a cochlear prosthesis, this device converts sound waves into electrical currents that are delivered to a wire implanted in the child's inner ear. With the headline, *New Hope for Deaf Children: Implant Gives Them Hearing and Speech*, the magazine *American Health* enthused, *Results promise to be even more dramatic for very young children* than they have been for adults. *The implants will actually allow them to speak.* (Weiss 1990) The modern miracle of biotechnology you say, as do the media, and yet: The National Association of the Deaf has called the FDA approval *unsound scientifically, procedurally, and ethically* (National Association of the Deaf 1991, p. 1). Audiologists and otologists, experts who 'have only the best interests of Deaf children at heart', proclaim a dramatic advance; yet the American Deaf community, whose members could not love Deaf children more, proclaim a dangerous setback to their interests.

Cochlear implantation is a surgical procedure, lasting about three-and-a-half hours under general anesthesia, and it requires hospitalization from two to four days. A broad crescent-shaped incision is made behind the operated ear and the skin flap is elevated. A piece of temporalis muscle is removed. A depression is drilled in the skull and reamed to make a seat for the internal electrical coil of the cochlear implant. A section of the mastoid bone is removed to expose the middle ear cavity. Further drilling exposes the membrane of the round window on the inner ear. Observing the procedure under a microscope, the surgeon pierces the membrane. A wire about 18 mm long is pushed through the opening. Sometimes the way is blocked by abnormal bone growth in the inner ear; the surgeon will generally drill through it but may have to settle in the end for only partial insertion of the wire. The wire seeks its own path as it moves around and up the coiled inner ear. The exquisitely detailed microstructure of the inner ear is often ripped asunder as the electrode weaves its way crushing cells and perforating membranes; if there was any residual hearing in the ear it is likely to be destroyed. The auditory nerve itself is unlikely to be damaged, however, and the implant stimulates the auditory nerve directly. The internal coil is then sutured into place. Finally the skin is sewn back into place over the coil.

Will the typical Deaf child, who was born deaf or became so early in life, be able to understand ordinary conversation after undergoing the surgery and a lot of training? Probably not. Will he or she be able to speak intelligibly? Probably not. Will the child learn English better than he/she would have without the implant? Probably not, but we do not know. Will the child be able to attend school with hearing children? Probably not. Will she or he then always have a severe loss of hearing? Yes (Lane 1991, 1992).

Although the implanted deaf children will not move easily in the hearing world, there is a danger that they will not move easily in the Deaf community either. So there is a real danger that they will grow up without any substantive communication, spoken or signed. The children may develop problems of personal identity, emotional adjustment, even of mental health – this has not been studied. You may well ask: If the benefits are so small and the psychological and social risks so great, why did the FDA approve general marketing of the device and why do surgeons implant it?

Why indeed? Why would such heroic medicine be practiced on young Deaf children who, moreover, cannot give their consent? For this to have happened, the plight of the Deaf child must be seen as truly desperate. Just as surgical removal of part of the brain – temporal lobotomy – seemed justified by the desperate plight of mentally ill people before the discovery of psychoactive drugs. Just as a surgeon removes a gangrenous limb to save the rest of the body. In hearing society, deafness is indeed stigmatized. The sociologist Erving Goffman distinguishes three kinds of stigma: physical, characterological, and tribal (Goffman 1963, p. 128) .

There is only one complete, unblushing male in America (...). [He is] a young, married, white, urban northern heterosexual Protestant father of college education, fully employed, of good complexion, weight, and height, and a recent record in sports.

Any deviation is likely to entail a stigma and we tend to impute many when we find a single one. All three categories of stigma are ascribed to Deaf people: physically they are judged defective; this is commonly taken to give rise to undesirable traits such as concreteness of thought and impulsive behavior; and hearing people may view Deaf people as clannish – even indeed an undesirable world apart, social deviants.

Even if the American Deaf community were known for what it is, a linguistic and cultural minority with a rich unique heritage, it would still be subject to tribal stigma as is, for example, the Hispanic-American community. It is not hard to see how a disinterested observer, a reasonable layperson, might arrive at the stereotypes with which we stigmatize Deaf people and at the conclusion that their plight is therefore desperate. It comes from an extrapolative leap: to imagine what deafness is like, I will imagine my world without sound. A terrifying prospect, and one that conforms quite well with the stereotype we project onto those in the Deaf community. I would be isolated, disoriented, uncommunicative and unreceptive to communication. My ties to other people would be ruptured.

The hearing extrapolation to what deafness must be like, in a world without sound, without facile communication, is not entirely without a counterpart in the real world, for each year thousands of hearing Americans lose substantial hearing from illness, trauma and old age. A few may take steps to integrate into the Deaf community, to learn American Sign Language (ASL), make friends in that community, join Deaf organizations, attend a Deaf club and so on; most do not. Growing up Deaf, as have most users of ASL, is quite another matter. To grasp that world of the Deaf community, extrapolation from the hearing world is of no use at all.

Is it better to be Deaf or is it better to be hearing? Anthropologist Richard Shweder asks, *Is it better to have three gods and one wife or one god and three wives ?*(Shweder 1984, p. 55). Of course, the question makes no sense except in relation to a cultural 'frame'. To know what it is to be a member of Deaf culture is to imagine how you would think, feel and react if you had grown up Deaf, if manual language had been your main means of communication, if your eyes were the portals of your mind, if most of your friends were Deaf, if you had only learned that there were children who couldn't sign after knowing dozens who could, if the people you admired were Deaf, if you had struggled daily for as long as you can remember with the ignorance and uncommunicativeness of hearing people, if . . . , if, in a word, you were Deaf.

The disinterested layperson is also misled, as countless parents of Deaf children have been misled, by the experts in otology, pediatrics, audiology, school psychology, special education, and rehabilitation – what I will call the audist establishment. The vocabulary and conceptual framework we have been using with regard to Deaf people, based as it is on infirmity, serves us and the members of the Deaf community less well than a vocabulary and framework of cultural relativity. We need to replace the normativeness of medicine with the curiosity of ethnography.

What makes the American Deaf community more like Hispanic-Americans than disabled Americans is, of course, its culture, including its language. Membership in the Deaf community is not decided by diagnosis; in fact, it is not decided at all, any more than membership in the Hispanic community. Various culturally-determined behaviors, and foremost among them language, reveal whether an individual belongs to a language minority or not.

Anthropologist Roy D'Andrade observes that significant cultural concepts like marriage, money, theft, are not givens but require the adherence of a group to a 'constitutive rule'.

Different cultures have different constitutive rules. Debates about abortion (at what age is a fetus a person?), about what age defines a minor, and the like, are debates about constitutive rules – they can only be pursued within a given cultural frame (D'Andrade 1984). 'Smart' is such a concept, so is 'on time', 'successful', and 'disability'. Because there is a Deaf community with its own language and culture, there is a cultural frame in which to be Deaf is not to be disabled; quite the contrary, it is an asset in Deaf culture to be Deaf in behavior, values, knowledge and fluency in ASL. If we respect the right of people in other cultures, including those within our borders, to have their own constitutive rules which may differ from ours (and we can refuse to do so only at the risk of being impossibly naive), then we must recognize that the deafness of which I speak is not a disability but rather a different way of being.

History, like ethnography, reveals that what we thought were surely fundamental and absolute values are in fact the product of time and place; it allows us to discover the variations in constitutive rules. We can then imagine rules other than the ones we have always taken for granted. Those other rules may serve us better, or an awareness of them may enrich our appreciation of the rules we now accept, or we may look with awe and admiration on the diverse ways of being of humankind.

I am concerned here with a language minority; a community that consequently has a rich culture and art forms of its own, a minority history and social structure. What is in dispute intellectually is the use of one type of description rather than another for this language minority, a cultural description rather than one based on infirmity.

To apply an infirmity model to members of a group is to regard them and interact with them particularly with respect to our cultural conception of bodily defect. This conceptual framework, which one normally acquires in the course of acculturation, is implicit; it entails issues, values, and reference to societal institutions. Some of the issues that naturally arise when a certain way of being or behaving is construed as an infirmity are: by what criteria and by whom is this construed as an infirmity; how did that infirmity arise; what are the risks and benefits of the available treatments, if any; what can be done to minimize the disabling effects of the infirmity? The values invoked are largely negative; we may admire someone's accommodation to their infirmity or their courage in struggling with it, but the infirmity itself is generally considered undesirable; at best we are ambivalent. The institutions that are part of this conceptual framework include notably the biological sciences, and the health and social welfare professions.

To apply a cultural model to a group is to invoke quite a different conceptual framework. Implicit in this posture are issues such as: what are the interdependent values, mores, art forms, traditions, organizations and language that characterize this culture? How is it influenced by the physical and social environment in which it is embedded? Such questions are, in principle, value neutral, although of course some people are ill-disposed to cultural diversity while others prize it. The institutions invoked by a cultural model of a group include the social sciences, professions in a mediating role between cultures such as simultaneous interpretation, and the schools, an important locus of cultural transmission.

An examination of the American Deaf community, for example, promptly provides evidence of the fit of a cultural model. There is now a very large literature that describes this culture, its language, its art forms, its organizations and social structure, its means of cultural transmission, its particular values, its cultural artifacts, the patterns of behavior that are culturally appropriate in various situations – its mores, its history.[1]

We have come to look at Deaf people in a certain way, to use a certain vocabulary of infirmity, and this practice is so widespread among hearing people, and has gone on for so

---

1 Some illustrative, mostly recent, references: Rutherford 1988; Schein 1987; Schein 1989; Bienvenu/Colonomos 1989; Padden,/Humphries 1988; Jacobs 1980; Wilcox 1989; Eastman 1974; Bragg/Bergmann 1982; Bragg 1989; Gannon 1981; Gannon 1989; Van Cleve (ed.) 1987; Van Cleve/Crouch 1989. On language, see, for example, the journal *Sign Language Studies;* Sternberg 1990; Lucas (ed.) 1989; Wilbur 1987; Eastman 1989; Baker/Cokely 1980; Klima/Bellugi 1979.

long, and is so legitimized by the medical and paramedical professions, that we imagine we are accurately describing attributes of Deaf people rather than choosing to talk about them in a certain way. If we but consult history or Deaf people for five minutes, we will be reminded of the error of this 'common sense' position.[2] There was a time in American history (as in European history) when hearing people viewed culturally Deaf people predominantly in terms of a cultural model. It went without saying at that time – the better part of the last century – that you needed to know the language of the Deaf community to teach Deaf children, that Deaf adults and Deaf culture must play a prominent role in the education of this minority. Deaf people published newspapers and books and held meetings that were focally concerned with the Deaf community, and they discussed the pros and cons of having their own land, where Deaf people lived and governed, perhaps some land grant from the federal government in the newly settled West. There were many more late-deafened children then and it seemed a pity not to maintain their skill in speaking English, so those children who could profit from it were given an hour or so of speech training after school a few times a week. There were no special educators; the requisites of a good teacher were a good education and fluency in ASL; nearly half of all teachers were Deaf themselves. There were no audiologists, or rehabilitation counselors, or school psychologists, and, for the most part, none apparently were needed. The Deaf child was not parametrized in the terms of those professions: so many decibels of hearing loss at such and such frequencies; a profile on the Minnesota Multiphasic Personality Inventory; an IQ score. Instead, Deaf children and adults were described in cultural terms: where did they go to school; who were their Deaf relatives, if any; who was their deaf spouse and Deaf friends; where did they work; what Deaf sports teams and Deaf organizations did they belong to; what service did they render to the Deaf community (see Lane 1984)?

II

I want to describe how the medicalization of Deaf people takes place, how an infirmity model of Deaf people is promulgated when it is grossly inappropriate. Let us shift the focus from the person labeled infirm and his or her etiology to the social context in which the infirmity label was acquired. If we ask culturally Deaf adults how they first acquired the label 'handicapped, disabled, impaired', we commonly learn that some circumstance of heredity, of birth or of early childhood, marked the child as different from its parents and created an initial breakdown in communication between parent and child. The parents then see this as deviant relative to their norms and take the child to the experts – the pediatrician, the otologist, the audiologist. It is they who legitimate the infirmity model. Why do they do it? Because that is precisely a core function of their profession, to diagnose infirmity.

How do the experts medicalize the child's difference into deviance? First they characterize the difference in great biological detail and often only in stigmatizing ways. Much will be said about impairment of spoken language, little may be said about acquisition of ASL. Much will be said about hearing loss, nothing about gains in visual perception and thought (Bellugi/O'Grady/Lillo-Martin/O'Grady-Hines/van Hoek/Corina 1990). Second, while pursuing the infirmity model, the experts commonly remain silent about the cultural model; they may not even mention the community of adults who were once children much like their client. Otologists and audiologists are often poorly informed about the Deaf community and its language; that knowledge is not a required part of their training; moreover, the audiologist works for a clinic under the jurisdiction of an ear doctor. If the professional

---

2 Rorty calls thinkers who have doubts about their vocabulary, since they are impressed with those of others and have seen all such vocabularies change in time, ironists. The opposite of the ironist view is called common sense (*The ironist takes the unit of persuasion to be a vocabulary rather than a proposition;* Rorty 1989, p. 78).

person does describe the Deaf community, it may well be in terms that are so concise that the parents do not really grasp an alternative conception of their child's status and destiny. The professional expert and the parents generally share the same hearing culture; they tend to evaluate and label the Deaf child from the perspective of their shared hearing culture.

The labeling is a prelude to profound life-changing events, to special practices at home, to a 'special' education, to training in some skills and not others, to studying some subjects and not others, to specific patterns of social relations, to the wearing of technological stigmata (electronic devices and wires), possibly to surgery, to the development of a certain self-image as a consequence of all these forces. The audiologist passes the healthy Deaf child-become-patient to the special educator; the child is now tagged with an infirmity model and has acquired a second persona, the child described in the accompanying dossier. The job of the educator is not to educate; it is to find an educational treatment for what the otologist and audiologist could not treat, the child's failure to acquire English normally. A difference has been identified; now a massive campaign begins to eradicate it.

The right to define a problem and to locate it within one social domain rather than another – to construe it as a problem of medicine, education, rehabilitation, religion, politics – is won by struggle and enterprise. The medicalization of the Deaf community is marked by a long history of struggle between Deaf people and the hearing people who profess to serve them (Lane 1984).

Toward the end of the last century, hearing teachers seized control of the profession of Deaf education and banished ASL and deaf teachers. With the cultural frame changed, the Deaf pupil was now an outsider. Spoken language in the classroom and speech therapy failed to make the child an insider while driving out all education, confirming that he or she was defective. Unsuccessful education of Deaf children reinforced the need for special education, for experts in counseling of the Deaf, and in rehabilitation of the Deaf. Finally and most devastatingly, Deaf children in America, starting in the late 1970s, were increasingly placed in local hearing schools. Cut off from the Deaf world, unable to communicate substantively with parents, peers and teachers, Deaf children have a greater need to be hearing children than ever before in American history. The typical Deaf child, born deaf or deafened before learning English, is utterly at a loss as he or she sits on the deaf bench in the hearing classroom.[3] What is the teacher saying? How can I make my own thoughts clear to her? What can I do to be accepted by the other children? Is there someone here who could explain things to me after school? The infirmity model has become more plausible applied to the young Deaf child; with academic integration, the medicalization of cultural deafness gained major ground. This latest development illustrates a principle of oppression articulated by Jean-Paul Sartre: *Oppressors produce and maintain by force the evils which, in their eyes, render the oppressed more and more like what he should be to deserve his fate* (Sartre 1966, pp. 35-36).

Representation is a political act. If the native is a child, he or she needs the European's guidance. If his actions are immoral and heathen, he needs the missionary. If he is uncivilized, only European intervention can raise him or her up to the status of civilized person. Deaf children and adults, in becoming the technical objects of psychometric investigation, make the audist establishment possible and seemingly legitimate its control over them. The representation of Deaf people is intimately bound up with the conduct of their education and training and the program of surgically implanting them. The portrayal of Deaf people as socially isolated, intellectually weak, behaviorally impulsive, and emotionally immature makes school psychology and counseling, special education and

---

3 A 1985 survey found only one Deaf child in four in integrated school settings had a teacher who used signs; 'using signs' is not the same thing as using ASL (Allen/Karchmer 1990) .

4 The development of special education was made possible by the technology of educational psychology (see Quicke 1984, p. 123).

rehabilitation appear necessary[4]; the failure of deaf education makes desperate and ill-founded medical intervention more appealing. If there is to be a treatment, and a treatment establishment, there must be a syndrome. Overly active and inattentive children did not receive amphetamines for more than a decade after this class of drugs had been shown to calm such children; this medical intervention, promoted by the drug manufacturer, required a syndrome to become widely practiced; hyperkinetic impulse disorder was conveniently 'discovered' (Conrad/Schneider 1980).

Preposterously invidious descriptions of Deaf people issued with authority by hearing people in the audist establishment have thus enjoyed a long and protected history. The practice continues. The award for the zaniest defamation may go to the educator of Deaf college students who reported in 1988 a *failure of hearing-impaired* (college) *students to conceptualize changes over time and space*, as if such students didn't keep appointments, couldn't find classrooms, had not used for most of their lives a language that requires subtle temporal and spatial discriminations, and had not relied on temporal and spatial understanding in much of their pre-college education (Senior 1988, p. 277). These invidious descriptions are designed to confirm the audist belief in the Deaf child's 'special needs' – above all, the special need for the audist establishment. The notion of need, as the need for food and the need for love, has been extended metaphorically here and we may well ask why. *The needs of the blind*, writes sociologist Robert Scott in his classic, *The Making of Blind Men*, (are those) *blind people must have if they are to fit into and be served by programs that have arisen for other reasons* (Scott 1981, p. 103).

According to the audist, the Deaf person is not only different from us, and different in starkly negative ways according to psychometric science, but also those differences are absolutized, they are inherent. This is an act of mystification (Tomlinson 1982) to obscure the true power relations. The intrinsic nature of African-American inferiority, fueled by Darwinian evolutionism, also seemed to justify the treatment of African-Americans as slaves (McCarthy 1983). Contemporary claims of the native inferiority of African-Americans arise in the context of the manifest educational and social inequalities between the majority and African-Americans in our nation. Political scientist James Q. Wilson and psychologist Richard Herrnstein, in their 1985 book *Crime and Human Nature*, contend that men with a certain body type – square-like, barrel-chested, muscular – are predisposed to crime, and that more young black males fit this type, called mesomorphy, than do young white males (Wilson/Herrnstein 1985, p. 469).[5] In the same vein, psychologist Arthur Jensen has contended that IQ scores of African-Americans reflect their biological inferiority to Caucasians (Jensen 1985), and when Dr. William Shockley was asked on the television program 'Firing Line' what could be done about the alleged inferiority, he replied: *I have this voluntary sterilization bonus plan (...) depending upon genetically carried disabilities (...) $1000 for every point you score below 100 on an IQ test* (Shockley quoted in Manion/Bersani 1987, p. 235).

The native is natively incapable, observes Memmi (Memmi 1984, p. 107). And so it is with the audist's characterization of Deaf people. Either their sorry state is the result of the practices of the audist establishment, which is unthinkable, or it is the result of the Deaf person's constitutional inability to profit from those practices. The tenet of the native inferiority of deaf people shores up the entire audist establishment. Thus psychologist McCay Vernon writes (1982, p. 24):

> *It is now apparent that behavior noted as characteristic of deaf children* [is] *often an interactional effect of both the loss of hearing and of other central nervous system lesions associated with the condition causing the deafness.*

---

5 *Among whites, being a mesomorph is an indicator of a predisposition to crime. Young black males are more mesomorphic (5.14 on Sheldon's scale) than are young white males (4.29) (...);* the authors also qualify these remarks; see chapters 3 and 18.

No wonder Deaf personality, socialization and cognition are in such poor repair! No wonder the professionals of the audist establishment are so urgently needed! No wonder Deaf education is largely failing at its task! These children have brain lesions! Not demonstrable brain lesions, mind you: a tiny percent have those (2.1 % in one survey; Wolff/Harkins 1986); but inferred brain lesions, the same as may be inferred from the allegedly poor performance of African-Americans on IQ tests. With the same line of reasoning, a British psychologist reviewing the translated classics in Deaf education, *The Deaf Experience,* which I edited, rejected my claim that deaf children were better educated in the era that proceeded on a cultural model of the Deaf community: *It is not the lack of* (sign language) *in the schools,* he wrote, *which is responsible for the deaf experience of social isolation and impoverished opportunity: it is deafness itself* (Webster 1985, p. 250).

Audism has a supplementary reason for believing in the constitutional inferiority of culturally Deaf people, beyond self-legitimation and mystification. For the audist establishment, unlike the colonialists and white supremacists, has a sector devoted to treating this constitutional flaw, to measuring it, modifying it, surgically correcting it; this is the medicalization of cultural Deafness and it requires a biological theory of Deaf inferiority.

The desperate plight of Deaf people portrayed by sham psychometrics, the design and failure of special education which that portrayal is invoked to justify, and the desperate cure undertaken with highly experimental surgical implants are interrelated and inter-legitimating programs of the audist establishment. The connections are not only intellectual and abstract, they are also administrative and operational.

If cultural Deafness were not medicalized by psychometrics and audiology, there would be no special education, but simply bilingual education for children whose primary language is ASL. If the members of the Deaf community were characterized in cultural terms and bilingual education was largely successful, there would be little motivation for parents to seek a surgical intervention of little value and unassessed risk to most Deaf children.

The three-pronged endeavor takes control of the body of the child psychometrically, educationally, and surgically. The service orienters and the service providers are in league: audiologists are sympathetic to oral education programs; otologists to audiologists and speech therapists. Deaf people must be kept away from orienting roles. Michel Foucault was right when he said that in such social struggles bodies are the battlefield. Cochlear implantation requires that the children be parametrized in terms of audiological, intellectual and psychosocial measures. It dictates their communicative relations with their parents and others and shapes their home environment; it influences the school to commit itself to non-academic goals and specific methods in striving to reach them; and it implants experimental electronic devices in the children's skull that continually affect their sensory milieu, their relations with those around them, and their image of themselves. The intervention is comprehensive and long-term. The National Institutes of Health Consensus Conference on Cochlear Implants said it clearly:

> *Children with implants still must be regarded as hearing-impaired* (and) *will continue to require educational, audiological, and speech and language support services for long periods of time.* (Kohut (ed.) 1988, p. 16)

This is bio-power (*bio-pouvoir,* Foucault): massive intervention in the life of the child in support of the majority's rejection of minority language, culture, and values.

There is a revealing irony here. In the aftermath of the Gallaudet Revolution rejecting audism and affirming the cultural values of the Deaf community, a sympathetic U.S. Congress passed a law creating a special institute devoted to the concerns of Deaf people. It was placed under the National Institutes of Health, named the National Institute on Deafness and Other Communication Disorders, refused requests from Deaf community leaders to delete the word Other from its name, and proceeded to devote a vast portion of its budget to research on cochlear implants.

The medical specialty of otology has been expanding its traditional clientele beyond adventitiously-deafened hearing people who seek treatment, for whom an infirmity model is appropriate, to include members of the Deaf community, for whom it is not. There is no prospect of medicalizing the million or so Deaf adults in America's Deaf community – they reject the claim that they have a medical problem (Evans 1989). This apparently came as a surprise and a great disappointment to the early manufacturers of cochlear implants who envisioned selling some three hundred thousand devices (sales of four and a half billion dollars) in the United States alone (House 1990). There is, however, the possibility of medicalizing culturally Deaf adults while they are young, while they are still children. That is because of a remarkable fact about this cultural and linguistic minority: most members have hearing parents who do not transmit and will not share the linguistic and cultural identity of their Deaf children. The children themselves are too young to refuse treatment or to dispute the infirmity model of their difference. Their hearing parents, frequently beset by guilt, grief and anxiety, and largely ignorant of the Deaf community, commonly accept the infirmity model uncritically, and consequently turn for help to the related social institutions, such as medicine, audiology, and special education.

III

Desperate and useless medical measures to address what we hearing people see as the desperate plight of culturally deaf children have a long history. French otologist Prosper Ménière captured the audist medical view well, writing in 1853:

> *The deaf believe that they are our equals in all respects. We should be generous and not destroy that illusion. But whatever they believe, deafness is an infirmity and we should repair it whether the person who has it is disturbed by it or not.* (Ménière qoted in Houdin 1855, p. 14)

It was necessary for Ménière to make this outrageous affirmation precisely because Deaf people were not disturbed by being deaf. On the contrary, in the last century as in this one, culturally Deaf people thought Deaf was a perfectly good way to be, as good as hearing, perhaps better. Jean-Marc Itard, the first physician to write a treatise on diseases of hearing, and thus considered a founder of otology, undertook the most extravagant medical procedures with culturally Deaf children, once his many years of trying to teach them oral skills had utterly failed. He started by applying electricity to the ears of some pupils at the Paris school, since an Italian surgeon had recently found that a frog's leg would contract if touched with charged metal. Itard thought there was some analogy between the paralysis of the hearing organ and the paralysis of a limb. He also placed leeches on the necks of some of the pupils at the school founded by the abbé de L'Epée and directed at that time by his successor, the abbé Sicard, in the hope that local bleeding would help somehow. Six students had their eardrums pierced, but the operation was painful and fruitless, and he desisted. Not soon enough for one student who died following this treatment. At first, however, his ears discharged some foreign matter and he reportedly recovered some hearing and with it some speech, which led Itard to think the deaf ear might be blocked up rather than paralyzed (Itard 1825).

It was said that the postmaster at Versailles had cured his own hearing loss by inserting a probe in his Eustachian tube, which leads from the throat to the ear, and *flushing out the lymphatic excrement* (Corone 1960, p. 41-42). The method had been widely tried by physicians and abandoned as impracticable and ineffective. Itard made improvements to the probe and then subjected to the treatment one hundred twenty pupils, almost every last one in the school save for some two dozen who would not be subdued. Nothing at all was accomplished. Itard dispensed a secret brew into the ears of every pupil in the school who was not born deaf, a few drops a day for two weeks – without effect (Itard 1821/1842, p. 342). With other students Itard tried a regime of daily purgatives; still others had their ears covered with a bandage soaked in a blistering agent. Within a few days, the pupil's ear lost all its skin, oozed pus and was excruciatingly painful. When it scabbed, Itard reapplied the bandage and the wound reopened. Then Itard repeated the cycle and applied caustic soda to the skin behind his ear. All of this was to no avail. Itard tried fracturing the skull of a few pupils, striking the area just behind the ear with a hammer. With a dozen pupils he applied a white-hot metal button behind the ear which led to pus and a scab in about a week. Yet another of Itard's treatments was to thread a string through a pupil's neck with a seton needle, which caused a suppurating wound that supposedly allowed feculent humors to dry up (Ménière 1853, p. 47). It was all a miserable failure.

> *'Medicine does not work on the dead', Itard concluded, and as far as I am concerned the ear is dead in the deaf mute. There is nothing for science to do about it.* (Quoted in Esquiros 1847, p. 412)

Medicine made no further inroads against cultural Deafness in the 19th century but two developments in biology, the Darwinian revolution and Mendelian genetics, gave rise to the eugenics movement which sought to improve the race and eliminate the Deaf community by selective breeding. If the members of the Deaf community indeed suffered from an infirmity, as the medicalization of cultural Deafness would have it, and if that infirmity ran in families as it clearly did at times, then it stood to reason for many audists that Deaf people should be discouraged from reproducing. The most famous audist in this period was Alexander Graham Bell, and he devoted his great wealth, fame and prestige to these measures. When the Breeders' Association created a section on eugenics *to emphasize the value of superior blood and the menace to society of inferior blood* (quoted in Lane 1984, p. 355), Bell agreed to serve. Bell published a warning in 1920 that Americans were committing race suicide, for *Children of foreign born parents are increasing at a much greater rate than the children of native born parents* (Bell 1920, quoted in Lane 1984, p. 355). As selective immigration laws had been only partially successful, he argued, restriction on marriage or child bearing might be necessary:

> *It is now felt that the interests of the race demand that the best should marry and have large families and that any restrictions on reproduction should apply to the worst rather than the best.* (Bell quoted in Lane 1984, p. 356)

Bell was opposed, however, to laws forbidding marriage of deaf people and other undesirables (as he called them).

> *This would not produce the desired improvement,* he wrote, *for even were we to go to the extreme length of killing off the undesirables altogether, so that they could not propagate their kind (...) it would diminish the production of the undesirables without increasing the production of the desirables.* (A.G. Bell to David Fairchild, Nov. 23, 1908, quoted in Winefield 1987, p. 83)

Bell specifically engaged the issue of eugenics and the Deaf population beginning in the 1880s, shortly after the congress of Milan. Sign language and the residential schools were creating a Deaf community, he warned, in which Deaf people intermarried and reproduced, a situation fraught with danger to the rest of the society (Bell 1883; Bell 1884, p. 66). He sounded the alarm in a *Memoir Upon the Formation of a Deaf Variety of the Human Race,* presented to the National Academy of Sciences. Since there are familial patterns of deafness, *It is to be feared that the intermarriage of such persons would be attended by calamitous results to their offspring* (quoted in Lane 1984, p. 357). Congenitally Deaf people without Deaf relatives also run a risk in marrying, as do people deafened adventitiously who have Deaf relatives. If these persons marry, Bell reasoned, and some of their children marry congenitally deaf people, and then some of theirs do, and so on, the proportion of deaf children born of such marriages will increase from generation to generation until nearly all their children will be born deaf. These families *would then constitute a variety of the human race in which deafness would be the rule rather than the exception* (ibid.).

In his recommendations, Bell considered repressive and preventive measures. Under the first heading, a law prohibiting Deaf adults from marriage might only promote deaf children born out of wedlock. A law prohibiting just congenitally deaf adults from marrying *would go a long way towards checking the evil* (ibid.) but it is difficult to prove whether a person was born deaf or not. *Legislation forbidding the intermarriage of persons belonging to families containing more than one deaf mute would be more practical. This would cover the intermarriage of hearing parents belonging to such families* (ibid.). But more data are needed before we can justify the passage of such an act, he said.

Thus, for the present, Bell found that preventive measures must suffice. *We commence our efforts on behalf of the deaf mute by changing his social environment* (ibid.). Residential schools should be closed and the Deaf educated in small day schools. Coeducation with hearing children would be the ideal *but this is not practicable to any great extent* (Bell quoted in Lane 1984, p. 358). Sign language should be banished. Currently only 14 percent of the Deaf use speech in the classroom. Deaf teachers are to be shunned yet presently a third of the teachers are Deaf (ibid.). As an audist par excellence, Bell believed speech to be the highest possible value for Deaf people. When the Conference of Principals of Schools for the Deaf placed on its agenda the question *What is the importance of speech to the deaf?* Bell was flabbergasted:

> *I am astonished. I am pained. To ask the value of speech? It is like asking the value of life! (. ..) What is the object of the education of the deaf and dumb if it is not to set them in communication with the world?* (Quoted in Conference of Executives of American Schools for the Deaf 1884, p. 178)

This belief persists in the audist establishments of many nations, and the desperate educational plight of Deaf children in those nations makes them particularly vulnerable to 'heroic' medicine. For example, British experts on Deaf education write: *Developing deaf pupils' ability to communicate, preferably in an oral way, is the central goal of deaf education* (Hegarty/Pocklington 1982, p. 120).

Bell's *Memoir upon the Formation of a Deaf Variety of the Human Race* received wide newspaper coverage. There was much consternation among Deaf people contemplating marriage, and many letters to the press, as well as journal articles, vigorously repudiated Bell's views. Whatever his intention, his actions led many to believe that there would be, or already were, laws prohibiting Deaf marriage. Proposals to segregate congenitally Deaf adults were made, as were counterproposals to allow them freedom as long as they did not reproduce (Johnson 1918, p. 6). News of Bell's memoir spread rapidly among parents of Deaf children, *their family physicians, and among surgeons generally throughout the world*, a contemporary observer wrote, *and suggested to them a senseless and cruel procedure – the sterilization of children born deaf.* This pastor of the All Angels Church, Baltimore, had come to know many deaf couples who were childless and unhappy as a result of having been sterilized in infancy; he laid the blame on Bell (quoted in Mitchell 1971, p. 355).

A 1912 report from the eugenics section of the Breeders' Association cites Bell's census of blind and deaf persons and lists 'socially unfit' classes, including deaf people, whose supply should, if possible, *be eliminated from the human stock* (American Genetic Association, Eugenics Section 1912, p. 3). The section drafted a model sterilization law to be applied to these classes; it was designed to satisfy the courts while purging the United States of its *burden of undesirable germ-plasm* (ibid.). By the time of World War I, sixteen states had such sterilization laws in force (Haller 1963, p. 133). By 1940, thirty states had such laws, providing for compulsory sterilization of 'sexual perverts', drug addicts, drunkards, epileptics, *and other diseased and degenerate persons*, including the feebleminded (May/Hughes 1987, p. 215). Physicians were actively involved in this eugenics movement (Conrad/Schneider 1980, p. 12). We are shocked at the extremity of the measures that our society was willing to take; but our surprise at some of the classes of people to be sterilized teaches an even more important lesson. What 'common sense' and medical science plainly show to be an illness in one culture and epoch, are plainly considered not to be in another place and time.

IV

Among the biological means for regulating and, ultimately, eliminating Deaf culture, language and community, cochlear implants have historical antecedents, then, in medical experimentation on deaf children and reproductive regulation of deaf adults.

One leading scientist studying childhood cochlear implants, Mary Joe Osberger of the Indiana University Medical Center states:

> *Given the limitations of any cochlear prosthesis at this time, it can be predicted that the performance levels of nonauditory children might match but not exceed those of profoundly hearing-impaired children with residual hearing who use hearing aids.* (Osberger 1989, p. 279)

My detailed inspection of the data that are available leads me to conclude that children who were born deaf or became so within the first few years of life (nine out of ten deaf children; Brown 1986)[6] are unlikely to profit from implants materially. Cochlear implants are still highly experimental devices for early-deafened children, with unknown consequences for their quality of life; experimentation on such children in these circumstances cannot be justified ethically.

There is now abundant scientific evidence that, as the Deaf community has long contended, it comprises a linguistic and cultural minority. Many Americans, perhaps most, would agree that as a society we should not seek the scientific tools nor use them, if available, to change a child biologically so he or she will belong to the majority rather than the minority – even if we believe that this biological engineering might reduce the burdens the child will bear as a member of a minority. Even if we could take children destined to be members of the African-American, or Hispanic-American, or Native-American, or Deaf American communities, and convert them with 'bio-power' into white, Caucasian, hearing males – even if we could, we should not.

Members of the American Deaf community affirm that what characterizes them as a group is their shared language and culture and not an infirmity. When Gallaudet University's president, I. King Jordan, was asked if he would like to have his hearing back, he replied:

> *That's almost like asking a black person if he would rather be white (. . .). I don't think of myself as missing something or as incomplete (. . .). It's a common fallacy if you don't know deaf people or deaf issues. You think it's a limitation.* (Quoted in Fine/Fine (producers) 1990)

Our story has come full circle. If the birth of a Deaf child is a priceless gift, then there is only cause for rejoicing, as at the birth of a black child, or an Indian one. Medical intervention is

---

6 Jensema/Mullins 1974 reports 90% of deaf schoolchildren in a large sample became deaf before age three (Jensema/Mullins 1974).

inappropriate, even if a perfect 'cure' were available. Invasive surgery on healthy children is morally wrong. We know that, as members of a stigmatized minority, these children's lives will be full of challenge but, by the same token, they have a special contribution to make to their own community and the larger society. On the other hand, the more we view the children born deaf as tragically infirm, the more we see their plight as desperate, the more we are prepared to conduct surgery of unproven benefit and unassessed risk. Our representation of Deaf people determines the outcome of our ethical judgment.

Scholarship does not provide reliable guides on where to draw the line between valuable diversity and treatable deviance. In the course of American history, health practitioners and scientists have labeled various groups biologically inferior that are no longer considered in that light; these include women, Southern Europeans, blacks, gay men and lesbians and culturally Deaf people. What scholarship does tell us is that there is increasingly the well-founded view in America, as around the globe, that the Deaf communities of the world are linguistic and cultural minorities. Logic and morality demand that where there are laws or mores protecting such minorities they extend to the Deaf community. In America, this recognition of the status of the Deaf community, fueled by the civil rights movement, is leading to greater acceptance of Deaf people. The interests of the Deaf child and his or her parents may best be served by accepting that s/he is a Deaf person, with a rich cultural and linguistic heritage which can enrich her/his parents' life as it will her/his own. We should heed the advice of the Deaf teenager who, when reprimanded by her mother for not wearing the processor of her cochlear prosthesis, hurled back bitterly: *I'm Deaf. Let me be Deaf.*

References

Allen, T. /Karchmer, M. (1990): Communication in classrooms for deaf students: student, teacher, and program characteristics; in: H. Bornstein (ed.): *Manual communication: Implications for education.* Washington DC: Gallaudet University Press. pp. 45-66.

American Genetic Association, Eugenics Section (1912): *American Sterilization Laws. Preliminary report of the committee of the eugenics section of the American Breeders Association to study and to report on the best practical means for cutting off the defective germ plasm in the human population.* London: Eugenics Educational Society.

Baker, C./Cokely, D. (1980): *American Sign Language: A teacher's resource text on grammar and culture.* Silver Spring MD: TJ Publishers.

Bell, A. G. (1920): Is race suicide possible? *Journal of Heredity,* 11, pp. 339-341.

Bell, A.G. to David Fairchild, Nov., 23, 1908. Bell papers, Library of Congress. Quoted in Winefield, R. (1987): *Never the twain shall meet.* Washington DC: Gallaudet University Press.

Bell, A.G. (1883): *Memoir Upon the Formation of a Deaf Variety of the Human Race.* New Haven: National Academy of Sciences.

Bell, A.G. (1884): Fallacies concerning the deaf. *American Annals of the Deaf,* 29, pp. 32-69. (Reprinted: Washington, DC: Gibson, 1884.)

Bellugi, U./O'Grady, L./Lillo-Martin, D./O'Grady-Hines, M./van Hoek, K./ Corina, D. (1990): Enhancement of spatial cognition in deaf children; in: Volterra, V./Erting, C. (eds.): *From gesture to language in hearing and deaf children.* Berlin: Springer Verlag. pp. 279-298.

Bienvenu, M. J./Colonomos, B. (1989): *An introduction to American deaf culture.* Burtonsville MD: Sign Media Inc.

Bragg, B. (1989): *Lessons in laughter: The autobiography of a Deaf actor.* Washington DC: Gallaudet University Press.

Bragg, B./Bergmann, E. (1982): *Tales from a Clubroom.* Washington DC: Gallaudet College.

Brown, S. C. (1986): Etiological trends, characteristics, and distributions; in: Schildroth, A. N. /Karchmer, M.A. (eds.): *Deaf children in America.* San Diego CA: College- Hill, pp. 33-54.

Conference of Executives of Am. Schools for the Deaf. (1884): *Proceedings.* Jackson, Miss: Clarion Ledger.

Conrad, P./Schneider, J. (1980): *Deviance and medicalization: From badness to sickness*. Columbus: Merrill. Reprinted 1985.

Corone, A. (1960): Contribution à l'histoire de la sonde d'Itard. *Histoire de la Medecine,* 10, pp. 41-42.

D'Andrade, R. (1984): Cultural meaning systems; in: Shweder, R. /LeVine, R.A. (eds.): *Culture theory.* New York: Cambridge U. Press. pp. 88-122.

Eastman, G. (1974): *Sign Me Alice.* Washington DC: Gallaudet College.

Eastman, G. C. (1989): *From mime to sign.* Silver Spring MD: TJ Publishers.

Esquiros, A. (1847): Les Sourds-Muets; in: id., *Paris au XIXième siècle.* Paris: Imprimerie Unis. Vol. 2. pp. 391-492.

Evans, J. W. (1989): Thoughts on the psychosocial implications of cochlear implantation in children; in: Owens, E. /Kessler, D. (eds.): *Cochlear implants in young deaf children.* Boston MA: Little Brown. pp. 307-314.

Fine, H./Fine, P. (Producers) (1990, March): *Sixty Minutes.* New York NY: Columbia Broadcasting System.

Gannon, J. (1981): *Deaf Heritage.* Silver Spring: National Association of the Deaf.

Gannon, J. (1989): *The Week the world heard Gallaudet.* Washington DC: Gallaudet University Press.

Goffman, E. (1963): *Stigma, notes on the management of spoiled identity.* Englewood Cliffs, NJ: Prentice Hall.

Haller, M. (1963): *Eugenics: Hereditarian Attitudes in American Thought.* New Brunswick: Rutgers University Press.

Hegarty, S./Pocklington, P. (1982): *Integration in action.* Windsor: NFER-Nelson. Cited in: Booth, T. (1988): Challenging conceptions of integration; in: Barton, L. (ed.): *The Politics of Special Educational Needs.* Philadelphia: Falmer Press. pp. 99-122.

Houdin, A. (1855): *De la surdi- mutité; examen critique et raisonné de la discussion soulevée a l'Académie Impériale de Médecine de Paris, séances des 19 et 26 avril 1853 sur cinq questions.* Paris: Lube.

House, A. (1990, January): Cochlear implants in children; past and present perspectives. Address to the Third Symposium on Cochlear Implants in Children, Indiana University School of Medicine, Indianapolis IN.

Itard, J. M.G. (1821): *Traité des maladies de l'oreille et de l'audition.* Paris: Mequignon-Marvis. Second edition: Paris: Mequignon-Marvis fils, 1842.

Itard, J. M. G. (1825): Rapport de M. Itard fait à l'administration le 8 juillet 1825. Unpublished manuscript, Archives de l'Institution Nationale des Sourds-Muets. Paris. Reprinted: Premier rapport... sur divers traitement contre la surdi-mutité. *Revue médicale française et étrangère et journal de clinique,* 2/1827, pp. 27-38.

Jacobs, L. (1980): *A Deaf adult speaks out.* Washington DC: Gallaudet University Press. Second Edition.

Jensema, C./Mullins, J. (1974): Onset, cause, and additional handicaps in hearing-impaired children. *American Annals of the Deaf,* 119, pp. 701-705.

Jensen, A. R. (1981): *Straight talk about mental tests.* New York: Free Press.

Jensen, A. R. (1985): The nature of the black-white difference on various psychometric tests; Spearman's hypothesis. *The Behavioral and Brain Sciences,* 8, pp. 193-263.

Johnson, R.H. (1918): The marriage of the deaf. *Jewish Deaf,* pp. 5-6.

Klima, K. /Bellugi, U. (1979): *The signs of language.* Cambridge MA: Harvard University Press.

Kohut, R. I. (ed.) (1988): Cochlear implants. *National Institutes of Health Consensus Development Conference Statement,* 7, 1-25.

Lane, H. (1984): *When the mind hears: A history of the deaf.* New York: Random House.

Lane, H. (1991): Cultural and disability models of Deaf Americans. *Journal of the American Academy of Rehabilitative Audiology,* 23, 11-26.

Lane, H. (1992): *The mask of benevolence: Disabling the Deaf community.* New York: Alfred Knopf.

Lucas, C. (ed.) (1989): *The Sociolinguistics of the Deaf community.* New York: Academic press.

Manion, M. L./Bersani, H. (1987): Mental retardation as a Western sociological construct: a cross-cultural analysis. *Disability, Handicap and Society,* 2, pp. 231-245.

May, D./Hughes, D. (1987): Organizing services for people with mental handicap: The Californian experience. *Disability, Handicap and Society,* 2, pp. 213-230.

McCarthy, M. (1983): *Dark continent: Africa as seen by Americans.* Westport CO: Greenwood.

Memmi, A. (1984): *Dependence.* Boston MA: Beacon Press.

Ménière, P.(1853): *De la guérison de la surdi-mutité et de l'éducation des sourds-muets. Exposé de la discussion qui a eu lieu à l'Académie Impériale de Médecine, avec notes critiques.* Paris: Baillière.

Mitchell, S.H. (1971): The haunting influence of Alexander Graham Bell. *American Annals of the Deaf,* 116, pp. 349-356.

National Association of the Deaf, Cochlear Implant Task Force, Cochlear implants in children (1991): *A position paper of the National Association of the Deaf.* February 2, 1991. Reprinted: The National Association of the Deaf *Broadcaster,* 13, March, 1991,1.

Osberger, M. J. (1989): Speech production in profoundly hearing-impaired children with reference to cochlear implants; in: Owens E. /Kessler, D. (eds.): *Cochlear implants in young deaf children.* Boston MA: Little Brown. pp. 257-282.

Padden, C./Humphries, T. (1988): *Deaf in America: Voices from a culture.* Cambridge MA: Harvard University Press.

Quicke, J. (1984): The role of the educational psychologist in the post-Warnock era; in: Barton L./Tomlinson, S. (eds.): *Special education and social interests.* London: Croom Helm.

Rorty, R. (1989): *Contingency, irony and solidarity.* New York: Cambridge Univ. Press.

Rutherford, S. (1986): *American culture: The deaf perspective.* San Francisco CA: Deaf Media Inc.

Rutherford, S. (1988): The culture of American deaf people. *Sign Language Studies,* 59, pp. 128-147.

Sartre, J.P.(1966): Introduction; in: Memmi, A.: *Portrait du colonisé.* Paris: Pauvert. pp. 31-38.

Schein, J. (1987): The demography of deafness; in: Higgins P. C./Nash, J.E. (eds.): *Understanding deafness socially.* Springfield IL: Thomas.

Schein, J. (1989): *At home among strangers.* Washington DC: Gallaudet University Press.

Scott, R. A. (1981): *The making of blind men.* New Brunswick: Transactions.

Senior, G. (1988): Temporal orientation in hearing-impaired people. *Disability, Handicap and Society,* 3, pp. 277-290.

Shockley, W. (1971): Models, mathematics and the moral obligation to diagnose the origin of negro IQ deficits. *Review of Educational Research,* pp. 369-377.

Shweder, R. (1984): Anthropology's romantic rebellion against the enlightenment; in: Shweder, R./LeVine, R.A. (eds.): *Culture theory.* New York: Cambridge U. Press. pp. 27-66.

Sternberg, M. L. (1990): *American Sign Language: A comprehensive dictionary.* New York: Harper and Row.

Tomlinson, S. (1982): *A Sociology of special education.* Boston: Routledge and Kegan Paul.

Van Cleve, J. V. (ed.): (1987): *Gallaudet encyclopedia of Deaf people and deafness.* New York: McGraw Hill. 3 vols.

Van Cleve, J./Crouch, B. (1989): *A Place of their own; Creating the Deaf community in America.* Washington DC: Gallaudet University Press.

Vernon, M. (1982): Multi-handicapped deaf children: types and causes; in: Tweedie, D. /Shroyer, E.H. (eds.): *The multihandicapped hearing impaired.* Washington DC: Gallaudet University Press. pp 11-28.

Webster, A. (1985): The Deaf Experience, edited by Harlan Lane. *History of Education,* 14, pp. 237-250.

Weiss, G. (1990): New hope for deaf children: implant gives them hearing and speech. *American Health,* 9, p. 17.

Wilbur, R. (1987): *American Sign Language* Boston: Little-Brown.. 2nd ed..

Wilcox, S. (1989): *American Deaf Culture: An anthology.* Silver Spring MD: Linstok.

Wilson, J. Q./Herrnstein, R. (1985): *Crime and human nature.* New York: Simon and Schuster.

Wolff, A. B./Harkins, J. E. (1986): Multihandicapped students; in: Schildroth A. N./Karchmer, M.A. (eds.): *Deaf children in America.* San Diego CA: College-Hill. pp. 55-82.

Optical Allusions XI
Lively Speech – Deadly Apparatus?

Ill. 103: Learning to listen at the Institute in Groningen, Netherlands, in 1951.

Ill. 104: A geography lesson (?) at the Institute in Groningen, Netherlands, in 1912.

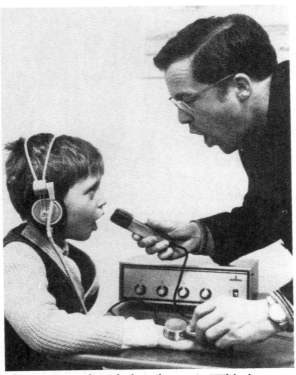

Ill. 105: Learning to speak with the vibrator in Wildeshausen, Germany.

Ill. 106: Injections to the Eustachian tube (19th century, France).

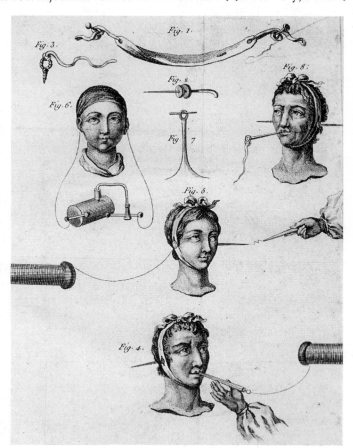

Ill. 107: Treatment by electricity (18th century, France).

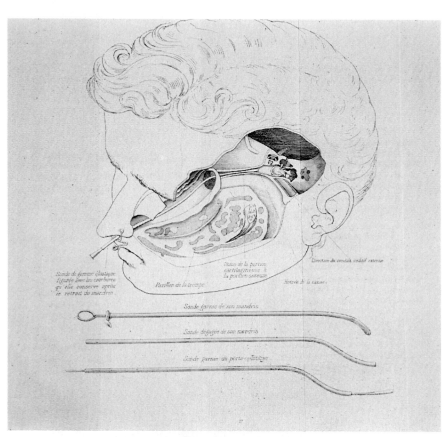

Ill. 108: Catheterization of the Eustachian tube (19th century, France).

Optical Allusions XII
Experiments on Animals

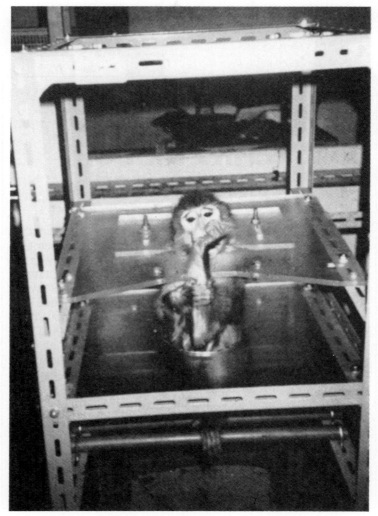

Ill. 109: A monkey at Kyoto University Primate Lab, Japan.

Innumerable experiments on animals are carried out all over the world in the domains of sign language acquisition and use, speech, voicing, and audition, among others. One of the first documented cases of this kind is the fate of an orang-outan transported to Europe in the 17th century by colonizers (see also ill. 101. p. 426). These experiments have ranged, and still range, from most cruel neurological procedures to allegedly harmless ones which place language learning in 'kind' settings in captivity.

Repeatedly, the animals are afterwards sold for further experiments (e.g. experiments on pharmaceutic drugs). Getting hold of the animals is a cruel affair, too. Most undergo the mechanisms of so-called laboratory animal trade. For quite a few experiments, baby animals are wanted by the experimenters; to get hold of one baby ape born free, several adult apes are slaughtered; and to have one baby ape survive being taken captive and shipped to the site of the laboratory, several others are equally taken captive initially.
Ethical issues are rarely raised...

BRIGITTE BARDOT SPEAKS UP FOR CHIMPANZEE

Brigitte Bardot, the French movie actress, has started a campaign to get Chloe Chimpanzee moved from the   basement of a Japanese laboratory where she has lived for several years.

Chloe and an orangutan named Doudou were sent from France to the Primate Research Institute of Kyoto University in 1984. They were to be used in sign language studies. Doudou has since died in still mysterious circumstances, and Chloe now lives in a basement cage. When Shirley McGreal of IPPL and Dr. Bernadette Bresard visited Chloe in August 1990, they found her alone in a cage. Several chimpanzees were living together in an adjoining cage. The cages were dismal and the outdoor parts of the units were surrounded by a pit full of debris.

Brigitte Bardot would like to see Chloe sent to a good zoo or to a rehabilitation center. If you agree, please write:

The Director, Primate Research Institute
Kyoto University
Inuyama City, Aichi, 484, Japan

Ill. 110

500

Methodological and
Theoretical Issues of
Deaf History

Günther List
Gleiszellen, Germany

Life Histories of the Deaf in an Oralist World

Preliminary reflections on a pilot project

Summary · Zusammenfassung

By documenting examples of life histories of the Deaf the pilot project BISSGEN announced here reacts to the need for information in the social science sector caused in Germany by the oralist tradition. Beyond their documentary character biographical texts, thanks to their dense, coherent and discursive form, seem to be most appropriate to stimulate further questions in a broader spectrum between history and linguistics. In the reflections developed here to prepare the project, some approaches of sociological Biography Research are discussed in their relevance to the societal problem of deafness. On the other hand, an interpretative frame is suggested for life histories of the Deaf which allows the hearing majority (still) dominating most interaction with the Deaf to be included as a substantial subject of research.

Das hier angekündigte nordrhein-westfälische Pilotprojekt BISSGEN geht mit der exemplarischen Erhebung von Lebensgeschichten Gehörloser auf den sozialwissenschaftlichen Informationsbedarf ein, den die oralistische Tradition in Deutschland hat entstehen lassen. Dabei erscheint die inhaltlich dichte, kohärente und diskursive Form biographischer Texte über ihren dokumentarischen Wert hinaus besonders geeignet, Fragestellungen in einem breiten Spektrum zwischen Geschichte und Linguistik anzuregen. Die hier publizierten Vorüberlegungen diskutieren einerseits die Anwendbarkeit einschlägiger Ansätze der soziologischen Biographieforschung auf das gesellschaftliche Problem Gehörlosigkeit. Sie visieren andererseits für die Lebensgeschichten der Gehörlosen einen interpretativen Rahmen an, der die hörende Majorität, da sie die meisten Interaktionsräume der Gehörlosen (noch) beherrscht, substantiell mit zum Thema macht.

I The project's historical and thematic background

The fresh approach to the manual communication of Deaf communities, initiated by American linguistics (Stokoe 1960), has also led to fruitful studies of German Sign Language (Prillwitz et al. 1985; Ebbinghaus/ Heßmann 1989). However, so much remains to be done in the linguistic domain, that the complementary social and historical studies have scarcely begun.

Instead, German educational and psychological studies are continuing to be turned out, all of which assume the traditional medical orientation toward deafness as predominantly a physical handicap or as a social deviance which should be treated (Fengler 1990; Jann 1991). This point of view has been long discarded by American scholars, who have tried to *'depathologize'* research on deafness (Woodward 1982, Lane 1988). Within the medical-pathological model, language issues are treated solely in the frame of the oral language and without benefit of modern linguistic analyses. The result is that, exactly in those professions most directly concerned with deafness in Germany education and social services, the social, cultural and linguistic dimensions of the German Deaf community are not recognized, much less addressed. Under these cicrumstances, the sources of information concerning the social issue of deafness in today's Germany are far from satisfactory. Germany not only lacks a body of social and historical theory concerning deafness; it also lacks a useful data base.

If we compare this present situation in Germany with the large amount of research activity in the United States on the Deaf community there, its language and culture (summarized, for example, in Van Cleve (ed.) 1987), we recognize that the Americans have had the advantage in this field of beeing able to draw upon an historically more well developed Deaf infrastructure, both within the educational system as well as within the Deaf communities themselves. In Germany, in contrast, any tendency to view the Deaf using a cultural-linguistic rather than a medical paradigm has not only consistently been blocked by a widespread institutional incrustation of oralism's official educational and welfare policy. The German Deaf community has correspondingly also been prevented from reaching its full potential in increased cultural self-awareness and in the gathering of factual information about itself. The oralists, by refusing to allow the language of the Deaf community to be used in the education of the Deaf and by refusing to recognize the cultural standing of the Deaf community, have effectively excluded Deaf people from academic discussions of Deaf concerns. This has resulted in a long-term deterioration of a potentially broad natural basis for cooperative research activities, in which Deaf and hearing researchers together gather information about the minority Deaf culture and society existing within the hearing world.

On the other hand, the German public is now beginning to view Deaf people in a new way, displaying a positive kind of curiosity about the everyday life of this group of people within their midst. What do their lives in the hearing society look like? How does sign language work in its social context? Questions such as these, asked by the hearing majority and by Deaf people themselves, marked with a growing self awareness, point the way toward an exploration of a hidden minority community within Germany. However, investigations of such questions depend, to a greater extent in Germany than in North America, on special initiatives from hearing social scientists and on well planned proposals of interdisciplinarity.

In order to meet this need for interdisiciplinary research on the German Deaf community, the Forschungsarbeitsgemeinschaft Gehörlosengemeinschaften und Gebärdensprachen (Research Group on Deaf Communities and Sign Languages) was founded in 1990 in the state of Nordrhein-Westfalen, subsidized by the Ministry of Science. This team of scholars from the most diverse fields, such as semiotics, cognitive psychology and functional linguistics, sociology and the history of education are planning future projects in cooperation with Deaf people. As a first approach to future research this forum decided to launch a pilot project on Deaf biography.

Biographical sources such as letters and autobiographies have always been important to social scientists -- although originally they were studied mainly in order to understand how individual leading personalities were motivated in their actions. In more recent times, the life of everybody has gained in importance as a means of understanding all social strata and thus biographies have become the subject of broader sociological interest (Szepanski 1972; Bertaux (ed.) 1981; Kohli 1981; Gestrich et al. 1988). At the same time, there is great appreciation of the value of non-written communication such as that elicited in oral interviews. Within so-called Oral History (Niethammer (ed.) 1980), one deals no longer with the official literate tradition of history, but rather with people who are exemplars of the history and typology of social and mental structures. Logically enough, the subjects of these Oral History studies are often the 'silent classes', forgotten by written history. Biographical texts, collected in interviews, this seems to be the source which may allow the most direct and comprehensive access to the world of the Deaf as social group. This type of text corresponds to the profound need for authentic information and rightly claims the status of contemporary documents in a changing state of public consciousness.

Books on deafness purchased by the general reading public often deal with biography. It is helpful for historians and sociologists to read accounts by hearing children of Deaf parents (Walker 1986), descriptions of the struggle to raise a Deaf child, written by hearing parents (Pellman Glick/ Pellman 1982), or the histories of the difficult experiences of being Deaf, written by successful Deaf individuals (Bowe 1986). We may be surprised to discover that even in the United States, the link between this biographical literature and the needs of social research is not yet firmly established. Biographical information about Deaf people obtained through interviews has been studied by classical social research mainly with a concern for special themes of social welfare (Owens 1981; Foster 1987), an approach that does not make visible the specifics of one's whole life narration. On the other hand, conventional autobiographical writing as a means of self-expression does not seem to be a common form of social communication for many members of the Deaf community. When Deaf people undertake a conscious, public, scientific analysis of their own biographical trajectory within Deaf culture, they are more likely to use the tools of sociology or anthropology than the tools of biographical analysis (see, for example, Kannapell 1977; Padden/ Humphries 1988). Indeed, biographical interviews with Deaf people seem not to have played a role in its own right until the recent Oral History activities reviewed in the present *Reader*.

In the United States, it is possible to conduct Oral History studies within a framework of already existing historical and sociological research which allows each individual's life to be viewed on its social background. Oral History, in this situation, acts as a kind of complement to structural insights by providing case studies. In Germany, in contrast, it is up to the pilot biographical studies themselves to provide the first data in an area which, until now, has been totally unexplored by the social sciences. Research studies in this situation entail different emphases. In a way we too intend to document the life stories as such, and thereby continue the documentation begun in Germany a few years ago by the journal *Das Zeichen* in which short biographical reports by Deaf people, originally delivered in sign language, are translated in written German (*Das Zeichen* 1, 1987 sq.). Beyond this, our biography project will have to furnish a basis for principal reflections on how to undertake social research about a Deaf community. The Ministry of Science of Nordrhein-Westfalen launched our pilot project precisely with this goal: production of a few materials apt to prepare those next steps in interdisciplinary research which would then lead from merely linguistic questions to the questions of social context: 'biographies of linguistic socialization of Deaf people in Nordrhein-Westfalen' (Biographien zur sprachlichen Sozialisation Gehörloser in Nordrhein-Westfalen = BISSGEN). In this paper, I wish to present some of the methodological premises we worked on while preparing our small sample of interviews.[1]

---

1 This text having been written in April 1991 represents the phase of preparing the interviews; the team will report on its experiences with the interviews in the near future.

We have begun with the assumption that language issues always loom large in most biographies of Deaf people and that social research in this area will have to focus on the sociolinguistic situation of Deaf people living within the hearing world. The biographical interviews must be undertaken in a way which produces, on the one hand, the most authentic texts possible and, on the other hand, allows the corpus to be used for a wide range of interpretations. By conducting the interviews in German Sign Language, a language which has so long been treated as inappropriate for serious discourse, we feel there is the greatest chance for the central issues of Deaf culture to emerge spontaneously. Autobiographical narration can be considered as a relatively natural form for personal experience to express itself vis-à-vis a systematic scientific interest. This narration will not necessarily proceed in the strict chronological order of life events, but it should reveal the whole trajectory of life and deliver at the same time a sufficient amount of details (Fuchs 1984). Such biographical texts can, from the perspective of the social sciences, offer privileged access at different levels to the lives and culture of Deaf people.

Integral life history, as expressed in the text of biographical narration, combines two opposed structural elements that organize life events: the potentially open form of narrative discourse (Hoffmann-Riem 1980) and the relatively closed frame of biologically predisposed life course. Texts with both these elements contain concrete information which facilitates comparison across interviews. Biographical narration falls midway between the well known two poles of 'quantitative' and 'qualitative' sociological analysis (Esser 1987) and thus qualifies their opposition. Sociological analysis that puts a premium on quantification proceeds by extracting isolated data from integral life histories and applying statistics in order to evaluate specific hypotheses. Advocates of qualitative social science, on the other hand, have protested that such quantifying methods destroy the unique constellation that is the biographical narrative, and some scholars have gone so far as to claim that subjective data, such as an autobiographical account, simply cannot be cumulated across individuals.

Our framework of integral life history rejects both these extreme approaches to biographical material, utilizing instead a productive interrelation of individual text interpretation (hermeneutics) together with a typologizing interpretation across texts. The first phase of the interview will be a narrative which should be as open as possible. This is then followed by a second phase, in which more specific details can be drawn out and explored. The second phase of the interview should be well prepared, using information from the first phase and necessarily will have to be conducted at a somewhat later point in time. With this second phase, we hope to lay the groundwork for a typological comparison (although we realize that our small sample in this pilot study will be far from quantitatively 'saturated').

Our basic criteria for persons directly involved in the interview situation are as follows: All interview partners should be Deaf, a criterion which should not be determined by audiological evaluation of the person's hearing loss, but rather by the person's avowed commitment to the Deaf community and its sign language culture. Secondly, all interviewed persons should have hearing parents, so that the typical situation of living in Deaf and Hearing worlds is involved. Thirdly, all interviewees should be adults, living in their own home. This criterion is made in order to avoid factors related to dependencies on parents.

During the last fifteen years, an interest in biographical documents has developed on a broad scale in the social sciences (Kohli 1981; Fischer/ Kohli 1987). Besides Oral History, two other approaches have been developed, which take up the methodological challenge of qualitative-quantiative polarity: on the one hand, the sociological-hermeneutic 'Biography Research' (Biographieforschung) in a strict sense which has received considerable attention in Germany, and on the other hand, the Life Course Research (Lebenslaufforschung) which is established in the international literature. In the following two sections these two approaches are examined for what they can contribute to the project of life histories of Deaf people. In the case of Biography Research we concentrate on the openness of the narrative interview situation (Section II); in the case of Life Course Research we emphasize rather the pursuit of the general interpretative frame of reference (Section III).

II Biography research and openness of the interview situation

While there is a long tradition in linguistics of using informants, both to guide grammatical analysis and the study of language variation, our sociological and historical pilot project has to deal with the problem that in such a sensitive social field as sign language and Deaf culture, a 'naive' ethnological curiosity (for instance the so-called lebensweltliche Ethnography, Honer 1989) quickly reaches its limits. In this situation, it seems reasonable for the processes of text production to pursue a line of the so-called Biography Research - a form of investigation that has reached a high level of social psychological reflection. We feel this approach, at the same time sociological and hermeneutical, would be most fruitful in the first phase of our project – to the degree that it preserves these two aspects in their own right. Where Biography Research follows this line (Fischer/ Kohli 1987, Fischer 1989) it avoids perceiving individual life history as mere data, and at the same time, also avoids adhering closely to mere subjectivism.

Biography Research, then, respects the subjective 'sense' communicated by the individual's interpretation of life as an irreducible expression of the person. But it attempts at the same time to project the subjectively applied strategies of experience and patterns of interpretation to their social background. Thus a superimposed reference plane, the level of 'structure', is established in relation to which the lives of a social group can be interpreted and the members of this group can learn to interpret the systemic caracter of their life stories. Such a perspective appears adequately sensitive to social issues, as it recognizes that the individual's actions are shaped by systematic social and historical forces. Thus, such a structural analysis will not shrink from recognizing the constellation of a social handicap which has been forced on the Deaf people by oralism and which reaches well beyond the obligatory oral language at school.

Not the least of what narrative reconstruction can accomplish is to throw light on the exact moments and means whereby society actually makes its imprint on individual lives, lives extended in this way between 'sense' and 'structure', for the narrating person as well as for the group. Such information and insights can assist the concerned individuals in appreciating and shaping their own lives. Thus the interviews with Deaf people may prove helpful in breaking the individualising spell that the ruling oralism has cast. In presenting oral assimilation as an overriding goal for the Deaf person, oralism sets the stage for what is generally an inevitable failure of assimilation. On the individual biography, it imprints a deeper track of negative experience and thus passive suffering (Mottez 1977). Biography Research can confront this oralist program with the concept of 'construction' of a curriculum vitae – a model, that includes both a socially presupposed structure and whatever resources the person him/herself mobilises to realize life on his or her own, by becoming aware of that preexisting structure (Fischer/Kohli 1987).

The term 'construction' arises out of the tradition of symbolic interactionism, which beginning in the 1970s, has brought about a change in the perception of people with handicaps. 'Handicap' and 'deafness' are now viewed as social constructs (Barton/Tomlinson (eds.) 1984; Higgins/Nash (eds.) 1987; Liachowitz 1988 and others). A radical social political change has occurred in the relations between the Deaf community and the hearing majority in the Anglo-Saxon and Scandinavian countries, but this change has yet to occur in Germany. Admittedly, this fundamental change will not be brought about Biography Research alone. Nevertheless it is worthwhile to continue exploring the critical potential of this approach, which up to now has not really penetrated into the field of socially-defined handicaps (Schuchardt 1982), and to extend the approach to the issues surrounding cultural Deafness.

To the extent that we rely on the methods of Biography Research, our project design will certainly profit from the state of discussion in this area, but will not find any models directly applicable to the sector of 'deafness'. The concentration on workers' biographies predominant in the beginnings of Biography Research, does not encourage directly analogous procedures when dealing with a linguistic minority. The field of Biography Research has gone on to study various fringe groups (cf. the bibliographical overview in Heinritz 1988). However, no group studied so far includes crucial elements of the Deaf situation: the genesis of self-awareness of a minority group through paradigmatic transition of the problem from a medical one to one of language and culture. Among possible analogs to social handicap, the category of patients' careers comes closest to our subject, for the related studies make clear that incurable disease must not be understood simply as the collapse of the usual planning of life, since at the same time it mobilises strategies that organize survival biographically on a new basis (Gerhardt 1984). To deal appropriately with the Deaf experience, one cannot simply project such problems of individual handicap onto problems of a whole group. Rather, the cultural use of sign language places the problem in a perspective where pathology moves to the background and new resources of society's 'normality' arise.

When Biographical Research began, it first ran the risk of confounding hermeneutic and sociological principles. True, this first biographical school used narrative interview and claimed to specialize in procedures that are supposed to assure the utmost authenticity of texts (Schütze 1976, 1981). However, the 'openness' of the interview proclaimed by this school does not seem really aimed at letting factual history come through. Like the comparable school of so-called 'objective hermeneutics' (Oevermann et al.1978), this kind of Biography Research tried with narrative interview approach to fulfill quantitative sociology's high expectations of methodological perfection. This led to a double ambition: on the one hand the model claims that it is precisely narrative texts that allow capturing with absolute accuracy the authentic reality of the narrating subject; on the other hand it claims that such authentic account can only be worked out validly by inherent text interpretation. Critics are right when they argue that, by these double absolutes of authenticity and method, in reality 'naive empiricism' gains ground (Gerhardt 1985). As regards text production, the narrative model presupposes the identity of real and narrated life history, and it balks at including any non-narrative, spontaneous as well as reflecting statements (Bude 1985). As regards text content, where socially shared meaning comes into play and where plausible connections of textual statements with general social structures are wanted, the model leaves a vacant space for interpretation. Only slowly is Biography Research, while criticising earlier positions, filling this empty space, mostly returning to the typological method of description (Max Weber's *ideal typus*, Gerhardt 1984, 1985).

How important it is to break the spell of the myth of methodologically controlled authenticity, is most impressively reflected in programs that approach, for example, the Sinti and Roma, by means of 'narrative interviews'. Based on the romantic notion that biographies somehow give the reader direct access to the narrator's life, the authors of these studies believe they are able later to extract biographical ruptures of self-confidence and identity crises in the course of an in-depth hermeneutical interpretation. This is where the 'biographical illusion' Bourdieu warned against (Bourdieu 1990) takes on a particularly drastic form: social science mistakenly takes itself to be a diagnostic agency for the problems of the minority in a society – (redefined as patients' careers). Bourdieu considers the approach of Biography Research as such illusory since it leads to the construction of an 'identity' that amounts to what is required for being identified by the authorities. This exaggerated but necessary criticism can claim to be historically concrete, precisely in the social 'fringe areas'.[2]

---

2 Even Bourdieu's apparently burlesque insisting on the systemic action of giving an identity (and thus handing it in) by giving a name gains sense when we remember how politics dealt with the gypsies throughout the last one hundred years. Where the government and the police forces

Applying this to Biography Research in the social case of deafness, the BISSGEN project team has to ensure that the situation in which biographical information is elicited avoids the subject-object-relation that science likes so much when dealing with its 'subjects'. This is a relation which, in the past, was an extension of social repression using science to achieve identification of the groups to be oppressed. Within the biographical horizon of many Deaf people, there is still present an awareness of how educators and doctors helped to carry out the *law for the prevention of genetically defective offspring (Gesetz zur Verhütung erbkranken Nachwuchses)* dated July 14, 1933 (Biesold 1988), as the oralistic principle of assimilation went so far as to promote a eugenic extermination policy for the 'hereditary deaf'.

If scientists nowadays want to help, in light of these facts about oralism, to overcome the oralist paradigm and to openly present the subject of Deafness in its productive social dimensions, they have to steer a narrow course between Scylla and Charybdis. On the one hand any methodological positivism that would lead back into the old respective roles has to be avoided. Thus, it would not be appropriate if hearing scientists were to assault Deaf interview partners with previously elaborated questionaires or were to evaluate the texts coming from alleged 'open' interviews in the laboratory. But on the other hand, it would not serve either Deaf or hearing people to abandon what science has to offer, namely, results based on carefully controlled questioning. Some scholars, aware that scientific 'identification' played a big role in the transformation of human beings into 'objects', have tried to avoid this historical burden by identifying totally with their subjects. In so doing, however, they renounce the possibility of perceiving themselves as subjects with specific scientific socialisation. In order to avoid this mistake in our project we recognize the discursive process of mutual learning in which each side, hearing and Deaf, contributes its own possibilities.

Rejecting such defensive strategies as naive identification with the community under study, our project proceeds from the assumption that the very oralist structure, which is so well implanted in Germany, and the educational lag caused by it, demand special scientific effort. Our longer lasting task is to actively involve those people in the discourse who have been the victims of the oralist structure. In our program we cannot count on the collaboration of as many Deaf scholars with academic credentials as might be the case in the United States. Nevertheless, we consider the biographic approach particulary suited to assure the transfer between the two poles of personal experience and scholarly knowledge in a natural way. Moreover, the biographic approach chooses a type of text for analysis that does not serve merely for the extraction of information. At the same time, and much more effectively, it works as an instrument that allows for the narrators to determine the degree of commonality of their various histories.

The situation of the interview itself implies an arrangement in which not only hearing researchers, but also Deaf persons fluent in German Sign Language who lead the conversation, take over the decisive control functions. We, the hearing researchers, will not actively participate in the interviews for a fundamental reason that the situation requires that we relate the question of authenticity on the one hand, and of valid interpretation on the other, to the different partial discourses, within which the participation of both sides, the hearing and the Deaf, differs because of the division of labor. In the first phase, we are prepared to elicit a basically narrative form: the biographical narration determines its own beginning and course of reconstruction and it proceeds without suggestive 'outside' intervention – though without becoming obsessively 'automated'. Thus, we recognize that basically it is the discourse in sign language which regulates the course of the interview. We will thus situate, quite consciously, the narrative discourse in an openness which cannot be completely 'closed', even by refined pre-planning. Only during the second phase can the specific social scientific interest become relevant.

were concerned, they aimed at civil registration for the longest time thanks to their internal system of giving names and family relations.

III Life courses and life areas: the frame for interpretation

Beyond the straightforward need for further details, what can guide us in structuring in advance the renewed inquiry and hypotheses for the second phase of the interviews? This question should not refer us just to the methods of Oral History for these open out onto methodological considerations for the conduct of all historical investigation. Instead we should remain within the terms of biographical science: From this perspective, the relative roles of personal initiative and passive suffering within a lifetime are not determined exclusively on the level of social 'structure', nor exclusively on the level of subjective 'sense', but in the concrete interaction of both. Or, we could say, on a level in between both, where the specific expectations that a life and a society mutually address one another are negotiated 'functionally' (Fischer 1989; Fischer/Kohli 1987). This level is characterized in the case of the Deaf community, just as with other minorities, by asymmetrical interactions. Thus, when we speak of 'the world of the Deaf' and 'the world of the hearing' we refer not only to the different life contexts, but also to structural relations of social power. In such situations, structural pressure does not meet simply with counter-pressure, nor merely with individual strategies of interpreting the imbalance of power, we see rather the profile of a typical minority culture with its evolving potential for resistance (Vermès (ed.) 1988). We can presume that the individual life courses of Deaf people orient themselves with respect to that collective potential.

When we examine the range of different ways in which lives of Deaf people can take shape, we can discern, in some respects, a 'continuum'. This term is widely used in sociolinguistic research on signed languages and refers there to the several language varieties used by Deaf people, varieties that have developed between 'pure' American Sign Language and 'pure' American oral language (Markowicz/ Woodward 1982, Mottez 1990). By choosing to use a particular communicative variation within the sociolinguistic continuum, a Deaf person positions, as it were, her or his situational sole and social standpoint between an identity defined completely by membership in the signing community and an identity marked by total oralist assimilation. It would be appropriate to combine this concept of the continuum of social options with the biographical perspective as follows. A system of coordinates is established, wherein the continuum of social options is one dimension, and an individual life course with its decision processes is the other dimension. The decision processes will be different in the various communicative situations and life areas, but the overall course of life should show a typical biographical line.

The epistemological ideal type of such a line might not be, as one might think, a straight forward integration into Deaf community, but rather a life-long movement veering from one side to the other. Less than a tenth of all Deaf children have Deaf parents. For all other Deaf children, growing up in or rather, in between two different worlds determines every day life right from the start, beginning with primary linguistic socialization. That is why in Deaf biography the central life event is a self-chosen shift from the world of the hearing into the world of the Deaf, from the mostly orally-determined hearing family (as well as the oralist school) to the sign language community of the Deaf. This is especially true for those Deaf persons who developed awareness of their culture (cf. the life courses in *Das Zeichen* 1/ 1987 sq.). The opportunity to gain an identity and a fluent language after years of communicative frustration and language deprivation, puts the stunningly positive accent of personality evolution on the second phase of socialization and gives this radical biographical change the features of a real 'conversion' (see Hoerning 1985 concerning this concept in the context of Biographical Research).

The present is defined by its productive distance to the past; the future becomes projectable; one living space separates from the next; and it is the very self-confidence of being at home in one's own 'world' that grants the developing Deaf person a broader range of actvities and communicates to him or her the possibilities of dealing more sovereignly with the expectations that a life and a society mutually adress at one another. Cultural identity and social competence, viewed as personal life- and self-construction, belong to the classic scope of open Biographical Research. If, however, we are concerned with historically pre-defined interactions that model a life history, the so-called Life Course Research is a means of uncovering biographical material. This line of research concentrates on interpreting life histories in context and in interaction with secular and group specific prestructured patterns of life courses (Kohli (ed.) 1978). Using terms like role, status, transition, etc. (Meulemann 1985; Tölke 1989 and others), Life Course Research applies instruments that seem most appropriate to make visible the asymmetry of hearing and Deaf worlds along a very con-crete line: along the seam of interaction between hearing and Deaf in the biographically decisive situations of role assignment.

It seems clear that, from this vantage point, the ideal constellation of 'conversion', that biographically decisive transition from the world of hearing people to the world of Deaf people, is not being reduced to mark a specific event and unique point within the bio-graphy. 'Conversion' may in this sense better be understood as a change in direction, an existential one, but historically open in its realization, possibly life-long or perhaps never put into realization. Challenged with greater or lesser intensity at different periods and vari-ous situations during a lifetime, such change in direction refers to a much lesser degree to the individual person than to the conditions set from outside.

It is essential to stress this point of view of the methodology which Life Course Research uses for the transfer of individual data onto a level of typological comparability – a metho-dology which is not immediately applicable to our project. It consists in reflecting individual data directly to a group-specific life-course (one example of many: Girtler 1987) and this would in our case merely come down to an analysis of what a Deaf career typically looks like. That would again mean isolating Deaf biographies, exposing them to just an attribute-oriented analysis, which would clearly contradict the critical epistemological potential of that same Life Course Research (Gerhardt 1984; Keupp 1987). For example, identifying a 'conversion' would contraproductively come down to setting up some kind of biographical marker for typical or even 'successful' Deaf biographies. If we want to make use of the possi-bilities offered by the typological approach, we have to transcend the biographical perspec-tive, without obscuring its role as the source of the information. The concept of 'life history' which, even construed typologically, tends to stay fixed to the isolated life trajectory of the concerned individuals, must not entail a latent expectation that it will serve as reference for frustrating individual reality. Rather, the biographical perspective must from the beginning be combined with the societal perspective.

What this is aiming at is a decisive shift in emphasis. We shall follow the biographical narrations of the Deaf interlocutors with interest, allowing them to let us enter the worlds they went through. But as soon as we undertake to compare and align these different trajec-tories, one single life will no longer be the subject of inquiry – not even in form of a typical career. It will rather be the life areas themselves and the passage leading through them that become the subject, as well as the kind of people who populate those life areas and the interaction of the hearing majority with the Deaf minority. So what is at issue are the struc-tural chances that are being offered or refused to Deaf people in the course of their lives – chances for a change in direction from oralist repression to authentic culture, which may occur in the individual case as dramatic 'conversion'.

Our preliminary reflections connect with the outlines which have been drawn by Amer-ican sociology of Deafness. We cannot, because of the different preconditions, directly profit from the general advance of this research, all the more since, as mentioned before, there has been no striking interest in specific biographical research in the American litera-ture on Deafness. However, just as a general sociology of life course must describe biographical experience in typical social constellations (Clausen 1986), it seems to be within the inherent logic of a sociology of groups to organize its material in biographical order. Indeed American sociology of the Deaf, tracing the natural development from childhood to old age, lines up a sequence of life areas which differ characteristically in the scope and intensity of the possibilities for interaction that they contain, interactions guided by pre-programmed conflicts. Such a sequence of life areas reveals its classic profile first by examining subjective personal accounts; second, with the description of educational systems within the family and at school; third, with the description of conventional social programs of rehabilitation; and, finally, with an account of the segregation of Deaf communities (Watson 1973). Another scheme may start directly under the term of life-long socialisation, assigning the different life areas – family, school, Deaf community – to this superordinated concept (Higgins/ Nash (eds.) 1987). Finally, sociology may start to deal with Deaf community as a whole and transfer chronological aspects into the description of subgroups (Christiansen (ed.) 1987). The central point will always be the conflict which the Deaf people experience at home, at school, at work, – i.e. with parents, teachers, employers and colleagues – as they strive for their cultural identity as signers.

Some of the results of past American research in this field can probably be confirmed for the German situation. But the context of life areas as a whole in Germany is no doubt differently structured than in the United States. To describe this structural context, will be the task of a future historico-sociological research in our country, and for this purpose a corpus of Deaf biographies is needed as base material. Given, then, that single life histories shall not be obliterated in typological generalizations, a system of coordinates as outlined above will in any case be helpful. It permits us to characterize the respective life areas predisposed for Deaf people by hearing society, and to localize them according to their closeness or distance to the one or the other pole, oralism or sign language culture. Indeed, considering the longevity of oralist stereotypes, even deep-hermeneutical interviews – though with hearing persons – would be justified as a part of an inquiry into Deaf biography.

The fact that the weight of analysis here turns to the hearing side in the interaction, corresponds to the interest in Deafness as a societal problem, i.e., a problem residing for the most part in the determining social 'structure'. The pilot project described here can only allude generally to the need for analysis of oralism evoked by this perspective (Cuxac 1983, Lane 1984, List 1991). However, the discussion involves more than merely the advance of science. The hearing majority has its own fundamental interest in its encounter with the Deaf community and in critical confrontation with oralism. This interest is directed to the provocative way in which the Deaf mobilise the resource of their own language; not just another oral language, but an autonomous linguistic medium, that in the course of the evolution of mankind has been overshadowed, although it has always been present. Sign languages invite a consciousness-raising reflection by hearing people that goes deeper than mere instinct of benevolence. What is at issue is the validity of a fundamentally different linguistic symbol system, which radically questions the hearing person's conventional and monopolising perception of 'language'. This is what makes 'Deafness' a paradigmatic case, a decisive case for the society's grappling with the 'different' – much as in the cases of racism and antisemitism. This is what makes oralism a provocative case for intensive anthropological and historical critique.

Only if the 'social problem of Deafness' is defined in terms of the wide range of issues that concern hearing as well as Deaf people, can talking about this problem achieve the character of a social discourse. With our biographical pilot project we cannot possibly illuminate the whole scenario, let alone deal with it in its details. But it is indispensable for our project to at least indicate this scenario from the beginning, because we, the hearing scholars, must by no means assume the role of evaluating from the outside the achievement or non-achievement of Deaf careers and leave the Deaf alone to overcome oralism. Instead, we intend to contribute to this goal, at the very least by not reproducing socially caused inequality under the banner of science.

References

Barton, Len/ Tomlinson, Sally (eds.) (1984): *Special education and social interests.* London etc.

Bertaux, Daniel (ed.) (1981): *Biography and Society. The Life History Approach in the Social Sciences.* Beverly Hills/ London.

Biesold, Horst (1988): *Klagende Hände. Betroffenheit und Spätfolgen in Bezug auf das Gesetz zur Verhütung erbkranken Nachwuches, dargestellt am Beispiel der 'Taubstummen'.* Solms-Oberbiel.

Bourdieu, Pierre (1990): Die biographische Illusion; in: *Bios. Zeitschrift für Biographieforschung und Oral History* 1, pp. 75-81.

Bowe, Frank (1986): *Changing the Rules.* Silver Spring.

Bude, Heinz (1985): Der Sozialforscher als Narrationsanimateur. Kritische Anmerkungen zu einer erzähltheoretischen Fundierung der interpretativen Sozialforschung; in: *Kölner Zeitschrift für Soziologie und Sozialpsychologie* 37, pp. 327-336.

Christiansen, John B. (ed.) (1987): Deaf Population; in: Van Cleve (ed.), vol.III, 251-299.

Clausen, John A. (1986): *The life course: a sociological perspective.* Englewood Cliffs, New Jersey

Cuxac, Christian (1983): *Le langage des sourds.* Paris.

Das Zeichen 1/1987 sq. Hamburg: Zentrum für Deutsche Gebärdensprache.

Ebbinghaus, Horst/ Heßmann, Jens (1989): *Gehörlose, Gebärdensprache, Dolmetschen. Chancen der Integration einer sprachlichen Minderheit.* Hamburg.

Esser, Hartmut (1987): Zum Verhältnis von qualitativen und quantitativen Methoden in der Sozialforschung, oder: Über den Nutzen methodologischer Regeln bei der Diskussion von Scheinkontroversen; in: *Voges,* pp. 87-101

Fengler, Jörg (1990): *Hörgeschädigte Menschen. Beratung, Therapie und Selbsthilfe.* Stuttgart usw.

Fischer, Wolfgang/ Kohli, Martin (1987): Biographieforschung; in: *Voges,* pp. 25-49.

Fischer, Wolfram (1989): Biographieforschung; in: *Wörterbuch der Soziologie.* Stuttgart, pp. 99-102.

Foster, Susan B. (1987): Employment experiences of deaf college graduates: An interview study; in: *Journal of Rehabilitation of the Deaf* 21, pp. 1-15.

Fuchs, Werner (1984): *Biographische Forschung. Eine Einführung in Praxis und Methoden.* Opladen.

Gerhardt, Uta (1984): Typenkonstruktion bei Patientenkarrieren; in: Kohli/ Robert (eds.), pp. 53-77.

Gerhardt, Uta (1985): Erzähldaten und Hypothesenkonstruktion. Überlegungen zum Gültigkeitsproblem in der biographischen Sozialforschung; in: *Kölner Zeitschrift für Soziologie und Sozialpsychologie* 37, pp. 230-256.

Gestrich, Andreas/ Knoch, Peter/ Merkel, Helga (1988): *Biographie - sozialgeschichtlich. Sieben Beiträge.* Göttingen.

Girtler, Roland (1987): Die biographische Methode bei der Untersuchung devianter Karrieren und Lebenswelten; in: *Voges,* pp. 321-339.

Heinritz, Charlotte (1988): BIOLIT. Literaturüberblick aus der Biographieforschung und der Oral History 1978-1988; in: *Bios. Zeitschrift für Biographieforschung und Oral History,*1, pp. 121-167; 2, pp. 104-132.

Higgins, Paul C./ Nash, Jeffrey E. (eds.) (1987): *Understanding deafness socially.* Springfield.

Hoerning, Erika M. (1985): Biographie, Biographieforschung; in: *Evangelisches Kirchenlexikon. Internationale theologische Enzyklopädie.* Göttingen, vol. III, pp. 514-516.

Hoffmann-Riem, Christa (1980): Die Sozialforschung einer interpretativen Soziologie - der Datengewinn; in: *Kölner Zeitschrift für Soziologie und Sozialpsychologie* 32, pp. 339-372.

Honer, Anne (1989): Einige Probleme lebensweltlicher Ethnographie. Zur Methodologie und Methodik einer interpretativen Sozialforschung; in: *Zeitschrift für Soziologie* 18, pp. 297-312.

Jann, Peter A. (1991): *Die Erziehung und Bildung des gehörlosen Kindes. Zur Grundlegung der Gehörlosenpädagogik als Wissenschaft.* Heidelberg.

Kannapell, Barbara M. (1977): The Deaf Person as a Teacher of American Sign Language; in: *Proceedings of the first national symposium on sign language research and teaching, Chicago; Illinois may 30-june 3, 1977,* pp. 159-164.

Keupp, Heiner (1987): Psychisches Leid als gesellschaftlich produzierter Karriereprozeß; in: *Voges,* pp. 341-366.

Kohli, Martin (ed.) (1978): *Soziologie des Lebenslaufs.* Darmstadt/ Neuwied.

Kohli, Martin (1981): Wie es zur "biographischen Methode" kam, und was daraus geworden ist. Ein Kapitel aus der Geschichte der Sozialforschung; in: *Zeitschrift für Soziologie* 10, 273-293.

Kohli, Martin/ Robert, Günther (1984): *Biographie und soziale Wirklichkeit. Neue Beiträge und Forschungsperspektiven.* Stuttgart.

Lane, Harlan (1988): Is there a "psychology of the deaf"?; in: *Exceptional Children* 55, pp. 7-19.

Lane, Harlan (1984): *When the Mind Hears. A History of the Deaf.* New York.

Liachowitz, Claire H. (1988): *Disability as a social construct. Legislative roots.* Philadelphia.

List, Günther (1991): Vom Triumph der "deutschen" Methode über die Gebärdensprache. Problemskizze zur Pädagogisierung der Gehörlosigkeit im 19. Jahrhundert; in: *Zeitschrift für Pädagogik* 37, 245-266.

Markowicz, Harry / Woodward, James (1982): Language and the Maintenance of Ethnic Boundaries in the Deaf Community; in: Woodward, James (ed.): *How You Gonna Get to Heaven if You Can't Talk With Jesus. On Depathologizing Deafness.* pp. 3-9.

Meulemann, Heiner (1985): Statusinkonsistenz unbd Sozialbiographie. Eine Forschungsperspektive für die Analyse der Mehrdimensionalität moderner Sozialstrukturen; in: *Kölner Zeitschrift für Soziologie und Sozialpsychologie* 37, pp. 461-477.

Mottez, Bernard (1977): A s'obstiner contre les déficiences, on augmente souvent le handicap: l'exemple des sourds; in: Renaud, M. (ed.): *La gestion de la Santé. Health care managment. Sociologies et sociétés* 9/1, pp. 20-32.

Mottez, Bernard (1990): Deaf identity; in: *Sign Language Studies* 68, pp. 195-216.

Niethammer, Lutz (ed.) (1980): *Lebenserfahrung und kollektives Gedächtnis. Die Praxis der "Oral History".* Frankfurt a.M..

Oevermann, Ulrich/ Allert, Tilman/ Konau, Elisabeth/ Krambeck, Jürgen (1978): Die Methodologie einer "objektiven Hermeneutik" und ihre allgemeine forschungslogische Bedeutung in den Sozialwissenschaften; in: Soeffner, Hans-Georg (ed.): *Interpretative Verfahren in den Sozial- und Textwissenschaften.* Stuttgart, pp. 352-434.

Owens, Diane J. (1981): *The relationship of frequenzy and types of activity to life satisfaction in elderly deaf people.* New York.

Padden, Carol/ Tom Humphries (1988): *Deaf in America. Voices from a Culture.* Cambrige, Mass./ London

Pellman Glick, Ferne/ Pellman, Donald R. (1982): *Breaking Silence. A Family Grows with Deafness.* Scottdale/ Kitchener.

Prillwitz, Siegmund/ Leven, Regina/ Mayenn, Alexander v./ Zienert, Heiko/ Schmidt, W. (1985): *Skizzen zu einer Grammatik der Deutschen Gebärdensprache.* Hamburg.

Schuchardt, Erika (1982): *Soziale Integration Behinderter.* I: Biographische Erfahrung und wissenschaftliche Theorie. II: Weiterbildung als Krisenverarbeitung. Braunschweig.

Schütze, Fritz (1976): Zur Hervorlockung und Analyse von Erzählungen thematisch relevanter Geschichten im Rahmen soziologischer Feldforschung. In: Arbeitsgruppe Bielefelder Soziologen (ed.): *Kommunikative Sozialforschung.* München, pp. 159-259.

Schütze, Fritz (1981): Prozeßstrukturen des Lebenslaufs; in: Matthes, Joachim et al.(eds.): *Biographie in handlungswissenschaftlicher Perspektive. Kolloquium am Sozialwissenschaftlichen Forschungszentrum der Universität Erlangen* Nürnberg 1981, pp. 67-156.

Stokoe, William (1960): *Sign language structure: An outline of the visual communication systems of the American Deaf.* Washington.

Szczepanski, Jan (1972): Biographische Methode; in: *Wörterbuch der Soziologie.* Frankfurt a. M., pp.117-119.

Tölke, Angelika (1989): *Lebensverläufe von Frauen. Familiäre Ereignisse, Ausbildungs- und Erwerbsverhalten. Forschungsbericht.* München.

Van Cleve, John V. (ed.) (1987): *Gallaudet Encyclopedia of Deaf People and Deafness.* New York. 3 vols.

Vermès, Geneviève (ed.) (1988): *Vingt-cinq communautés.* Paris. 2 vols.

Voges, Wolfgang (1984): *Methoden der Biographie- und Lebenslaufforschung.* Opladen.

Walker, Lou Ann (1986): *A Loss for Words. The Story of Deafness in a Family.* New York.

Watson, Douglas (1973): *Readings on Deafness.* New York.

Woodward, James (1982): On Depathologizing Deafness; in: Woodward, James (ed.): *How You Gonna Get to Heaven if You Can't Talk With Jesus. On Depathologizing Deafness.* Silver Spring, pp. 75-78.

John S. Schuchman
Washington, USA

Oral History and Deaf Heritage

Theory and case studies

Summary

In this article, the author examines the use of Oral History interviews in relation to Deaf heritage. Much of the earlier history of the Deaf community can be described as elitist: a history of white men, predominantly those who could hear, who controlled or led organizations, schools, churches, and other institutions that dealt with Deafness or Deaf people. In the United States, these histories appear in written English.

Since elitist history depends primarily on written documents, this history naturally ignores the historical record of much of the Deaf community that communicates through the use of sign language. To get at the history of the underrepresented signing Deaf individuals, it will be necessary to turn to other methods of historical research - primarily videotaped Oral History interviews.

The author, who has conducted videotaped interviews since 1981, presents both the theory and use of Oral History with Deaf persons. Included as well are two case studies of actual interviews with Deaf informants from the author's research on the subject of American movies and the Deaf community.

I Theory and application

As we look back on the 1980s in the United States, it is clear that the decade reflected an increased awareness and interest in the importance of the *deaf heritage* by both historians and the Deaf community. The number of historical monographs that appeared during the decade as well as the conferences that occurred, such as *The Deaf Way* (1989) and the First International Conference on Deaf History (1991), demonstrate this interest. Despite this increased interest, however, major gaps remain.

The largest gaps in our history of the Deaf community are in social history, particularly in reference to the community's underrepresented elements: racial and ethnic minorities, women, gay men and lesbians, the poor, the oral Deaf, and generally the entire Deaf signing population that is not comfortable with standard written or spoken English. For the most part, these are groups for which we do not have much documentation in the form of written records. To get at the history of the underrepresented Deaf groups, it will be necessary to turn to other methods of historical research - primarily through Oral History interviews.

It is also clear that this historical interest is directly related to the perception, by Deaf people themselves and academic scholars, of the Deaf community as a linguistic minority group. The American Deaf community achieved significant political gains in the 1980s and early 1990s. The *Deaf President Now* protest (1988), for example, resulted in the installation of Gallaudet University's first Deaf president. Enactment of the Americans with Disabilities Act (1990) expanded American civil rights protections to Deaf people. It is likely that an increased historical interest in the Deaf community will continue to accompany these political gains.

For example, universities and school systems throughout the United States recently have begun establishing academic programs in Deaf studies, programs similar to the African American and Hispanic Studies curricula demanded by other racial and ethnic minorities. Although these programs tend to focus on the place of sign language in the curriculum, they all include some reference to the history of the Deaf community.[1] It is, then, appropriate to give some thought to the nature of historical inquiry and the Deaf community, in particular, the role of Oral History interviews for the heritage of the Deaf community. A quick review of the general history of Deafness will place Oral History within its context.

Historically, society has viewed Deafness primarily as a medical problem.[2] When doctors could not produce a cure, however, society assumed that persons who could not hear and who could not speak clearly were not as intelligent as the general population. Lacking a medical solution, other experts took over the responsibility of teaching Deaf persons to communicate. Until the 18th century, most of this instruction consisted of private tutors for Deaf children of wealthy parents. Adapting the natural signs and gestures of the Deaf people of Paris, France, a priest, the abbé de L'Epée established a school for poor Deaf children in Paris. From that date forward, educators of Deaf children have vied for the 'true' pedagogical system: oral or manual.[3] In our own day, various combinations of these approaches have been promoted as superior, but the underlying conflict, oralism versus manualism, remains. Despite the pedagogical dispute by experts, it is equally clear historically that deaf people throughout the world sought each other out and, communicating via a variety of sign languages, proceeded to establish loosely-organized communities. The abbé de L'Epée encountered one in Paris at the turn of the 18th century. In the United States, there were a sufficient number of individual Deaf communities to warrant the creation of a

---

1   The two largest university Deaf studies programs are located at Boston University and California State University, Northridge. Each enrolls approximately two hundred students.

2   For a survey of written documents relevant to the education of deaf students, see Scouten 1984.

3   For an excellent bibliographical survey of both American and European Deaf history, see Lane 1984, pp. 457-518.

national organization of Deaf Americans, the National Association of the Deaf, in 1880 (Van Cleve/ Crouch 1989). The new American organization had, as one of its goals, the preservation and perpetuation of sign language.

Despite this early and consistent support for sign language from Deaf people themselves, no substantial scientific support existed for sign language as a linguistic entity. Most persons, including many Deaf individuals, assumed that sign language merely substituted as a manual or gestural representation of spoken language. By 1965, Dr. William Stokoe, an American professor at Gallaudet University in Washington, D.C., provided linguistic evidence that sign language constituted a language, replete with its own rules of syntax and grammar. Other scholars soon confirmed Stokoe's work, with similar analyses of sign languages from deaf communities throughout the world.[4]

Once this linguistic breakthrough occurred, it was a short step to the conclusion that Deaf people shared much in common with linguistic minorities and that many of their past problems resulted from cultural oppression, not the medical fact that they could not hear. It was happenstance that this breakthrough occurred in the United States in the midst of the civil rights movement led by Martin Luther King. With the visible progress of African Americans before them, more and more Deaf leaders began to realize that solutions to their problems lay in the political arena.

Today, then, it has become acceptable for scholars outside of education, medicine, and rehabilitation, to analyze Deafness, along with other disabilities, from a cultural point of view in contrast to the older societal perception that viewed disability as primarily a medical or pathological problem. As noted earlier, historical studies of Deafness and Deaf people in the 1980s reflected this change in perception. This change is welcome; however, it is time for historians of Deafness to reflect upon and make explicit a premise of deaf community history that is common to the history of all racial and ethnic minorities.

Although university-based historians often distinguish between professionally trained historians and nonspecialists who are interested in a historical subject, this writer does not. For purposes of this article, a Deaf community historian is anyone (Deaf or hearing, university trained or enthusiast) who is interested in the heritage of Deaf people and Deafness and who is willing to share his or her research in any form: formal publication, exhibit, dramatic script, lecture, or storytelling.

It is tempting for historians of Deafness to celebrate the very real past achievements of deaf people. In many ways, *The Deaf Way* festival that occurred in the summer of 1989 was such a celebration. Such celebrations are necessary for the community's sense of achievement, heritage, and self esteem. Nevertheless, the historian is obliged to point out that all of the significant achievements of Deaf people have taken place within a political and economic structure and that it is clear that this structure in nearly all parts of the world is one that oppresses Deaf people. This structure of oppression provides a historical connection with the experiences of other racial and ethnic minority communities throughout the world.

On any demographic measure of Deaf people, it is apparent that the Deaf community shares characteristics of an oppressed minority. Deaf people are both undereducated and underemployed. Race and gender simply compound these problems.

This demographic reality must be at the core of Deaf history and Deaf studies. History is never neutral in its presentation of the past. American historian Charles Beard (1934) once reminded us of the interpretive nature of history; there are no facts, only historical facts. Any discussion or interpretation of the heritage of the Deaf community that does not account explicitly for the underlying structure of conflict and oppression does its subject a disservice. In this sense, historians are obliged to strike a balance between celebration of past achievements and advocacy for the liberation of all Deaf people from societal constraints that prevent a full measure of equality.

---

4 To obtain references to this literature, see Van Cleve (ed.) 1987, vol. III.

On the assumption that the best advocates for Deaf people are Deaf people themselves, historians must be sensitive to the need to return the results of their study to the Deaf community itself. Although dissemination of Deaf community heritage to the academy is necessary, it is insufficient. In order for any minority to achieve political and economic equality, it must have information and this certainly includes historical information. Historians, then, are obliged to return the fruits of their labor, in a way that is understandable, to the objects of their study - the Deaf community.

Although there was a dramatic increase in the 1980s, a substantial written account of Deafness and the history of American Deaf people existed previously. Much of this history can be found in the newspapers and magazines of the deaf community, such as *The Deaf Mute's Journal* and *The Silent Worker*, as well as in professional journals of educators of deaf children such as *The American Annals of the Deaf* and *The Volta Review*. Most of this history can be described as elitist, that is, it is a history of white men, predominantly those who could hear, who controlled or led organizations, schools, churches, and other institutions that dealt with Deafness or Deaf people. These published histories appear in written English.

Even when Deaf persons themselves wrote history, they communicated in written English. In fact, most of the American Deaf leadership traditionally has consisted of men who were born hearing, who became bilingual in English and sign language, and who shared many of the attitudes of their hearing colleagues on matters of race, gender, and class.

It is not surprising, then, that this history celebrates the achievements of these men, and promotes the maintenance of the status quo with a modicum of 'progressive' change. In fairness to this view, however, one should point out that this elitist perspective dominated much of the history written in the United States prior to the early 1960s.

There is a place for this elitist history in future studies of the deaf community. We need to know about the achievements of the National Association of the Deaf for example, but we also need to understand why that organization excluded deaf African-Americans for so long and why its leadership excluded women and prelingually Deaf men. Similarly, we need to know about the achievements of Deaf ministers in the Episcopalian Church, but we also need to understand the institutional barriers that the church imposed on its Deaf congregations. In short, an excessive focus on achievements is historically short-sighted. At best, it provides the historical material for celebration; at worst, it perpetuates discrimination and inequality for the larger Deaf community.

In order to achieve more balance in the historical record of the Deaf community, increased attention needs to be given to its underrepresented elements who do not produce much written documentation records. Oral History interviews can provide historians with two types of information. First, they can provide historical information that has not been recorded in writing. Hence, Oral History can supplement the elitist written record or provide testimony from the underrepresented majority of the Deaf community, individuals who do not feel comfortable with written English or written records. Since this information is limited to living remembrances, however, most historical data about past generations of the deaf community is simply lost. Nevertheless, this is an important area of historical research and needs to be collected for future study.

The second use of Oral History interviews is as folk history. We need to understand what the Deaf community believes to be its own deaf heritage. The Deaf community's belief about Alexander Graham Bell's attitudes toward marriage between deaf persons, for example, are just as important as Bell's actual written statements on the subject. We also need to understand how these historical beliefs and stories are perpetuated and transmitted between successive generations of Deaf people.

The Deaf community has always had its storytellers. Many of the written records of 'successful' Deaf individuals refer to Deaf community storytellers, usually when the individual learned sign language at a school for Deaf students or at a Deaf community club. Although these oral traditions need to be subjected to the analysis of specialists in folklore and ethnography, historians can benefit from an understanding of the popular culture of Deaf people.

Oral History

The practice of Oral History is one of the oldest forms of history, but it has experienced a popular revival since World War II. In the United States, historian Allan Nevins is credited with reviving interest in the use of tape-recorded (audio) interviews with living subjects as a way to supplement and document the written historical record. At the time (1950s), Nevins and his colleagues at Columbia University primarily were interested in tapping the memories of elite public figures: politicians and high-ranking military officers. But by the 1960s, an increasing number of historians expressed interest in the record of the heretofore voiceless minorities: African Americans, Indians, and women as well as average citizens. [5] Today, Oral History can be used profitably to collect and document the memories of persons who are deaf and do not communicate via oral speech.

Even though the pedagogical dispute in the United States between oralists (persons who advocate the use of speech and speech reading) and persons who use sign language extends back into the 19th century, the disagreement has no significance in the practice of Oral History. The operative word in Oral History is not 'oral,' but 'history.' Oral History is a communication event in which one person, guided by an interviewer, narrates his or her recollection of past events or persons. The term 'oral' simply signifies that the historical facts are collected from an informant through an interview process. The interviewer/historian, unlike the historian who collects historical facts from the written record exclusively, obtains testimony about the past through an interview with an individual who is knowledgeable about the time or subject of interest. Most importantly, the interviewer is able to interrogate the subject when the narrative is unclear, in dispute, or in need of amplification. The recorded interview is ultimately transcribed into written form. Today, we record this communication event through the use of an audio tape recorder or a video camera. How the communication occurs, through oral speech or sign language, is incidental. It is the individual's remembrance of the past that is important.

Whenever this writer uses the term *Oral History* with an audience composed of Deaf persons, it is explained, through the use of signs from American Sign Language, that 'oral' is not an 'o' handshape circling about the mouth which means vocally-produced speech but instead two linked 'f' handshapes moving in and out which means a story or a narration. In many respects, this signed explanation more accurately describes the craft of Oral History.

The products of Oral History are no better or worse than the products of a written historical record. Historians apply two general tests to all records, written or oral. Is the record authentic and is it credible? As long as these two tests are satisfied, oral documents are as reliable as written ones.

It is perhaps ironic that the American Deaf community has long understood the need for a different methodology for the preservation of its culture. Since sign language could not be adequately expressed through printed words, photographs, or illustrations, the National Association of the Deaf (NAD) quickly recognized the potential of motion picture technology as it evolved at the turn of the 20th century. One of the earliest fund-raising campaigns of the NAD occurred shortly before World War I and centered on a motion picture project designed to preserve sign language. These films have been described elsewhere but their central purpose was to document and preserve sign language as performed by some of the most prominent platform signers of the day (Van Cleve 1987).

---

5   For a survey of the origins of Oral History in the US, see: Dunaway/Baum 1984.

When Eastman Kodak and other companies made movie cameras and safety film designed for the home user in the 1920s/1930s, other amateur filmmakers added to our historical treasury of the Deaf community. Deaf filmmakers, like Charles Krauel of Chicago and Ernest Marshall of New York, regularly filmed events of importance in the life of the Deaf community. Even though these films and filmmakers are important resources for history, film by its nature remained inconvenient and expensive. Not until the widespread use of videotape and lightweight video cameras in the 1970s has it really become feasible to engage in Oral History interviews in the Deaf community. In short, the technology has caught up with what the Deaf community has always understood: in order to capture the history of Deaf people, it is necessary to turn to research tools that allow Deaf individuals to express themselves fully in their own language. Despite the power of the written word, it is simply inadequate to express the visual component of sign language.

If the Deaf community is a linguistic minority community, then its history cannot be adequately documented without substantial attention given to information expressed in a visual format. Since the ability to record this information has occurred only recently, historians need to account for this limitation in their studies of the past beyond that of the memories of the present generation. Historians, then, should be concerned about two types of documents in their search for evidence related to the heritage of the deaf community: 1. traditional written sources and 2. oral (signed) sources; Oral History interviews (living remembrances) and folk history (current interpretations of the community's past).

Application

In 1981, the National Endowment for the Humanities (United States) awarded this writer (Schuchman) a small grant to complete an Oral History project with Deaf persons who used sign language. The purpose of the project was to obtain substantive information about Deaf people's experience in the United States during the years of transition between the technologies of silent films and the new talking motion pictures, 1927-1929.[6] A second purpose was to establish appropriate techniques for the use of Oral History with Deaf persons.

By 1981, there existed a large body of literature and experience on Oral History; however, very few practitioners of Oral History utilized video cameras.[7] Nevertheless, the uniqueness of the project was not the videotaped interviews with Deaf persons per se but rather the effort to conduct interviews that met the professional standards of the Oral History Association (United States).[8] Although Gallaudet University provided access to its television facilities, the project was an individual research effort of one historian, myself - John Schuchman.

The Happy Hands Club is a senior citizens' club for Deaf persons that meets in Arlington, Virginia, (metropolitan Washington, DC) at St. Andrews Episcopal Church. Despite its location in Virginia, the club's members come from the entire metropolitan area. Due to the presence of employment opportunities with the federal government and Gallaudet University, the deaf population of Washington, D.C. has diverse geographic roots. A majority of the

6   Some of the information obtained from these interviews appeared in Schuchman 1984, pp. 58-78. This information was then expanded into a larger treatment of deafness and film in Schuchman 1988.

7   In the United States, the Oral History program at Baylor University (Waco, Texas), directed by Thomas Charlton, pioneered the use of videotaped Oral History interviews. At the present time, most major university Oral History projects endeavor to incorporate some videotape as a part of the overall interview process.

8   In May, 1989, the American Historical Association, which is the major professional association of historians in the United States, adopted an addendum on 'Interviewing' to the association's Statement of Standards of Professional Conduct. This statement, which reflects the practices of the Oral History Association, appears in the AHA Newsletter, *Perspectives* (October 1989).

Happy Hands members grew up elsewhere in the United States but moved to the Washington area as adults, where they sought jobs and education. Prior to the project, this writer did not know most members, with the exception of my father.

Parlaying this connection to the club through my Deaf father, I wrote a general letter to the members inviting them to participate in Oral History interviews. One of the major questions in any project is to determine who the interviewer will be: insider or outsider.[9] There are advantages and disadvantages to both approaches. In addition, however, with Deaf persons who sign, it is paramount that the interviewer be fluent with sign language. If not Deaf, the interviewer should be bilingual or at least comfortable with the sign communication of the Deaf interviewee. Since the grant did not include any funds for the training of interviewers and since one of the project's goals was to develop Oral History techniques, I personally conducted all of the interviews.

In point of fact, the actual communication style of the Happy Hands members ranged from signed English to American Sign Language. Since most of the interviews utilized two video cameras, it is possible to observe the language style of both interviewee and myself in order to evaluate the adequacy of the signs.

After the initial contact by correspondence, followed up by Telecomunication Device for the Deaf (TDD) calls, to explain the general purpose of the interview, I followed up with a home visit with each interviewee. There were several purposes for the home visit: to further explain the project in more detail, to evaluate the correspondent's physical and mental suitability for an interview, to obtain any documents (newspaper articles, letters, or photographs) that might complement or supplement the interview, to collect a demographic form which had been distributed earlier, and to explain their rights under American copyright law, the need for a legal release form, and the eventual disposition of the videotaped interview.

For reasons of health, a few Happy Hands members were not suitable subjects for an interview. One of the purposes of the home visit was to determine the mental alertness and communication style of the interviewee. A side benefit of this visit was to allow the interviewer to obtain an idea of the scope of experiences that could be discussed in future interviews and most importantly, to establish rapport without the pressure to complete an interview during the visit. Most individuals' initial response was to state that they did not have anything 'important' or 'interesting' for a history interview. This response simply provided an opportunity for the interviewer to explain Oral History and the value of obtaining different points of view about the past, not just the perspective of the political or social elite.

Another benefit of the home visit was the opportunity to obtain related historical documents. Often during an interview, the subjects would mention that they possessed a diary, a letter, newspaper clipping, photograph, or scrapbook. Although well intentioned, both interviewee and interviewer could forget to follow through if the materials were not readily available. The home visit was a practical and natural opportunity to search out such documentary evidence. Looking at photographs or scrapbooks was a particularly good way for an interviewer to develop questions for an interview guide, as well as rapport. Among several items obtained during home visits with the Happy Hands was a complete set of newspaper articles relevant to a school oral/manual controversy during the 1930s, which resulted in the dismissal of a superintendent, and a 'super 8' film record of a White House Ceremony (during the presidency of Harry Truman) which recognized the first American coast to coast airflight of a Deaf pilot. Most persons simply gave the material to this interviewer for archival deposit with the videotape. Where this was not possible, individuals loaned materials in order that archival copies could be made.

---

9   The literature for Oral History is extensive. For a good introduction to field work see Ives 1974. A videotape (Ives 1987) now supplements Ives' monograph (this writer negotiated the addition of open captions which should be specified when ordering). For a good introduction to Oral History in general see Dunaway/Baum 1984.

At the outset of the home visit, we reviewed a demographic form that had been mailed earlier. This form included basic demographic data as well as education and employment information. Although it was sometimes necessary to begin an Oral History interview with a general question about birth and schooling in order to calm a nervous interviewee, lengthy details of this sort are a waste of videotape and time. Interview time should be reserved for narration and reflection. Demographic data can be obtained in writing. Questions about this information can be covered in the home visit; however, if there is a substantive issue, it can be included in the interview guide.

One of the most important goals of the home visit was the explanation of the interviewee's rights (Neuenschwander 1985). The Happy Hands volunteered their time and it was important that they understood what they were being asked to do. Most people wanted to know if anyone was going to make money from an interview. This needed to be answered at the outset. In particular, I explained that I planned to write some articles and perhaps a book but estimated that research expenses would far outweigh any possible income.

It also was important that each individual understood that their videotaped interview would be deposited with the Gallaudet Archives and that the interview could be seen by other researchers in the future. This is often a sensitive issue with older persons (the average age of the members was 73); yet, none of the Happy Hands objected. Although Oral History interviews cannot be anonymous, I explained that interviewees had the right to place conditions on the interview, such as availability only upon death, or the expiration of a period of time. Again, no one asked for any such restrictions.

Archival deposit is also a sensitive topic for individual researchers. Quite often, individuals assume that they have exclusive rights to the interview; this is perhaps a natural desire. However, professional standards dictate that researchers arrange for eventual deposit of the interview with an archival repository. This is particularly important for videotaped interviews which are sensitive to possible damage from inattention to climate controlled storage.

The final task of the home visit was to arrange for the date and logistics of the interview. All of the interviews took place at Gallaudet University. Since not all of the Happy Hands drove automobiles, this interviewer arranged to transport approximately half of the interviewees. In one instance, I took one of the Happy Hands grocery shopping after the interview. In the real world of Oral History, interviewers can expect to 'help out' their interviewees.

Although Gallaudet University has excellent television studios as well as supporting technical staff, all of the interviews took place in a small self-study interview room. No one else was present during the interview. This researcher operated all of the video equipment. This was done for two reasons. Although the videotape was 3/4 inch, the goal of the interview was not production but research.[10] Thus the interview did not require the presence of technical support staff. The configuration of the interview room with two cameras, a switcher (permitting the split-screen display of both the interviewer and interviewee), microphone, and television monitor, was designed to facilitate use without the presence of technicians. The most important reason for excluding technicians, however, was simply to improve the chances for good rapport and trust during the interview.

There was one exception to the rule that no one else be present during the interview. One nervous spouse asked to sit in on her husband's interview so that she could see what it was like prior to her own interview scheduled for a later date. Although the interview quality was acceptable, the husband constantly deferred to his spouse, and therefore, she distracted him. Even though this sometimes cannot be avoided, it should be discouraged.

Attempting to eliminate the mystique of television and the video equipment, I initiated each session with 'hands on' exercises. In 1981, videocassette recorders (VCRs) were not as widely available as they are today (particularly since the availability of captioning deco-

---

10 Although somewhat dated (video technology changes rapidly), for a good introduction to the use of television for historical research see Jolly 1982.

ders); hence this was an important element of the interview. Demonstrating the equipment, I produced a sample image so that the interviewee would not be surprised by the end result. In a few instances, Happy Hands operated the equipment prior to the actual interview.

On the basis of the earlier home visit, I prepared an interview guide that listed the general topics for discussion. The goal in all interviews was to allow the interviewee to narrate her or his remembrances, with as little prompting as possible from the interviewer.[11] The interviews ranged in length from forty-five minutes to two hours. When interviews exceeded two hours, future appointments were scheduled. Nearly all of the interviews tired the Happy Hands.

Upon completion of the interview, both interviewee and interviewer signed a legal release (permission) form after an explanation, once again, that the videotape would ultimately be deposited with the Archives. The videotape was then played back for the interviewees to determine if any incorrect information had been included or if they wished to add any comments. All of the interviewees enjoyed this part of the process. Despite disclaimers that they appeared 'old', interviewees enjoyed seeing themselves on videotape. No one ever corrected a tape but a few added comments. Two or three Happy Hands, later, individually contacted me either because they had other stories they wanted recorded or because they had recommendations of other persons as possible sources for interesting interviews.

Once the interview was complete, a duplicate copy was made for research and transliteration use. The master videotape was deposited with the Gallaudet Archives.

In many ways, the interview was the easiest part of the Oral History process. Good Oral History practice, however, required that the interview be prepared for archival use. Oral historians differ about the next step: transcription. Some programs actually destroy the interview tape and rely exclusively on a written transcription that has been checked for accuracy by both the interviewer and interviewee. Others maintain that the tape is the primary document and prepare finding aids to permit researchers access.

The Happy Hands project posed several problems. Not only were the videotapes visual but the language of the interview was signed and sometimes not easily translated to written English. Even though a microphone was available in the interview room and I am hearing, the interviews, for the most part, did not include spoken English. Unlike typical Oral History projects, it was not possible for a secretary to listen to audiotapes and to transcribe the words into writing.

This researcher tried two approaches in order to produce English language transcripts. In the first, I personally voice-interpreted the Happy Hands interviews and produced audiotapes for transcription by a secretary. These voice interpretations required an average of seven hours for each hour of interview. Transcriptions required an additional day to produce a typed document. The typed transcription posed an additional problem because some of the Happy Hands were not comfortable with standard written English and clearly not with a transliterated Oral History interview. I opted not to send these translated documents to the Happy Hands. Anticipating this problem, all of the interview releases stated that the videotapes themselves were the primary documents, not the transcripts.

The second approach used by this researcher involved students. Since the original NEH grant did not include funds for interpreting, I sought economical ways to deal with the issue

---

11 Although subject to the limitations of time and budget, the interviewer needs to remember his obligation to other historians. Where possible, interviewers should ask questions designed to elicit other significant life experiences of the interviewee. The temptation for individual researchers is to focus on their specific research needs. For example, Schuchman recently interviewed a Deaf woman who had been a part of the cast for the only all Deaf-cast silent film, *His Busy Hour* (1926). In the course of the interview, it became clear that the interviewee's mother had been a private tutor of John Tracy, son of Louise and Spencer Tracy, namesake of the world-famous Tracy Clinic. Even though this topic had nothing to do with Schuchman's interest in silent film, this was an opportunity to collect historical data that was otherwise unavailable.

of interpreting. Moreover, I tried to establish a model for the future. This researcher concluded that if future Oral History projects or individual researchers were required to include transliterated transcripts, interpreting costs would be astronomical and thus limit Oral History to well-funded institutions. As a practical matter, required transliteration might impose substantial limits on the future collection or preservation of deaf community history. In an effort to avoid this result, I turned to students.

Sign language and interpreting classes often seek opportunities for practice. Approaching a Gallaudet faculty colleague, I offered the use of the Happy Hands videotapes to students in exchange for written transliterations. After one semester, this approach was abandoned. The students spent inordinate amounts of time on the project. It was clear that if interpreters were to be used, they needed to be experienced professionals in order to reduce the time expended down to the average seven hours.

Several years later, I obtained a small grant from the Gallaudet University Research Division to prepare a set of finding aids for the Happy Hands Project. Over a period of a summer, a graduate assistant and I reviewed all of the videotapes and prepared a subject index. Most of the procedures described here are still being used, with a few exceptions.

Today, nearly all of the interviews are conducted in the field in a non-studio setting, usually at the interviewee's home or place of residence (nursing home).

Since these interviews are conducted at a distance, they are scheduled over a period of at least two days. The first day serves as the home visit described above. Carrying my own equipment and continuing the initial commitment to a closed interview, this researcher now simply sets up a tripod-based camcorder shot over his head and focused on the interviewee. Other than the opening moments of the interview, when I introduce the date, site, and myself on camera, Schuchman does not appear in the interview; however, he voices his questions via the camcorder's microphone.[12] It is possible to do a wide-angle shot of both interviewee and interviewer but in this writer's opinion, it is more difficult to read the signs when this is done.

A major change in my procedure concerns interpretation or transliteration. This writer, as an individual researcher, no longer attempts to voice interpret videotaped signed interviews.[13] Lest I be misunderstood, however, I always would advocate that an 'ideal' Oral History interview should include a written transcript in order to make the results accessible to all historians, even those who do not understand sign language. Nevertheless, in a world of limited funds, this approach is not always possible.

Unless a project is well-funded, interpreting is not a good use of time or budget. Instead, once the interview is complete, it is important that the interviewer prepare a complete set of finding aids: 1. background of the interview and listing of any accompanying written or photographic documents, 2. interviewer's notes including description of the interview site and of the interviewee, 3. demographic form, 4. subject index of the videotape, 5. interview guide, and 6. summary description of the interview.

The Happy Hands Project demonstrated that videotaped Oral History interviews with deaf persons are both possible and worth doing. With the widespread availability and enhanced quality of videotechnology for the amateur, there is no reason why historians should not routinely include Oral History interviews, when appropriate, as a part of their research. Moreover, researchers who interview Deaf persons should be familiar with the

---

12 The obvious disadvantage to this approach is that a Deaf researcher needs to depend upon an interpreter for these questions. When the interviewer is also Deaf, this approach can not be used since the questions would be lost (this assumes that in a typical interview, many questions wil be spontaneous and that an interview will not adhere rigidly to an interview guide). In the instance of a Deaf interviewer, it is necessary to go to a wide shot. As indicated in the text, there are advantages to both approaches.

13 This advice is limited to an individual who is engaged in research that uses Oral History interviews. An Oral History program or project, ideally, should transcribe all interviews and should seek funds for that purpose.

standards of Oral History, particularly the obligation to arrange for archival deposit by institutions capable of maintaining and preserving records of the deaf community.

II Case studies

The preceding section dealt with the theory and general application of the practice of Oral History interviews to Deaf community history. This section examines specific Oral History interviews with two Deaf individuals: Joan Payzant and Ernest Marshall. Both persons occupy a special place in the history of American Deaf community films. Their oral testimony provides information that is not available in any other form.

Joan Payzant

In an earlier publication that dealt with the treatment of Deafness and Deaf people by Hollywood, this writer (Schuchman) had identified a film, *His Busy Hour* (1926), as lost (Schuchman 1988, pp. 23, 27, 117). The film's importance lay in the fact that it is the only silent era film with an all-Deaf cast. The presence of Deaf author Albert Ballin, who wrote *The Deaf Mute Howls* (1930), as a member of the cast added to its importance for Deaf community film history.[14] However, very little information about the film existed. Shortly after the appearance of his book, Schuchman received correspondence from Deaf persons which ultimately resulted in the receipt of a copy of the film from the daughter of a deceased cast member.[15] In addition to this major find, this writer identified at least one surviving cast member who could be interviewed, Joan Payzant.

The interview took place over a period of two days in December, 1989.[16] Only twenty years old when she participated as a minor player in the production of the film, Payzant now was more than eighty, and mentally alert. Correspondence over the preceding months with Payzant, who had resided in a nursing home for many years, clearly demonstrated that she looked forward to the visit.

Pointing out that she only appeared in the film briefly, Payzant denied that she remembered much about the film. In some ways, her judgment proved to be true; yet she provided important testimony about her own life as well as about her colleagues who performed in the film.

The director, producer, and scriptwriter of the movie was James Spearing, a hearing man who filmed the story at two locations: a residence and an isolated Southern California beach. Publicity for the film promoted its use of Deaf persons as natural actors.

Spearing also used the film in an effort to convince Deaf audiences to invest in a movie company of, by, and for Deaf people. He failed.

Although failing to convince potential Deaf investors, Spearing did produce a professional quality film. Videotape copies of the original film footage retain the mark of a serious film photographer. Even though the actors utilized a highly emotive style no longer popular, it is clear that these amateur Deaf players measured up to the professional standards of the day.

Payzant's interview indirectly provides insight into the failure. Despite the quality of the film and their professional expertise, Spearing and his hearing colleagues possessed very

---

14 Ballin's book has been identified as an early example of Deaf rage directed against hearing society (Batson/Bergman 1976, pp. 229-233).

15 Mary Balli donated videotape copies of the film *His Busy Hour* (1926) to this writer and the Gallaudet University Archives.

16 Joan Payzant, interviewed by John S. Schuchman (December 16-17, 1989). Videotape recording, Gallaudet University Archives, Washington D.C.

little knowledge of Deafness or of the Deaf cast members. As a result, their efforts to convince Deaf investors to create a movie company could not have been credible.

As a young woman, Payzant and her parents moved to Los Angeles, California. Her father worked as an accountant and her mother found employment as a teacher of Deaf children at the Mary Bennett School.[17] Payzant remained at home where she *took care of the house*. Enrolling in a special secretarial course for Deaf students, Payzant met other Deaf people in Los Angeles where she learned sign language. From this group of young deaf people came nearly half the cast for *His Busy Hour* (1926).

From the interview, it is clear that the young Deaf actors saw the project as an interesting adventure, *a lark;* they did not receive pay. Payzant participated in the filming at the residential site which actually was Spearing's home. Recalling that the Spearings were nice and that Mrs. Spearing provided lunch, Payzant knew nothing about Spearing's professional film background or the reasons for the production of the film.[18] *We laughed*, she remembered, at the efforts of the film's dramatic and pantomime coach, Gabrielle Ravenelle, who tried to convince the Deaf actors that enrollment in lipreading classes would improve their acting skills. It is ironic that Ravenelle would try to convince a young woman who had spent a lifetime acquiring speech and speech reading skills but who, as an adult, chose friends who signed.

During the visit and interview, Payzant had an opportunity to see the film she had participated in more than sixty years earlier. She enjoyed the film and expressed appreciation for the opportunity to see the Deaf friends of her youth. In the course of the interview, Payzant asked this interviewer several times if he agreed that the film depicted good acting and beautiful players. Despite her pleasure in seeing the film, Payzant refused all offers to show the movie to her fellow residents at the nursing home.

When asked how she communicated with Spearing and his hearing colleagues, Payzant commented that the director seemed *nervous around the deaf* and identified Albert Ballin as the interpreter for the Deaf group.[19] Payzant offered her mother, since deceased, as corroboration for Ballin's skill. At the end of the day's shooting, Payzant's mother picked her up for the return home and offered a ride to Ballin. Afterwards, the mother, a trained teacher of Deaf students, explained to Payzant that Ballin possessed excellent speech and speechreading skills.

Payzant's experience reflects a pattern that continues today. Filmmakers who are willing to take advantage of the perceived skills of Deaf actors rarely make any commitment to understand Deafness or Deaf people. Payzant offered valuable historical information about the film, particularly about the film's Deaf participants. The fact that she could not say much about the production or distribution of the film points up the inability or unwillingness of the filmmakers to include Deaf people in a significant way behind the camera.

The interview also provided some insight into the life of an orally-educated person. Previous correspondence and the interview demonstrated that Payzant had excellent written English; however, she lived a sheltered existence. A product of an 'oral' education, Payzant remained at home all of her life. Her mother trained to become a teacher of the Deaf at the Clarke School in Massachusetts and educated her child, Payzant, at home. During the course of the visit and the interview, Payzant spoke in a clear, soft, barely audible voice and signed English. Although she was a long-time resident of the nursing home and many of the staff and other

17 Now closed, the Mary Bennett School provided an oral education to deaf students enrolled in the Los Angeles public school system.

18 Spearing wrote scripts for Paramount Studios. He also contributed movie reviews for the New York Times. Robert Olson, the film photographer for *His Busy Hour*, also had professional Hollywood credits. Specific film credits for both men can be found in the American Film Institute *Catalogue* for the 1920s.

19 Throughout the interview, Payzant consistently referred to Ballin as 'Ballini'. When this writer pointed out to her that all written references used 'Ballin', Payzant insisted that she knew him as 'Ballini'; however, since we viewed the film together, it is clear we were identifying the same man.

residents smiled in recognition, no one engaged her in conversation. Payzant indicated that she depended upon lip reading and that no one else at the nursing home knew or used signs. Throughout the visit, this writer used signed English with her, and it was obvious that she required signs in order to understand the substantive questions in the interview. Never marrying or working outside her parents' home, Payzant chose to remain with her parents throughout her life. When her father died, Payzant and her mother returned to their home town. Shortly afterwards, they moved to a nursing home where Payzant has now resided for more than twenty years (her mother passed away a few years prior to the interview at age ninety-nine).

The Oral History interview and the opportunity to see the film brought Payzant a great deal of pleasure since it brought back memories of the thirty year period in her life when she had significant contact and interaction with the signing Deaf community in Los Angeles. In a letter to this writer, Payzant concluded: *My mother never learned sign language, because I talked all the time, but she understood that the deaf were happier that way, naturally. I can sign and spell and am glad of it, because I can mix with the deaf easily.* [20]

Ernest Marshall

Unlike Joan Payzant, Ernest Marshall came from the Deaf community. His parents, grandparents, and other relatives were Deaf. When he enrolled in the New York School for the Deaf (Fanwood), the other students, impressed that the little boy could sign so well, gave him the nickname, *Mr. Smart Signs*. Recognizing the young man's sign skills, the Deaf community recruited Marshall to perform in local New York theater productions. In 1937, Marshall made his first film, designed for Deaf audiences, and he would go on to make more sign language movies than anyone else (Schuchman 1988, p. 154).

This writer interviewed Marshall in October, 1981, when he was seventy one years old. The videotaped interview took place at Gallaudet University. The following edited transcript, originally twenty-one pages long, is one of the few sources of information about early Deaf filmmakers. [21]

Edited Transcript

Schuchman (hereafter *JSS*): So you graduated in 1931?
Marshall (hereafter *EM*): Yes, it was during the depths of the Depression.
JSS: And at the time you were 21 years old?
EM: Right, I was 21 years old.
JSS: That means that during your teenage years you were a silent movie fan?
EM: Yes, that's correct.
JSS: Okay. So silent films stopped about 1929-1930, which was just prior to your school graduation. Do you remember what it was like for you when you discovered the talking movies? Do you remember going to see your first talking movie?

20 Joan Payzant to John Schuchman (August 7, 1989), personal correspondence, Arlington, Virginia. Payzant's interview also resulted in a surprising tangent. During the interview, Payzant mentioned that her mother had been employeed by Spencer and Louise Tracy to tutor their son, John, for whom the world famous Tracy Clinic is named. It is clear from the interview that Payzant knew the Tracy family. In the interview, Payzant explained that John was painfully shy and that on the day of the dedication of the John Tracy Clinic building, he *drove home* rather than face the well-wishers.

21 Ernest Marshall to John Schuchman (October 6, 1981), transcript, videotaped interview, Gallaudet University Archives, Washington DC. Also, see a recent film: Ted Supalla, *Charles Krauel, A Profile of a Deaf Filmmaker.* Although he never made entertainment films like Marshall, Chicagoan Krauel filmed events of importance in the deaf community for more than a half-century.

EM: Hmmm...No...that was about 50 years ago and I don't remember that. But I can remember deaf people becoming depressed because we would go into the theatre to see the movies and there weren't any subtitles any longer and so we felt really left behind. So we decided we would start renting captioned films from the local film libraries and show them ourselves to make up for the loss we felt. Then the filmmakers went out of business, people were laid off, and later captioned films came into being, then we would show those regularly.

JSS: I know that later you became very involved with acting. When did you first get the idea of acting yourself? When did you begin making movies?

EM: At first I became involved in drama in high school, taking on some small parts in various plays such as *The Taming of the Shrew*, which was very exciting, and some Biblical plays. After having sat in the audience during one of my performances, John Funk [leading Deaf community actor] approached me and he asked me to join his club and be in his play that next fall. That fall he gave me the script.... Regarding the movies, I realized that deaf people were at a loss when they went to the movies. So in 1937 I began making movies.

JSS: Excuse me, 1937?

EM: Yes, 1937. And the deaf people were very happy about that and went to see the first film. So I continued to make movies and all together, I had about seven or eight.[22]

JSS: ...could you give us an idea of how you did this, could you describe what it was like, where you began, what you had to do?

EM: We had limited facilities and we had to direct ourselves as best we could.

JSS: Who is 'we' ?

EM: There was a group of people who were interested and the people selected from that group got together to do the films.[23] We knew it would take a lot of money for a big studio, yet we had limited financial means, though we still enjoyed (it).

JSS: Okay, how many people were involved in making a movie....

EM: When considering a script I chose one with a small number of characters, because if there were too many parts - say seven or eight - I felt that would be too many people to direct and have involved. If the story itself seemed good enough, then it did not matter if there were just a few characters.

JSS: Where did you get the money to make the films?

EM: I got the money from my own earnings. There were no grants that funded the films, nor were other people willing to invest into the making of the films. So I went ahead and used the money out of my own pocket.

JSS: Did you own a camera?

EM: Oh yes! You had to have a camera. That was one prerequisite for making a movie, so I bought one.

JSS: Where did you do the work on the titles?

EM: I did all of that in my own home. I worked on all of the measurements, figuring, splicing, and editing there, and I used a small manual splicer. It was not a machine like you see today, but a very small one.

---

22 Marshall retains possession of his original films; however as a result of this 1981 interview, he purchased his own video equipment. In the intervening ten years, he has donated videotaped copies of his films to the Gallaudet University Archives.

23 Marshall lived and worked in the New York City metropolitan area all of his life where he drew upon the talents of the local Deaf community. Although Marshall was the acknowledged film entrepreneur, the official title of the *group of people* he identified in the interviews is the, now defunct, *Independent Theatrical and Cinema Club for the Deaf.*

JSS: Did you teach yourself how to edit?

EM: Yes. I read a lot and practiced. I learned an awful lot from the books. The editing work itself was very, very difficult. First of all, there were only 20 foot reels to work with. So while filming, you would have to shoot and stop, shoot and stop, and continue to work with the film in these segments - 20 foot segments. We did not have the continuous reels of film like they do today. While editing the film you would have an even more difficult time because you had to make sure all the hand movements fit together correctly. You watch the shows they have today, and that was all easy work compared to what we had to do. We also had to write out and splice in all the title cards. And there would be as many as 400 title cards for one film. We would watch the footage and then have to match each one with the correct segment of the film. With over 400 of these title cards, it took a terribly long time to complete the movie, *The Debt*.

JSS: After you completed your movies, where did you show them? In clubs for deaf people?

EM: I showed them in deaf clubs all over the United States. I went to many states but did not get to all of them.

JSS: You were the producer as well as the owner?

EM: Oh yes, in fact I was considered the director, the producer, the editor, just about every imaginable title was given to me.

JSS: Now, is it true that you showed all the movies personally? You did not allow people to borrow them nor did you mail them out to anyone. Right?

EM: Right! I went with the movies everywhere. I enjoyed meeting the people who viewed them, seeing their reactions, and getting their feedback. There was one time at which I travelled 9,000 miles.

JSS: 9,000 miles?

EM: Yes, 9,000 miles. We began in New York, travelled to Akron, Ohio; Canton, Ohio; made our way to Dallas, Texas; and then over to Los Angeles, California. From there we went to San Francisco, California and then travelled to Chicago which was my last showing in 1964 on our way back to New York. That was probably the longest trip I had ever taken and we were gone for sixty days....That is one experience that I will **never** forget - one in which everyone thoroughly enjoyed themselves.

JSS: When you showed your films, did you sell tickets? Did you always lose money...?

EM: I would distribute the tickets in advance and the people at the places where I would show the films would sell the tickets. I had an agreement with all the places where I showed the films - and that was that I would get half of the proceeds and they would keep the other half. The money that I earned would go to cover my expenses.

JSS: Your movies were made for Deaf people, but was there ever a time when you tried showing them to hearing people?

EM: I tried that once. I distributed circulars and planned to have a showing for hearing people in the afternoon and a showing for deaf people that evening. A good number of hearing people came that afternoon and sat and watched the movie and watched the signing, but they depended on the subtitles throughout the film because they just were not used to seeing people sign. So I felt that it just was not worth it to show the film to hearing people who could not understand the signing.

JSS: So your movies were designed specifically for Deaf people?

EM: Yes.

JSS: So your films incorporated signs. And you know that today we have groups such as The National Theater for the Deaf. What do you think of their way of signing and their performance? Have you seen them?

EM: Yes, I have seen them a few times. From my perspective, some of the signing is too fast and it is very difficult to catch some, and I think that many deaf people miss a lot of the lines. I think that signs on the stage need to be clear and simple so that you are able to follow them.

JSS: So you really think that most Deaf people would enjoy your films better?

EM: Oh yes. See, my movies were asked for again and again, and I would have made more but the expense of them prevented that.

JSS: Did you try to get government funding at all?

EM: Emerson Romero wrote for grants but we failed to get funding, although NTD [National Theatre of the Deaf] did receive money.[24] Helen Menken, daughter of deaf parents, who was a former Broadway actress and who had established a school in New York, had heard about my movies and she wanted to see them. I brought the films to the movie house for her to preview and an interpreter explained to her what was occurring. She then discussed these movies with several filmmakers. These were new concepts to them, as they had never seen deaf actors perform in the movies before. She called me to her office and told me that she felt the filmmakers could help me out, probably CBS studios. Well, I thought that was great! Helen really pushed and encouraged me. Then, one day after getting home from work, I saw in the newspaper that she had dropped dead. That really hit me hard!

JSS: Do you still go to Deaf clubs?

EM: Oh yes, I go all the time. I am a member of the Union League Club for the Deaf, the oldest deaf club in America - I think it's 95 years old, yes, that's right...

JSS: You know about captioned TV. Do you own a decoder?

EM: No, I do not have a decoder. I only watch TV occasionally, but my wife watches it more often.

JSS: So you never see any of the captioned shows. What do you think of the captions...do they seem to be an improvement?

EM: Yes, I think they are an improvement, to some degree.

JSS: Do you think that they are as good as your movies?

EM: Oh, people grow up with TV nowadays. ...Really what we need is more movies and hopefully in the future people will get together and start making them again. Deaf people enjoy seeing 'our' people on the screen. You see hearing people on the screen all the time.

JSS: Would you encourage young people to continue making movies?

EM: Oh you bet I would! I really wish there was more motivation of that kind out there. If anyone asked me about it, I would encourage them. It's been fifty years since I began making them and we really need some more.

JSS: So you are looking for some 'new blood' to come and help, right?

EM: Oh, yes.

JSS: Thank you very, very much for the interview and all of your information.

EM: My pleasure to give it.

From the edited transcript, it is clear that Marshall is an articulate individual who had made a substantial contribution to the history of the Deaf community. When Hollywood proceeded to ignore the interests of Deaf people when they produced talking motion pictures exclu-

---

24 Romero, deceased, became a good friend and mentor to Marshall. Romero, one of the few Deaf actors who worked professionally in silent films, moved to New York City where he became active in Deaf community theater and pioneered efforts to obtain captions for commercially-produced talking motion pictures.

sively after 1929, Marshall was one of a small band of Deaf individuals who reacted in a positive manner. Without any outside financial support, Marshall produced sign language films for nearly thirty years. When he needed advice and support, Marshall turned to his Deaf peers. Viewed by Deaf audiences across America, Marshall's films both perpetuated the art of sign language actors and inspired other and future deaf filmmakers.

Yet, in 1981 (the date of the initial Oral History interview), very little information had been published about Marshall. In spite of its nearly encyclopedic account of Deaf people's accomplishments, the standard history of the American Deaf community did not mention Marshall (Gannon 1981).

The Marshall interview is a good example of the potential of Oral History interviews. He is from the working class, did not attend college, and did not participate in state or national political organizations of the Deaf community.[25] Although he collected and retained copies of advertisements for his movies in personal scrapbooks, traditional documentation of his achievements are limited. In effect, elite Deaf community history had ignored him.[26]

Joan Payzant and Ernest Marshall provide two of hundreds of life stories that need to be collected by serious historians of Deaf communities everywhere. Portable videotechnology has made the underrepresented constituents of the Deaf community accessible to historians. Although Oral History interviews are neither panaceas nor substitutes for traditional approaches, the craft of Oral History may no longer be ignored in the writing of future Deaf community history. Over time, much has been lost but much remains to be collected.

References

Ballin, Albert (1930): *The Deaf Mute Howls*. Reprinted in: *The Deaf Spectrum* (1974), vol. 5. Beaverton (Oregon): Spectrum Inc.

Batson, Trenton W. /Bergman, Eugene (eds.) (1976): *The Deaf Experience. An Anthology of Literature by and about the Deaf*. 2nd edition; South Waterford, Maine: Merriam-Eddy.

Beard, Charles (1934): Written History as an Act of Faith; in: *American Historical Review* (Jan. 1934), pp.219-229.

Dunaway, David K. /Baum, Willa K. (1984): Introduction; in: id. (eds.), pp. 3-36.

Dunaway, David K. /Baum, Willa K. (eds.) (1984): *Oral History. An Interdisciplinary Anthology*. Nashville: American Association for State and Local History.

Gannon, Jack R. (1981): *Deaf Heritage. A Narrative History of Deaf America*. Silver Spring, MD.: National Association of the Deaf.

Ives, Edward D. (1974): *The Tape-Recorded Interview. A Manual for Field Workers in Folklore and Oral History*. Knoxville: University of Tennessee Press.

Ives, Edward D. (1987): *An Oral Historian's Work*.Sheldon Weiss Production, color VHS, 33 minutes.

Jolly, Brad (1982): *Videotaping Local History*. Nashville: American Association for State and Local History.

Lane, Harlan (1984): *When the Mind Hears. A History of the Deaf*. New York: Random House.

Neuenschwander, John (1985): Oral History and the Law (Oral History Pamphlet No. 1)

Schuchman, John S. (1984): Silent Movies and the Deaf Community; in: *Journal of Popular Culture*, 17:4 (Spring), pp. 58-78.

---

25 However, Marshall is well known in the New York City Deaf community. As indicated in the interview, Marshall attended local Deaf clubs. In addition to his own movies, he served as a film projectionist for Deaf organizations throughout the city.

26 In addition to my own published work concerning Marshall over the subsequent ten years, this Deaf filmmaker has received increased attention. Most notably, the Deaf community television production company, *Beyond Sound* (now defunct), produced: *Moving Pictures, Moving Hands: The Ernest Marshall Story* (Los Angeles, 1987).

Schuchman John S. (1987): NAD Films; in: Van Cleve, J. V. (ed.), vol.III, pp. 279-280.

Schuchman, John S. (1988): *Hollywood speaks. Deafness and the Film Industry.*Urbana: University of Illinois Press.

Scouten, Edward L. (1984): *Turning Points in the Education of Deaf People.* Danville, Illinois: Interstate Printers.

Van Cleve, John V. (ed.) (1987): *Gallaudet Encyclopedia of Deaf People and Deafness*, 3 volumes; New York: MacGraw-Hill

Van Cleve, John V. /Crouch, Barry (1989): *A Place of Their Own. Creating the Deaf Community in America.* Washington D.C.: Gallaudet University Press.

Ill. 111: Abbé de L'Epée, after the portrait made by his Deaf pupil Paul Grégoire. France, 1959.

Ill. 112: An outer ear in relief, at the center of the 'waves', commemorating the International Congress on Education of the Hearing-Impaired, 1980. Germany, 1980s.

Ill. 113: Spelling D-E-A-F with the British hand alphabet. Great Britain, 1980s.

Optical Allusions
Iconography

Optical Allusions was completed by Renate Fischer
in collaboration with
Alexis Karacostas, Anne Oostra, and Joachim Winkler.

Special thanks go
to Gertrud Fischer, Hans Ballschuh, and Tomas Vollhaber,
to Maryse Bézagu-Deluy, Harlan Lane, Christiane Margull, Renate Poppendieker, Bernard Truffaut, and Yasemin Yetkin.

Ill. 1: In: *Illustrierte Gehörlosen-Welt* 2.3, 1930, p. 15. [Deutsches Institut für Internationale Forschung/ Bibliothek für Bildungsgeschichtliche Forschung/ Bibliothek für Hör- und Sprachgeschädigtenwesen, Leipzig. Photo: Hans Ballschuh]

Ill. 2: [Institut National de Jeunes Sourds, Paris. Photo: Studio de la Comète, Paris]

Ill. 3: [Archives of Gallaudet University, Washington]

Ill. 4: [Archives of Gallaudet University, Washington]

Ill. 5: In: *Illustrierte Gehörlosen-Welt* 4.1, 1932, p. 4. [Deutsches Institut für Internationale Forschung/ Bibliothek für Bildungsgeschichtliche Forschung/ Bibliothek für Hör- und Sprachgeschädigtenwesen, Leipzig. Photo: Hans Ballschuh]

Ill. 6: In: *La voix du silence* 8.1-4, 1964, p. 125. [Deutsches Institut für Internationale Forschung/ Bibliothek für Bildungsgeschichtliche Forschung/ Bibliothek für Hör- und Sprachgeschädigtenwesen, Leipzig. Photo: Hans Ballschuh]

Ill. 7: In: *Zwölfter Bericht des Verwaltungs-Ausschusses der am 28sten Mai 1827 gestifteten Taubstummen-Schule für Hamburg und das Hamburger Gebiet.* (1856) Hamburg. (ill. introduced after p. 129) [Universität Hamburg]

Ill. 8: In: *Eilfter Bericht des Verwaltungs-Ausschusses der am 28sten Mai 1827 gestifteten Taubstummen-Schule für Hamburg und das Hamburger Gebiet.* (1853) Hamburg. (ill. introduced after p. 188) [Universität Hamburg]

Ill. 9: Undated photo. [Institut National de Jeunes Sourds, Paris. Photo: Studio de la Comète, Paris]

Ill. 10: By Joseph Cochefer, born in 1849, Deaf. Undated. [Institut National de Jeunes Sourds, Paris. Photo: Studio de la Comète, Paris]

Ill. 11: By Bertrand. Undated. [Institut National de Jeunes Sourds, Paris. Photo: Studio de la Comète, Paris]

Ill. 12: Lithograph by Auguste Colas, Deaf engraver, representing the statue and bronze plaques by Félix Martin (1844-1916), Deaf sculptor. [Institut National de Jeunes Sourds, Paris. Photo: Studio de la Comète, Paris]

Ill. 13: In: Rodenbach, A. (1855): *Les aveugles et les sourds-muets.* Bruxelles.

Ill. 14: Undated anonymous engraving. [Private collection. Photo: Studio de la Comète, Paris]

Ill. 15: Lithograph by Langlumé; in: Docteur Deleau jeune (1825): *L'ouïe et la parole rendues à Honoré Trézel, sourd-muet de naissance, précédé d'un rapport fait à l'Académie des Sciences.* Paris. [Institut National de Jeunes Sourds, Paris. Photo: P.-A. Mangolte]

Ill. 16: Engraving by Deaf Frédéric Peyson (1807-1877), 1826, 'pupil at the Specialized Institution for Deaf Mutes directed by M. Bébian'. [Institut National de Jeunes Sourds, Paris. Photo: Studio de la Comète, Paris]

Ill. 17: In: *Illustrierte Gehörlosen-Welt* 4.3, 1932, coverpage. [Deutsches Institut für Internationale Forschung/ Bibliothek für Bildungsgeschichtliche Forschung/ Bibliothek für Hör- und Sprachgeschädigtenwesen, Leipzig. Photo: Hans Ballschuh]

Ill. 18: In: Ruth Schaumann (1934): *Der singende Fisch.* Mit 20 farbigen Tafeln nach Pergament-Miniaturen der Verfasserin. Berlin. [Deutsches Institut für Internationale Forschung/ Bibliothek für Bildungsgeschichtliche Forschung/ Bibliothek für Hör- und Sprachgeschädigtenwesen, Leipzig. Photo: Hans Ballschuh]

Ill. 19: In: Ruth Schaumann (1934): *Der singende Fisch.* Mit 20 farbigen Tafeln nach Pergament-Miniaturen der Verfasserin. Berlin. [Deutsches Institut für Internationale Forschung/ Bibliothek für Bildungsgeschichtliche Forschung/ Bibliothek für Hör- und Sprachgeschädigtenwesen, Leipzig. Photo: Hans Ballschuh]

Ill. 20: In: Ruth Schumann (1936): *Leben eines Weibes, das Anna hieß*. Eine Folge von Scherenschnitten zu einem Gedicht. Berlin. [Deutsches Institut für Internationale Forschung/ Bibliothek für Bildungsgeschichtliche Forschung/ Bibliothek für Hör- und Sprachgeschädigtenwesen, Leipzig. Photo: Hans Ballschuh]

Ill. 21: [Institut National de Jeunes Sourds, Paris. Photo: Studio de la Comète, Paris]

Ill. 22: [Museo Regional de Pintura JOSE A. TERRY, Tilcara, Argentina. Photo: Graciela Alisedo]

Ill. 23: [Deutsches Institut für Internationale Forschung/ Bibliothek für Bildungsgeschichtliche Forschung/ Bibliothek für Hör- und Sprachgeschädigtenwesen, Leipzig. Photo: Hans Ballschuh]

Ill. 24: [Koninklijk Instituut voor Doven H.D.Guyot, Haren]

Ill. 25: [Koninklijk Instituut voor Doven H.D.Guyot, Haren]

Ill. 26: [Deutsches Institut für Internationale Forschung/ Bibliothek für Bildungsgeschichtliche Forschung/ Bibliothek für Hör- und Sprachgeschädigtenwesen, Leipzig. Photo: Hans Ballschuh]

Ill. 27: Undated anonymous engraving. [Institut National de Jeunes Sourds, Paris. Photo: Studio de la Comète, Paris]

Ill. 28: In: *Illustrierte Gehörlosen-Welt* 2.3, 1930, p. 16. [Deutsches Institut für Internationale Forschung/ Bibliothek für Bildungsgeschichtliche Forschung/ Bibliothek für Hör- und Sprachgeschädigtenwesen, Leipzig. Photo: Hans Ballschuh]

Ill. 29: Undated engraving by A. A. Boclet. [Institut National de Jeunes Sourds, Paris. Photo: Studio de la Comète, Paris]

Ill. 30: Undated photo by van Wegner and Mottu, Amsterdam. [Koninklijk Instituut voor Doven H.D.Guyot, Haren]

Ill. 31: Photo by von Kolkow & Co, Groningen, 1870. [Koninklijk Instituut voor Doven H.D.Guyot, Haren]

Ill. 32: Undated anonymous drawing. [Institut National de Jeunes Sourds, Paris. Photo: Studio de la Comète, Paris]

Ill. 33: In: *Illustrierte Gehörlosen-Welt* 3.1, 1931, coverpage. [Deutsches Institut für Internationale Forschung/ Bibliothek für Bildungsgeschichtliche Forschung/ Bibliothek für Hör- und Sprachgeschädigtenwesen, Leipzig. Photo: Hans Ballschuh]

Ill. 34: [Deutsches Institut für Internationale Forschung/ Bibliothek für Bildungsgeschichtliche Forschung/ Bibliothek für Hör- und Sprachgeschädigtenwesen, Leipzig. Photo: Hans Ballschuh]

Ill. 35: Lithograph by E. Schlotter, 1836, after a drawing by Poetschke (Deaf), 1834. [Deutsches Institut für Internationale Forschung/ Bibliothek für Bildungsgeschichtliche Forschung/ Bibliothek für Hör- und Sprachgeschädigtenwesen, Leipzig. Photo: Hans Ballschuh]

Ill. 36: In: Teuscher, C.W. (n.d.): Grammatischer Sprachunterricht als Leitfaden für den Lehrer. Unpublished manuscript, pp. 2-3. [Deutsches Institut für Internationale Forschung/ Bibliothek für Bildungsgeschichtliche Forschung/ Bibliothek für Hör- und Sprachgeschädigtenwesen, Leipzig. Photo: Hans Ballschuh]

Ill. 37: [Deutsches Institut für Internationale Forschung/ Bibliothek für Bildungsgeschichtliche Forschung/ Bibliothek für Hör- und Sprachgeschädigtenwesen, Leipzig]

Ill. 38: [Deutsches Institut für Internationale Forschung/ Bibliothek für Bildungsgeschichtliche Forschung/ Bibliothek für Hör- und Sprachgeschädigtenwesen, Leipzig]

Ill. 39: [Deutsches Institut für Internationale Forschung/ Bibliothek für Bildungsgeschichtliche Forschung/ Bibliothek für Hör- und Sprachgeschädigtenwesen, Leipzig. Photo: Hans Ballschuh]

Ill. 40: Painting by E. Weser, 1836. [Samuel-Heinicke-Schule, Leipzig. Photo: Hans Ballschuh].

Ill. 41: Drawing by René Hirsch (Deaf), in: *La France silencieuse*. [Institut National de Jeunes Sourds, Paris. Photo: Studio de la Comète, Paris]

Ill. 42: Untitled caricature by Marié (Deaf); in: *Le réveil des Sourds-Muets*. [Institut National de Jeunes Sourds, Paris. Photo: Studio de la Comète, Paris]

Ill. 43: In: *Illustrierte Gehörlosenwelt* 4.4, 1932, p. 4. [Deutsches Institut für Internationale Forschung/ Bibliothek für Bildungsgeschichtliche Forschung/ Bibliothek für Hör- und Sprachgeschädigtenwesen, Leipzig. Photo: Hans Ballschuh]

Ill. 44: [Bamberg dome, tympanum of the Portal of the Princes (detail: 'The Damned'). Photo: T. Lehmann]

Ill. 45: In: Czech, F.H. (1836): *Versinnlichte Denk- und Sprachlehre, mit Anwendung auf die Religions- und Sittenlehre und auf das Leben*. Wien, table 8 (detail). [Universität Hamburg]

Ill. 46: In: Czech, F.H. (1836): *Versinnlichte Denk- und Sprachlehre, mit Anwendung auf die Religions- und Sittenlehre und auf das Leben*. Wien, table 8 (detail). [Universität Hamburg]

Ill. 47: In: Czech, F.H. (1836): *Versinnlichte Denk- und Sprachlehre, mit Anwendung auf die Religions- und Sittenlehre und auf das Leben*. Wien, table 2 (detail). [Universität Hamburg]

Ill. 48: [Institut National de Jeunes Sourds, Paris. Photo: J.-P. Chalvin]

Ill. 49: Undated photo (to the earliest, of 1898). [Foyer du Sourd Champenois. Photo: Studio de la Comète, Paris]

Ill. 50: Lithograph in: *Paris ignoré*, p. 465. [Institut National de Jeunes Sourds, Paris. Photo: Studio de la Comète, Paris]

Ill. 51: [Private collection. Photo: Volkmar Jaeger]

Ill. 52: [Private collection. Photo: M. Mauersberger]

Ill. 53: [Private collection. Photo: H. Lane]

Ill. 54: [Private collection. Photo: C. Margull]

Ill. 55: In: (anon.) (1793): *Versuch über die im fränkischen kreise bekannte sogenannte Fingersprache, nebst einer illuminirten kupfertafel, ein schärfchen, zu verminderung menschlichen elends und zum besten armer verunglükkter*. Nürnberg. [Deutsches Institut für Internationale Forschung/ Bibliothek für Bildungsgeschichtliche Forschung/ Bibliothek für Hör- und Sprachgeschädigtenwesen, Leipzig. Photo: Hans Ballschuh]

Ill. 56: [Koninklijk Instituut voor Doven H.D.Guyot, Haren]

Ill. 57: [Koninklijk Instituut voor Doven H.D.Guyot, Haren]

Ill. 58: [Institut National de Jeunes Sourds, Paris. Photo: Studio de la Comète, Paris]

Ill. 59: [Koninklijk Instituut voor Doven H.D.Guyot, Haren]

Ill. 60: [St. Johannis-Eppendorf, Hamburg. Photo: Hans Ballschuh]

Ill. 61: [Photo: Renate Fischer]

Ill. 62: In: Stammbuch von C.G. Reich (loose sheets, started in 1812). [Samuel-Heinicke-Schule, Leipzig. Photo: Hans Ballschuh]

Ill. 63: [Deutsches Institut für Internationale Forschung/ Bibliothek für Bildungsgeschichtliche Forschung/ Bibliothek für Hör- und Sprachgeschädigtenwesen, Leipzig. Photo: Hans Ballschuh]

Ill. 64: [Samuel-Heinicke-Schule, Leipzig. Photo: Hans Ballschuh]

Ill. 65: Stammtafel der Familie Heinicke, by J. Winkler. [Samuel-Heinicke-Schule, Leipzig. Photo: Hans Ballschuh]

Ill. 66: Undated postcard. [Institut National de Jeunes Sourds, Paris. Photo: Studio de la Comète, Paris]

Ill. 67: Undated postcard distributed by German self-help groups, about 1991. [Private collection]

Ill. 68: Undated postcard (publicity for hearing-aids). [Koninklijk Instituut voor Doven H.D.Guyot, Haren]

Ill. 69: In: Czech, F.H. (1836): *Versinnlichte Denk- und Sprachlehre, mit Anwendung auf die Religions- und Sittenlehre und auf das Leben*. Wien, table 6. [Universität Hamburg]

Ill. 70: In: Czech, F.H. (1836): *Versinnlichte Denk- und Sprachlehre, mit Anwendung auf die Religions- und Sittenlehre und auf das Leben*. Wien, table 4 (detail). [Universität Hamburg]

Ill. 71: In: Comite oud-leerlingen Guyot 200 (eds.)(1990): *200 jaar doveninstituut. Van gebaar tot gebaar. 1790 - 1990*. Groningen, p. 44. [Koninklijk Instituut voor Doven H.D.Guyot, Haren]

Ill. 72: Undated engraving by Borricelli. [Private collection. Photo: Studio de la Comète, Paris]

Ill. 73: Undated photo (about 1900 ?). [Centre Augustin Grosselin, Paris. Photo: Studio de la Comète, Paris]

Ill. 74: Undated photo. [Municipal archives of Groningen]

Ill. 75: Painting by J.-E. Lenepveu (1819-1898); in: Couturier, L./ Karacostas, A. (eds.)(1989): *Le pouvoir des signes. Sourds et citoyens*. Paris, p. 103.

Ill. 76: In: Czech, F.H. (1836): *Versinnlichte Denk- und Sprachlehre, mit Anwendung auf die Religions- und Sittenlehre und auf das Leben*. Wien, table 4 (detail). [Universität Hamburg]

Ill. 77: Undated photo by R. Schoenberg; in: Gannon, J. (1981): *Deaf Heritage. A Narrative History of Deaf America*. Silver Spring: NAD, p. 64.

Ill. 78: Undated photo. [Institut National de Jeunes Sourds, Paris. Photo: J. P. Chalvin]

Ill. 79: Undated photo. (after 1900). [Koninklijk Instituut voor Doven H.D.Guyot, Haren]

Ill. 80: Undated photo. [Municipal archives of Groningen]

Ill. 81: Undated photo. [Institut National de Jeunes Sourds, Paris. Photo: J. P. Chalvin]

Ill. 82: In: Comite oud-leerlingen Guyot 200 (eds.) (1990): *200 jaar doveninstituut. Van gebaar tot gebaar. 1790 - 1990*. Groningen, p. 67. [Koninklijk Instituut voor Doven H.D.Guyot, Haren]

Ill. 83: In: *Gehörlosenschule Wildeshausen 1820-1970. Festgabe zur Feier ihres 150jährigen Bestehens am 30. Mai 1970*. (n.d.) Wildeshausen, p.37. [Universität Hamburg]

Ill. 84: [Private collection]

Ill. 85: In: Czech, F.H. (1836): *Versinnlichte Denk- und Sprachlehre, mit Anwendung auf die Religions- und Sittenlehre und auf das Leben*. Wien, table 72. [Universität Hamburg]

Ill. 86: In: Emmerig, E. (ed.) (1927): *Bilderatlas zur Geschichte der Taubstummenbildung*. Mit erläuterndem Text. München, p.12. [Deutsches Institut für Internationale Forschung/ Bibliothek für Bildungsge-schichtliche Forschung/ Bibliothek für Hör- und Sprachgeschädigtenwesen, Leipzig. Photo: Hans Ballschuh]

Ill. 87: [Municipal archives of Groningen]

Ill. 88: Painting by Augustin Massé (Deaf), after Joseph Cochereau (Deaf), 1814. [Musée des Beaux-Arts, Chartres]

Ill. 89: Drawing by F. Engel. [Deutsches Institut für Internationale Forschung/ Bibliothek für Bildungsge-schichtliche Forschung/ Bibliothek für Hör- und Sprachgeschädigtenwesen, Leipzig. Photo: Hans Ballschuh]

Ill. 90: Undated postcard. [Institut National de Jeunes Sourds, Paris. Photo: Studio de la Comète, Paris]

Ill. 91: In: Hill, M. (n.d.): Bildersammlung. Leipzig, 5th ed., sheet 3 (detail). [Deutsches Institut für Internatio-nale Forschung/ Bibliothek für Bildungsgeschichtliche Forschung/ Bibliothek für Hör- und Sprach-geschädigtenwesen, Leipzig. Photo: Hans Ballschuh]

Ill. 92: Undated postcard. [Institut National de Jeunes Sourds, Paris. Photo: Studio de la Comète, Paris]

Ill. 93: [Municipal archives of Groningen]

Ill. 94: [Institut National de Jeunes Sourds, Paris. Photo: Studio de la Comète, Paris]

Ill. 95: In: Vatter, J. (1911): *50 Jahre Taubstummenlehrer*. Lebenserinnerungen. Frankfurt/M., p. 83. [Uni-versität Hamburg. Photo: Hans Ballschuh]

Ill. 96: [Koninklijk Instituut voor Doven H.D.Guyot, Haren]

Ill. 97: [Deutsches Institut für Internationale Forschung/ Bibliothek für Bildungsgeschichtliche Forschung/ Bibliothek für Hör- und Sprachgeschädigtenwesen, Leipzig. Photo: Hans Ballschuh]

Ill. 98: Anonymous etching, undated. [Deutsches Institut für Internationale Forschung/ Bibliothek für Bil-dungsgeschichtliche Forschung/ Bibliothek für Hör- und Sprachgeschädigtenwesen, Leipzig. Photo: Hans Ballschuh]

Ill. 99: [Bibliothek für Hör- und Sprachgeschädigtenwesen, Leipzig. Photo: Hans Ballschuh]

Ill. 100: In: Aquapendente (1600), part 'De aure auditus organo Liber', p. 11 (detail). [Deutsches Institut für Internationale Forschung/ Bibliothek für Bildungsgeschichtliche Forschung/ Bibliothek für Hör- und Sprachgeschädigtenwesen, Leipzig. Photo: Hans Ballschuh]

Ill. 101: In: Aquapendente (1600), part 'De Larynge vocis instrumento Liber', p. 19. [Deutsches Institut für Internationale Forschung/ Bibliothek für Bildungsgeschichtliche Forschung/ Bibliothek für Hör- und Sprachgeschädigtenwesen, Leipzig. Photo: Hans Ballschuh]

Ill. 102: van Helmont (1657); frontispice, coverpage, and table I. [Deutsches Institut für Internationale For-schung/ Bibliothek für Bildungsgeschichtliche Forschung/ Bibliothek für Hör- und Sprachgeschädig-tenwesen, Leipzig. Photo: Hans Ballschuh]

Ill. 103: [Koninklijk Instituut voor Doven H.D.Guyot, Haren]

Ill. 104: [Municipal archives of Groningen]

Ill. 105: In: *Gehörlosenschule Wildeshausen 1820-1970. Festgabe zur Feier ihres 150jährigen Bestehens am 30. Mai 1970*. (n.d.) Wildeshausen, p.42. [Universität Hamburg]

Ill. 106: In: Docteur Deleau jeune (1838): *Traité du cathétérisme de la trompe d'Eustachi, et de l'emploi de l'air atmosphérique dans les maladies de l'oreille moyenne*. Paris. [Institut National de Jeunes Sourds, Paris. Photo: P.-A. Mangolte]

Ill. 107: In: Le Bouvyer-Desmortiers, U.R.T. (an VIII): *Mémoire ou considérations sur les Sourds-Muets de naissance et sur les moyens de donner l'ouïe et la parole à ceux qui en sont susceptibles*. Paris. [Institut National de Jeunes Sourds, Paris. Photo: P.-A. Mangolte]

Ill. 108: In: Deleau, L. (1863): *De l'emploi des douches d'air et du cathétérisme de la trompe d'Eustache dans le traitement des maladies de l'oreille*. Paris. [Institut National de Jeunes Sourds, Paris. Photo: P.-A. Man-golte]

Ill. 109: In: *International Primate Protection League Newsletter* 17.3, 1990, p. 26.

Ill. 110: In: *International Primate Protection League Newsletter* 17.3, 1990, p. 6.

Ill. 111: [Private collection]

Ill. 112: [Private collection]

Ill. 113: [Private collection]

Index of Names

This index was completed by Katharina Kutzmann.

List of Contributors

Igor A. Abramov, Seliverstov per. 8, Russia - Moscow 103045

Graciela Alisedo, Avenida Las Heras 1660 P.B., Argentina - 1018 Buenos Aires

Yves Bernard, 101, av. des Bleuets, F - 91400 Orsay

Maryse Bézagu-Deluy, 3, rue Pierre Guignois, F - 94200 Ivry-sur-Seine

Horst Biesold, Universität Bremen, Fachbereich 8, Postfach 33 04 40,
D - 2800 Bremen 33

Serena Corazza, Istituto di Psicologia/CNR, Via Nomentana, 56, I - 00161 Roma

Renate Fischer, Universität Hamburg, Romanisches Seminar, Von-Melle-Park 6,
D - 2000 Hamburg 13

Polina Fyodorova c/o Howard Williams

Brian Grant, Eden Hill, Armathwaite, UK - Carlisle CA4 9PQ

Alexis Karacostas, 73, av. Ledru-Rollin, F - 75012 Paris

Harlan Lane, 15 Rutland Square, USA - Boston MA 02118-3105

Günther List, Winzergasse 9, D - 6749 Gleiszellen

Gertrud Mally, Pählstr. 51, D - 8000 München 70

Patrick McDonnell, Centre for Language and Communication Studies, Trinity College,
IRE - Dublin 2

Bernard Mottez, 3, Villa Joany, F - 92250 La Garenne-Colombes

Anne Oostra, Koninklijk Instituut voor Doven H.D. Guyot, Rijksstraatweg 63,
NL - 9752 AC Haren

Laura Pagliari Rampelli, Ist. Statale Sordomuti, Via Nomentana, 56, I - 00161 Roma

Paola Pinna, Ist. Statale Sordomuti, Via Nomentana, 56, I - 00161 Roma

Susan Plann, 1653 South Hayworth Ave., USA - Los Angeles, CA 90035

Jean-René Presneau, 21, rue Albert Mallet, F - 63000 Clermont-Ferrand

Gloria Pullen, University of Bristol, School of Education Unit, 22 Berkely Square, UK - Bristol BS1 5HP

Maria A. Rodrígez González, Calle Josep Balari 14-16 6ᵉ D, E - 08022 Barcelona

Paolo Rossini, Ist. Statale Sordomuti, Via Nomentana, 56, I - 00161 Roma

Helena Saunders, Irish Deaf Society, Carmichael House, North Brunswick Street, IRE - Dublin 7

Odd-Inge Schröder, University of Oslo, Institute for Special Education, Box 55, N - 1347 Hosle

John S. Schuchman, Gallaudet University, Dept. of History, Kendall Green, 800 Florida Ave. NE, USA - Washington, D.C. 20002-3625

Carlos Skliar, Calle Hipolito Yrigoyen 3083 2° C, CP, Argentina - 1207 Buenos Aires

Aude de Saint-Loup, 9, rue de Varize, F - 75016 Paris

Rachel Sutton-Spence, University of Bristol, School of Education Unit, 22 Berkely Square, UK - Bristol BS1 5HP

Bernard Truffaut, 2, rue Abbé Dugué, F - 45140 St. Jean de la Ruelle

John Vickrey Van Cleve, Gallaudet University, Dept. of History, Kendall Green, 800 Florida Ave. NE, USA - Washington, D.C. 20002-3625

Virginia Volterra, Istituto di Psicologia/CNR, Via Nomentana, 56, I - 00161 Roma

Jonna Widell, Danske Døves Landsforbund, Fensmarkgade 1, DK - 2200 København N

Howard G. Williams, 94 Quantock Rd., UK - Weston-super-Mare Avon BS23 4DW

Joachim Winkler, Pfaffendorfer Str. 50, D - 7010 Leipzig

Avraham Zwiebel, Bar-Ilan University, School of Education, Israel - 52900 Ramat-Gan

Siegmund Prillwitz and Tomas Vollhaber (Eds.)

Current Trends in European Sign Language Research

Proceedings of the 3rd European Congress on Sign Language Research, Hamburg 1989

ISBN 3-927731-03-X • 406 p. • paperback • DM 45,-

William Edmondson and Fred Karlsson (Eds.)

SLR '87

Papers from the 4th International Symposium on Sign Language Research, Lappeenranta 1987

ISBN 3-927731-06-4 • 280 p. • paperback • DM 40,-

Siegmund Prillwitz and Tomas Vollhaber (Eds.)

Sign Language Research and Application

Proceedings of the International Congress, Hamburg 1990

ISBN 3-927731-12-9 • 304 p. • hardcover • DM 40,-

McQuarrie/Beattie; in **Sign Language Studies** 76, 1992:
The papers presented at this conference attest to the current depth and breadth of active research on the language, cognition, and culture of deaf people around the world. Even skeptics questioning the role and use of a natural sign language in the education may find "Sign Language Research and Application" a refreshing contrast to the emotional anti-speech, anti-hearing, sentiment found in some recent literature. This book's value lies in its ability to provide practising teachers or researchers with an overview to the theories and research associated with bilingualism. Operating from the premise that theory informs practice, these proceedings will undoubtedly give readers a base on which to validate the decisions they make as teachers or clinicians. Hopefully, this volume will add impetus toward improving both the social recognition of sign language and the life situation of deaf people.

Signum Press

Hans Albers-Platz 2, D-2000 Hamburg 36
Tel. ++49 - (0)40 - 3192140, Fax: ++49 - (0)40 - 3196205

Distributor for the United States:
Gallaudet University Press, Kendall Green, 800 Florida Ave. NE, Washington, DC. 20002-3695